T0380751

NOT FOR THE BOYS

Preteen edition

PAMALA LAVAN

author HOUSE

AuthorHouse™ UK
1663 Liberty Drive
Bloomington, IN 47403 USA
www.authorhouse.co.uk
Phone: 0800 047 8203 (Domestic TFN)
        +44 1908 723714 (International)

Published by AuthorHouse 12/18/2019

ISBN: 978-1-7283-9656-9 (sc)
ISBN: 978-1-7283-9657-6 (e)

Library of Congress Control Number: 2019920310

Print information available on the last page.

Any people depicted in stock imagery provided by Getty Images are models,
and such images are being used for illustrative purposes only.
Certain stock imagery © Getty Images.

This book is printed on acid-free paper.

CONTENTS

ABOUT THIS BOOK — NFTB (NOT FOR THE BOYS) — PRETEEN EDITION

This book is aimed at schoolgirls from 6-year old plus (but teenagers may enjoy it too)
This book should only be read by girls or ladies -
If it is a girl reading this book or her Mummy, then all is well.
However, if it's a boy or man they are obviously sissies -
If it's a boy, then he's to admit to liking skipping, playing dress-up, dollies, etc.
If it is a man, then I hope you enjoy reading this in a sweet bra, panties under your frock
In both case hair ribbons and mincing with your handbag are optional -

The stories in this book are all made up, but should make you laugh
while you imagine your brother, cousin, boy next door or from school
being put in the precarious situations and under control of girls.

This preteen book has no sexual contentHowever, when girls play dress up, with boys, they'll sooner or later, spy
his baby-pee-pee. So, there will be sections mentioning a boy's 'baby-pee-pee'!

This book is pure fiction
Please girls! Don't try out any of the techniques on your brothers or friends
They would be mortified if they ended up in dresses or carrying a handbag around town

It might be good for your Mummy's to read the book first to check if it's ok for you girls

This book is split up into various sections –
Initial sections – explain about ways to trap a boy, into coming under your control and being nice and kind and
doing what he's told – helping with housework and maybe even playing with his sisters or other girls.

They say, about tricks you can play on him, to make him look and sound girly, in front of his Mum, a neighbour,
his Aunty or female cousin. Imagine him being offered the choice of going out the back garden to play football or
slip into a pretty apron to do the dishes, housework, help with the laundry.
But he actually chooses the latter.

You can start off slowly and steadily increase the girly things, he does, with his embarrassments steadily growing
day by day or hour by hour – it's up to you.

The main part of the book contains stories about boys of various ages, but for this PT (preteen) book it is mostly
about **boys between 5 and 10 or 11**.

The **full book** contains more about boys, from 11 up and men, especially concerning the cases, when boys have
become men and is for, girls from 11 up and ladies, with suggestions for them, to have fun with their older brothers,
boyfriends and husbands too.

Although as you little girls know, playing dollies, shouldn't be the reserve of the young boys, there's no reason, why your big teenage brothers, shouldn't have fun, dressing and undressing your dollies and wheeling them about in a doll's pram! Boys of any age should be shown how to dress and undress dollies, so when they grow up and their wives have children, they can help them changing the baby's clothes and even changing their nappies and wheeling them about in prams or buggies!

Each story – I try to have a brief summary at the top of each page
I list the first few page summaries to give an idea of what the story concerns
How long are the stories – they never end, but get each boy in embarrassing situations.

PS Girls – try and keep this book and the stories and techniques a secret from the boys
As it is entitled 'NOT for the Boys!'
If a boy finds out about the book and it's contents – he might be on his guard for what you or one of your girlfriends might try on him!

About the Book

The book is totally fiction, but should make you laugh as you imagine your brothers, cousins or local boys in the same situations that the boys in the book find them in.
Although I don't think you should try any of the techniques on a boy, as it would be terribly embarrassing for him.
The book starts with various sections, about controlling boys by various girly means – a how to guide and also various suggestions of things to do with them, when under your control, before reading the stories themselves.

The main section contains about 12 stories, with boys of ages from 6 to 12 or so, but the main story of 8-year old **Tom** and his young 7-year old sister, **Pam**, is very large and so is interspersed, between the other stories with

Tom Continued – Part B to J, to stop you getting bored, with the one boy, being put through his paces by his sister.

The Main Index

If you wish to gather the main parts of each story quickly, then go to the back of the book where you shall be able to read each story in a matter of minutes, gathering the main section titles which make up each story.

The index below – **Index NFTB** only gives a title for each story or sub-story whereas the main index gives much more detailed of each!

NFTB (NOT FOR THE BOYS) AND BOOK PREVIEW

Preteen edition 1
Pamala Lavan - Published 2019 December
pamala.lavan@hotmail.com
 www.nftbbooks.com

Note by going to the website www.nftbbooks.com
you can obtain
a FREE 70+ page preview of the ebook with the 1st of 19 stories

 The Paperback and Hardback versions of the book are
Available from AuthorHouse.UK

https://www.authorhouse.com/en-gb/

They are also available from Barnes & Noble and Amazon

   ©NFTBbooks

www.barnesandnoble.com
www.amazon.com

Future NFTB books - There will be future books in this NFTB series
There will be other versions of this book with other hilarious stories

 The full version
A full book – for teenage girls and ladies
This will contain some sexual content – (although not a lot)
Again, there will be other versions with different stories

There may be books containing pictures
There may be online versions too

10 STORIES -APART FROM THE MAIN STORY OF TOM AND PAM

1: 8-year old Tom with his sister Pam 7 have lots of adventures
She has lots of embarrassing fun with him in hundreds of girly situations

2: The **Questionnaire** leads to the first boy **Toby 7** being trapped, to the delight of his young sister Francesca who's just 5.

3: 10-year old Harry – is getting out of control and his neighbour Sally traps him and turns him into a nice helpful boy, helping his Mum and her with housework, but he's then seen by Abi 6 and he ends up in dresses and worse.

4: Tania prepares her Mum to transform Peter by showing Harry off

5: Tania 8 at same school as Abi, traps, her **7-year old brother Peter**, but at school, he is taken to the kinder garden, where after dealing with him,

6: 14 year old Katie(full book) shows her girly boyfriend off to Suzie 7, who traps her **9-year old brother Robbie**

7: Francesca helps his Mum transform **Gerry 9** – His Mum and some ladies have heard what happened to Toby and thought it might be fun to get their big boys under control and acting girly.

8: Several **6 year old boys** are trapped one morning, with girls asking them individually, to teach them to play football, but they all end up in dresses and Sissy Football, mincing with handbags while kicking the ball in the back garden.

9: Ian one of the 6-year old's tells his Mum, but she then enlists the young girl next door to have fun with her boy and then also gets another of the boys Larry to join them.

10: TV Stories about boys being turned into sissies – acting in a girly way

8 YEAR OLD TOM WITH HIS SISTER PAM 7 - EXAMPLE

Pam initially plays a trick on Tom and he then finds himself playing football
    in shorts with frills sewn to the legs and Pam shows his mates
However, their Mum asks Pam to stop her friends messing with Tom and she does

However, his Mum realizes he's still being a MSP, not helping them with the housework
    and decides to embarrass him a little, to change his attitude
    Pam However, accidentally discovers what she's done to Tom and …

Pam decides to take it slowly with outing her brother Tom, to school friends
    but accidentally starts a chain reaction.

She calls him Nancy and makes him carry a doll around the house from room to room
    telling him off loudly – any time he forgets Baby Suzie
Tom then (accidentally) outs himself, to their neighbour, June, who makes Nancy
    wheel his dolly about the back garden, in Pam's apron and headscarf
Pam then gets their Mum to agree that Tom aka Nancy, can help with the laundry
    using a handbag and purse to hold his clothes-pegs
Pam tricks Tom who wets his panties and let's Mum know he's wearing Pam's panties
    Pam gives his dolly Baby Suzie a handbag to carry about the house too
    also leads to his Mum realizing Pam is making Tom ask before playing footy
Pam asks their Mum if they can play shopping using a handbag and purse
Pam then deputizes her Mum to checking he's wearing her panties to go out
    Pam then plays a trick on him and supplies baby plastic pants to wear instead
Pam thinks of girly things for Nancy to do
    Homework with his handbag and/or shopping bag dangling from his elbow
    Get their Mum to teach him needlework, embroidery and dressmaking
    Pam can teach him ballet in one of her tutus

Pam then thinks of Nancy joining her and their Mum to play football
    but it's actually Sissy Football with him in apron, mincing with a handbag
    However, he ends up in a worse situation playing Baby Football in nappies

This is all without girls at school or locally and especially his football mates realizing.

However, he's eventually outed to more and more girls, especially Julie and then her
little sister Tina and then girls at school and then his mates
Pam has recordings of him saying, girly things and plans to let Tina hear him asking
    She has Julie and Tina over, and they hear 'Pam will you play dollies with me?'
He ends up wearing a dress and pinafore to school and mincing with his handbag/shopper, but even worse –

TAMING UNRULY BOYS (PRETEEN)

You may have a disobedient boy who tries to do what he wants and disobeys your smallest request. He may think he rules the roust if there's no man in the house. He may be rude to you or his sisters and sometimes swear and be nasty and even hit you or them. He may lock himself away and you worry about what he's doing or getting up to.

Going out all the time with his mates, to play or whatever.
Staying out late when he wants to and hanging out with a bad crowd.

However, you might want some token help, with the housework now and then
or for him to do his homework for school and be more studious for later life.

The Solution to him mending his naughty ways

Using the techniques mentioned in this book will have him doing most things you ask, but in a nice sweet way. Obeying most of your requests!

The earlier he's brought under control the better
and especially for young boys it will have lasting effects.

Imagine your boy
No longer being rude or disobedient!
Complementing you and his sisters on their clothes or looks – maybe daily
- Oh, that's a nice skirt or dress or apron! Is that handbag or those shoes new?
- You're looking nice today! I like your hair!
- To which a nice curtsy and a sweet kiss would be a nice embarrassing response

Doing his homework before going out to play
Letting you take the key of his bedroom to be able to check what he's up to
Letting you see what he's up to on his computer or phone
Asking can he help with the washing up (with or without apron – is up to you)
Asking can he help peg out the laundry (with or without apron – is up to you)
Maybe other housework too!

The laundry will maybe take a bit longer, but you will laugh your head off at the sights in front of you - See, later in the book

Helping you with the shopping – carrying a shopping bag or basket for you, or …
Asking can he go out to play, but obeying you when you ask him to

- Help you with some housework
- Stay and do some homework first

- Come in early and not stay out late – when you ask
- Do something else you request
- Not hang out with some bad influences

Saying, "Thanks Mum!" or "Thank you Mummy!" when you say, he can pop out for a short while
Being nice to his sister(s) or younger brothers and maybe even playing with them when you want.

You can amaze a neighbour or relation when they come around by asking him does he want to go out to play footy in the garden or stay and help with some housework and the visitor be amazed when he asks to help you with some housework (with or without an apron is up to you)!

A female neighbour can help bring your boy under control, him dreading a secret/photo getting out
If you have a male partner/husband – he might not agree to the things you have your boy do and so a female neighbour can help to have him doing some of your ironing or her housework for.

Whether you take it as far as the girls or mothers/ladies in this book, is up to you, though the boys, do bring a lot of laughter and giggles to them and many girls.

Girls birthday parties

Once a boy has come under control of a girl or girls, he'll look forward being invited (NOT) to lots of little girl's birthday parties – as the only boy dressed in a party frock, having to mince around and being teased by all the little girls!

Calling happy birthday to the girl and having lots of the girls telling him, they'd invite him to their parties too and him dreading it. However, Pam then thought if they have some niece's birthdays, they can bring Nancy up and most will be completely oblivious.

An example of Tom being embarrassed

Pam is making her big bro Tom 8 do whatever she wants and one of the things she does is make him change into various panties, when he gets home from school. She is kind though and let's him go out to play with his mates. However, he has to ask her 'Please Pam, can I where your pretty pink frilly panties, out to play footy with my mates?' to which she can give a range of replies.

However, Pam then realized, she might not be there, all the time, when he got home from school. Hence, she asked her Mum would she deputize for her, but then giggled, as she asked her Mum, to ask to see his panties, before she said, yes. Once she'd got her Mum to agree, to checking his panties, she then got Tom to one day, not have any panties on, when he dropped his trousers, but have them in his handbag,

She told him that their Mum had to put them on for him, before he asked and then went out to play. She then extended this to him, not seeing the panties, till she put them on, to hilarious consequences.

PRELUDE — SUGGESTIONS OF WAYS TO HAVE FUN WITH YOUR BROTHER OR BOYFRIEND

Imagine a situation where a macho **young boy** who would normally be football mad, sometimes playing with his trains or building Lego, but wanting a skateboard for his birthday, suddenly starts helping his Mum or sister or other little girls and their Mum with the housework. Slipping into a **pretty apron** to help with the **housework**, whereas he'd normally have screamed blue murder and thrown a tantrum, had his Mum or sister asked him, to help with the washing up or any kind of housework. He starts playing **skipping** or even **dollies** in secret, with his sister or girls next-door or even playing **dress up** and **ballet**. Why you may ask is he letting his sister control him. To his mates he's the same macho bullying boy they've always known, playing football and cowboys and Indians or whatever, but in secret in the house, under the control of his sister or other girls, or even his Mum, he's doing something girly to amuse them. This doesn't just apply to **7 or 8 -year old young boys**, but to **teenagers** and **men** too., but they will be even more embarrassed at what you make them do – (see the full book)

You just have to find some way to get a **young boy** under your control and **he'll end up doing anything you want.** Not by violence, but by embarrassments and gradually increasing this to higher levels. **You start off small, but you can gradually increase his embarrassments,** bit by bit, each time, his 'fun' gets him into more and more embarrassing situations. Imaging a 7 or 8-year old boy slipping into a pretty apron and popping out back to **wheel his dolly around the garden, a handbag dangling from his arm** as he minces around the garden, with his arm outstretched looking a complete sissy. Even more embarrassing if he's to slide his arm or arms out the sides to do extreme mincing.

He's not a sissy, but is being coerced into doing anything his sister, or girlfriend asks and is blushing bright red, dreading being spied by neighbours or anyone else. However, imagine the embarrassment he'll have it **he's not 7 or 8, but a 12 or 15 o16 year old boy** doing the same thing, wheeling his dolly about the garden, with his **handbag** dangling from his arm as he minces around in a **frilly apron**. See the full book for this and more!

You can have him in a **pretty apron** and teach him how to curtsy with it, gripping the sides of the apron and **bobbing down to curtsy** and then tell him that any time you or his Mummy speaks to him, he's to **bob a sweet curtsy** and when you give a signal to him, he's to say, to his Mum, "**Mummy I'm practicing my curtsies with my pretty apron, so I can play curtsies properly with Suzie later!**" causing your Mum to giggle and curtsy back and probably say, "It's much easier in a skirt or frock dear!" He can have fun in **hair ribbons** – in a frock, but even when in boy's clothes, coming down for breakfast before school in ribbons, where he'll look a real **sissy**.

You can then enhance his fun to popping him into a **pretty frock over his trousers** and **show him off to a neighbour or girlfriend** and him being given the choice of removing his frock or trousers, he'll say, he want to keep his frock on and is having fun. You – the reader, may say, that any macho boy would rather remove his frock, to walk about as a boy, but any boy in the same situation, will ask to keep his frock on and sound a complete sissy. Why? You may ask – He's dreading the lady or girl, spy what undies he's wearing. However, all this could apply to your macho husbands too, with even more embarrassments felt, as you show him off to **neighbours** or even around the **shops**.

There are **many storylines** involving several young boys, but then teenage boys and even men (full book) and how girls or ladies, get control of them, with **them willing to do almost anything they want**, due to them **dreading embarrassing secrets be let out**. The embarrassments felt, can get ten times worse for **teenage boys** or **men** due to things not applicable to younger boys. Here's some **IDEAS**

Girly Aprons

Wearing a pretty apron to help you and your Mummy with the housework –
- If he complains- get **a small apron** from when you were very young to teach him a lesson
- For any wet work- get a pretty PVC apron from a few years ago – so it looks silly on him
- Hence, he wears a **PVC pinny** over floral cloth one for washing up or pegging out clothes
- Teach him to **curtsy** with his aprons, any time his Mummy or you speak

Complements with Curtsies and Kisses

Dependent on age– kisses can be embarrassing for a boy especially if doing something girly
- Little girls like kissing –, but not little boys especially from their Mummy
- Little boys normally hate kisses from their sisters or Mummies
- Even boys of 9/10 who starting liking girls or teenagers hate kisses from their Mummies
- You make him complement a girl, a lady, his Mum or you on your look
  - Imagine him in a pretty apron, but having to complement a girl/lady about her skirt, dress, apron or handbag
  - to which he receives a curtsy and then receives a kiss
- But you then complement his pretty apron,
  - to which he's to bob a curtsy back and kiss you
  - but of course, you tell him
    - it's much easier to curtsy in a skirt or frock
    - as you demonstrate with your own.

Housework

Get your young girl's toys to **play housework** – dolls tea set, washing bowl, vacuum cleaner
- Teach him how to do vacuuming with **toy vacuum,** peg out some skirts and frocks, etc.
  - using the toys and telling him off when he does something wrong
- Then to the **real housework** – washing up, vacuuming, dusting, polishing, laundry
- Hanging out washing or just clothes to air, using a handbag to hold his clothes pegs
- Bring a lot of handbags out to the garden for him to wash and peg up on the line - After washing a handbag, he's to mince it around the garden before pegging it up.

Nighties

Make him wear a **pretty nightdress to bed** – initially without his Mum knowing
- Then get him to let your Mum spy him in his nighty – causing her to giggle
- If she doesn't like it and tries to stop you, let him wear PJs till she has checked
  - He's then to remove his PJs and get back into the nightdress and panties
- You can make him wear the nighty under his boy's clothes for playing footy too
- Don't let him tuck it into his trousers and so he's to hide it with an apron around the shops

Skipping and other girly games

Get him to join you and a girl to play skipping out the back or in the street
- Just skipping around the garden or using a rope to
- Make up a girly rhyme to sing out to embarrass him while skipping
- Ring a ring of rosies – where he's to fall down, with you or some other girl
- Doing handbag twirls with handbags dangling from his elbow, doing spins
- Sissy tag, where he's to chase you and girlfriends about in apron and carrying a handbag

Dollies

Make him **play dollies** – with you and then your Mummy – sometimes when you are out
- **Carrying a dolly about the house** from room to room and then tie a handbag to it
- Get him to say, he's played dollies since **3 or 4,** stealing your dollies to play with
- He's to **wheel his dolly** around the garden in your dolly pram and then a real pram
- To ask his Mum to play dollies, but give her some big clothes to treat him as a dolly
  - Saying, his dollies are too small for her big hands and puts a frock on him
- Get him a dolly carrier to show his dolly off

Shoppers and handbags

Adding a **pretty shopping basket** to his arm and then **handbag** too for mincing
- Saying, its good practice for helping Mummy with shopping to hear him wail
  - "I'm not carrying a girly basket around the shops!"
    - but you say, about his handbag
- Swapping his baskets and handbags for other shopping bags and handbags to mince about the house or garden
- Have him do **handbag twirls,** with his handbag dangling from his elbow as he spins
- If you get him shopping with his Mum, you can get him to hold your basket or bag
  - You can take him over to help you choose a skirt, dress or handbag
- Make him have a **pretty apron on,** under his jumper or over it, hidden by his jacket
  - Then when you reach the shops, cut, buttons from his jacket to expose it

Saying, girly things

Saying, girly things to you, your **Mummy or female neighbours**
- Mummy that's a pretty skirt or dress, is it new?
- Mummy can you get me a tutu to play ballet with Suzie
- Mummy can you get me a new dress – and after a pause - for my dolly

Dress up

Get him to join you to play dress up -
- Making him play **dress up** with you in your bedroom
- Then in front of his Mum who may or may not like it and may stop you from continuing –, but you can find a neighbour to let you continue teasing him
- If she won't – you can be helped by the **neighbour** to play dress up with him
- Him asking to play dress up in his **Mummy's clothes** – slipping into shoes and bras
- Getting him to ask his Mum to buy him a skirt or dress to help play dollies with you

TOOLS TO BRING YOUR MSP BROTHER OR SON UNDER CONTROL

A boy won't normally want to slip into a pretty apron, play dollies or mince

What are the tools of the trade to let the girls take control of the weaker gender?

Candidates for being brought under control

1. First and most important tool is having a proper MCP (Male Chauvinist Pig) boy or man
   a. Who refuses to help with the washing up or help with any kind of housework?
   b. Running a mile from any kind of apron, especially one of your girly aprons
   c. It's not as good if it's a girly effeminate boy or man as there is little embarrassment

2. Try to not rush things! Take things slowly, when having fun with your boy, man
   a. Once you've him under your thumb – keep it secret from his friends
   b. So! To his mates, he's the same macho boy they've always know, but in-doors …

3. Ensure that when you eventually out him–making him wear a girly apron or frock outside
   a. That you have a girl or lady with him– at all times
      i. So, he's not picked on by other boys or men
   b. If you hear or see a boy being nasty to your sissy brother or boyfriend, then
      i. They should be an ideal subject to trap + get under your thumb as a lesson
      ii. Imagine the bully boy having to slip into a frock to apologise to your bro

THE TOOLS -

Frilly girly aprons are a major tool when it comes to embarrassing boys or men

1. Slip up behind him and slide a frilly apron over his head and quickly tie it
   a. If he reaches back, to try to remove it, you tie his hand(s) behind him
   b. Taken out a back garden a handbag slid around his neck and photos taken
   c. You tell him he's to help with washing, as you take pegs from his handbag
   d. Maybe add a headscarf to stop neighbours realising its him, in a frilly apron
      i. But then add hair ribbons and take photos of him, maybe with a smiling neighbour who has spied him.
      ii. After a while, ask why he wants ribbons,
         1. what's he disguising himself as - a girl

2. Make him give girls or females complements
   a. To which he gets curtsies and a kiss
      i. But when in an apron – he's complemented
         1. and has to bob a curtsy and give a kiss
   b. He's to complement his dolly
      i. Then she gave, him a complement
         1. He's to curtsy back and give her a kiss

3. You can use a **shirt** with its sleeve cuffs tied or sewn together behind him.
   The same applies to a **blazer or jacket**
   a. You, your Mum or a neighbour, pretend to have a new shirt or jacket
   b. You get him to remove a jumper and he can try it on over his own shirt
      He slides his arms into the sleeves, as you, button or tie his shirt at the front and he's trapped, with his arms pinned behind his back, at your mercy.
   c. He can then be dressed up in aprons, skirts, hair ribbons + photos taken.
      Imagine your MSP coming down next morning sliding his sister's apron on
      Asking Mummy can I help you with the washing up or housework
   d. He'll beg her and you not to tell and be willing to play dollies or dress up

4. It doesn't have to be a shirt with its' sleeve cuffs tied together
   a. It can be his school blazer or a jacket
      i. With a couple of pieces of string tied to the front out of sight
         Once he slides his arms in and is trapped
         Quickly take the 2 strings at the front and tie them together
         He should be trapped and unable to escape
         He's then free to slide into pretty aprons, hair slides etc.

5. Young boys love of playing footy and wanting to show off with the ball
    a. Tell a boy that you girls, want someone to teach them to play football
       He joins you in a back garden, where he sees some young girls and a ball
       Then a couple of older - bigger girls come from the house to join you
    b. He's trying to show you how easy football is – dribbling + passing the ball
       However, they get him down, onto his back and hold him down,
    c. He's tied into an apron and a handbag slid up his arm tied to the apron
       Given the choice of going out to the street or playing Sissy Football
    d. You stop him being recognised by adding a headscarf or ribbons

6. Sewing some frills and lace to the inside of a pair of his shorts
    a. See him run out, oblivious to girly frills which soon appear

7. If you can get him into a nighty then he'll then be at your mercy
    i. Though this is much easier for Mum's to do with your Daddy's. As explained in the full book

Once trapped

8. If you've your brother or boyfriend with his hands bound behind his back
    a. Tie a frilly apron around him, but then remove his trousers and undies
    b. You pull a pair of frilly panties up and then a pair of trousers to hide them
       But the trousers came from a charity shop and have a hole in the front
    c. Take photos of him and threaten to show his mates| girls at school unless
    d. Hence, when taken down to show his Mum, he can't remove his pinny
       Even to go out to the back garden and eventually the street or the shops

9. Get several pieces of string and if when his hands are behind his back
    a. Slide basket handles up one hand + tie it to a pram or dolls pram handle
    b. Slide handbag handles up his other hand + tie his hand to side of trousers
    c. You can cut the string or ties, sewing his hands together behind his back
       You can slide the basket handles up his arm and sew it up to his shoulder
    d. You can tie string to his wrist and move it to raise hand up to shoulder
       His handbag can be slid down to his elbow so he's ready to mince along

LEVELS OF CONTROL (FOR HIS MOTHER OR SISTER)

Once you have your boy willing to cow-tow to your requests
You have options on how you want him to look, to the neighbours etc.

0: Your boy just willing to do the washing up and a little housework in doors without any kind of an apron.

1: Your boy just willing to do the washing up and a little housework in doors with a boy's apron.

2: Your boy just willing to do the washing up and a little housework in doors with a boy's apron, but a PVC pinny over it for the dishes.

3: Your boy just willing to do the washing up and a little housework in doors, but also the laundry without any kind of an apron.

4: Your boy just willing to do the washing up and a little housework in doors, but also the laundry with a boy's apron.

5: Your boy just willing to do the washing up and a little housework in doors, but also the laundry with a boy's apron with a PVC pinny for any wet work.

6: Your boy just willing to do the washing up and a little housework in doors with a girl's apron.

7: Your boy just willing to do the washing up and a little housework in doors with a girl's apron and a girly PVC pinny to protect it for the dishes.

8: Your boy just willing to do the washing up and a little housework in doors, but also the laundry with a girl's apron.

9: Your boy just willing to do the washing up and a little housework in doors, but also the laundry with a girl's apron and a pretty PVC pinny for any wet work.

10: Your boy just willing to do the washing up and a little housework in doors, but also the laundry with a girl's apron, but a pretty **headscarf** as a disguise

11: Your boy just willing to do the washing up and a little housework in doors, but also the laundry with a girl's apron, but a pretty **hair ribbons** as a disguise

12: Your boy just willing to do the washing up and a little housework in doors, but also the laundry with a girl's apron + PVC pinny, but a pretty **headscarf**

13: Your boy just willing to do the washing up and a little housework in doors, but also the laundry with a girl's apron, but a pretty **hair ribbons** as a disguise

14: Your boy just willing to do the washing up and a little housework in doors, but also the laundry with a girl's apron + PVC pinny, but pretty **hair ribbons**

15: Your boy just willing to do the washing up and a little housework in doors, but also the laundry with a boy's apron with a PVC pinny for any wet work and a **shopping basket/bag** to hold his clothes-pegs

16: Your boy just willing to do the washing up and a little housework in doors, but also the laundry with a girl's apron + PVC pinny, but a pretty **headscarf** + and a **shopping basket/bag** to hold his clothes-pegs

17: Your boy just willing to do the washing up and a little housework in doors, but also the laundry with a boy's apron with a PVC pinny for any wet work and a **handbag** to hold his clothes-pegs

18: Your boy just willing to do the washing up and a little housework in doors, but also the laundry with a girl's apron + PVC pinny, but a pretty **headscarf** + and a **handbag** to hold his clothes-pegs

19: Your boy just willing to do the washing up and a little housework in doors, but also the laundry with a girl's apron + PVC pinny, but pretty **hair ribbons** + and a **handbag** to hold his clothes-pegs

20: Your boy just willing to do the washing up and a little housework in doors, but also the laundry with a girl's apron with a PVC pinny for any wet work and a **handbag and purse** to hold his clothes-pegs

21: Your boy just willing to do the washing up and a little housework in doors, but also the laundry with a girl's apron + PVC pinny, but has a pretty **headscarf** + and a **handbag and purse** to hold his clothes-pegs

22: Your boy just willing to do the washing up and a little housework in doors, but also the laundry with a girl's apron with a PVC pinny, but pretty **hair ribbons** + and a **handbag and purse** to hold his clothes-pegs

23: Your boy just willing to do the washing up and a little housework in doors, but also the laundry with a girl's apron with a PVC pinny, but pretty **hair ribbons** + and a **handbag and purse** to hold his clothes-pegs, **wheeling his dolly** around the garden between pegging each item of the washing

GIRLY GAMES

Once he's under control

Ring a ring of rosies

Curtsies
- And girly PVC pinny
  - With ribbons
    - Carrying a dolly
    - Carrying a handbag
    - Carrying a handbag and dolly

Dollies tea party
- And girly PVC pinny
  - With ribbons
    - Carrying a dolly
    - Carrying a handbag
    - Carrying a handbag and dolly

Playing house
- Play ironing
- Play vacuuming
- Washing up
- laundry

Play shopping
- And girly PVC pinny
  - With ribbons
    - Carrying a dolly
    - Carrying a handbag
    - Carrying a handbag and dolly

Skipping around the garden
- In a girl apron
  - And girly PVC pinny
    - With ribbons
      - Carrying a dolly
      - Carrying a handbag
      - Carrying a handbag and dolly

Girly Games - continued

Sissy Football
- And girly PVC pinny
  - With ribbons
    - Carrying a dolly
    - Carrying a handbag
    - Carrying a handbag and dolly

Sissy Tag
- And girly PVC pinny
  - With ribbons
    - Carrying a dolly
    - Carrying a handbag
    - Carrying a handbag and dolly

Sissy Laundry
- And girly PVC pinny
  - With ribbons
    - Carrying a dolly
    - Carrying a handbag
    - Carrying a handbag and dolly

Pass the handbag with the music stopping at certain times
- Whoever has the handbag has to mince around the garden or up the drive

Dollies – dressing/undressing – carrying about/ wheeling in dolly pram

Dress up – in pretty skirts and dresses – play dress up in Mummy's clothes/shoes

Ballet – doing pirouettes as you spin with your aprons or skirts with arms above head
- In skirt or dress
- In tutu skirt
- In tutu dress

TAPE RECORDING OF SISSY OR GIRLFRIENDS

You can have fun listening to lots of tape recordings, of your sissy brother or other boy you have under your control, by having the tape running, recording him, hidden under your bed, or wherever and then can listen to it before bed etc.

You can even adjust the tapes and have another recorder, to modify the recording, to fit whatever purpose you want.

> Can I
> Play dollies
> Play dress up
> Play ballet

Mummy will you buy me

> A pretty basket to help you shop
> A handbag
> A purse
> A frock
> A tutu
> Hair ribbons

Babying your Sissy using recordings.

Making your sissy wet his panties – leading to nappies and plastic baby pants, etc.
However, he will be dreading you let a girlfriend into the house or room to see him dressed up or playing dollies, etc.

You invite some girlfriends over to your place to play dollies, without him being around and make a recording of some of them. It could be just the general sound of their voices, or you try and get them to say, certain things for you. Once you have these recorded, like mentioned above, you can take a second recorder and select parts of their recordings to modify certain phrases to scare him silly.

Hence, when you bring him into a room to play dollies in your panties and maybe a frock or pretty apron, but you might want to have some plastic down on the carpet or a changing mat down. You then switch on the recorder, but have a gap so after a minute, he suddenly hears girls' voices saying,

> Pam! Who is this?
> XXX, Can I come in?
> XXX, Can I play too?

Causing your sissy to wet his panties – leading to Nappies and plastic baby pants!

GIRLY SAYINGS

Once he's under control

- He's to ask his sister to let him skip with her
- Ask her to let him play dollies with her
- Ask her to let him wear hair ribbons or bows
- Ask her to let wheel his dolly around the garden
- Mummy will you teach me how to do the housework in a pretty apron
- Mummy can I help you with the housework in my pretty apron
- Mummy can I help with the laundry in my pretty apron
  As your Mum Says, well don't forget your PVC pinny
  However, she might show him a fun way using a basket/handbag for the pegs
- Mummy will you teach me embroidery
- Mummy will you teach me to crochet
- Mummy will you teach me to knit
- Mummy will you teach me dress making

Get his Mum to have a female neighbour around visiting
If you have taught him or trapped him by using Sissy Football
In a pretty apron, with a handbag dangling from his arm and hair ribbons

You invite a neighbour around and ask
XXX which would you rather do – go out to play football (Sissy Football)
Or be a good boy and slip into your apron to help with the dishes/housework

GIRLY SAYINGS - CONTINUED

Of course, he'll dread going out to look a sissy boy kicking the ball and amaze the neighbour by donning the pretty apron and ask to do housework When he appears in a pretty apron and has to say "Thank you Mummy for showing me how much fun a pretty apron is to help with the dishes and housework!" As the neighbour laughs and his Mum bobs a curtsy "Thanks XXX!" but Says, "Come here a tick!" and then "That deserves a kissy!" as she kisses him, to a gasp from the neighbour. However, then your Mum Says, "I'm glad you're enjoying your pretty apron, but don't forget your pretty PVC pinny, if doing any wet work, like the dishes or laundry!" as he Says, "I won't Mummy!" as she Says, "Here's some dishes and cups here! Why don't you run the water and do some washing up now, to show my friend, what a good boy you've turned into!" as the neighbour gasped and giggles. He has to pop into his pretty PVC floral pinny over his girly apron and then run the water and start the washing up, with the neighbour coming in to join his Mum and laugh at his girly look.

After the dishes, you could arrange with his Mum that she tells him he's to pop around to get Sally next door and to remove his aprons. However, he can't as he'll be displaying frilly panties, a nighty or something even more embarrassing if he removes both aprons. Hence, the visitor is amazed when he Says, "It's ok Mummy! I'll keep these on to pop around to get Sally!" but adds "I'll just make sure nobody is around!" as the laughs "Oh is he shy?" as he nods and they see him slip out nervously checking the street and stop when he spies someone and his Mum sees it's a girl, so tells him to get around., but if it's a boy, she lets him wait till their gone and head around after.

Another time or a bit later, he thanks his Mum for showing him how much fun dollies are as he walks in holding a dolly in front of the neighbour, of course begging her not to tell on him, as she giggles., but then scolds her for not getting him dollies when he was a little boy to play with, not to mention a dolly pram, to screeches from the female visitor.

Making him give complements to the lady or girl who has to bob a curtsy back along with a kiss
But then when in his apron, he's complemented for his pretty apron and has to bob a curtsy back along with a kiss of course

RHYMES FOR LITTLE SISSIES — ONCE YOU HAVE THEM UNDER YOUR CONTROL

Once your brother or other boy willing to done aprons, play dollies or dress up with you, then you should realize you can get him to say, anything you want to your Mum, a neighbour, a female relation, a girlfriend or girl's at school. Hence, another fun thing to do is to make up rhymes for him to memorize and to have to repeat to whichever girl or lady you wish. You should make them short, as they will be more easily memorized by him, but it also means you can create tens if not hundreds of them over the years to embarrass the boy. You create them to the rhythm of a popular children's song or rhyme or make up your own. Note, the verses don't need to rhyme, but it's a lot better and funnier if they do. He could say, them while skipping, before bed in his nighty or ….

Examples

1:
I'm a

Little sissy boy, sissy boy, sissy boy
I'm a

Little sissy boy
XXX is my name

I love

Dressing my dollies, in pretty skirts and frocks, pretty skirts and frocks
I love

Dressing my pretty dollies

C

I love

Dressing my dollies in skirts and dresses, skirts and dresses, skirts and dresses
I love

Dressing my dollies in skirts and dresses

C

I love

Carrying my dollies, around the house, around the house
I love

Carrying my dollies around the house
In a pretty apron

I love

Wheeling my dollies, in their dolly pram, in their dolly pram

I love

Wheeling my dollies around the garden

C

I love

Skipping around the garden, around the garden, around the garden

I love

Skipping around the garden
With ribbons in my hair

I love

Wearing pretty pinnies, pretty pinnies, pretty pinnies,

I love

To protect my pretty aprons

C

I love

Wearing frilly panties, frilly panties, frilly panties

I love

Wearing frilly panties

C

I love

Wearing pretty ribbons, in my hair, in my hair, in my hair

I love

Wearing pretty ribbons and bows

C

I love

Mincing with my handbag, with my handbag, Mincing with my handbag,

I love

Mincing around the shops

C

I love

Wearing skirts and dresses, skirts and dresses, skirts and dresses

I love

Mincing around the shops

C

I love
     Playing Sissy football, in a girly apron, girly apron, frilly apron
I love
     Playing Sissy football
     Mincing with my handbag

I love
     Helping Mummy with the laundry, with the laundry, with the laundry
I love
     Pegging up the washing
     Taking pegs from my handbag and purse

I love
     Wearing a dress and pinafore, dress and pinafore, dress and pinafore
I love
     School in a dress and pinafore
     Mincing with my handbag

C - All day long

2:
I'm a little sissy boy XXX is my name,
Playing with my sister's toys playing girly games
Playing dollies and dress up any time she wants,
Playing footy with my mates, to try and look non girly,
Looking and sounding a normal boy kicking the ball about,
But having to wear frilly panties hidden in my trousers,
Often with a pretty apron hidden by my jumper,
Dreading my sister play a joke and show me off as a girly whirly

3:
I love playing dollies, dollies are my game,
Dressing and undressing them trying not to get a name,
Wheeling them in her pink doll's pram, initially in the house,
But soon I was wheeling her around and around the garden,
Dreading neighbours spying me and teasing me something rotten
Carrying a dolly from room to room, to please my little sister,
She adds a pink handbag to my arm, to enjoy mincing better
Dreading being seen by anyone, but especially mates from footy,
But she helps my disguise with hair ribbons to stop me looking a sissy

4:
I'm looking forward to getting back to school,
     Wearing a dress and pinafore
     Wearing ribbons in my hair
     Skipping in the garden

Carrying my books in a pretty shopping bag
Carrying my books in a large pretty handbag
Doing cookery with the girls
Doing needlework with the girls
Doing dance with the girls
back to school

5:
I'm a little sissy boy (Not!) Dollies are my game
Carrying my Wendy doll from room to room trying not to get a name
Sometimes wheeling her around the back up and down the garden
Dreading being found out and teased something rotten
Wearing pretty aprons indoors and outback
To heighten my blushes As, my pretty sister, insists I carry out her wishes
Washing up the cutlery and the dishes Wearing pink rubber gloves and pinny
Looking a right sissy ninny
Sometimes she asks, do I want to stop carrying my dolly when I nod
Am rewarded with a pink dolly carrier attached to my pinny to hold my dolly
And told that will teach you for being a sissy ninny in a pinny
Taken out to wheel my pink pram – dreading who can see me
She taught me to mince with my arm outstretched – like she learns at ballet
Adding a handbag up my arm to the elbow to carry
Hating my girly look when a female neighbour spies me mincing
Saying, I should wheel my pram around to hers to have fun prancing
Using a handbag to hold my clothes-pegs Pegging out the washing
When out playing football with my mates
She'll sometimes wheel my dolly past in her dolly buggy
But she Says, 'Don't worry sissy! I'm sure Lucy will wheel u back home dolly
When teatime comes and my mates go home
There in the garden – what do I spy, but the pink pram with my dolly –
My sister opening the window and telling me to pick her up and carry her in
Wheeling the pram – I beg to no avail and dread who will see me
But on picking up my dolly - I then see my dolly is tied to a frilly pinny
But she also has a handbag tied to it,
And told if I want in, I've to don the apron and slide the handbag up my arm
And turn to bob curtsies checking up and down to make sure it's clear
I pull the apron over my head and slide the handbag up my arm
Before bobbing curtsies to the street trembling with fear
I then look over across the street to see a laughing neighbour.
In her own pretty apron, bobbing curtsies back
My laughing sister Says, I should pop across to ask her not to tell on me
But adds ribbons and a headscarf to disguise me
As I have to push her dolly pram quickly across the road to the laughing lady

6:

I'm a little sissy boy – I'm a little sissy boy – XXX is my name
(I'm a little sissy boy – I'm a little sissy boy) repeat with
Who likes to wear a pinny
Who likes to play dollies
Who likes to play skipping with the girls
      In the back garden,
      in the street
Who wheels his dolly in it's pram
      Around and around the house
      Around and around the garden,
      Up and down the street
      Down to the shops
      All around the town
Who likes to wear ribbons and bows in his hair
      Around and around the house
      Around and around the garden,
      Up and down the street
      Down to the shops
      All around the town

Who likes to play dress-up
      Mincing in a pretty skirt and blouse
      Mincing in a pretty frock
            Carrying a pretty
                Shopping bag | Shopping basket | Handbag
            Around and around the house
            Around and around the garden,
            Up and down the street
            Down to the shops
            All around the town
Who likes to wear pretty panties and an apron
Who protects his panties in case of accidents
      With plastic baby pants
      With plastics and nappies and a big diaper

7:

I love pegging out the washing, or clothes to air, clothes to air,
      Wearing a pretty apron and PVC pinny
      Wearing a pretty tabard apron
      With the pegs in a pretty
            shopping bag
            shopping basket
            handbag
            purse
            purse, closing up my handbag before mincing around the garden

Have him repeat a girly rhyme while skipping

I love playing ballet, it looks so much fun
Pirouetting around the room in a pretty leotard and ballet skirt
Copying my sister or girls at school spinning on one foot
But even more when in a pretty tutu ballet dress

As you write more and more rhymes, you will probably find yourself getting better at the rhymes to make it easier for your sissy to remember.

8:
I love wearing pretty aprons to help my lovely Mummy,
Asking what housework she'd like help with, in my little pinny,
Bobbing a little curtsy, making her laugh and giggle,
Especially if while doing the dusting and polishing, I give a little wiggle,
When doing any wet work like dishes or the washing,
I've been taught to protect my pretty apron with a PVC pinny,
But she offers me a disguise, so I don't look a ninny,
Wearing a pretty headscarf or ribbons in my hair,
As I'd rather neighbours think me a girl, than a little sissy,
However, she asks what I'm disguising myself as with ribbons in my hair,
As I eventually say, a girl and so she calls me Missy,
She sometimes asks what do little girls like to wear, as she bobs a little curtsy,
As I stammer skirts and dresses and am rewarded with a frock.
Change the words of a girly rhyme when playing a girly game
Ring a ring of rosies a pocket full of posies, with a sister or one of her girlfriends
        I kiss you (instead of a tissue)
        I kiss you (instead of a tissue)
We all fall down
Playing football with some girls or his Mum or ladies in the back garden
But it's Sissy Football

8 YEAR OLD TOM'S STORY - TOM AND PAM

He's a bully and MSP – considering housework is girls work

Tom is a bully to his sister Pam and a MSP about housework

Tom is a bit of a bully to his sister Pam and never helps their Mum or Pam with the housework, not even with the washing up, considering only girls do that. Pam plays a trick with his shorts and their Mum sees how easy it is to bring him under control and so traps him, when Pam is out, but Pam accidently discovers what she's done and the gloves are off, with her putting him into more and more girly situations.

Pam tricks Tom into wearing frilly shorts and then fibs to girls that he's a sissy boy

> **Pam traps Tom by sewing lace and frills to the bottom of his shorts**
> **Pam gets a young girl to watch for his frilly knickers showing**
> **His mates get him down and Pam tells him he's not to wear her panties**

Main Story =

Pam sews lace and frills to the inside bottom of Tom's shorts

With Tom – a young 8-year old boy, his embarrassments came about due to him bullying his sister Pam 7 and never helping her or their Mum with housework, thinking only girls did that. Pam was tired of him calling her names like Ug and hitting her arm or pulling her hair, if he thought she was annoying him. She thought of a trick to play on him, to teach him a lesson, not realizing what it would lead to. She got a pair of his shorts into her room and carefully sewed some white lace and pink frill to the inside, near the bottom, with it naturally hanging down an inch below the bottom. However, she ironed the frills up, so that they initially would stay hidden, but gradually fall down to show his frills while he ran about. She split them at the sides, as she realized his shorts, were loser around the back, compared to the front and so he wouldn't realize anything was showing, till it was too late.

One day she made sure she had got home from school before him and hid his other trousers, leaving this one pair of shorts in his drawer and knowing he normally changed into shorts to play footy with his mates. Tom comes home after school and slips upstairs to change out of his uniform, into the shorts and comes down saying, to his Mum he's off out to play footy with his mates.

Tom removes his school uniform and slips into the shorts for football

Pam appears in her pretty apron and Says, "Not want to help Mummy and me with some housework?" as he says, "Ha Funny Ug!" and thumps her arm with her Mum telling him off, but not punishing him. He has a quick drink of Coke and a few biscuit's and exits, getting his football from the garage, he runs out to find some mates. Pam complains "Mum you should get Tom to help with the housework too!" but his Mum laughed "You know he'll just throw a tantrum!" but "Pam Says, - I owe Tom, for being nasty to me and have a plan to teach him a lesson!" as her Mum said, "Watch it, he'll hit you!" as Pam said, "Can you make sure he doesn't?" adding "threaten to smack his botty if he hit's me!" as her Mum laughed "Now Pam! I only do that if he's very naughty!" as Pam laughed "You should make him help with the housework!" but then Says, "If he can't find an apron, I've some sweet pinnies, he'd look lovely in!"

Pam said, "I'm just popping out, but might pop around to Alice's in the next street later, once I've paid Tom back for hitting me!" as her Mum asked, "How?" as she giggled, "Wait and see!" as she exited and saw Tom with a couple of mates, kicking the ball about down the street.

Pam and a young girl sit down to watch Frilly Knickers Tom

She saw a young 5 year old girl Tammy in the street and called her over and asked, "Want to see something funny?" as the girl nodded, and she said, "Do you know my big nasty bro, Tom?" as she nodded, and heard Pam say, "We'll just go down and watch Frilly Knickers playing with his mates!" as she giggled, "Do you call him that?" as Pam said, "Don't say, anything, but we'll sit down and watch him playing with his mates, for a short while!" as they walked down and sat on a wall, nearby the boys.

She heard Tom call "Pam you bug off – we're playing here!" as she laughed "It's a free country, Tom!" as she watched and saw nothing had shown yet, from his shorts. She talked to Tammy, saying, "Keep an eye on my big bros shorts at the back and you might see something pink and white!" She giggled, "What frilly knickers!" as Pam laughed "Keep quiet, till we see!" as they watched him run about after the ball and slowly, but surely, she spied the frills come down, at the back of his shorts and giggled, "Look Tammy can you see frilly knickers - Tom!" as she giggled, "Yes I see!" as Pam walked down towards the boys and again heard Tom tell her, to bug off.

She whispered to one of his mates, if you can get Tom down on his back, I'll show you all, something funny!" as Tom looked and wondered what she was doing. He was about to ask Pam, when he felt his mates pulling him down, on his back. Tom cried "What to heck are you doing?" when Pam and the little girl appeared and she said "I've told you Tom!" adding "You aren't to wear my frilly knickers outside for football or going shopping or pushing your dollies around in their dolls pram, without asking!" She fed her hand down to the bottom of his shorts at the front and pulled the frills out.

His mates get him down and Pam shows his frilly panties

The little girl giggled, "Frilly Knickers Tom!" as the guys laughed and Tom cried "I'm not!" but then sat up and looked down, dismayed at the sight. He cried "What to hell's that, Pam?" She and the little girl ran off a She fed her hand down to the bottom of his shorts at the front and pulled the frills out, as he got up and heard his mates say, "You can see them at the back of your shorts now too!" as he cried "I'm not wearing her knickers!" as his mates called "Frilly Knickers Tom!" He got up and went to run after Pam, but started sobbing, with embarrassment and ran back into the house to tell his Mum. He ran in crying and his Mum asked, "What's wrong, Tom?" He said, "Look what that witch Pam, has done!" as he turned to show his Mum the frills at the back and then turned to face her and pulled out the frills at the front, causing his Mum to gasp, but then giggle "Oh Tom! I heard her say, she wanted some pay back for you hitting her!" but added "No calling her names!" as she giggled, "Oh Tom!" as he

wailed "and she showed my mates and a little girl too and said, "I was wearing her frilly knickers and they started calling me 'Frilly Kickers Tom' too!" She inspected the shorts and laughed "She said, she wanted some pay back, on you, but didn't tell me, what she'd done!" as she pulled his shorts down and off, leaving him in his underpants. She laughed "The naughty girl, must has sewn some lace and pink frills, to the inside of your shorts! Didn't you notice, when you were putting them on?" as he shook his head "No way! Those weren't showing when I pulled them on! You'd have seen and my mates too! They must have come down, while I was running about!" He said, "I'm going up and cutting those lacy bit's off!"

She laughed "You'd better prove to your friends you weren't wearing her panties! Go up and get a pair of trousers and then you'd better take these out and show your mates, how she tricked you! Adding and that little girl too!" as he said, "I don't know, where she lives!" Her Mum said, "I think Pam said, she'd be popping around to Alice's, I think it's Number 16 the Gardens!" He went upstairs and changed into his trousers, checking there weren't any frills on them, first, before pulling them on. He did them up and picked up the shorts, grimacing at the sight, as he pulled them inside out. He went downstairs and held out them out to her, saying, "Well give me a bag to hide those away in!" as his Mum went to fetch a carrier bag, but on seeing one of Pam's yellow handbags, she appeared with her hand on her hip and the handbag dangling from her arm and asked, "Will this bag do, Tom?" as he huffed "Very funny Mum!" as she handed him, a plastic carrier bag and saw him hide the frilly shorts away. He blushed as he exited and on reaching the street, heard his mates call "Oh Frilly Knickers is in his trousers!" as Tom huffed "Funny! Wait to you see what my stupid sister, did to my shorts?" He pulled them from the bag and turned them inside out and showed his mates. They gasped "'Gosh what a nasty trick!' She really stitched you up!" as the other mates laughed "Get it? Stitched you up!" as his mates laughed "You owe her!" as he said, "I'll get her and Mum will give it to her, for playing that nasty trick!"

Pam goes to Alice's with the little girl and fibs about him being a sissy

One of the guys said, "Tom! We won't laugh! Why don't you get back into them! It might be fun to play in frillies!" as he called "You watch it Jamie!" adding "I'm serious!" as they laughed. Pam and Tammy had run around to Alice's and they were led up to her bedroom where they told her about Frilly Knickers Tom. Pam said, "I got Tammy to join me, watching my nasty big bro Tom play footy with his mates! We were watching, when we saw his shorts were showing his frilly knickers, at the back!" as Alice gasped "Never! Does he wear your frilly knickers?" Pam nodded, "I try and keep it a secret, from his mates! but he hit me and so I owed him one!" as she gasped and giggled, "He doesn't wear your skirts and frocks too?" as Pam nodded, "I keep having to tell him off, for slipping into my pretty frocks and playing with my dollies too!" as Tammy giggled, realising she was fibbing, to Alice. Alice giggled, "Gosh I'd never have thought your big brother, was a sissy!" as Pam laughed, knowing she was on a roll - "He tries to keep it a secret from his mates and at school, but loves wheeling his dollies around the back garden, where he can only be seen, by us or the neighbour June!" Alice laughed "What in a frock too?" as Pam laughed "Not always, sometimes he likes a skirt and blouse!" as they giggled, and Pam said, "He adores handbags and often helps Mum and me peg out the washing using his!" Alice asked, "What do you mean?" as Pam said, "Mum has shown us, how to pop our clothes pegs, into a handbag for pegging out or collecting in the washing and Tom loves mincing about the back garden, carrying his, but Mum let's him wear a headscarf, or my ribbons so he's not so recognisable as a sissy boy!" to more giggles and laughter from Tammy. She added "I'm sure, if he comes around!" not thinking she'd see Tom around at Alice's, she continued "He'll love to help you and your Mummy peg out the washing, as your garden is bigger and more open than ours!" She added "Now! He insists on wearing, a pretty frilly apron, when doing housework and a pretty PVC pinny to protect his apron and dresses if the washing is wet, or any other kind of housework, where his frocks might get wet!".

Alice called her Mum up and when she entered her bedroom she said, "Pam's been telling us about her sissy big brother Tom!" as her Mum laughed "Pam stop teasing him! What does he do?" Alice said, "He wears her frilly

knickers and skirts and frocks too and plays with her dollies pushing them around the back garden in their dolls pram!" as her Mum laughed "Oh Alice! I bet she's joking!" Pam said, "Tammy! Didn't we see Frilly Knickers Tom, playing and showing off his frillies, to his mates?" as Tammy nodded, "He had big frilly knickers under his shorts!" and they called him Frilly knickers Tom!"

Pam tells them the fun way to do the laundry using a handbag for his pegs

Alice said, "Apparently he likes to slip into pretty aprons over Pam's frocks to help her and her Mum with the washing and loves handbags too!" as her Mum laughed "He doesn't?" Pam said, "Mum's taught us to put our clothes pegs into our handbag, so we don't have to bend down, to get the pegs, from a bucket on the ground!" as her Mum laughed "We'll have to use handbags, for our washing from now on!" as Alice giggled, "Especially if Frilly Knickers Tom, comes around to play dollies with me!" as her Mum laughed and said, "Pam! This is a joke!" adding "Isn't it?" Pam said, "Ask Tammy?" as they giggled. Pam Says, "Anyway! Mum tells him, that using his handbags, for the washing, will be a good help, for taking him shopping, to use his purse and handbag, around the shops!" as they screeched with laughter. She added "Mum makes him, zip his handbag up, between getting a peg, or putting some back, so when we go shopping, he'll know to close his handbag after use, so his purse isn't stolen from his handbag!" to more laughter.

Tom thumps her complaining to his Mum wrt her sewing lace to shorts

However, when Pam was heading back, he was looking out for her from her bedroom and on seeing her around the bend, he went downstairs and hid behind the chimney stack. Pam went to ring the bell but saw Tom at the side door and heard him call "Mum wants you in this way!" She got up to the side door and Tom punched her arm hard and yanked her hair really hard and called "You witch! Bloody well sewing frills to my shorts and then showing me off to my mates!" as Pam cried "Mum Tom hit me! And it hurt!" with real tears in her eyes and saw him run off out the drive to join his mates at football again.

She entered the side door and her Mum heard her call "Mummy! Tom thumped me and pulled my hair really hard, just because I played that trick on him earlier!" as her Mum cuddled her and sat her down saying, "I've warned him not to hit you!" adding "He'll get a spanking when he comes in for that! "as Pam said, "You know it never does him any good! He just ignores you and does what he wants!" adding "He never helps us with the washing up or housework! You should make him!" as his Mum said, "He'd just scream blue murder!" Pam said, "Seeing he didn't like wearing frilly shorts and looking girly, you could play on that and make him wear something of mine!" as she added "Maybe one of my pretty aprons and PVC pinnies, to do the washing up or housework!" as her Mum laughed "Now Pam! Keep your clothes away from your brother!" as Pam wiped her eyes and said, "What a fab idea Mum! Pop him into one of my skirts or frocks!" as she gasped and heard her add "I bet he'd not run out to play footy with his mates if he was wearing something really girly!" as her Mum laughed "Now Pam! Stop that!"

His Mum spanks him and he's to apologize for hitting Pam

Tom returned from footy and his Mum said, "Right young man! Follow me or else!" as he sobbed "Mum! I owed her for that trick, she played on me earlier and the teasing I got from my mates, about wearing her knickers and them calling me Frilly Knickers Tom!" as his Mum said, "That's no excuse for hitting her and yanking her hair!" as she led him into the bedroom and pulled down his trousers and underpants, she pulled him down across her lap and spanked his bottom hard. Tom sobbed "Not fair Mum! You should spank her, for her horrible trick on me!" She let him up and said, "Right get dressed and wash your face! Then come downstairs and apologize to Pam for hitting her!" He dressed again and washed his face, thinking "Now bloody fair!"

He descended the stairs and saw Pam, sitting there and cried "That wasn't funny Pam about those shorts!" as he said, "I've shown my mates and they realize, the horrid trick you played on me!" His Mum said, "Apologize to your sister, for hitting her and pulling her hair!" as he grimaced and mumbled "I'm sorry!" but his Mum stood there and looked sternly, at him and said, "Look at your sister and don't stammer!" as he huffed "I'm sorry for thumping you and pulling your hair!" as Pam gasped "Never having heard him apologize before and laughed "I didn't hear that! Say, it again!" as her Mum said, "Now Pam! He's said, sorry!" She said, "I don't want to hear of you hitting Pam again like that or else!" as Pam added "And Mum Says, you've to help with the dishes and housework!" as he said, "No way! You can stick the dishes where the sun don't shine!" as his Mum said, "Watch it Tom, or you get another smack!"

His Mum then said, "I thought you were going around to Alice's to show them Pam's trick on your shorts!" as he huffed "I didn't like the sound of going around there and several girls being there to jump me or something!" as Pam laughed "What Tom! You were afraid that us little girls, might try and dress you up?" as her Mum laughed "Now Pam! Stop teasing!" Pam laughed "Now Tom! I owed you for hitting me and calling me names!" as her Mum said, "Now Pam! No more sewing frills or stuff to your brother's clothes!" as she said, "Oh Mummy! I need practice with my embroidery and sewing skills!" as he huffed "Ha! Funny ha!" She then said, "Mum! Boys should learn needlework too! You should teach Tom to do embroidery and maybe some knitting and even dressmaking!" as he cried "You bug off Pam!" as her Mum laughed "Now Pam! You're pushing it with Tom!" as she laughed "Needlework is good fun, especially making your own frocks!" as he ran to catch her, and she ran upstairs and locked her bedroom door. Tom ran up after her, but heard her door shut and lock, as he called "I'll get you later!"

Pam calls "Little Tammy thought you were wearing my knickers and told some of my other girlfriends" as he cried "Oh no! Who?" adding "Didn't you tell them it was a joke?" as she laughed "If I don't go around soon to tell them all, they'll all be telling other girls and boys at school about Sissy Tom or Frilly Knickers Tom!" as he sobbed "Please tell them Pammy!" as she said, "You promise not be nasty to me anymore?" Tom cringed and said, "Ok!" but then her add "And help Mummy with the housework!"

Pam tells her Mum the fib she told the girls, but must tell them the truth

Tom cried "No way! That's flaming girls work!" as he stumped into his room. Pam thought she was safe from him, for a while and so unlocked her door and opening it, she popped downstairs and into the kitchen. She entered and picked up her favourite pink apron, but also a pretty PVC pinny too and popping into the living room, saw her Mum and said, "Mum! Tom's promised to be nice and not hit me!" adding "But Says, he'll help us with the dishes and housework from now on!", but she then added "I'll lend him an apron and pinny to help us!" as she gripped her apron and bobbed a curtsy, to her laughing Mum. Her Mum gasped and giggled, "Now Pam! Stop teasing Tom about your pretty aprons and pinnies!"

Tom came down and saw Pam and their Mum and cried "Pam! Please go around and tell them!" as his Mum asked, "What?" as she laughed "He's wanting me to go back to Tammy's and Alice's and tell them, that he's not a sissy boy and doesn't wear my frilly panties!" as she laughed "Why?" as she laughed "Little Tammy told them that Tom was wearing my frilly knickers and I forgot to tell her it was a trick!" adding "So at the minute they all think, he likes to be a girly!" as she gasped "What do you mean?" as she laughed "I possibly hinted he played dollies with me!" as he sobbed "Oh no! Pam you didn't?" as he ran upstairs, sobbing to his room.

Her Mum said, "You naughty girl!" as Pam laughed "I suppose I'd better bring the shorts around to show them, my little trick!" as her Mum said, "You'd better!" as she laughed "It's well he can't hear this bit!" as her Mum asked, "What?" as she laughed "They asked me if he wore my skirts and frocks and I kind of hinted he did!" as her Mum gasped "Oh no Pam! That will be terrible, if it gets out around here and especially the school! You head

around now!" adding "You're in big trouble if it gets out!" as she said, "Ok Mum!" adding "Where are his frilly knickers? Sorry I meant frilly shorts!" His Mum fetched them and held them out and saw her pop them into her yellow handbag. She exited and her Mum laughed, as it was the same handbag, she'd offered to Tom, to hold the shorts, when he was proving to his mates, he wasn't a sissy. She called him down the stairs and said, "I've sent her around to show the girls and tell them it was all a trick and you're not a sissy!" as she laughed "She's hidden them away in that yellow handbag I offered you!" as he blushed "Funny!" She added "It would be terrible, if it got out!" as he huffed "Yea! With girls thinking I flaming play dollies with her!" as she laughed "I think it got worse than that!" adding "I think Tammy suggested you played dress up in her skirts and frocks!" as he cried "I'll flaming kill her!" as his Mum hugged him and said, "Look!

No being naughty! Don't you dare hit Pam or any of her friends!" adding "or I bring Pam back and you might very well end up, in one of her frocks playing dollies and wheeling them about the place in a pram!" as he sobbed "Not flaming fair, Mum!" She giggled, "You wouldn't like that would you?" as he shook his head "It would be horrid Mum!" She said, "Pam's going to tell them all it was her joke and that you're not a sissy!" adding "She'll show them the shorts" as he huffed "They'd better not tell or tease me later!" as she said, "I'll get Pam to ask them not to mention it again!"

Pam calls at little Tammy's house and tells them Tom's not a sissy

Pam called at Tammy's and rang the bell. Her Mum came to the door and called "Tammy! It's Pam!" adding "What's this I hear about your brother being a sissy!" as Pam laughed "Actually I'd played a joke on him!" as she took the shorts from her handbag and turning them inside out showed her. Tammy came into the room and giggled, "Hi Pam!" as she laughed "Mum's sent me around, to show you the trick I played on Tom!" as she asked, "What?" as she saw the shorts and laughed as Pam explained "I took his shorts here and sewed lace and frills, to the inside legs!" as her Mum laughed "So Tom's not a sissy!" as Tammy laughed "Oh Poo! I was looking forward to playing dollies and dress up with him!" adding "Wearing one of Pam's frocks!" as they giggled, and Pam pulled the shorts up under her skirt and removing it, she showed her Mum saying, "Tom came home from school and changed out of his uniform into these, without checking!" as her Mum laughed, as she saw the frills and lace and giggled, "What a wonderful trick!" as Pam explained "I turned the shorts inside out and ironed the frills up, at the front and back, cutting them at the sides and got Tammy to join me, watching Frilly Knickers Tom. Her Mum laughed "Oh the poor boy!" as Tammy called "We sat down and eventually saw some frills show from the back of his shorts!" as they laughed, but then heard Pam say, "I asked one of his mates, to get him down on his back and I insinuated, he was wearing my frilly knickers and they believed me, too!" adding "Didn't you Tammy?" as she nodded, "I thought he was wearing them and played dollies and dress up with you, Pammy!" as her Mum laughed "Oh! That was a naughty trick!"

Pam said, "Now! Around to Alice and tell her and the other girls, about Frilly Knickers, not being a sissy!" as she pulled her skirt back on and was about to remove the shorts, when she laughed "Why not? Just to let me experience the fun, Tom had wearing them, to play silly football!" as they all laughed. She took her handbag and said, "I suppose us girls could join the boys playing football!" but slid her handbag over her elbow and said "We could play Sissy Football and tell Tom, to play you must mince with a handbag on your arm and wear an apron or skirt or dress with ribbons being optional!" adding "Or frilly shorts!" as Tammy and her Mum screeched with laughter.

Tammy's Mum was wearing her apron in the kitchen and Pam laughed "That could be part of the uniform for Sissy Football!" as she asked, "What Pam?" as she gurgled "One of my frilly girly aprons and maybe a really girly PVC pinny on top!" as Tammy's Mum giggled, "Oh Pam! Could you imagine your bro wearing a girly apron and pinny to play footy!" as Pam nodded, "With a handbag dangling from his elbow and hair ribbons and Alice band in his hair!" as they screeched with laughter. She then added "Even better if instead of my big aprons, it was Tammy's

6

little ones, which would really look stupid and girly on him, to more laughter and giggles. Her Mum laughed "I might get her a football and we'll get her young friends to play in their aprons with handbags, while kicking the ball about!" adding "So they'll be experts at Sissy Football, for when you send your big brother around to play with them!" as they screeched again.

Pam heads around to Alice's to show her the trick she'd played on Tom

Pam gasped "Are you serious?" and saw her nod and kissed her bye. Tammy kissed Pam bye and her Mum opened the front door to show her out, with Pam mincing along and up the street, with her handbag, dangling from her elbow. Tammy and her Mum gurgled at the conversation they'd had with Pam, as Tammy returned to playing with her dollies and her Mum in the kitchen. Pam skipped around to the Gardens and rang at Alice's house. Her Mum came to the door and smiled as she saw Pam, standing there and asked, "What have you been up to, Pam? Not playing dollies or dress up with your big brother?" as Alice came to join her, followed by a few other girls, that were there when Pam and Tammy told about sissy Tom. They were led into the sitting room, as she said, "Mum wasn't pleased about me telling on Tom!" as she laughed "Actually it was all a big fib!" as her Mum laughed "I thought so!" as Alice cried "Oh Pam! We were all thinking how much fun it would be, playing dollies and dress up, with your big sissy brother!" as she laughed "I've just been around at Tammy's and she'd said, the same thing, but I can now show you, the naughty trick, I played on my nasty big bro!" as she raised her skirt and then pulled it off, as she showed them the shorts.

They all giggled, and heard her say, "Mum suggested he bring them around here to show, the trick I'd played, but after showing his mates that he wasn't a sissy, he thought twice about showing you girls!" as her Mum asked, "Why?" as she laughed "He thought with you and us girls, we might get him down and dress him up and he'd be really under our control, to play dollies and dress up all over the place!" as they all screeched with laughter. She said, "I was tired of Tom hitting me and never helping Mummy or me with housework! Not even the dishes!" adding "He considers it girls work!" adding "As part of the deal, for me telling you girls he's not a sissy, he's promised to stop hitting me and hopefully will join Mum and me, doing the dishes and housework!" as they laughed "Oh Pam!"

She said, "So what I did was, I took a pair of his shorts, here and sewed some lace and frills to the inside of each leg and then ironed it up, so that he wouldn't realize, till it was too late!" as she pulled the frills out from the shorts and heard them giggle "What a fab trick!" as she said, "I saw him exit in the shorts, but the naughty boy hit me again, when I suggested he help Mum with some washing up and so that was it! His goose was cooked!" as they laughed as she continued "I then saw Tammy playing and enlisted her to join me, watching Frilly Knickers playing footy, with his mates!" as they laughed. She said, "We sat down and soon enough, his frills came down at the back, unseen by his mates, for a while!" adding "However, I whispered to one of them to get him on his back, to give them a laugh!" as Alice and the girls gurgled, but her Mum gasped "You showed him off to his mates?" but Pam said, "It was ok! Afterwards Mum got him to take the shorts out in a carrier bag, to show them my trick!" as she laughed "That's ok then!" She giggled, "When he was down, I pulled the frills from the bottom of his shorts and told him off for borrowing my frilly knickers and playing dollies and dress up with me!" as her Mum gasped "Oh Pam! It could get out to school!" as she laughed.

Pam suggests they play Sissy Football together to prepare for Tom

Pam said, "That's why I'm showing you girls now!" as they laughed and Alice said, "What a fab trick Pam, to play on your nasty bro!" as Pam laughed as Alice asked, "So he doesn't even play dollies, with you?" as she laughed "He'd break them, if I even showed him one or put one near him!" as they laughed "Your Mum should stop him and make him play with you!" as another girl asked, "He doesn't even play dress up?" as they screeched and saw Pam shake her head and heard her say, "I wish! It would be great to have a hold over him and make him play dollies

and dress up and lots of other girly games with me and my girlfriends here!" as they all laughed and a young girl said, "Oh poo!" Alice gasped and ran to the phone and rang around to Jen, a girlfriend and said, "You know that Sissy boy Tom, I told you about, wearing panties and playing dollies and dress up?" as she laughed "Yes! Why?" as she laughed "His sister has just come back around to tell us, its' all a fib!" as she gasped "Oh drat! I was looking forward to playing dollies with a big boy, in a frock and taking him shopping!" as Alice screeched and heard her friend call "Mum! It's all a fib, about that sissy boy Tom!" as her Mum laughed and said, "I thought so Jen!"

Alice said, "His sister Pam here, apparently was practicing her sewing and accidentally attached some pretty lace and frills to a pair of his shorts, ironing them up, without him knowing and he changed into them, to join his mates playing!" as her friend giggled, "Fab Alice!" as she continued "Next thing her and Tammy were sitting down to watch her brother and sooner or later, they saw the frills appear, at the back of his shorts and then she got the boys, to pull him onto his back and she then pulled out the frills at his front and told him not to borrow her frilly panties, without asking!" as Jen screeched "Fab trick! I'll have to try it on my big brother!" as she called "She's still here and is telling us something else to have fun and tease boys with!" as Jen called "Ring back later! Bye!" as she said, "I will!" and rang off.

Luckily Jen hadn't told any girlfriends, but had tried to phone one Julia, but she was out and so she'd luckily for Tom, had not had any time to tell anyone else. Alice joined Pam and the girls back to hear Pam say, "It's about us girls playing football!" as they all called "You must be joking Pam!" and Alice said, "Count me out!" as Pam explained "The idea came to me while wearing FKs shorts here, but carrying my handbag that we could play Sissy Football, but to join us, you have to carry a handbag, wear a skirt or frock and hair ribbons and Alice band are optional!" as they laughed as she said, "I then saw Tammy's Mum in a pretty apron and thought instead of skirt or dress, initially a pretty apron and possibly PVC pinny on top could suffice, so as not to totally embarrass the boy!" as they laughed, as she said, "We could practice ourselves initially kicking a ball about, but eventually get a boy to join us!" as they asked, "What for?" as she laughed "We can pretend we're starting a football team and need an expert to show us!" adding "We'll tell him, the other boys said, he was the best!" She continued "So he joins us in the back garden and sees a little girl or two with a ball kicking the ball about and runs to join them! Telling us how easy it is to dribble or pass the ball!"

Pam tells the girls how they can trap a boy to being, a sissy to play dollies

They listened and asked "What next?" She laughed "If then bigger girls appear and get him down on his back!" as they laugh "And do what?" as she giggled, "We slide an apron onto him and tie it up behind his back and then slide a handbag up his elbow and tie it to the apron and he'll be trapped!" as they screeched. She continued "He wouldn't dare run out into the street, to be seen in a girly apron and carrying a pretty handbag!" adding "And he won't be able to remove either handbag or girly apron, which are tied together and so he'll be trapped at our will!" She then thought "Though the poor boy will be dreading being recognized by neighbours, or houses at the back and so we'll be kind and offer him a disguise!" as they asked, "What?" as she laughed "A pretty headscarf!" as Alice asked, "Hair ribbons!" but she said, "Slowly does it girls! Start off with the headscarf, to give him more of a disguise!" She then said, "We then start kicking the ball about, with us all wearing pretty aprons and mincing with our handbags, too!" adding "Although, we'll have our hair ribbons of course!" as they giggled.

Pam then Says, "However, after ten minutes or so, of playing Sissy Football with Tom! I mean the boy, we chose first to join us playing footy!" adding "We ask him why he wanted the headscarf!" as they laughed and she replied, "He'll of course say, to stop the neighbours recognizing him, as a sissy boy!" but added "We then ask him what he was disguising himself as!" as she asked, "So girls what would our macho boy reply to that, question!" as they screeched and said, together "A girl!" as she nodded, and laughed "After which we can of course help our little sissy's disguise, by popping him into a skirt and then a dress and then maybe, something instead of his smelly undies!" as they screeched and Alice's Mum said, "Now girls! No touching his trousers or undies!" as Pam laughed

"Well if you are there, to help us, we'll let you pop his frilly panties on, in place of his smellies!" as she blushed "Pam! You are so naughty!" adding "You mean I'll have to remove his trousers and then his underpants and pop him into panties?" as she nodded, as Alice laughed "Bags second!" as her Mum said, "No way, Alice!" as several other girls called "Bagged third!"

Pam laughed "Once we have the boy under our thumb, with a few photos dressed up in skirts and dresses, he'll be willing to play dollies, dress up and anything else we want!" as they giggled, "Fab Pam! When can we try with your, Sissy Tom?" as she laughed "Now girls! Just try playing footy together and get reasonable, so when the boy joins us, we won't look silly!" adding "At the minute, if any one of us, tried to kick the ball, we'd look silly and so we'll get ourselves some practice playing Sissy Football, till I give the word and we try on Tom or should I say, some boy of our choosing!" as they laughed and patted her on the back, saying, "If this works Pam, it will be great, having girly boys to play dollies and dress up with!" as Alice giggled, "Not to mention, shopping with his handbag and baskets, girls!" as they screeched at the thought. Pam laughed "We can eventually get him playing ballet too, but then get, several of his mates dressed up too!" as they screeched "Oh fab!"

Pam gets Tom to help with the washing up and wear her PVC pinny

Pam leaves and returns home and after having their dinner, she said, "Tom's promised to help with the washing up!" as he cried "I didn't?" as she asked, "Want me to tell the girls to ignore, what I said, and treat you as a sissy?" as her Mum said, "Now Pam!" but she then said, "They had plans to have you join them playing dollies!" as he huffed "No way!" as she added "That wouldn't be so bad, but it's what you'd be wearing while wheeling your dolly about the street, that might be a little embarrassing!" as he asked, "What?" as his Mum said, "Don't, Pam!" as she took her skirt and bobbed a curtsy to him and said, "Or even a frock!" as he said, "No way, Pam!" as her Mum said, "They couldn't make him!" as Pam laughed "Want to bet?" as she laughed "He'd probably end up wearing a pretty frock out shopping!" as she laughed and saw her Mum's handbag and stood up, she lifted it and said, "Carrying one of these!" as her Mum said, "Now Pam!" as she laughed "And guess what you'd be wearing underneath your skirt or frock?" as her Mum said, "No way!" as Pam gurgled "Frilly Knickers!" and so you would actually be Frilly Knickers Tom!" as he sobbed "Not fair Pam!"

His Mum said, "Tom! Just help with the dishes tonight ant that will appease Pam, for a while!" as Pam huffed "He should help with housework, too!" as her Mum said, "Slowly does it, Pam!" as she huffed "Not fair! He should do everything we do, like the washing up, dusting and polishing and the laundry too!" as her Mum laughed "Now Pam! Let's try the washing up, tonight!" as she said, "Ok! He washes and I'll dry!" as he huffed "Ok!" but added "He's to do it like us! Ok Mum?" as she wondered what she meant, as she said, "Ok! Pam!"

Their Mum ran the hot water and poured the Fairy liquid into it and soon it was bubbling and ready for him to start. Pam pulled a turquoise apron around her, over her blouse and skirt, but then held out her pink floral apron to him and heard him say, "No way!" but her Mum went and fetched his blue and white, boy's cookery apron and held it out for him, as he cried "I don't need a flaming apron!" but she said, "Either this or you will wear Pam's pink apron!" as he huffed "Not fair!" and took the apron and pulled it around himself. He said, "There!" and approached the sink and took a few plates and set them into the water. However, Pam said, "Mummy you've said, he must do it like you or I!" as she reached for the back of the door and took a floral PVC pinny, as her Mum gasped "Pam! He's being good and wearing an apron!" but Pam insisted and said, "Mum you promised!" as his Mum took the pinny and tied it around him, as he sobbed "Mum! Get that off me!" as she said, "It will only be for a short time, while doing the dishes and I'll help too!" as she took a large PVC pinny and tied it around her own apron!" as Pam laughed at him in her girly PVC pinny, as he said, "Where's your pinny?" as she laughed "I don't need them for drying! It's only for washing up, you need a pretty pinny!" as he said, "I'll dry then!" but she said, "No way, girly!" and tied his pinny in another tight knot, to his trousers, saying, "Remove your pinny and your trousers come off, to show me your frilly knickers!" as he cried "I don't wear them!" as his Mum laughed "Come on Tom and I'll get

you out of your aprons after!" Pam laughed "Oh Mum! Can't he play dollies with me, in his pretty pinny?" as he blushed and said, "No way, Pam!" as her Mum took some pink rubber gloves and pulled them on, but then took a pair of Pam's yellow gloves, as he cried "No way! I'm not wearing rubber gloves!" as they laughed.

Tom pulls on Pam's yellow gloves and helps his Mum washing up

Pam said, "If you don't, I'll bring Julie and Tina, to sit and tease you silly, while you do the washing up and then play dollies!" as he sobbed "Not fair!" and pulled the yellow gloves on and started the washing up. Pam let him wash a few plates and cutlery and was doing ok, when she went to the living room and returned and asked, "Mummy! We should stop hairs, getting onto the plates!" as she held up a pink headscarf, towards him, as he cried "No way, Pam!" as her Mum laughed "Now Pam! No! He's doing well, so let him be!" as she laughed "Just trying to help his disguise from the neighbours at the back, seeing him!" as he realised and tried to pull them closed, but his Mum stopped him and heard him cry "But they can see me!" as Pam giggled, "Oh Tom! If you try my scarf on, they won't recognize you!" as she held it out again to him, as her Mum laughed "Oh Pam!" He looked up and said, "Nobody looks to be there, so I don't need it now!" as she shrugged her shoulders, but then said, "What's going to happen, when you help with the laundry!" as he said, "I'm not going outside, wearing a flaming girly apron!" as they laughed and his Mum said, "Pam! We'll keep any housework indoors!" as she huffed "Mummy! We have to go outside to do the laundry and so should Tom!" His Mum said, "Take it slowly Pam! Let him get used to doing some in doors first!" as she laughed "My headscarf will be ready, if he asks me sweetly for it!" as he said, "No way!" as she laughed "You might, if you don't want to be disguised, if a lady or girl is looking down on you wearing my pretty aprons!" as he huffed "After this! It will be just my apron to do housework!" as his Mum said, "Yes Pam! He only needs a PVC pinny, for any wet work!" as she laughed "Ok, Tom!" adding "And my pretty headscarf or ribbons, when he's being spied by neighbours!" as her Mum laughed.

Pam said, "I'll be back in a minute!" as she slipped upstairs and fetched her camera and hid it away in her apron, for to get photos of Sissy Tom, in her PVC pinny. She returned and was drying some plates and cutlery and said, "See Tom! It can be fun to do the washing up!" as he huffed "Ha!" His Mum was doing more washing than him, but Pam noticed and said, "Come on Tom! You've to do more washing! Mum's done most of it!" and said, "Mum! You rest!" as her Mum sat down to leave Tom, to do more of the dishes. He huffed "Not fair!" as he continued, but heard her say, "Wash the plates properly, Tom!" and so he washed the plates a bit harder, to laughter from his Mum. He thought he'd finished, but then Pam said, "What about the saucepans?" adding "Do you think the washing up, fairies do them?" as he blushed and huffed "Funny!" and so had to work on a saucepan. He huffed "This is hard!" as she laughed "Mum! He'll need more practice!" as she laughed "Right! I'll finish up!" as Pam huffed "Oh Mum! He was having fun!" as he tried to remove his aprons and reached around to untie his aprons, when Pam took the apron ties and tied his hands up.

Pam ties his hands and pops him into the headscarf and photographs him

Tom cried "Oh no!" as Pam giggled, and taking the headscarf, she reached up and tied the headscarf around his head, under his chin, as he cried "Oh no! Get it off me, Mum!" as his Mum turned and saw her boy, in the pink headscarf and giggled, "Oh Pam!" as Pam said, "Don't be wetting my good headscarf, Mummy!" as she said, "Sit down Tom and I'll get it off you, in a tick, once I've finished the saucepans and pots!" as Pam giggled, "Tom! Mummy will help you sooner, if you help her!" as he sobbed "How can I! You tied my hands behind my back, to my aprons!" as his Mum laughed "She didn't?" adding "I wondered why you were still in her headscarf!" as he cringed "Not fair! Take my headscarf off?" as she laughed and saw him sitting there, looking at his Mum at the sink, as she took the camera and took a few photos of him, in the pink headscarf and pretty PVC pinny over his apron!" She hid it away again, to stop him seeing it.

Pam laughed "Ok! I'll remove your headscarf!" as she thought "Pity I haven't got a tape recorder on, to hear him pleading to take his headscarf off!" She approached him and said, "Come on in and I'll remove your pretty headscarf!" adding "Mum! I'm just taking him into the living room, to remove his headscarf and knots in his aprons!" as her Mum said, "Ok Pam!" as she led him out of the kitchen, where she closed the door and led him into the living room and heard him say, "Hurry up Pam!" but then whispered "Actually upstairs!" as she led him up the stairs, smiling at him looking girly, in the pretty headscarf and pinny, as their Mum continued with the washing up. Pam led him up to her bedroom and locking the door, sat him down by the window, as she said, "Keep quiet or I tell on Frilly Knickers!" as he cried "Oh no! I'll be seen!" as she laughed "Don't worry! No-one will recognize you, with your headscarf!" but then added "Or Alice band and ribbons!" as she quickly removed it and taking her Alice band, she slid it onto his head, as he cried "Oh no, Pam!" as she gurgled "Now Tom! It's not the end of the world, looking girly!" as he lay down on his back to try and hide from view. She took the camera and took a few more of him, now in the Alice band, without him realizing. She then took some hair ribbons and fed them into his hair too, as he sobbed "Not fair!"

She smiled and realized her Mum couldn't protect him, or stop her as she took an elasticated skirt from a chair and seeing he was lying back on the bed, with his legs raised, she slid the skirt up his legs and then pulled him up, as he cried "Don't show me off Pam!" and quickly pulled the skirt up to his waste. He cried "Oh no! Not a skirt Pam!" However, she then slid herself under his skirt and he cried "Not my trousers Pam!" as she laughed and undid his trousers and the zip and pulled them down, as he cried "Not fair!" but then gasped, as he felt his underpants coming down. Pam giggle as she raised his skirt to let more light on the subject and giggled, as she saw his small willy on show and reaching up touched it, as he cried "Don't you dare, Pam!" as she tickled it, causing him to sob "Not fair! I'll tell Mum!" as she came out from under his skirt and laughed at her brother in her skirt.

Pam takes him to her room and pops him into a skirt, frock and panties

She opened a drawer and fumbling in found a pair of yellow and white, lacy frilled panties and turned around and showed him, as he cried "No! Not fair Pam!" as she fed them up his legs again and pulled him up on show to the window. She laughed as she slid them up again, touching his willy and then fed them over it, into place. She said, "I'll take you back from the window if you let me pop a frock on you!" as he sobbed "Not fair!" as he said, "Ok!" as she took the camera and he cried "Not a photo?" as she nodded, "Don't worry! I won't show, if you're a good boy!" as he huffed. She led him back from the window to her wardrobe and opening it, took a pretty pink frock out, as he cried "Oh no! That's really little girly!" as she gurgled "Oh fab!" as she said, "I wish I could see you wearing it properly, but will start with it slid over your bound arms!" as he quietly sobbed "Not fair! Please don't tell the girls on me!" as she laughed and kissed his lips as he cried "Oh no! I don't like kisses!" as she kissed him again. She took the pink frock and fed it down over his head and then down his body and gurgled as she fed it down over his skirt.

She clapped with laughter and took several other photos, of her sissy brother. She said, "Don't worry I won't tell and won't even make you do the washing up or housework!" as he asked, "Promise?" as she nodded. She asked, "Can I undo your arms to get you into the frock properly?" as she said, "Don't worry! When I take you down, you'll be dressed as a boy!" as he huffed "Ok!" as she laughed "Apart from your panties or Frilly Knickers of course!" as he cried "Not fair!" as she laughed "We won't tell Mummy!" as he blushed. She undid the knots from the apron strings and eventually had his hands undone and pulled the apron and pinny off him. She said, "Now any playing up and I tell!" as he sobbed "Ok!" and felt her pull the dress over his head, but then said, "Slide your arms into the sleeves again!" He fed him arms into the sleeves of the frock and fed his hands through, as she pulled the dress back down again and giggled, as she took more photos, but then removed his Alice band and hair ribbons, to look like a real sissy boy in a pink frock. She had him try to bob curtsies to her, as she took more photos.

She heard their Mum call them and she said, "Let's get you out of your frock and skirt and then down to show Mummy!" as she pulled the dress over his head and his arms out of the sleeves, as he was left in the skirt over the yellow panties. She said, "Right remove your skirt and back into your trousers!" as she said, "Remember! The panties stay on, till I get them back tomorrow morning!" as he sobbed "Not fair!" He pulled down his skirt and grimaced at the sight of his frilly panties and pulled up his trousers and did them up, pulling his zip up. She said, "Just tells Mum! I took ages to get your knots undone!" as he huffed "Ok!" and she kissed him again. She then said, "I want you to complain to Mum, about me tying you up and say, "Not flaming fair Mum! I don't want to do the dishes and won't let her tie my hands again!" adding "Complain saying, flaming several times protesting about your apron!" She added "You can even complain about me!" She said, "I will even let you hit me softly and I'll complain to Mum ok?" as he nodded, "Ok Pam!" as she unlocked her door and let him out again.

Tom must wear the panties under his trousers playing footy with mates

They exited and Pam took his underpants and slid into his room to hide them in his dirty clothes basket. She stopped him and asked, "What's your name, just for me?" as he said, "I don't know?" as she gurgled "Frilly Knickers Tom!" as he sobbed "Not flaming fair! I'm Frilly Knickers Tom!" as she kissed his lips and patted on his bottom to send him down the stairs. Their Mum heard them coming down the stairs and heard him complain "Not flaming fair Mum! She took ages to undo the knots in my apron strings!" as she laughed and saw him out of his apron and Pam's PVC pinny. She asked, "Not bring your aprons down!" as Pam said, "I'll get them Mum!" as she went upstairs. He sobbed "It wasn't fair Mum, making me do the washing up!" as she laughed "Oh Tom! It wasn't the end of the world!" as he huffed "I'll make sure she can't tie my hands back, like that again! She flaming-well took ages to get me untied!" as she laughed.

He sat down in the living room and heard Pam come down and leave the PVC pinny back in the kitchen, but then came in carrying his blue apron and handed it to him. He huffed "Thanks!" as his Mum asked, "Not leave his apron in the kitchen?" but Pam said, "Just in case he wanted to wear it to school!" as he gasped "What?" as she added "I meant for his cookery lessons!" as his Mum and him sighed, that it wasn't a tease.

He asked, "Can I go out to play footy?" as Pam said, "Ok with me, for being a good boy and helping with the washing up!" as his Mum laughed "See Tom! Pam's being nice too!" as he blushed and said, "I'll be back around nine!" as his Mum called "Ok Tom! Bye!" as he exited the front door, hating the fact he was playing footy, still wearing Pam's panties.

When he'd gone out, his Mum laughed "I hear you took a while to get the knots undone!" as Pam laughed "Yea Mum! When I saw his hands reach around to get himself, out of his pretty pinnies, I couldn't resist tying him up!" adding "Didn't he look sweet in my pretty headscarf and my pretty pinny, Mummy?" as she nodded, laughing, but said, "Now Pam! No more dressing him up!" as she gasped "Mummy! I wouldn't dare! He'd hit me!" as their Mum laughed, not realizing she had dressed him up in skirt and frock and hair ribbons. She said, "But he should help with the washing up and housework more!" as her Mum said, "Go easy on him! He's not used to it!" as they both laughed. They watched some TV film and Pam did some homework, as she knew she could make Tom do lots of things, but would take it slowly. She thought "I'll get him to be naughty and say, bad things to her and their Mum!" adding "She'd try and get their Mum to take the reins and think it's her who is controlling him!"

Tom had a good game of footy, even though he blushed a bit more than usual, especially when one of his mates mentioned 'Frilly Knickers' as he yelled "Look! You bloody well know, it was Pam who tricked me!" as another said, "Let's drop that guys!" and they continued playing without any other incident. He finally had finished the game and went up the street with a few of the guys and saw them continue, on up the street as he called "Bye" and entered his driveway.

Pam Says, the girls are going to play too but hands him a nighty for bed

He rang the bell and his Mum went up and let him in the door and said, "I've got the supper out, for the two of you!" as he went in and saw Pam in the living room smile towards him and ask "How was your game?" as he said, "Yea good! I scored a few goals!" as she laughed "A few of us girls were talking about taking up football too!" as he laughed "You must be joking! You girls are no good at footy!" as their Mum entered and Tom called "Pam made a joke, Mum!" as she asked, "What?" as she laughed "Her and some friends, are thinking of starting footy!" as her Mum laughed "Oh Pam! You tease!" as she laughed "Honest Mum! We were talking about it earlier!" as Tom said, "Us boys will always be, better than you girls!" as she laughed "We'll need some practice, but some time we'll have a game, against you boys!" as he laughed "No chance! You'd be in for a thrashing!" as her Mum laughed "I'll look forward to seeing you playing Pam!" as Pam laughed "Mum! We could maybe teach you too!" as she laughed.

Their Mum set out the tea and biscuit's and they all tucked in, with Pam kissing their Mum calling "Bye Mum!" and him going up ahead of Pam, he headed up to wash and clean his teeth. He went into the bathroom and did his ablutions and exited to see Pam put her finger to her mouth, for him to be quiet and whispered as she showed him a nighty and said, "Hide that in your bed, till Mum reads your story!" as he huffed "A flaming nighty!" as she laughed "Over your panties, for me to check in the morning or else!" but also heard her say, "PS You've to refer to me as Ug, to get told off, till I say!" as he said, "Ok Ug!" as she laughed and said, "Big kiss!" as he blushed as she kissed him and took the nighty into his room and slammed the door. Pam locked her bedroom door, taking the key with her and slipped into the bathroom and locked that door. She did her ablutions and unlocking the door, she slipped past his room and unlocked her bedroom door and entered, locking it again to undress and get into her nighty. He too undressed down to the panties and got into his PJs, until his Mum read his story when he'd to swap into Pam's nighty.

Pam ran down the stairs a bit and called "Mummy! We're ready for our fairy tale stories!" Tom heard and grimaced as he lay there in bed waiting for his Mum to come in. Their Mum knocked and heard him call "Ok Mum!" as she entered his rom and smiled at him, in his PJs and sat down on his bed to read him his story. He said, "Close the door Mum!" and saw her close it, as he huffed "Today was terrible, with Ug sewing those frills to my shorts and then showing me off to my mates and saying, I was wearing her frilly panties!" as he blushed, at realizing he was now wearing them, but she laughed "It was very naughty! but less of calling her Ug!" adding "If she hears you, she might tell!" adding "Although you might be ok, as they know she fibbed earlier, to them!" He blushed as she said, "That was good with you, helping with the dishes!" as he huffed "Think well of that!" as she laughed "Now! It didn't hurt!" as he huffed "It did! Only girls normally do it!" as she laughed "I bet your mates do it, too!" as he huffed "Ha!" as she laughed "Although you probably were wearing a prettier pinny, than them!" as he grimaced, with a large beamer, as his Mum laughed and red him the story.

Their Mum reads Tom and Pam their bedtime stories and fairy tale

She kissed him goodnight and turned out the light, closing his door, as she went into Pam's room and saw her lying there in her pretty nighty and asked, "How was Frilly Knickers?" as her Mum shut her door and said, "Now Pam! Less calling him that! You know, he doesn't wear them!" as she giggled, and thought to herself "Want to bet, Mummy?" as she said, "I'll read your fairy tale!" as she asked, "Did you read him the same one too?" as she laughed "I read him a bedtime story Pam! Less treating him like a girl!" as she laughed "Oh Mummy! He so hates looking girly!" as Pam laughed "If you'd have seen his face, when his mates got him down and I pulled the frills from his shorts! It was comical!" as her Mum laughed "That was so naughty, sewing frills to his shorts!" as Pam laughed "It worked out brilliantly!" adding "I removed all his other shorts and trousers, hoping he thought you had them in the wash!" as her Mum laughed "What! You only left him, the one pair and he didn't suspect?" as

Pam nodded and laughed. She said, "I couldn't believe it had worked, as I followed Tom out, getting a thump on the arm for something I'd said and so looked forward to his just reward as I joined little Tammy, to watch the lace come down on show from the back of his legs. She said, "I realized the front of his legs were tighter, than the back and so had cut the frills at the sides to separate the front from the back and it worked great!"

Her Mum read her the fairy tale and heard Pam say, "It was great, that he helped with the washing up tonight, but especially when I made sure he wore my pretty PVC pinny over his own silly boy's apron!" as her Mum laughed "I think he'll think twice about trying on your apron and letting you tie his hands up, like you did tonight!" adding "I couldn't believe, when I saw him in your headscarf!" and scolded "Now Pam! Tom's a boy! So no putting him in headscarves!" as Pam giggled, "Ok Mum! Hair ribbons then!" as her Mum gasped "Now Pam, less of that!" as she said, "Promise not to tell your girlfriends, about what happened today and especially tonight!" as Pam nodded, "I promise Mum!" but then said, "He still hasn't lost his MSP ways!" adding "When I released his hands from his aprons, he called me a flaming Ug and thumped my arm!" as her Mum gasped "He didn't!" as she turned out the light and closed the door, as she heard Pam lock the door, in case Tom came in. She thought to herself, she hadn't heard Tom lock his, but just went downstairs to watch some TV before heading down.

Tom of course had waited for his Mum to enter Pam's room and quickly turned on his bedside light, he removed his PJ jacket and trousers and then blushed, as he saw his panties in the mirror, but then pulled the turquoise nighty, over his head and turning out the light, he slid back into bed again. He lay there sobbing, about the terrible day and how Pam had tricked him and then after doing the dishes, he ended up in a skirt and then a flaming frock. He hated the fact, she had photos of him, dressed up and hoped she'd not show them to anyone. He then remembered her flaming changing his panties and touching his willy, as he blushed. Their Mum watched some TV and then went upstairs and got herself ready for bed and went to sleep, laughing at Pam's trick on Tom and the fact, he'd actually helped her with the dishes and worn her pinny too.

Morning and Pam slips in to take her nighty and panties back from Tom

Pam could have used her dressing him up to make him do anything she wanted, but she wanted her Mum to get involved and think she's the one, who he's afraid off. In the morning, she'd got up and gone down to do their breakfasts and called them, to get up for school. Pam got up and giggled, as she slipped quietly into Tom's room and smiled as she saw him turn, still in her pretty nighty. She laughed "Right Frilly Knickers, out and ten curtsies!" as he blushed and pulled the bedclothes back, he slid out of bed and saw her raise his nighty to check his panties, but gasped, as she laughed at the wet patch on the front and gurgled "Naughty baby wet his panties!" as he cried "It's just a little bit damp!" as she laughed "Maybe at some time in the future, I might have to invest in nappies and plastic baby pants!" as he gasped "Oh no!" as she gurgled "Only joking!" as she kissed him and said, "I'd better take my panties back, unless you want them for school!" as he blushed and pulled down her panties, but then he gasped as she pulled the nighty over his head, leaving him with his hands pulled down to cover his privates, as she giggled and took them back, closing his door.

He got himself dressed for school and exited to the bathroom to get himself washed and came down for breakfast, to see a smiling Pam, already down at the table, in her pretty apron, over her school dress and pinafore. She said, "Tom called me 'Ug' again, Mum!" as he cried "I didn't?" but his Mum said, "Now Tom! I wouldn't, in case Pam tells at school about her trick!" but she said, "Honest Mum! I won't!" as she said, "He's going to show me, how to play footy and I'll let him off, being nasty!" as she laughed and he gasped "Not fair!" adding "Well! It won't be in the street!" as Pam laughed "Ok! Deal!" They had their breakfast and went up to clean their teeth and then picked up their school bags - Pam with her yellow zipped up shopper and Tom with his satchel.

Tom asked, "Can I go on ahead?" as his Mum said, "Ok!" and Pam called "Bye Tom! Have fun at school" Her Mum said, "Remember Pam! No telling at school!" as she said, "Mum! I've promised and normally done even see him at school!" as ten minutes later, she left for school and joined a few girlfriends to chat about this and that. Tom had run on too and apart from spying Alice who saw him blush as he ran on past her, but luckily, she didn't say, anything about him. School went on as normal with Tom having good games of football and Pam skipping with her classmates.

They went home and their Mum had their refreshments ready and saw Pam enter first and kissing her Mum, she said, "School was fine!" as she headed up to change into the pink dress, he'd worn the previous night. Tom got in and his Mum asked, "How was school Tom?" as he called "Ok Mum!" adding "Is Ug in?" as Pam heard and laughed "Watch it! Get changed and ready for ten minutes playing footy with me!" as he saw her in the pink dress and blushed as he saw her and ran up the stairs saying, "Not fair!" He went into his bedroom and locking the door, he changed out of his uniform into his shirt and trousers and into his plimsoles. He bounded down and had a quick drink of Coke as Pam had mineral water and said, "Get your ball Tom and I'll see you out the back, as her Mum laughed "You were serious Pam?" as she nodded, "Told you so!"

Tom tries to show Pam some football passing in the back garden

Pam exited waiting for Tom to appear and saw him exit and enter the garden and kick the ball over to her. She took the ball and steadied herself and kicked it but skewed it a bit with Tom laughing "Ha!" as he ran and got the ball and said, "Try again and kick it to me, at the far end of the garden!" She steadied herself again and kicked it slightly to the left of Tom and heard him say, "Not bad!" They played along with him trying to help her when he said, "That's ten minutes up!" as she laughed "Ok!" as he asked, "Can I go?" but heard her say, "When I nod, you say, loudly "Ug! You're bloody hopeless!" as he shrugged his shoulders and kicked the ball a bit more.

as she waited till their Mum was looking out the window and heard him call it loudly!" as her Mum laughed and said, "Now Tom! It will take her a while to learn!" as he entered the side door. She asked "How did she do Tom?" He called "She's hopeless!" as his Mum laughed with him saying "I'm off to play footy with my mates!" as he exited the front door. Pam ran in saying, "He could have stayed another five minutes!" as her Mum saw her enter and laughed "Not the traditional football uniform dear!" as Pam curtsied to her and laughed "I might help him learn to play something in return!" as she asked, "What?" and heard her giggle "Dollies!" as she said, "Don't you dare, Pam!" as she laughed "Got you Mum!" as she ran up to her bedroom and peered out, to see Tom with his mates, but giggled, as she thought of him, running about in her pretty apron, maybe eventually over a frock, mincing with a handbag while kicking the ball.

Pam came down and saw a few cups and glasses and asked, "Want some help with the washing up?" but her Mum said, "I can leave that till after dinner!" as Pam laughed "Maybe Tom will help, like last night!" as her Mum laughed "I don't think you'll get him into an apron again!" as she laughed and said, "Ok Mum! You and me can do them, but he shouldn't be such a MSP and laughed "I know what you could do, to make him change!" as her Mum asked, "What?" as she laughed "If I'm out and you ask him to do the washing up and he makes some sexist comment, you know how he hated wearing my pretty apron and a headscarf?" as her Mum laughed "You mean I pop him into your girly apron and headscarf!" as Pam laughed "If he's very naughty and rude you could help him enjoy himself, by popping the apron over a pretty frock!" as her Mum laughed "Now Pam! I'm not dressing your brother up, in your clothes!" as she laughed "Now Mum! It would change his attitude!" adding "And if I was out, I'd not know anything about it!" as she laughed "Less of that talk!"

Tom returned from footy with his mates and said, "That footy was great! Much better than with Ug!" as his Mum said "Watch it Tom, or she'll tell!" as he huffed "She'd better not try that washing up crap, like last night!" as his

Mum said, "Watch it or you'll be sorry!" as he blushed and said, "Ha!" They had their dinner around 5pm and afterwards Pam has Tom, upstairs and Says, "I'm going to ask you to help with the washing up!" as he said, "No way!" but then added "I want you to pretend to thump my arm and pull my hair!" and call "You know where you can stick your washing up!" and run out to join your mates. He asked, "Why!" as she laughed "Just to please me!"

Tom reverts to his MSP, but Says, he'll do the dishes over the weekend

Hence, Pam heads down and a few minutes later Tom comes down and sees Pam in her pretty apron and their Mum running the water for the washing up. Pam Says, Tom I've a pretty apron for you again!" as cried "You bug off Ug!" as he hit her on her arm and yanked her hair, as his Mum said, "Stop that Tom!" as he cried "You know where you can stick that washing up, where the sun don't shine!" adding "I'm going out!" and stormed up the hall, but his Mum caught him and said, "I thought you had promised to be nice to Pam!" and taking his hand, dragged him up the stairs and into his room. He sobbed "Mum not fair!" as she pulled down his trousers and underpants and spanked his bottom, causing tears and him to sob, even though it didn't hurt that much.

She said, "You go down and apologize to your sister! No more hitting her, ok?" as he sobbed "Ok Mum! Not fair!" as he got dressed again and was led down the stairs and into the kitchen, where he said, "Sorry Pam! I hit you and pulled your hair!" as his Mum asked, "What about calling her Ug!" as he sobbed "Sorry for calling you Ug!" as she said, "Ok! Head on out!" and saw him exit the side door. Pam asked, "What about the dishes?" but his Mum said, "I've punished him and will let him go for now!" as she said, "He should really help us with housework too, over the weekend!" as her Mum said, "Let's leave it for now!"

The next evening, Pam got him up to his room and whispered "I'll head over to Julies in a while and when I'm out, I want you to say, 'Pam's been saying, I should help with the washing up and I'll help with the dishes over the weekend!'" as his Mum asked "Promise?" as he nodded, "Ok Mum!" as she said, "Saturday after dinner!" as he huffed "Ok!" but added "Don't expect me, to wear a flaming apron!" as his Mum laughed "You afraid of Pam or me, tying you into it?" as he nodded, "Yea! I won't fall for that again!" as she laughed.

Over the next few days Pam was helping her Mum, with the washing up and some housework with Tom refusing to help them and was still calling her Ug!" She had him join her in the back garden kicking the ball and she gradually got a little bit better, being able to kick the ball towards him, with her right foot. He said, "You have to be able to do it, with your left foot too!" She whispered to him "Pull my hair and call me a 'Stupid Ug' so I can complain to Mum again and then run out to join your mates!" as he huffed "Ok!" and pulled her hair, harder than she wanted, as she cried "Tom that hurt!" as he said, "You're a stupid Ug!" He ran out to join his mates and Pam ran in, with fake tears in her eyes and cried "Mum! Tom pulled my hair again and called me a 'Stupid Ug!'" as she asked, "Where is he?" as she looked out the back, but heard Pam say, "He ran on, to play stupid football!" as she said, "I'll see to him, when he gets back!" Pam said, "Mum! You should make him help, with the dishes every night!" as she said, "He's promised on Saturday night! So! We'll leave it at that!"

She looked forward to the day when she could show Tom how to play Sissy Football, with him in pretty apron and a headscarf and mincing around with a handbag, kicking the ball. However she'd then soon have him in hair ribbons and dear knows what?"

Saturday arrives and Pam tells him to swear and refuse to do the dishes

It came to the Saturday where he said, he'd help with the dishes that evening. Pam got him up, but just before heading off to ballet with her friends, she got Tom to pretend to thump her and pull her hair and cried "Mum! Tom thumped my arm and pulled my hair again!" adding "Just because, I suggested he join me at ballet class!" as she

cuddled her Mum, who said, "I'll deal with him, when you've gone!" and soon the car arrived and Pam dried her crocodile tears and exited, kissing her Mum bye, as she ran to the car and got in to head to the class.

His Mum ran upstairs and called "Tom! Here right now!" as he exited his bedroom and she called "What do you mean, by hitting your sister and pulling her hair!" as he sobbed "I didn't hit her hard and hardly touched her hair!" as his Mum took him onto the bed and pulled down his PJ bottoms, followed by his underpants and smacked his bare bottom. He of course sobbed crocodile tears, to try and get her to let him off and go easier on him. She said, "Any more of that nastiness and you'll be sorry!" adding "And you might well, end up joining Pam at ballet lessons!" as he cried "No way! You know where she can stick her stupid ballet!" as she gasped and smacked him harder.

Her Mum got herself ready and handing Tom some money for fish and chips, she left to pick Pam up after her class and then they headed to town shopping. Pam suggested that it wouldn't hurt Tom, to join ballet, causing her Mum to laugh. She said, "Don't forget, Mum! He's promised to help with the washing up and housework tonight!" as her Mum laughed "If he does the dishes properly, I might let him off the housework or postpone it to Sunday!" as Pam said, "I hope he wears an apron and pinny, like the other night!" as her Mum laughed "I think he's worried about you or I tying him into it, like the other night and him being helpless for you to pop a headscarf or ribbons on his head!" as Pam laughed "He did look sweet in my pinny and headscarf!" but added "I'm sure he'd look even sweeter in a few of my clothes" as her Mum laughed "No way!" as Pam laughed "It would really bring him to heel and obey your slightest wishes, if he ended up in a pretty skirt or frock for being naughty!" as her Mum laughed and she said, "I'll just leave a few things on my bed, which you might find handy, to make the big MSP, more obedient and willing to help us around the house!" as her Mum said, "He's promised to do the dishes tonight, so they shouldn't be needed!" as Pam laughed and flicked her wrist.

Saturday before dinner and Pam gets Tom upstairs and tells him "I'll be heading over to Julie's for a while and Mum's going to ask you to do the washing up, with her!" as he huffed "Ok!", but she laughed "But I want you to flatly refuse and call out loudly 'No way, Mum! I'll do it tomorrow night!', but then add 'That's bloody girl's work!'" as he huffed "Why?" but just heard her laugh "I just want to hear that Mummy gave your naughty bum-bum, a good spanking!" as he huffed "Ha!" She warned him "Don't you dare tell her, I've made you refuse!" as he huffed "Ok!" but if she spanks me, it better not be any harder than usual!" as she laughed "She normally doesn't hurt that much, when you start your crocodile tears!" as he cringed "Ha!"

Tom's refuses to do the washing up saying 'It's girl's work!' and pays for it

After dinner, Pam said she was popping over to see Julie, but said "Mum! Tom's promised to help with the dishes! Bye" as her Mum thanked her for helping her all afternoon with the housework and saw her exit. His Mum ran the hot water and added the Fairy liquid and called "Tom! Come on! You've promised to help me with the dishes!" adding "Pam's helped me all week!" as he called "**Mum! I shouldn't have to do the bloody washing up!**" but added **"It's flaming girl's work!"** and went towards the front door and said, "I'm going out to play footy!" She gasped at him swearing to her, having only used the word 'flaming' before, but now had used 'bloody' and thought to herself "I'd better nip this in the bud, before it gets out of hand!" as she ran and dragged him back and decided to teach him a lesson and take Pam's advice.

She knew he had hated Pam tricking him into the frilly shorts and so takes him upstairs for a spanking, initially into his own room, where she pulls down his trousers and then pants, as usual, but this time, removes them fully. She Says, "I'm going to have to teach you a lesson, to stop you being such a MSP!" adding "and no swearing to me! Ok?" as she smacked his bottom as usual, causing him to cry fake tears, to try make her stop. He sobbed "Mum! Let me go! Sorry I swore!" but she instead, pulled his jumper off, followed by his shirt, to leave him in just his socks, as he cried "What are you doing Mum!" as she said, "Pam's out and I've locked the side door, to

keep her out, while I deal with you!" as she picked up his clothes and heard him call "Eh Mum! I need those!" as she exited. He wondered what she was up to and thought she had taken them to stop him going out, to play footy.

She entered Pam's room and smiled as she saw girly clothes on the bed and realized there was a full package of yellow panties, white tights, a petticoat and to top it all her favourite yellow frock. However, she also had added a yellow Alice band and some hair ribbons. She smiled as she lifted the clothes, but left the frock, as she exited and entered his room. Tom was sitting there, wondering whether to get other clothes from his drawers, when his Mum came in with Pam's undies and heard him cry "No Mum! Don't!" as he really sobbed "Not fair, Mum!" as she pulled him back across her lap and gave him another spanking, but this time harder, causing him to really sob. She pulled the yellow panties up his legs and pulling him up, pulled them up over his willy, as he cried "Don't dress me, in Ug's panties!" but gasped as she took the tights and said, "Sit down and pull these on!" as he cried "Not fair!" and sat down and saw her scrunch the tights up, for him and helped him pull them onto his feet and then up his legs and over his panties!" all the time, with him sobbing with embarrassment!"

She said, "Now Tom! I won't tell Pam what I've done and after you've helped with the dishes, I'll let you out of her clothes! Ok?" as he cried "Not fair!" but she then took the petticoat and pulled it up his legs, with him crying "But Mum! Someone will see!" She pulled him up and led him out and into Pam's room at the front of the house and over to the dressing table mirror, near the window and heard him cry "Mum! Close the blinds! I'll be seen!" but she laughed "They can't see below your waste!" as he blushed.

His Mum adds Pam's yellow dress over his petticoat, tights and panties

He gasped at the sight in the mirror, of the petticoat over the white tights, but cried "Oh no!" as he saw the yellow frock and cried "Mum! Don't put me into that!" but she closed the blinds a bit and said, "Arms up, or else I open them!" and saw him raise his arms, as she fed the dress over his head and slid his arms into the sleeves and finally pulled it down his body and over his petticoats. He sobbed "Mum close the blinds fully!" as she fed the Alice band and hair ribbons into his hair and showed him his look in the mirror, with him dreading someone like Julie or her neighbours spying him through the partially open blinds, as he sobbed.

She then said, "Now, for the washing up!" and he realized she was going to bring him downstairs and screamed "Don't take me downstairs like this Mum! I'll be seen!" but she dragged him out along the landing and downstairs into the kitchen, where he was dreading being recognized, by the houses at the back or Pam walking in the back door.

She asked, "What do we need to protect our pretty dresses?" as he saw her lift Pam's pretty pink apron and pull it around his dress and slide his arms into it, with him crying "Not fair Mum!" as she tied it behind him in a bow. However, she then took Pam's pretty PVC apron and held it up, but said, "Ok! I'll leave that, as her apron is pretty enough over your frock!"

He sobbed "Not fair, Mum!" but she said, "**Right My Girl! As washing up is girl's work! Get on with it!**" as he cried "Close the curtains! Them at the back will see me!" but she refused and laughed, "Anyone looking in, will just think, it's a sweet young girl, helping her Mummy! So hurry up, before your sister comes back, with Julie!" as he gasped and cried "Not fair!" He sobbed as he started the dishes, looking down, trying to hide his face, but peering out every so often, to check that nobody was looking in. He washed one plate and sobbed "Aren't you going to help?" but his Mum shook her head "Pam often does it all and if you'd volunteered earlier, I would have done most of it, but now you've forced my hand, you'll just have to do it all and learn your lesson!" He continued washing the plates and heard her scold him, when he didn't do it right, causing him to repeat and wash the item more thoroughly. She said, "For being so naughty and rude to me earlier, you will be helping Pam and Me with

the washing up every night!" as he sobbed "Not fair, Mum!" as she added "Wearing an apron! Though I'll maybe let you off with your boy's one, if you're a good boy!" but said, "If not then you'll definitely be a good girl and wear Pam's pretty apron, you are in now!" as he sobbed "Ok! That's cruel!" as she laughed "Get on with it!" He washed another plate and was just doing some cutlery, when the bell rang!" He jumped back, away from the sink, trying to hide by the door.

Pam returns early and nearly catches him, but his Mum let's him escape

He cried "Oh no! His Mum laughed and opening the kitchen door, she peered up the hall to see Pam's silhouette, through the frosted glass of the inner porch door. She laughed "It's Pam!" Tom quickly removed her apron and hung it up again. He begged her not to show him off and she said, "Ok! When I call her around the side, you run upstairs to your room, but you mustn't remove anything, till I come up and speak to you! Ok?" and saw him nod. She said, "Get ready!" and saw him peek up the hall, as Pam rang the bell again. Her Mum opened the side door and called "Pam Dear! The side door's open!" and Tom saw her outline disappear.

He opened the kitchen door fully, as she walked up the side of the house, totally oblivious of what she'd have seen, had she stayed. Tom took his chance and ran up the hallway and then turned, at the inner porch door, to bound up the stairs. Pam came in the side door and heard Tom's feet, going up the stairs and a bedroom door slam shut and lock, as her blushing, smiling Mum said, "You're back early from Julie's!"

She closed the back door and said, "Yea! Julie could only chat for a short time, as she was off to her Aunties!" Pam laughed "Well! Did you take my advice?" but her Mum shook her head and said, "I did have to give him a few smacks, but he's learnt his lesson and helped me with the washing up!" She asked, "Can you watch TV a tick while I go upstairs! I need to speak to Tom!" Pam saw the half-finished washing up and asked, "Want me to finish the dishes, Mum?" as she laughed "Thanks dear!" as she saw her Mum ascend the stairs. Pam pulled on her pink apron and felt it was a bit damp, as she pulled on a pretty PVC pinny, on top and giggled "Mum must have made him wear my pretty apron! He mustn't have worn a pinny to protect my good apron!" as she does the rest of the dishes and things. She washed them all and then emptied the water, to rinse all the items and soon was drying and putting it away in the cupboards.

His Mum let's him out of Pam's clothes, but makes him wear her panties

His Mum knocked and he let her in as she locked it again and said, "You can remove Pam's clothes, bar the panties to keep you in check!" as he gasped "Oh no! Not fair!" but nodded. She said, "Get out of the frock, petticoat and tights and I'll take them back before she realizes they're missing!" and saw Tom, try to pull it over his head, but his Mum had to help him and soon had it off. He pulled his Alice band off and the hair slides, as she laughed "I never said, you could remove those!" as he cried "Oh no!" as she laughed "Just, my little joke! Could you imagine Pam's reaction, if she saw you in her hair ribbons and Alice band?" as he begged "Keep quite Mum, she'll hear!" as she hugged him and took them from him. She then pulled down his petticoat and smiled at the small bulge in the tights and pulled them down too. However, his panties came partially down, causing him to gasp, as she giggled, at his small willy on show and he quickly pulled the panties up again. She laughed "I've a feeling those might need to be washed, before being returned to Pam!" as he blushed and pulled on his trousers.

His Mum exited and on entering Pam's room, she replaced her petticoat and frock, as well as popping her tights into the drawer and put the Alice band and hair slides, back onto the dressing table. She then took another pair of yellow panties and placed them on the top of her panty pile, so Pam shouldn't realize what he's wearing. She laughed to herself "That was so naughty of me, dressing my little Tom up, in his sister's clothes and hair ribbons!" but then said, "It's his own fault, for those MSP comments about 'What was girls work' that led to my punishment!" She

laughed "At least in future, he will be much more obedient and help with washing up and housework!" thinking "He will be dreading, I even hint, about him dressing up or wearing panties!" as she flicked her wrist towards his room, giggling at what she'd made him wear. She exited downstairs and saw Pam had finished the washing up and said "I take it, he tried to get out of helping with the washing up?" as her Mum nodded "He did and got more smacks on his botty!" as Pam laughed "Well done! You should have put him into those things, I left out!" as her Mum laughed "Now Pam! I've put them away! I couldn't believe the full outfit, you expected me to put your brother into!" as Pam laughed "Pity!"

Tom goes down and tries to go out to play, but must apologize to Pam

Around 7pm, Tom had come down the stairs and entered the living room, where he saw Pam and his Mum, sitting on the sofa, watching TV and chatting. Pam saw him stump in and said, "I'm not staying in tonight, if he's going to be here!" He scowled "Don't worry! I'll be going out to play in a minute!" as he sat down on the floor. He then heard his Mum say, "First of all! Is there something you want to tell your sister?" and saw Tom, blush and turning his face away, he mumbled "Sorry, I hit you!" and then turned to his Mum and said, more audibly "There! I've said, it! Can I go now?" She looked down on her blushing, brother and called out "That thump, hurt my shoulder and you pulled my hair!" but heard him yell "Well! Don't go into my room, then!" His Mum looked at him and said. "Tell Pam! You won't hit her again, or else!" as he dreaded, her telling Pam, what she'd just done to him and mumbled "Ok! I won't hit you again! Promise!"

Pam heard her Mum add "You'll be nice to Pam from now on! Won't you?" as he nodded, and huffed "Ok!" and heard his Mum add "Even if she goes, into your room, without your permission!" He cried "What? That's not fair! I don't go into hers!" Pam said, "I caught you in my room, one day last week!" as he replied, "I just looked out, to see if any of my mates were about!" as she huffed "You can go into my room, so why couldn't I go into yours?" as he huffed "Cause I say, so!" but knew he'd to obey and stammered "Ok! You can go into mine!" Pam wondered had her Mum actually taken her advice and dressed him up, realizing he was scared stiff of their Mum and would do whatever she wanted. She went upstairs and checked but sure enough, there was her frock back in the wardrobe, along with the petticoat and even saw the white tights in a drawer. She opened her panty drawer and saw yellow panties, not realizing they were a different pair from the one's she'd left out for Tom and so didn't realize he was in them.

Pam teases Tom and he calls her 'Ug', but has to apologize again

Up to now, he'd been nasty to, both of them, ignoring what he was told and being insolent. However, he now seemed a changed boy, having actually, apologized to her, for hitting her, earlier and now this. Pam got up and smiled "I think I'll go upstairs for a minute!" as she stood up and as she exited the room, laughed as she ran up the stairs and entering his room. She looked out of Tom's window!" Pam called "Mum! His room's so untidy! He should really tidy it!" Tom went to get up, but heard his Mum warn him, "Sit there and let Pam be!" adding "She is right! You should be tidier!" Pam looked at his untidy room, with some toys on the floor and clothes on the bed. She saw the back of the houses in the next street and a few young boys, playing ball in a garden, a few doors up and a few girls, in another garden, wheeling a doll's pram about. She saw their next-door neighbour June, hanging out some washing and waved down to her, but wasn't noticed. She opened Tom's window and called out "Hi, Mrs Makepiece!" June looked up and called "Hi Pam! Just taking advantage of the nice evening, to do my washing!" Pam called down "I'm just taking advantage of being able to go into horrid Tom's bedroom, without being hit for it!" adding "It's so untidy!" and heard June laugh.

She closed the bedroom window and returned downstairs.

Pam entered the living room and scolded "Tom! Your bedroom's such a mess! You should be tidier and put your toys and clothes away!" Tom yelled "You're for it, when Mum goes!" but heard his Mum say, "For that! You'll stay in, all night and show Pam, you're sorry, for threatening her and being nasty!" He cried "Mum! That's not fair! I want to go and join my mates!" as tears started to trickle down his cheeks, dreading having to sit there, with his stupid sister.

He gulped, as he heard Pam say, "Mum! Whatever have you done to him? Normally he'd have just gone out or yelled at both of us!" Tom's face lit up and their Mum blushed a bit, as she remembered why Tom, was being so placid and she explained "When you were out, I just had a few stern words with your brother and made him understand, that I wasn't standing for any more of his naughtiness, towards me or you!" adding "I did have to give his legs a bit of a hard smack too!" 7.15 Pam giggled, "You've done that before, but it never used to do any good! He'd just cry a bit and be back, being nasty Tom, in no time at all!" and turning to Tom, asked him "Did naughty Tom, get his botty spanked?" and heard him yell "You bug off, Ug!" as his Mum gasped and said, "Naughty boy!" His Mum added "I don't want you calling your sister any more names, either!" as more tears flowed down Tom's face and his Mum said, "Now apologize to Pam and tell her she's a pretty little sister and you like her!" Tom wiped his eyes and cried "What?" as Pam gasped and giggled, "Go on Tom! Let me hear you?" He cried "Mum! Don't make me?" but she said, "Hurry up! The sooner you learn to be nice to her, the easier it will be!" He stammered "Sorry I called you UG!" and mumbled "Your very petty and nice!" as he tried to fudge the words. However, his Mum said, "Look at Pam and speak clearly!" Pam giggled, "Come on Tom! Say, it again! I didn't hear you!"

Pam cuddles her new nice brother and gives him a kiss

He sobbed, as he said, "Sorry I called you names and I think you're very pretty" and sob "I think you're a nice sister!" Pam screeched "Oh Tom! I never thought, I'd have heard you say, that, not in a million years!" as their Mum laughed "Now Tom! Was that hard to say?" He cried "Yes it was! It's not fair!" as tears rolled down his cheeks and Pam giggled. Pam wanted to play on Tom's plight and got up off the sofa, planting herself down on the floor, edging nervously towards him. He was rubbing the tears from his eyes and face and so didn't spot her edging towards him, as he heard her voice, behind him. He suddenly heard her say, "Don't cry Tom! I'll let you be my friend!" causing him to gasp and turn to face her. He yelled "Get away, Pam" as he saw her hand, reach up and drop onto his shoulder. He threw himself away from her attempt at a cuddle and cried "Mum! Tell her to get back over there! I don't want her near me!" Pam giggled, "I was just going to give you a cuddle!" as her Mum laughed "Tom! She won't bite!" as Pam laughed "Come on Tom! Give your pretty little sister a nice hug!"

Pam realized Tom wasn't attempting to hit her, or even yell at her, instead he was just pleading to their Mum for help. This gave her more bravado and so she moved quickly over to him and put her arm around his shoulder, for a hug. His head just turned away, as she said, "Tom! I've given you nice hugs! Come on! Give me one back!" as he cried "Mum! Stop her!" His Mum laughed "Pam Don't!" but then said, "Now Tom! It won't hurt! Give her a quick hug!" as he shook his head "No way!" and moved further away. 7.30 His Mum pointed to the sofa saying, "Come up here onto the sofa!" as Pam giggled, and stood up, holding out her hand for Tom and saying, "Come on Tom! Take my hand and we'll sit with Mummy!" as he cried "No way! Mum! You sit in the middle of us!" and heard her laugh "Ok! You sit here Pam and Tom can go there!" as she moved to the centre of the sofa.

Pam complained "Mum! I want to sit beside my lovely brother! I don't normally get a chance, to sit with him!" She sat down beside her Mum, trying to push her over to make room for Tom, but her Mum giggled, "Quick Tom! Sit down here!" Tom got up and quickly sat on the far side of the sofa, glad to have his Mum between him and Pam. Pam stood up and giggled, as she skipped around and planted herself on his lap, saying, "Mummy! I never realized how comfy his lap is!" as her Mum gasped and giggled, "Oh Pam!" and moving up, she said, "There Pam! There's room for you down there!"

Tom tried to shove her off his lap, saying, "Get off! Or I'll thump you!" but heard his Mum threaten "I wouldn't, if you know what's best!" and heard him sob "Mum! Not fair!" as he felt Pam's arm slide around his neck and around his shoulder again, only this time, perched on his lap. Their Mum laughed saying, "Ok Pam! Get off his lap and leave your brother alone!" Tom moved up to the middle of the sofa and Pam slid down off his lap, but kept her arm around his shoulder, saying, "Come on Tom! Give me a nice hug back and I'll take my arm away!" He cried "Mum! Stop her!" Pam said, "Mum! You too, a nice three-way hug!" as her laughing Mum, popped her arm around Tom's shoulder and she said, "Go on Tom! Just for a minute! Give her and me a hug!"

Pam suggests a girly game and that Tom be her pretend sister 'Nancy'

Tom huffed "Not fair, Mum!" as he raised both arms, to put them around first Pam's shoulder and then his Mum's back. He huffed "There! Can we stop now?" Pam couldn't believe her nasty horrid brother, was acting so sweet and although, hating the thought of doing it, knew he'd hate it, ten times worse, as she leant over and gave Tom a kiss on the cheek. Tom pulled his arms from around his Mum and Pam's shoulders and cried "Mum! She kissed me!" causing both Pam and their Mum to screech, with laughter, as he blushed, bright red and slid back down onto the floor, with more tears flowing down his cheeks, as Pam said, "Yuk!" but added "Sorry Tom! I couldn't resist kissing my sweet big brother!"

Pam laughed "I just gave you a peck on the cheek, to say, thanks, for being so nice and giving me a hug!" but asked, "Don't I get one back?" as he cried "No way!" as his Mum laughed "Pam! You can stop now! Just sit still and you can watch the TV!" She looked up and said, "Mum! I suppose Aliens didn't come, when I was out and replaced my horrid brother Tom, with a nice sweet look-alike!" Her Mum shook her head and laughed "No Pam! He's the same brother as always! Just a much better behaved one!" Pam laughed "Mum! I don't know how you did it, but you've worked a miracle on him!"

7.45pm They sat in front of the TV, with Tom trying to concentrate on the program, but Pam trying to think of ways to embarrass and tease him. She then turned to face him and said, "Come on Tom, let's play pata-cake?" as he huffed "No way! Please don't?" Her Mum laughed "Pam! He probably doesn't know how!" as she giggled, "Don't boys play that?" as he shook his head. She said, "I'll teach you!" as she said, "Hold up the palms of your hands, like this!" Tom cried "Mum! Make her stop! I'm not playing a girl's game!" as Pam giggled, "It's not that girly! I can think of lots more girly games for us to play!".

Her Mum gasped and said, "Now Pam! Tom's your brother, not?" as she stopped herself, but Pam giggled, "You mean 'Not my Sister!'" adding "That's right! You could be a pretend sister, for me! I've always wanted a little sister, to play with!" as he cried "No way!" She continued "Then when Julie's not around, for me to play with, I can teach you, lots of girly games like skipping, patta cake, dollies!" as her Mum said, "Stop that, Pam! You know he won't play girly games with you!" as he cried "No way!" and tried to get off the sofa, but his Mum held him down, saying, "Pam's just teasing! Ignore her!" Pam giggled, "Pity it's so late, or we could go out to the garden, to skip!" as her Mum scolded "Not outside, Pam!" as she laughed "Ok! I can think of lots of girly things, for us to play inside!" Tom cried "No way! I'm a boy! Not a flaming girl!" Pam giggled, "Mum! I'd even thought of a name for my little sister!" as her Mum went to scold her, but couldn't stop her, shouting out loudly "NANCY! Isn't that a sweet name for her, Mummy?"

He runs upstairs and his Mum tries to calm him down, scolding Pam

Tom couldn't stand anymore of Pam's teasing and jumped up, crying "I'm not going to be your flaming sister!" as Pam giggled, and his Mum scolded "Pam! That was naughty!" as they saw Tom run out the door and heard his feet, stumping up the stairs. He threw himself down on the bed, sobbing at his sister's teasing, but also what his Mum

had done to him earlier. It was worse now, with Pam teasing him, as being her sister 'Nancy'. His Mum goes up after him and knocking on his door, said, "Let me in, Tom! I'll try and stop her teasing you!" as he unlocked the door "Mum! Let me go out and get away from her, she knows I'm doing anything you say, and she's now wanting me to be her flaming sister!" as his Mum locked his door again. She laughed "Are you still wearing her you know what's?" as he nodded but she reached to his trousers and pulled down his zip and reached her hand in, as he gasped "Not fair, Mum!" as she pulled out the yellow material and laughed "Just checking!" as she pushed it back again and pulled his zip up again, His Mum laughed "I didn't think, keeping you in and being nice to your little sister, would lead to this!" adding "I'll try and stop her, teasing you!" She said, "Wash your face and come downstairs!" as he cried "Please Mummy! Let me out to play?" as she laughed "What! In your panties?" as he huffed "Nobody should realize what I'm wearing!" as she laughed "Oh Tom!" and bending down, she gave him a kiss on the lips.

Meanwhile, Pam stayed downstairs, laughing, as she thought of her tease about making him her pretend sister, Nancy and wondered could she take that further, with him joining her skipping, in the back garden and maybe helping her and their Mum with the laundry. She giggled, at the extremely girly way, they did it, as she gurgled with laughter at the thought of her macho brother pegging out the washing, but especially if she could get him wearing a few of her pretty aprons too and thought "Whatever would June next door say, if she saw him looking so girly, pegging out the clothes?" adding "I bet she'd want my new sister, to do her laundry too!"

She chuckled "June might even want him to dress as my sister, as she stood up and gripped her dress and bobbed a curtsy!" She then gasped and laughed "That's right, he would hate having to bob a curtsy, but knew her Mum wouldn't let Pam make him wear a skirt or frock. She then laughed and ran in, taking her pink floral apron, she pulled it on and bobbed a curtsy and then thought "Maybe, even if he wears his blue boy's school pinny, he could bob a curtsy in it, too!" Pam then thought of her dollies and giggled, "Wouldn't it be great to make him, or should I say, HER, play dollies with me?" She hadn't played dollies herself, for a year or so, thinking it was too little girly, but now thought "If I can get Nancy to play dollies with me, I think I'll be getting lots of my old dolls out again!" She then laughed as she thought of her friend Julie, whose little sister Tina was always pestering them, to play dollies with them and thought "Wouldn't little Nancy love to play dollies with Tina too?" She thought how nasty Tom had been to Tina and her friends in the past, calling them names and realized they'd love to have the nasty bully boy, play dollies with them.

Pam thinks of him playing dollies and curtsies but checks her clothes

She realized how he'd hate playing dollies with loads of little girls, especially if it included pushing a doll's pram, around the back garden and then added "Or even the driveway!" and "Eventually the street!" adding "How would he explain that to his mates?" However, she thought "Slowly does it!" adding "I'm sure I can keep Nancy a secret from my friends!" as she gurgled "For a while!" His Mum unlocked and opening his door, she descended the stairs and called "Pam! Less of the teasing, Tom! Especially about being treated as your sister!" as Pam giggled, "Oh Mummy! It's not that bad!" adding "It would be different if I was suggesting he wear skirts and frocks and join Julie, Tina and me to play skipping and wheel a dolls pram around the streets!" as her Mum gasped "Watch it Pam or it's no ballet!" as she said, "Just joking!" Pam giggled, "You gave me an idea, for if Tom is really bad again!" and heard her Mum ask "What?" as she giggled, "It would help him with his curtsies!" as her Mum gasped and said, "Now Pam! He can't!" Pam whispered, "He could join me on Saturday mornings at the ballet class!" as her Mum put a hand to her mouth and gasped "Pam! You are, a little tease!" Pam laughed "It's ok Mum! He wouldn't have to wear the same as me!" as her Mum said, "I hope not!" Pam gurgled "The little fairies-group are allowed to wear tutus!" as her Mum screeched "Oh Pam!" She laughed "I'll go up and apologize for teasing him!"

Pam goes up and calls through his bedroom door "Sorry Tom, for teasing you about being my sister!" as he called back "You bug off! I've had a terrible night, with you and not playing with my mates!" as she laughed "Don't

23

worry! I won't tell my friends or at school anything about what happens here, in the house!" adding "No matter how girly you are!" as he cried "I'm not girly!" as she laughed "Come on down and we'll watch TV till supper time!" as he said, "You go down and I'll be down soon!" as she said, "Ok!"

and decided to check her clothes, she'd left out earlier for him.

She opened her wardrobe and sighed as she saw her yellow frock and petticoat, thinking "Mummy is such a poo bum! Not dressing Mr MSP up, in my frock!" as she checked her drawers and saw her white tights back in place and the pink panties, only giving them a cursory check, not realizing they weren't the ones, she'd left out and that Tom was actually wearing them. She closed the drawers and wardrobe and was about to go back down, when she had a naughty thought and smiled, as she picked up two large dolls, that she hadn't, actually played with, for a year or so, but were just lying in a basket beside her wardrobe.

She slipped downstairs and on reaching the sitting room, she hid them behind the sofa. His Mum was in the living room and soon was joined by Pam, with her saying, "I said sorry and promised I wouldn't tell Julie or anyone at school of any girly things that happen!" as her Mum said, "Now Pam! No making your big brother do girly things! I'm warning you!" as Pam said, "But I'm allowed to play girly games myself and just let Tom watch?" as her Mum laughed "He can just watch you play!" They then heard steps on the stairs and saw a teary eyed, Tom, enter the room and sit down in an armchair.

Pam will give Nancy dolls for birthday, but asks how to know it's Nancy

Pam said, "Sorry Tom! Sorry for teasing you, like that!" and heard him huff "Ok! I just want to watch TV!" She beckoned him over to the sofa beside her, saying, "Come on! Sit with me and I'll not tease too much!" Pam then giggled, "Mummy! That's right! On Tom's birthday, it will be Nancy's birthday too!" adding "So you can get her a dolly!" as her Mum laughed "Now Pam! No way! It would be money wasted!" as Pam laughed "Oh you big meany!" adding "I know Mummy! I'll give you one of my dollies and then we both can, give her a dolly each!" as he cried "No way Pam! Please don't give me dollies?" as she giggled, at him, not exploding and hitting her, or running out the door. Pam laughed "Don't worry Tom! I know you wouldn't want a dolly, for your own birthday!" but added "We'll give my sweet sister Nancy, my dollies, as her birthday pressy and I'll make sure, she has lots of pretty skirts and dresses to play dress up with!" as her Mum gasped "Pam don't?" as she said, "I meant her dolly! Not Tom!"

She laughed "I know, she'll love to play dollies with me!" adding "That way, we don't need to spend any money on her!" as her Mum gasped and laughed "Now Pam, don't?" as he cried "Oh no! Mum don't let her?" Her Mum said, "Pam that's naughty!" as she said, "You know he won't want to play with a dolly!" as Pam said, "He won't want to play with me, Mummy! It will be Nancy playing dollies with me!" as he cried "No way!"

Pam knew her Mum was making him behave and said, "Tom! Do you want me to introduce my dollies to you or Nancy?" as he cried "Oh no! Mum stop her!" as her Mum scolded "Now Pam! Don't?" She asked, "How can I distinguish them apart?" as she got up and ran into the kitchen and returned holding her pink apron.

Tom cried "No way Pam!" adding "Mum stop her!" She said, "It's either my pretty apron, or I'll let Nancy wear her twin brother Tom's, boy's apron!" as his Mum said, "I'll get it!

It's better than yours!" as Pam whispered "To play curtsies!" as he cried "Oh no!" as she laughed "It's better than the alternative!" as she gripped her dress and bobbed a curtsy to him, as he cried "Not fair, Pam!" as she laughed "Curtsying in frocks, is lots more fun!"

His Mum brings his blue boy's apron and hands it to Tom and saw him pull it around him and tie it up. Pam took her own apron and tied it around herself as she said, "Mummy! I think Nancy will prefer to play something else,

instead of dollies!" as her Mum asked, "What?" Pam giggled, "Curtsies!", as she gripped her own apron and bobbed a curtsy to him. Her Mum said, "No Pam!" adding "Tom! Give me your apron!" but Pam giggled and explained "Mummy! If you take Nancy's boy's apron, I'm sure I could persuade her, to wear something else to play!" as she gasped, as she saw her grip her dress and bob a curtsy with it, laughing. Her Mum let go of Tom's apron and said, "Well! Don't be making him play curtsies outside!" as he cried "Not fair Mum! This is getting worse!" as she said, "Ok Mum! Go on Nancy! Give me and then Mummy a sweet curtsy like this!" as she bobbed another curtsy to him.

Tom says he's Nancy when in an apron but then has to play curtsies

Tears appeared in his eyes, as he gripped his apron and tried to bob a curtsy with it, but saw Pam demonstrate another curtsy, but then said, "Mummy! Show Nancy!" as her Mum gripped her own skirt and bobbed a curtsy to him. He again tried a few curtsies, with his boy's apron, blushing as both Pam and their Mum giggled, at his attempt at his curtsies. His Mum said, "I'm off to the toilet!" but added "Be good Pam!" as she exited the room to ascend the stairs, leaving the blushing Tom to the teasing and threats of his little sister.

Pam takes her chance and whispers "Now Nancy! I'll keep this a secret indoors and promise not to tell at school, or even Julie and her little Tina, but it's better we swap our aprons!" He cried "Oh no!" as she undid her apron and said, "Better here, than playing with my friend Julie, but could you imagine her little sister Tina coming over, what she'd make Nancy play with her, probably wheeling his doll's pram in the street or even to the shops!" as he gasped and cried "Oh no!" as he removed his blue boy's apron, as Pam giggled, and handed him her apron. He took hers and pulled the pink apron on and tied it behind his back, as Pam giggled, and tied his apron around her own back, saying, "Just say 'Nancy will be easier to recognize in my pretty apron to play curtsies!'" as he blushed and sobbed "Not fair, Pam!" as she laughed "It could be dollies!" as he begged "Please don't!"

Their Mum came down the stairs a few minutes later and entering the hall, she heard Pam telling Tom how to bob a curtsy, saying, "Just dip down and take one foot behind the other!" as she walked along laughing at Pam making Tom bob curtsies, but gasps as she spies Tom, in Pam's apron and laughed "What's this Tom?"

Pam looked at him and he stammered "Mummy! It's easier for me to be Nancy in Pam's pretty pinny, than in my silly blue one!" as Pam gasped, at it being even more girly a statement than she'd planned. She giggled, "What a sweetie, Nancy is!" as she threw her arms around his neck and kissed his lips, causing him to cry "No kissing Pam!" However, Pam said, "Mummy! Isn't my sister, sweet?" adding "Doesn't she deserve a nice kissy, from her lovely Mummy, too?" as his laughing Mum bent down and kissed him too. Pam laughed "Mummy! I think we should help Nancy practice her curtsies!" as she asked, "How?" as she laughed "I get a lot of practice curtsying, on Saturday mornings!" adding "Especially when I was a young girl of three or four!" as her Mum gasped and Tom remembered what she did every Saturday morning and called "I'm not going to ballet classes!" as Pam and her Mum both screeched with laughter.

Pam said, "Mummy! I've promised I'll keep Nancy a secret from Julie and the girls at school!" as her Mum said, "Promise?" as she nodded, "Honest! I'll keep her a secret! It will be lots of fun, having a secret sister to play with!" as he cried "Oh no!" adding "Just for curtsies Pam!" She gurgled "Oh Nancy! You enjoy playing curtsies, do you?" as he blushed and nodded but heard her giggle "There's so many in-door games, us girls love playing!" as her Mum laughed and pleaded "Pam! Don't make him!" as he cried "Please Pam don't make me?"

Pam adds her Alice band for Nancy and then shows him the dollies

She laughed "We'll see how well you play curtsies with Mummy and me!" as he asked, "What do you mean?" as she whispered "Complement Mummy on how nice she looks in her dress and apron!" as her Mum wondered, what

25

she was whispering. Tom suddenly Says, "Mummy! That's a nice skirt and pretty apron!" as his Mum gurgled and heard Pam say, "Now Mummy! A sweet thank you with a curtsy, to your sweet Nancy!" as her Mum gripped her apron and skirt and called "Thank you Tom!" but Pam scolded "Mummy! Don't you recognize her! This is your sweet little daughter Nancy!" She removed her Alice band and said, "It seems, we'll need something, to help you recognise her!" as she fed it onto his head, as he cried "Oh no! Not fair, Pam!" as his Mum laughed "Pam! That's ok! I recognize your sister Nancy!" as Pam said, "Just while we're playing curtsies, Mummy!" She laughed "Ok! but take your Alice band back when his curtsies are over!" as Pam laughed "As soon as her curtsies are over, I'll take my pretty hair band or ribbons back!", as she reached into her hair and removing a flower, she slid it into his hair, as he sobbed "Not fair, Pam!" as she added "But she'll need her pretty apron for Mummy to recognize her daughter!"

Hence, he now had to stand there as his Mum gripped her skirt and bobbing a curtsy giggled, "Thank you Nancy!!" as Pam giggled, "And reward her, with a kiss too!" as her Mum laughed and he cried "Not fair!" as his Mum bent down and kissed his lips, as he blushed and grimaced. Then Pam said, "Now for me!" as he stammered "Pam that's a pretty apron over your dress too!" as she laughed and gripping her dress and the blue apron, called "Oh Nancy! What a sweet big girly, you are!" as she reached her arms up around his neck and kissed him again on the lips. However, then Pam said, "Oh Nancy! You are a sweet big sister! That's a pretty apron and Alice band and ribbons you're wearing!" as he blushed and gripping her pink floral apron, he bobbed a curtsy and almost got it right. However, then he had to reach his hands around her and kiss her lips, as she called "Yuk!" adding "Only joking Nancy! Your kisses are much better than my horrid bro, Tom's" as her Mum laughed "Stop teasing him Pam!" as she clapped "Well done, Mum!"

She then said, "As we have my sweet little sister Nancy here, I'll just introduce her to our dollies!" as her Mum said, "No Pam! Don't!" as he begged "Please Pammy?" as she reached over and gave him a kiss. Pam then left the room a tick and returned holding two dollies and saw the look of fear, in Tom's face. He cried "Oh no! Not dollies!" as he tried to get up, but his Mum laughed and said, "Stay there, Tom! Pam's just playing on her own!" as she said, "Mummy! You said, Tom had to watch!" as he cried "Oh no!" She said, "Now Pam! Tom can't play dollies!" but she said, "I just wanted them beside me! I know my nasty brother Tom, won't want to play dollies!" but added "But my sweet sister Nancy, will love to play with my dollies!" as she sat down on the sofa, pulling them down onto her lap, beside Tom, who cried "You bug off Ug! Keep them away from me or else I'll break them!" as his Mum said, "Now Tom! Less of that!"

Pam introduces Baby Suzie and Wendy and makes Tom take the doll

Pam said, "Right Nancy! This dolly is Baby Suzie!" as she held it out to him and saw him take it in his hands and heard Pam ask "So Nancy! What's your dolly called "As he stammered "Baby Suzie! But you said, not until my birthday!" as Pam screeched and giggled, "I might be nice and give you an early birthday pressy!" but then corrected herself "I mean Nancy, an early birthday pressy!" adding "Unless Tom, doesn't get jealous and steel Nancy's dolly!" as tears welled in his eyes and he huffed "Not funny!"

Her Mum tried to stop her, but she said, "Look on the bright side, Mummy!" as she asked, "What?" as she laughed "All my dollies will get used again and not have gone to waste!" adding "Just like when I was a little girl, but this time they'll have double the fun with Nancy and me!" as he cried "No Pam! Please don't make me?" as his Mum cuddled him and laughed.

He then heard her say, "This bigger dolly was my favourite dolly and is called 'Wendy!'" as she asked, "What's my dolly called?" and he stammered "She's Wendy!" as their Mum laughed "Pam, we shouldn't!" Pam laughed "Now let's give our dollies a kiss!" as he sobbed "Oh no!" as she raised Wendy and kissed her and asked, "Want me to

get Tina over to show you how to kiss your dolly?" as he raised the doll and tried to miss it, but she said, "Kiss your dolly properly!" and saw him kiss it's face, as they giggled. Tom sobbed "I'm not your sister!" and threw the dolly down, as Pam warned "If you don't play properly, I'll bring Tina to pick up your dolly!" adding "Imagine what she would say!" He sobbed "Not fair!" as she picked the doll up and handed it back to him, again. He took it onto his lap, and she made him kiss it and say, sorry for throwing her down. Her Mum laughed and scolded "Pam!" but heard her say, "Now we'll swap dollies and you can kiss my favourite dolly, Wendy!" as he held out her Suzie doll and took Wendy from her and kissed it, as Pam kissed the other dolly.

Pam sat there, with the dolls on her lap and just watching TV with her Mum and Tom, but occasionally, she picked up a doll and let it fall on part of Tom's leg, causing him to cry "Mum! Tell her to keep them away from me!"

Pam held the dolls towards him and said, "No playing with my dollies when I'm away!" as she threw the two dollies down, beside him. Pam returned from the bathroom, but had also picked up a few dresses for her dolls and enterinf the living room, she sat down on the sofa and picked up both dolls and said, "I'll just change our dollies frocks!" as he said, "They're your dollies! You'd better keep them away from me!" as she laughed "Mummy Says, you've to watch!" Her Mum laughed "I suppose it won't do you any harm watching Pam change her doll's dresses!" as he blushed and sobbed "Not fair Mum!" Pam laughed "Don't worry Tom, you can watch the TV!" as he turned to concentrate on the program and her Mum thought, she was being nice to him, but heard her add "But Mummy want's Nancy, to learn how to change her dolly's dresses!" as he cried "Not fair!" as her Mum laughed "Pam! You are naughty!"

Pam shows Nancy in Alice band + apron how to change a doll's dresses

Pam said, "I'll start with Baby Suzie!" as she said, "I just turn her onto her front and undo the Velcro of her dress here!" as she pulled it and they saw it come lose. She said, "Then I just pull the dress off its, arms and voila, her dress is off!" as her Mum laughed and saw Tom look over and blush. Pam said, "I then take another frock and slide my dolly's arms into each sleeve!" but saw Tom try and watch TV as she said "Nancy watch or you join me playing!" as he turned to look at her dolly, as his Mum laughed. She said, "After pulling its arms into the sleeves, I just pull the dress around dolly's front and do the Velcro up at the back!" adding "See Nancy! That wasn't hard was it?" He shook his head and sobbed "Please don't make me, play dollies?" as she stood up and sat back onto his lap and cuddled him again, but gave him a kiss on the cheek, as he sobbed "I don't like kisses!" as her Mum gasped and heard her say, "Look of course, Tom doesn't play dollies!" but added "But Nancy can and will play with me!" She added "But it will be our secret in doors! I won't tell Julie or at school!" He blushed and her Mum laughed "Pam! You promised to keep your dollies for yourself!" as she laughed "Ok! Mum!"

She said, "I've an even prettier dress for my Wendy doll, but it's a bit more difficult to get her dress on and I might need some help!" Tom said, "No way!" but she added "I meant from Mummy!" as her Mum laughed as Pam brought her Wendy doll over and undid the Velcro, like before and pulled the dress off her dolly. She then took the other princess dress and showed him, saying, "See this frock has a princess neckline!" as her Mum laughed at her explaining dress details to her big brother. Tom again tried to look at the TV but she said "Keep watching Nancy or you'll be no good when you try yourself!" as her Mum gasped and heard her explain "I meant with her dolly's skirts and dresses!" as her Mum scolded "Watch it Pam!" She turned it round and showed him, saying "It has hooks and eyes, instead of the Velcro, so is more difficult to get onto our dollies!" as he forgot himself and nodded, as his Mum laughed "Now Pam! I'll help you! Keep your dolly away from your brother" as he blushed. Pam got the doll's arms into the frock sleeves and pulled the dress around its body. Her Mum helped get the hooks and eyes done up with Tom trying to watch TV, but Pam saying "Watch Mummy closely, Nancy! You might have to try yourself!" as her Mum said "Now Pam! He's not going to!" Her Mum said, "Pam! That's enough! Take those dollies upstairs, now!" Pam protested "Can I keep Wendy down here? I'll leave Baby Suzie, upstairs! I promise to

keep Wendy with me and not make Tom or even Nancy play with her!" Her Mum said, "Ok! but keep her away from Tom!" Tom cried "Mum! You know she'll tease me!" as he removed the hair slide and Alice band and then pulled her apron off as she huffed "Oh look Mummy! We've got naughty Tom back here again! I preferred sweet Nancy in my pretty apron and hair ribbons!" as he blushed, as she slid the Alice band and hair slide back into her own hair and removing the boy's apron, she put her Apron on again as her Mum laughed.

Pam teases him and has to put her dolly to bed, but hides it in his bed

Pam giggled, "Sorry Baby Suzie! I've got to put you to bed now! Say, good night to Mummy and nasty Tom!" as she made a funny voice and said, "Nighty night Mummy! Nighty night Tom!" but then Pam said "Sorry, I forgot! It was my sweet big sister Nancy that kissed you earlier!" as she giggled and said "Nighty night, Nancy!" and then said, "Wish Baby Suzie sweet dreams, Tom" Her Mum scolded "Pam! Take her up now!" and saw her set the Wendy doll, on the sofa, beside Tom, saying, "Don't dare touch Wendy doll, unless you want to give her a cuddle!" as he huffed "Only Nancy, plays!" as she gurgled "Good answer, Tom!" She then said, "Baby Suzie wants to say, nighty night to Nancy!" as he cried "What?" as she said, "I'm waiting for Tom to make up his mind, as how I'm to recognise Nancy!" as she removed the apron and hair slides again, as he sobbed and took her apron and pulled it on again, followed by her Alice band, as Pam screeched taking the doll over said, "Nancy! Kiss Baby Suzie good nighty!" and his Mum gasped "Oh Tom!" as he kissed the dolly and she cuddled him and scolded "This is so naughty Pam!" Pam stood up, holding Baby Suzie out for Tom to see, waving an arm towards him, calling "Bye Nancy!" before slipping out the door.

Pam slipped upstairs, giggling her head off, that she'd got Tom into her pretty apron and wearing hair slides and an Alice band and pretending to be a girl, doing curtsies as she returned Baby Suzie to her own room, when she had a lovely wicked thought. She entered Tom's room and tried to think, where to put the dolly. She didn't want him to see it, but wanted him to discover it, either in the morning or even better though the night. She tried slipping it into the bed, but saw the obvious bulge, which would give it away, right off. She then saw his two pillows and slipped the dolly down between them, making sure both were covering it. She whispered "Good night Baby Suzie! Nancy will be up to sleep with you soon. Just the way I used to!" as she checked it was well hidden from initial view. She lay down on his bed and rolled over and felt the lump, realizing that if he didn't spy her, he'd do the same thing and have to turn on the light, to check and would probably yell out and call for Mummy!" She checked everything was ok, before she closed the door and then popped into her own room. Pam entered the living room, where her Mum was sat beside Tom, with the Wendy doll on her other side, along with her pink apron and the hair slides too, him having removed them as soon as she'd left to take her doll upstairs.

Her Mum picked it up and warned "Now Pam! Here! Keep your dolly to yourself! Tom's had a terrible evening!" as Pam took the doll and sat down on the floor, facing both her Mum and Tom. Tom huffed "Can't you take that over there? Take her away from me!" Pam laughed "Tom! She won't bite you! She's just my dolly!" as he tried to watch the TV and ignore his teasing sister. She whispered "Wendy! That's my nasty brother Tom!" as she put on a voice and said, "Is he not nice?" but then changed to her own voice "Not normally! But tonight he's been extra nice and I think Mummy has threatened him, with something, if he didn't behave!" Her Mum gasped and said, "Pam! Stop teasing! I'm going into the kitchen to get your supper!"

Pam makes Tom swap into her pink apron but ties it up, to do the dishes

Around 9pm as their Mum slipped out of the living room, not wanting Pam to tease her about whatever, she'd done to Tom, but realizing Tom would be left at her mercy. She called "Tom! Want to be a good boy and help me get the supper?" as Tom realized if he stayed, his sister would tease him with her dolly, but knew it would be embarrassing for him, to help his Mum in the kitchen. Pam giggled, "Well Tom! Want to stay with us and play dollies or go and help Mummy?" as he huffed "You bug off! Keep your doll away from me or else!" as he left the

room and entered the kitchen. Pam called out "Mummy! Tom threatened to break my dollies!" as his Mum looked at him and heard him plead "I didn't! I just warned her to keep them away from me!" She called back "He Says, he'll leave them alone! What do you want to drink? Anyone for tea?" Pam called "Mineral water and a couple of wafers, please Mummy?" and Tom called "Coke and choc-y biscuits!" as his Mum reminded him "Please!" and heard him add "Please Mum!" She put on a kettle to make tea for herself and then poured out glasses of water and Coke, before putting biscuits onto a plate. His Mum lifted up a blue tabard-apron with white spots and heard him whisper "No Mum! Don't, please? She'll tease!" but saw her point to some of Pam's aprons, saying, "I think you'd prefer Pam to wear that one!" as he quickly pulled the tabard over his head, dreading Pam's reaction, to seeing him in his boy's apron.

His Mum said, "Bring this apron in for Pam!" as he huffed "She'll laugh!" but took the pink apron and slipped out the door and into the living room. Pam looked up and screeched "Oh Tom! Don't you look pretty!" as he held out the pink apron and said, "That's yours!" Pam giggled, "Mum! Did you want me to wear my blue pinny, or Nancy's pretty pink one?" and heard her Mum come in and laugh "Pam! Put on your pinny! I'm bringing in your supper, in a minute!" Pam took the pink apron and pulled it over her head, giggling "I'm sure Tom would have suited, this pink pinny!" as Tom huffed "Funny!" Pam giggled, "I wonder what Julie, or your mates will say, if I tell them about macho Tom, wearing a pretty apron!" as he huffed "Please don't tell, anyone Pam?" She laughed "Of course, I won't Tom!" but after a pause she added "As long as you do something for me!" Tom grimaced and asked, "What?" Pam whispered "Swap pinnies, to surprise Mum! When she comes in! I'll let you swap back, as soon as she sees us!" as she removed the pink apron and held it up for Tom.

Tom huffed "Not fair!" as he pulled the tabard over his head and grimaced, taking back the pink apron. Pam helped pop it over his head and fed his arms in, before turning him around, to tie the apron strings at his back, making sure it was a tight knot. She then took the tabard and pulled it on, just in time, to hear the wheels of the trolley, trundling out of the kitchen.

His Mum gets the knot from his pink apron, but ties a bow in it

Their Mum wheeled in the trolley for them and burst out laughing, when she saw Tom in the pink apron, as he huffed "There Pam! You said, I could remove this, when Mum came in!" Pam smiled and said, "Mum! Tom asked could we swap aprons, thinking Nancy's apron was prettier!" as he cried "I didn't! She said, she'd tell Julie and my mates, if I didn't swap!" as he reached behind him to fiddle with the apron strings and then realized Pam had tied them in a knot. He cried "Mum! Get this off me!" as Pam held out his blue tabard for him, giggling "I'm waiting! Don't you want to swap then?" as his laughing Mum said, "Let me see?" as she sat down, on the sofa and turned him around, to get at the knot. However, she realized it was too tight and said, "You'll have to wait, till I've had my tea! I'll need scissors to undo that!"

Pam pulled the tabard, back over her head and said, "Oh well! Don't worry Tom! It's just an apron!" He sobbed "Mum! This is too girly!" as Pam giggled, "I must admit, 'I never realized how much, like a dress, my pink apron looks, from the front!'" adding "You do suit it, Tom!" as he cried "It's not a dress! Is it Mum?" as she shook her head, laughing and agreed "No! It's not, Pam! Stop teasing Tom! You're going too far!"

She sat him down and hugged him again, saying, "Get me some scissors from the bookcase, Pam!" Pam huffed "I hope you aren't going to cut my good pinny?" as she opened a drawer and retrieved the sharp pointed scissors, but heard her Mum say, "No! I'll just use the point, to undo this knot, that you tied in his pinny!" Tom cried "It's not my pinny! It's hers" to laughter.

His Mum said, "Drink your Coke and I'll get this knot undone. Tom took a slurp from his glass and bit into a few biscuits, while his Mum was fiddling with the knot, using the point to try and prize the knot lose, scolding Pam

29

for tying it so tightly. Pam giggled, "I didn't realize I'd tied it so tightly! Sorry Tom!" She fiddled for a minute, before she eventually got it lose and said, "There! At last!" She took the two apron strings and tied them again, but this time in a normal bow. Tom cried "Hey! We've to swap!" A giggling Pam said, "Too late! We've almost finished and we've both seen you in your apron dress, so don't worry!" Pam laughed "Anyway Tom! That will come in handy when you're acting as my sister Nancy!" as her Mum gasped "Now Pam! Less of that! I told you!" Pam said, "Anyway Mummy! He'll need my pretty apron to help with the washing up!" as he cried "No way!" but his Mum said, "You started them earlier!"

Pam gasped "I thought you were joking Mum!" as she laughed "He actually did the washing up?" as she nodded. Pam said, "You should have made him finish!" as her Mum laughed "You came back early and so I let him off, with him dreading you tease him about wearing his boy's apron!" as she laughed "See the difference Mum that tonight's made! The old Tom was worried about wearing his own boy's apron, whereas the new Tom doesn't mind slipping into my pretty pink apron!" as he cried "I do!" as she gurgled "Nor transform into Nancy at the addition of hair slides!" as her Mum laughed.

Tom has to help with washing up, but Pam holds up a PVC pinny too

She laughed "Anyway Tom! It's not as bad as it could be!" as she added "Is it Mummy!" as she saw her grip her dress and bob a curtsy to him and giggle "We don't mind wearing a pretty apron to protect our pretty skirts or dresses!" His Mum said, "Just help Pam with the washing up and you can then remove your aprons!" Tom blushed at remembering how he looked. Pam gasped "How on earth did you make him?" as she laughed "I had to give him a few smacks! But as part of our deal, to do with him being a good boy and not being nasty to us, he offered to help with the washing up!" adding "Haven't you Tom!" but then asked "Or will Nancy do them instead?" as Pam reached up for her Alice band and hair slides. He grimaced and nodded "Ok!" not wanting her to add his ribbons or Alice band and his Mum not to squeal to Pam, about his up session.

Pam said, "You wash, and I'll dry!" as Tom started putting the plates, cups and glasses into the water. His Mum handed him a pair of yellow rubber gloves and heard him say, "I don't need those!" but Pam asked, "Haven't you got a pink pair to match his apron dress?" as he cried "Mum! Stop her!" He pulled on the yellow gloves and started washing the dishes. However, Pam then took one of her PVC pinnies and said, "Nancy! I mean Tom, I don't want you wetting my good apron!" as he turned and cried "Oh no! Not fair!" as he saw her holding up a pretty floral PVC apron, as his Mum gasped "Oh Pam!" as Pam said, "I'll let him wear his boy's PVC pinny, if he has one!" but her Mum laughed "You know he doesn't have one!" Pam laughed "That sounds the first thing to get him, when you take him shopping, tomorrow Mummy!" as he cried "I'm not going shopping for a flaming pinny!" as his Mum laughed "Now Tom! I think you'd prefer to choose your own, boy's PVC pinny than, to leave the decision, to your sweet sister here!" Pam gurgled "Oh Mum! You don't think I'd choose the prettiest of all PVC pinnies, for my big macho brother here?" as he cried "Not fair! Ok! I'll join you to town!" as they laughed.

Pam giggled, "I never realised the power of a little PVC pinny!" Pam had a thought and asked, "Sure you don't want to wear this pretty pinny to protect your apron dress?" as he shook his head and saw her run up the stairs as her Mum called "What are you up to young lady?" His Mum said, "I don't know what she's up to!" as he begged "Let me out of this?" as he fed his hands back to untie the bow, but his Mum said, "Watch it or next time I tie your hands back and leave you at Pam's behest!" as he quickly returned his hands, to his front and cried "Not flaming fair, Mum!" They heard her feet on the stairs and saw her enter the kitchen with a large smile on her face and her hands behind her back. Her Mum and Tom looked and both gasped as she pulled them around to her front and showed them a little PVC pinny, from when she was around 4 or 5 and she giggled, "I've found Tom a PVC pinny, to protect his aprons!" as he cried "No way!"

Tom wears Pam's PVC pinny, due to her showing him a little girl's one

Her Mum laughed "Pam! You are so naughty! Tom can't wear that! It's so small from, when you were really young!" Pam laughed "It will be perfect for little Nancy, to play with me, when her apron dresses or frocks might get wet!" adding "She'll just need her Alice band and hair ribbons!" as he cried "No way, Pam!" as he grabbed her PVC apron and quickly tied it over her apron!" as his Mum gasped "Oh Tom!"

Pam said, "Honest Mum! I'll keep quiet and help Tom with the dishes!" as she said, "Ok!" His Mum Says, "Just finish the washing up and Pam laughed "Now what's Julie's phone number?" Her Mum laughed "Don't you dare, Pam!" as she laughed "Just joking, Mum!" as she added "Anyway! I want to keep Nancy to myself, for a while!" as her Mum scolded her, and he pulled a face. Pam took a drying clothe and said, "Mummy! This is the way it should have been all along, with Mr MSP here, helping with the dishes!" They soon had finished the dishes and put them all, back in the cupboards, when Pam said, "I'm sure you haven't told me all, that went on! I can't see Tom, cowering just because of that threat!" She removed the tabard and hung it up, saying, "But Mum! You must agree, my nasty male chauvinist pig of a brother, did look very cute, in my pink apron dress and especially my pinny?"

Tom huffed "Not fair Mum! Can't I go up to bed?" as his Mum said "You can remove Pam's apron and go into the living room to watch a bit more TV, as he huffed "Ok!" and saw him remove Pam's apron, saying "That's been horrid!" and hang it up, before he exited. Pam giggled, "It's not horrid! It's a lovely apron! If you're quick next time and rush to get into the pinny, you might beat me to my blue apron and not have to wear your pretty pink one! Although it does look sweet!" 8.15 as he turned on the TV and tried to ignore his sister.

Her Mum said, "Now Pam! I think Tom's been teased enough!" Pam replied, "Mum! I didn't tease him that much! Anyway, he's been so nasty to me, hasn't he? Thumping me earlier and all the times he shouted and was horrible to me!" Her Mum said, "Go easy on him! He's promised he's changed his ways and won't be nasty anymore, to either of us!" as Pam giggled, "Yes Mum! I know you've done something! He didn't just change over teatime! He's scared stiff of you! What did you do?" and saw her Mum blush again and stammer "I told you! I just had a stern word with him and gave him a good smacking!" Pam asked, "Did it have something to do with his birthday? Did you threaten not to get him that skateboard he's after?" Her Mum saw a way out and took it, saying, "Something like that!" Pam asked, "Go on, Mum! Tell me! How did you get him to behave?" but heard her reply "I told you! I just had a stern word with him!" adding "Along with giving him much harder smacks!" as she laughed "Well I don't know what you did, but it's been fabulous!"

Pam Says, he should do housework in aprons but dons the little pinny

Pam then added "What about housework! I hope he'll be helping us, with that too!" as Tom cried "No way! Mum only said, the washing up!" His Mum said, "Shush you two! Let me sleep on it?" as Tom sniffled and Pam said, "Don't worry Tom! You'll soon get the hang of housework, like Mum and me?" as her Mum corrected "Mum and I" as she joked "That was a quick decision, Mummy!" as her Mum laughed "I haven't said, Yes or No, yet!" His Mum Says, "If Tom's a good boy and is well behaved, I might let him off housework, for a while!" Pam huffed "Mummy! That's sexist! There's no reason a boy can't help, with the housework, nor wear a pretty pinny!", but added "Though he doesn't seem to have a problem, with wearing a pretty apron and a pinny!" Tom cried "Stop teasing, Pam!" He huffed "Funny! I'm going to bed!", but then heard her add "and I'm sure with a little coaxing, he'll be great at slipping in and out of nighties and frocks too!" as he cried "You bug off!" as her Mum said, "Now Pam! Stop that!" as Tom sobbed "Not flaming fair Mum!" and stumped up the hall and up the stairs into his own room with Pam's giggles filling his ears. Pam apologized "Sorry Mum! It's just a little tease!" adding "I didn't mean to be so cruel to him, but I just remembered him being so nasty, to me and don't forget how, he shouted back to you?" Her Mum said, "I know, he was getting out of control, but I think I've that sorted that now!" adding "He'll be

much better behaved from now on!" Pam said, "Mummy! Wouldn't you prefer to have him and me playing quietly in the house and not arguing, compared to him banging his drum and shouting at both of us, like he used to do?" Her Mum laughed and said, "Yes! But you can't make him play girly games! Whatever will it grow into, in later life?" Pam giggled, "At our age, it's ok Mum! I agree if he was playing dollies at 15, it might be a bit funny, but it's ok at our age!" as her Mum gasped "I never said, he could play dollies!" Pam took her pink apron but then the little PVC pinny from when she was 4 or 5 and pulled it on over it to show her Mum and laughed "If Tom refuses to help with the washing up, this would be a wonderful look for him!" as her Mum gasped and giggled "Pam! I couldn't!" as she laughed "Especially if you added playing dollies with me as his punishment for being a MSP again!" as she laughed "I couldn't!" She then said "You know he hated wearing those frilly shorts Mummy?" as she nodded and asked "Why?" as she said "What would really bring him to heel, if he'd to wear my pretty apron and this little girl's PVC pinny, over one of my pretty frocks!" as her Mum gasped and said "No Pam! I won't do that to your big brother!" as Pam gurgled "Mummy! He'd really do a beamer and do anything you wanted!" as she laughed and shook her head "No Pam! That would be too cruel!" although, knowing she'd actually popped him into her frock, a few hours earlier.

Tom hides the yellow panties under his pillow not spying Baby Suzie

Her Mum watched her enter the living room and saw her exit with her Wendy doll, before she skipped down the hall and heard her slip up the stairs. Tom had gone upstairs and cleaned his teeth and gave his face a quick wash, before entering his room and locking the door. He went around to his chest of drawers and found a pair of his underpants, but as he turned, he caught sight of himself and grimaced as he saw the yellow panties in the mirror. He quickly pulled the panties off and thinking "Where can I put these flaming things?" as he quickly shoved them under his far left-hand pillow, not realizing Pam's dolly, was between his two pillows. He pulled the underpants up, followed by his PJ bottoms and then the top and jumped into bed. He lay there thinking of the horrid night, first his Mum taking him upstairs and spanking his bottom harder than she usually did. However, far worse was her taking him into Pam's room and putting him into the panties and then petticoat and flaming frock. Then the hair ribbons and being taken down to do the flaming girls work in Pam's apron and the fact that Pam nearly caught him dressed up, as he stuck his fingers up at both his Mum and Pam in a V sign. He then remembered his Mum making him keep the panties on and making him apologize to Pam for hitting her and then be a goody two shoes and sitting with her and then all the teasing Pam had given him with her dollies and even flaming hugs and kisses too! The final straw was having to wear her girly apron and then the PVC pinny.

Tom has to promise only touch, her dolly to cuddle or play with them

Pam went upstairs and did her ablutions in the bathroom, before slipping out and trying Tom's door. He said, "Go away Pam!" She giggled, "How did you know? Listen Tom! I won't tell Julie or her Tina, about tonight, but I want you to promise me something!" He asked, "What?" and heard her explain "I was worried when you threatened to ruin my dollies or toys!" He huffed "Ok! I won't break them!" as she said, "I won't tell Julie, if you promise to only touch my dollies, to either cuddle or play with them!" He huffed "Don't worry! I won't be touching your flaming dollies at all!" She said, "That's ok then! Nighty night!" as he huffed "Yea! Good night!" Pam giggled, as she entered her own room and locked the door, before removing her skirt and blouse and slipping into her nightdress and then to bed, waiting for her Mum to read her a fairy tale.

He complains about everything and is told about Pam's ballet suggestion

Pam heard her Mum come upstairs and knock on Tom's door. She heard him call "Is she about?" and heard his Mum say, "No! She's in her own room!" as Tom slipped out of bed and unlocked the door, before returning under the bedclothes, ready for his bedtime story. His Mum entered and closed his door, locking it, in case Pam sneaked in and smiled, as she saw Tom snuggle down under the bedclothes.

He blushed and huffed "Mum! Tonight, has been terrible – having to sit in with her and then her teasing me with her dollies and finally having to do the dishes and wear aprons!" She laughed "Well apart from the aprons! That was very naughty of Me and Her!" as she cuddled him saying, "Sorry Tom!" and gave him a kiss!" as he huffed "I don't like kisses, Mum!" She However, said, "As for aprons, although it will probably be your blue boy's apron, that you will wear to help with the dishes and some housework!" as he gasped "Not fair Mum!" She said, "It was refusing to do housework and dishes that got you into that situation downstairs young man!" adding "Wasn't it?" as he sobbed "Sorry Mum! but you shouldn't have kept me indoors with Ug!" She said, "No more calling names, or she might call you Nancy, outside!" as he gasped "Mum please, stop her!" as she laughed "I'll try! I couldn't believe how quickly she took to towering over you and having you under her thumb!"

She did mention "I did threaten to stop her going to ballet, if she kept it up!" as he said, "Good!" but heard his Mum laugh, but unfortunately it gave her an idea for you, if your naughty again!" He asked, "What?" and heard her giggle "Make you join her to ballet class!" as he grimaced and said, "That's not funny!" as she laughed "She is so naughty! She said, not to worry, you wouldn't have to wear the same as her!" as he huffed "No way am I going to do ballet!" She gurgled "See the little girls are called the Fairies and they are allowed to wear tutus!" as he blushed and pulled the bed clothes over his head in embarrassment. His Mum bent down and kissed him goodnight, as she turned out the light and closed his door. He scrambled back out of bed and turned his key, before slipping back under the bedclothes again. Her Mum exited and laughed as she knocked!

Pam Says, she'd heard Tom get up in the night and disturbing her sleep

Pam heard her Mum exit Tom's room and knock on her door. She asked, "You alone Mum?" as her Mum laughed "Yes Pam! I'm alone!" as she unlocked her door and sat down on the bed, waiting for her Mum to come and brush her hair. She saw her smiling Mum enter. She said, "Now Pam! No more dressing him up! That was terrible the teasing you gave him, with your dollies and stuff tonight!" as she said, "Sorry Mummy!" but added "He does deserver a little payback, due to all the naughty things and refusing to do any housework for us!" as she laughed "Just a little!" Pam laughed "Wasn't I good, stopping my friends teasing him or dressing him up, after me fibbing to Alice about him being a sissy boy, last week, as her Mum said, "I'm glad you've been a good girl and told your friends, it was a fib!" as she huffed "I wish I could!" as her Mum said, "Don't you dare young lady!" and added "I know he absolutely hates doing anything girly and blushes so easily, at the slightest sight, of one of my dollies!"

Her Mum laughed "Naughty girl!" Pam asked, "How was sleeping beauty?" adding "Did you read Nancy her fairy tale!" Her Mum scolded "Less of the Nancy and girly talk about Tom!" as she said, "Tonight must have been the worst night of his life!" as Pam laughed "Mum! I don't know what you did, but it's completely changed his attitude and life with him and her, will be so much fun from now!" Her Mum said, "I think he's, settled down for the night!" as Pam wondered whether to say, "Want to bet!" but held off.

She scolded her again "Pam! That was naughty! All that teasing you gave Tom tonight!" Pam said, "Sorry Mum! I'll try not to and anyway, it's only, us three, know about his dollies!" Her Mum said, "Now Pam! Keep those dollies away from Tom or I'll get rid of them!" as she complained "Mummy! You wouldn't get rid of Wendy!" as she pulled it up from her bed and gave it a kiss and a cuddle. Her Mum said, "I think you can put your dolly down for a few minutes! I thought, you'd given up dollies, as they were just for little girls!" Pam giggled, "I've changed my mind! Isn't that a girls perogative!" as her Mum laughed and corrected her "Prerogative dear!" Pam set the doll to her side and said, "Don't worry Wendy! I'll cuddle you to sleep, in a minute!" as she enjoyed getting cuddles by her Mum. Her Mum asked, "Pam! What was that about earlier?" as she giggled, "What Mum?" and heard her explain "Something about Tom not getting a good night sleep!" She laughed "I thought I'd heard Tom get up, in the middle of the night, a few times, lately!" adding "And it woke me up!" as her Mum said, "I didn't hear him! He's not mentioned it to me!" as Pam said, casually "I'll call you, if I hear him tonight!" as her Mum carried on

combing her hair. A minute later, she asked, "Ready for your fairy tale, dear?" and saw Pam turn around and nod, before slipping her legs under the bedclothes, with her and her Mum cuddling each other, as her Mum read the story.

Her Mum realizes Baby Suzie isn't around and gasps as she realizes ...

Her Mum laughed "Where's your other dolly, you had earlier? I hope you aren't going to neglect her! Sure! You don't want to cuddle her, too?" Pam giggled, "I'd like to, but I can't remember, where I put her!" as her Mum laughed and was about to ignore it, when she gasped and asked, "You haven't put her in Tom's room?" Pam giggled, "I don't think so! Do you think, we should wake Tom up and ask, has he been playing with my baby dolly?" Her Mum scolded "Now Pam! Tell me you didn't!" Pam laughed "Should we pop in and ask has he seen her?" as she laughed and said, "No!" Her Mum said, "Turn around and I'll comb your hair!" Pam sat up and felt the brush glide through her long dark brown hair. She casually lifted her doll up and cuddled it. Her Mum finished combing her hair and Pam got into the bed, ready for the fairy tale. Her Mum started reading the fairy tale, with Pam cuddling her dolly in bed with her.

She giggled, and said, "Mummy! I hope you read Tom a fairy tale too!" as her Mum said, "Less of the interruptions, young lady!" as Pam giggled, at the thought of him being read stories, about princesses and princes. She soon had finished the story and was kissing her "Sweet dreams, darling!" before Pam slid down under the bedclothes and called "Night Mummy! This evening was a lot of fun!" as she pulled Wendy down under the bedclothes, for a cuddle with her dolly.

Pam said, "Sweet dreams too!" as her Mum laughed and turned out the light and closed the door. Pam quickly slipped back out of bed and turned the key, before climbing back in to cuddle her dolly and have a giggle. She turned on a small bedside lamp and spoke softly to her dolly "Don't worry, Wendy! Baby Suzie will soon be cuddled, too!" She didn't want to go to sleep, too soon, as she was sure that Tom, would eventually find Baby Suzie and cry for Mummy, when she'd go in to tease him silly, as her Mum went into her own room, wondering what she should do.

Her Mum locked her door and changed out of her clothes, into her long nighty, before sliding into bed to ponder. She could go into Tom's room, to search for the dolly. However she realized that even if Pam was only joking, she would tease Tom rotten, about her searching for a little dolly in his room. She thought to herself "He should be ok, tonight, as he's in bed, with his door locked and there was no sign of it there, or he'd have found it, already and created a row!" She decided to read for half an hour and then turned her own light off and slid under the bedclothes, to get some sleep.

Tom had locked his door and slid back into bed under the bedclothes, lying down on the righthand side of the bed, still unaware of the dolly, in the middle of the two pillows. He lay there, thinking of the horrid time, with his Mum after tea, when she'd taken him upstairs to give him a smack for being naughty, refusing to help her with the washing up and yelling at her. However, this time she'd taken it much further and dressed him in Pam's clothes, before taking him down, to do the washing up, with her pink pinny over her yellow frock. Luckily Pam wasn't in and when she came back early, he was able to escape upstairs and change back into Tom's clothes. Then his Mum had made him say, nice things to Pam and stay in for the night.

Tom rolls over and realizes a baby doll is between his pillows

Pam had teased him rotten about playing with her and now she was teasing him about aprons and dollies. He was tossing and turning, on the right side of the bed, for about half an hour, without traversing to the left-hand-side. He'd heard his Mum leave Pam's room and go into her own and the house fall silent. He rolled over and felt something lumpy, under the pillow, but tried to ignore it, as he rolled over to the left side of the bed. However, after more

tossing and turning, almost an hour later, he was near the centre of the bed, when his head turned to feel a definite lump, under the pillow and he reached up to feel. Tom felt the cotton head and then some material over a lumpy hard material and then something thin, sticking out and pulled it down to try and see what it was. However, the room was pitch black and so he pulled back the bedclothes and slipping out of bed, he turned on his light and let out a cry "Mum!" and threw the dolly down on the bed and sobbed "Not fair!" A laughing Pam unlocked her door and called out loudly "Mum! Tom's up again!"

Her Mum unlocked her own door and exited, knocking on Tom's door. He unlocked it and let her in, crying "Look what she'd put, under my pillow! Not flaming funny!" as his Mum held him to her nighty, to give him a hug and said, "That was naughty!" A giggling Pam entered and said, "Now Tom! You promised not to ruin or touch my dollies, unless it was to cuddle, or play with them!" adding "So you've given your dolly a nice cuddle in the night!" Her Mum said, "Now Pam that was naughty!" Pam said, "I took Wendy to bed with me too! It's our secret!" as he sobbed "She'll tell if I sleep with a dolly!" Pam laughed "Honest! I won't! As long as you're a good boy and do what I say!" as her Mum said, "Pam! I thought, you'd just put the dolly in his toy box, or something!" Pam shook her head "No! She was right in-between the two pillows, but underneath!"

Tom huffed "I felt something lumpy, as I rolled across a few times, but didn't twig, till a flaming minute ago, when I turned on the light!" as Pam giggled. Pam lifted the doll up and placed her the way, she had her before, giggling "Good boy! I had her like this, so you must have given our dolly, a few kisses, as you rolled over, back and forth!" He sulked "I didn't!" as her Mum said, "Come on Pam! Take your dolly back?" but Pam said, "Mum! Can you give me a minute with Tom, and I'll sort this!" Her Mum looked at her and said, "Ok! But don't be naughty!" Pam sat down on the bed and said, "Come and sit here Tom!" He sniffled and sat down beside her, as she put her arm around him and though he wanted to shove her away, but knew she could tell. Hence, he sat and listened. She said, "Now Tom! You've been sleeping with my dolly for an hour now and so I can tell Julie or Tina about you, whether I take it back or not!" She said, "But you'd please me, if you keep my dolly in your bed tonight!" Tom sobbed "I don't want to sleep with a flaming doll!" as she laughed "Too late!" and reached over his bed and popped the doll under the bedclothes, resting on the left pillow.

Her Mum scolded, but Pam insisted he sleep with her dolly

Pam Says, "Look! I'll put the dolly there! On the far side of the bed! So! You shouldn't have to cuddle her! You'll have the rest of the bed to move in!" He huffed "Not fair, Pam!" as he slid back into the right-hand side of the bed, pulling the bedclothes back over himself. She asked, "Can I turn out your light?" as he nodded, and said, "Close the door!" Pam said, "I won't make you kiss Baby Suzie, to sleep, but I want this door unlocked, for the morning!" as he cried "Why?" as she explained "I want to check, you haven't thrown your dolly, out of bed in the night" She said, "In the morning I'll just bring her back in, when you let me in!" He huffed "But you might see me change!" as Pam laughed "I'll make sure you're still in bed!" as she turned off the light and said, "Sweet dreams Tom and Baby Suzie!"

Pam closed his door, smiling, as she put a hand to her mouth, to stop herself giggling, but then called "And Nancy too of course!" She knocked on her Mum's door and heard her say, "Come in Pam! How is he?" as she entered and closed the door too. She whispered "I think I've sorted it out! I've promised to keep it a secret, as long as he's a good boy and does what I say!" Her Mum asked, "Have you taken your dolly back?" but saw Pam smile and shake her head "I've popped her over to the far side of his bed, so he won't have to cuddle her, in the night!" adding "Unless he wants to that is! Wendy knows how much fun a cuddle is!" as her Mum gasped.

She scolded "Your brother can't sleep with a girly dolly! If it ever gets out, he'll die!" as Pam laughed "I won't tell on him Mum and it will keep him under control!" as her Mum asked, "What do you mean?" Pam said, "Well it

seems you have something on him and now I have something too!" as her Mum gasped "I hope you know what you're doing, Miss Pamela Crothers!" Pam sat down and gave her Mum a cuddle "Mummy! I'm sure between us, we'll turn Tom from a horrid MSP bully boy, into a nice young man, who is thoughtful and caring!" as her Mum shrugged her shoulder and heard Pam add "Not to mention, great fun to play dollies with!" as she exited the door and fled back to her own room, giggling at her joke.

Her Mum decided to check on Tom and tried his door and was surprised to find it unlocked, as he cried "Get away Pam!" She said, "Don't worry Tom! It's only me Tom, as she turned on the light and smiled at the doll's head, sticking out, from the left-hand side of the bed. Yet again Tom forgot to give her back the yellow panties, which were to seal his fate, in the morning when Pam entered to check for his dolly and accidentally spies them. He sniffled and said, "She'd better not tell!" as his Mum asked, "Will I take her dolly back?" but heard him say, "No Mum! It's ok! She knows I've already had her in bed, with me for an hour! If you take her, she can already tell and it would be horrible, especially if it got out in school!" She stroked his head and kissed it and said, "Sweet dreams Tom!" but joked "or is it Nancy?" as he blushed and grimaced "Ha!" She said Ok! I'll speak to her tomorrow!" She turned out his light and closed the door, but didn't hear the customary key turn, to stop Pam or her entering.

Morning Pam checks he's still with his dolly, but then spies the panties

In the morning, Pam awoke and went in to check, that Tom still had his dolly in bed with him. She slowly opened his door and smiled as she saw Tom still asleep and not stirring, facing the doll, his head only a foot away. She thought to herself "So! My big bully, macho, nasty MSP brother, slept with a little baby dolly, all night long!" adding "I wonder what he'd do to stop me, telling Julie or little Tina?" as she tiptoed inside and closed the door, still without him stirring. She reached for his doll and pushed it, over, so it was only an inch away from his mouth. She saw Tom, stir and move his hand up towards his mouth, to clear the obstruction away, but instead pushed the doll further into his face. Pam saw his eyes open and him pull his head away, simultaneously pushing the doll away, as a giggling Pam, said, "Morning Nancy!" as he grimaced and cried "Get out! You go away! I'm Tom!"

She laughed quietly, not wanting to alert her Mum, to her being in Tom's room. She giggled, "Ok Tom! Kiss your dolly good morning and tell her you love her!" He pleaded with her "Please go!" but she giggled, "Go on! You've slept with your dolly, so you might as well!" Tom grimaced and pulled the doll towards his mouth and kissed the doll, mumbling "I love you! Baby Suzie!" causing Pam to giggle "Good girl! I mean boy!" He huffed "Go on then! I've done it!" as she asked, "Did you like sleeping with your dolly?" as he turned away and pulled the blanket over his head, feeling really embarrassed. He begged "Please Pam! Don't tell anyone, about this?" as Pam sat down on the edge of his bed and laughed "Now Tom! It will be our secret, as long as you're a good boy and do what I tell you!" as he asked, "What do you mean?" She smiled "I'll have to think about that! You're definitely going to help Mum and me, with the washing up, from now on and wear an apron and a pinny!" as he grimaced, but nodded, "Ok!" She held up the dolly and said, "And play dollies with me!" as he pleaded "Please don't Pam? I've had her with me all night! Please take her back?"

Pam was about to return to her own room, with her baby dolly, having forced Tom to kiss his dolly, when she caught sight, of the yellow material, peeking out from under his pillow and pulled on it, asking "What's this?" and gasped, when she realized, it was the pair of her own panties, she'd left out for her Mum. She held them up to show Tom, asking "What were these doing, under your pillow?" as Tom blushed and mumbled "Mum must have put them there, by mistake!" She whispered "Right! Mr yellow panties! Tell me why, you were wearing them, or I'll bring Julia over to ask!" and saw him turn away, sobbing and mumbled "Mum made me!" as she giggled, "Mum, made you wear my knickers!" as she added "So! That's why you had to do what she said, or she'd tell me!" as he nodded, hoping she'd leave it at that, but she didn't. However, she then asked, "Is that all, she made you wear?" as Tom said, "Yea! Just those!" but heard her threaten "If I ask Mummy and find out you've lied to me, I'll be very

annoyed and punish you!" as Tom flushed and sobbed "Not fair! It's not fair!" but nodded, "She was horrid to me!" Pam giggled, "So she made you wear other stuff "What, tights?" and saw Tom nod, as she giggled, "Great! Wait! I want to hear this from Nancy!"

Tom wears a nighty and panties to tell Pam the full story

Pam tiptoed around his bed and out the door, back to her room. Pam picked up her Wendy doll, her pink nightdress and a pair of pink panties, but also an Alice band and hair ribbons and closing her door, quietly, she entered Tom's room and closed his door. She knew her Mum had stopped her dressing Tom up, when she'd found out about the frilly shorts and then aprons and headscarf but now her Mum had actually dressed him up herself, she knew she had him and could do anything she wanted. She sat down on the edge of his bed and set the doll and nightdress down, giggling "Right Tom! Nancy wants to wear her nighty!" as he pleaded "Please Pam! Don't make me?"

But she laughed "Quiet! We don't want to let Mummy know, that I've found out about you?" adding "Remove your pyjama top!" He grimaced, as he unbuttoned his top and pulled it off, as Pam handed him the nightdress and giggled, as he stared at it and pulled it over his head and down to his waist. She said, "Remove the bottoms too!" and heard him plead "But I've got nothing underneath!" as she smiled "Don't worry! I've thought of that!" and pulled the pair of pink panties, from behind her back and held them out, saying, "I'm sure, these should fit! They're the same size as Nancy's yellow panties!" He sobbed "Won't, this do?" but she shook her head. She giggled, as she saw him reach down under the bedclothes and struggle to remove his pyjama bottoms, as he huffed "Not fair, Pam!" as he pulled the pyjama bottoms and pushed them off, with his feet.

He then took the pink panties and reached down, he pulled the panties up his legs and into place, pulling the nighty down to cover himself, huffing "There!" He softly cried "This isn't right, Pam!" as she giggled, "Is Nancy dressed?" He nodded, and she pulled back the bedclothes, to hear him cry "Eh!" and see him pull his nighty further down to cover himself, as Pam laughed and let the bedding go and say, "Ok Nancy! You're dressed and can tell me and our pretty dollies, the full story, of what our lovely Mummy did to you!" He pulled the bedclothes back to cover himself and started his tale of woe. He huffed "You had left, and Mum asked me to help dry a few dishes! I gave my normal reply and said, "Washing up was girls work!" She suddenly got annoyed and said, "She was going to teach me a lesson!" adding "It was terrible!" as Pam laughed "What did she do?" He continued "I thought she meant just a smacking, but she took me up to my room and after undressing and smacking me, she took my clothes away to leave me naked. She flaming well, returned holding some of your clothes!" as she gurgled "What?" as he cringed and said, 'Your yellow undies there!' but then added 'Flaming tights and a petticoat!'" as she gurgled. He was about to continue, when they heard footsteps on the stairs and Pam put a finger to her mouth, to be quiet. She lifted her Wendy doll and pushed it under the bedclothes, into Tom's body and saw him cuddle it, looking up at her, wanting to cry, but keep quiet. He didn't want his Mum coming in to spy him, in Pam's nighty and so kept quiet, although it couldn't have made the situation much worse. Their Mum assumed they were asleep in their own beds and just quietly entered her own room, before returning to carry on with their breakfast.

Pam Says, that when their Mum discovers she knows, it's an action replay

Pam smiled and said, "You won't want Mum to know, that I know your secret!" as he huffed "Why?" She said, "As soon as Mummy finds out that I know, I'll want her to give me an action replay step by step of what she did to you, but with me, standing right beside you laughing away!" as he gasped and pleaded "Please don't, Pam? That's cruel!" She said, "Mum's gone! Continue!" as Tom shoved the doll out, saying, "She's yours!" But she laughed "I might double your dolly collection!" as he grimaced "Not fair Pam!" He lifted both dolls and saw Pam pull the bedclothes down to see him cuddling them.

He sobbed "Not fair, Pam!" as she giggled, "Hurry up, Nancy!" as he huffed "Anyway, she pulled my pants off and pulled those yellow things up my legs! She then made me pull on your white tights and then a flaming petticoat!" as Pam gasped "Not petticoats too?" as he nodded. She giggled, "I didn't see any bulge, when I came back, later!" as he blushed "I'd only your panties on then!" as she said, "Continue!"

He blushed "She took one of your flaming dresses from your wardrobe and put it on me!" as Pam took hold of his bedclothes and shoved them in her own mouth to stifle a scream of laughter. She calmed herself and asked, "Which one?" and heard Tom huff "A stupid yellow one!" as Pam giggled, "Mum put you into my pretty yellow frock?" as she stuffed a hand into her mouth to stop herself screaming. He tried to turn away, but she said, "Face me and carry on!" Tom huffed "She put a hair band, on me and I hoped she'd just threaten to tell you, if I didn't do what she wanted, but she was really cruel!" Pam giggled, "What did she do, with you dressed like that?" He grimaced and muttered "She flaming-well took me downstairs to the kitchen, with the curtains still open and I dreaded being spotted by someone out the back!" causing her to gasp "She didn't?" trying to stifle a scream, in case their Mum heard. Tom continued "Mum said, 'I'd still to do the dishes - As washing up was girl's work, I could now do it!" as Pam giggled, "Fab!" as he added "She put me in your pink apron, too!"

Continuation of Tom and Pam's stories – after stories 2 to 10

with him getting into more and more embarrassing situations.

- **Part B** - Pam plans girly things for Tom, horsies, dollies and do housework
- **Part C** - Tom and the next-door neighbour **June** sees Nancy and dolls pram
- **Part D** - June gets him a boy dolly and **June, Brenda and Clare** go to town
- **Part E** - Plastic carrier bag dance and Nancy does, the laundry
- **Part F** - Play Shopping and Pam tells Julie a fun way to do laundry
- **Part G** - **Julie + Mum** sees Nancy and Pam deputizes Mum to check panties
- **Part H** - Pam makes Tom wet his pants – Nappies – Sissy + Baby football
- **Part I** - **Tina** realizes Tom is Nancy and June gets him into her pram
- **Part J** - Tina's friend **Becky's** birthday party and Becky's dolly and Shopping

THE QUESTIONNAIRE TO TRAP BOYS – TOBY 7

Some girls design a questionnaire to trap boys

The girls decided to draw up a questionnaire to see which boys, might be suitable for transformation. They decide to choose boys, with at least one sister and no male parent around – so it's just the mother, boy and daughter(s). A small group of girls took copies of the questionnaire to school with them and then put it onto the internet and sent emails out, to their schools. Most girls didn't realize what it was for, but those with brothers, passed them on and said, they'd a chance to win £10 for filling it in. Response was slow, but soon speeded up, with the internet responses and soon the organizers had about two hundred replies, with more and more coming in daily. Some girls filled in the forms and made up answers for a boy in their class, or their brothers, for a giggle.

Based on the answers, they grouped responses into sections, wondering could they put their plan into action. The girls planned, so that several girls would pop around, to the boy's house, but ensure they were a few years older than him, so an 8-year old, boy, would have girls 8-11 attend and a 12-year old would have girls 12 to 15 etc. This would mean that they should be bigger and be able to control him, easier than if they were younger.

They scan the answers selecting young Toby who has a sister - Francesca

They dismissed all the ones without Mum's or sisters and concentrated on those, who only lived with their Mum and sister(s). There were several boys who lived with their Mum and sister(s), some Dad's having divorced, and others died. They decided to speak to about 6 boys and their sisters and initially selected a boy Toby who was 7, who had a younger sister Francesca who was almost 6. They phoned their home and spoke to Toby and said, he was in with a good chance of winning a prize, for filling in his questionnaire, as he said, "Great!" as his Mum came on the phone and asked who it was. Jenifer said, "Toby was in for a chance to win a prize, for filling in a questionnaire that they had on life-styles.

His Mum said, "Yes he showed me, and I helped him fill it in!" but laughed "He baulked, at some of the possible answers – like did he play dollies with his sister?"

Jenifer laughed "We just popped it in, for a laugh, realizing most boys don't!"

Jenifer added "Some cheeky girls filled in fake forms for their brothers or boys they knew and made them sound real sissies, playing dollies, dress up, wearing their sister's aprons to help with housework and doing needlework!" as his Mum giggled, "The naughty girls!" She continued "That's why we need to phone up and confirm the boy has actually filled in the form himself!" as his Mum laughed "So what's next then?" as Jenifer said, "Is it ok if we meet him and his sister?" as his Mum said, "Fine!" as she told her their address and arranged a meet up one early Tuesday evening.

The Questionnaire – for boys -
Prize of £10 or £5 in a raffle for completing 25 questions

Our phone is,
Email – sarah.jones@hotmail.com
Date today –

Name -
Phone No.

1. Who do you live with?
   a. Mum + Dad
   b. Just Mum
   c. Just Dad

2. What age are you?
   a. Years
   b. Months

3. Do you have any sisters?
   a. None
   b. Older with ages
   c. Younger with ages

4. Do you ever be nasty to your sisters?
   a. No
   b. Call them names
   c. Swear at them
   d. Pull their hair
   e. Hit their arm
   f. Other

5. Do you like to play football?
   a. Yes
   b. No
   c. Sometimes

6. If you have sisters – do you ever play with your sisters?
   a. Yes
   b. No
   c. Sometimes

7. If yes or sometimes - What do you play with them?
   a. Football
   b. Chase
   c. Ball games
   d. Skipping
   e. Dance

f. Dollies

g. Other

8. Do you help your Mum / sister make the breakfast/dinner?

   a. Yes

   b. No

   c. Sometimes

9. Can you cook or bake?

   a. Yes

   b. No

   c. A little

10. Do you help your Mum / sister with the dishes – washing up?

   a. Yes

   b. No

   c. Sometimes

11. Do you help your Mum / sister with the housework?

   a. Yes

   b. No

   c. Sometimes

12. Do you help your Mum / sister with the Vacuuming?

   a. Yes

   b. No

   c. Sometimes

13. Do you help your Mum / sister with the dusting/polishing?

   a. Yes

   b. No

   c. Sometimes

14. Do you help your Mum / sister change the bedding?

   a. Yes

   b. No

   c. Sometimes

15. Do you help your Mum / sister do the windows?

   a. Yes

   b. No

   c. Sometimes

16. Do you help your Mum / sister with the laundry?

   a. Yes

   b. No

   c. Sometimes

17. If yes or sometimes What do you use to hold your clothes pegs?
    a. Bucket?
    b. Plastic bag
    c. Drawer
    d. Other – state

18. Do you help your Mum / sister cut the grass?
    a. Yes
    b. No
    c. Sometimes

19. Do you wear an apron to help with housework?
    a. Yes
    b. No
    c. Sometimes

20. Do you wear a PVC apron for wet work?
    a. Yes
    b. No
    c. Sometimes

21. If you wear an apron?
    a. I don't wear one
    b. Is it your own
    c. Your sisters
    d. Your Mum's
    e. Other

22. Can you do needlework - Sew, Knit, Embroider, Dress-making?
    a. Yes
    b. No
    c. Sometimes

23. Do you help your Mum/sister with the shopping?
    a. Yes
    b. No
    c. Sometimes

24. Do you help carry your Mum/sister's shopping bags?
    a. Yes
    b. No
    c. Sometimes

25. When shopping do you bring any kind of bag with you?
    a. No
    b. Carrier bags
    c. Shopping bags

Three girls pop around to see Toby and his family and bob curtsies

Jenifer who was 9 and two younger girls, Fiona 8 and Trish 7 arrived in Jenifer's Mum's Wendy' car and rang the bell. His Mum answered with Toby and his young sister behind and invited them in. She asked did they want a cup of tea or something and she sat them down in the sitting room. Jenifer's Mum said, "This is my Jenifer whose 9!" and saw her curtsy to Toby's Mum Kathy as she laughed, as Wendy continued "and this is Fiona who's 8", and saw Fiona bob a curtsy too.

His Mum laughed and bobbed a curtsy back to her. Wendy continued "And this young girl is Trish 7, her friend who's roughly Toby's age!" as Trish curtsied too and saw his Mum, bob a curtsy back, as she said, "This here is my Toby 7!" and his young sister Francesca who's 5 nearly 6!" Trish called "What, no curtsies?" and whispered in her ear and saw Francesca grip her skirt and bob a curtsy and saw the three girls, grip their dresses and bob curtsies back, to laughter. Wendy explained "The girls learn to curtsy at ballet classes! I do think, it looks very sweet!" as his Mum Kathy laughed "I love the way you girls curtsy! I'll have to start Francesca curtsying, too!" as Francesca gripped her skirt and bobbed another curtsy to her Mum, who bobbed a curtsy back!" Toby said, "You all look stupid!" as her Mum laughed "Now! Don't be cheeky, Toby?" as his Mum asked what they wanted to drink and went to get it ready. He asked, "How much have I won?" as his Mum heard and called "Don't be cheeky, Toby!"

He said, to his sister "Francesca! You don't need to be here, so scat!" as Jenifer said, "Now Toby! Your sister needs to be here, too!" as he huffed "Well! She's not getting any of my money!" as she said, "Not fair!" Jenifer called Toby over and said, "Sit down here, on the Sofa, beside me and I'll check this!" as he sat down and she took his questionnaire out from her handbag and asked, "Did you fill this in, yourself?" as he said, "Mum helped me, a bit!" as she asked, "Didn't Francesca help, too?" He huffed "You must be joking, she's stupid!" as the girls gasped "You are naughty!" Francesca called "Mummy Says, I'm not stupid so there!" as she stuck her tongue out to him.

They sit Toby down to check his answers, but let Francesca stay

Fiona then sat down on his other side and said, "We've had lots of boys, replying to the questionnaire and you are very lucky to have been chosen "Toby!" Toby asked, "When do I get my money?" as the girls laughed "We just need to check some of your answers! and see if they need to be corrected!" Jenifer laughed "I suppose you don't want to try to curtsy too, Toby?" as Francesca screeched "Oh! I'd love to see him curtsy!" as he huffed "Funny! You only curtsy in skirts or flaming dresses!" as Fran gripped her skirt and bobbed a curtsy towards him. Trish whispered in Francesca's ear "Can we see some of your pretty aprons and a PVC one too!" and saw her run back, into the kitchen, as her Mum asked, "What are you after?" and said, "Just showing the girls my pretty aprons!" as she took four or five, from the door and returned with four floral clothe aprons and a floral PVC one.

The girls said, how pretty her aprons were and Fiona asked, "Toby! Do you have any pretty aprons?" as Francesca gurgled. He said, "Just my blue one, for school!" as Trish giggled, "Well I'm sure, Francesca will lend you one of these, if you ask, sweetly!" as he cried "You must be joking!" as he went to get up, but the girls, held him down and said, "Look Toby! We won't be long!" Francesca giggled, "I'd love to see him in one of my pretty aprons!" as she pulled a frilly apron around her body and asked, "Will you tie me up, Trishy?" as Trish tied it behind her back. Trish said, "You can curtsy in a pretty apron too!" and saw Francesca grip her apron and bob a curtsy to her.

Franny was showing the girls other aprons and Fiona said, "Oh how pretty! Can I try one on?" as Francesca nodded, and saw the 8 year old girl, pull the floral apron around her and tie it up, as Francesca laughed "That looks funny on you, as you're bigger than me!"

Fiona said, "It's fun to curtsy in aprons too!" as she gripped the apron and Trish asked, "Can I try one too?" Jenifer saying, "Me too!" as she nodded, and saw Trish pull the other one around her, with Fiona removing her apron

43

and handing it to Jenifer who pulled it around her and curtsied and heard Francesca gurgle "Oh that looks even funnier on you Jenifer!"

Jenifer said, "Trish! These apron's are more your size!" as Trish gripped the apron and curtsied and said, "I'm about the same age and size, as your big brother Toby here!"

Jenifer said, "Oh Toby! There's something on your back! Just turn around, a tick!" as he asked, "What?" and turned around on the sofa, to let her check.

Jenifer ties a pretty little apron around Toby's front and a PVC pinny

She took the pretty apron from Fiona and quickly fed it down Toby's front and quickly tied it behind his back. He cried "No don't girls! Get this off me!" as he struggled with the apron, trying to remove it, but to no avail as he stood up to run out, but Jenifer helpd him still. Francesca screeched "Oh fab!" as Fiona quickly took a photo of him and put her camera a way. His Mum came running in and gasped and giggled, as she first of all saw big Jenifer, in her daughter's little apron, but then gasped and screeched, as she saw her big boy in one too!" Toby cried "Mum! Quick! Get me out of this apron!" adding "Look! She's tied me into it, and I can't get if off!" as she laughed "Oh girls! That's naughty!" as he tried to leave., but Jenifer held him still and kept hold of his apron strings. He cried "Oh no! The blinds are open and I can be seen, from the street! Let me down!" but a giggling Jenifer and Fiona held him on show, as Francesca laughed "It's fun to wear a pretty apron, Toby!" as she said, "Go on Toby! Give me a curtsy, with your pretty pinny!"

Trish said, "Toby thought he could only play curtsies, if he wore a skirt or frock, but look Toby, you can bob a curtsy, in your sister's pretty aprons, too!" as she gripped the apron and bobbed a curtsy to him!" His Mum laughed "Oh girls!" as Jen whispered, "We'll let you down, if you bob a curtsy!" His Mum and sister gasped, as he gripped his little sister's floral apron and bobbed a kind of curtsy to them. Francesca screeched "Oh Toby! It's going to be fun playing curtsies with you, from now on!" as her Mum said, "Now Francesca! I'd better get your big brother, out of your pretty apron!" as Francesca laughed "Don't worry, Mum! I'll find him some skirts or dresses, to play curtsies properly with me!" as her Mum gasped "Naughty girl, Francesca!" to giggles from the girls and their Mum Wendy. Jenifer's Mum Wendy said, "I'll pull the blinds and try and get him out of it or stop him showing off in it, if you bring the drinks in, as she laughed and left the room. Wendy pulled the blinds and said, "There Toby! You can't be seen from the street, in your sister's apron!" as he begged "Please get me out of this?" Fiona said, "We said, we'd stop you showing off in your sister's pretty apron!" as Trish whispered to Francesca "Stick your hand in your mouth, to stop yourself screaming!" She took the PVC pinny from his sister, behind her back and asked, "Will I open the blinds?" as he begged "Please don't?" as she said, "Kick up a fuss and we open the blinds on you, Tinkabelle!" as Francesca giggled, "What a fab name, for my big brother! I mean sister!" Fiona fed the PVC apron, around him and saw Francesca stuff her hand into her mouth, to stop screeching, as Fiona took another few photos of him. He sobbed "Not fair, girls! I look a real sissy, like this!" as Trish asked, "While we're dealing with Toby, can we see, some of your dollies?" as Francesca gurgled and ran out of the room.

Jenifer said, "When your Mum comes in, say, you're just protecting your good clothes and it's ok!" as he gasped "Not fair!" as she said, "Or we show you off to the street!" as he cried "Not fair girls!"

Fran fetches some dollies and they make Toby kiss one

Next thing, Francesca ran in with 2 dollies and heard giggles, but protests from Toby "Not dollies! Don't make me play dollies with her?" as they giggled, and Fiona took one and said, "Just a quick Sissy kiss!" as Francesca gurgled, as he sobbed and kissed it, as Fran laughed "It's going to be lots of fun, playing dollies with Toby, from

now on!" as he cried "No way!" but heard Jenifer laugh "Francesca can tell, girls at school or even your mates, about what pretty aprons you wear and how you like to kiss her dolly!" as he sobbed "Not fair!" He then gasped as Jenifer took an Alice band from her handbag and slid it onto his hair!" as Francesca gasped and gurgled "Oh fab!" but even more, as she took her yellow handbag and slid it around his neck, as he sobbed "Oh no! Not a handbag?" and Fiona took another photo of him, as Franny gurgled "Oh yes! I've always wanted a sister to play dollies with!" as he cried "Please don't make me, Franny?" as she added "But it's even more fun playing dress up!" as they applauded her and patted her on the back, as he sobbed "Not fair, girls!" Next his Mum was wheeling a trolley of drinks, out of the kitchen and they quickly removed his Alice band and handbag, from around him.

She wheeled the trolley into the room and gasped and giggled, as she saw her big Toby, now in his sister's apron, but also a floral PVC apron on top!" as Jenifer said, "Toby's wanting to protect his clothes, with some pretty aprons! Aren't you Toby?" He sobbed and nodded, "Yea!" as his Mum giggled, "Was this some kind of joke?" as they laughed. Their Mum said, "Can we have tea and then I'll explain the girl's plan!" as Francesca giggled, "Mummy! I think I'll have someone to play dollies with, from now on!" as her Mum said, "Now Francesca! As soon as he's out of your aprons, I doubt he'll want to play with you!" adding "He's footy mad!" as Trish asked, "Francesca! Do you not play footy, with your big brother?" as she said, "I hate football!" as Toby cried "I'm not playing with her?" as Francesca laughed "Just dollies!" and then added "And dress up and ballet too!" as he cried "Mum! Stop her!" He protested "She's saying, I've to join her, doing stupid dance and flipping dollies!" as Francesca called "It's not stupid! You'll soon find out, Tinkabelle!" as the girls laughed and his Mum gasped "She'd never have had the nerve, to call him a name before, or he'd hit her!" Jenifer called "Toby you hit Francesca again and we will have a suitable penance, for you!" as he grimaced and heard her say, "Promise you won't hit, your sweet little sister, anymore!" as Franny looked at him sternly and he huffed "I promise not to hit you, Franny!" His Mum can't believe the change in her big boy, and laughed "I can't believe the change in my boy, since you got here, girls!" as Francesca called out "Mummy! They're lots of fun!" adding "And so will Toby be, from now on!" as he cried "Please don't make me? Please?" to more laughter and giggles.

Jenifer whispered into his ear "Tell her and then your Mummy, how you like their aprons and pretty outfits!" as he cried "No! Don't make me!" They asked, "What?" and heard him stammer "Your apron and skirt looks nice, Francesca!" as she screeched "But heard Trish say, "I think that deserves a nice curtsy, to your sweet big bro, now!"

Toby has to complement Fran and his Mum to get curtsy back

They saw Francesca grip her skirt and giggle as she bobbed a curtsy to him. However, Jenifer said, to her "A nice kiss too!" as she said, "No way!" but Trish whispered, "He'll hate it, even more than you!" adding "Especially seeing he's in your pretties!" She said, "Ok!" as he sobbed "Mum! Don't let her kiss me?" as the girls held him still and Francesca threw her arms around him and kissed his cheek, laughing, as he blushed and said, "Yuk!", but Fi said, "Only the lips count, Francesca!" as she gurgled, and her Mum gasped and said, "Don't Francesca!" but she approached her big brother and kissed his lips, as he cried "Not fair, Mum!" as he sobbed. Jen said, "What about your lovely Mummy!" as he blushed and said, "Your pretty aprons nice too and I like your dress Mummy!" as she gasped and giggled, as Fi laughed "That deserves, a nice curtsy and kiss too!" as his Mum blushed and gripping her own apron, she bobbed a curtsy "Thank you Toby!" to him. She tried to get out of the kiss, but the girls egged her "Now! It's only fair that since, he gave you such a sweet complement, in his pretty aprons, that you give him a sissy kiss too!", as Franny screeched "Oh yes!" He cried "I'm not a sissy!" as his sister gurgled "You're wearing my girly apron and pretty pinny and kissed one of my dollies too!" as her Mum gasped "He didn't?" as they all nodded, and she laughed "Oh Toby!" She giggled, as she approached him and gave him a kiss on his lips, to laughter around the room and clapping from Francesca, as he blushed and sobbed "Not fair Mum!"

Jen complements him and he's to bob a curtsy and give a kiss

However, then Jenifer said, "Toby that's a lovely little pretty apron and pinny, you are wearing!" as he looked at her, wondering what she wanted and heard Francesca giggle "Oh yes! He's to give a curtsy and a kiss!" He cried "Don't make me?" adding "Mum! Stop them!" as his Mum said, "Just a quick curtsy and kiss!" as he bobbed down, but not a proper curtsy and heard Trish called "Francesca and your Mummy, will have to give Toby lots of practice, curtsying tonight!" as he cried "Don't Please?" Francesca giggled, "I will!" but then said, "He might want to remove my pretty aprons, later!" as he said, "Your darn right, there!" as she laughed "I'll have to find him something, he can play curtsies better in!" as she gripped her skirt and bobbed a curtsy to him!" Toby gasped and cried "No don't, Francesca! Don't dress me up?" as she gurgled "Oh fab! We can play dress up!" as he cried "No! Don't make me! That's not fair girls!" as Trish cuddled him and gave him a kiss, saying, "Don't cry Toby! I might let you be my boyfriend, if you're a good brother to your sweet little sister!" Toby gasped "What?" as she gave him a kiss on his lips, as he cried "Oh no!" and his Mum laughed "You girls are terrible!" His Mum said, "Don't worry Fran, your dresses won't fit him!" as she giggled, "Mum! I know what we can do!" as she asked, "What?" as she laughed "Until I've borrowed some big frocks for him, from my big girlfriends!"

Toby's Mum prepares clothes for the laundry some of his and Frans

He begged "Please don't?" but heard her add "Or else his sweet Mummy goes out and buys him, some skirts and frocks, to play dress up in!" She gasped "I couldn't get your brother, girly clothes?" as Franny nodded but smiled "Until then! We'll just have to use your old, dress up box, with your clothes in it!" as the girls screeched, and Toby cried "Oh no! Don't Mum? You wouldn't?" as they all dared her, as she laughed "We'll see!"

They tucked into the food and said, "Can I hear what this was about?" as Jens Mum asked, "Can I talk to you, in the living room?" as she said, "Well girls! Don't be naughty with Toby!" as they promised "We won't open the blinds, if he's a good boy!" as Francesca ran and fetched some dresses for her dolly and returned, as Toby begged "Please don't make me, play dollies, Francesca?" She laughed "Oh Toby! It's so much fun, hearing you beg me, not to play dollies!" as the girls giggled. However, then Jenifer took one of the dresses and asked, "Can I dress your dolly?" as the girls giggled, and saw her hold it, towards Clarabelle, but then hold it up to Toby and say, "Now dolly! I think this dress, is just a tad small for you!" as Francesca gurgled "Oh fab! Yes! He can be my big dolly, to dress and undress!" as he gasped and cried "Please don't, Francesca?"

Jen's Mum Wendy was led into the living room and said, "See the girls have realized, there a lot of boys, who don't help their sweet Mummy's or sisters, with the housework and are MSPs!" His Mum laughed "Yes! He's been a bit of a chauvinist, up till now!" as they laughed, and she continued "Now! Your boy will probably be completely changed now and help you and Francesca with housework, in a pretty apron, but can you bear with us, for a few minutes and we'll show you some things, to make you and Francesca laugh and will change your life?"

She asked, "What?" as she asked, "Does Toby ever help you with the washing?" as she shook her head, saying, "Francesca often helps me, but not Toby!" as Wendy asked, "What if we get him to peg out, just a pair of trousers and a pair of his pants?" as his Mum laughed "I can't see anything wrong with that!". Wendy said, "He's to pay a penance, if he refuses!" as Kathy asked, "What?" as Wendy said, "To peg 6 things of yours and 6 pretty things of Francesca's up!" as she laughed "I think he'll stick, to his own pants and trousers!" Wendy then said, "And then we'll let him play footy, after!" as she laughed "I'm sure he'll be relieved at that!" Wendy asked, "Will we call him in, to start some of the dishes, as he's dressed the part and you get his washing for him, along with your and Francesca's washing!" as she said, "I've none washed yet!" but Wendy said, "Just get some pretty clothes, to air in the garden!"

Toby has to complement his dolly and then change her dress

Meanwhile, Francesca laughed as she held up a large doll said, "you haven't complemented your dolly, Clarabelle, on her pretty dress and apron?" as he called "Mum! Don't let her?" as she laughed "I could bring some girlfriends around, to play dollies with us!" as the girls gasped "Oh Francesca!" He sobbed "Hi Clarabelle that's a pretty apron and dress!" as his giggling sister gasped and said, "Did you hear that, dolly! My big brother Toby, just complemented your dress and apron!" She took the doll and bobbed a kind of curtsy with her dress and held it up to his mouth and said, "Kiss your dolly, Tinkabelle!" as he sobbed and kissed it, to more laughter. She then said, in a squeaky voice "Oh Toby! What a pretty pinny over your apron dress!" as the girls giggled, "Good one, Franny!" as he sobbed "Not fair!" as he gripped his apron and bobbed another curtsy, to his dolly and giggling sister, as she laughed some more.

She then held out a dress to him and said, to him "Remove your dolly's dress and get her into her new frock!" as he cried "Oh no! Don't make me dress her?" but she laughed "Will I bring Lucy in, to help you change your frock!" as the girls laughed and Trish said, "I think you're getting the hang of this, Francesca!" as she laughed "I'm so glad you girls, came over tonight!" She said, "Turn your dolly over and carefully undo the Velcro, from your dolly's dress and then slide her into her new frock!" as he sobbed and turned the doll over onto it's front and woefully undid the binding and soon had slid the doll out of her dress. His sister gurgled "Right Tinkabelle, slide the dolly back into her new frock!" Trish added "The same way you'll slip into a frock yourself, later!" as they all giggled, with him still begging "Pleas Franny! Don't make me play dress up?" He took the dolly and slid it's arms into the dress sleeves and then slid the dress over its head and down it's body and finally did the Velcro together, as his sister screeched "Oh fab!" as she took the doll and standing up, she ran out and into the room and showed her Mum Saying, "look Mummy! Toby just changed his dolly, into a new frock!" as both Wendy and his Mum giggled, and his Mum laughed "Oh, the poor boy!" as the young girl slipped back out of the room.

Wendy returned to the sitting room and giggled, as she saw Toby on the floor with Fran trying to change her doll, with her clapping with Joy and saying, "It's going to be so much fun, playing with Tinkabelle, dollies and dress up!" as he cried and begged "Please don't make me, Francesca?" as she reached over and kissed his pouting lips, to more giggles. Wendy said, "Now Toby! I don't think you're enjoying dollies and so we'll give you a rest from them, till later!" as Franny said, "Oh pooh! I was enjoying seeing him, with my dollies!" However, she then heard her add "We want you to start the dishes, with your sweet sister!" as he cried "No way!" but she asked, "Francesca! Do you know some sweet girls, who would like to join your big brother, playing dollies?" as she gurgled "I know lots!" as he sobbed "Not fair! Ok!" as she said, "Ok! Into the kitchen and you get a PVC pinny too, Francesca!" Francesca ran and got another PVC pinny and pulled it on herself, giggling, as the girls led Toby into the kitchen.

Toby has to start the washing up, but sees his Mum with the wash basket

He cried "Close the curtains girls! I'll be recognized!" as they laughed "I'm sure Francesca doesn't mind being seen, in a pretty apron!" as she laughed "No! I love wearing pretty aprons, over my skirts and dresses!" Fi asked, "Well Toby! You're enjoying your pretty aprons too, aren't you?" as he cried "Not fair! Yes! I'm having fun!" as Francesca giggled, at him. Jen started the water and the Fairy liquid into the bowl and soon, it was frothed up, as she asked, "Any rubber gloves Fran?" as she pulled out the gloves and said, "Here Toby!" as he cried "Please don't make me?" but next thing was pulling a pair of his sister's pink gloves on and grimaced, saying, "I hope nobody sees me!" as the girls laughed. He was handed some plates and cups and put them into the bowl and started washing them, with his sister giggling away, teasing him, about her aprons.

He hated doing the washing up but got on with it and saw his little sister, helped by Trish and the girls dry them. He asked, "Can some of you girls help me?" but they shook their head saying, "You need the practice Toby!" as Franny giggled, "Yes Toby! You never normally help, Mummy or me!" as he blushed and grimaced.

His Mum had gone upstairs and fetched the clothing for Toby and Francesca, smiling as she entered the bedroom and selected some skirts, dresses and lingerie to air, in the garden. She also went into Franny's room and got some of her pretty skirts, dresses and some undies too and finally went and smiled as she selected a pair of his underpants and trousers too, thinking "It's not going to be the end of the world, if he's to peg out these!" as she returned downstairs and gasped as she saw her big boy still in the apron and PVC pinny but wearing Fran's rubber gloves at the sink washing the cups and saucers. She laughed "I can't believe it girls!" adding "Well done Toby! It's about time you helped with the dishes!" as he sobbed "They made me Mummy and wouldn't close the curtains and I can be seen!"

They saw his Mum come down with a large basket of clothing and set the basket down for later. Francesca saw her Mum and said, "Are you putting some washing on, Mummy?" as her Mum laughed "Just popping some of our stuff out, to air in the garden!" Toby finished washing the last cup and saucer, when Jenifer said, "Well! We want you to peg out some washing!" as he cried "I'm not going out, in these flipping aprons!" as his Mum said, "Just a pair of your pants and trousers!" Francesca called "He should peg out, my frocks too!" as he sobbed "Mum! Don't make me? It will be terrible, if the neighbours spy me, pegging out washing!" Meanwhile Trish took over, from Francesca, saying, "I'll join my sweet big, boyfriend, Toby here, drying the washing up!" as she reached over and gave him a kiss, as he gasped and heard more giggles, as Francesca removed her aprons and handed them to Trish and giggled, "Thanks Francesca!" as she reached up and kissed him again, as he huffed "Not flaming-well fair, Francesca!"

Fiona got Francesca, to fetch a pretty pink handbag and saw her run off and return with one around her neck, as Fi said, "Just slide it up your arm, like this, to mince!" as Francesca giggled, and slid her handbag, up her arm and laughed "Oh, I see!" as Fi said, "It's much more girly, like that!" as she giggled. She then heard Fi say, "Just mince up to the front door and back!" as Francesca giggled, but turned and saw Fi, had slid her arm out to the right and mince towards her, as Francesca copied her and said, "That's even more girly!" Fi whispered "It will be fun to teach your brother later, in the house or back garden or around the shops!" as Francesca gasped and gurgled "fab!"

Trish said, "Can I have a word with him?" as she led him from the kitchen, into the living room and said, "Now! You know we could tell lots of girls, around here, about you or even show you playing dollies!" as he sobbed "Not fair!"

Toby wears a headscarf to peg out his trousers and pants

She laughed "Now you only need to hang up 2 items of yours on the line, but you don't want the neighbours to recognize you, in your sister's pinnies?" as he shook his head, but gasped, as she removed the headscarf, from her handbag. She said, "If you wear this, it will disguise you and you'll be finished in a jiffy!" as he gasped, but then saw her remove an Alice band and ribbons and say, "I'll give you 10 seconds to decide and then it's hair slides for Tinkabelle!" as he nodded, "Ok!" and felt her tie the headscarf, around his head. Trish gave him another kiss and led him into the kitchen and heard his sister screech "Oh fab!" and more laughter and giggles. His Mum then spied him in the pretty headscarf and couldn't believe her eyes, as he entered in both the aprons, but with the girly headscarf around his head and tied sweetly at the back.

His sister screeched, as he sobbed "Mum! She threatened to put me into ribbons, if I didn't wear this!" as his Mum, ran and hugged him "Oh you sweetie!" as Francesca called out to him "Don't worry Toby! I'll save hair ribbons for when Tinkabelle is playing dollies and dress up with Mummy and me!" as he sobbed "Oh no!" as she kissed him and he cried "I don't like kisses!" as they all laughed and a few flicked their wrist, towards him effeminately. Jen said to him "All you have to do, is peg out your pants and trousers and we'll let your Mum and sister, peg out their girly stuff and then we'll let you play footy!"

He huffed "I can't wait to get out of these stupid aprons and play footy!" as Jen asked, "Where's your football, Toby?" and he said, "In the cupboard, there!" His Mum went and fetched his football and asked, "Where do you want your ball, Toby?" as Wendy said, "Just throw it into the garden, for later!" as his Mum opened the window and threw his ball, into the garden and saw it bounce a few times before sitting still, in the grass in the center of the garden. Francesca called "Count me out, of playing football, with him!" but Fi whispered "You'll adore the way, he now plays football with you!" as she asked, "How?" but Fi giggled, "Wait and see?" She said to her "Just slip into another apron, to help peg out the washing!" and saw her run and slip into another pretty apron.

Wendy said, "See! In a pretty headscarf or ribbons, he won't be recognized, as a boy helping his Mum and sister, in the garden to peg out the washing or clothes to air!" as Kathy laughed "It is cruel, making him wear a pretty girls, headscarf!" as she laughed "He thought it was better, than hair ribbons!" His Mum laughed "Oh! You girls are naughty!"

Wendy asked her "Where's his clothes pegs?" as his Mum opened a drawer and took out an old clear plastic bag, saying, "That's some here and others are on the line!" as they smiled. Wendy called "Fiona! Just pop out and bring those pegs on the line, back in, will you?" as Kathy said, "But it's quite handy, to have them there, on the line, beside us!" as Fi slipped out with her handbag and began popping the pegs, into her own handbag. His Mum looked and saw what she was doing and gasped, as Wendy, put her finger to her mouth, to be quiet!" Wendy said, "Ok Toby! Let's bring the basket of clothes out and you get your undies and trousers ready, ok!" He said, "Well! Make sure that nobody sees me, in these aprons, when I go out! Mum you check!" as his Mum stepped out and saw the street was clear and said, "Ok Toby!"

His Mum sees Fiona pop out to put the pegs into her handbag

She saw him step out with the basket, of clothes and run around the back to the garden, followed by the giggling girls. He took the basket to the center of the garden and setting it down, he reached in and rummaging, eventually found both his trousers and underpants. However, Jen had taken the plastic bag of pegs and quickly emptied them, into her handbag and asked "Will you give him, his clothes pegs Fi or will I?" as she held out her handbag, as she laughed. Toby set the basket down and said, "Just my stuff! None of Francesca's or Mum's!" as they nodded, "Fine Toby!" as he asked, "Right! Where's the pegs, Mum?" as a smiling Jen said, "Right Toby! If you refuse, to peg out your trousers and pants, or even complain, then there's a penance!" He asked, "What?" as she laughed "You promise to peg out your sweet little sisters and Mummy's pretty clothes too!" as he cried "No! Don't make me!" She laughed "We won't! You'll be a good boy and peg out your own trousers and pants and we'll let you play football after, ok?" as he huffed "Ok! I'll do them!" However, Jen then held out her handbag and asked, "Do you want to use my pegs, or Fiona's pegs?" as Fiona held out her handbag to him, as he cried "Oh no! Don't make me?" as Francesca screeched "Oh fab! He's to use a handbag, too!" as Jen laughed "Choose or you peg out, all the pretty clothes!" and saw him take Jen's handbag and hold it there, to giggles from the garden.

Jen said, "You won't be any use like that, with the laundry, Toby!" adding "Now, let me slide it up your arm!" and taking the handbag, she slid it up his arm, to the elbow, as Francesca screeched "Of fab!" She gasped at his look and added "Just like I see, Mummy, carry her handbag, to do the shopping!" as her Mum gasped and laughed. The girls laughed and Trish said, "Our Mummy's say, this is good practice, for when we join her shopping, too!" as Franny screeched "Yes Mummy! Tinkabelle can help us shop!" adding "With his pretty handbag!" as he sobbed "Please don't, Mum?" His Mum giggled, "Oh girls!" as her big boy stood there in aprons, headscarf and with the handbag on his elbow and Jen said, "Right Toby! Reach into your pretty handbag and take out 2 pegs, for your trousers!" as he sobbed and reaching in, he pulled out 2 pegs and then went to set the bag down, as he picked up his trousers and pegged them up, to giggles from the garden but Fi said, "Sorry Toby! You must have your handbag, dangling from your elbow, for all the washing!" as he grimaced and heard her say, "Pick up your pretty handbag!"

Toby sobbed and reaching down, he picked up the handbag and slid it up his elbow again, to more laughter. Trish said, "Unpeg your trousers and pop the pegs, back, into your handbag, ready for to start again!" as his sister giggled, "Fab!"

Francesca gurgled "Mummy! We'll have to use a handbag from now on, for the washing or any laundry!" adding "And airing any of our pretty clothes!" as her Mum nodded, "We certainly will!" adding "I thought I was being clever, about leaving the pegs on the line, but I must admit, this is more fun!" Francesca called "But I'll need Tinkabelle's arm, to carry his handbag, when I need the pegs, from now on!" He said, "No way! I won't!" but then changed and begged again "Please don't dress me up Franny?" as she ran and gave him another kiss laughing.

They suggest a handbag as a birthday present and he's to swap handbags

He sobbed as he unpegged his trousers and popped them back into the basket, and slid the pegs back into his handbag, to more giggles. **However, Jen said, "Just peg them up by the ankles, deary!"** Trish said, "Francesca would you like to hold your big brother's basket, for him?" as she laughed and said, "Ok Tinkabelle!" but then saw her hold out her handbag and say, "Better hold this, for me then!" as he cried "But I've already got, this bag on my arm!" as she laughed "I could bring a few girlfriends in, to hold my bag for me!" as he took her pink handbag. She laughed "Such a greedy boy, wanting two handbags!" as she laughed "Mummy! At least you know what he'll be wanting, for his next birthday or Xmas presents from now on!" as he cried "Not fair!" as her Mum laughed "What, a handbag?" as she nodded, along with pretty skirts and frocks too!" to more laughter and giggles. She said, "Slide your handbag up your other arm, Sissy!" as he cringed and slid her bag up his right arm, to leave him with 2 handbags now dangling and saw her lift the basket and say, "It's a bit heavy! Hurry up and get your pegs from your handbag, Sissy!" He sobbed "She's calling me sissy!" as her Mum scolded her "Now Francesca! This is bad enough for him!"

His sister said, "Sorry Tinkabelle!" and saw him reach into his handbag and get 2 pegs again. They saw him then dip into the basket, for his trouser again and taking them by the legs, he pegged them up on the line, to applause. His Mum said, "You did that very well, Toby!" as Francesca giggled, "She did! Didn't she, Mummy?" as he huffed "Funny!" Jen said, "Now, for your undies!" as Francesca laughed "Oh! He should have some pretty panties, like us, Mummy!" as he said, "Ha!" as Francesca said, "You should use my handbag for your clothes-pegs!" adding "Just take all the pegs from Jen's handbag and pop them into my pretty handbag first!" He cried "Not fair, Francesca!" as her Mum gasped "Gosh! Its brought out a really naughty side, to my little girl here!" as she saw him dip his hand into Jen's handbag, to get some pegs and then reach over and pop them into Francesca's little handbag, as they giggled.

However, he heard Trish say, "Mummy taught me to zip my handbag closed, after use, in case my purse was stolen, when shopping with her!" as the girls screeched and heard Francesca call "Zip your handbag up, Tinkabelle!" as he blushed and grimaced as he zipped her handbag up, calling "Not fair girls!" He again reached into Jen's bag for the rest of the pegs and then he had to unzip Francesca's handbag again, to more giggles as he deposited the pegs back into it. He said, "There! They're all there!" but Fiona said, "Zip your handbag up again!" and saw him, zip the pink handbag up again. However, then Jen said, "Oops! I've got some of your Mummy's pegs here!" as he cried "Oh no!" but saw her mince up the garden and say, "Come and get the rest of your pegs sweetie!" as he cried "Don't please?" but was pushed up the garden by Fi, Trish and Francesca. He reached her, as the girls held him still, but then a laughing Francesca, pulled his headscarf off.

They remove Toby's headscarf and replace it with ribbons

He cried "Don't Francesca! Leave my pretty scarf alone!" as Jenifer ran up and said, "Your sister, is so naughty!" as he cried "Give me that back, Francesca! That's not funny!" However, she then reached into her own handbag

and took out the Alice band and some ribbons, as he cried "Oh no!" as she slid the Alice band onto his head, followed by some slides. Francesca screeched "Oh Toby! You look fab! Just like my big sister, would look!" adding "Mum! Doesn't she look like a sister, if I ever had one!" as her Mum nodded, and laughed "I suppose so!" to more laughter. Francesca gurgled "This just gets better and better with my sissy brother!" as he sobbed "Not fair Mum!" as he had to reach into Fiona's handbag and get the pegs and then unzip Francesca's handbag and pop the pegs back inside. His Mum, "Girls! Let him off! This must be terrible for him!" as he quickly popped the rest of his pegs into Francesca's handbag and said, "Off you go Tinkabelle!" as he walked towards the washing basket.

However, Francesca called him back and saw him walk back with the 2 handbags on his arms and when he reached her, she whispered into his ear and he cried "Please don't?" as his Mum watched him slide his elbows, to his waist and then slide his arms out to the side and extreme mince, as the whole garden broke into screeches, at him mincing towards his laughing Mum. Francesca called "Mummy! That's the way Tinkabelle, has promised to join us shopping around the shops!" as he cried "No way! I wont!" as she laughed "It will be the frock, you're wearing, you won't like!" as the garden erupted with laughter. His Mum ran and cuddled him and said, "I never expected tonight, to be so funny!" He finally dipped into the basket and picked up his underpants and huffed "Ok! I've got them and reached up and unzipped Francesca's handbag and got a clothes-peg and pegged them up again!" as he cried "You've promised that was it! If I was a good boy, I could play footy!" as Francesca said, "She should peg up, all the girly washing now, using his handbags!" as her Mum shook her head.

Wendy said, "He's been such a good boy! I think he can play football now, as Francesca called "Boo! Not silly football!" as he called "Ok! Take your bags back and let me get these ribbons and aprons off!" as Jen took her handbag and kissed him "Thank you, Toby, for looking after my pretty handbag!" She saw him still with Francesca's handbag on his arm and him hold it out to her. Jen asked, "So Toby how long do you want to play football for?" as his Mum checked the time and said, "It's 8pm!" and said, "You should be in by 8.30, but heard him beg "Mum! Can't I play footy till 9.00 please! I've been a good boy this evening and it's been terrible, prancing about like a flaming, big fairy!"

Francesca heard and gurgled "Oh Tinkabelle! Being a little fairy at ballet, is lots of fun!" adding "When will you get him his ballet outfit, his skirt and tutu?" as he cried "Please don't, Mum?" She laughed "The girls at ballet will adore you!" adding "especially the young girls, who'll be dressed the same as you, in tutu's too!" as the girls giggled, at the prospect. Francesca laughed "Mummy! Hasn't this evening been wonderful and I'm looking forward to lots of fun times, with my new big sister!"

Franny teases him about being a fairy and joining ballet class

Trish giggled, "Now Francesca, she's actually your little sister, as she'll do anything you want?" as Francesca gurgled and her Mum, gasped "Oh girls!" Trish whispered into Toby's ear, but nothing happened until a few minutes later, she gave him the nod and he called out "Mummy! Francesca stole my big dolly!" as Francesca screeched and gasped "Mum! I've wet my knickers!" as her Mum gasped and giggled, "Oh Toby! Naughty boy!" as the rest of the girls and Jen's Mum, laughed, as she ran indoors. He cried "Not flaming fair!" Jen asked, "Can I bring Toby in a minute!" as his Mum laughed and nodded. He begged "Please don't do anything more to me?" While Francesca was upstairs changing her panties, Jen took Toby into the hallway and taking some panties from her handbag, said, "Quick! Into the cloakroom and change these panties for your undies, or else I let Francesca see!" as he sobbed and quickly went in.

He removed his trousers and then pulled his pants down and removing them, he then pulled the frilly panties up his legs and got back into his trousers again. He hid his underpants away in the cloakroom, for later and exited, as Jen smiled and asked, "You ok?" as he nodded, "I've put them on!" as they heard Francesca coming down the

stairs, laughing. He heard her call "You're a naughty boy Toby, making me wet myself?" as Jen asked, "Toby! Have you wet your panties?" as Francesca laughed, thinking it was a tease as she laughed "I'm going to make sure, you wear girly panties, from now on, even to school!" as he begged "Ha! Mummy won't let you!" as she giggled, "Want to bet!" as he begged "Please don't make me, Francesca?" as she laughed and kissed him again, knowing it really embarrassed him. Jen said, "Francesca! Get another handbag for yourself!" as Francesca got herself another handbag!" as she led him back. Meanwhile Jenny had slipped into the sitting room and popped a nighty, inside a frock into her largish handbag and slid it back again.

Toby then asked, "When can I go and play footy with my mates?" adding "This has been terrible!" as his Mum said, "I'm sure the girls will let you go, soon!" but the girls laughed and Jen explained "Now the rules for football!" as he called "I know how to play footy!" as his Mum wondered why, they'd have to tell him the rules. However, she then laughed "It's not normal football! We'll be playing, Sissy Football!" as he cried "Oh no! What's that?" to laughter, as his Mum said, "Better wait for Francesca, girls!" Francesca returned and laughed "I'm not taking my handbag back, he's to keep that with him to play silly football!" Trish giggled, "It's ok Franny!" adding "See! Your sweet brother and us will be playing 'Sissy football'" as she explained "I'm just about to explain the rules and the uniform!" He cried "Please don't make me play, girly football?" to more laughter. Jen explained "To play Sissy Football, you have to wear a pretty apron, mince with a pretty handbag on your arm, wearing hair ribbons or a headscarf are optional, but so is a frock!" as the garden erupted with laughter and screeches, as Fran laughed "Mummy! I definitely will be playing football with Toby lots more, from now on!" as he begged "Please don't Franny?"

Trish makes him remove his shirt, jumper and wear a frock

She asked Toby "So Toby! Do you still want your hair ribbons in, to play football?"

He blushed and nodded, "Not fair!" but said, "Yes, please!" as she joked "We don't mind if you want to join your mates to play, instead!" as Fran screeched "Oh! His mates would love to see Toby play in my pretty aprons and his hair ribbons!" as he sobbed "Not flipping fair!" They kicked the ball to each-other, but the neighbour Sylvia, came out and then screeched, as she saw Toby in hair ribbons, his sisters pretty aprons and mincing with a handbag and they explained, having tricked him into being a girly, for his Mum and sister. However, then Fiona asked, "So Toby! Why did you want to wear the pretty headscarf earlier and those pretty hair ribbons?" as they all laughed and he replied, "To stop you and the other flaming neighbours, seeing me dressed up, as a flaming fairy?" She asked, "So! What are you trying to look like, in hair ribbons or your pretty headscarf?" as he gasped "Oh no!" adding "A flipping girl!" and heard giggles. Trish gurgled, as she took her chance and asked, "Can I have a word with him a tick and calm him down?" as she minced him to behind the garage and said, "Quick Let me get you out of that pretty apron and handbag!" as he said, "Thanks Trish!" and pulled them off him. However, she said, "Remove your shirt and jumper!" as he gasped "What?" as she undid his jumper and then his shirt, with him begging "Please don't, do anything more?" She then removed the frock from her handbag and said, "I'm going to let you remove this, in a few minutes, but to please me, arms up, as he gasped and whispered "Not a dress?" as she fed the frock up his arms and over his head. She laughed "I think, your sister will be playing dress up with you, lots from now on!" as he swallowed and reddened and felt her pull the dress, but also the nighty, down his arms. He sobbed as he was left, in the dress, but she said, "Just add the pretty apron and handbag and I promise to let you remove them and get back into your boy's clothes to play with your mates, if you want, in a few minutes!" and he wiped his eyes and said, "Promise?" as she nodded, and gave him a kiss.

She saw him pull the apron with the attached pink handbag, over his frock. He signed as he thought to himself "At least, it's just for a few minutes of embarrassment, being shown off, to my sister and Mum, but then will be allowed back into my boy's things to play footy properly!" However, it was a naughty trick and just before returning to

show the garden, she giggled, as she undid his trousers, but kept the belt up. Jen raised his frock and laughed "See Toby! If you remove your frock, they'll spy your frilly panties!" as he cried "Oh no!", but then he felt her reach under his dress and into his panties and gasped as she pulled out his willy and left it on show, sticking down from his panties. She gurgled "Your sister will spy that, too!" as he gasped and cried "Oh no!" as she pulled down his frock again and led him out to screeches, from the garden.

They all laughed, and Francesca screeched "Oh great! He's in a frock now!" as his Mum laughed "You are naughty, Trish!" She then said, "Look girls! I've told Toby it's to give us and Franny a laugh! He just needs to mince about in his frock for a few minutes!"

She laughed "When I heard him say, he wanted to look like a girl! I remembered I'd this pretty frock in my handbag and thought Franny would have a laugh at seeing him!

Franny called "He's to stay in that dress all day or else!" as her Mum laughed "Now Franny, let him remove it after he's played a bit more Sissy Football with us!"

The garden explodes at seeing him in a frock but refuses to remove it

Fiona added "And I've told him for being such a good sport, we'll let him then remove his girly dresses and aprons and ribbons and handbag, to go and join his friends playing footy, in five minutes time!" as Franny complained "No! He's to stay and play as my sweet little sister!" to more laughter and her Mum scolding her. She said, "Aren't I nice Toby?" as his sister said, "No! He's to stay here as a girly and play Sissy Football with us!" as she laughed "Now Franny! Don't be cruel! Just let him kick the ball with us, playing Sissy Football, but then, let him change into his boy's clothes after!" as she shook her head. As her Mum thought Jen was being kind to Toby and laughed "Now Francesca! Toby's had a really embarrassing time here, with all the girls, looking a complete sissy!" as the girls giggled.

Jen took the ball and kicked it to him and said, "See girls! Sissy Football is lots of fun!" as they continued kicking the ball about with each lady and girl kicking it back to Toby, who was told to dribble the ball about, to show off his football skills, in his frock, ribbons and aprons mincing with his handbag.

However, Franny reminded them "Girls! Remember, it's his Sissy Football skills!" to more laughter. His Mum laughed "Oh Toby! This has been embarrassing!" as he nodded, "It's been terrible Mum!" as they kicked the ball between the ladies and girls. After about five to ten minutes his Mum said, "Right girls! I think Toby's time is up!" as Franny and the ladies complained "Mummy! This is lots of fun! Just another half an hour!" but she shook her head and said, "No! Let him change and play with his mates for a while!" Trish asked, "Well Toby! Do you want to continue playing Sissy football with your Mummy and sister and us, in your pretty dresses and hair ribbons or change back into a boy again, to join your friends?" as Francesca said, "I want Sissy to stay here and play with me!" as she looked at him and said, "He'd better!" However, she gasped as he stammered "Can I keep my pretty dress on, to play Sissy Football with all you!" as the place erupted with laughter, as she screeched "I can't believe it! He's obeyed me!" thinking that her threat had done the trick and forced her brother to keep his frock on.

They all ran up and gave him kisses and hugs, as he sobbed "Not fair!" as his Mum said, "Francesca! Let him change back into a boy!" as Jen called "I'm sure he's actually, having fun!" adding "Aren't you, Toby!" He called "It's ok, Mummy! I'm having fun in my new frock and aprons with my handbag!" as his Mum gasped, as did the neighbour, who called "I'll look forward to having your two around here, to play as Francesca laughed "I'm going to have lots of fun with my new little sister, Tinkabelle!" as they all laughed. She of course added "I think this will be his new uniform, for playing dollies with me in the house!" but added "Then wheeling them around the garden

and the drive!" as he cried "Oh no!" as she gurgled "Playing Sissy Football with me in the garden and the drive!" but then added "Not forgetting the streets!" as he cried "No way!" as the place erupted.

The girls modify his questionnaire answers to sound a sissy

His Mum said, "We'd better get him back inside, but they all reminded her "He said, he wanted to play footy till 9 o'clock!" as Francesca said, "Yes Mummy! He said, he wanted to play footy till at least 9pm, but was hoping for 10!" He grimaced "Not fair, Franny!" She then whispered to him "Better tell Mummy, you want to stay out in your frock, or I bring a few girlfriends around to play with you!" He called "Mum! You said, I could play footy till 9pm!" as Francesca giggled, "At least! Though it wouldn't hurt to play till 10!" as the girls laughed. His Mum laughed and realized Fran was making him say, that, but wondered why he didn't want to change out of his girly gear and join his mates as a boy.

They said, "We'll have to head back soon, but as long as Tinkabelle, promises to play till at least 9 in his new frock!" as he huffed "Not fair!" Jen added "Is it ok, if he has that frock, as his present, instead of the £10?" as his Mum laughed and nodded, and he cried "You mean, I don't even get money now!" adding "Not flipping fair!" to more laughter. Francesca giggled, and said, "There you were, wanting the money, all for your greedy self and now you have it!" adding "See I've my own frocks, to play dress up in, so I'll be letting you have that frock, all to your sweet self!" as they all giggled. She added "Every day after school, until Mum takes us out, to get you lots of pretty skirts and dresses, to play dress up!" as her Mum laughed "Oh Fran! I couldn't!"

His Mum laughed "You, poor boy!" Jenifer then took a pad from her handbag and said, "I think we need to adjust his form from earlier!"

6   If you have sisters – do you ever play with your sisters? Yes
7   What do you play with them – dollies and it's about to be football too?
10   Do you help your Mum / sister with the dishes – washing up? Yes
11   Do you help your Mum / sister with the housework? Yes
12   Do you help your Mum / sister with the Vacuuming? Yes
13   Do you help your Mum / sister with the Dusting and Polishing? Yes
14   Do you help your Mum / sister with the Bedding? Yes
15   Do you help your Mum / sister with the laundry? Yes
16   If yes or some-times? What do you use to hold your clothes pegs?
17   – a handbag | shopping bag/basket
18   Do you wear an apron to help with housework? Yes
19   Do you wear a PVC pinny for wet work? Yes
22   If you wear an apron it's my sister's pretty aprons?
23   Can you do needlework?
24   Do you help with the shopping? Yes
25   What type of bag or basket? –

Sylvie comes around to hear how they transformed Toby

The girls got their stuff and handbags and kissing Toby, Francesca and her Mum bye, they left, reminding them that Tinkabelle should finish pegging out the washing, in the morning. The three of them left with Wendy but Sylvie joined Toby around in the garden, giggling at the blushing boy in his frock with his handbag and ribbons. She laughed "How did this come about?" as Kathy laughed "It all came about due to a Questionnaire about boys,

helping about the house and helping with housework. I helped him fill it in and he answered in his usual MSP self, saying, he never helped with housework or shopping or played with his sister. His Mum added "Next thing they phoned saying, Toby had possibly won a prize, asking could they come around. Anyway, I invited them around not expecting anything on=toward!" Sylvie asked, "So what happened when they arrived?" as he sobbed "It was terrible!" as his sister kicked the ball to him "Oh Tinkabelle! This Sissy Football is so funny!" His Mum continued "The three of them arrived with Jenifer's Mum Wendy and I invited them in, and they wanted to check, if he'd filled it in himself!" She added "He was trying to get Francesca to leave, telling her she wasn't needed and saying, she wasn't having any part of his prize, not realizing it actually was going to be his pretty frock there!" as Sylvie screeched "Oh fab!" She said, "They complemented us on our outfit's and when we complemented them, they curtsied and told us it was fun to curtsy!" adding "Of course, Toby thought we were stupid!" Francesca heard her and laughed "But he just loves to curtsy now in his pretty frock!" adding "Don't you Tinkabelle?" as he begged "Please don't make me?" but she nodded, and blushed and gripping his frock and aprons, he bobbed a curtsy with them, to more laughter. She continued "They asked Toby if he could curtsy and he swore at them and said you only curtsy in skirts or dresses. However they then tied him into one of Francesca's pretty aprons and he was sunk!" Francesca gurgled "I couldn't believe it, when I saw my big macho brother in my pretty apron and then bobbing a curtsy!"

He cringed, as she added "They then got me to bring in some dollies and made him kiss it, and then play dollies with me!" as she giggled. She laughed "Toby! How come you didn't want to remove your frock, when Trish, told you that you could?" He huffed "It's not fair!" as his Mum laughed "Did she threaten to embarrass you?" as he nodded, still not wanting them to know, about his panties, but worse was his willy, sticking out of them!

She added "They made him offer to do the washing up, in her pretty aprons, but also her rubber gloves and thought that was bad, but didn't realize they wanted him to also peg out a few of his boy's clothes, on the washing line, adding 'Just his trousers and a pair of his underpants!'" as Sylvie laughed "What could be wrong with that?" His Mum then explains about them, taking the pegs from the plastic bag and popping them into a handbag and then those from the line too, to pop into another handbag as she asked, "Why?" as his Mum laughed "Can't you guess?" as she added "Toby brought the basket of washing out to the garden being told he'd only to peg out his trousers and underpants but wondered where the pegs where!" as she gasped "You don't mean he'd to use a handbag to peg out his clothes?" His Mum nodded. She gurgled "Next thing the girls had slid a handbag up his arm to the elbow and he'd to dip his hand into his handbag to get pegs out!" as she screeched as Franny gurgled "He looked just like Mummy does, when shopping and so will be great to take around the shops as my little sister!"

They play Sissy Football till 9 when his Mum brings them in

He cried "Don't Mum, please?" as they all laughed as she added "It's his frock he won't like wearing around the shops!" She added "Finally he thought they were letting him go to play silly football!" as his sister laughed "I always thought football was silly, up till now!" adding "But now realize how much fun it is, if I can get the boys to play in frocks, mincing with handbags and wearing hair ribbons!" as Sylvie screeched "Oh fab!" Hence, they played Sissy football till around 9 when his Mum giggled, "It's quite light, sure you don't want to play on, Toby? We don't mind!" as he called "No Mum! Please let me in and out of these clothes to go to bed?" adding "Today has been terrible! I hope tomorrow, we can forget it and get back to normal!" Francesca laughed "Well except for playing dollies with me, playing dress up, playing sissy football and not forgetting pegging out some pretty clothes in the morning in your frock and using my handbag!" adding "Just for starters!" as her Mum and Sylvie screeched "Oh Franny, you going to make him be a girly?" She nodded, "Oh yes! She's going be my little sister!" as her Mum said, "Now Francesca! He can't be girly all the time, let him go out with his mates and play football properly sometimes!" She laughed "I'll think about it! He's got to say, really nice things to me and you if he wants

55

out with his mates!" adding "And giving us lots of curtsies with his aprons and frocks too!" He cried "Oh no! Franny! Don't make me?" but she nodded, "Oh yes, Tinkabelle!" Francesca then gurgled "What about school?" as he begged "Please Francesca! Don't tell anyone at school, or in your class?" as she gurgled and asked, "Mummy what about a dress and pinafore, for Tinkabelle!" as his Mum laughed "Now Francesca, keep his dress up and stuff to home!" She added, "Please? Don't tell at school?" as his neighbour kissed him and then Francesca and her Mum good night.

Francesca called "Watch out Aunty Silvie, in the morning, before school for Tinkabelle, pegging out some washing in a fun way!" as Sylvie laughed "In a frock?" as Kathy called "Wait and see! It surprised Francesca and me!" as she laughed and said, "I'll look out!" as his Mum led them inside and locked up. Francesca said, "Just some supper Mummy and then put us to bed!" as he called "I go to bed on my own!" but she said, "Either Mummy or I, put you to bed, with your dolly!" as he sobbed "Oh no!" His Mum laughed "Oh Fran! Hasn't he had enough?" but she shook her head and whispered in his ear and he suddenly said, "Mummy! Will you put me to bed and read me a fairy tale?" as his Mum screeched "Oh Toby! Whatever next?" She got their drinks ready and then a few sandwiches, which were soon eaten and after she'd kissed Toby sweet dreams, her Mum took her up to bed and soon had her into her nighty and read her a fairy tale.

His Mum spies the nighty inside his frock before a fairy tale

Francesca said, "Don't forget to read Tinkabelle a fairy tale too, Mummy!" adding "We'll have to get him a nighty for bed, unless you want to let him sleep in one of your big nighties, till you take him shopping to try out a few in the girl's department!" as his Mum laughed and kissed her nighty night. His Mum went down and giggled, at him, pulling his trousers up, as she asked, "What are you doing?" as he huffed "You know Jen told me I could remove my dress, Mummy?" as she nodded. He sobbed "I couldn't remove it, or everyone would see me!" as she asked, "Why you had your trousers on?" as he huffed "She had pulled my trousers apart, but left my belt done up, so if I removed my frock, my panties would be spied, as she gurgled "Oh! She didn't?" as he nodded. However, he then added "Do you know what she also did, to me?" as she shook her head with a large smile on her face and listened. He said, "She reached into my panties and took my willy out on show, under the leg of my panties!" as she screeched "Oh fab!" as she giggled, "Oh! She didn't?" as he huffed "I didn't want all the girls, but especially Franny and you, to spy my willy and girly panties!" She hugged him "Oh what a wonderful trick, to play on you! Let's get you up to bed and see what you can sleep in. He huffed "Don't let Francesca know. what I'm wearing or why I couldn't remove my frock!" as she laughed "You realize, she and all the girls think you enjoy wearing a frock?" He cringed and nodded. She turned out the lights and led him upstairs to his bedroom and heard him call "Lock the door, Mummy!" as she laughed and turned the key.

She said, "Let's get your frock off!" He cringed and heard her giggle, as she pulled it over his head and gasped, as she spied his nighty and laughed "Oh Look! She's even given you a pretty nightdress, your size too!" He cried "Oh no!" as his Mum laughed "For a second there, I thought, I'd have to let you sleep in one of my big ones!" as he huffed "Not fair!" as she said, "Off with your trousers too?" as he huffed "Can I do it, alone?" However, his Mum laughed "Franny's orders - I've to read Tinkabelle his fairy tale!" as he cringed and turning around, he pulled down his trousers and took them off. She laughed as she raised his nighty and saw his frilly yellow panties and said, "Make sure Francesca doesn't spy your privates" as he cringed and got into bed. His Mum took the fairy tale and started reading from Francesca's book. However, then she heard Francesca call "Mummy let me in, to give my sweet little sissy sister, a kiss and cuddle!" He begged her not to, but next thing she'd unlocked the door and his sister ran in giggling "Did you find him a nighty?" but she also had a large dolly in her hands and said, "Here Tinkabelle! You forgot your dolly!" as he cried "Oh no! Not fair!" and took the doll from her, as his Mum laughed. His Mum said, "Jenifer had given him a nighty, too!" as Francesca screeched and pulling back the bedclothes,

jumped into bed, with her big brother, as her Mum laughed "Naughty girl! Well keep your arms up, out of the bed, while I read him, his fairy tale!" as Franny said, "Cuddle your dolly, she wants to hear too!" Francesca laughed and said, "Just a few kisses for my sissy!" as he turned to face her and let her kiss him and throw her arms around him as she gurgled "Oh what a pretty nighty, for my sissy brother!"

Fran gives his Mum the choice of shopping or her girlfriends

He huffed and heard his Mum say, "Let me finish his fairy tale!" as she said, "Go on Mum, Read Sissy his fairy tale!" as his Mum read him the fairy tale about the princess. Fran said, "Tomorrow night you should read him a tale all about the adventures of Tinkabelle the fairy!" He huffed "Not fair, Francesca!" as his Mum laughed and took her daughter out of bed, as she pulled back the bedclothes and gurgled "I saw sissy's panties!" as he sobbed "Not fair!" Her Mum put her back to bed and kissing her again, she turned out the light. Francesca then explained to her Mummy that if she doesn't buy him frocks, then she'll have to get lots of skirts and frocks from her girlfriends, but they'll want to see her sissy brother. She then said, "I don't think he'll want the alternative!" as her Mum asked, "What?" as she gurgled "I approach lots of big girls I know and ask them for their old frocks for my sissy brother Tinkabelle here!" as he cried "No don't!" and his Mum screeched "Oh no!" She giggled, "But it's going to be fun in the shops! Having him actually try, the skirts and dresses on!" as he cried "Oh no! Please don't dress me up, in the shops?" as they all giggled. Both Francesca and her Mum laughed themselves to sleep, thinking about the evening and all the things that had happened to Toby, that night and the games and fun they could have with him. He lay there, sobbing and wondering "How to hell, am I to get out of this?" adding "I should have run out to play with my mates, when those girls arrived and left them with Mum!" He grimaced "I hope she doesn't tell anyone at school or tell any of my mates!" adding "That would be terrible!" He looked at the doll and flung it out of bed, hating it. However, he thought "I'd better get it in, or she'll tell!" as he clambered back out of bed and turning on the light, he found it and turning if off, he cuddled it again, dreading her tell on him. He thought "It's bad enough playing dollies inside with her!" but it's ten times worse in the garden, where I might be spied by anyone!" He hated the girly way to peg out the washing, but even worse was playing Sissy Football in a frock and mincing with a flaming handbag.

In the morning Francesca laughed, as she heard her Mum downstairs and knocked on his door, saying, let me in or I phone lots of girls, to tease you silly, on the way to school!" as he woke and begged "Please Francesca, let me alone!" but she insisted and heard the key go and opening the door, saw him jump back into bed again to hide his panties and nighty. She laughed as she saw his dolly in the bed and gurgled "Did you cuddle your dolly all night?" as he said, "Yes Franny! Honest I did!" as she said, "Let me see you kiss it and don't forget to bring it down to breaky!" as he cried "Not, to show Mum?" as she nodded, "It will just make her laugh!"

She then said, "I want to dress Sissy, for doing the laundry, before breakfast!" as he begged "I've to get dressed for school!" but she said, "You've to ask, to peg out the washing, Mum's got ready for you, but also ask Mummy 'Do you think they'll let me wear my party frock, to school today, instead of my dress and pinafore?'" as he sobbed Oh no!" She added "PS, to please me, you'll wear the panties and nighty under your boy's clothes or else I tell lots of girls!" as he sobbed "Not flaming fair!"

Morning and before breakfast, Franny helps take his basket out

She then said, "Pull up your nighty, till I see something!" as he gasped "No! You don't want me to?" but she nodded, and saw him pull up his nighty, as she gurgled "Oh what pretty panties!" as he sobbed "Not fair!" He then gasped, as she pulled his panties down and giggled, "Oh Toby! Is that your baby-pee-pee?" adding "Why do you call it that?" as he cringed and said, "Because it's the size of a baby boys pee-pee!" as she giggled, and reaching out touched it and said, "It does look really funny!" She added "Don't forget to call it that, if Mummy or any of my

girlfriends ask!" as he begged "Please Franny, don't tell any of your girlfriends on Toby!" adding "I mean Fairy Tinkabelle!" as she gurgled and gave him a big kiss causing him to blush. She said, "Ok let me get you dressed in your ribbons, frock and pretty apron, ready to go down for breaky and pegging out the washing for Mummy!" as he sobbed "Not fair!" but heard her "Better remove your nighty Toby!" and saw him woefully remove it, to leave him in the girly panties, as she laughed "Let's play a trick on Mummy?" as she pulled the panties down to leave him naked, as she gurgled, at her blushing brother. She took some hair ribbons and giggled, as she slid them into his hair, laughing at her naked brother, in hair ribbons. She took his frock and said, "Arms up Sissy!" and saw him raise his arms, as she pulled the dress down over his head, laughing away, as she pulled it down to hide his willy. She laughed and pointed "Mustn't forget your pretty aprons, to protect your frock, sissy!" as he took her aprons and pulled them on and heard her call "Don't forget your dolly?" as he blushed and took the dolly, as he entered the bathroom and washed his face and hands, before going downstairs.

Franc had got herself into her dress and pinafore and had donned her pretty apron to join her Mum at breakfast and heard Toby coming downstairs. He turned at the bottom of the stairs and sped into the hall and then entered the kitchen, carrying her dolly, as his Mum gasped "Oh Toby! I thought you'd be dressed for school!" His sister laughed "Mummy!

Couldn't you imagine my big brother, attending school in his pretty frock, ribbons, carrying his dolly and a handbag?" as she shook her head and laughed "No! Don't be cruel!" adding "And no telling tales at school young lady!" as she laughed "Would I, Mummy?" and giggled. However, she heard him stammer "Mummy!" as she said, "Yes dear!" and heard him stammer "After pegging out the washing, do you think I could wear my pretty frock to school, instead of the boring dress and pinafore?" as his Mum gasped and gurgled "Oh Francesca!" as she hugged and kissed him and said, "You naughty girl!" as she laughed "What's he done now?" She giggled, "Won't it be great, if he can attend school in a dress and pinafore, Mummy?" as her Mum said, "She's, such a tease!" as he cringed at the thought. She then said, "Look at the advantages, Mummy!" as she asked, "What do you mean, dear?" as she gurgled "I could wear his hand-me-downs and so you'll only need to buy our school dresses once!" She gasped "Oh Franny!" as he huffed "That's, not funny! You know they wouldn't let me!" She laughed "It depends how much I persuade you to plead?" as her Mum gasped. Francesca said, "He's promised to peg the rest of the washing out!" as his Mum said, "He won't have time before school, just a few of yours and my things dear, say, four of each!" as she said, "Ok!"

Fran shows Tinkabelle off to 2 young girls doing the laundry

His Mum said,Ok! I suppose you can do a little of the washing for us, but be careful when you go out the side door, that nobody spies you!" as Francesca giggled, "Oh Mummy! It's so much fun to show off, in your pretty frock!" as she laughed and took the washing out of the machine for him. Francesca laughed "I'll help him with his basket!" as she said, "You take one end and I'll take the other!" as his Mum laughed and heard her say, "Don't forget the clothes pegs Toby?" as she handed him, her pink handbag and heard him huff "Not fair!" as he took the handbag and slid it up his arm to the elbow, to giggles as her Mum, watched Francesca open the door for him. He begged "Please Fran! Make sure no one is about to see me, dressed up?" as she laughed and exited and saw some girls coming up and said, "Ok Sissy!" and saw him step out timidly, as she pulled on the basket and said, "Come on!" and saw him edge out, as she saw him with his handbag and ribbons with her apron over his frock and saw him try to push her on, into the garden, but she laughed "Hi Carol!" He gasped and turned to look at, who was there and gasped, as he was looking into the street, at two young girls and their Mummy, at the end of the next gate and one saw the look on his face and giggled, "I think that's a boy in a dress!" as Francesca giggled, and nodded, as he tried to get back inside, but she took hold of his apron string and pulled him back, as the two little girls about her age, or younger laughed and then screeched "Oh! Is that a big boy?" as Francesca laughed "Do the washing

and I'll ask them not to tell on you!" as he cried "Not fair, Fran!" She then said, "Give the girls a curtsy and then around the back, to peg out all the clothes using your handbag!" as she watched him stand and gripping his dress, gave the girls, a quick curtsy and heard them screech.

Toby then took the basket around the back and started pegging it up, dipping into his handbag. Francesca ran and laughed "Can you girls not tell anyone, on my sissy big brother, as she laughed "Want to see him peg out, the washing?" as she led them up and got them to be quiet, as they sneaked up to the edge of the garden and saw the boy, reaching into a handbag on his elbow, to get pegs, with Silvia next door laughing and flicking her wrist to him, as he reddened. He then sobbed "Oh no, Francesca! Don't tell on me!" as she giggled, "These sweet girls won't tell on sissy, Toby!" as her Mum opened the door and scolded "Oh Fran, I told you to keep him a secret!" but she said, "He showed himself off, in his pretty frock and gave a curtsy to these sweet girls and their Mummy!"

Fran added "Don't worry! They won't tell anyone about my sissy brother Toby, if he plays dollies with them!" as they giggled, and their Mum apologized, and his Mum laughed "The poor boy!" Hence, after the very embarrassing laundry session, in front of the 2 young girls and their Mum and Sylvia not to mention Francesca and his Mum, dipping into his handbag and having to say, how much fun, using a handbag was and wearing his frock and hair ribbons, to more laughter.

Toby heads down to breakfast still carrying his dolly

But also having to bob curtsies, with his frock between each item of washing, knowing if he raised his dress too high, they'd spy his willy., but even more embarrassing was half-way through, Francesca went over and removed his Alice band and ribbons, to leave him as a sissy boy, to more screeches. His Mum scolded her, but she whispered in his ear and called "It's ok Mummy! I want to peg out the rest as a big sissy in a frock!" as they all giggled, but especially when Francesca said, "That deserves a kissy for my big sissy!" as the girls called "Yuk!" as she said, "Go on, Mum!" and saw her Mum bend down and give him a kiss, as she whispered "He'll hate you girls, kissing him, more than you!" as the girls ran over and kissed him on the cheek, but heard Francesca say, "Only the lips count!" and so they both kissed him, to more giggles followed by their Mum and then Sylvie, as he gasped, as he was on show to neighbours.

He carried his handbag and dolly upstairs to change for school, dreading Franc expose him to classmates or girls from his own class. Hence, he removed his hair ribbons and then his apron and frock, but pulled his panties and nighty back on over himself, before pulling on his trousers and then his shirt and jumper. He hated the fact, he'd to have girly things to school and hoped she'd not expose him to anyone. He checked in the mirror and ensured nothing girly, could be seen, as he descended the stairs, carrying his dolly and saw his Mum smile and laugh "Oh! Are you bringing your dolly to school?" as his sister giggled, "It would make my day, if he did!" adding "Although, even better if he wore a dress and pinafore like me!" as she gripped her dress and bobbed a curtsy to him.

His Mum handed him an apron and set out the breakfasts for the both of them. They tucked in and she teased "I thought you might be in your dress and pinafore like Francesca!" as he cringed and said, "Not funny, Mum! I hope she won't tell, any of her class or worse my class!" as his sister giggled, "Would I Tinkabelle?" as she laughed at his look and said, "In future make sure you don't wear your boy things till after breaky just before school!" as he cried "Not fair!" His Mum hugged him and gave him a kiss saying, "I've asked her not to! I've told her to keep your dressing up to home!" as he huffed "She loves teasing me and showed me off to those 2 girls and their Mum in my frock earlier!" She laughed "It's brought out a new side to her!" as he cringed and huffed "I can't believe how they've got me to sound and look so girly!" as she laughed "I know! I never realized how easy it was to turn a macho boy, into a girly!" as he blushed. Francesca gave him a kiss and said, "Ok! Remove your pinny and give your dolly a kiss goodbye!" and saw him kiss her dolly. Her Mum said, "Now Fran, I'll let your big brother head

on to school ahead of you!" as Francesca kissed him bye but whispered "Sissy better wait around the corner at the top of the Gardens or else! Don't tell Mum!" as he gasped "not fair!" and kissed his sister bye.

Toby heads to school, but has to wait for his Mum and Franny

However, before Francesca went on to school, she swapped her books into a girly carrier bag and set it into a pretty shopping basket, whereas she'd normally have just used a large girly bag. She also ordered Toby not to tell their Mum, but he'd to wear his panties and nighty under his school clothes or else, she'd tell lots of girls at school. He grabbed his satchel and ran on and saw some mates and started chatting to them, on the way around too school. Her Mum saw her young daughter, with a pretty shopping basket and her books in a Miss Selfridge carrier inside and said, "That's a prettier basket, than you normally carry your books in!" as she gasped "No getting your big brother to swap and carry his books in either of those! That would be terrible Francesca! Please don't make him?" as she gurgled "Oh Mummy! How on earth could I make my big brother carry a girly basket or bag like this?" adding "Anyway, you always told me, it's fun to carry books about in a pretty bag or basket!"

She added "Now where's his pink handbag, for his pencil case!" as her mum scolded "No way!" as she took her own handbag and shopping basket and escorted her to school. Fran was chatting away with her Mum, but minced with her basket over her arm and saw a few girls from school and called out "Hi Sarah!" as she walked over with their Mum and called "Hi Francesca!" as they joined her and her Mum, up the street and saw her with the pretty basket on her elbow. Sarah said, "I don't usually see you with a basket, Francesca!" as she laughed "Oh I thought it was prettier, than my other shopping bag!" as her Mum laughed, as she minced up the street, but she then extreme minced, with it too, sliding her arm out to the side. Her Mum laughed "What a pretty girly way, to carry your basket!" and saw Sarah copy her, with her own shopping bag, as both Mum's laughed. As Kathy asked, "Will we join the girls, as she and Sarah's Mum, copied the girls with their handbags and shoppers. They all minced along and got some funny looks from other children and Mum's, when they turned the corner and her Mum gasped, as she spied Toby chatting to a mate, before he said, "I've to wait for my Mum and sister!" Her Mum said, "Francesca you didn't make him wait for you?" as Francesca giggled, "Mummy! How on earth could I do that?" as Sarah saw her big brother and called "I don't like Toby, he's a nasty big boy and sometimes hit's us, calling us names!" as Francesca laughed "Mum! Hear that?"

He blushed bright red, at seeing the two girls and Mum's, all extreme mincing, along the street towards him. He thought "Oh no! She's got a friend with her too!" as they reached Toby and Francesca said, "Now Toby! My friend Sarah here, has told me, you were a naughty boy, who hit her and called her names!" as he huffed "Sorry!" as she laughed "I think to make up for it, you should do something for her!" as her Mum said, "Francesca! Don't please?" as she whispered in Sarah's ear "Let him carry your pretty bag for you!" as she asked, "He wouldn't?" Francesca said, "Offer to carry Sarah's bag for her!" as he stammered "Can I carry your flaming bag for you?" as Francesca whispered, "Say, pretty or else!" He asked, "Can I carry your pretty bag for you, Sarah?" as she giggled, and held out her orange shopping bag, as her Mum gasped "Gosh! What has she on him?" His Mum laughed "Oh Francesca! You are naughty!" as Francesca said, "Sarah! You take his stupid bag!" as she huffed "Oh! Can't he carry both?" but heard Francesca say, "Don't worry! You can show Toby, a sweeter way to carry his bag!" adding "for when he takes it back!"

His Mum realizes Franny is making him mince with the bags to school

Francesca whispered "1st Mincing and then extreme mincing!" as she giggled, and slid his satchel up her arm, to the elbow. She said, "See Toby! How I carry your satchel?" as he cringed and said, "Ha!" but then said, "But a sweeter way is like this!" as she slid her arm out to the side and extreme minced along to screeches, from both Mum's as Francesca laughed "Oh Sarah! What a fun way to carry his satchel!" as she said, "Toby why don't you try?" He

60

begged "Mum! Stop her!" but then saw her, take the satchel from Sarah and said, "Go on Toby! Try with your own satchel first? before too many school kids spy you!" as he cringed and took the satchel and sliding her bag over his shoulder and slid his satchel, up his arm to the elbow, as Sarah's Mum gasped "Oh Fab!" as he cried "Mum! Make sure none of my mates, can see!" Sarah giggled, and saw him slide his arm out in front of him, and step forward as they screeched and he tried to take it down, but then heard Francesca say, "Now extreme mince, Tinkabelle!" as he sobbed "She called me Tinkabelle!" as Sarah laughed "What a fab name, for him!" as he looked around and saw none of his mates, were around. So next thing slid it back up his arm to the elbow and sliding it out to the right, minced back to them, as Francesca ran up and kissed him on the lips, to a gasp from Sarah, as the ladies laughed and Francesca said, "Mummy! Sissy wants a kissy!" as he cringed and saw her bend down and kiss him.

However,Francesca giggled, and whispered "He hates kisses Sarah!" as she said, "No way!" but Francesca begged "Please and he'll really hate it too!" as she said, "Ok just one!" as her Mum gasped "Don't you dare?" but saw her kiss him, as she broke away giggling, but then heard Francesca's Mum said, "I dare you!" as her Mum said, "Count me out!" as Sarah laughed "Spoilt-sport!" as Francesca took his satchel back and heard Sarah say, "Oh pooh! I enjoyed seeing him walk with his satchel!" but then heard Francesca say, "Try again with Sarah's pretty bag!" as he sobbed "Mum stop her!" as she laughed "You could be swapping your books into her bag, to carry all day around school!" as he sobbed "Not fair!" and next thing had slid her shopper down to his elbow and walked forward and Sarah and her Mum both screeched "Oh fab!" as Francesca said, "Just till the next gate!" but then you've to extreme mince back, or else it's to the next post box!" as her Mum laughed "Now Francesca! Don't Please? Stop embarrassing your big brother!" as they all minced to the next gate, giggling at him, but then saw him check. He gasped "Oh no! There's some boys coming up!" as Fran said, "Mum stand to block sissy's view!" as Fran said, "Quick Toby!"

Sarah makes Toby swap her books into her girly bag

His Mum stepped to the side and saw him extreme mince with Sarah's bag, as they all giggled, and Sarah said, "Oh fab!" and kissed him again, as he gasped "Not fair!" and then she said, "Thanks for letting me use your satchel for school today and you'd better look after your pretty shopping bag or else!" Francesca giggled, "I dare you!" as she laughed and heard Sarah say, "If you don't want me to tell your mates, about you mincing and extreme mincing! Swap your books into my pretty bag!" as her Mum laughed "Don't Sarah, wouldn't that be cruel! He can't carry a girly bag about school, all day! What would his mates say?" as Francesca laughed "Oh Mum! It won't do him any harm! and I'll ask the girls to go easy on her and let her skip with them!" Sarah screeched "Oh fab! Is he going to skip with the girls, at the breaks!" as he cried "No!

Don't Francesca?" as she said, "Look! The boys won't let you play with them, if you're mincing about with a pretty handbag on your elbow!" Her Mum laughed "Now Francesca! He can't!" as she laughed "Unless she'd prefer to carry his books, in my pretty basket, here!" as he cried "No don't, Francesca?" as she held it out and said, "Just try with my basket, till we see how you look?" Sarah's Mum laughed "I dare you!" and saw him sob "Not fare!" as he took it, in his other hand and heard giggles from them all.

Francesca whispered to Sarah "Borrow your mummy's handbag a tick! I don't think Mummy will play along!" as Kathy said, "Mummy can I see your handbag a tick!" as her Mum asked, "What dear?" and taking her purse, handed it to her. Francesca took it and said, "Now! No running off, with Sarah's Mummy's handbag!" as she slid the basket and then the handbag up his arm, as he sobbed "Oh no! Not fair, Francesca!" as she said, "Just up to the next gate and then extreme mince back girly!" as her Mum said, "Oh Francesca! You are pushing it!" Sarah gurgled "Oh Mum! Isn't she fab!" as her Mum said, "Look after my handbag missy!" as he minced on towards the next gate, with Francesca mincing with her hand on her hip and then they turned and he extreme minced back,

to screeches as Sarah and Francesca, gave him a kiss and then her Mum too and took her handbag back, saying, "Gosh! Whatever Francesca has on him, must be bad!" as his Mum laughed and nodded.

However, then Francesca took him up the street and whispered something to him, as next thing, she'd taken a girly half apron out and said, "Just for a few minutes with my pinny!" as he cried "Oh no, Francesca don't!" as she tied it around him, but reached her hand under it and unzipped his spur and pulled out his nighty. He cried "You didn't?" as she nodded, "Nighty night!" as she turned him and heard screeches, as Sarah and her Mum saw him, in the little girls apron and saw him run back, mincing with the basket and girly shopper, as his Mum laughed and heard her say, "I suppose Mummy will want you to remove my girly apron!" as her Mum gasped and realized what Francesca had made him wear and if she removed his pinny, they'd spy his nighty and maybe his willy and gasped "Oh Francesca! You are being really cruel, to Toby!" as she said, "Can I see him a minute, but Francesca said, "No Mummy!" She said, "Tell Mummy how you enjoy wearing my pretty aprons and it's ok!" or else remove your pinny yourself!" as he sobbed "Not fair! I enjoy wearing Francesca's pretty aprons!" as she laughed "He's always borrowing my aprons, to help Mummy and me with housework, isn't that right Mummy?" as his Mum laughed "Well yes, just since last night!"

She slides a half apron on over his trousers, but pulls out his nighty

Sarah laughed "Why! You look so sweet in Francesca's pretty apron, with your baskets!" as she gave him another kiss, as he begged "Please take your bag and basket back, girls!" Francesca laughed "I know what she needs Mummy!" as her Mum asked, "What?" and saw her remove a hair slide and said, "Here sissy!" as Sarah screeched and saw her slide it into his hair, as she gasped. Her Mum asked, "She doesn't dress him up, does she?" as he gasped and cried "Oh no!" as Francesca pulled the pinny, from him and they screeched, as they saw the nighty peeking out, from his trousers and Francesca laughed "Naughty boy! Wearing his pretty nighty to school!" He tried to push it back into his trousers, but she said, "Just for 30 seconds, Tinkabelle! Let me show Sarah, as he cried "Oh no!" as she pulled hard on the nighty and felt more of it come out, of his trousers. She then pulled him towards the giggling Sarah and her Mum, who ran towards him, as they looked and said, "Oh what a pretty nightdress!" as did her Mum.

His Mum said, "Oh Francesca! This is terrible! I don't know, if I should let him change out of them!" as Sarah's Mum asked, "Them, what else?" as Sarah asked, "What?" as his Mum laughed and whispered "I bet she's made him wear girly panties!" as Sarah's Mum gasped "Oh you little, sweetie!" Francesca gurgled and Sarah asked, "What else?" and then said, "Tell me or else sissy!" as he sobbed "Panties!" as Francesca giggled, "Frilly pink ones!" as he cried "They're yellow!" as Sarah screeched "Oh fab! After school! I want you down to play dress up, with me and Francesca!" Francesca laughed "Not dollies too?" as Sarah nodded, "Oh yes, Dollies too!" as he sobbed "Not fair!" His Mum reached down and slid his nighty back into his trousers and did his zip up again.

Sarah's Mum gasped "Has Francesca seen his, you know what?" as Francesca giggled, "Toby tell us what is in, your frilly panties!" as he sobbed "Not fair!" as he said, "It's my, baby-pee-pee!" as they screeched "Oh what a wonderful name for it!" as Francesca asked, "Why do you call it that?" as he sobbed "Because it's the size of a little baby boys pee-pee!" as Sarah and her Mum gasped and screeched "Oh fab!" She then asked, "Franny! You haven't seen it?" as her Mum said, "I changed him last night and am trying to hide it, from her!" but then Francesca laughed "I had fun changing my big dolly this morning and dressing her up in her frock, for pegging out the washing!"

Sarah gasped "You didn't?" Francesca asked, "Didn't I diddum's!" as he sobbed and nodded. She laughed "You didn't put his panties on, too?" as she laughed and said, "I actually pulled them off and then slid his dress on, as he wanted to get some air, around him, while pegging out the washing!"

She laughed "I had him bobbing curtsies to us and 2 little girls and their Mummy, using his handbag to get pegs for the laundry!" She laughed "What? A handbag to peg out the laundry?" as her and her Mum giggled, "Three girls came over last night and showed us a fun way to do the laundry!" She laughed "Two little girls spied him when he bobbed some curtsies to them, when he exited the side door with the wash basket.

Toby has to tell about his Baby-pee-pee and say, why he calls it that

Her Mum gasped "I didn't realize, he'd no panties on in the garden!" as Franny laughed "It's just as well he didn't raise his dress any higher, when bobbing curtsies to the two little girls!" Francesca laughed "Mummy! You are naughty not letting Tinkabelle wear her dress and pinafore to school!" as Sarah laughed and said, "That would be fab! If we can get him some!" as he begged "Please Francesca! You promised not to tell, please don't tell any other girls or especially boys!" Francesca laughed "Now! You are so lucky that Mummy is here, to protect you, from Sarah and me!" as Sarah laughed "Think well of your trousers Missy!" as he begged "Please don't make me?" as his Mum gasped "Now don't you dare! They won't let him?" as Francesca giggled, and they minced on, with some extreme mincing. Then a girl gasped "Is that you Toby?" as he sobbed "Oh no! Please take your girly bags back!" as she ran over and saw his sister flick her wrist, effeminately and say "Toby was jealous of our pretty bags and baskets!" as she laughed "I love his hair ribbon!"

as he'd forgotten it and cried "Oh no! Take it back! Please Francesca?"

She took it, from his hair!" as Janet booed "Oh she suited his hair ribbon!" as he begged "Please don't tell, on me?" as she laughed and Francesca called "Sissy wants a kissy!" as she threw her arms around him and kissed his lips, as the girl gasped, but then saw Sarah call "I want to give your sissy, a kissy too!" as the girl gasped and heard Francesca say, "We dare you?" as she said, "No way, girls!" but Francesca whispered "You'll have the time of your life, with my sissy brother, if you do!" as she said, "Ok!" and said, "Come here sissy!" He sobbed and she gave him a kiss, but instead of just a peck, she kissed him for about 5 seconds and heard the girls giggle "That was a proper kiss!" as she blushed and asked, "How come, he's acting so girly!" as the girls giggled, and Francesca laughed "Oh my big brother has been playing dollies and dress up with me for years!" as he cried "Only since last night!" She whispered, "Do you want me to tell lots of girls, about your nighty and knickers?" as she said, "Now Toby! You've been playing dollies and dress up with me, since you were 3 or 4, weren't you?" as her Mum gasped, and he cried "Not fair!" and nodded, "Yes Francesca!" to giggles and more kisses. She then whispered something into his ear, again and a few minutes later, they couldn't believe it, when he called out "Francesca! You stole my big dolly!" as Janet and Sarah both screeched and gasped "Oh Toby!" and then "Oh Francesca! This is so funny!"

Sarah goes to a friend's and gets him school dress, pinafore and handbag

Sarah realized where they were and said, "Girls can you hold on a tick? I've to see a friend in here!" as she rang the bell and a lady answered and she asked, "Is Flo in?" but she said, "Sorry she's gone on to school!" as she asked, "Can I come in a tick!" as she led her in. She said, "Look my friend Francesca has her sissy brother with her and we've had him carrying girly bags and baskets and hair slides, on the way to school, but if would be much better, if he is dressed properly!" as she giggled, "I know Flo's about 8, would you have an old dress and pinafore, I can borrow, that would fit a six or seven-year old!" as her Mum gasped "You going to dress him up?" She giggled, "He's already in a nighty and frilly panties!" as she gasped "Never! Will he wear them here?" but she shook her head!" His mummy's here and won't let us! We'll have to wait, till she's gone and then we can take control!" as she led her upstairs and opening a wardrobe. Her friend's Mum, pulled out a dress and pinafore asking "Should this fit?" as she held it up against the young girl and saw it was a bit bigger and said, "You'll have to show me and Flo afterwards!" as she nodded, "We will!" as she popped them away in a carrier for her, but then she asked, "Did she have a pink handbag for him?" as she fetched one of Flo's and slid it in the satchel along with the dresses.

Sarah exited and was asked, "Why did you need to go into Flo's?" as she said, "I just wanted to check something about ballet class, on Saturday!" as Francesca laughed "Mummy! That's right! Maybe while shopping in town this morning, you can get him a tutu ballet dress!" as her Mum said, "Now Francesca! You have a couple!" Francesca gurgled "But my tutus, won't fit Toby!" as he cried "Mummy! Don't, get me a tutu!" as they all giggled, and Sarah whispered in his ear and heard him stammer "Mummy will you get me a pretty tutu, ballet dress, for Saturday!" His Mum gasped, as did the others and screeched "Oh Toby! You will look adorable in a tutu!" as they hugged and kissed him more. Sarah called "Thanks girls and sissy!" as Janet scolded "Now Sarah! Don't call him sissy!" as she said, "Sorry Tinkabelle!" as he blushed and begged "Please take your bags back! Boys are around and will see me!" as they laughed and said, "We don't mind carrying pretty bags or baskets! Do we Mummy?" as her Mum shook her head as she added "Nor wear pretty skirts and dresses?".

His satchel was quite heavy with his handbag and dresses and she asked, "Mummy would you carry his satchel for me?" as she laughed and nodded, and took it saying, "His books are quite heavy!" as he said, "They aren't that bad!" as he didn't realize the trick she'd played and was about to play. Sarah whispered to Francesca "I've his uniform in his satchel!" as Francesca giggled, "Great!" and continued on towards the school. His Mum kissed him and Francesca and tried to hold Francesca while he went on ahead, but Francesca called "You wait for me, with your girlfriend Janet! and Sarah" as Janet gasped and giggled, "Oh! It would be nice to have a sissy boyfriend!" as he blushed "Not fair girls!" Her Mum laughed "Now Francesca! Don't be cruel to Toby!" adding "It's going to be terrible, if all the girls at school know about him!" as she laughed, and Sarah kissed her Mum bye and taking his satchel and passed it to Janet.

They take him to the loo to change into dress and pinafore for school

She asked, "Can you hold his satchel a tick!" and said, "Oh! Today will be so much fun at school!" as her Mum laughed, as she kissed Toby, but whereas, it was just a peck earlier, this time she kissed him, like Janet for about 5 seconds. Her laughing Mum scolded "No kisses, Sarah! Leave that, to big Janet!" and saw the girls and a blushing Toby mince on. Sarah whispered "Janet! Can we get him into the girls, to get dressed properly?" as she gasped "You haven't got him a dress and pinafore?" as she nodded, "In his satchel!" as she gasped and giggled, as they entered the girls loos at the end of the school and saw girls giggle, as they spied Toby, with the girly bag and basket. Sarah said, "I'll just try and commandeer this toilet here!" as she went in and asked some girls to leave or if they stay, they've to help her, with a little dress up!" as they all agreed and hid quietly in the loo, as she exited and said, "Coast is clear, girls!" Fran said, "Now Toby! Do what we say, and the girls will look after you, ok?" as he asked, "What do you want?" as she laughed "Just come in here?" She led him into the girl's toilets and he saw them empty, but then heard Sarah say, "Now Toby! Remove your trousers and silly boy's clothes and get into this pretty dress and pinafore, I've borrowed for you!" Suddenly the other girls, exited and giggled, "You dressing him up?" as they laughed and Francesca said, "Jane his girlfriend here, will look after my sissy brother, Tinkabelle in class!" as he tried to struggle, but felt the big girls hold him, as Francesca pulled his spur down to gasps and giggles, but then more as they saw her pull his nighty out and soon had his trousers down. He cried "Leave my trousers girls!" but they soon had his blazer, jumper and shirt off, to leave him in just the socks, nighty and panties.

Sarah then produced the dress and pinafore and said, "Arms up girly!" and as he raised them up, she pulled up his nighty and they giggled, at his frilly yellow panties, but then gasped as Fran pulled them down, to flash his willy to them. He sobbed "Not fair!" as she asked, "What do you call that Sissy?" as he sobbed "My baby-pee-pee!" as she asked, "Why?" as he sobbed "Because it's only the size of a baby boy's pee-pee!" as they all screeched and Janet fed the dress down his arms and then his body. His panties were pulled up again, as the pinafore dress was pulled down again.

However, then Francesca said, "I know you think, he's ready!" but she then pulled his trousers up his legs, under his dresses, as they asked, "Why?" as she laughed and did his belt up, but then left his trousers undone. Francesca said, "See girls! We will ask Tinkabelle in front of lots of girls, but also teachers, if he wants to change back, into his boy's clothes, or just stay in his dresses and if he doesn't want everyone to spy his frilly panties, then he'll say, he's wanting to keep his dresses on and mince like a big girly!" as a cheeky Janet reached in and pulled his panties down at the front and slid his willy outside of his panties and laughed "I think he'll hate the girls, spying his baby-pee-pee too!" Francesca gurgled "Oh fab!" as he begged for some hair ribbons as she slid her Alice band onto his head and a few girls, copied her and slid ribbons into his hair.

PART B

PAM PLANS GIRLY THINGS AND HAS HIM PLAY DOLLIES AND HORSIES

Nancy has to do housework and push a doll's pram

Tom tells how Pam nearly caught him in the kitchen in her frock and pinny

Pam giggled, "Mum did that?" adding "Made you wear my pretty yellow frock? What a great punishment for a MSP, like you!" He huffed "It was horrid! She shouldn't have done that!" as Pam reached over and put an arm around his shoulder and gave him a hug, whispering "I've always wanted a sister, but I'll keep your secret!" adding "We're going to have lots of fun, together! Carry on!" Tom wanted to push her away, but knew she was in complete control and dreaded her telling Julie or even worse, someone at school.

He huffed "I was sobbing, dreading being seen or you entering the side door!" as Pam giggled, "I wish I had! I might even have had Julie with me! Whatever would she have said?" as she laughed "That's right! I rang the bell! And so, you were there, in the kitchen, in my pretty frock and apron?" and saw him nod. Tom huffed "I heard the bell and nearly fainted!" adding "Mum called you, to the back door and let me remove your pinny and open the kitchen door, to escape upstairs!" as Pam realized "You mean, I'd have seen you, in your full pretties! Damn!"

Tom said, "Mum told me, she'd not tell you, but I'd to be nice and do what she said, or else!" adding "I thought she'd let me change fully, but she made me keep those panties on!" Pam giggled, "Fantastic! So, all night, you were worried that she'd mention to me, about your panties or pull your trousers down to show me?" as he nodded, and she gurgled "Oh fab!"

Pam pulls his panties down to spy his willy and calls it a baby-pee-pee

She then looked down at the dolls and giggled, "Wonderful! Isn't it, girls'?" as she pretended to be the dolls and changing her voice "Oh yes! I bet Tom looked really pretty, in your yellow frock!" Pam giggled, "I bet he did, but we might have to wait a while, to see him, re-enact the dress up session, as it's a secret from Mummy, that we know!" adding "Don't you dollies, tell Mummy, that we know, his frock secret!" She gurgled "As soon as Mum realizes, that we know, then we'll see Tom dress up as a girl!" as he asked, "What?" Pam giggled, "See! I'll want Mum, to repeat, everything that happened last night, but with me standing right beside you!" as he gasped "Please don't, Pam? She wouldn't?" but Pam nodded, "Want to bet?"

He then gasped "But when she stripped me, my flaming willy, was on show!" as Pam gurgled "Out of bed a tick or else!" and heard him beg "Please don't?", wondering what she'd do. He slid his legs out of bed and she pulled

him up saying, "When I'm dressing and undressing my big dolly, Nancy, I'm bound to accidently spy, his little baby-pee-pee!" as he gasped "No Pam! Please don't?" She raised his nightdress and said, "Hold that up and keep quiet!" as she smiled at the small bulge in his pink panties and slowly pulled them down, taking her time, as she looked at his blushing face and soon saw a bit of it appear, as She blushed herself and giggled, "Oh Tom! What a little pee-pee!" as she pulled them completely down, giggling at the sight in front of her. He sobbed quietly "Not fair Pam!"

Pam pulls Tom to window in nighty and holds him on show to curtsy

She reached out and touched it and laughed "What a funny looking thing!" She laughed "It looks like a little baby's dummy!" as he blushed and said "Ha!" as she took the yellow panties and pushed them into his mouth and he let go of his nighty and cried into the panties "Not fair, Pam!" as she said, "Take those out and I tell!" She took hold of his willy and pulled gently and was amazed, at how fast he moved to follow her, as she pulled him to the window and opened the blinds, pulling them up fully, as he cried "Oh no!" into the panties, as she removed them from his mouth and ducked down, still holding his willy and pushing his bottom, to stop him ducking, out of sight. She said, "Ten curtsies with your nighty and I'll let you go!" as he gasped at being on show to the back houses in a nightdress. He gripped his nighty and started bobbing curtsies, to the window, oblivious to who might see and recognize him. He was glad he'd her Alice band on his head, to partly disguise him, but when he got to five, she stood up and pulled it off, to leave him on show, as a sissy boy!" as she ducked down again and said, "Continue your curtsies, Sissy Tom!"

He blushed and heard her giggle "It might be fun to play dollies with the two of you!" as he heard her add "Sometimes as Nancy, but other times as Sissy Tom!" as he blushed and finally got to ten and said, "Ten! Please let Sissy Tom go?" as she laughed and let go and standing up kissed him and waved to the imaginary onlookers.

Tom gasped as he saw a woman at her upstairs window, smile and wave back, as he went to run back, but Pam held him and raising his nighty, she lifted him up, to expose his little willy, to the laughing woman, as he gasped and cried softly "Oh no! She saw!" as she let go and waved, flicking her wrist effeminately, as he ran back and jumped into bed, sobbing "Now fair, Pam! Some woman saw me!" as she laughed and continued waving to her. She laughed "I wonder will she want to meet Nancy or Sissy Tom!" as he begged "Please close the blinds and go!" as she laughed "Now Nancy! You shouldn't be so shy!"

Pam giggled, "Anyway! Now you know why you'll not want, to squeal to Mummy, about me making you do anything!" as he huffed "Like what?" as she giggled, "Don't worry! I'll think of something!" as he sobbed, blushing, dreading what she'd make him do. Tom realized he'd to keep Pam's knowing about everything, a secret from his Mum. She giggled, talking to her dollies and said, "Now girls! This is Nancy my sister, who's cuddling you! Not Tom! My nasty brother! Look at her pretty nightdress!" as Tom grimaced and heard her say, "Sorry Nancy! We thought you were a boy!" Pam asked, "Tell your dollies! Are you a boy or a girl, wearing your nighty!" as he huffed "I'm a boy!" as she giggled, "So Sissy Tom, likes to wear nighties! Does he?" as he huffed "No! Please Pam don't? Ok I'm Nancy, your sister!" as she laughed "Hear that girls?" as she laughed "She doesn't seem to know, if she's a boy, or a girl!" Tom huffed "Not fair! Please go and take these with you!" as he held out the dollies to her.

Pam tells Tom he's to replace his PJs with a nightdress at bedtime

She giggled, "Ok! I'll go now, but you've to your pink panties on all day!" as he pleaded "Please don't Pam?" She said, "You can hand Mummy back my yellow panties!" Pam realizes that she'd to keep it from her Mum, that she knows about her dressing Nancy up.

She'll need to take things slowly and hide what she's making Tom, do. She then giggled, "As well as wearing my panties to bed, you'll be wearing something else to please me!" as he asked, "What?" as she laughed and pointed to his nighty!" as he cried "Oh no! But Mum will see!" She laughed "You'll wear your PJs over my panties, to let Mummy read you a fairy tale, I mean bedtime story, but as soon as she's gone, you'll remove your PJs and slip into the nighty, that will be hidden in your bed" adding "She'll of course hear you turn the key, to lock it and keep me out, but then later, you'll unlock the door again, so I can check on Nancy, in the morning!" as he sobbed quietly "Not fair, Pam!" However, she added "But Nancy also wears an Alice band and ribbons!"

She then thought of enlisting the help of June next door, as her Mum wouldn't let her take things too far with Nancy. Around at her house, she could play any games she wanted, with her sissy brother, without her Mum or anyone else seeing. She could have him do some housework in her aprons too, before getting him going outside, dressed up, as she gurgled. She thought "I can make him say to Mum, he's off to play footy, but he'll actually pop around next door, where I'll join him to play dollies and dress up and lots of other girly games!"

She said to him "I'll take my Wendy doll, but Baby Suzie is your early birthday present, who you'll carry, all about the house, with you! I won't make you take her out to play, unless you're naughty!" as he sobbed "Not flaming fair, Pam!" and saw him blush. She said, "You'll bring her down to breakfast with Tom and thank me, for your birthday present and pull on your blue pinny, asking "Mummy! Can I do any housework for you!" He sobbed "Not fair! I normally play footy on Sundays!" as she laughed "There'll be a lot less footy from now on and much more dollies, for you Tom boy!" as she added "I know if Tom refuses, to do something for me, then my sweet sister Nancy, will jump at the chance to do it!" but gurgled "But then, she'll want to wear some pretty skirts or dresses!" as he gasped as she corrected herself "I meant my pink apron!"

Tom nodded, "Ok! I'll do what you want!" but added "Please keep me indoors, so I'm not seen, doing anything girly?" She laughed "Oh Nancy! It's so much fun, being a girl!" as he grimaced. She said, "Ok Nancy! Remove your nightdress and I'll take Wendy back, once you've given her a kiss and told her and your dolly, they're pretty and you love them!" He kissed each dolly in turn and said, "I love you dollies!" to giggles from Pam, as he handed Wendy to her. She laughed "Playing dollies is good fun!" as she gurgled "Ask Julie's little sister, Tina!" as he begged "Please don't tell Julie!" adding "And especially not, little Tina!" as she added "Tina loves prancing about with her doll's pram in the driveway or even the street and would adore to teach you dollies!" as he sobbed "Please don't tell on me?" as she giggled and gave him another kiss.

Tom returns the nighty to her, but must keep the pink panties on

He then adjusted himself and pulled the nightdress over his head and handed it to her, with her saying, "Each night, before or after Mummy's read you your story, I'll provide Nancy with a pretty nightdress, before he gets into his PJs!" adding "You'll hide them in bed with you, till Mummy leaves and then you remove both tops and bottoms, to slip into the nighty, to become my sweet, sweet sister Nancy!" as he blushed and nodded.

Pam added "Once, Mummy knows about Nancy wearing a nighty to bed, we'll have to get her to buy you, your own pretty night clothes and undies!" adding "But of course, you'll be there with her in the shop, to make sure your nighty fits!" adding "and then we can see to some skirts and frocks, too!" as he cries "Oh no! Don't Pam! Not fair!" as she kissed him. She giggled, "See you a breakfast, my sweet, sweet, brother Tom" and exited the door, giggling, as she slipped into her own room and bounded onto the bed, laughing to herself, at what she'd heard from Tom.

Their Mum called them down for breakfast and Pam got herself up and out, lifting up some clean undies, a skirt and blouse, but Tom, was already in the bathroom, washing his teary-eyed face. He heard Pam knock on the door and call "Hurry up, Tom! You can come in. after me!" and grabbing a towel, dried his face quickly before

69

unlocking the door and pulling it open. She saw he was back in his pyjamas again and whispered, "You suited my nighty better!" and then said, "Come on out! Let me in?" He grimaced, saying, "But I was here, first!" as Pam brushed past him, saying, authoritatively "From now on, your lovely pretty sister, Pam, takes precedence! Do you hear?" and saw him sniffle and nod. She then realized he hadn't Suzie with him and smiled as she reminded him "And I see you've forgotten something!" He asked, "What?" and heard her call out "Tom! You forgot your dolly!" He blushed "Sorry!" and heard Pam say, "Imagine, if you're upstairs and your dolly is downstairs. How loudly I will shout that!" He cried "You mean I've to carry my doll, wherever I go?" as she smiled and nodded, "Oh yes! Mummy will get lots of fun out of seeing you, carrying Baby Suzie, about the house!" He realized what she meant and stammered "I'll remember my dolly and bring her with me!" as she giggled, "Good boy! Dollies are lots of fun! You'll soon learn how much fun!" as she entered the bathroom and locked the door to get cleaned and dressed.

Tom returned to his own room and slammed his door shut, locking it securely, before throwing himself down on the bed and quietly sobbing to himself, as he looked at the doll, beside him. He picked it up and threw it to the floor, wanting to rip it to pieces, but knowing he couldn't, for fear what his horrid Ug of a sister, would tell Julie or Tina or make him do. He hated the hold, she had over him and realized, that he'd to do what she said, for fear her telling anyone about his dolly, but worse of all, of his wearing her frock and undies. He wiped his eyes and removed his pyjamas and blushed, as he saw the pink panties on show. He quickly took the pair of under-pants and pulled them up, over the horrid panties. He followed this, by his trousers and a tea-shirt and then his jumper.

Tom goes to breakfast carrying the Baby Suzie dolly and his Mum sees

He pulled on his socks and slippers and was about to leave, when he remembered the doll and picked it up of the floor, hating how much of a sissy he'd look, carrying a large baby doll, about the house and dreaded being seen by anyone.

He then remembered that Julie, Pam's friend from across the road, sometimes comes in to play with her and thought "Oh no! She doesn't mean, I've to carry it about, when Julie's here!" He got up to complain, but then remembered the doll and took it with him, calling "Pam! What about Julia?" as she heard him and giggled, loudly, so he could hear through the bathroom door "Let me think about that! Don't you want to play dollies with Julie?" adding "Her little sister Tina, loves playing dollies! Wouldn't you like to play with her, too?" as he sobbed "Pam! Not so loud! No! Please don't?" She giggled, and finished her dressing, as she exited the bathroom, carrying her nightdress and smiled at the sight of Tom, dressed as a boy, but carrying the dolly, as she said, "Good boy, Tom! Look after your new dolly! Carry her with pride!" as he huffed "Please Pam, don't?"

She said, "Ok! Tom! I've finished! See you at breakfast! Don't forget to thank me, for your dolly and pinny!" as she popped into her own room. She put her nighty away, in the dirty clothes basket and then picked up Wendy to exit and descend the stairs, to breakfast.

Pam greeted her Mum with a kiss and called "Morning, Mummy! What a wonderful night, that was?" Her Mum laughed "Morning Pam! Is he up?" and heard her giggle "Well I saw him slip into the bathroom, as I left, so he shouldn't be long!" He did look sweet sleeping beside his dolly, this morning!" as her Mum laughed "He wasn't?" as Pam nodded and heard her scold "You shouldn't make him, sleep with a dolly! If anyone finds out, they'll rib him to bits!" as she giggled, "How will they find out? Unless they see him in bed, or we tell!" Her Mum scolded "Pam! You wouldn't?" as Pam giggled, "Not unless he reverts to his old ways! If he's a good boy and does what he's told and helps with the housework, I won't tell on Nancy!" as they heard footsteps on the stairs and Pam waited, for their Mum's reaction.

Tom braced himself, as he turned into the hall and then reached the kitchen, holding the doll behind his back. Pam called out "Tom! No hiding your dolly away!" to hear her Mum laugh, as he pulled it out and plunked it down on

top of the washing machine, beside Pam's doll. He sat down and blushed, as he stammered "Thank you Pam, for my early birthday present! She's a very pretty dolly!" Pam giggled, "I thought you'd like your dolly, Tom!" as her Mum laughed "Pam! You shouldn't have! Tom can't play dollies!" Pam replied, "Mummy! That's sexist! It will be our secret! Won't it, Tom?" as he huffed "I'm not going to flaming tell anyone!" to laughter. Tom remembered the apron and asked, "Mummy! Where's my blue pinny?" as his Mum took the blue and pink one and said, "Pam! You'd better put yours on!" as Pam grabbed for the blue one and heard Tom plead "Please Pam! Let me wear the blue one?" as she laughed "Ok! As long as, you'll be a good boy!"

His Mum realizes he's got to carry Baby Suzie all about the house

He took the blue tabard and pulled it over his head and tied it at the side and huffed "I will!" as Pam pulled on her pink floral one. Tom swallowed, hating what he had to say, next, as he stammered "Mummy! Is there any housework, you want me to help with, this morning?" and heard his Mum laugh saying, "Gosh Pam! What have you done to him?" as Pam giggled, "Who me?" as they both laughed. His Mum said, "Well! I've to change the bed linen and get the washing on. You can help Pam and me, with that!" as Pam added "After you've done the washing up!" Tom tucked into his breakfast and tried to ignore their teasing, till he remembered Julie and he cried "Pam! What about Julia?" Her Mum asked, "Pam! You won't tell Julie, will you?" as Pam laughed "Tom's worried about Julie seeing him, carrying his dolly, if she comes over to play with me or us!" as her Mum said, "You can let him off, while any friends are here!" as Pam giggled, "You can hide in your room or the cupboard under the stairs!" as her Mum gasped "You'd be too tempted, to get her to look inside, for something, Pam!" as she giggled, "Who me?" Her Mum said, "While Julie's here, you can let him off, his dolly!" as he blushed at the mention of his dolly. Pam laughed "I'm sure she wouldn't tell!" but added "Her and especially her little sister Tina, would love to join you, playing dollies!" as her Mum said, "Stop that, Pam! You'd better not tell on him!" as Tom sobbed "Mum! Stop her teasing!"

Tom got up with tears streaming down his face and ran out the door, but was halfway up the hall, when he heard Pam giggle "Oh Tom! You've forgot your dolly!" and her Mum scold "Pam! That's naughty!" as they saw Tom run back and pick up the doll, to laughter as he stomped off. His laughing Mum, got up to console him, calling "Pam! That's cruel! Stop teasing your big brother!" She ran after the sobbing Tom and up the stairs to his room and on entering, she gave him a cuddle, saying, "She doesn't mean it! She won't tell!" as he huffed "She's making me carry this dolly, all about the house!" as she gasped "She's not?" as he nodded and heard her laugh "Naughty girl!" She took his hand and led him downstairs again and scolded "Pam! He can't carry that dolly, all about the house with him!" but heard Pam giggle "He can, and he will, or I'll be annoyed! Only in the house! I'm not making him carry his dolly outside, unless he's a naughty boy!" Her Mum led him in and said, "I'll have a word with her and see if she'll let you off! Come on and finish your breakfast!"

Tom returned holding the dolly and threw it down on the washing machine, to hear Pam warn "Be careful with your dolly or I'll have to take you to the toy shop, to get a new one! You wouldn't like that?" He shook his head and stammered "Sorry Pam! I'll look after my dolly!" to laughter from both Pam and their Mum. Pam Says, "It wasn't me, you threw down, like a brick! Apologize to your pretty dolly and tell her you love her and will be gentle with her, from now on!" adding "Don't forget, a nice kiss!" as her Mum laughed "Pam don't!" but saw him take the doll and say, "Sorry Baby Suzie! I'll be gentle with you, from now on!" adding "I love you!" as he kissed the doll and heard screeches from both Pam and her Mum, as he sobbed "Not fair!"

Tom does the dishes in apron and PVC pinny, but also does housework

They finished their breakfast and Tom asked, "Who will I help with the washing up?" but heard Pam say, "Mum and I normally did it! So! It's your turn!" Tom grimaced as he approached the sink and dreaded being seen by

anyone in the blue apron. He asked, "Can I pull the curtains?" but Pam said, "No way! There's nothing wrong with a boy wearing an apron, especially a blue one! Now if you were wearing this pretty pink one, you might have a point!" Tom went to the sink, but Pam took the floral PVC pinny and said, "If you slip this on, I'll help tie it, but if you don't then it's my little girl's one and I'll make sure you wear it all day!" as he blushed and took the girly PVC pinny and tied it around his back, over her blue apron. His Mum laughed "Now Pam, won't his apron do?" but she shook her head "It's the way you taught me Mummy and it will protect his apron from getting wet!" but added "And it will make him want us to go to town, sooner rather than later, shopping to get a boys PVC pinny!" as her Mum gasped, at her bullying daughter.

He pulled on some rubber gloves, lifting some dirty plates and heard his Mum say, "Scrape any food into the bin, first! That's a good boy!" smiling at Tom's compliance and Pam's hold over her normally bullying brother. She certainly was showing another side to her character. Tom popped the plates, cups and cutlery into the bubbling water and soon had washed most of it, when his Mum reminded him "Don't forget the frying pan!" as he looked at the smiling Pam, holding the two dolls and say, "Look girls! Tom is being a good boy and doing the washing up!" as she then said, "Is Tom my new Mummy?" and then replied, "Yes! Suzie!" adding "Tom's your new Mummy!" adding "But likes to be called Nancy!" as her Mum laughed "Pam! He's not her Mummy!" as Pam giggled, "It's just pretend Mummy! We all know he can't be a real Mummy! She's just his dolly!" as Tom huffed "Funny!", hating the conversation, about him being a Mummy. He finished washing the frying pan and eventually dried and put everything away, indicated by his smiling Mum, with Pam saying, "Didn't you know, where those go?" adding "He certainly needs a lot of practice, girls!" as she cuddled the dollies again.

Pam asked, "Right Mummy! What housework do you want us to do now?" to hear Tom complain "But, I've just done the dishes! I'm tired!" as Pam giggled, "Us girls normally do, lots of housework, before we rest! Don't we Mummy?" as her Mum laughed "She is right, Tom!" and heard him huff "But you're…!" He went to say, "Women!", but then heard Pam say, "What was that, Tom? You weren't going to say, we're women and only us do housework?" and then "Mummy! He still hasn't learnt his lesson!" adding "We must keep on teaching him, to be helpful with the housework!"

Her Mum laughed "Well! I'm sure the bedrooms need tidying and I want the bedding to wash!" Pam said, "Off you go, Tom!" but saw him undo the PVC pinny saying "I don't flaming need this!" as he hung it up. They saw him stomp up the hall, to then remember his dolly and run back, saying, "You aren't going to trick me!" Tom took the doll from his giggling sister and said, "Give me my, dolly, then!" to screeches from both Pam and his Mum.

Tom returns panties to his Mum, saying, he hid them under his pillow

Pam handed him the doll, saying, "Make sure you look after Baby Suzie!" as she picked up her dolly and followed Tom and said, "Let's do my room first!" and heard Tom huff "Not fair! I want to play footy?" but heard Pam say, "Your mates will only laugh at your pretty apron" He got to the landing and heard Pam say, "Stay here a tick, till I check it's ok!" as he remembered the yellow panties in his pocket and asked, "Can I go down to give Mum your yellow panties?" She nodded, "Ok! Remember, I don't know about them!" as he blushed and slipped downstairs, still carrying Baby Suzie, to his Mum. His Mum said, "That was quick!" as she then saw him pull the panties from his pocket and heard her laugh "I wondered about those!" as she laughed "I take it, you don't want to wear them today!" as he huffed "Funny!" although knowing he was wearing frilly pink panties instead. She said, "Where did you hide them?" adding "Don't tell me you kept them on, all night, under your PJs?" as he said, "No way! I took them off, as soon as I got into my bedroom and hid them under my pillow!"

His Mum gasped "Weren't you afraid of Pam spying them?" as he huffed "I didn't think she'd come into my bedroom!" as she laughed "Just as well, she didn't pull the pillows off, when showing me, where she hid your dolly!"

as he thought "At least you'd have known and stopped her controlling me!" as he nodded. She laughed "I'd have thought, you'd have given them back to me, when I read you your story or when I checked later on, if you wanted to sleep with your dolly, or not!" as he blushed and said, "I forgot, with all Pam's teasing about dollies!" He added "You know she's making me, sleep with that flaming dolly every night!" as she laughed "She's not?" as he nodded.

He thought to himself "I wish I flaming-well had returned them, when you had come into the bedroom!" adding "Why was I that stupid?" as she laughed "Ah well! No harm done!" as she popped them into the washing machine, which was half full. She laughed "So Baby Suzie, hasn't turned you, into a complete girly boy?" as he huffed "She hasn't! I'm not a sissy!" as she laughed "What's your dolly, called?" as he huffed "Baby Suzie!" as his Mum, laughed "I rest my case! Better take your pretty dolly, back up to help Pam!" as he huffed "Not flaming fair!" as she laughed and saw him run up the hall holding his dolly.

Meanwhile, Pam went into her bedroom and giggled, as she saw her nightdress and the one, she'd made Tom wear, that morning. She opened her wardrobe and pulled out a few skirts, blouses and frocks, scattering them on the bed and bedroom chair, for Tom to put away. She left her yellow frock inside, in case her Mum saw it and guessed, that she knew his secret.

She threw the Wendy doll down on the bed and said, "Ok Tom! Come on in!" as she opened the door for him. She also pulled the blinds up fully so he'd be on show to anyone looking in, helping her tidy her room with the thought of maybe making him do more curtsies, at her window, at the front of the house and outing him to Julie and Tina, but slapped her own wrist saying "Naughty girl!" and thought to herself "No! I'll take it slowly and try to keep Nancy to myself for a while!" as she giggled.

Pam makes him pop her dirty clothes away and then hang her dresses up

Tom entered and immediately hit the floor, crying "Pam! Close the blinds! I'll be seen!" as Pam giggled, "Now Tom! You're wearing blue, not pink and won't be recognized!" He huffed "Ok! But I'm not going near the window!" as she laughed "We'll see!" She said, "First thing to do, is put any dirty washing away, in the clothes basket!" as she pointed to her nightdresses and saw Tom grimace, as he picked up the two girly items and heard her giggle "Just pop them in the basket! They won't bite!" He huffed and picking them up, he popped them into the basket and said, "There! What now?" Pam ordered "Right! Now pick up my undies!" He sobbed "I'm not picking your flaming undies, up?" and heard Pam giggle "Mum and me, have had to pick up your horrid smellies and not complained!" She saw Tom pick up some tights and use them, to pick up her knickers, saying, "Yuk!" as he deposited them into the basket.

She said, "Now for my pretty clothes! Check your hands are clean!" as he cried "I've just done the washing up!" as she said "But you'd rubber gloves on!" as he went and washed his hands again, before returning to her. She giggled, "Hold on a tick! Wait for me before you start!" as he blushed and saw her exit, as he turned around from the window and sat down on the bed, hating having to do housework and wear a silly apron, even though it was his boy's one.

Pam went down stairs into the kitchen, "We've started in my room and he's just put my dirty washing into the wash basket!" adding "My nighties and panties!" as her Mum gasped "He hasn't!" as Pam nodded, "Although he pulled such a face, when he'd to pick up my dirty panties!" as she added "using a pair of my tights, to pick them up! Though I said, you and I have had to pick up, his smellies lots of times!" as her Mum laughed at Pam's comments. She then added "He's now putting my pretty skirts and dresses away!" as her Mum scolded her and said, "Pam keep him away from your clothes!" as she giggled, "Mummy! How on earth is my sweet housemaid, meant to learn her housework duties?" as her Mum gasped "Pam, he can't!" as she laughed at Pam's cheek. Her Mum said,

"Don't forget the bed-linen!" as she replied, "I'll call, if she needs any help!" as her Mum laughed "ok!" and saw Pam disappear, up the stairs again.

Pam returned to her bedroom to see Tom sitting on her bed, facing away from the street and laughed "Oh yea! I forgot to check! Are you wearing, my you know what?" as he blushed and nodded, "I am!" She giggled, "Let me see?" as she giggled, "Just unzip your trousers!" as he cried "No way!" but she insisted "Just sit down on the floor and I'll take a peek!" Tom sat down and unzipped his trousers, to see Pam sit down and peer at his front, as he pulled the black underpants to the side, to then show the pink of her panties. She said, sternly "What are those?" as he huffed "Your panties!" but she scolded "I never said, you could wear your silly underpants!" as he huffed "But someone might see!" She laughed "They won't see, so long as you don't remove your trousers or play swapsies with your mates!" He cringed and heard her say, "Right! Into the bathroom and get those horrid undies, off! I'll be in to check, in a minute!" as he sobbed "Not fair Pam!" as he stood up and exited.

Pam checks he's in her pink panties under his trousers, but ...

He disappeared out, to hear Pam call out "Oh Tom! You forgot your dolly, again!" and saw him run back and grab the dolly, as he heard his Mum laugh, on hearing Pam call out to him, but Pam said, "Every time you forget your dolly, she cries and so you must kiss her and tell her your sorry and that you love her!" He picked up the doll and hugged it, saying, "Sorry, I forgot you Baby Suzie! I love you!" as Pam giggled, "Ok! Take her in, but don't embarrass your little dolly!" as Tom exited, taking the doll with him and locked the bathroom door. He blushed as he removed his trousers and his underpants, to be left in the pink panties, partially covered by his tea-shirt and the blue apron. Two minutes later, Pam checked her Mum was still downstairs and knocked "Let me in!" He whispered "I can't! I'm just in your thingies!" but she giggled, "Just a peek!"

He unlocked the door and saw her enter, as she quickly locked the door again. She giggled, as she saw one leg of the pink panties, showing from under his blue tabard and picking up his underpants said, "Right! Unless you want to do the housework like that, get your trousers on!" and unlocked the door, to leave him to get dressed. He pulled his trousers on, over the pink panties and tucked his tea-shirt in, before doing them up. He grimaced, as he picked up the dolly, before opening the door and exiting to join his giggling sister.

He entered her room but saw that she'd removed her pink apron and was petrified, when she held it up and said, "For trying to wear those pants without permission, you must pay a forfeit!" Tom gasped and sobbed "Not fair Pam! Please don't? I can't wear that apron, not in here, at the front!" adding "Please Pam! I'll be seen!" adding "Wait till we're in my room at the back!" She said, "Well ok! I'll be nice this time, but you must promise to wear my pink apron, as soon as we're finished with my room!" as he nodded, "Ok!" and sighed with relief, as he retied the blue tabard again and huffed "Ok! What now?" She said, "See Tom! I'm not that cruel! As long as you're a good little boy and do what I say, I'll be nice to you!" as he grimaced, seeing her smile, at her power over him.

She laughed "When I was downstairs and mentioned to Mummy about you hanging up my pretty skirts and dresses!" as he blushed and heard her say, "She did scold me, but I then asked, how on earth my new housemaid Nancy, was to learn her duties!" as he cried "Not fair, Pam!" as she laughed, hugging him and gave him a kiss on the cheek.

Pam said, "Alright! We'll just put my clothes onto that chair, for now, till we get the bedding for Mummy to wash. She said, "Carefully lift any clothes, from my bed and put them over that chair!" Tom looked down and grimaced at the clothes, on top of the bed. He lifted a skirt and blouse, causing Pam to giggle "Nice choice of outfit!" as he huffed "Pam! Stop teasing!" as he threw them down onto the bedside chair. She warned "I said, carefully!" He

huffed "Ok!" and picked up a dress, causing her to giggle "Not quite as pretty as my yellow frock, but I'd love to see which looked prettiest!" as he placed it over the skirt and blouse on the chair.

Pam gets Tom to change the bedding but has to swap pinnies as Nancy

He asked, "Aren't you going to help?" but just heard her laugh "I'll help when we're doing the bed!" He took the last dress and the two dollies, off the bed and popped them onto the chair, shoving the dollies under the clothing. Pam said, "Right Tom! We've to take the quilt and bedclothes off, to get at the pink bed sheet! You go around the other side!" as he cried "But I'll be near the window!" as she closed the blind a bit and saw him go round to help pull the bedding off and throw it onto the chair, on top of her clothes. She said "Now for the bottom sheet!" and he helped her pull one side off and soon she'd taken it and popped it onto the floor, outside her bedroom door.

She said "Now for a clean sheet! Just try the chest of drawers there!" and saw him open the bottom drawer and reached his hand in, to see what was there. He asked, "Pam! What colour?" as he fumbled with the folded-up sheets. Pam realized they weren't the bed sheets, she was after, but were eiderdown and bed throws, from when she was younger, with themes, 'My little Pony' and saw Tom fiddling in the drawer. She smiled and thought of a wonderful tease for him later. She said, "Oops, wrong one! Try the middle!" and saw him close the bottom drawer and open the middle one, to see various coloured sheets and pillowcases. Pam said, "I'll have the white sheet, with the pink satin flowers on it!" He pulled it out and she helped put it on, followed by the rest of the bedding. He then had to change the pillowcases and took the matching cases, out of the drawer with Pam putting the old ones, outside on the floor, ready for her Mum to take. He then popped the pillows into the new cases and soon Pam was satisfied.

Pam smiled and opened the blinds again but then pulled them up and saw him run out the door, but she of course called "Oh Tom! You've forgotten your dolly!" and saw him run back, but then turned and walked backwards to try and hide his face from view, as he picked up his dolly. She said, "Come on and we'll let Nancy, do your room, now! We've to get the bed sheet and pillow-cases down to Mummy!" as he grimaced.

However, she stopped him at the door and said, "Aren't we forgetting something?" Pam called "Tom! Bring my Wendy doll for me, too!" as he cringed at having to pick up both dollies and carry them out of her room, with the possibility of being seen through the window by someone or even Julie or Tina in the houses, across the road.

However, his embarrassment was doubled, when he exited the room and saw his giggling sister, holding out the pink pinny, saying, "I also meant we've to swap pinnies! You promised!" Tom huffed "Not fair!" with tears in his eyes, as he set the dolls down on the floor and untied his blue tabard, pulling it over his head. Pam took it and he blushed as he took the pink apron and pulled it over his head and down his body.

Pam did the blue tabard up and said, "Turn around and I'll tie up your pink pinny!" He cried "No! You'll tie it in a knot!" as she giggled, "You'd better go down and get Mummy to tie it for you!" as he realised he'd have to go downstairs in the pink floral apron and show it off, to his giggling Mum. Pam said, "Just tell Mum, that you were naughty and have to wear it, to change the bedding in your room!" as he picked up Baby Suzie and slipped, nervously downstairs, to giggles from Pam.

He's to go down to ask his Mum to tie a bow in Pam's apron

He got to the bottom of the stairs and dreaded being spotted through the front door, in the girly pink apron. tabard!" His Mum was in the kitchen and turning around, broke into a giggle, at seeing Tom, in Pam's pink apron, holding the dolly. He huffed "Mummy! Can you tie a bow in this pinny! If she does it, she'll tie a knot!" and heard her giggle "I thought you were in the blue apron!" as he blushed, "She let me wear it, to do her room at the front but

for my room I've to flaming wear hers!" She laughed "I see!" and tied a pretty bow in the apron strings, laughing "There! You look very sweet!" He huffed "Mum! It's bad enough with Pam teasing me! Can't I stop now? I've helped Pam change her bedsheets and pillowcases. She said, "Good boy!" adding "If you help her for another half hour, I'll see if she'll let you go and play!" He huffed "Ok!" and turned around, still holding the dolly, causing her to add "I see she's not letting you, get rid of your dolly!" and heard him huff "She's making me carry it into each room, we go in!" as he disappeared up the stairs again.

Pam had watched Tom disappear downstairs and ran over to her drawers and looked in the bottom drawer, giggling at the girly top sheets, she had on her bed, as a little girl. There was 'My Little Pony', but best of all, underneath it was 'pink Barbie Girl' top sheet, with a large Barbie Doll on the front, a couple of smiling girls faces and 'Barbie Girl' in large letters and thought, I'll keep this one till Nancy appears, in a week or so!" She thought "I'll surprise Tom later, with the My Little Pony! I'll be able to tease him, by saying, "Off you go! Giddy up, Neh and Gee up!" as she returned to wait for him in his own room.

Tom stomped up the stairs in the pink floral apron, still holding the dolly and heard Pam giggle "What did Mummy say?" He huffed "She laughed and asked why I was wearing your pinny!" She said, "Come on and let's get your bed-sheets changed!" as she entered the room, with a blushing Tom following her. He ran to the wall, saying, "Pam! Pull the blinds! Someone in the back street, will recognise me, in this flaming thing!" She giggled, "You promised you'd wear my pinny and help change the sheets!" but then added "Hold on! I'll see, if I can find something!" as she ran out and entered her own room. Tom sat down on his chair out of sight, waiting to see, what she'd suggest.

He looked up and saw Pam enter the door, with a large smile and then pull a hand from behind her back, holding a floral headscarf and giggling "This should stop anyone from recognising you!" He cried "You bug off! No way!" as she huffed "Ok! I just thought it would disguise you a bit! Come on then! Nobody will look!" as she stood at the far side of the bed. Tom was glad he didn't have to go near to the window, but was worried, as he'd be facing it, whilst changing the bed and dreaded being spotted in the pink apron.

They pulled the top sheet and then the rest of the bedding and soon had the blankets off his bed, to get at the under-sheet. They whipped the sheet off and then Pam had Tom remove the pillowcases and then heard their Mum coming up the stairs. She entered the room and smiled at seeing Tom, still in the pink apron and Pam in the blue tabard, as Pam called "Hi Mum!" She asked her "How's things going, Pam?"

Pam said, "We've got my sheet and pillowcases, at my door and there's Tom's there!"

Her Mum said "Now Pam! Tom's done well so far! Let him out to play with his mates!" as Pam complained "Mum! Not fair! He should do more" but said "Ok!"

Tom is let out to play footy, but Pam puts a girly bedsheet on his bed

Tom exited and stomped downstairs into the kitchen, undoing the apron strings and pulling it over his head, before flinging it down on the kitchen table, along with the baby doll. He exited the side door, hating his sister and how she'd embarrassed him. He was glad to be able to escape, from Pam and housework for a while, wanting to hit her or call her nasty names, but knew Pam could easily tell anyone about his dolly or dress up.

He ran around to the next street and found Pete and Dave standing chatting together and when they saw him, they called "Hi Tom! Where were you, last night?" Tom blushed a bit, remembering his Mum dressing him up and then Pam making him stay in with her. He fibbed "My relations called around and I'd to stay in!" Pete said, "We had a wicked game of footy, down in the big car-park!" We played the guys from James Street and they just beat us!" Dave said, "We could have done with you!"

Tom grimaced "I wanted to come, but Mum made me stay in!" as he blushed at the thought of what had happened.

Meanwhile Pam decided to take advantage of his absence, by putting a girly bedspread on top of his bed. She asked, "Mum! What have you to do this morning?" She replied, "The washing's nearly done! If you want to help me!" She said, "Fine! I'll just finish up here and join you downstairs!" Her Mum said, "Thanks!" and returned downstairs to the kitchen. Pam took the chance to get the bedspread and opening her bottom drawer. She chose the 'My Little Pony' bedspread and pulled it out, smiling at the choice, as she took it into his room and pulling the top sheet off the bed, she replaced it with the girly bedspread. She smoothed it out and giggled, at the sight that would greet her macho brother, later. There were the words My Little Pony, a smiling girl's face and a few pink and yellow horses, with long manes and various headdresses, with other frilled adornments. She thought to herself "Before he discovers my little joke, I'll tell him he's to play horsies with me and pretend to be a horse!" adding "He'll prefer it to playing dollies!" adding "although I will want my horsy to be nice and pretty and so she'll end up wearing lots of headscarves and hair ribbons!" as she giggled to herself. She laughed and thought "I'll end up calling him 'My Little Pony' and then introduce him to his new girly bedsheet!" which he can then show to our lovely Mummy.

She looked around the rest of the room and thought how untidy it looked, thinking to herself "I could tidy it up and replace his toys with lots of dollies and girl's toys!" She laughed at the thought but didn't want to rush things. She laughed as she took his door key and closing his door, locked it, not wanting Tom to enter and discover her secret, till she was ready. She smiled and thought of his reaction when he saw what he'd have to sleep in, that night, not to mention the nighty, I'll make him wear. She hid the key in her room and skipped downstairs, to join her Mum who was just getting the washed bedclothes out of the machine. She said, "About time, Missy!" and Pam said, "Sorry Mum! I was just finishing off upstairs!"

Pam uses the handbag of pegs to help her Mum with the laundry

Her Mum asked, "Want to swap back into your pinny, since he's finished with it!" Pam giggled, "Oh! Didn't he want to wear it to protect his clothes playing footy?" causing her Mum to scold "Pam! Stop teasing!" as Pam removed the blue tabard and popped on her pink and yellow apron. Her Mum said "The washing will take about half an hour! You can rest for a while and watch TV or something!" as Pam switched it on and started watching a film. Her Mum joined her and asked "Pam, go easy on him! Let him off carrying that dolly about the house?" but she shook her head "Mummy! Isn't it funny, seeing my big MSP of a brother carrying a dolly from room to room?" as she laughed and nodded "Yes! But it isn't right!" as Pam laughed "Especially when he wears my pretty aprons and pinnies!" adding "You should have let me pop him into that little girl's one!" as her Mum laughed "No Pam!" They waited and soon heard the washing machine finish and saw her Mum get up to open it up and get the washing.

Pam said, "I'll get the clothes pegs Mummy!" She opened the cupboard and retrieved the old plastic purple handbag, which her Mum used to hold the clothes-pegs. She swung it over her arm and said, "Pity Tom's not here to help! We could show him how to hang out the washing!" Her Mum looked up and laughed at the handbag, dangling from her young daughter's elbow, saying, "I hope that handbag wasn't in your plans?" Pam giggled, "Mummy! You did teach me to carry it, when hanging out our washing! So, I don't have to bend down to get at the pegs!" Her Mum laughed "I think he'd rather bend down, to holding that handbag!"

She said, "Now Pam! Don't let him be seen outside, as a girly boy!" as Pam huffed and said, "You're too soft on him, Mummy!" as her Mum stood up, with the basket of clean bed-sheets and pillowcases, along with a few items of clothing, that had been popped in.

Pam opened the door and stepped out, followed by her Mum with the wash-basket, as she then closed the side door and joined her in the back garden. She reached into the peg bag and retrieved two pegs, as her Mum set the basket

down and pulled out a large bedsheet. Pam handed her a few pegs and taking the far end of the sheet, she pegged it up, as her Mum pegged up the other end. They carried on pegging out the pillowcases and rest of the laundry, using the handbag, to get the pegs again.

It was Sunday afternoon and her Mum thanked her and said, "Right! I'd better get the lunch on! You can rest if you like!" Pam followed her in the side door and replaced the peg-bag in the cupboard, saying, "Hopefully Tom will help us collect the washing in, this afternoon!" as her Mum laughed "Now Pam! Not outside" but Pam laughed "I'd ensure he wasn't recognized!" as her Mum asked "How!" and saw her hold up a headscarf as her Mum gasped "No Pam! Don't!" She said "He helped make the beds this morning!" Pam said, "Mum! He should help with all the housework! He used to leave it all to you and me! You shouldn't have let him go out and kept him at housework!" adding "I'm sure if he'd had to keep my pinny on, he wouldn't have gone to play!" Her Mum said, "Pam!

Don't make him go out, in the garden, in your pinny or anything!" adding "I don't want June or the people in the back streets, to see him dressed up!"

Tom in his apron helps lay the table and is told he's to play horsies

Pam laughed "Mummy! He probably was seen, when doing the housework this morning, in my pretty pink apron!", knowing at least one lady, waved to him, doing curtsies to the back and giggled. Her Mum laughed "Don't be cruel to him!" Pam said, "He's to tidy up my room and put my clothes away!" Her Mum scolded "Pam! You put your own clothes away! Don't make him go near your clothes! Anyway, he'd just ruin them!" Pam giggled, "Mum! I wouldn't let him out in them! At least not to play football!" as her Mum gasped "Pam! Stop teasing! You know, what I meant! It's bad enough you making him carry that dolly, about!" to more giggles.

Around 12.50, Tom finished playing with his mates and returned home, entering the door he complained "Mum! I missed a really good game of footy last night!" Pam giggled, "You could have told your mates you had a really good time playing dollies! I'm sure they'd have been dead jealous!" He cried "You bug off! I didn't! I just held it!" as his Mum said, "Come on children! Stop bickering!" and "Pam! Stop teasing!" Pam giggled, and saw him pick up his dolly, stumping out of the kitchen and into the living room, as she called "I'd to help Mummy hang out the wet bed-sheets and pillowcases on the line, so you can help us collect them in, this afternoon!" as he cried "But I made the flaming beds and did the washing up earlier!"

Pam said, "Look ok! Mummy doesn't want the neighbours to see you, outside and you might be seen, if you collect the washing in!" as she added "So instead, you can play horsies with me!" Tom cried "Mum! I don't have to! Do I?" She said, "Pam! He did help make the beds! Let him off?" She smiled and said, "If he agrees to play with me after lunch!" He cried "I'm not playing dollies with you!" as she giggled, "I didn't mean dollies! Unless you want to!" He asked, "What do you want to play?" as she laughed "I just want to play horsies!" as he huffed "But that's stupid!" Her Mum said, "Pam! Only for fifteen minutes!" She huffed "Ok!" but thought to herself "Then I'll make him play dollies for another fifteen minutes, after tea!"

He huffed "What do you mean horses? I'm not playing with Julie or anyone else!" She giggled, "Oh! Julie enjoys playing horsies!" as he cried "Mum! She's trying to make me play with Julie!" as her Mum scolded "Pam! Just the two of you can play horses!" as Pam huffed "Oh! Mum! Ok! I was just joking!" She smiled "I've got him! It will be a laugh making him canter around the room, pretending to be a horse! It won't be that embarrassing, till he sees his bedsheet! I'll be able to say, "Giddy up and Neh!" as Tom wondered what she had in mind.

Her Mum said, "Can you lay the table for me?" and Pam said, "You'd better get your blue pinny on or would you prefer the pink one?" and saw Tom return to the kitchen still holding his dolly and take the blue apron, setting his

dolly down, till he'd pulled it on and tied the string. Pam said, "I'll take the table-cloth and you take the knives and forks!" She took the cloth and saw Tom open a drawer and get some cutlery. She entered the living room and laid out the clothe, over the dining table, watching for Tom to enter. He came in with his hands full of the cutlery and set it down on the table.

After dinner Pam teases Tom doing the washing and prepares for horsies

Pam said, "Lay it out for Mummy!" and saw him set out the knives and forks at the three places. She waited till he'd finished and then she walked into the kitchen and called "Tom! You forgot your dolly!" and heard him run back in, as he cried "Not fair! I had my hands full!" as she giggled, "I'll find you a bag to carry your dolly in! That will leave your hands free!" Her Mum called "Pam! Let him off, while he's laying the table!" as she huffed "Ok! But don't be long!" She took the salt and pepper and told Tom to bring in some cups and glasses. Tom hated having to obey his horrid sister, but knew he had to do what she said, or she could tell Julie about him. Their Mum got the dinner out and brought it in, to them, telling them to sit down and eat. Pam asked, "So Tom! What did you get up to this morning, whilst Mummy and I were doing the washing?" He huffed "Just messing about with some mates, playing footy! They said, I missed a good match last night!" Pam retorted "You play too much football! You've got to spend more time helping Mummy and me about the house!" turning to her Mum saying, "Isn't that right, Mum?" Her Mum laughed "Well a little more help, wouldn't hurt!"

Her Mum reminded her "Horsies is just for ten, or fifteen minutes Pam! Remember! Then you've to let Tom go and do his own thing!" She huffed "Ok!" and heard Tom protest "Mum! She'll tease me!" but heard Pam warn "Watch it or We'll play dollies instead!" and saw him pull a face and take a mouthful of food. They finished dinner and Pam helped her Mum bring in the dishes, as Tom pulled on her PVC pinny again, running the water and started washing up.

Her Mum said, "Want to help dry some dishes, as Pam said, "Ok! It will help make sure he washes them properly!" and saw Tom pull another face. What made it worse, was Pam's teasing whilst he washed up, saying, "It's good that all three of us wear aprons and do the housework now! Isn't it, Tom?" and "Sure you wouldn't like to swap pinnies with me?" and "Look Tom! Your pretty dolly is watching you, doing the dishes!" He wanted to thump her but dreaded the consequences and so just cried "Mum! Tell her to stop teasing!" but with no results.

Pam reminded him "Almost finished?" as she dried and put away the last few things. Tom nodded, and heard her say, "We'll soon have a lovely game of horsies and then I'll let you go and play!" Tom didn't like it, but thought it better than playing dollies. He finished the last few sauce-pans off and Pam dried and put them away, before saying, "Ok Tom! I'll let you rest for five minutes, but then you've to come up and play with me!" He huffed "Just for ten minutes!" as Pam said, "Fifteen minutes will do for now!"

Tom removed the PVC pinny and then his boy's tabard and went into the back room to rest, but of course heard her call out "Tom! You've forgotten your dolly again!" and saw him run back and pick it up with Pam and her Mum both laughing, as he cried "Not Fair!"

Pam pops Tom into headscarves and an Alice band to be her little pony

Pam ran upstairs and got some things ready for their game. She got some girly scarves out of her wardrobe and then had another idea, as she got her tape recorder and plugging it in, she turned hid it away and got ready to start recording a conversation with Tom. She waited a few minutes and then called "Tom! Come on up to play horsies!" really loudly and heard him cry "Not so loudly Pam!" as she heard his footsteps on the stairs, as she turned the tape recorder on. She smiled and thought to herself "I hope this works!" Tom hadn't forgotten his dolly and so

was carrying it, as he got to her door and called "Pam! Close the blinds! I don't want to be seen!" She reached up and pulled on the chord, which closed the blinds shut a bit, saying, "Ok! There! Seeing you were a good boy this morning!"

She added "I'm glad you didn't forget to bring your dolly with you! There's lots of girly games you don't know how to play! Dollies! Pushing them in prams! Dress up – oops you know that one! Skipping and Lots more!" as he huffed. She giggled, knowing or hoping, it would be on the tape, that should be recording everything they were saying.

She opened drawer and pulled out another smaller headscarf and heard him cry "No way, Pam! Please don't?" She giggled, "My horsy has to do, as he's told or I'll be annoyed and make Nancy come and play dress up!" as he cringed and said, "Pam! I'm a boy horse!" She giggled, "Boy horses can wear pretty things, too! Can't they?" He grimaced and nodded, "Ok! But not too much!" She took the headscarf and tied it around his head, giggling as she said, "There's My Little Pony's pretty main! You like your pretty main! Don't you?" and heard him mumble "Yes! Your little pony likes it!"

She showed him how to place his hands, up near his throat, as if he was holding reins of a horse as she demonstrated and cantered up and down her room to show him. She said "Off you go my pretty pony!" and saw him try to copy her walking up and down her room, causing her to giggle "You make a sweet little pony!" as he blushed. She loved it and carried on gigging around the room, with Tom in front, but this time, with him wearing a pretty headscarf. She had him gig around the bed and back again, before stopping by her drawers and saying, "See Tom! If you're afraid of being recognized wearing my pretty apron dress, whilst doing the housework, you can borrow one of my headscarves, instead of needing to close the blinds!" He blushed and cringed "Pam! Not fair! Is the time nearly up?" She took an Alice band and a hair ribbon and heard him cry "Please Pam! Don't make me wear those?" and heard her say, "They aren't for Tom! They're for My Little Pony! If he's a good little pony I'll let him go out to play in the paddock with the other ponies!" as he cringed and felt the headscarf being pulled off his head and the Alice band, being put in its place.

She then led him over to the mirror and asked, "What does my little pony think of his Alice band?" Tom cringed as she asked, "Is this the same Alice band, Mummy put on you last night, when she put you into my yellow frock?" and saw him nod. However, she wanted it on tape and said, "Tell your dolly!" He huffed "Yes Suzie! It's the same Alice band that Mummy put on me when she dressed me in your pretty frock last night!" as Pam gurgled.

Pam supplies her horsy with a large handbag to carry his dolly about in

She said, "Hold still, till I get My Little Pony's hair ribbon tied up and then he can go for a canter!" as she fed the ribbon under his chin and around the top of his head, where she tied it in a large hair bow. She said, "There! How do you like your hair ribbon?" and Tom wanting to get out of there asap and not wanting to annoy her, stammered "It's very pretty! It matches my hair band!" Pam gasped, surprised at his answer and gave him a hug, saying, "You are a sweet brother Tom! I wish I'd have had you to play dollies and dress up, years, ago! You'll be even better and much more fun, when you act as my sister, Nancy!"

He cried "Pam! I was nice there! Please don't tease me, anymore!" She giggled, "Ok! Let's canter up and down a couple of times and then it will nearly be time to let you go!"

He turned and placed his hands up to hold the pretend reigns and heard her say, "Giddy up there, 'My Little Pony!'" but then asked, "What are you?" and heard Tom say, "I'm your little Pony!" Pam had him canter around her room like a little pony with his hands by his chest. Pam gurgled "No Tom! You're my pretty little pony, now you've got

your hair ribbons in! What are you?" and heard him echo "I'm your pretty little pony!" as he turned at the door and cantered back again to the window. He turned again and cantered to the door, with Pam behind him, with the long scarf, as she said, "Almost finished! Just downstairs to show our lovely Mummy!" He gasped "Please don't?" adding "Take my ribbons out first?" and in an effort to make her stop, he said, "I've forgotten my dolly!" as she giggled, loudly "I think you're getting to enjoy playing dollies, Tom!" at his statement and turned to let him get his dolly. He picked it up and went to continue, holding it in his hand, but Pam said, "Now Tom! You can't hold your dolly and play horsies, at the same time!" He asked her "Will you bring her down for me?" but Pam opened the wardrobe and pulled out a shoulder bag, saying, "Let's pop your dolly into this handbag and then your hands will be free!" Tom cried "Please Pam! Don't make me carry that?" Pam took the dolly and popped it into the large floral handbag, so that it's head was sticking out and giggled, "Now Tom! You're my little pony! Not my horrid brother and so you won't mind if you carry a handbag about with you!" as she slung the strap over his neck and down his side, giggling as she stepped behind him, taking the scarf in her hands and said, "Gee up!" and saw Tom return his hands to the horsy position and continue along the landing and nervously down the stairs, taking it slowly, for fear of tripping, but also for fear, anyone might call at the front door.

He got to the hallway and heard Pam gurgle "Come on! Don't forget to tell Mummy what you are!" as she geed him up and they cantered into the living room. Her Mum turned and let out a shriek of laughter at seeing Tom, with an Alice band and hair ribbon, carrying a handbag with his dolly's head peeking out the top of it and with Pam behind, holding reigns around him and him pretending to be a horse. Pam giggled, "Tell Mummy what you are!" Tom grimaced "I'm your pretty little pony!" Her Mum scolded "I wondered why you wanted to play horses with Tom!" Tom cried "Look what she made me wear!" as his Mum stood up and pulled the hair ribbon and Alice band off his head, saying, "Pam! That was very naughty!" as she giggled, "Mummy! I didn't put them on Tom's head! I put them onto My little Pony's!" as her Mum saw Tom raise the handbag straps over his head and she then saw the doll's head sticking out and giggled, "Pam! A handbag too?"

Pam shows Tom the My Little Pony bedsheet and he shows his Mum

Pam said, "Horses don't mind wearing pretty ribbons or carrying pretty handbags!" adding "See Mummy! It holds his dolly, while his hands are busy, holding the horse's reins! Just like we use them around the shops, when holding skirts or frocks!" as Tom huffed "Mum! It was terrible!" His Mum said, "Ok! You can go on now! She's had her fifteen minutes with you!" and saw him stump off. Pam leads Tom upstairs saying, "I've a nice surprise for you, but no telling Mummy yet!" as he huffed "What?" as she led him along and unlocking his door, she opened it and led him to his bedroom, to show him, as he cried "Oh no!" but she put her finger to her mouth "Keep it a secret from Mummy a tick, till I've gone!"

He saw the pink 'My Little Pony' sheet on top of his bed and cried "Not fair Pam! That's terrible!" as she laughed and hugged him and said, "Just tell Mummy, that it will be ok and act as a sweet reminder of playing horsies with my sweet sister Pammy, as My Little Pony!" as he blushed and sobbed "Not flaming fair, Pam!" She told him "I'll be popping out soon, but it better be still there, when you show Mummy!" as she kissed his cheek and skipped downstairs.

At around 11 o'clock Tom came downstairs after her and heard Pam say, "Tom! Are you sure you don't want to do more housework for Mummy!" as he cried "Please let me off? Can't I go and play footy?" as his Mum then said, "I think he's done enough housework for now, Pam!" She huffed "Mum! I'm sure he'll start to enjoy his housework, just like us?" adding "Not to mention, wearing pretty pinnies!" as her Mum laughed at her comment and Tom huffed "Ha!" Pam relented and undid her pink apron and then his tabard to say, "Give your dolly, a kiss and put her in the kitchen to pick up, when you return from footy!" Tom grimaced, as he kissed the dolly and took her into the kitchen, where he set it down on the washing machine.

She said, "I'm about to go out too! I want you to wait till I've gone and then you can show Mummy your bedsheet, telling her, it will remind you of playing horsies with me!" as he blushed and cringed "Not fair, Pam!" She gave her Mum a kiss on the cheek and a hug, saying, to her Mum "I'm going across to Julie for while!" adding "I think Tom has something to show you Mummy, before he goes!" Her Mum asked, "What, dear?" but she said, "I'm not sure, but it's something to do with playing horsies!" Her Mum laughed and saw her skip off and out the front door, closing it shut. His Mum asked, "What have you to show me then Tom?" as he cringed "You'd better come up the stairs Mum!" as she followed him up and entered his room and gasped and laughed "Oh no! She didn't?" She said, "I'll remove it and put one of your normal bed-covers on!" but heard him say, "No Mummy! Just leave it, as nobody else will see it and it will just be a nice reminder of playing horsies with Pammy as My Little Pony!"

Pam tells Julie she did housework and started playing dollies again

His Mum laughed and hugged him, saying, "I never thought she'd take it this far!" adding "You go on now and have fun with your mates!" as she kissed him, bye. Tom exited and was relieved to be out of the house and away from his horrid sister and her dollies. He went down and called for Dave and then the two of them went around to call for Jim.

Pam had exited the driveway and saw Tina and a couple of young girls in the driveway, pushing a pram and playing with some dollies. She laughed at the thought of Tom having to play with them and knowing how embarrassed he'd be, playing like a little girl. She called "Hi Tina! Is Julie in?" Tina called out "Yea! I think she's watching TV or up in her room. Pam rang the bell and saw Julie's Mum answer the door, calling "Julie! It's Pam!" as she opened the porch doors. Julie joined her and called "Hi Pam! Want to come in?" as Pam stepped in asking "What are you up to?" and followed her into the living room. Julie said, "Just watching TV and I've some homework to do for tomorrow! What have you been up to?" Pam giggled, "I helped Mummy with housework, making the beds and hanging out the washing!" Julies Mum asked, "Hear that Julie! Pam helps her Mum with the housework! You should follow her example!" Julie replied, "I help a little! I do the washing up!" as her Mum laughed "Sometimes, but not that often!"

Pam said, "I also played with my dollies a bit!" as Julie asked, "What? I thought you'd given them up, saying, they were just for young girls!" as Pam giggled, "I've changed my mind and realise how much fun, I used to have with them! Have you still got yours?" Julie laughed "I gave most to Tina! She'd love it, if I started playing dollies again! She's always wanting me to play with her!" She called "Hear that Mummy? Pam's started playing dollies again!" Her Mum laughed and brought a trolley of some biscuit's and mineral water into the living room, saying, "I suppose that means, you'll be playing dollies again too?" as Julie giggled, "Well! I did used to love playing! It was just because Pam stopped that I did too!"

Her Mum said, "I suppose if Pam stuck her hand into fire, you would too?" as she replied, "Don't be silly!" Julie asked, "Mummy! Where are my dollies, the ones Tina, hasn't taken?" Her Mum said, "You gave most to her, but I think you've still got some up in the wardrobe!" Pam mentions her dolls pram and Julie gasped and giggled, "Now Pam! I don't think I'd want anyone in the street to see me playing dollies! They'd take the mick out of me!" adding "I think I'll keep that to the house!" as Pam laughed "Not even the back garden?" as Julie giggled, "Pam! What's got over you?" as they both laughed.

They chatted away with Julie saying "Tina will really love it, if we join her to play dollies and stuff!" as Pam giggled "Now Julie, you must remember how much fun we used to have playing dollies and wheeling them about in their doll's pram!" as she laughed but with a bit of a blush on her face.

Pam listens to her tape of Tom saying girly things and about his dolly

When she'd finished playing over at Julie's, she returned home and saw her Mum in the sitting room, dusting. Her Mum laughed "That was a naughty trick with your My Little Pony bed cover on his bed as Pam giggled "It does look sweet and is a nice reminder for him of playing horsies with me!" Pam said, "Sorry Mum! I couldn't resist doing his hair for horsies!" Her Mum scolded "That's naughty! He's your brother, not your sister! So less of the ribbons and Alice bands and especially no handbags!" Pam sat down and laughed "Mum! You're always telling me how useful they are!" as her Mum gasped "Yes for shopping!" as Pam giggled, "Well! I'm just giving him some practice before we go!" as her Mum said, "No way, is he carrying, a handbag, shopping!" as Pam huffed "That's sexist!" as she said, "I'll be back down in a minute!" She played the tape recorder and heard Tom saying, girly things and laughed at the thought of going to bed, listening to Nancy's sweet words putting her to sleep. She ran back down the stairs and joined her Mum in the living room, watching TV. Her Mum gurgled "When I got you to change the bedding, I never thought you'd take advantage and put a girly sheet on his bed!" as she said "I've hidden the other girly sheets away, to stop you really embarrassing your brother!" as Pam giggled "Oh Mummy! I remember loving my, Barby Girl and Princess bed covers and I'm sure Nancy will adore them!" as she laughed "I know his dolly used to love sleeping beside me in my pretty nighties, under the pretty bedding!" as her Mum shook her head and said "No, my girl!"

Pam giggled, "Mummy! As long as he is nice to me and plays with me, I won't tell anyone and so nobody should discover his girly secrets!" Pam added "Didn't he look pretty in my Alice band and ribbons, this afternoon?" Her Mum giggled and nodded, "Yes! but it's not right, to do that to a boy!" Pam replied, "At our age, it's not a problem! We're just playing children's games!" Her Mum scolded "Pam! No more doing his hair up like a girl's!" as Pam giggled, "Could we not see how he'd look as my sister?" causing her Mum to gasp and saying, "No! We cannot! Get that thought straight out of your head and keep your pretty clothes to yourself!" She said, "Just because you made him wear your pink pinny, there's no reason to think, I'll let you do anything more to him!" adding "That trick you played with his frilly shorts, was very naughty!" Pam laughed "Now Mum! It's just indoors I'm making him carry my dolly and sometimes wear my pretty apron!"

Pam apologised "Sorry Mum! but Tom was so nasty to me, for all these years and I do deserve a little pay back!" Her Mum said, "If he's naughty, you can threaten to make him wear your hair ribbon! but only if he's naughty!" Pam giggled, "Mum! Can't we include a handbag too, like earlier?" and heard her Mum laugh and shake her head, saying, "No handbags! He'd die if someone saw him carrying a handbag, around the house!" as Pam giggled, "Don't worry! I'll keep that, for when we take him shopping!" and heard more laughter from her Mum. Pam reminded her "That's right, Mummy! He never usually helps with the shopping! We'll have to teach him, how to help and make him come shopping, next Saturday!" Her Mum said, "We'll see! but I don't want you making him carry anything girly, about town!" as Pam giggled, "Mum! Would I?" Her Mum laughed "If it was up to you, you'd have him carrying a bag and basket!" Pam said, "There's nothing wrong with a boy carrying a shopping bag, or basket!" Her Mum said, "Let's change the subject! You're making me blush!"

Tom's out when Pam finds her pink doll's pram for Nancy to have fun

She asked, "Don't you want to go out to play, with Julie, or something?" adding "What homework have you for the weekend?" Pam replied, "I did some on Friday and I'll get on with some English tonight! I might do some Sums later!" Pam decides to do some homework. She closed the door and locked it, as she got out her maths books, but also retrieved the tape from its hiding place. She popped it into the tape recorder and stuck the headphones into her ears, before starting the tape playing. She lay back on her bed, smiling, as she heard her own voice teasing Tom and then his replies and girly comments. She soon burst into soft laughter and giggles at the conversation between her and Tom, about him wearing her clothes and hair ribbons and his dolly and thought "He'll die if Julie

or anyone hears this tape! I'll have to get more on him! He'll do anything for me then!" She lay there listening and giggling for about ten minutes, till the tape went blank and then sat up and returning the tape to her wardrobe. She thought to herself "If I got Julie or even her and Tina over and up to my room and then slip into his and turn on the tape recorder and get them to listen, he could be saying "Can I play dollies with you or even saying Can I play dress up with you Pammy!" as she giggled and realized he'd be outed to them and have to join Tina to wheel her doll's pram about dreading being spied by his mates.

She started on with her maths, occasionally peering out to check, if Tom or anyone was about the street. She saw Tina and some of her young girl friends, pushing a pram about and playing with her dollies and giggled, at the thought of Tom having to join them, with Baby Suzie and his doll's pram.

Tina would really give it to him for being such a bully and make him push his dolly around the streets!" She thought "She'd probably make him wear hair ribbons and hair slides too!" as she thought "I can't wait to see it but I must take it one step at a time! Slowly does it! At some time, Julie must discover his girly secret!"

Whilst he was out, Pam had an idea for her and Tom, playing dollies and ran up to the spare-room and opening a wardrobe giggled, at the sight in front of her. Her old toys from when she was younger, other dollies, games for playing house, and an old dolls pram. She pushed some things to the side and pulled down the doll's pram, she'd discarded as being for little girls, a year or two earlier and set it down in front of her. It was around 2.5 ft tall, by 2.5 ft long and a foot wide. She closed the wardrobe and taking her Wendy doll, she put it into the pram and wheeled her out, before lifting it up and carrying it downstairs.

Her Mum was in the living room and heard her on the stairs and didn't think anything of it, till the door opened and she turned to see Pam standing there giggling. She asked, "What have you been up to, young lady?" as Pam giggled, "I found a new home for our dollies!" as she turned and wheeled the pram into the room, as her Mum gasped and screeched with laughter. She giggled, "Pam! No! Don't! That would be cruel! He can't push his dolly around in a pram!" Pam said, "Mum! You know, you can't play dollies properly, without a doll's pram!" as her Mum laughed "Pam! He'll be mortified!" but Pam said, "Think of when he grows up and gets married and has children!" adding "By dressing and undressing his dollies, he'll be able to help his wife (Yuk I pity her), from having to do all the work of changing them, in and out of dresses and stuff!" Her Mum said, "Pam! What if he has a boy?" as Pam gurgled "Like father like son! Only joking!" as her Mum gasped, adding "It's not right!" as she continued "And by getting practice with my

Pam suggests Tom play with the play 'house' games she had as a little girl

little doll's pram, he should be fine helping his wife, wheel his children, around the garden, drive, street and then to the local shops!" as her Mum gasped, till she gurgled "and then around the shops in town!" adding "Just like you showed me when I was a little girl, wheeling my dolly proudly around the shops, with a pretty handbag and purse to act like a real Mummy!" as her Mum screeched "Very funny Pam!"

Her Mum said, "Now Pam! He's a boy! You can't treat him like a little girl!" but heard her giggle "That's sexist! Don't worry Mummy! I wouldn't expect Tom to wheel his dolly and mince around town like I did!" Pam gurgled "I'll let Nancy, take his place and add ribbons to go with his frock and handbag, while wheeling Suzie around the shops!" as she ran giggling up the stairs, followed by her laughing Mum, saying, "Naughty girl!" Her Mum said, "Don't you dare say, that to him! That would be too cruel Pam!" as she laughed "Oh Mum! Bye the way! You should teach him how to change nappies too! You can't expect to leave it all to his wife!" She added "Tom should have practice changing both boy and girl baby dollies too!" as her Mum gasped "Now Pam! I've only shown you a bit!" as she laughed "Mum, wouldn't it be great killing 2 birds with 1 stone and teaching us together!" She said, "It

will stop him from being the horrid boy, who wouldn't help with any housework and was a real bully and ruined my life, up to now!" She giggled, "Anyway! I'm letting him be a boy, in his blue pinny, so long as he plays right!" She then added "Mum! While looking for this pram, I noticed the 'play house' games and toys, I had when I was a young girl and thought it would help him, to learn how to do the housework better!" adding "If we start him practicing with toys, then he'll learn quicker! It was naughty not making Tom play 'house' with me!" as her Mum laughed "I can see he's going to have a lot of fun with you!" as she nodded, "Thanks Mummy! Life with him is going to be a lot of fun now, for me!"

Tom came home for his lunch around 12.30 and opening the side door, he dreaded seeing his sister and her dolls again. Pam was in the kitchen with her Mum, both wearing aprons and Pam greeted him with a cheery "Good afternoon Tom! Did you have fun with your mates?" as he nodded.

Next thing, Tom asked, "Where's, my dolly?" causing Pam and her Mum both, to burst out laughing. Pam asked, "Pop on your pinny Tom and we'll see, if we can find your dolly!" He took the blue tabard and pulled it over his head, dreading being seen by anyone. He looked to see if the doll was hidden in the kitchen but couldn't see any sign of it, or even Pam's Wendy doll.

Tom then spies the doll's pram for the dollies and cries out in fear

She giggled, "I think your dolly might be with Wendy in the sitting room!" Tom cried "But that's at the front and I'll be seen in my pinny!" as her Mum laughed and said, "Pam! Don't show him off, in his pinny!" as she giggled, "Look Tom! You'll be in and out in a few seconds! Just run in and bring the dollies out!" He huffed "I'm crawling along the floor, so nobody will see me!" as Pam huffed "Ok! You'll be just the right height, to see our dollies!" Tom opened the sitting room door and asked, "Whereabouts are they?" as he crouched down and crawled in and then cried "Oh no!" to giggles from the kitchen, as Pam ran in to see him staring, at the pink doll's pram, in the centre of the room.

Pam giggled, "Well Tom! Do you like the new pram for our dollies?" He huffed "I'm not pushing a doll's pram!" as she giggled, "You'd better check, that they're in the pram first!" as he sobbed "Close the blinds! Someone might be looking in and see me with the pram!" but she giggled, "Hurry up! Our dollies are lonely!" as she put her foot on his bum and pushed him forward, towards the pram. He cried "That's not fair, Pam!" as he edged forward, in the pinny, peering up at the window, dreading someone's head pop up and laugh at him. He edged further towards the pram, with Pam's giggles filling his ears, as he reached the head of the pram and pulled it over towards him and the door, to protests from Pam, saying, "You didn't check on your dollies, first!" He bobbed up and checked "They're ok!" as he then realized, only Wendy was there and cried "Only your Wendy doll is there!" as he pushed the pram back behind him to Pam. She giggled, "Your dolly, must be playing hide and seek!" He huffed "You could leave, her, but then I might call out and ask where your dolly is!" He sobbed "Not funny! Where is she?" as Pam giggled, "She's definitely in here! Try and find her!" as she took hold of the pram handle and wheeled it to the sofa where she sat down and looked out, as she pushed the doll back and forth, like she'd a real baby in it.

She giggled, "Come and find your dolly!" as he huffed. Next-thing their Mum peered in and laughed at Pam pushing the pram and said, "Dinner's ready, children!" as Pam giggled, "We'll be in, in a minute! Tom's just getting his dolly!" as he begged "Not so loud!" Her Mum said, "Don't be long!" Tom huffed "She's making me search all over the room, for my dolly!" to giggles from Pam, who watched him crawl under the window to the other armchair and smile, as he retrieved his Baby Suzie doll and said, "There! Can we go into dinner now?" Pam nodded but said, "Just pop your dolly in the pram and then you can wheel her, into the living room!" Tom crawled around by the wall and then over to the pram and popped his dolly into it, before pushing it out, followed by his giggling sister. Their Mum looked back and giggled, as she saw him stand up again and push the pram out of the room and into the hall and laughed "Pam! He must be so embarrassed!"

STORY 03

MARGY'S RUDE 10-YEAR OLD SON HARRY

Margy complains to Sally about son Harry being a, MSP and swearing

Harry is a disobedient MSP boy who never helps his Mum with housework and she mentions to her neighbour Sally who offers to bring him under control. His Mum asks how, but she won't say, but invites them around.

Margy was a divorced mother of Harry, a ten-year old boy, who was getting far too big, for his britches and as well as, never helping with any kind of housework, was getting very rude and nasty to her. He'd even sworn at her telling her to F off, when she asked him to tidy hid room, which took her back, wondering what she could do, to mend his ways.

His father and her had divorced, when he was only 4 and so there was no male role model and although his Dad was keeping up maintenance payments, he'd moved abroad.

She happened to mention about Harry's bad behaviour, to her next door neighbour Sally who said, "I'm sure I can help transform him, to being a nicer son, if you give me a day and I'll invite you two around, for a cuppa and a chat!" as Margy nodded, and said, "I don't know how you can help!" Sally smiled and said, "We'll see!" as they both continued pegging out the washing. Sally laughed "You might get him to help you peg out the washing!" as Margy laughed "See that flying pig?" as they both laughed.

Sally goes to the supermarket shopping for girly clothes and aprons

That afternoon around 3pm, Sally drove off to the large supermarket and taking a trolley, started adding items which although knowing she was spending money on Harry, she knew it would be worth it and Margy would probably offer, to pay some if not all of it back, if she wanted. She found a couple of girly aprons for a 10-year old girl, but also a frilly apron for a 4 or 5-year old, which would look really silly, on him. She then got a pink PVC apron with large daisies all over it which was for a 7 or 8-year old girl, but which would look very sweet over the larger aprons and make them look like dresses. She also got some pink rubber gloves for the washing up and wet work. Next, she trotted along to the underwear department, but was tapped on the shoulder by a lady she knew, who saw the pretty aprons and asked, "I don't normally see you in the young children's section!" Sally laughed "No! I've a niece coming over and wanted to surprise her!" as Rosie said, "I'm just getting my seven-year old Julie and five year old Becky, some pants and stuff!" as Sally laughed "I'll maybe bring my niece around to play with your girls!" as Rosie asked, "What age is she?" Sally laughed "Oh, about ten!" as she called "See you again!" as she continued her shop and got some panties but knew she could sew some lace and frills to the front and back, to make them look much girlier than normal.

She then giggled, as she saw bras and got a white training bra, which should fit him too.

87

She then saw some pretty dresses and realised they were on sale and added 2 dresses, one for a 10-year old and another for a large younger girl, which was even more girly, as she gurgled, at the thought of Harry wearing any or all of these items. She then added a lot of ribbons and bows and an Alice band to the trolley and wondered what else. She looked around the supermarket, wondering what else to get the little boy, trying to think of other girly things that would look sweet on him.

Sally buys a dolly and a dress to play dollies and tells the girl it's for a boy

She then thought about sleeping and went to get him some nighties. She got a long one and a shorter prettier baby-doll nighty, which would stop around his waist, to show off his panties, prettily. She was about to finish, when she then thought "What do young girls, like playing?" and skipped along to the dolls section and selected a large pretty dolly in a floral dress and added one extra dress, which would fit her. Hence, he could have fun changing his dolly, in and out of its dresses. With that, she was at the till and when the lady asked, why she was laughing. She explained "All the pretty clothes, are for a very naughty boy, to become better behaved!" The lady gasped "You wouldn't? What age?" as she laughed "I'll not say, too much, but you can guess by the size of his dresses!" as she gasped "Not a 10 or 11 year old?" as she nodded, and the lady laughed "Oh the poor boy, will be so embarrassed!" as Sally nodded, "Exactly!" as she paid for the shopping and returned home.

She got home and after unpacking and putting the stuff away, wondered how to plan her attack on the naughty Harry. She took some lace and frills and sewed them to a couple of the panties, one pink and the other yellow, giggling at the girly look of them. She then asked his Mum for one of his shirts and would pretend, she'd got him it, as a present. His Mum asked, "Why the shirt?" as Sally laughed "I'd prefer to keep it, as a surprise for you and especially him!" adding "When you bring him around later, for a cup of tea and his present!" adding "Can you stay down here and watch TV and not come up, no matter, what!" as his Mum laughs "I can't understand, why!"

His Mum supplied her with the white shirt and said, "When were you wanting him around?" as Sally laughed "He should be home from school soon, so in about half an hour, bring him around for tea, but could you wear a pretty apron around too!"

She took the shirt and slipping around home she took her sewing box and sewed the two sleeves together at the wrists. However, she also sewed some string to either side from the chest which would stop him trying to struggle out of it and Hence, be at her mercy to dress up.

She waited and soon heard the bell go and opened the door to his Mum in her own apron, as she called "Come in Margy! Come in Harry!" Harry huffed "I don't know why you flaming-well wanted me, around here!" as Sally said, "I have a present for you!" He huffed "It's not my birthday, or anything!" She led them into the living room and asked, "Tea or Coffee?" as Marge said, "Coffee please, Sally!" as Harry said, "I'll have Coke!" as his Mum said, "Please!" He huffed "I'll have Coke, please!" as Sally went to put the coffee on and soon had returned, wearing a pretty apron, wheeling the trolley, with two coffees and a glass of Coke. She engaged Harry and said, "So Harry! How do you like school?" as he answered gruffly "Not a lot!" as Sally laughed "Isn't he very studious?" as Margy shook her head and said, "No! He's football mad!" adding "Aren't you, Harry?" He said, "Yea! Can I go and join my mates?" as his Mum said, "Don't be rude, Harry! You've just got here, and you haven't seen your present yet!"

Sally led him upstairs and slips him into his new shirt, but he's trapped

They continued chatting and Sally said, "Your Mum has told me you've been a good boy and help her about the house!" as Marge gasped and laughed "See that flying pig!" and he huffed "You must be joking! That's women's work!" as she laughed "Oh! What a, MSP!" as she continued chatting about this and that. They finished their

coffee and he'd drank his Coke, as Sally wheeled the trolley out of the room and said, "I suppose you don't want to help me, with the washing up, Harry?" as he said, "No way! I don't even help Mum!" His Mum said, "It's ok Sally! I'll do them!" as she followed her, into the kitchen and heard Sally whisper "Stay downstairs here and watch TV, no matter what you hear!" as his Mum smiled and nodded and returned to the living room. Sally said, "Ok Harry! Come upstairs and I'll check if your present fits!" as he followed her upstairs and she said, "Just remove your jumper and I'll check the shirt for size, over your tea-shirt!" as he removed his jumper and saw her hold up a white shirt, as she said, "I'll hold it and you slide your arms, into the sleeves. She'd also sewn some strings to the front of the shirt, to be able to tie them together at the front to stop him removing it.

He slid his left and then right hand into the sleeves and he pushed them further down to try and get them out, but saw Sally take the string and quickly tie it together, in a knot, so he couldn't remove it. He then realised, he couldn't remove his arms from the sleeves and they were pinned behind his back and cried "Hay! What to heck, are you doing?" as she smiled and locking the door, she pushed him down onto the bed and said, "It seems you are not being very nice, to your Mummy and need to be taken in hand, young man!" He said, "You can bug off! No matter what you do! I'll do what I want!" as she smiled "Will you, indeed?" as she opened the wardrobe and retrieved a girly floral apron and showing him, heard him gasp "Keep that away from me, you witch! I'll tell my Dad!" She laughed and pulled it over his head and heard him call "Mum! Get her off, me!" as she laughed and tied it around his back in a bow.

She took a camera and flashed a photo of him, as he said, "Hey! What are you doing?" as his Mum heard and wondered "What on earth, is she doing, to my boy!", but just watched the TV and turned the volume up, to try and drown out his calls. Sally said, "I bet by the time I'm finished with you, you'll beg to wear this pretty apron and even wear it around home, to your house!" as he said, "No way! You're completely mad, if you think I'd wear this stupid thing, in doors or especially outside!" as she smiled and took him over, to see himself in the bedroom mirror. He gasped at the girly apron, hanging down his body, She took her camera and said, "Smile Lucy!" as he gasped "What do you mean, Lucy?" as she laughed "Oh! I thought it would be a sweet name for you, when you're naughty!"

Sally asked, "So Harry! You don't like your big pinny?" as he shook his head and she removed it and set it, onto the bed. She then took the little girl's apron, from a 4 or 5 year old and held it up, laughing "Isn't this little apron, pretty?" as he gasped and begged "Please don't, Mrs?" as she fed it down his front and tied it around him and saw him cringe, as he saw the girly apron, stop around his waist, making him look a real sissy, as she took another couple of photos.

She pops ribbons in his hair and then shows him the panties

She then took out some hair ribbons and showed him, as he sobbed "Please don't do my hair up, like a girl?" as she laughed and slid one ribbon into his hair and giggled "Oh Harry! How sweet!" as he sobbed "Not fair!" as she slid more ribbons and bows into his hair, as he looked in the mirror and sobbed "Please don't show anyone the photos!"

adding "Take them out!" as she laughed "I bet at some stage, you'll actually ask for a headscarf or hair ribbons, outside!" as she shook his head "No way!" as he saw the camera flash again.

She then said, "You'll do what I say, or I show some of Lucy's photos, to girls or even boys in the street!" as he begged "Please don't, Mrs! What do you want me, to do?" as she smiled. She opened a drawer and pulled out a pair of pink lacy panties, as he gasped and cried "Oh no! Not panties?" as she nodded, "Ask me to pop these pretty panties, on you!" as he sobbed and called "Mum! Stop her!" as his Mum heard him call, but again, ignored his pleads.

He huffed "Will you put those panties, on me?" as she said, "Aunt Sally?" as he grimaced and repeated "Will you pop those frilly panties on me, Aunty Sally?" as she smiled and bending down, she gave him a kiss on the cheek "Good girly!" as she reached down and as the apron was short. She was able to get at his trousers and soon had them down, to his ankles, but then he gasped, as she pulled down his underpants and giggled, at his willy on show. He cried "Not flaming, fair!" but heard her say, "You call that, 'your baby-pee-pee' and when your Mummy asks why, you call it that? You say 'Because it's the size of a little baby boys, 'baby pee-pee'!" He sobbed "Oh no! That will be terrible!" as she smiled and removing both his trousers and the undies, she then pulled the frilly panties, up his legs and over his willy, to hide his embarrassment.

She of course took some more photos of him, in the frilly panties, with him blushing away, dreading his Mum spy him. She said, "I suppose you'd like to have something to hide your pretty panties?" as he nodded, "Please Mrs!" as she smiled and said, "Please! Aunty Sally?" as he grimaced. However, he then saw her take a frock from the wardrobe, as he sobbed "Oh no! Not a frock!" as she put a finger to her mouth, to be quiet!" as she laughed "It's just in front of me! We'll keep a secret, from your Mummy!" He cringed and felt her remove the small apron, but then feed the dress down over his head and he soon saw himself, in the mirror, in the girly frock.

He begged "Please don't tell anyone, Aunty Sally?" as she smiled and bending down kissed him on the lips, causing him to gasp "I don't like, kisses!" as she laughed. She took another few photos of him, still with his hands behind his back and so the dress sleeves hung limply down, each side and didn't look right. She added the little girly apron and he grimaced, as it looked even more girly, on him, as he asked, "Can I have the big apron, Aunty Sally?" as she laughed "I told you, you'd enjoy wearing your pretty apron!" as he nodded. She then took a handbag and slid it around his neck and said, "Smile into the camera and tell me, you're enjoying your dress and handbag!" as he made the embarrassing statement and grimaced, but tried to smile, as she videoed him on her phone.

She unties his hands and has him try the frock on properly for photos

She asked, "Will I untie your hands, Lucy?" as he nodded, "Please will you, Aunty Sally! I'll be a good boy, from now on!" as she smiled "You'll do what Aunty Sally, Says, at all times!" He nodded, "I will Aunty Sally!" as she laughed "You'll do anything your Mum wants!" adding "You call her Mummy, all the time – No Mum!" as he huffed "But it sounds really girly!" as she said, "You'll complement her clothes and apron when you see her! Won't you?" as he nodded, "I will, honest!" as she laughed and me too, as he nodded.

He huffed "Give me my big apron!" She then said, "No playing up, when I untie you, or you never know, who, I'll show the photos to!" She took some scissors and cut the thread, tying his wrists together and soon he'd brought his hands around to rub his wrists and huff "That was a nasty trick, you played on me!" She laughed "You'll eventually thank me, for showing you your stupid ways and will be much nicer to your Mummy, from now on!" as he nodded, "Please don't show the photos, or tell on me, Aunty Sally?" as she smiled and said, "Let's get that pinny and your frock off!" He said, "Thanks Aunty!" as she saw him remove his pinny and then the frock, waiting for to be dressed as a boy again and taken, downstairs. She then undid the string tie from his shirt and undid it, but also his tea shirt too, as he was left, bare chested. She said, "You know to obey me, or your Mum will be shown!" He said, "I will Aunty!" as she then produced the long nighty, coming down, to about his thighs, as he gasped "Not, a nighty?" as she smiled and nodded, deciding not to use the training bra yet, as she said, "Just let me, to check your nighty for size, Lucy!" as she fed the nighty over his head and saw him slide his arms into the sleeves, as she flashed a few more photos of him. She then tied some ribbons around the sleeves, as he asked, "What are you doing, Aunty Sally?" as she smiled "You will be sleeping in your nighty and panties tonight!" as he gasped and cried "No! You aren't serious?" as she nodded, and said, "Don't worry! We'll not let your Mummy know and it will be our secret!"

He grimaced, as she added "In the morning, if the ribbons are still tied around your nighty, I'll let you remove it for school and change into your normal undies, ok?" as he gasped and nodded, "Not fair!" She then said, "Now

your arms are free, you can try your frock on, properly!" as he huffed "Oh no!" as he took the dress and pulled it over his head, sliding his arms into the sleeves, as she gasped at how quickly he'd got it on. She laughed "Gosh Lucy! You got your frock on quickly! Have you been playing dress up, in your Mummy's frocks?" as he gasped and said, "No way?" but she slid a handbag over his neck and asked sternly "Have you been playing dress up, in your Mummy's frocks, Lucy?" He blushed as he stammered "Yes! I've been playing dress up, in my Mummy's frocks, Aunty Sally!" as she turned the phone camera off and knew she had him, under her control. She said, "Good boy! Right remove your frock and handbag and pull your shirt and jumper on to hide your nighty!" as he gleefully removed his dress and pulled on his shirt and then jumper to hide the nighty.

His Mum gasps as she spied Harry in the girly apron

She said, "Get your trousers on too!" and saw him pull the trousers on, over the frilly panties and do them up. She then said, "Right! Remove your hair ribbons and pop them into your handbag!" and saw him obey and soon, he was looking like a boy again.

However, she then took the apron and pulled it over his head and then tied it tightly, around his body. He huffed "Do I need it, Aunty Sally?" as she said, "Let me see your trousers, a tick?" as he gasped "What do you mean?" as she smiled and reaching out to his fly, she unzipped it and pulled his nighty out, on show, saying, "See your small pinny, won't hide your nighty, from your Mummy, spying it!" adding "So Lucy! What does sweet Harry want to wear, to hide his pretty nightdress?" as he huffed "Not flaming fair! Can I wear the big apron please?" as she added "Don't worry! I'll tuck your nighty away in a while!" adding "I'll let you remove your aprons, later on, Ok?"

She said, "Let's get you down and show your Mummy your new look and don't forget to complement her on her clothes and apron and me too!" She added "However, at some stage, I will ask you 'How long have you been playing dollies and you'll answer 'Since I was 4 or 5 Aunty Sally'" as he begged "Please don't make me, play dollies, or say, in front of Mummy?" as she unlocked the door and followed him down the stairs.

His Mum heard them coming down and called "I was about to send a search party, out for you two!" as she looked around and then saw Harry enter, in a girl's floral apron and gasped and giggled. Sally said, "I went shopping earlier and after you saying, 'Harry didn't have any aprons, to help you with the washing up', so I saw this pretty apron and couldn't resist the thought of your Harry helping you, about the house in it!" as his Mum gasped "Gosh Sally! How on earth, did you persuade him, to wear that pinny?" She laughed "I don't know, what you mean! His eyes shot open with delight, when he saw how pretty it was!" adding "Didn't they?" as he swallowed and nodded, "Yes, Aunty Sally!" as his Mum laughed. She asked, "Will you keep your pretty apron on, to help your Mummy with the washing up, or want to be a silly Ninny and want to remove your pinny?" as she giggled, "Hear that, a rhyme?"

His Mum nodded, "Ok! Remove it, Harry!" and expected him to remove the pretty apron in a flash but gasped as he grimaced and stammered "It's ok, Mum! I'll keep it on, to show I'm a good boy and help with the washing up!" as his Mum screeched "Have aliens replaced my macho MSP Harry, with a robot?" He said, "Just Mum! I realized, how silly I was being!" as Sally laughed "At least that pretty apron, will mean, he can protect his clothes, while helping his lovely Mummy, with her washing up or even housework!" as he swallowed and looked at her, as she smiled and heard him say, "Ok!" as his Mum laughed "Gosh Harry! What on earth has come over you?" as he blushed some more.

Sally complements his Mum and gets him to copy for a curtsy and kiss

He then heard Sally say, "Margy! That's a pretty skirt and blouse!" as she looked at Harry and heard him say, "Yes Mummy! That's a pretty skirt and blouse!" adding "And I like your apron too!" His Mum giggled, "Gosh!

Where's the on/off switch?" as he said, "That's a pretty dress and apron too, Aunty Sally!" Sally laughed and said, "Oh you little sweetie!" as she bobbed a curtsy and said, "Come here, sweetie! That deserves a kiss!" as she bent down and gave him a kiss on the lips, as his laughing Mum gasped. However, she heard her say, "He deserves a curtsy and a kiss too, from his sweet Mummy for his complement!" as his laughing Mum bobbed a little curtsy "Thanks Harry!" and bending down, she kissed him on the cheek, but Sally said, "Only the lips, count!" as his laughing Mum kissed his lips. However, then Sally laughed and said, "Harry that's a pretty apron, you're wearing, to help your lovely Mummy, with the washing up!" as his Mum looked at them and gasped "Oh! You don't mean?" as she said, "I'm waiting!" His Mum couldn't believe it as he gripped his apron and bobbed a sweet curtsy to her, as they both screeched with laughter, as she bent down and said, "Now for my kissy!" as she kissed his lips, with him blushing bright red.

Sally said, "Your turn Margy!" but she said, "I'll leave my complement for later, around at our place!" as Sally giggled, "Chicken!" and then said, "Well! He might be out of his aprons by then!" as he said, "You bet, I'll be!" She laughed "If he can't find his aprons to play curtsies, I'm sure one of us, could find him a few other things, to play curtsies in, Margy!" as she gripped her own dress, bobbing a sweet curtsy to him. Margy screeched "Oh Sally! Stop teasing Harry about wearing a frock!" as he huffed "Very funny!" as Sally said, "I bet he'll rush, to get into his apron, if the alternative is a pretty skirt or frock!" adding "It used to be so much fun as a little girl, playing dress up in Mummy's clothes, playing curtsies!" as Margy screeched again and he begged "Please don't, Mum?" as she cuddled him and gave him a sweet kiss. She laughed "It might encourage you, to do your homework, if the alternative if to play curtsies!" as he blushed, and Sally laughed "I can see him being very studious!" as she gurgled "or a model!"

She laughed "Ok! Seeing you, 've finished playing curtsies with your pretty apron, let's get you started with the washing up and I'm sure, your sweet Mummy, won't mind helping you dry them!" as his Mum laughed, wondering would he. Sally said, "Come on!" as they entered the kitchen and they saw him approach the sink, but cry "Close the curtains, Aunt Sally! Them in the back houses, can see me!" as they laughed and heard her say, "Look! What's going to happen, when you're in the back garden, helping your Mummy with the laundry?" as he gasped "Not outside! I can't go outside in this, Mum!" as she looked at his pretty apron. Sally laughed "I've a solution that might solve his dilemma!" as his Mum wondered what it was, as she reached into her handbag and pulled out a floral headscarf and heard him cry "No don't?" as his Mum gurgled "Oh Sally! He can't!" as she laughed "Look! Come here a tick and let us check! You shouldn't be recognized by anyone in this!" as he blushed and stepping forward, felt her tie it around his head and under his chin, as his Mum gurgled "Oh Sally! Oh Harry!"

They enter the kitchen and see's the window and is offered a headscarf

She laughed "See, they'll just think it's my niece, over helping me!" as he blushed red and his Mum said, "She is right Harry! No one will realize!" as Sally laughed "It could have been worse!" as his Mum asked, "How!" as she laughed "Hair ribbons!" to screeches. He said, "Very funny!" as he turned on the hot water, squeezing the liquid into it, till it was full of bubbles. She took some pink rubber gloves and holding them out to him. His Mum gasped, as he meekly pulled them on, but she then pulled out the little girl's PVC apron with daisies and said, "Right Lucy! Mustn't get your pretty apron wet!" as his Mum screeched, with laughter. He turned and sobbed into her apron "Oh no! Don't call me Lucy!" as she laughed "Now! Don't be a silly ninny in a pinny!" adding "Now! Let me slip you into this, pretty pinny!" as his Mum laughed and said, "It's just in here, Harry! Only us two, can see you!" He grimaced and let Sally tie it, around him, with his Mum gasping, as she saw it was smaller, than the big apron and looked really girly on him, as she laughed "Oh Sally! That little PVC apron, over his pinny, make his pinny, look like a dress!" He cried "No! Get it off, please, Aunty Sally?" She laughed "Look Harry! The neighbours will just think you're a little girl!" as she handed his Mum, her own PVC pinny and pink rubber gloves and said, "Look! Your Mummy, doesn't mind wearing pretty aprons, pinnies or gloves!" as his Mum laughed.

He grimaced, as he approached the sink and she said, "You start washing Harry and your Mummy will dry! Eh Margy?" She nodded, laughed "I still can't believe, the change, in my big boy! However, did you persuade him to change?" Sally laughed "Oh! It's just saying, the right words!" adding "Isn't that right Harry? You just needed a good talking to!" as he nodded, "Yes, Aunty Sally!" as Marge laughed and said "It never worked, for me! How come?" He continued washing the dishes, which his Mum started drying, smiling, as she watched her son, diligently at the sink, in the two girly aprons. She laughed, as he passed her a clean cup and she said, "I could get used to this!" as he blushed and said, "Not fair, Mum!" as she laughed "What's up?" but he just said, "Nothing!" He continued the washing up and they soon had finished and his Mum dried the last saucer and put the drying clothe back, on the rail, as he emptied the water and removed his rubber gloves. His Mum removed the PVC pinny saying, "Thanks Sally!" as Sally hung the pinny, back up again. His Mum said, "Thanks for the coffee and his drink and of course his pressies!" as his Mum said, "Ok, Harry! Better get your aprons off, to join me, around home!" as Sally said, "Right Harry! Remove those and your Mum, can take them!" as he looked at the smiling Sally, who said, "As part of our deal, Margy, I've asked Harry to wear his new pretty apron around home!" His Mum laughed and heard her say, "You or I don't mind wearing our pretty aprons, to pop next door and it shouldn't do him any harm, either!" as his Mum laughed "Go on Sally! Let him out of it?" as she laughed "Ok! But I think it does look sweet!" as his Mum agreed and said, "Right Harry! Remove those aprons!" However, he surprised her, by saying, "It's ok, Mum! I'll wear my new apron around home!" adding "I'll just remove this silly PVC one! I don't need it, now!"

His Mum can't believe that he wants to keep his aprons on to go home

Harry was dismayed when Sally said, "Oops, Sorry Harry! I've accidentally tied it, to your big girly apron!" as he begged "I can't wear both, around home?" as his Mum laughed and knew Sally had some hold on him, as Sally said, "I'm only joking Harry! If you want to remove both aprons now, just pull them over your head and let your Mummy take them!" He blushed and stammered "It's ok! I'll keep them both on, as long as I can disguise myself with this flaming scarf!" as they gasped, and Sally laughed "So Harry! Why did you want to wear, my pretty headscarf?" as he huffed "To stop being recognized!" as she added "So! What are you disguising yourself as?" as his Mum gasped and giggled, as he stammered "A flaming girl!" Margy gurgled "I think you've got yourself a new daughter, to have fun, helping you, with housework, Margy!" as she laughed "Oh Harry! Whatever next?" Sally asked, "Sure you want to go around like that?" as he nodded, and said, "Just to prove, I'm no longer the MSP, I used to be!" as his Mum gasped and giggled and flicked her wrist to him and saw him blush and nod. Sally said, "Don't worry, Harry! If you want to keep your pinnies on, around home, I'll come around later, to let you out of them!" adding "But you've to promise, to keep them on, till then!" as he looked at her and said, "Ok! But, make sure, none of my mates, or anyone is about, to see me!" as his Mum gasped and picking up her handbag and said, "Gosh! You are surprising me, Harry?"

His Mum would have been happy with just this change, in his behaviour, but things were going to get much worse, for little Harry, as he had to keep his aprons on, to go home.

Sally said, "Lead him up and into the porch and I'll call, when it's safe, to take him around home!" as his smiling Mum, led him up and opening the inner door, she tried to get him out, but he held back and said, "Wait for Aunty Sally, to say, it's safe!"

His Mum laughed "Oh! Nobody will see!" Sally looked and saw a boy go up the street and around the corner, but then a lady and her young daughter, coming up towards them. She waited till they were about 40 feet away and exiting the sitting room, she saw Harry, hiding indoors and called "It's safe to go around, now!" as she pushed him out, as he gasped, at being in the porch, in the two girly aprons and headscarf and sighed "Hold on Mum and check the street!" Sally said, "Be a good girly and help your Mummy with some housework!" as she closed the inner door on him and his smiling Mum, pulled him out from the porch, to the front of the house. Sally skipped

up the stairs and opened the window, as she saw the reluctant boy, edging down her drive, to the gate and gasp as he saw the mother and young girl, walking up towards him. He said, "I'm waiting here or running on!" adding "I don't want them, to see me!" as his Mum laughed, but heard Sally say, "Hurry up Lucy and take your Mummy's hand! Be a good boy or else!" He saw his smiling Mum hold out her hand and take it, as Sally laughed "He could hold his Mummy's handbag, to help his disguise!" as she laughed "Now Sally! Don't embarrass him!" as they edged towards their gate, but, also the mother, who had noticed the big girl, in the floral aprons.

Five-year old Abi and her Mum spy the boy in girly aprons

They got a bit closer and Abigale's Mum Caroline then realized, it was a boy and laughed and said, "Look Abigale, at this boy in his girly aprons and pretty headscarf!" as the young girl looked more closely and called "That boy, calls us names and threatens me and my friends!" as she started laughing, at the big boy, in his pinnies and girly headscarf. They came up and Sally called out "Thanks Harry! For helping me with the housework and am pleased, you love your new aprons!" as she called "Margy! Let Harry remove his pretty aprons?" as the young girl and her Mum laughed and called "Oh! He suits his pretty aprons!" as his Mum said, "Well Harry! Want to remove your pretty aprons?" as he stammered "It's ok, Mummy! I'll keep them on!" as the Mum giggled, and flicked her wrist and said, "Gosh! He must like his pretty aprons!" Sally laughed "I wonder why he wanted to wear my headscarf, for helping with the dishes and then going around home?" as his Mum gasped and knew what was coming. She called "Ask him! Why he wanted some hair ribbons or my pretty headscarf?" as he sobbed "Oh no!" as they all laughed, and Caroline queried "So Harry! Why the headscarf?" He cried "Mum! Let me go on?" as Sally called "Tell them, Lucy!" as they heard and Abi giggled, "Oh yes! He'll be Lucy from now on!"

He begged "Please don't call me that, in the street?" as she giggled, and Sally said, "Tell them, Harry!" as he stammered "I didn't want to be recognized as a boy, in these and wanted to look like a girl!" as they screeched, with laughter. Sally laughed "I'm sure, if your little girl doesn't tell on Lucy, she'll come around to play with her!" as he cried "Oh no!" She asked, "What does she like playing?" as Abi called dollies!" as he cried "No! Don't make me!" Caroline called "I've seen him playing footy in the street, but never suspected I'd see him enjoying such girly aprons, nor the headscarf!" adding "They're almost as pretty as yours, Abigale!" Abi laughed "I love wearing my pretty aprons, to help Mummy around the house! Don't I Mummy?" as she nodded and laughed "Yes! My cherub! But I don't think this boy would like to run about the streets, like you, in your pinny, wheeling your dolly about!"

Sally laughed "On the contrary Harry! What age did you start playing dollies?" as his Mum gasped but thought he'd just laugh and rebuke her question, but couldn't believe it, when she heard him stammer his reply. Harry knew what she wanted him to say, and stammered "Oh no! Not fair!" as he said, "Since I was 4 or 5, Aunty Sally!" to a gasp from his Mum, who knew it was a fib and heard screeches, from the giggling girl and her Mum. Abi's Mum said, "If he'd like to come around and play dollies, with my Abi, I'm sure she'd oblige!" adding "We live at number 73, around the corner" as he cried "Please don't make me?" as Sally called "If he doesn't want his secret let out, to his mates, I'm sure he'll agree to come around to play dollies!" adding "He insists on always wearing an apron, when playing dollies!" as he laughed it off, saying, "Ha!" thinking she was joking. Harry said, "Come on, Mummy, please? This is terrible! My mates, might spy me!" Abi's Mum said, "We'd better head on home, too!" but then said, "Pity we couldn't have an escort, up the street, in his pretty aprons!"

His Mum laughed "I think he's had enough fun, for the day!" Abi laughed "Oh Lucy! Join us, around to our place!" as his Mum laughed "Oh Abi" as she guided him past, but on passing her Mum, he felt his headscarf being pulled off, as he cried "Oh no!" and heard a screech from Abi, at the obvious boy, in the two girly aprons and without a disguise, as a real sissy.

Harry tries to go home but feels his headscarf removed and held on show

He tried to run on, but Caroline held his apron strings. His Mum laughed "Oh Caroline! Let him go! His mates or someone else, might spy him, in his pinnies!" as she laughed "You don't mind mincing around home in your pretty apron and neither should your boy!" as Abi gurgled, at the big boy, sobbing. She laughed "The big cry baby should be put back in nappies and baby pants!" as they gasped, and she then added "Anyone, got a dummy!" as her Mum laughed "Now Abi! Stop teasing him, like that!" Sally saw him being held on show and slipped downstairs, picking up a carrier bag and her own handbag, she opened her door and exited down to the gate.

Sally called "Harry! Come here a minute!" and Caroline let him go and saw him walk towards Sally, who turned him to face them. She scolded "Caroline! You naughty thing! Removing his pretty headscarf! Someone might recognize him!" as she held him, still facing them and added "Don't worry, Harry! I'll help you!" and opening her handbag, took an Alice band and slid it onto his head. His Mum gasped and Abi and her Mum screeched with Abi calling "Oh fab!" as Sally added a few hair ribbons to his hair, as he sobbed "Not fair!" as Abi gurgled "Lucy will be fun to play dollies with!" but added "Mummy! We'll have to find her a pretty frock, to join me and my girlfriends playing dollies and dress up!" as he cried "Please don't!" as they laughed.

Sally then reached into the carrier bag on her arm and retrieved a large dolly and a frock for it and called "Harry was dressing his dolly with his Mum and me, earlier!" as he cried "I wasn't!" She added "He forgot them but has promised to play dollies with his Mummy after dinner, tonight!" His laughing Mum gasped, as she saw the dolly and small frock and Abi, and her Mum screeched, and the little girl called "So it's true! You do play dollies!" as tears appeared again in his eyes. She handed him the large dolly but also the other frock for it and let him head back. His Mum said, "I'd better get him home, before he's spied by someone!" as he sobbed "That's not fair, Aunty Sally!" as Caroline apologized "Harry! Sorry for taking your headscarf! Come here and I'll return it and you can show Abi your pretty dolly!" as he walked up to her and felt her turn him to face Abi and put her finger to her mouth, to not say. His Mum wondered what she was doing, when she hid his headscarf away, in her handbag and pulled out, her own plastic floral, rainhat. She fed it around his ribbons and tied it behind his neck, so he wouldn't realize, his ribbons were on show, along with the Alice band. Sally laughed "I think that deserves, a curtsy!" and saw him grip his pretty apron and bob a curtsy to Caroline and Abi, as they giggled, as Sally added "He was playing curtsies with his Mummy and me earlier, with us all bobbing curtsies with our pretty aprons and dresses!" as Abi gripped her skirt and bobbed one back, to the blushing boy, as did her Mum.

He's to bob curtsies to Abi and her Mum, admitting to playing dress up

However, Sally said, "Naughty Harry admitted something to his Mummy, earlier!" as they asked, "What?" as she laughed "He used to play dress up in his Mummy's clothes, as a little boy, without her knowing!" as his Mum scolded her "Sally! You shouldn't tell!" as they gasped, thinking it was the truth, as he cried "Not fair!" Abi screeched "Oh fab! I love dressing up, in Mummy's clothes, too!" she asked, "Didn't you tell your Mummy that earlier, Lucy?" as he nodded, "Yes! Aunty Sally!" as Caroline laughed "Seems Harry will have lots of games to play with you, around at our place Abi!" as she gurgled "Oh great!" Sally said, "He especially loved mincing along with his Mummy's handbags, as he gasped and cried "Not fair!" as a laughing Caroline, took her handbag and slid it up his arm, to his elbow, saying, "Now Lucy! Look after my pretty handbag!" as they all laughed, but especially Abi who said, "Yes Lucy! You'll be fun to play shopping with!"

Sally laughed "Right Lucy! Now you're disguised as a little girl again, with ribbons, headscarf and handbag, you can show little Abi your pretty dolly, Cissilia, and your frock!" as he held out the dolly, towards the smiling girl, who said, "Oh! What a fab dolly, to play with!" as her Mum laughed "You talking to Harry, or his dolly?" as they giggled, and he cried "Not fair!" She asked, "So Harry! What do you play with your dolly?" as he shrugged

his shoulders and Sally called "He loves changing his dolly into new frocks!" adding "Don't you, Harry?" as he nodded, "Yes Aunty Sally!" as she laughed "He's a bit annoyed, he hasn't a doll's pram, to wheel his pretty dolly about in, like you Abi!" as she laughed "I'll lend him my dolly pram, as long as he plays dollies with me!" as he cried "Please don't make me?" Her Mum laughed "Oh Harry! We'll make sure your friends don't recognize you!" as she laughed "We'll make sure your disguised, just as you are now!" adding "With a headscarf over your hair ribbons!" as he blushed, as Sally laughed "And you'll let him wear a pretty apron, too!" adding "To protect his frock!" as Abi screeched "Oh yes! You'll have to wear a frock and carry a handbag too, like me and Mummy!" as he cried "I can't! Please don't make me!" as they laughed.

His Mum wanted to say, something to him, about the trick, but thought "It does still disguise him, more than his ribbons and Alice band and he still looks more like a girl than without!" Abi giggled, "Yes Mummy! If he's my big dolly, I can dress and undress her!" adding "And take her walkies!" as he cried "No way!" as they laughed. She added "Mummy, can we get some big skirts and dresses for me and my friends to dress Lucy in and then we can take her walkies!" Her Mum laughed I'm sure Jenny next door, who's about twelve will have some of her old skirts and frocks, that would fit him, and she'd lend you a hand and help you control her!" as he cried "Oh no! Don't tell a big girl about Lucy?" Sally laughed "I'm afraid he wouldn't fit in your doll's pram, like your other dollies!" as he huffed "Funny! Ha Ha!" She then added "Now Abi! If you're taking your dolly walkies, you might need baby reigns, to stop her running off!" as she thought to herself "and maybe his ankles tied up too!" as she laughed at the thought.

His Mum takes Harry home and he leaves the doll and ribbons upstairs

His Mum said "I'll take him home, now!" as Abi cried "Oh Can't we take Lucy with us and return her later!" His Mum shook her head and said "I'm sure she's tempted but we'll leave it for now!" as she led Harry in the gate and then unlocked the front door and then the inner door, where he ran upstairs to his room, locking the door and burst into tears, at what had happened that afternoon. He wanted to rip the panties and nighty off, but dreading the photos, being shown to his mates and girls he knew. He then reached up, to pull the headscarf off and gasped as he saw the plastic rainhat and then saw his girly Alice band and hair ribbons and pulled them off too. His Mum sat down giggling and thought "I can't believe what has happened to my big macho boy and how come, he's appeared to be so girly and that Sally definitely, has done something to him and he's scared stiff, of her!" His Mum called him down and heard his door open and heard his feet on the stairs and then the hallway, expecting to see him without his aprons, but saw him, still in both pretty aprons and asked, "What happened to your dolly and hair ribbons dear?" as he huffed "You know I don't play dollies and Sally made me sound, a complete sissy, to that little girl and her Mum and am dreading them telling my mates or girls they know!" She laughed "Sorry Harry! I just wanted you to change your attitude and mentioned to Sally, but never thought, she'd force you, to sound and look so girly!"

Harry must bob a curtsy to his Mum and then get another kiss

She laughed "Can you tell me, how she got you to wear the apron and stuff?" as he huffed "I'm not allowed to say, yet!" as she laughed "Pop up and bring your dolly and her frock down but to please me, pop your ribbons back in!" as he begged "Please don't make me play dollies, as a girl?" as she laughed "I could send you around to play dollies, at Abi's" Harry stumped up the hall and then the stairs and entering the bedroom, he slid his Alice band back on and then added his hair slides and returned downstairs carrying the dolly and its frock, as she laughed "Oh fab!" but as he entered the room and saw a flash of the camera, as he cried "Not you, too, Mummy!" as he sobbed and sat down on the sofa, crying, His Mum sat down beside him and cuddled him and then gave him a kiss on the lips, as he cried "I don't like kisses, Mummy!" as she laughed "I do think your new look is lovely, dear!" as he stammered "Ha!" However, he heard her giggle "Now what does that complement, deserve?" as he gasped and cried "Not a curtsy?" as she nodded, and saw him stand and grip his apron and tentatively bob a curtsy, but he didn't do it right., but then heard her say, "And a kissy!" as he blushed and kissed her on her lips, causing him to blush.

His Mum said, "You haven't quite got your curtsies right, darling!" and demonstrated "It's like this, dear!" as she stood back to show him and said, "You take one foot behind the other and bob down, gripping your skirts!" as he huffed "Ok Mummy!" He copied her, with his apron and heard her giggle and screech "Oh Harry!" adding "We'll maybe play a game of curtsies later, to help you improve your curtsies!" as he huffed "Don't Mum!" She then added "In some of my old clothes!" as he cried "Don't dress me up in skirts and dresses?" as she gurgled "It's my old bra's, which will be especially funny on you!" as he gasped and cried "Oh no! Please don't Mummy?"

Sally invites Abi and her Mum in to fib about girly Harry

She added "All little girls like to act as their Mummy's, when playing dress up, with their Mummy's and in their old clothes!" She laughed "Well! I'll let you remove the PVC one, for when any wet work, has to be done, ok?" as he nodded, and she tried to untie it, saying, "I may have to remove both, till I get the PVC one untied!" but heard him gasp "No Mummy! Try and untie it and leave my pretty clothe apron, be!" as she laughed and heard him add "She Says, I've to keep this flaming thing on, till she comes around, to untie it!" His Mum gurgled and fetching some scissors eventually got the knot undone and removed the PVC apron, saying, "I'll just hang it up, in the kitchen, till you're helping me, with some washing up or the laundry!" as he gasped "Not outside, Mummy?" He gasped and cried "Not the laundry too?" as she nodded, "Oh yes! You are going to make up, for the years, you never helped me with housework, young man! but now in your very pretty aprons!" as he grimaced, as she took the little pinny and entering the kitchen, smiled as she hung it up on show.

Meanwhile Sally had invited the laughing Abigale and her Mummy in, for another coffee, but now to expand on the white lies, of his sissy antics and have him completely at their mercy and playing dollies and dear knows what. She got Abigale some orange juice and her Mum some coffee and said, "Harry was such a sweetie and helped his Mum and me, do the dishes, after having some coffee earlier!" adding "Although I let him play dollies, for a while, first!" as they laughed. She said, "When they first moved in, I actually thought, she had a little girl!" as her Mum gasped "Why! He wasn't wearing a frock?" as Abigale giggled, but she shook her head and said, "I looked out one day, to see him wheeling a dolly in a pink dolls pram!" as Abigale called "I've one too!" as her Mum giggled, and said, "He never was?" She nodded, and added "I then saw him mincing with his arms in girly positions, as she said, like this, around the garden!" as she showed them, with his arm outstretched from the waist!" as they giggled, as she added "but then saw him pick up a pretty pink handbag, to mince too!" as they screeched with laughter, as she picked up her own handbag and minced up and down the room, pretending to be copying him, as Abi and her Mum gasped "Hi didn't?" She continued "However, then I saw him splay his arms out like this for what I'd call, extreme mincing!" as she slid her arms out to the side, as Abigale's Mum laughed "Abi! You'll have to get Harry to show you, how to mince and then do some extreme mincing with his handbag!" as she giggled, "Oh Mummy! That will look funny!" as Sally laughed "Can you try, to not tell anyone on him, yet?" as they nodded but weren't sure if they'd be able to keep it a secret!"

Sally said, "When he comes around to play dollies with you Abi, ask him did he not bring his big apron around to play?" as they laughed and listened, as she continued "He'll shake his head and say, 'No!' and you can then lend him one of your pretty aprons, Abi, which will look really funny on the big boy!" as they both laughed.

Sally suggests a way to embarrass Harry when playing with his mates

She added "He'll be dreading being spied playing dollies and stuff, so you can offer him a disguise!" as she added "Don't forget his hair ribbons or headscarf!" as they screeched with laughter. Sally said, "Tell you what you can do to make his day?" as they asked, "What?" as she said, "If you see him playing footy in the street, with his mates!" adding "You can call at his house to borrow his dolly and pop it into your dolls pram and wheel it down the street, past him and stop a tick and say, loudly "Don't worry Jamima! Big Lucy will be around to my place later, to play,

with you and wheel you back home again in your doll's pram!" as Abi gurgled "Oh yes Mummy! Can I?" Her Mum laughed "You are naughty, to that big boy Harry!" as she laughed "I'm sure your Abi and you, can think of lots of other girly things, to do with him, to give him fun!" Her Mum laughed "I take it, you were joking about his frock!" but she ran up the stairs and came down, with the pink floral frock, as they asked, "Can we take it around, to be ready for him, coming around to play dollies?" as she nodded, and handed it to her, as Abi laughed "Oh fab! I bet he'll love slipping into this pretty dress to play dollies with me!" as her Mum laughed "Not wheeling them in your doll's pram?" as she nodded, and heard Sally add "Not around the street?" but Abi nodded, "Oh yes! That big sissy is going to have lots of fun, playing dollies in his frocks!"

Abi's Mum said, "Here, take our phone number to warn us, when he's coming around to play!" as Sally wrote it down, giggling away as she put it into her handbag and said, "Here's mine too!" as Abi's Mum noted it down and popped it away. She said, "If he refuses to go out to the garden to push your pram, I'm sure you have some baby reigns, to tie around him and possibly tie his hands up, to!" adding "Then Abi should be able to take him walkies!" as Abi giggled, "What! To the shops?" as her Mum gasped "We couldn't, could we?" as Sally laughed "Make sure, she has some pretty ribbons, to disguise her, for anything outside, where he might be spied!" as they giggled.

They soon had left and were mincing home with Abi mincing like Sally had shown her and then did some extreme mincing with her Mum's handbag. She laughed "Won't it be fun having Harry around to play dollies with me!" as her Mum laughed "I think most of what Aunt Sally told us about Harry, was a complete fib!" Abi asked, "What do you mean, Mummy?" She laughed "You know that dolly she made him take and show us?" as Abi nodded, "Well I'm pretty sure, it was the first time, he'd seen that!" as Abi asked, "Why did he take it then and sound such a girly?" Her Mum laughed "I don't know! Sally must have something on him, and he'll do anything, she Says!" as they laughed and her Mum said, "We'll try and discover it, later!" as Abi said, "Great, Mummy!"

Meanwhile his Mum had done the dinner, with Harry helping, to lay the table for dinner. She had a constant smile on her face, as she saw him in his pretty floral apron and occasionally burst out into giggles, with him grimacing "Not funny, Mummy!" as she said, "Oh! I forgot my curtsies!" as she bobbed one to him, but then bent down and kissed him again, as he huffed "I don't like kisses!" as she giggled.

Abi and her Mum go home and she says, that Sally was fibbing wrt him

However, she then said, "Harry! That's a pretty apron!" as he said, "Ha!" as she said, "Now! What should you do, when given a complement?" as he gasped "Not a curtsy?" as his Mum said, "And a kiss!" as he grimaced and gripped his apron saying, "Thanks Mummy!" and bobbed a curtsy, but she said, "Foot back and to the side, as you stoop down!" and saw him repeat. She giggled and saw him purse his lips, as she kissed him again, saying, "It is much easier in skirts and dresses, though!" as he huffed "Stop teasing! You know Aunty Sally, was just joking about a frock!" She said, "Now admit it, Harry! You were turning into a very naughty boy, even swearing at me and wouldn't even help me, with the washing up, even without an apron!" She continued "I just happened to mention to Sally, when we were pegging out our washing, about you turning into a bit of a naughty boy, when she said, she'd have a go at helping you to mend your ways!" but added "She said 'You'd maybe even help me with the laundry' and of course I said, 'See that a flying pig!' Never thinking in a million years, she would she transform you" as he grimaced. He cried "You shouldn't have said, anything to her! She was terrible!" as she giggled, and asked him "Whatever did she do, to you?" as he stammered "I'm not allowed to say, yet!" as she cuddled him and gave him another kiss.

He stammered "Mum! You wouldn't make me go out to the garden?" as she laughed and said, "Don't be silly! It's just Sally and me, could see you!" as he pointed out and cried "But them 2 houses from the back street, can see me and realise I was in girly aprons!" as his Mum laughed and said, "Don't worry! We'll add your ribbons

and headscarf!" as he begged "Not ribbons outside?" as she laughed "Let me think on it and we'll see!" as she continued with their dinners.

However, she giggled, "I might just go shopping and wonder, what size would fit you!" as he gasped "Mum! You wouldn't dare! Please don't get me a dress?" as he sat down and sobbed into his hands, as she laughed "Oh Harry! I'm just joking!" as she sat down and put her arms around his shoulder and cuddled him, saying, "Today, has turned into the funniest day of my life!" as he huffed "Its' been the worst day of mine!" He hated having to wear the pretty apron and hair ribbons, in the house with his Mum, teasing him, about how sweet, he looked in it. He knew he could remove it and tuck the nighty into his trousers, but didn't want to annoy Sally, in case she showed the photos or something else! Hence, his Mum called him in for dinner, asking 'Do you want your PVC pinny to protect your pretty apron?' but he shook his head, as she dished it out and soon, they were tucking into it. They ate their food, with his Mum smiling at his pretty apron.

She said, "I can't believe Sally, getting you, a girl's apron and not a boy's one, instead!" as he blushed and said, "Yea! Why did she have to get me, such a girly one!" as his Mum laughed "I thought it was bad, until she produced the little girl's, PVC pinny, which looked really silly!" She laughed "Though it does look so sweet and gives me a laugh, too!" as he stammered "Ha Funny! Ha!" as they continued eating the meal.

Harry's Mum Says, about going shopping for a dress

He added "I think it was to embarrass me and teach me a lesson, for not helping you with the flaming washing up!" as she laughed again and said, "I wish I'd have thought of getting you pretty aprons, all those years ago!" She laughed, as she added "Just think back, to when you were three or four, I could have had you helping me, since then, wearing sweet little aprons, about the house!" as he huffed "Ha!" as she added "And maybe, had you playing dollies too!" as he cried "Not funny, Mum! You know, I'm not a sissy boy!" She flicked her wrist to him and said, "No! Not at all! In your pretty girly aprons, hair ribbons and bobbing curtsies to Sally and I!" adding "You don't look like a sissy, at all!" and saw him blush and stammer "Flaming! Sally is making me!" as she again asked 'How?', but to no reply.

They soon had finished and said, "I can't flaming go out to join my mates, as Sally Says, I've to keep this pinny on!" but then, saw his smiling Mum hold up the PVC pinny and say, "You've to help me with the washing up first, young girl, anyway!" adding "So let's get your pretty PVC pinny on!" as he grimaced and pulled it on, saying, "Not fair!" as his Mum tied it around his back, with him saying, "Not in a knot, Mummy!" as she laughed and tied it in a bow. She said, "I'll then see if Sally will let you remove your aprons for playing footy!" Adding "Though I'm sure you'd look sweet, playing footy in your pretty aprons!" as she gurgled, and he blushed "Funny, Mummy!" as she gave him a kiss. They started the washing up, with him again washing and his smiling Mum drying. He asked, "Can I close the curtains, Mum!" adding "Them out the back houses, might see me, in these flaming aprons and ribbons and they'll laugh!" She giggled, "Now Harry! They'll just think you're a sweet little girl, Lucy, helping her Mummy!" adding "It's not the end of the world!" as he grimaced and heard her continue "And they're bound to see you sometime, especially when you help me with the laundry!"

He cried "No Mum! Don't take me outside in these?" as she laughed "Considering, you walked right around the front earlier, in both those pretty aprons and hair ribbons, I don't think here, or even the garden, are going to be such a challenge!" as she laughed and saw him pull a face and continue washing the dishes. They'd just finished, when he heard the bell go and ran to the back room to hide, as his Mum laughed and looked up the hall. She called "I think it's only Sally!" adding "Not want to go and let her in?" as she went up and opened the door in her apron, on the smiling neighbour.

Sally calls around after dinner to let him out of his aprons

Sally entered and said, "I think I've been too cruel to Harry! I'll let him remove his pretty aprons for an hour or so and go out to play footy, with his mates!" Harry came out and she laughed "Oh I see, you've still got both pretty pinnies, on!" as his Mum laughed "I did let him remove his pretty PVC pinny, for a while, but put him back into the PVC pinny, to do the dishes!" Sally laughed "Well done, Harry! I hope you're starting to enjoy your aprons and realize how useful they are?" His Mum laughed "What's your answer to Aunty Sally?" as he said, "Yes! Aunty Sally! They are fun to wear and to help Mummy with the dishes!" as they both laughed and Sally and then his Mum, kissed him. However, Sally said, "It's not just the washing up, you'll be helping your sweet Mummy, with! It's the housework too!" as he blushed and huffed "Ok! Not fair!" as she added "And especially the laundry in the back garden!" Harry huffed "I hope none of them, in the back houses, see me!"

He begged "Please let me out of the ribbons?" to more laughter from both of them! He huffed "That wasn't funny what Abi's Mum did earlier, taking my headscarf and putting that stupid plastic hat on to show off my hair ribbons!" as they screeched and his Mum laughed "I was tempted to tell you, but thought it did make you look a bit more girly and so didn't!" Sally asked, "Where is it Lucy? Can I see how you look to do the dishes?" as he cringed and cried "Not fair!" His Mum asked "Where is it?" as he huffed "In my room on the dressing table!" and saw her run up the stairs and returned holding it and passed it to Sally who said "It's such a pretty rainhat! I hope you'll thank Caroline for lending you it, when you pop round to play dollies with Abi!" as he cried "Please don't make me?" as they both laughed and she said "Just till we have a giggle and then I'll let you out of your aprons, to go and play footy with your mates!" as he grimaced and felt her reach up and feed the rainhat around his head and then tie it, behind it, over his hair ribbons, as they both screeched. His Mum led him to the mirror and heard him cry "Oh no! Mum don't?" as he tried to pull it off, but Sally took it and retied it around him and said, "Just keep it on, till I let you out of your aprons, to play footy!" as he cringed and cried "Be quick and let me out of these, please?"

Sally removed it a tick and handed it to him and said, "Have a go Harry!" as he took the headscarf and fed it around his head and tied it under his chin, as they laughed and Sally said, "That's an old fashioned way, under your chin!" adding "Try tying it behind your head!" and saw him remove it and retie it on his head and with a bit of trouble, eventually tied the bow behind his head in a bow, to applause and laughter from his Mum and Sally. His Mum laughed and said, "He's been practicing his curtsies with me and has given me lots of kisses!" as she added "I did say, how much easier they are in skirts or frocks!" as Sally screeched "Oh Margy! You are naughty embarrassing your big boy here!" as he thought "Mum! Embarrassing me! Sally's been flaming ten times worse!"

She then laughed and said, "What a good boy! I bet you've enjoyed the new Harry!" as he grimaced and heard his Mum say, "I've had a constant smile, since we came around and couldn't help bursting into fits of giggles, at his new look!"

Sally pops Harry's nighty back into his trousers and removes his aprons

Sally said "Let me see you do the washing up in your rainhat!" as he blushed and sobbed "Not fair!" as she led him into the kitchen and sat down to watch, as his Mum laughed "You wash and I'll dry!" as Sally pulled out the pair of rubber gloves and said "I've got his pink rubber gloves to help you Margy!" as he cringed and pulled them on as they laughed.

He started washing the dishes with his Mum rinsing and drying them. Of course Sally took her camera and took a few photos of him and then called "Lucy!" as he turned and cried "Oh no!" as he saw her videoing him and his smiling Mum, as she said "Caroline and Abi will love to see you putting her rainhat, over your hair ribbons to good use!" as he cried "Not fair Aunty Sally!" as his Mum laughed "It might be useful for helping me with the laundry too!" as he cried "Not out the back too?" as they laughed.

Sally laughed "When you bring her rainhat round to Caroline, it might be nice to thank her for lending you it and ask her can you have it, to help your Mummy and us with housework, as its very pretty and can you do some laundry for her!" as he cried "Oh no! Not fair Aunty Sally! Please, don't make me!" as his Mum laughed "Oh Sally! I dread to think what Abi's Mum will make him wear!" as she laughed "Oh! I bet she'll just have him play dollies with Abi!" as he dreaded the thought.

He turned back to the washing up and continued the dishes with more photos being taken, till he'd finally finished the washing up.

Sally said "Oh Harry! Aprons are fun to wear and mince about the place, especially when carrying a handbag!" as she added "Margy! Remember Harry saying he used to play dress up in your dresses, without you knowing?" as she nodded and remembered him saying when Abi was there. He cried "Not fair!" as she asked, sternly "Didn't you, Harry?" as he nodded, and bobbing a curtsy, said, "Yes! Aunty Sally! Yes Mummy!" as his Mum laughed "I thought some of my frocks had moved, a few times, but now that explains, it!" as he huffed "Not fair!" Sally slid her handbag around his neck, with his Mum screeching, as he begged "Please don't, Aunty Sally!"

She then gave in and said, "For being a good little boy for your Mummy, I'll remove your pretty aprons and let you go and play footy?" as he said, "Thanks! Aunty Sally!" as she pursed her lips and saw him grip his pinny and bob a curtsy. He then realised he'd be playing in the frilly panties and his nighty and cringed, as he said, "Thanks Aunty Sally!"

Sally said, "Margy! Can I have a word with Harry a tick in the living room?" as she took him into the back room and slid her hand under his aprons and slid his nighty, back into his trousers, pressing her hand onto his willy and zipped his trousers up again. She smiled "How's your baby-pee-pee?" as he grimaced and said, "It's ok, Aunty Sally, thanks!" as she giggled. She laughed "Don't I get a curtsy with your pretty apron?" as he gripped it and bobbed a curtsy to her, as she sad "When you finish playing footy, I want you up to my place and not to your Mummy's, ok?" He said, "Ok, Aunty Sally!" as she led him back to his Mum and saw him remove the rainhat and return it to his Mum and then pull the PVC pinny off and then his pretty apron, to leave him looking as a boy again, ready for joining his mates later.

Sally laughed "It might be fun, to teach him to curtsy tonight, that's when you aren't teaching him how to play dollies!" as his Mum laughed, and he cringed "Please don't Mummy?" as they both laughed. She said, "When you come in at 7.30 or 8.00, you'll slip into your pretty apron and keep your apron on till bed time, playing dollies and curtsies and mincing with a handbag, for your Mummy, till when you kiss your Mummy sweet dreams and go up to bed for a nice sleep.

He cried "Not a handbag, too?" as she nodded, "It will make your Mummy laugh as she shows you various ways to carry one about!" adding "Whether she'd slip you into one of her frocks too, I'll leave up to her!" as he begged "Please don't, Mummy?" as they both laughed. However, she added "All little girls love slipping into her Mummy's shoes to play at being a Mummy!" as his Mum screeched "Oh Sally! You are getting worse!" as Sally laughed "I dare you to bring down a frock, just till we see him try one on!" as he cried "Please don't, Mummy?" but she'd gone and heard Sally say, "Now! If you're sweet Mummy is providing a frock, I'd better provide something too!" as she stepped out of her yellow shoes and said, "Just slip out of your shoes and try mine on, to give Margy a laugh!" as he sobbed "Not flaming fair!"

Harry's to wear Sally's shoes and handbag and get into his Mum's frock

He blushed as he removed his shoes and stepped into hers, one foot at a time and had to hold onto her, momentarily for balance, not being used to the slightly higher back end of the shoe, but it wasn't too high and he was soon

standing in them without too much trouble, as she gurgled "I wonder what your Mummy, will say!" as she slid her handbag over his neck again. They heard his laughing Mum, come down the stairs holding a yellow dress, not realizing what Sally had got him to do. She turned into the hall and screeched as she saw Harry, now in the yellow shoes, but also with her handbag around his neck. She laughed "Oh Harry!" as she held out the frock to him and said, "We're very coordinated "Yellow shoes! Yellow handbag and here a pretty yellow frock too!" as he begged "Please don't, Mummy?" but she said, "Just for a few seconds and we'll let you go!" as he cringed "Not fair!" She took his handbag and returned it to Sally and then slid his arms into the dress sleeves and then fed the main part over his head.

Sally screeched "Oh Margy! He looks adorable, as she fed the dress down his body over his trousers and gurgled "Oh Harry! We will have to play dress up, a lot more often!" as he begged "Please don't, Mummy? That will be terrible!" Sally popped her handbag back over his head and laughed "Now Margy! You did tell him earlier, he should be able to curtsy better in a frock!" as he cried "Not flaming fair!" as his Mum giggled, "Oh yes! Right Hariot! Let's see your curtsies!" She saw her blushing boy, grip the skirt of his dress and bob several curtsies to them, as they giggled. He sobbed "This is terrible making me into a sissy!" as his Mum kissed him and removing the handbag to Sally and pulled him out of her shoes, she then removed his dress, as Sally laughed "Margy, he could have removed your dress himself!" adding "After all the years playing dress up, in your skirts and frocks as a little boy!" as he blushed and said, "Ha!"

He called "Bye!" as he stepped out of the porch and ran out into the street, glad to be out of the girly aprons. Sally looked out and smiled as she saw Harry and then several of his mates gather and start kicking the ball about the street.

Sally laughed as she joked with his Mum about how macho he looked playing footy, with her knowing about his nighty and panties, but his Mum not. His Mum laughed "We've been terrible to my big boy, putting him into girly aprons and ribbons, but now a frock, shoes and even your handbag, Sally!" as she laughed "Now Marge! It's just in doors, apart from when he helps a bit, with OUR laundry!" as his Mum laughed "Has he to help you too?" as she laughed and nodded, "He'd better or else!" adding "Anyway! It should improve his skills! I'm sure he'll be all fingers and thumbs playing dollies and dress up!"

His Mum laughed "That was terrible making him wear a frock!" as Sally laughed "At his age, there's no harm!" as she kissed her bye. Sally finally exited and skipped around home to phone Abi's Mum and said, "You know that sweet boy, earlier, he's out playing footy with his mates!" as Abi's Mum heard and giggled, "Abi! Harry's playing with his mates!" as Abi gurgled "Right! I've my doll's pram in the porch ready, with my dolly!" Her Mum got the laughing Abi out and had her wheel her pink dolly pram, around to Harry's and rang the bell. His Mum came to the door and laughed "Oh you aren't going to tell on him, about his aprons!" adding "Are you?" but her Mum said, "Trust us! Abi's promised not to say!" but added "Can we borrow Lucy's dolly, for a short while?" His Mum went and fetched the dolly and asked, "His dolly's frock too?" as her Mum nodded, and saw Abi take them and pop them into her dolls pram, with his Mum saying, "I'll keep a look out, upstairs!" as Abi wheeled her dolls pram down, beside her Mum. Harry was playing away with his mates, kicking the ball about, when he suddenly spied the young girl, wheeling her dolls pram, beside her smiling Mummy, but he was dreading what they might say.

Harry sees Abi on her way down to Sandy's but on her return wets himself

He tried not to look, but then saw Abi take the dolly out and realised it was his dolly, that Sally had given him and heard her say, out loud "Don't worry Cissilia! Big Lucy will be around later to wheel you home in your dolls pram!", before popping her back into the pram and wheeling her on. He gasped as he realized Abi was talking about him, although his mates didn't know anything at all. His face reddened and the ball was passed to him,

his mates called "Gosh Harry! You haven't half, gone red!" as he made an excuse "I just remembered, an Aunt is coming around!" Abi called "He wouldn't get so red, if he played dollies, instead of stupid football!" as they gasped and said, "Ha, funny!" Her Mum laughed "You, naughty girl Abi!" as she pushed her on down the street. They watched the smiling young girl, wheel her dolly on down, wondering why she'd had a joke with them. Harry was glad to see them go, but dreaded them coming back up and what she might say, to him. Her Mum scolded her "That was so naughty Abi!" adding "Now, let's wait a while before outing him! We can maybe out him to some of your girlfriends or neighbours!" as she laughed "Ok Mummy! I can't wait!" as they called at a girlfriends house and asked, "Did she want to help push, her new dolly up the street?" as the girl Sandra asked her Mum "Can I go out for a short while with Abi? I'll get my pram too!" as her Mum nod and she ran and fetched it from the garage. Abi giggled, "This afternoon has been so funny!" as she asked, "Why?" as Abi laughed and said, "It's a secret, for now!" Sandy ran and fetched her doll's pram and wheeled it back to Abi and her Mum, as Abi asked, "Sandy! Do me a favour and when we reach these boys, start laughing and giggling, as if I've told you something funny!" as she said, "Ok! but I don't get the joke!"

Harry, then saw the two girls coming back with their doll's prams and heard the other tried to ignore them, but then heard the little girl start laughing and giggling at something and thought Abi had told her on him. He reddened again and couldn't help himself and wet his panties, saying, "Guys! I need to go home for something!" as he ran off, with Abi joining the little girl, laughing too. Her Mum laughed "Oh Abi! He must be so embarrassed, thinking you've told on him!" as Sandra asked, "What! Something about that big boy?" as they nodded. Her Mum said, "Now Abi! He must have nearly wet himself!" as she gasped and started laughing herself. Abi gasped "Mum you don't think he wet himself?" as they saw him run up the street towards his house, but then run past and into Sally's driveway. His Mum saw him run up and expected him to pop into his house but saw him run up to Sally's and ring the bell, thinking "He must have gone to complain, about Abi having his dolly or something!" The boys never noticed and just continued playing ball, but Abi and her Mum noticed him running up to Sally's. He rang the bell sobbing and said, "Not fair Aunty Sally, that little girl told her friend on me and they were laughing, as they wheeled my dolly past me!" She led him in, but heard him say, "I've flaming wet my panties!" as she screeched "You haven't? Have you?" as she added "Oh why didn't I get nappies too?" as he cried "You wouldn't?" as she led him into the kitchen.

They plan to diaper him, Caroline returns shows them Abi's diaper bag

She removed his trousers and then gasped as she heard the bell go. He begged "It's not Mummy, is it?" as he pulled the kitchen door to and dreaded who it might be. Sally opened the door and gasped and giggled, as she saw a laughing Abi and her Mummy and another little girl. Her Mum asked, "He didn't did he?" as she nodded, and heard her say, "Why the big baby!" as he sobbed "Not fair don't tell on me!" as Sally said, "I don't happen to have anything for a naughty baby, would you?" as Abi's Mum gasped "You wouldn't dare would you?" as she nodded. Abi's Mum asked, "Can you keep an eye on my Abi and her friend Sandra, while I fetch something for our big baby!" as she took her handbag and exited said, "Try not to embarrass him, too much, till I come back!" as she slipped around to her own house, to get Abi's old diaper bag.

Her husband wondered why she was laughing, but just heard her say, "Just around at some friends of Abi dear!" as she fetched her old diaper bag and on looking inside gurgled as she saw nappies, diapers, baby bonnets, large plastic baby pants and wondered would they fit him and nappy pins, but also a pink dummy and some baby bottles and gurgled "Oh fab!" as she also saw the baby reigns and gasped "Would she?" as she called "bye darling back in an hour or so!" Sally had taken the young girl's prams around her back and into the garage, as she got Harry to pull his trousers up again to not embarrass the girls. She sat them down in front of the TV as Abi was telling Sandra all about Sissy Harry who enjoyed wearing girly aprons even in the street, as she laughed and having played dollies since he was 4 or 5 and how he liked to mince with a handbag, but said, it was a secret to his friends.

Abi said, "Sandra could have fun playing dollies with him too!" as she giggled, at the thought.   Sally led him up to the bathroom and took his trousers down and then his panties as she saw his nighty wasn't too bad and pulled it up under his shirt and jumper, to stop it getting any wetter. Caroline said, "What a big baby! Wetting his panties and nighty!" as he sobbed "Don't tell them or let them see, please?" as she took a cloth and running some hot water into the sink, told him to wash his baby-pee-pee and botty clean, for when she came up again. He grimaced, as he was washing his loins and then heard the bell go and dreaded who it was. A smiling Caroline came in, holding Abi's old diaper bag and showed the laughing Sally the contents, who led her up the stairs and then into the bathroom, to see the semi-naked boy. She gasped as he was on show to the laughing woman, as Sally asked, "Is baby's pee-pee clean and his botty clean?" as he nodded, "They are, Aunty Sally!" as she led him out and into the bedroom. Caroline gasped "You aren't going to really diaper him?" as Sally laughed "Well actually, No!" Sally laughed, but then heard her add "See! I'm not the baby changing expert, among the two of us!"

Harry then sees the diaper bag and realizes she's going to diaper him

She said, to her "Caroline! Can you help protect our big baby, while I see to the girls!" as Caroline gasped and giggled, as she added, "You might want to strip him first!" as she gasped and giggled. He pleaded "Please don't Mrs?" as Sally got him down on his back and pulling up his shirt and jumper, pulled down his nighty, causing Caroline to gasp "Oh fab!" Sally pulled his jumper off and then undid his shirt and pulled it off to expose his nighty and then said, "Hands back baby!" as she tied his hands back, behind him. She then said, "Your turn Caroline, to diaper baby Harry!" as he cried "Oh no! Not fair! Please don't?" The laughing Caroline then showed him the baby bag causing him to cry "Oh no! Not nappies!" as they giggled, and Sally went down, to see the girls.

Caroline remembered the dummy and baby bottle and taking them into the bathroom, she washed the dummy and baby bottle, before running back and popping it. into his protesting mouth, but then giggled, as she added the baby bonnet, to his head, causing her to gurgle. She laughed "Will I call the girls up?" as he begged her not to. She turned him over and gave his botty some light smacks, before gelling his bottom and then applying talcum powder, over it and finally added the disposables to his bottom. She then blushed, as she turned him over and smiled at his little willy, as she took some gel in her hand and gelled it, saying, "Baby better not tell, what I've done today!" as he blushed and sucked on the dummy, nodding. She applied the talcum powder and then his disposables and gurgled "They just about cover your baby-pee-pee!" as he blushed. She then folded the diaper in a triangle and gurgled "Its' been a few years since I diapered, Abi!" as she pulled it around him, but found it was too small.

She turned him over and called Sally up and saw Sally followed, by the two little girls, as she heard Caroline say, "Sorry! Abi's diaper was a tad, too small!" as Sally laughed and said, "I'll get a towel!" as the girls peeked in and screeched, as they saw him, sucking on a dummy and wearing Abi's old baby bonnet, but with nappies on his bottom. As Abi gurgled "Is Harry, a big baby girl, now?" as her Mum shoed her and Sandra downstairs. Her Mum took the towel and folded it into a triangle, before folding it around him and pulling it up, she pinned it into place and gurgled "Oh Baby Harry! You do look funny!" as she called Sally up, as she ran up and screeched as she saw him, in the diaper and laughed "Oh Fab!" as she asked, "What about the plastics?" The girls entered and screeched, and he sobbed "Not fair! Letting the girls see me, in my diaper!" Caroline took some of Abi's old plastic baby pants and pulled them up his legs, as the girls giggled, and saw they were a bit tight and stopped, part way down, as she pulled him up.

They heard him complain "The plastic pants are too small, Aunty Sally!" as she said, "Try walking baby!" as she stuck his dummy back, in his mouth, to more laughter.

He huffed "It's hurting my legs, the plastics are really tight!" as the laughing Sally said, "I've a feeling me and Aunty Caroline, will be shopping tomorrow, for extra-large baby plastics!" as the girls giggled, and Abi said, "You

mean, baby won't be protected for school tomorrow!" as he cried "I can't wear nappies, to school! Please don't girls?"

Harry complains about the baby pants and is popped into a carrier bag

Sally said, "I've thought of a solution!" as she took a Laura Ashly carrier bag, as they wondered what she was doing. She then made two holes in the corners, saying, "This should protect baby!" to more laughter and giggles, as he cried "Please don't? That will be terrible!" She pulled his plastics off and slid the plastic bag up his legs, to screeches and over his diaper, to laughter from them all and sobs from him. He was led down and into the front room, as he stood there, in the nighty over his nappies. Sally then untied his hands and removed his wet nighty, to leave him in the bag, over his diaper, but she then took some scissors and cut a few large holes, in the plastic bag at each side, to expose the diaper through it, to more laughter. She then handed him the short baby doll nighty, to more laughter, as he pulled it over his head, to giggles, as she tied the ribbons around it, at the shoulders, to ensure he kept it on, as her and Sally took photos.

Then Caroline asked about his frock and he begged her not to make him wear it, as Sally fetched it, but also his training bra, to screeches, as she said, "Pop your bra and frock on and we'll let you go and play footy after!" Abi giggled, "In his frock?" as he cried "I'm not playing footy in my frock!" to more giggles, as more photos were taken. However, then Sally thought of a wonderful trick, to play on him, which would seal his fate, with his Mum, as she said, "Hold on girls!" as she added more hair ribbons and then a head scarf and said, "Now baby! Don't play up, or we'll tell!" as she said, "You're well disguised, as a big girl and I'll walk in front of you!" adding "We'll mince you around to show your Mummy!"

He sobbed "Please don't take me out in my frock?" as she said, "Girls make sure, you don't mention his nappies to his Mummy!" adding "And you'd better not tell her either, baby!" as he huffed "Not fair!" as she got his trousers. She said, "We'd better remove his plastics, so his Mummy doesn't hear them" and pulled them off his diaper. She then took his trousers with the slightly damp patch, where he'd wet his panties, but they weren't too bad, as she added "I know they're a bit wet, but you're well protected in your diapers, as she got him to pull them up his legs, but she said, "Let me!" as she pulled them up, but pulled them apart, to expose his nappies, as she did his belt up and let his frock drop down over it. She said, "See girls, when offered the choice of playing football in his frock or removing it to play out the back in his trousers, he'll ask to play sissy football with us, in his frock, as she picked up his handbag and slung it over his elbow and said, "Let's go around girls, to show his Mummy!" as he sobbed "Not fair girls!" The giggling girls followed with Caroline and Sally picking up their handbags, but Sally saying, "Let's pop out the side door, so the girls can get their dollies and prams. She let Harry pop out, in his frock with him begging "Please don't let, my mates see?" as she locked up the back door. She said, "Look Harry! Caroline and I'll be walking in front of Lucy!" and then "Girls! Don't say, anything to his mates, Ok?" as they nodded, and wheeled their dollies out, smiling, as they saw the boys still playing footy in the street. Sandra laughed "Don't you want, to play footy, in your pretty frock and handbag!" He begged "Please Sandy! Don't tell on me?" as he minced behind the smiling Caroline and Sally.

She shows the girls his trousers and he's taken around in the frock

They entered his gates and he gasped, as he was momentarily on show, to his mates, but they didn't notice as they led him up the driveway to the side and then around the back to the back garden. Sally rang the bell and his Mum soon was opening the inner door and then the outer door and said, "That was funny earlier!" adding "Is he still playing footy with his mates?" as she replied, "No! I've had him play dollies for a while with Abi and her Mum, but thought he'd prefer to be back playing football!" Sally laughed and said, "We're letting him play football, but think it will be more fun with us!" as his Mum gasped "Me play football?" as she nodded, and asked, "Can you

bring his ball and apron out and then your handbag and then lock up?" His Mum fetched his ball and handed it to Sally as she set it down and untied his two aprons from the door knocker. His Mum fetched her handbag and then picked up both aprons from the porch as she locked the backdoor, she then exited the front pulling it tight, expecting to be going around to Sally's house, as she peered down at the boys playing footy. She said, "I saw him run up to your house, probably to ask to play footy till later on!" as she went to walk down the driveway, but saw Sally walk up and said, "Folly me dear!" as his smiling Mum, followed her up her own drive and heard giggles from Abi and Sandra and on reaching the entrance to the back garden gasped, as she saw Harry in the pink frock and hair ribbons carrying a pink handbag and she screeched "Oh Harry! What have they done to you?" as she ran over and threw her arms around him and kissed his sobbing lips!" She asked, "And who is this?" as Sandra laughed "I'm Sandy one of Abi's friends and live down the street!" adding "Abi called down for me and we wheeled our prams up past the boys playing football!" Abi's Mum Caroline stopped her elaborating saying, "I thought it might be more fun if as well as us around the next street! He has someone down the street, to play dollies with!" for fear she mention about him, wetting himself. His Mum laughed "You girls are naughty!" Sally then said, "I've told Harry that he's had enough fun in his aprons and frock and he can remove his frock and ribbons, to play footy as a boy in his trousers!" as his Mum laughed "I'm sure, he'll appreciate that!" but then heard Sally add "But he'd please the girls, if he wants to play Sissy Football in his frock, mincing with his matching handbag and ribbons!"

Sally asked, "Well Harry! Do you want to play footy with us as a boy, or please these little girls here and play Sissy Football, in your frock and then play dollies with their dolls prams!" His Mum looked at him and expected him to remove his frock and ribbons and start kicking the ball as a boy. However, she gasped and giggled, as he stammered "It's ok Aunty Sally I'll play Sissy Football in my frock and mince about with my handbag and ribbons!" as the girls screeched. His Mum gasped "I can't believe it Harry! Are you enjoying your new frock?" as Sally looked at him and saw him nod, as Sally said, "I think that deserves a kiss and curtsy to all of us!" as he bobbed a small curtsy to his Mum, who bobbed one back and bent down and kissed him. Then to Sally who bobbed another curtsy back and kissed his pouting lips, then to Caroline who bobbed one back and said, "My hubby, better not hear, I've kissed you!"

His Mum puts his aprons back on over his frock

She kissed him and then he bobbed a curtsy to Abi. They heard Abi call "I don't like boys!" but then said, "As Harry is enjoying himself, as a sweet big girl called Lucy, I'll let him kiss me!" as she pursed her lips and saw Harry bend down and kiss her, as she blushed and said, "Yuk! Horrible! You owe me sissy!" as he grimaced and then he bobbed the last curtsy to Sandra, who bobbed one back to him and giggled, as she let him kiss her and said, "That's my first kiss by a boy!" as Abi said, "A girly boy!" as they all laughed. His Mum said, "I suppose you should protect your pretty frock with your pinnies!" as he huffed "Not fair!" as she said, "But we've told you, you can remove your frock and play as a boy!" as he said, "Ok! I'll wear my pretty aprons!" She went to the porch and retrieved the aprons that he'd tied up earlier to the knocker and taking the floral one, she pulled it over his dress followed by the PVC pinny, to cheers from the garden. Sally said, "I think that will be a perfect look, for his return from school and 10 minutes playing Sissy football with his Mummy and sometimes me, before she can let him remove his girly clothes, to then join his mates!" She added "Or if she has some housework for him, then he'll be dressed the part, to have fun doing some housework for his lovely Mummy!" She giggled, "Or me!" He sobbed "Not every day! Not fair!" as she nodded, and said, "Marge you'll be kind and let him remove his frock, for a few days to have fun with his mates?" as she laughed "If he's a good boy and does what he's told!" She laughed "I must admit you do look cute in that frock and ribbons!" as the girls giggled, and Sandra called "She does!"

She added "She'd better be wearing them and dressed like that when she comes around to play dollies with me!" as he cried "Not in the street?" but heard Abi say, "For me too or else it will be the shops in a really short dance

106

skirt!" as he gasped at her meaning his nappies would be showed off. Caroline added "He's promised to let you teach him how to play dollies later!" as she laughed "Have you darling?" as she said, "Abi! Could you do me a favour and lend Lucy your dolls pram to play with later with his Mummy!"

She giggled, "Well! He'd better bring it around to me in the morning or else!" as he cried "I can't! All the school kids will see me!" as they laughed and said, "Harry you wouldn't be recognized, in your frock!" as he huffed "I'm not going to school, in a flaming frock!" to more laughter. Sally said, "Now Lucy you can't wear your pink frock to school!" adding "Have you his school dress and pinafore, ready for the morning, Margy?" as the garden erupted with laughter and he sobbed "No way!" His Mum said, "They're just joking Harry! Come on let's play football!" as Sally reminded her "It's sissy football dear!" as they spread out and Harry kicked the ball to Sally, who tried to kick it to Abi, but it screed off, to Caroline as Harry stood there with his handbag dangling from his elbow, as Sally called "Other hand on your hip dear, to look a proper sissy!" as he obeyed to more laughter. Abi then said, "That's right he used to do mincing and then extreme mincing!" as he listened and wondered what she meant, as she said, "Aunty Sally told us that, when you were about 4 or 5, you used to mince about the garden with a handbag like you are now, well without a frock!"

They start playing Sissy Football mincing and extreme mincing

Adding "But then you used to splay your arms out to the sides like this!" as she showed them all, to giggles. Sally said, "Go on Lucy! Show us the way you used to mince and then do some extreme mincing with your handbag!" He blushed as he minced up the garden and around and then heard her say, "Now extreme mincing!" as she demonstrated and saw him splay his arms out, to the sides, with his elbows at his waist, as he minced around with the whole garden in fits of laughter and screeches, at his girly antics. Caroline said, "That's a good way for him to mince after school, with you Margy!" as she laughed "Oh girls! I can't believe you're doing this to my big macho boy!" However, Sally laughed as she added "It would be the perfect look for helping his Mummy with some shopping!" as he cried "No you wouldn't Mummy?" as she shook her head, but then said, "I'll think about it!" His Mum then said, to Sally "When I told you of my naughty rude young boy, I never expected him to have turned into this!"

Sally bobbed a curtsy and said, "It's funnier than I ever expected Margy!" adding "I think your Harry has realised, how much fun it can be to wear pretty aprons and frocks"

She then asked, "Isn't that right Harry?" as he bobbed a curtsy and said, "Yes, Aunty Sally!" She expanded "You've suddenly realised how much fun, being a girly is" and added "and are having lots of fun in your pretty frock, mincing about with your pretty handbag and hair ribbons?" as he bobbed another curtsy and said, "Yes Aunty Sally, it's lots of fun!" as his Mum laughed. She added "Though as he's just a beginner, I've left his bra unpadded!" as his Mum screeched and ran over and fed her hand down his dress and giggled, as she felt the bra and giggled, "A bra too!" He sobbed "Not fair!" as Sally said, "It's not actually, your first bra is it Harry?" as his Mum looked at him and wondered as she continued "When playing dress up in your Mummy's old frocks, you sometimes used to slip into her bra's too?" as she added "Even popping socks into them to pad them out, to make yourself into a big girl!" as they giggled, again. He sobbed "Not fair!" as he nodded, "Yes! Aunty Sally!" to screeches from the garden. Sally said, "Maybe you could have fun with him tonight in your old bra's Margy and a few of your frocks too, playing dress up, like other little girls like to?"

Margy laughed and nodded, "That might be fun!" as he begged "Please don't Mummy? Leave it to, playing dollies!" as they screeched. Caroline said, "Shopping in a pretty frock is lots of fun too!" as he sobbed "Please don't take me shopping as a girl or do girly things Mummy!" as they giggled, at the effeminate looking boy asking not to be taken shopping as a girl. His Mum laughed "I'll think about it, you've to be a nice obedient boy and do what your

told and no more being rude ok?" as he nodded, "Sorry Mummy for being a naughty boy and sorry for all the nasty things I said!" as Sally said, "Bob curtsies and repeat to your lovely Mummy!" as he gripped the apron and dress and bobbed some curtsies to her as he repeated the same apology. As she added "And what about apologising for slipping into her bras and frocks without asking her?" as they giggled, and he apologised to his Mum for the fake dress up. Caroline said, "I'd better get the girls back home!" as Sandy laughed "Oh can't I stay and play with Sissy!"

They mince their prams down to Sandy's house to tell her Mum about him

Abi said, "Mummy can't we stay?" as her Mum said, "Sorry dear! We'd better get Sandy down to her Mummy and then you back home!" She said, "Pooh!" as he begged "Please Sandra! Please don't tell your Mummy or anyone else on me?" as she giggled, "Oh Harry! I'm sure she won't tell too many ladies about b - sissy!" as she almost said, about baby, but remembered his Mum didn't know about him wetting his panties and nappies. Caroline and the girls kissed him bye with Abi reminding him to have her dolls pram around in the morning, with your own dolly, as she picked up her own small dolly to carry around. Her Mum said, "Now girls! Not a word to the big boys playing footy, about Harry ok?" as they nodded, and heard her say, "Why don't you mince your pram down the street Sandra and you can do extreme mincing Abi!", adding "Sandy tell your Mummy, but keep it a secret from your Daddy ok?" adding "He might think it too cruel to do all these things to a big boy!"

She nodded, "Ok!" as she minced her pram down towards the boys playing footy. Abi had both arms stretched out with her Mum carrying her dolly, as they passed the boys. She asked her Mum should I tell them he's been playing footy with us but saw her shake her head and they minced on. The boys continue their game, wondering what had happened to Harry, but hope he'll appear soon. It was about 8 when they reached Sandy's house and rang the bell and her Mum came to the door and said, "It's past your bedtime dear!"

Sandy gurgled "Mummy you'll wet yourself when you hear what's happened!" as Caroline said, "Sorry for keeping her out so long, but Sandra is right!" Her Mum said, "Leave your dolls pram around in the garage and then join us in the front room Sandra!" as she invited Abi and her Mum inside to hear the tale of Harry. Sandra popped her pram into the garage and taking her dolly out, ran in the side door and into the front room. She sat down beside her Mummy and held her arm and said, "Listen to this Mummy!"

Gloria asked could she get them something to drink or eat, but they shook their head and Caroline giggled, and said, "I think when you hear our story you might need new panties!" as the girls giggled, knowing about Harry wetting his. She laughed "It can't be that funny, can it?" as they nodded. Caroline said, "I was escorting my Abi here, up the street before tea, when who do we spy, but you know that big 10 year old Harry from about 10 houses up the street?" adding "He often plays footy in the street with his mates!" as she stood up and pointed to the guys playing footy outside and saw Gloria stand and look at the boys and ask "Which one is he?" as they laughed and Abi called "He was playing earlier, but then ran off, when we wheeled our dollies bye them!" Caroline giggled, "Anyway, there he was walking around from Sally's next door with his Mummy, but wearing a girls pretty apron, with a little girls daisy print PVC pinny on top, making his apron look like a dress!" as Abi giggled, "And wearing a pretty headscarf!" as Gloria gasped "He wasn't?" Caroline continued "He was blushing away, dreading us recognise him!" adding "Hoping his headscarf would disguise him as a girl!" as Gloria gasped "He wasn't?" as they nodded. Abi giggled, "He had a dolly too!" but her Mum said, "Let me tell the story and get the timing right!"

Caroline added it was due to Sally next door that he asked to keep them on

She continued "Anyway I realized it was a boy, but not exactly who and started laughing and told Abi, who recognized him as one of the boys who play footy but call her and her friends names and chase them!" Gloria asked, "Why was he dressed as a girl?" as they laughed and Caroline said, "I think it was due to his next-door

neighbour Sally!" She said, "Him and his Mum were around at hers and were walking back when we spied him!" as she added "She called down to thank him for doing her housework and asked his Mum, to let him out of his girly aprons!" as we laughed. She continued "We booed and wanted him to stay, but couldn't believe it when he said, he was having fun in them" as Gloria laughed "Never! What a little sissy!" as she laughed "That's what we thought!"

adding "But we're pretty sure he's not and Sally is making him sound girly!" Her Mum laughed "He wasn't?" As Gloria gasped and giggled, "Wait till I see him, I'll have to get him to come down to show me his pretty aprons!" Caroline said, "I'm sure he wouldn't mind helping you and me with some housework!" as they all laughed at the thought.

She continued "Then Caroline called "What age did you play dollies from Harry?" and we were amazed when he said, "Since I was 4 or 5" as they all giggled. However, then Sally called him back and handed him a large pretty dolly and a frock to change it into to!" and we saw the look of horror on his face and I've a feeling he hadn't seen the doll before!" adding "But he had to show Abi and me his dolly and we giggled, our heads off, with Abi saying, he can come around to play dollies with her at our place!" with him begging us not to tell his mates or anyone on him. Anyway, his Mum took him on home and Sally invited us into her house to tell us about the girly boy!"

She told us "At first when he was 4 or 5, she thought he was a little girl with short hair, as she peered out to see him mincing about the garden with a handbag, dangling from his arm, first mincing and then extreme mincing!"

Gloria asked, "What do you mean?" Abi took her Mum's handbag and said, "Sandy get a handbag too!" as Sandra ran and fetched a handbag and returned with a turquoise handbag and slung it over her arm up to her elbow and then they minced up and down with her Mum and Caroline giggling. They then splayed their arms out and did some extreme mincing with her saying, "You'll have to mince like that when we go shopping girls!" as they giggled and nodded, "Especially if we can get girly Harry to join us!" She gasped "He wouldn't, would he?" as she added "Not carrying a handbag?" as they nodded, and Sandy called "Listen Mummy!" as she waited to hear. They giggled, "He's playing football in his back gardena with his Mum and Aunty Sally from next door, as you'll understand later!" Sandy and her Mum asked, "You mean she was lying?" as she nodded, and said, "I don't think he'd even played dollies, before and it was all Sally's plan!" as they giggled, and asked, "Why did he say, he'd played dollies then?" and heard her say, "I think she had something on him, some photos or something!" as they giggled. Anyway, she then said, we could make his day, while playing football with mates!" as Gloria gasped "You didn't out him to his mates?" as she shook her head "No they haven't a clue!"

Sandy's Mum spies Harry in nappies and a diaper

She added "She told Abi she could call at his house with her dolls pram and borrow his dolly and then mince his dolly down past him playing with his mates and say, "Don't worry Cissilia! Lucy will be around later to play with you and then wheel you back home to play dollies with her Mummy!" Gloria gasped "You didn't! Did you?" as she said, "After tea she let him remove his aprons to go and join his mates, but then phoned us and told me that he was playing footy in the street. Hence, I got my Abi here with her dolls pram to mince around to his house. We borrowed his new dolly and Abi minced it down and embarrassed him and I saw his face glow bright red, as we minced on down to your place. Gloria giggled, "The poor boy must have been so embarrassed at seeing his dolly in your pram!" as she continued "Wait till you hear it gets better!" as she listened on.

We collected your little Sandra here and Abi was so naughty as she said, "She didn't tell on him, but told Sandy to laugh at the top of her voice as if she'd been told something funny!" as Gloria giggled, "The poor boy!" He must have nearly wet himself!" as Caroline gurgled "That's what I said! And then gasped as I saw him run up, not to his Mummy, but to Sally and I realised he must have wet his pants!" Gloria giggled, "Why the big baby!"

as Caroline added "Exactly, next thing I was around at my house collecting Abi's old diaper bag and guess who gelled and talked him, with the girls downstairs off course!" as Gloria laughed "Thank goodness for that I'd not have been pleased if Sandy had spied his you know what!" Gloria giggled, "Is he still up there in the back garden in his frock?" as they nodded, and she said, "I'll pop up to see!"

Caroline laughed "Remember! His Mum doesn't know about the nappies!" as she nodded, and said, "You pop upstairs to bed and get undressed and when I come back, I'll put you to bed!" Sandy asked, "Can I come up?" but her Mum said, "No darling, you've had enough fun! I just want to see for myself and I'm sure he'll give us lots of fun, in the days to come!" as Sandy gave Abi and her Mum a kiss bye and said, "Thanks for my fun!" as they exited with her Mummy telling her hubby, she'd be back in 5 minutes and joined them up the street, smiling, as she saw his mates still playing footy. At Harry's, she split from them and called bye and walked up to the back and he gasped, as another lady saw him in the dress and mincing with his handbag!" as she laughed "I couldn't' believe it, when my Sandy told me about your sweet boy here!" His Mum laughed "It's come as a bit of a shock to me!" She asked, "Can I have a word with him a tick around the back of the garage?" as his Mum nodded, and she took him around the back and said, "Let me see baby!" as she raised his frock and giggled, at his diaper, as she let his frock fall down again and she led him back out again. She laughed "I just asked him was he enjoying himself and he told me he was!" as she said, "Can I see him mincing before I go" Sally said, "Off you go Lucy!" and saw him mince and then do the extreme mincing around the garden to screeches from Gloria. She bent down and kissed him" adding "I'd better head back to put Sandy to bed" as she minced back home, giggling at what she'd just seen, especially when she passed his mates.

Morning he's hoping his Mum won't spy his nighty or nappies for Abi's

Sally whispered to his Mum "Can you leave playing dress up with him in your clothes, till another time, when I'm there?" as she huffed "Oh I had planned some dress up this evening, but ok! I suppose dollies and curtsies and mincing!" Sally said, "Don't forget his kisses!" as they both laughed and Sally said, "I'll pop around and borrow some of Abi's dollies to give him some variation!" as they both laughed. She said, "I'd better be heading back girls!" as she kissed Harry and Gloria bye and minced out and back around to next door. Margy laughed "Better pop Abi's pram back in the garage, till the morning unless you want to play dollies with it before bed!" He quickly wheeled the pram into the garage and was told to take his dolly with him. He picked up the doll and followed his laughing Mum in doors where they sat down, and she got him something to drink and some biscuits but had him playing with his dolly and then sent him up to bed. He went up to bed carrying his dolly and locking his door, undressed down to his horrid diaper and nighty. He thought, how could he have been so silly, letting her next-door trap him and now it's absolutely terrible that the young girls have seen him dressed up and then in flaming nappies. He slipped into a deep sleep. His Mum wasn't far behind him and called "Don't forget to wear your pinnies down in the morning!" as he called "Ok Mummy!" as she added "Give your dolly a nice cuddle to sleep, as he huffed "Funny!" as she laughed and went to bed herself. In the morning he awoke and realised he was still in the nighty and nappies and hoped they'd let him remove them for school. He got himself dressed in school shirt, with his jumper over it and trousers.

He then donned the floral apron and washed his face and then cleaned his teeth, as he then brought his dolly and the PVC pinny down with him. His Mum smiled as she saw him enter the hall wearing his floral apron and carrying his dolly and PVC pinny and said, "Not wearing your little pinny too?" as he huffed "I only need it for helping with wet stuff!" as she smiled and dished out his breakfast and said, set your dolly down on the washing machine. She laughed "You haven't forgotten Abi's dolls pram?" as he cringed "Mum please don't let them make me! I'll be spied by girls or even mates and teased rotten!" as he tucked into his cornflakes and then a fry up. His Mum handed him the pink rubber gloves and his PVC pinny and smiled as he donned the small daisy apron over his bigger clothe apron and then the gloves as he started washing the dishes.

He dreaded the neighbours out back spying him and asked, "Can I close the curtains Mum?" but she said, "I'd think you'll be more worried about seeing you with your dolls pram out the back and mincing with your handbag!" as he blushed and continued.

She smiled and said, "If your quick and wheel your dolly around the garden they might let you off, wheeling it around to Abi's!" as he cringed and soon had finished the washing up. His Mum handed him his dolly and his pink handbag and heard him beg "Can I have a headscarf or some hair ribbons?" causing his Mum to screech "Oh Harry!" as she bent down and gave him a kiss on the lips. His Mum said, "You are turning into such a sweet boy since the other day!" as he blushed. She handed him some hair ribbons and asked, "Will I do your hair darling?"

Sally collects Harry's doll's pram to take around to Abi's for him

Harry nodded, and felt her slide the ribbons into his hair, giggling away. She saw him open the back door and peer out checking no kids or anyone could see him, but his Mum pushed him out and saw him speed around the back garden and then open his garage to pop his dolly into the dolls pram and start wheeling it around the garden. His Mum gurgled and called "Don't forget to mince and extreme mince with your pretty handbag Lucy!" as he blushed and started mincing with his handbag and then slide his arm out to the side to extreme mince around the garden. He had only been there for 5 minutes, when a smiling Sally saw him, from her bedroom window and skipped down and picking up her handbag and locking up, she exited and minced around next door and up the drive, as she laughed "I see you're putting your naughty boy through his paces Margy!" His Mum laughed "Yes he's such a changed boy since yesterday!" Sally laughed "Are you Harry?" as he nodded, and bobbed a curtsy to her with his aprons, saying, "Yes Aunt Sally I've been a good boy and done the dishes and slept with my dolly!" as they gurgled and she bent down and kissed his pouting lips and then got his Mummy to repeat, as he bobbed a curtsy thanking them.

Sally said, "I'll collect Abi's dolls pram if he likes!" as his Mum laughed "Thanks Sally, he was a bit worried about being seen by girls from school or his mates!" as she laughed "Oh I'm sure they wouldn't' recognise you Lucy, in your pretty hair ribbons, if you get your frock on again!" He sobbed "I can't I'm off to school Aunty Sally!" as she laughed "Ok I'll take Abi's dolls pram around, but let me see you do some handbag twirls?" and saw him turn and twirl with his handbag spinning around too!" causing his Mum to laugh. Sally said, "That could be fun when you take him around the shops, Margy!" as his Mum gurgled, "Ok! Come on sissy! Let's get to the shops!" as she took his arm and then said, "Just joking, Harry!" He huffed "Funny!" as she said, "Abi wants you to bring both your aprons around for after school and help her Mummy with some housework!" He cringed and said, "Ha! Not fair!" as his Mum said, "You can pop them into your school bag for your trip around to Abi's!"

However, Sally reminded him "Don't forget you don't remove your aprons till in your porch, facing the street!" as he said, "Mum's said, I don't have to in the morning!" as she scolded "Spoilt sport, Margy!" but was glad when he saw Sally wheel the pram with his dolly out the garden and down the driveway. He said, "I'm glad that's gone, as she giggled, and said, "Another few minutes mincing with your handbag Lucy and then up and get ready for school!" His Mum giggled, "Now where's that dress and gymslip!" as he said, "Funny Mummy!" as he minced around the garden and did some more handbag twirls before finally being let back in. He ran upstairs and quickly removed his ribbons and then his aprons and picked up his blazer and schoolbag and descended the stair and called "Bye Mum!" as his Mum gurgled and giving him a kiss, said, "Not want to wear your pretty aprons to school darling?" but entered the sitting room and looked out to watched him go.

Harry spies Sally chatting to a woman but she says about Harry's aprons

Harry exited the gate, hoping to get away from any girls in case Abi, her Mum or Sally said, something girly to him and get around to change out of his nappies and his baby doll nighty. He nervously edged past Sally's house

and was relieved when she didn't appear to embarrass him. He walked on up and his Mum smiled as she peered out the window and wondered would Abi and her Mum tease him or something. He walked up the street and saw a few boys ahead of him and heard a few older girls coming up on the other side of the street and a few young girls, some with their Mum's too behind him, as he peered back, dreading someone tease him. He ran around the corner out of sight of his Mum, but gasped, as he spied the smiling Sally stopped at a gate, chatting to another older lady and he wanted to escape onto Abi's., but Sally called him over and said, "Abi asked you to wheel her dolls pram back to her place at 75!" as he blushed "Not fair! I'll be seen!" as the lady laughed "Oh the poor boys, not going to wheel that dolls pram!" but heard her giggle and nod. Sally said, "At least I saved him the embarrassment of wheeling the dolly pram out his driveway and up the street, with those schoolgirls teasing him silly!" She laughed "I think that deserves, a thank you!" as he blushed and knew what she meant as he cried "Oh no!" as the lady wondered what was wrong. She said, "He was around at my place with his Mummy yesterday afterschool and after we'd something to drink, the little sweetie, did the washing up in an apron and even donned a PVC pinny, to stop it getting wet!" as she lady said, "Good boy Harry! It's good that you help with the washing up and protect your clothes with pinnies!" as he huffed "Ha!"

Sally asked, "Did the girls spy you in your pretty aprons?" as he shook his head "No! Mum let me pop them away!" as the lady giggled, as she asked, "Did you bring them with you?" as he nodded, "Please don't tell Mrs?" as she gurgled "Oh my word!" as he removed the floral apron. He heard Sally say, "Remove your blazer and done your pretty apron to thank me properly!" adding "And show Angela how you look!" as he blushed and begged "Not here! I'll be spied by some kids who know me!" as they giggled. He removed his blazer and took the floral apron and pulled it on, to giggles from the older lady and young girls passing bye who said, "Oh he suit's that pinny!" as he huffed "Can I add my blazer quick?" but Sally said, "Aren't we forgetting something!" as she pulled out the PVC apron and said, "Abi wants you to do her dishes, so better protect her pretty apron!" She pulled pinny around him and heard the girls giggle and Angie said, "Oh that pinny makes his big apron look like a frock!" as he blushed and sobbed "Not fair! Can I have my blazer?" but she shook her head. He then asked, "Have you a headscarf Aunty Sally?" as she laughed "Angela Here! Might have some hair ribbons, to help disguise yourself, Lucy!" as she gurgled "He doesn't want a frock too?" as he huffed "Not fair!" as Angie removed some hair ribbons from her handbag and slid them into his hair to giggles from Angie and flicked wrist.

He calls at the wrong house, but has to wheel the pram back towards kids

He asked, "Can I have my blazer?" but she said, "I'll bring it up to Abe's and ask her to get you dressed for school!" as he started wheeling the dolls pram and dolly up the street, with the girls screeching at the big sissy boy in the girly aprons, hair ribbons pushing the doll along in its pram. Sally smiled and as she saw a girl of about 8 or 9 across the road, said, "I bet he'd love you to call out 'Harry you can't wheel your dolly to school today!" as the smiling lady called loudly "Oh Harry, you can't wheel your dolly to school today!" Sally said, "We'll just mince up to little Abi's, to return her dolls pram!" as he wheeled the dolly on up with the little girls teasing him and giggling at his look. He reached 75 and wheeled the pram up and rang the bell and saw someone come to the door and then saw another lady, he didn't recognise and said, "I've got Abi's pram here!" as she smiled and saw the lady and young girl at the gate, as she laughed "How sweet!" as the lady laughed "She lives next door sweetie!" He gasped as Sally said, "Oops I must have got their number wrong!" as he grimaced and pleaded "Please don't tell on me Mrs?" as he wheeled the dolls pram down the driveway and turned to return to Abi's, but gasped as he was now facing lots of school girls and boys as Sally whispered "He'd hate a kiss girls!" as she held his dolls pram and onto his pinny to stop him running up and a girl then reached her arms around his neck and kissed him, causing her to giggle and him to blush and say, "I don't like kisses!" as she let him wheel his dolly up the drive and ring Abi's bell. Her and her Mum came to the door and giggled, as they saw Harry, but also Sally and an older girl and said, "Oh Harry must have another girl friend!" as her Mum opened the door and heard Abi say, "Did you wheel your dolly around in my dolls pram Harry! I mean Lucy!"

He was led in and heard girls call "We'll catch you after school around here Harry to play dollies and dress up!" as they all giggled, and he sobbed "Not fair girls!" as Caroline led him in and he sobbed "I've to remove my diaper and baby doll nighty!" as they giggled. Sally entered and said, "I suppose as he's been a good girly boy for his Mum and me, we'll let him remove his diaper and nighty!" They laughed and Abi called "Oh Harry wants to go to school in his nappies and carry his dolly!" as he cried "Please Abi I've been a really good girly boy and baby too!" as she giggled, "You going to tell the girls that?" He begged "Please don't baby me in front of them?" adding "That would be terrible!" as they giggled. Her Mum shoed Abi out of the room and said, "Can you wait downstairs Abi, while we see to cleaning baby up!" as he cringed and she protested "Can't I watch Mummy?" but Sally took her down the stairs and left her Mum to clean him up. Caroline smiled as she pulled his trousers down and saw his diaper still in place, asking "Did baby wear his diaper all night?" as he nodded, "and I wore the baby doll too!" as she removed his aprons and then the jumper and the shirt to leave him in the baby doll nighty and his diapers. She giggled, "I suppose we can't send you to school in your nappies or baby doll!" as he sighed and felt her undo the ribbons attached to his nighty and remove it and then the diapers, giggling at his disposable nappies, but said, "I think baby can keep his nappies on! You don't have PE today?"

Harry's to wear his aprons, but carry his books in a girly shopping bag

He cringed "Not fair!" as she took 2 new disposables, she removed his and washed him and then added gel, talcum powder and then applied the new disposables, but then added a plastic carrier with 2 holes to cover them, as he cried "Oh no!" as she smiled "Not a word to Abi or Aunt Sally!" Caroline pulled a pair of frilly panties up over the bag, as he cringed, and she pulled the trousers and shirt and then added his jumper before leading him down the stairs. Sally and Abi protested "Oh Harry suited his pretty aprons!" as he huffed as Caroline asked, "Are you ready to head on to school?" as Abi called "I've your dolly here!" as he cried "I'm not carrying my dolly to school!" to more laughter. He got his blazer on and went to pick up his school satchel, when he saw a smiling Abi pick it up, but he then saw a pink handbag attached to the outside as he cried "No I can't carry my handbag!" as she then held up a girly shopping bag and Sally said, "I'm sure you can think of a suitable excuse for having to carry your books to school in a shopping bag!" as he sobbed "Oh no! You aren't serious?" but Sally said, "I'd head on if you don't want Abi to tie your handbag to your shopper!" and saw him woefully go to head out but remove his blazer and try to hide the shopper.

Caroline said, "He's trying to hide his shopper with his blazer!" as Sally laughed "Just Pop your aprons on and you can go!" as he woefully sobbed "Not fair girls!" as he pulled the floral apron and then the PVC apron over his jumper and quickly donned his blazer with the shopping bag over his shoulder, dreading being seen carrying the girly bag, but worse wearing the girly aprons. He ran on and heard a girl giggle "Harry is that your shopper?" as he cried "Oh no!" and ran on with giggles in his ears!" as he found a side street and quickly removed his blazer, but then was trying to remove the PVC apron, when a girl from his year at school stepped out a side gate and saw him in the 2 girly aprons and gasped "Gosh what on earth?" as he sobbed "Oh no! Not fair!" as he quickly reached around and untied the PVC apron and then pulled the cloth apron over his head as she giggled, "Oh you suited your pretty aprons! You're in my year, aren't you?"

He begged "Please don't tell! Someone tricked me into wearing the aprons to stop me hiding my bag!" as she looked and screeched "Oh fab! What a pretty shopping bag?" as she asked, "Why's this happened?" He cringed "I was a bit of a MSP, and some stupid neighbour has tricked me into carrying that bag!" as she flicked her wrist towards him and said, "The girls will adore your bag! If you're a good boy, I'll ask the girls to protect you from the boys!" as he cringed. She said, "Pop your pinnies back into your bag girly and wear our blazer to join me!" as he huffed "Can't I hide my bag?" but she shook her head, as he walked along with the bag over his shoulder. Hating it and dreading being spied by girls or especially mates. She asked, "So what's your name?" as he tried to

say, James, but she said, "If I find you've fibbed, I'll tell the girls to hand you over to the boys and not let you skip with them!" as he begged "I can't skip with the girls!" as she laughed "The boys won't let you play with them with your girly bag!" as he huffed "Not fair!"

Natalie spies Harry and makes him wear her pinafore and then her dress

He said, "I'm Harry and in 6B" as she smiled and said, "I'm Natalie! I know a few girls Karen and her friend Jenny in that class and they'll adore you!" as she laughed. She led him on with some girls calling "Hi Natalie, is that your boyfriend?" as he gasped and Natalie giggled, as she called "Is she carrying your bag for you?" as Natalie gurgled "No He's carrying his own pretty bag!" as she giggled, "Never!" as he blushed and she ran off to tell other girls. He huffed "How can I hide this girly bag?" as she laughed "Now where are you first?" as he said, "J1 for English!" as she said, "I'll escort you and we'll say, you've been tricked into carrying your books in the girly bag and I'll ask them to look after you!" as he led her on with several girls gasping and whispering about the boy and his girly shopping bag.

They rounded the corner and heard gasps as they saw Harry with the girl from a higher class!" and Karen laughed "Natalie, Harry's not your boyfriend is he?" as she blushed and laughed and said, "What my sweet Harry!" as she threw her arms around him and kissed him on the lips to gasps from Karen who screeched "Oh Natalie!" as the guys called "Go for it Harry!" as she smiled and said, "Look Karen, he's going to be teased by the boys soon, but can you and the girls look after him and realise he's being tricked into carrying his girly shopper!" and maybe a few other embarrassing things, but just have a giggle at him!" She giggled, "You can get him to be an honouree girl!" as she gasped "What?"

However, she asked, "Can you get some prefects to escort him down to the needlework department at 11am break time, with his girly bag of course?" as she asked, "Why?" but was told "Wait and see!" as she skipped off. Harry joined the boys saying, "Natalie and some girls tricked me into carrying my books in it!" as some called him "Woofter! No girl could make me carry a girly bag like that!" as Karen heard and said, "Come on Harry You can join us, to stop the boys teasing you!" as he went over and joined her and the girls, as she giggled, "You can be an honorary girl!" as he cringed "Ha!" as the teacher Mrs James, came and opened the door. The girls entered with Karen pulling him with her and sat Harry down beside her with the girls as the boys entered and called "Harry's joined the girls!" as she asked, "Why are you there Harry?"

Karen called "Miss! His girlfriend has tricked him into carrying his books, in a pretty shopping bag, as she held it up and said, "The boys are teasing him Miss and so he can sit with us!" as the teacher laughed "Ok Harry, but no playing up!" as he nodded.

However at break time they get a prefect to march him down to the girls gym, where Natalie is there sobbing and saying "He stole my good aprons and they're in his bag!" as the laughing teacher took them out and asked what he was doing with them. Of course Natalie said "I've thought of a suitable punishment!" as they asked "What?" as she said "He's to wear my aprons to class!" as he cried "No don't!" but then she added "Over my pinafore!" as she removed her blazer and then her pinafore and the prefects got him into the pinafore and then tied the pretty aprons on over it, followed by the PVC pinny.

He hated having to wear the pinafore and aprons to classes, but at lunchtime Natalie had phoned her Mum to bring her Summer dress and a pink handbag in and next thing he had to slip into it, under the pinafore and then the aprons, and he'd to mince with his handbag to look really girly in the last two classes.

PART C

TOM'S HAS TO CHANGE BABY DOLL'S NAPPIES

Nancy outs himself to June and wheels his dolly in the garden

Pam Says, why wheeling his dolly in a pram is useful for life wrt married

Pam then Says, to her Mum "Look Mum, Tom wheeling his dolly about in her pram will be good practice when he grows up and is married and has his own babies!" adding "Yuk!" She laughed "Will it indeed?" as she said, "It means he won't leave his wife to do all the wheeling baby, around the place!" He cried "I'm not wheeling my dolly around the streets!" to screeches of laughter, as Pam said, "Now Tom! We can start off in the house here and then give you practice around the garden!" Tom cried "But neighbours and her next door, will spy me, wheeling her about!" as Pam giggled, "I've thought of a solution!" as her Mum asked, "What?" Pam then pulled a headscarf from her skirt and said, "He can dress as Nancy, in my pink apron and with a headscarf and then June next-door or the neighbours, will probably think she's me!" as he cried "I'm not wearing that flaming scarf!" adding "No Mum! Don't let her make me?" His Mum cuddled him and scolded "Now Pam! You can't dress him up as a girl, outside!" as Pam laughed "Well I thought he'd prefer a pretty headscarf, to the alternative!" as her Mum guessed and said, "No way! He's not wearing hair ribbons, in the back garden as a girl!"

Pam giggled, "Now Mummy! I gave Nancy some practice earlier, as My Little Pony, wearing an Alice band and hair ribbons!" as her Mum laughed "Now keep Nancy inside! No making her go outside, dressed up!" as he sobbed "Mum! She's getting worse!"

She giggled, "He won't be very useful helping his wife with wheeling his babies about, if he only knows how to wheel his dolly around the garden!" adding "I think she'll thank us, if you give Tom practice playing dollies – dressing and undressing his dolly into different pretty frocks and then wheeling her about the place!" as her Mum laughed "Pam stop this conversation! This is so naughty!"

She giggled, "I remember you letting me wheel my dolly about the streets and then take her shopping to the shops and around town!" as her Mum scolded "No way, Pam!" as he huffed "Very funny, Pam! No way am I going to push that pram around the streets!"

She giggled, "I had so much fun, acting as a Mummy, wheeling my dollies and carrying my handbag, to help Mummy, shopping!" as her Mum gasped "You are pushing it Pam!" as she looked at her brother with the doll's pram with his dolly in it and gurgled "Mummy! I can't wait to get Nancy shopping, with us!" as he sobbed "No way!" adding "Although she might need a better disguise than my apron!" as she gripped her skirt and bobbed a curtsy to him. He cried "No way Pam!" as he ran out of the room but heard her call "Oh Tom! You've forgotten your dolly!" as he ran back and picked it up from the pram and exited again, sobbing up the stairs

Pam finds a large baby doll in nappies for Tom to diaper

Pam then rummaged in the spare room and found a large baby doll in nappies and plastic baby pants in its' box, with spare disposables and other baby stuff - "A dummy that fitted in its' mouth, a baby bottle that it could drink and it also wet its nappies, when you pressed a, button. She found her diaper bag and brought the bag and dolly in its' box down to show her Mum. She gurgled at the thought of her big brother having to change another baby doll, but this time in and out of nappies and plastic baby pants, giving it it's dummy and baby bottle and popping it in and out of baby dresses too! Her Mum was watching TV when a smiling Pam came down and first of all showed her the diaper bag, as she gasped "Why have you, your old diaper bag out for, Pam?" as she laughed "Don't worry Mummy! It's not for Tom! Although it would be fab, if you put him back into nappies and plastic baby pants!" as her Mum scolded "Watch it or it might be you, who ends up a baby!" as she laughed "Oh Mum!"

She then said, "You know I mentioned us getting some experience at changing nappies?" as her Mum nodded, and saw her produce the box with the large baby dolly and nappies, etc. Her Mum gasped "Oh Pam! He'll die!" but she asked, "What's going to happen when he's married and has a baby! You expect him to leave it all to his poor wife?" as her Mum laughed "I suppose you are right, but it's a bit naughty!" Pam said, "After dinner! Ok Mummy?" as she laughed "I suppose it won't hurt, but you've to let him run on after to play with his mates!" adding "You can't have him acting as a girl, all the time!" as she laughed "I don't see why not! It hasn't done you or me, any harm!" as her Mum gasped and they both laughed.

Tom comes down for dinner and Pam handed him his blue apron, with him thankful he didn't have to wear her pink apron and sat down as his Mum dished out the food for their evening meal. He tucked in as Pam laughed "What did you think of your wonderful dolly pram to have fun with Baby Suzie?" as he cringed "It's not fair Pam! I might be seen, pushing that flaming thing about the house!" Pam giggled, "Tina across the street, thinks it much more fun to wheel your dollies about the driveway or even the street!" as he begged "Please Pam keep me in-doors! Don't take me outside with my dolly and especially that flaming pram!" as his Mum heard and giggled, "Pam stop teasing Tom about his dolly and doll's pram!" Pam laughed "It's going to be fun tonight!" as he cried "What?" as his Mum smiled "I'll leave it till after we've done the dishes!" as Pam laughed "Oh Mum! It's going to be so much fun!" as he cried "Please don't! What is it?" but she just laughed "It's an essential task that both boys and girls should be taught, by their Mummy's!" as her Mum laughed. He huffed "But I thought I could go out to play footy tonight!" as Pam laughed "It depends how fast you are with the task!" as he blushed, wondering what it could be.

Tom realizes he's to learn how to change a baby doll's nappies

After dinner he pulled Pam's floral PVC pinny on over his own blue apron, with Pam asking "Sure you don't need the pink one Tom?" as he shook his head and they did the washing up, without him worrying about a pink headscarf to hide him from neighbours.

They finished and Tom asked could he go and play footy, but Pam said, "After our Mummy has shown us how to change a baby doll's nappies!" as he cried "Oh no! That's not fair!" as she took the diaper bag and laid the changing mat down on the living room floor and the dolly on top of it and giggled, "This will be fun!" Tom gasped as he now realized what the task was and cried "Not fair Pam!" as she fetched the large baby doll, in nappies and plastic baby pants and showed him, saying, "Tom! I mean Nancy! This is Baby Jane!" He sobbed "Don't make me?" but his Mum said, "It shouldn't take very long and then you can pop out to join your mates!" He blushed and Pam held out the dolly to him and said, "At least it gives you a rest from carrying your Baby Suzie, all about the place and look Tom! This dolly even can suck a dummy or baby bottle and even wet itself!" Her Mum said, "Make sure you put the baby changing mat down, when changing baby's nappies!" as Pam gurgled "Hear that Tom?" adding "Or is it Nancy?" as he blushed and said, "Ha Ha!" but then asked her Mum "Will our big baby, fit on that little mat,

Mummy!" adding "Mummy! You said, I could have a go at changing Baby Tom in and out of nappies, after!" as he gasped, and her Mum scolded "I did not! You watch it Pam, or you'll be the one who ends up in nappies!" as Tom said, "Ha Ha Ha!"

Pam takes a dummy and pops the dummy into its' mouth and holds up the dolly's baby bottle and asks "Mummy! Can we have some milk for Baby's bottle?" as she added "Tom's still a bit thirsty!" as Tom huffed "Funny, Pam!" as her Mum laughed "Pam! Stop that!" as she put some milk on the boil. However, while she was in the kitchen, Pam whispered "Just a joke for Mum, when she comes back in?" as he asked, "What?" as she said, "Just be sucking the dummy!" as he pleaded "Please don't, Pam?" but she nodded, and took the dummy and popped it into his mouth, as tears appeared in his eyes.

A few minutes later, their Mum returned with the baby bottle of milk and gasped as she saw Tom with the small dummy in his mouth and heard Pam gurgle "I just pacified Baby Tom!" adding "That's good! You've got his baby bottle!" as her Mum laughed "Take that out, Tom!" and saw him remove it as he cried "She's terrible, Mum!" as she said, "Watch it or Nancy will replace Tom or maybe replace Baby Jane!" as her Mum gasped "Don't you dare, Pam!" as she giggled, at her blushing brother's embarrassment.

Pam took the dummy and said, "Tom! You can have some practice giving your new dolly it's baby bottle!" and saw him take the bottle and pop the teat into the doll's mouth, but Pam said, "Now Tom! What have you done wrong?" as he said, "I don't know!" as she said, "You must always check the temperature of the milk, to make sure it's not too hot for baby!" as her Mum said, "Pam don't" but saw Tom take the bottle and give it a suck, saying, "Horrid!" as they both screeched and his Mum laughed "You just normally feel it!"

They get Nancy to change his dolly's nappies

Pam laughed "I knew he was thirsty for his baby bottle!" as he sobbed "Not fair!" as Pam held up the dummy and said, "At least this is something we can use, to stop Tom protesting too much, Mummy!" as her Mum laughed "Pam! Stop that!" Pam said, "Now Tom! Just take the bottle out and then replace Baby Jane's dummy and a few minutes later give her that bottle again!" as he cringed "Not fair, Mum!" as he removed the bottle and replaced it's dummy into the dolly's mouth and then removed it and a few minutes later, he replaced the baby bottle, to clapping and laughter from both her Mum and little Pam. Their Mum said, "Now children! Now to change your dolly's nappies!" as she said, "Just press here, to make dolly wet her nappies!" as she showed Tom the button and he saw it was just below its head, on one of its shoulders. She said, "Go on Tom! Press here!" as he swallowed and pressed as Pam gurgled "Tom! You've made your dolly wet her nappies!" as he sobbed "She said, that really loud!" adding "Please talk softly when we're playing dollies?" as they both laughed.

His Mum handed Pam and then Tom some rubber gloves and saw them both pull them as she said, "Right Tom! Pop your dummy back in and then try and pull down your dolly's plastic baby pants!" as he blushed and said, "She's not my dolly! I only have Baby Suzie!" as Pam gurgled "If you ask nicely I might add Baby Jane to your dolly collection!" as her Mum laughed and taking the doll, he pulled the plastic pants, as Pam gurgled "Oh fab!" as the dolly was left in the diaper, which had just Velcro, to keep it together and not nappy pins. Pam said, "Now Tom! Remove your diaper! I mean your new dolly's diaper!" as he cried "What about you?" as she laughed "I'm more an expert than you!" as he cringed and said, "Ha! Funny! Ha!" as he unstuck the Velcro and saw it come away and reveal the small wet disposable nappy. His Mum said, "Remove the diaper and pop it onto the mat beside you, to replace it after you've changed dolly's disposables!" with Pam giggling at the red glow on Tom's face, as he changed her dolly's nappies.

Tom went to pull the disposable off, but his Mum said, "Turn her over first! You always start with the bottom and then do it's front!" Hence, he turned the dolly over and saw the disposable on his bottom wasn't wet and said, "I don't need to change the back one, it's not wet!" but his Mum said, "You must always change both front and back disposables, in case there is a little bit of poo, has leaked out and you don't want your baby, to get nappy rash!" Pam said, "You'd better explain Mum about wet wipes, baby gel and talcum powder, for baby!" as she corrected "Sorry Mum! For Tom!" as he huffed "Tom's not doing this! It's Nancy!" as she laughed and took her pink apron and said, "Pop this over your pinny, then!" as he pleaded, but took the pink apron and popped it on over his other aprons and said, "There!" Pam gurgled "Mum! He'd learn so much faster, if he had to change his own nappies and diaper!" as he huffed "You're not funny Pam!" as her Mum laughed "Now Pam! Stop that now!"

They get Tom to replace its disposable using wet wipes on its bottom

His Mum said, "Right now gently pull it's disposable off, checking if it's soiled or not and then pop it onto the newspaper or carrier bag out of the way!" He pulled the disposable off and set it down on the newspaper and saw his Mum hand him some wet wipes, as she said, "Just give the baby's botty a nice wash clean with those!" They saw Tom rub the wet clothe over the baby doll's bottom, as Pam said, "Wash it all over its botty! Between the legs too!" as her Mum nodded, "Quite right Pam!" as she smiled and saw Tom rub it's bottom, over each cheek and then underneath. His Mum said, "Well done Tom! I mean Nancy!" as Pam gurgled "Mummy don't you know if he's a boy or a girl either?" as he cried "Mum Stop her!" as they laughed. His Mum then handed him the baby gel and said, "Now rub that gel over baby's bottom!" and saw him take the gel and squeezing some onto his hand, he rubbed the gel over the doll's bottom again and underneath too.

Pam took the powder and said, "I'll sprinkle some over baby's bottom!" but pushed Tom down onto his front and sprinkled the talc over his bum, as he cried "No don't!" as her Mum scolded "That powder better come out young lady!" as he cried "Oh no! It better not show!" as Pam giggled, "Nancy! You can just say, you were showing Tom how to change his nappies!" as her Mum laughed "Stop that Pam!" Tom got up and said, "Not funny, Pam!" as he smacked the bottom part of his trousers but didn't get it all off. She then added the talcum powder to the doll's bottom and said, "Nancy! Your dolly is just about ready for its disposable again!" as she handed him the disposable from its bottom.

Tom took the disposable and pushed it back down onto the dolly's bare bottom and said, "There dolly is into a clean nappy!" as Pam screeched "Oh Mum! This is so much fun!" as Tom blushed.

His Mum took some news-paper and said, "In the case of a real baby, you'd maybe have a wet nappy on its front and even a dirty nappy on its backside and so you throw them onto the newspaper or pop them away in plastic carrier bags, for disposal afterwards, but in this case we'll just wash the nappies and reuse them the next time!" as Tom cried "There won't be a next time!" Pam laughed "It might give him practice, if he gets to change his nappies, every Sunday night after dinner!" as she corrected herself "I mean his dolly's nappies after dinner!" to more laughter. His Mum then tells him to now do the baby's front and said, "Pam and I will watch and see if you can do it all, without any help!" as he blushed and turned the doll back onto its back, but Pam said, "I want a commentary while Nancy is changing her nappy!" He said, "I popped dolly onto her back and then just remove its disposable here!" and saw him remove the nappy, to expose the doll's naked front, but sighed as he complained "It's all wet!" as his Mum laughed and said, "Don't worry! It's just milk!" as Pam gurgled. He then took the packet of wet wipes and pulled one out and said, "I then take a cloth here and wash dolly down, to clean her front!" as he took the doll and started wiping it down from the waist down and even between the legs as he said, "There is a clean dolly!" as Pam giggled, "Yes Tom! Your baby dolly is nice and clean!"

Tom must change his doll's disposable nappy on his own

Tom then said, "I then take the baby gel!" as he squeezed some onto his glove and rubbed it over the front of the doll. He said, "I then take the talcum powder and sprinkle it over dolly's front!" His Mum asked, "Do you know why you need the talcum powder?" as he shook his head and heard her say, "It's to stop the nappy sticking to it!" as Pam screeched as her Mum said, "You meant to your dolly!" Pam laughed "Keep on going Mum! I wish I had this on record!" as he then took the talc and went to sprinkle it over Pam, but his Mum stopped him and said, "Just finish off your dolly!" as he sprinkled it over the doll's front. He then asked, "Pam! Have you a clean disposable for my dolly?" as she screeched and threw her arms around him and kissed his lips, as he cried "I don't like kisses!" to more laughter, as Pam giggled, "Sorry Tom! You are coming out with some funny statements, as Nancy!" as he blushed.

She took a disposable from the box and handed it to him and saw him open the tabs and stick it down on the doll. He was about to take the diaper, when Pam took it and held it up, saying, "Just get into your diaper and baby pants and you'll be protected to go and play with your mates!" as her Mum screeched and he huffed "Funny!" He grabbed the diaper and struggled as he had to take the sides and then the front up to stick the towel down properly, as his Mum hugged him and said, "Not very tight, but you'd normally use nappy pins!" as Pam gurgled "Mummy! Baby might prick something!" as he cried "Not funny!" s his Mum laughed "Not bad for your first go!" as Pam giggled, "I'm sure with a lot of practice he'll be good enough, to join me babysitting!" as he cried "I'm not ding flaming babysitting!" as they both laughed.

His Mum said, "And finally baby's plastic baby pants!" and saw Tom take the small plastic pants and pull them back up the dolly's legs again and pull them over the nappies as Pam gurgled "Well don't Nancy!" adding "She did very well Mum, didn't she?" as he asked, "Can I go out now?" Pam said, "Who just changed her baby doll's nappies?" as he huffed "Nancy did!" but she said, "I think Tom can now have a go himself!" adding "Just give me my pinny back!" He sobbed "Oh no! I've to do it all again!"

However, her Mum stopped her and said, "Now Pam! Tom's done very well for his first go! Don't be mean?" as she huffed "Oh Mum! It was so funny seeing him changing his dolly's nappies!" He blushed and begged "Please Pam! Let me go and play footy?" as she laughed "Won't they laugh at your aprons?" but said, "Ok! Go and hang them up and then you can ask me!" as he blushed and taking his Baby Suzie doll, he ran off to remove the aprons and hang them up. She said, "For being a good boy and changing his new baby dolly's nappies, I'll let him play footy with his mates!" as she asked, "What's your new baby doll, called?" as he cringed and said, "Baby Jane!" as she gave him another kiss and asked, "What do you want to ask me?" as he cringed and said, "Can I wear your pink panties out to play footy with my mates?" as she giggled, and said, "Off you go!" and saw him slip out.

Tom joins his mates for footy, but they mention the mark on his trousers

Pam went in and gurgled "Wasn't that fab Mum, seeing my big macho brother changing his dolly's nappies?" as she nodded, and laughed "He must be so embarrassed!" However, her Mum gasped "You know what we forgot?" as Pam shook her head and she replied, "His trousers with that talcum powder!" as Pam screeched "Oh fab!" Tom had ran out and found his mates down the street and started kicking the ball with them when he turned and one guy asked, "What's that mark on your trousers?" as he gasped and realized it was the talcum powder, from changing his dolly's nappies and reaching around, he rubbed and smacked his jeans hard and said, "My flaming sister, Pam, spilt something, on my trousers and I forgot to clean it!" as they saw him hit it some more, till they said, "It's gone!" but of course, he had a massive beamer on his face.

Pam then gurgled "Wouldn't it be fab it we got him back into nappies and plastics!" as she added "Look on the bright side!" as her Mum said, "No way! What?" as she laughed "I could say, I've got experience changing both girls and boy's nappies and plastics!" as her Mum screeched "Pam you are terrible!" Pam hung her uniform up to then locked her bedroom door. She threw herself down on the bed and giggled, to herself, thinking of what had evolved, over the weekend and her MSP of a brother, wearing her nightdress and panties to bed and playing dollies. She loved the way, things were going, but wanted to let someone else, in on his sissiness. She wouldn't tell anyone at school, yet, as that would be too cruel.

She thought about Julie and would love to tell her but wanted to hold back a while. She was trying to think of someone, when she considered "Why not let our neighbour Aunty June know!" She thought of ways, to tell her or hint and thought "I could mention that he's started helping Mum and me with the housework!" She then thought of a way for Tom to out himself to her, as she giggled, "If I can persuade her, to pop around, for a chat with Mum, just before he gets back from school" adding "Then big macho Tom comes in and asks 'Mummy! Where's my dolly?" and she hears, that would be brilliant!" She decided to try and speak to June, next-door asap, to set the trap.

Morning and she heard her Mum call "Right Children! Time to get up for breakfast!"

Pam ran into the bathroom, with her wash things and quickly cleaned herself up, before returning to get dressed. She heard Tom exit his bedroom and enter the bathroom and peeked out to see, he'd forgotten his dolly and called out "Tom! You've forgotten your dolly!" and saw the bathroom door open and him run back to his bedroom and exit, again holding Baby Suzie, sobbing "That's not fair Pam!" but she said, "Now Kiss her and say, sorry for leaving her behind and tell her you love your dolly!" He blushed as he raised the doll to his lips and kissed it, before stammering "Sorry Suzie for leaving you behind! I love my dolly!" as Pam giggled, "Good boy!" as she shut and locked her bedroom door and heard Tom lock the bathroom door again. She removed her nightdress and undies and put on clean underwear, before pulling on her school dress and gymslip, loving how girly they looked and giggling at the time, when she'd force Tom to try them on. Pam screeched at the thought of him attending school as a girl.

Pam plans to get June, next door to discover Tom's dolly secrets

Tom got down and huffed "Mum! Will you let me, run on ahead of her, this morning! If she comes with me, she'll tease me the whole way to school!" as her Mum laughed.

Pam said, "That's ok Tom! You can run on ahead! I don't mind! I've promised not to tell at school and if you're a good boy, I won't!" This played into Pam's hands as she wanted to try and chat to the lady next door, although she wondered if she'd be up or not. She went up and got her blazer and yellow school bag, checking she'd all the books for that day and had packed the homework she'd done over the weekend. She'd love to make Tom carry a girly bag to school.

She thought "Slowly does it! Plenty of time to embarrass my sweet sister, Nancy!" She waited in her room, tidying a few things and making her bed, to wait for Tom to leave. Tom finished drying the dishes, for his Mum and asked, "Can I remove this now?" as she whispered "If only you'd been a nice boy, on Saturday, I wouldn't have had to do that to you and you wouldn't have to wear a pinny, not to mention play dollies!" as he blushed. He huffed "It still wasn't right! What you did to me!" Tom went to collect his school satchel and books, but luckily his Mum reminded him "Aren't you forgetting something. Tom? Your dolly!" He huffed "Mum! It's bad enough her teasing me, without you, too!" as she laughed "I was just trying to help! You know her! She's liable to sneak back and if she finds you without your dolly!" adding "You know what she'd call out, if you were upstairs, without her? At least I said, it softly!" and saw him pick up the doll and ascend the stairs.

Pam took the pram and placed it into the sitting room, where her Mum would often entertain guests. She then popped her dolly and hid Baby Suzie underneath it, in the pram, giggling "If Aunty June sees him take his dolly from the pram, she'll laugh!"

Pam called "Mum! I've put Wendy away in the sitting room!" Her Mum laughed "Ok dear!" not thinking, to ask about Tom's doll.

Pam warned "Mummy! I might be a bit late as I'm going around to a Rachel from my class's house after school! I'll be back by 4.30!" and heard her Mum say, "Ok dear!" as she asked "Mum! but please don't mention to Tom! It will keep him on his toes!" as she laughed. Pam picked up her school bag and her pink lunch box, thinking I'll maybe have to swap lunch boxes with Nancy!" as she kissed her Mum Bye and ran out the front door.

Her Mum waved and then closing the door, she returned to the kitchen to tidy up, but glad her Mum had stopped watching her, as she slipped back across the road and down to her neighbours. Pam rang the bell and saw June come up the hallway in her dressing gown and smile, as she opened the porch doors, to little Pam. She whispered "Hi! Aunty June! Can I speak to you a minute?" as June, led her in saying, "Of course, Pam! Come on in!" as she led her into the living room. Pam sat down and she said, "I'm trying to pay my brother back, for being such a, MSP and nasty to me and thought you could help!"

Pam asks June next door to go around to speak to her Mum at 4

June listened and laughed, saying, "Is he still not helping, about the house?" but was surprised when Pam giggled, "Well actually Mummy made a break-through this weekend and he's started helping with the housework!" as June laughed "Well done Doreen!" Pam then said, "I was wondering could you pop around, to have a chat to my Mum, around 4 pm just before Tom arrives and hopefully, he won't realize, you are there!" adding "Try not to say, I've spoken to you! If you can think of an excuse, for a chat, it would be great!" June asked, "What if I go around and she doesn't invite me in?" as Pam laughed "I hope she will!" as June asked, "What am I to do?" Pam explained "Just make sure you stay out of sight but listen to what my big macho brother Tom Says! It should make you laugh and be embarrassing for my MSP of a brother!" June laughed, wondering what it could be and asked, "Can't you, give me a hint?" but Pam shook her head and giggled, "It would spoil the surprise!" adding "But it could be so much fun from now on!" as she added "I'd better be going! I hope Mum doesn't spy me, leaving here!" as June laughed and led her out, watching her slip up, their side of the street, before darting across to run on to school.

Pam tells Tom at school she's hidden his doll beside her Wendy dolly

Tom had a normal day at school, playing footy with his mates, at the break and lunch, but after lunch, he saw Pam waiting for him and nervously approached her. Pam is as good as her word at school, not even giggling as she mentioned Tom. She met Tom at the lunch time and said, "I've kept completely stump about Baby Suzie and you!" as he huffed "Thanks Pam!" as she added "But when you get home, you've to try and find where I've hidden her with my Wendy doll!" but added "Mum might know where Wendy is!" as he cried "Not fair!" as she said, "Now Tom! I've been a good sister and not mentioned Baby Suzie or Nancy to anyone!" He blushed and stammered "Thanks!" as she continued "I'm just reminding you, not to forget her, when you get home! I'll be around at a girlfriend's house and so, won't be in till later! You'll be able to join your mates at footy!" as he said, "Ok!" as he thought "That's good Ug's away!" as she told him "Just ask Mummy! She might have found them, while tidying up!" She finished by saying, "Bye the way! I've left something in your grey toy-box, for Nancy to change into, when she gets home! Make sure you wear them to play footy!" as he nodded, and she giggled, "Ok! You can run on to class now! See you at home later!" as she ran off giggling, to her own lesson. Tom thought to himself "At least that means, I can go out and play footy, with my mates! Even though, I've to wear her flaming undies!" and

then thought 'it was mean, her hiding my dolly!' as it meant, that if he hadn't found it, by the time, she came home, she could call out "Tom! Where's your dolly!" with the possibility, of his mates or one of Pam's friends, hearing her. Hence, he was more concerned with finding the doll, when he got home, than worrying about anything else.

Tom outs himself to June about his dolly and she teases him silly

June picked up her handbag and locked up, as she popped next door and rang the bell. Her Mum came to the door and called "Hi June! Come on in!" June said, "I just wondered how things are! Sorry! I meant to call earlier but got stuck into something!" as Doreen showed her into the sitting room and offered her a cup of tea!" She called "I had a bit of a blow up with Tom on Saturday, with him refusing to dry some dishes and seem to have sorted him! He ended up agreeing to help with the washing up and even some housework on the Sunday!" as June laughed "Well done Doreen! I'd heard you complain about him, not helping before! How's little Pam?" as her Mum laughed "She's her normal helpful self, but seems to enjoy teasing Tom, now that he's started wearing an apron, to help around the house!" June laughed "Now Doreen! There's nothing wrong with a man or a boy, wearing a pinny!" as June laughed "I know! I suppose, it's just his old male chauvinist attitude, that makes him, wearing an apron, seem worse than usual!" She returned to the kitchen to pour the tea out and set some biscuits on the trolley, before wheeling it into the sitting room for June. afternoon double cookery with the boys, with him wearing a blue apron, finished and he made his way home from school, checking to see if Pam was about, but pleased, not to see any sign of her. He entered his street was chatting to Ricky from down the street, who asked, "Playing footy this afternoon?" and heard Tom say, "Yea! See you in ten minutes or so!", as he knew Pam wasn't there. His Mum then noticed Tom coming home, chatting to a mate and said, "Speak of the devil! There's my Tom now!" June asked, "Shall I go?" but his Mum said, "Not at all! He'll probably shoot out to play footy!", as she thought "At least Pam's not here, to tease him about his dolly!" as she got up to unlock the side door and waited. June waited to stand up, not wanting Tom, to see her, from the street, to spoil the surprise, Pam had promised. She heard him at the side door and stood up, walking over to the door and listened to what Tom would say, wondering what it would be, that Pam has said would make her laugh.

He bounded up to the side-door and opened it, to hear his Mum say, "Hi Tom! Had a nice day! Don't worry! Pam's out!" She was about to add "June from next door is here!" He saw his smiling Mum in her apron and swallowed before stammering "Mum! Have you seen my dolly! Pam Says, she's hidden Suzie, with her Wendy doll!" and heard a gasp and laugh from his Mum, but also one, from the sitting room and then saw June exit and smile, as she said, "Hi Tom! Your Mum's just told me you've started being a good boy helping with the housework!" He looked at his laughing Mum, who said, "Sorry! I was about to say, "June is here!", when you blurted that out!" as he tried to make an excuse and stammered "Pam asked me to see, if you knew, where her dolls were!" as her Mum laughed "Well I think she said, her Wendy was in the sitting room!" as June laughed "That's nice of you Tom! Helping Pammy with her dollies! Come on in and see if they're here!"

His Mum tells June about Pam making him carry a doll about the house

Tom didn't know what to do and was blushing bright red, setting his bags down, he passed his smiling Mum and entered past June, as he saw the pram and peered in, to say, "Wendy's in the pram!" He then noticed Baby Suzie and huffed "Her other doll's there too!" as his Mum joined the smiling June and giggled, "Tom! June won't tell anyone, on you!" June giggled, "Does he play, with Pam's dollies?" as his Mum laughed "She made him play a little, last night and next thing, she'd forced him, to have one, himself!" Tom sat down on the floor and sobbed "Please Mum! Don't tell! That's not fair!" as June sat down on the sofa, beside him and pulling him up laughed "Don't cry Tom! I won't tell! I think it's very sweet, that you play dollies!" as he blushed again. She said, "I don't have any children, or know anyone, to speak to about it! Your secret's safe with me!" as he wiped his eyes. His Mum said, "Show June your dolly!" as he cried "She's not my dolly! She's Pam's!" to hear her say, "Just show her

122

to June!" adding "After that, you can run up and change! Wash your face and calm yourself down!" He reached into the pram and took out the baby doll and said, "There! She's Pam's!" as June asked, "What's she called?" and heard him stammer "Pam calls her Baby Suzie!" as his Mum laughed "Give her a cuddle! Go on Tom!" He cried "No way!" and ran out of the room, to arounds of laughter from both women.

He bounded upstairs and into his room, flinging himself on the bed, sobbing "That wasn't fair! Mum should have warned me that June was there!" He then wiped his eyes and another thought, crossed his mind "What if Pam comes in now and finds me without my dolly! She might shout up the stairs 'Oh Tom! You've forgotten your dolly'

in front of June and then dreaded, his mates hearing her, too. He thought to himself "Her next door knows, about my doll, so I might as well bring her up, with me, just in case!" as he returned downstairs and back into the room. June was still holding the dolly, chatting and laughing to his Mum, when she saw him return and ask "Can I borrow the doll, for a few minutes?" as she asked, "You aren't going to ruin it, or break it? Are you?" and saw him blush, as he stammered "No! I'm just bringing it up to my room!" as his Mum laughed "I think he's worried, that Pam might come in! She makes him carry her, wherever he goes!" A laughing, June, held her out to him and said, "Ok! Let me see you, cuddle your dolly!" and saw Tom kneel down, on the floor, begging "Mum! Would you close the blinds? Someone might look in and see me!" as they both laughed. He took the doll and held it against his chest, as his Mum said, "Give your dolly a quick kiss, before you take her upstairs!" and saw him turn away from the window and raise the doll to his lips and kiss her cheek, as June giggled, "Oh Tom! You do look so sweet!" Tom crawled along the floor and out the door, getting up, he ran upstairs. His Mum explained "See! If Pam came in and found him, without his dolly, she can then call out in a loud voice "Tom! You've forgotten your dolly!" and he's dreading, his mates, or Julie across the street, calling at the door and hearing her tell about his baby doll!" June laughed "What a wonderful tease!" as his Mum laughed "Pam told me, she'll be around at a girlfriend's house, till about 4.30! So! He could have left his dolly down here, but I forgot to say!" causing June to giggle "Oh Doreen! You tease!" as they both laughed and took a drink of their tea.

Tom changes into Pam's panties and June tells him how to play dollies

Tom threw the doll down on his bed and locking his door, he drew the blinds, as he proceeded to get undressed, out of his school uniform. He then remembered about Pam's comment about the toy box and lifted out a few toys, to discover a pair of her lace trimmed, turquoise panties and grimaced "Not fair!" He removed his underpants and replaced them by her panties, quickly, pulling on his jeans over them. He pulled on a tea-shirt and then his jumper, before unlocking his door and going into the bathroom to wash his face. He ran back and picked up the doll, to bring her into the bathroom, just in case, Pam returned early. He finished washing his face and heard his Mum call "Tom! Come on downstairs!" as he called down "I've homework to do!" but his Mum said, "Come on Tom! June won't bite!" as June laughed "Just a little nip!" as they both laughed. A blushing Tom descended the stairs, holding the dolly and as he reached the door, he knelt down on the floor and pushed the door open. June laughed "Over here Tom! Let me see you play dolls?" He huffed "Mum! I want to go out to play footy!" as June laughed "I take it, she doesn't make you play dollies outside?" as Tom blushed, shaking his head and his Mum tittered "Now June! There's no way, I can see him ever playing dollies outside! If Julie, Tina or his mates saw him, they'd rib him to bits!" as June laughed "Come on over here and let me see you playing!" He huffed "I don't know how, to play with dolls! Pam just makes me carry it around and occasionally hug and kiss her!" as he crawled over to her, realizing he was on view to a few of the houses, across the street and trying to hide the doll, from view, as he moved.

June laughed "There's lots of things you can do with your dolly! Isn't there Doreen?" as his Mum laughed "I suppose so!" as June said, "You can dress and undress her, into pretty skirts and dresses! Have you any doll's clothes for her?" and heard his Mum say, "I think Pam has some upstairs!" to hear Tom plead "Please Mum! Don't bring them down?" June said, "Then there's something over there, which is a necessity, when playing dollies!" as Tom

123

cried "I'm not pushing a pram!" as his Mum laughed, saying, "Go on Tom! I'll close the blinds!" and standing up, she adjusted them, to close a little more. He stood up and said, "Close them shut!" and heard her laugh "Ok! I'll have to turn the light on!" as she closed them fully and turned the light on. June giggled, "Spoil sport Tom!" as he walked over to the pram. He took the Wendy doll out and heard June laugh "What a pretty dolly!" as Tom huffed "She's Pam's!" as her Mum said, "That's Pam's favourite doll, she called Wendy!" and watched, as Tom shoved his doll into the pram. June scolded "Set her gently down! Just like you'd do, a real baby!" as his Mum scolded "Hopefully, not for many years, June!" She asked, "What about him baby-sitting!" as Tom huffed "No way! That's just for girls!" and heard his Mum laughed "Pam persuaded me to teach, both of them last night, to change her dolly baby Jane's nappies!" adding "So we gave Tom a go!" as he cringed "That was terrible Mum!" Pam teased me rotten and as a joke she sprinkled talc over my trousers!"

June's told how Pam and her Mum taught him to change a dolly's nappy

June giggled, as his Mum laughed "Afterwards Tom ran out to play footy and completely forgot about his talc on his trousers and so they saw it!" as June gurgled "What did you say!

I said, it was Pam playing a joke and quickly rubbed it off!" as they laughed. June said, "Wheel your dolly around the room! Is it ok, Doreen, or would you rather he take his doll's pram outside?" as his Mum laughed "No! Inside is ok! I think, the wheels are clean!" as Tom huffed "Funny!" June said, "Now Tom! Every few steps, you should take your baby out and give her a kiss and a cuddle and tell her you love her!" as Tom huffed "Mum! Tell her to, stop teasing! She's worse than Pam!" His Mum replied, "It's just between the three of us!" as he picked up Baby Suzie and hugged her, before kissing her and saying, "I love you Baby Suzie!" and then, set it back carefully in the pram. June laughed "Well done Tom! Now push your dolly along and repeat!" He huffed "Please! Not so loud! If one of my mates, call, they'll hear!" as he pushed the pram around, before stopping again to repeat hugging and kissing her. June said, "Anyway it's important, that young boys, get some practice with a doll's pram and dollies!" as he huffed "Why?" as she said, "So when you get married and have some children of your own, you don't expect your wife, to be the only one pushing the baby's around and changing nappies too!" as he huffed "Ha!" She laughed "Well! Let me see you wheel your dolly around the place and into the hall to show, you'll be a good Dad and get practice with dollies and wheeling them about!" as he sighed "Not fair!"

June Says, a doll's pram is important when playing dollies, but Ricky calls

He then gasped as he heard the bell go and Ricky was at his door, with his ball at his feet, waiting for Tom to join him. He shot down on the floor, beside the pram, with June laughing and his Mum standing up and exiting to see who it was. She saw the silhouette and called "I think it's one of your mates, Tom!" as she went to the door and opened it, said, "Hi! Tom's a bit busy at the minute!" as he said, "What! He can't come to play footy?" as she shook her head and said, "His cousins Wendy and Suzie have called around!" However, a smiling June had gone to the window and opened the blinds again, as Tom gasped "Oh no!" and whispered, "Please don't!" as he was sat there, petrified, but June pulled him up and said, "Why don't you say, hi, to your mate!" and pushed him out the door of the sitting room and up the hall, to join his Mum. Ricky said, "Ok! Maybe catch him tonight, after tea!" but then saw Tom's silhouette, beside his Mum at the door and said, "Hi Tom! I hear you can't come out, with your cousins being here!" as he stammered and called "Yea! See you later" Ricky turned and was halfway down the drive, when Tom heard June call "Oh Tom! You've forgotten your dolly!" as he gasped and his Mum laughed and quickly shut the door, to stop his mate, seeing his horrified reaction. Tom cried softly "Oh no! He might have heard!" as he ran, back, but knew not to enter the sitting room, in case Ricky saw him and ran into the kitchen instead. Ricky was exiting the driveway, when he heard a woman call to Tom and something about a dolly and turned and saw a lady, in the sitting room, standing there holding a doll and thought it was some kind of joke and kicked his ball across to pop around to see other mates.

His Mum squeals about Pam calling him Nancy as her sister

Tom sobbed "Not flaming fair! I think he heard!" as June called again, but this time out of earshot to Ricky, who was now halfway up the street. Tom ran in and shot down on the floor and took the doll from the laughing June and sobbed "That wasn't funny! I think he heard!" His Mum ran in and closed the blinds again and cuddled him "June you are awful!" as June laughed "Just my little joke! I'm sure Pam will have a giggle, when she hears!"

His Mum said, "Pam calls him Nancy, when being her sister!" as he huffed "Mum don't tell!" as they giggled, and June said, "Nancy! That's a pretty name!" adding "Since your little friend has gone, you can continue wheeling your dolly about!" as he blushed and wheeled the doll around more. He wheeled the doll around the room a few times, having to lift his doll out and give her a cuddle and kiss on each time around, with his Mum and June teasing him and him blushing his head off.

June asked, "What other games does she play with him?" as his Mum laughed "She just tries to get him to do housework, but wearing her pretty aprons and PVC pinnies, which he hates!" as June laughed "Now Tom! There's nothing wrong with helping your Mummy or Pammy with housework!" as he cringed and his Mum said, "It was his MSP way, that got him under Pam's control in the first place!"

June laughed "She doesn't try to play dress up with him?" as his Mum said, "Now June!

Although I let her make him wear her aprons, I won't let her put him into dresses or anything!" as June laughed "Spoilt-sport!" adding "At his age, it wouldn't be any harm!" adding "And look on the bright side Tom!" as he asked, "What?" She replied, "It would stop anyone spying you playing dollies, just thinking you were a little girl, if they saw you in a pretty frock and hair ribbons!" as he cried "No way!" and his Mum laughed "June! You're ten times worse than Pam!" She laughed "I know if when I was a young girl and made my brother play dollies, I'd have no problem, getting him into skirts and frocks, to play dress up with me!" as she added "If my Mummy wouldn't let me, I'm sure I'd know a kind neighbour!" as she bobbed a curtsy and continued "who would love, to see my brother, dressed up in lots of pretty skirts and dresses, not to mention tutus and things!" as he cried "Not fair June!" as her Mum begged "Please June! Don't suggest to Pam, she might try and take you up on that!" adding "And I don't know what I'd do!" as she laughed "Ok Nancy! We'll keep the joke between the two of us!" as she kissed him, and he blushed bright red. He wheeled the doll out of the sitting room door and up to the inner porch door and she stood up and quietly opened the blinds, pulling them up, fully, but gestured to his Mum, to keep quiet.

June gets Nancy to wheel his dolly into the porch and garden

June saw him at the front door and saw him turn the pram to return, when she stepped up and opened the inner porch door and he cried "No don't!" at seeing the sunshine from the street and dreading being spied, with the doll's pram. He quickly ran past her, back to the

kitchen but heard June call "Oh Tom! You've forgot your pretty dolly!" in a very loud voice. He sobbed and cried "Oh no! Not fair!" He stepped back, towards the pram and gasped, as he saw a lady walk by and look in, to see the doll's pram and the young boy and smile, but then June pushed the pram forward, into the porch. He cried "Oh no! Don't please!" as he stepped forward and begged "Please don't, Aunty June!" as he stopped, but heard her say, "I'll keep calling that out, if you don't get your dolly!" and saw him step nervously forward, into the porch. His Mum came out of the room and gasped "Oh no, don't June! He'll be seen!" as she saw his pram in the porch and Tom step out and giggled, "Oh June! You're worse than Pam!" and tried to call him back in, saying, "Tom! Get back in here!" but was too late. Tom got to the door, checking the porch and street ahead, but then June shoved him out, and said, "Wheel your baby doll, around to the back garden, or else!" as she closed the door on him and heard him cry "Oh no!"

He nervously looked out into the street, hoping he'd not spy any mates or other children about and was lucky, as he checked up and down and opened the outer door, trying to get the pram out, without being seen. Tom wheeled the pram out of the porch and turned it out to the driveway and quickly along and into the garden, where, he gasped, as he realized neighbours, from the back houses, could see him and quickly pushed it up, to the far end. June had called his Mum and they were watching, giggling as he wheeled the dolls pram up the garden to the back. June opened the kitchen window and said, "Well done Tom! I mean Nancy!" as he cringed and sobbed "I might have been seen, wheeling that flipping pram out, the porch and up the driveway!"

Brenda spies him with his doll's pram and tells Claire from up the street

However, the lady Brenda, who'd spied him, in the hallway, had stopped up the street, to chat to another lady, Claire in her garden and was looking down occasionally, as they chatted, when she saw the doll's pram being pushed out and a tentative figure, of a young boy, appear behind it and hurriedly, push it out to the driveway and then up, around the corner and out of sight, as she laughed "Did you see that?" Claire laughed "What?" as she said, "A young boy of about 8 or 9, wheeling his dolly in a pink dolls pram, out the front door and up the drive!" as the lady shook her head and ask, "Which house?" Brenda pointed to Tom's house as she laughed "Yes! Young Pam and her brother Tom live there! Sure, it wasn't Pam?" as she shook her head "It was definitely a boy!"

Tina sees Tom in headscarf with the dolls pram and calls Hi Pammy

She laughed "I often see her big brother Tom, playing football in the streets! You think, it was him?" as Brenda nodded. She laughed "Some boys will be girls!" as they giggled.

Brenda laughed "I've seen him playing football too, but didn't think, he'd have played dollies and pushed a pram about!" as Claire laughed "Now Brenda, we all remember how much fun we had as little girls playing dollies and pushing them about in their doll's prams!" adding "Maybe Tom has realized too and plays with his little sister Pam!" as they giggled.

His Mum led June out the back door and giggled, "His Mum had picked up the headscarf and Pam's apron and holding them out the window, she called "Here! As we seem to have Nancy out the back, she'll need these to wheel her pram around the garden!" June giggled, and he sobbed "Not fair Mum!" as he took Pam's apron and pulling it on, he then took the headscarf and tied it around his head, as June giggled, "Oh fab! Doesn't she look sweet!" He wheeled the pram up and around the garden and heard June call "Doreen! Do you remember when we were young girls, wheeling our dollies up and down the street?" as his Mum said, "Yes!" as she added "Then to the local shops and then all-around town, showing off as good Mummies!" His Mum screeched "Now June, stop embarrassing my Tom!" His Mum added "This must be terrible for him! At least Pam keeps him in doors, while playing dollies!"

He blushed "Not fair Mum! Can I come in?" as she said, "I think he'd better get back in doors June!" as June laughed "Spoilt sport! At least Pam can now, extend his fun to the garden!" adding "As this has set a sweet president!" as his Mum said, "Now June! He might be spied by his mates!" He sighed as she led him back in and wheeled the pram back from the garden, out to the driveway and timidly checked the street, that nobody was there, to see him in Pam's apron, but also a headscarf, wheeling the doll's pram about. He sighed as it seemed clear and he got it to the side door, but June called "Around the front Nancy!" His Mum gasped "He can't! He'll be spotted!" as June laughed "She's got a good disguise, with Pam's headscarf and her pinny!" as his Mum ran and opened the front doors and checking the street, she called "Quick Tom! Get your pram back inside, while nobody's about!"

Tom grimaced as he wheeled the doll's pram, up to the front, checking from inside the pink headscarf left and right, that nobody was about and gasped as he saw Tina, Julie's sister across the street. He quickly turned the pram

away from her, as he heard Tina call "Hi Pammy!" as his Mum laughed and called "Hi Tina! Pam's in a bit of a rush!" and helped get the pram, up the step and into the porch, saying, "Keep it here and get in! The wheels are dirty from the garden!" A blushing Tom, ran indoors, pulling the headscarf off and sobbed "Not fair, Mum! Tina caught me!" as she laughed "She thought you were Pam!" as June approached and cuddled him, saying, "Sorry Tom! That was a naughty trick, I played on you!" adding "What? Tina thought you were Pam?" as she laughed "Thank goodness for pretty headscarves and aprons!" as he blushed "Not fair!" Tom couldn't believe his afternoon, was turning out this way.

Tom in his blue apron, wheels the trolley into the kitchen

Meanwhile Brenda was still chatting to the lady Claire, when they gasped as they saw Tom return, but now in the pink apron and headscarf and his Mum usher him in, after speaking to little Tina. They laughed "Do you think that was big Tom, in his sister's apron and headscarf?" as Brenda nodded, "We'll have to speak to him later, if he goes past" as Claire laughed "What will we say?" as she replied, "Oh say, how sweet he looked, playing dollies and wearing his pretty apron and headscarf!" as Claire laughed "He'll die of embarrassment!" as she nodded. Tom was being consoled by his Mum, but still teased by June, when she said, "That was a lovely cup of tea Doreen!" but added "I wonder who's, going to be a good boy and wash up for you?"

Tom huffed "Mum! That's not fair!" as his Mum laughed "At least it will give you a rest, from playing with your dolly!" as he huffed "Not fair, Mum! Showing me off in front of her!" as his Mum laughed "It wasn't me, who blurted out 'Where's my dolly'?" and saw him blush and sniffle. She said, "You can take the trolley in!" as he huffed "Do I need the apron?" June laughed "There's nothing wrong with a boy, wearing an apron!" as his Mum said, "I'll get your boys one!" as she went in and brought it back and held it up, with June giggling "Go on Tom! Keep the pink one on!" He cried "That's Pam's!" and quickly grabbed the blue one and removing Pam's, he pulled it over his head.

His Mum laughed "Spoil sport!" Tom entered the sitting room to get the trolley, wearing his own blue apron, but gasped as he saw the blinds up and him on display, to the street and cried "Oh no! Who opened the blinds?" as he tried to run out, but his Mum said, "Wheel the trolley in!" as he grimaced and peering out. He was glad he didn't see anyone and quickly took the trolley and pushed it out of the room and into the kitchen. He ran the hot water and poured some liquid into the bowl and soon had it ready for the washing up.

However, he had still been visible, in the sitting room, to the ladies up the street, who said, "Oh look, he's changed into a boy's blue pinny now!" as they laughed "Not sure if he's a boy or a girl!" His Mum laughed and said, "It's well Pam wasn't here!" as June asked, "Why?" She'd have realized he'd forgotten his dolly and called out "Tom!

You've forgotten your dolly!" and heard June call "Oh Tom! You've forgotten your dolly!" and saw him run back from the kitchen and cry "Not fair!" as he then realised his doll, was still in the pram, in the porch and cried "Oh no! Mum get it for me?" but she laughed "Want your headscarf again? Just in case Tina is about!" as he nodded, and took it from her, as June giggled, "Oh Nancy's back again!" but said, "If she wants her headscarf, then she's to get back into Pam's pinny!" His Mum laughed and he cringed "Not fair!" as he took Pam's apron and pulled it over his own blue one. He went to the front door and opened it and checked the street, as he sighed, as Tina was wheeling her pram down her driveway. He stepped out, into the porch and reaching in, he grabbed his doll, but of course June had run up and pushed the inner door shut and called "Nancy! Back around the side door!"

Brenda and Claire notice Tina calling to Tom and plan some dress up

Tom cried "Oh no!" as he was left standing in the porch, in Pam's pretty apron and her headscarf, holding the baby doll. He grimaced as he checked the street and especially Tina and turned as he saw her wheeling her doll,

back up her driveway, towards him and heard her call "Hi Pam! Bring your dolls pram over, to play with me!" He sighed and not wanting to chance her, running across the street to see him. He stepped out the door holding the doll and around the side to the driveway and ran up to get in the side door. Tina wondered why big Pam, was acting so strangely, but shrugged it off and just turned her doll's pram to wheel her Cindy doll, on up towards the garage again, saying, "Don't worry Cindy doll, I'm sure Pam will come over and play dollies with me and Julie later on!" The ladies again had spied the figure back in the pink apron and headscarf exit, into his porch and then out and disappear up his driveway, carrying his dolly.

However, they did notice Tina down the calling across to him, thinking "Oh dear! That little girl has spotted him!" adding "I wonder what she'll say!" as they laughed, but were surprised, when she didn't screech and run over to tease him silly.

Brenda laughed "I think she must have thought, it was his sister Pam, in her apron and headscarf, carrying her dolly about!" as Claire laughed "Oh Brenda, he must have been nearly wetting himself, when she called over to him, asking him to play dollies with her!"

Brenda laughed "He'll dread her realize, it was him in his apron and headscarf, with Pam's dolls pram!" Claire asked, "You going to tell?" but she laughed "I'm sure if we keep stumps, he'll do something for us!" as Claire asked, "What?" as she laughed "I don't have any children! Do you?" as she shook her head and heard Brenda say, "It might be fun to have our niece Lucy, around to play dress up and dollies in front of us!" as Claire screeched "You don't mean at my place?" as she nodded., but she said, "At mine too!" explaining "We can get some dress up clothes and dollies from charity shops and have him come in, to play with us!" as she gurgled at the thought "Oh the poor boy!"

Brenda then said, "Talking about wetting himself, at some time, he might be spied prancing about in frocks, in our sitting rooms or even the garden and have a little accident!" as Claire gasped "You don't mean?" She nodded, "I doubt baby will tell, on us and so we should start each session, at our place, with a diapering session, to stop our carpets being ruined!" Claire screeched "Oh the poor boy!" as she asked, "When will we go shopping?" as Brenda said, "Tomorrow morning?" as they agreed ten am. They asked each other had they any nappy changing experience and both had done babysitting for girls, with only Brenda having babysat for a few baby boys before. She laughed "It's probably going to be a bit embarrassing for us, seeing his tinkle, for the first time, but after that it should be plain sailing!" Claire giggled, "Embarrassing for us! What's it going to be like for him! He'll be so embarrassed he'll light up the city!" as they laughed.

Pam enters to hear of June having fun with Tom and Nancy and Tina

He sobbed as he entered and called "Tina nearly caught me again and thought it was Pam and called me over to play with her!" as June screeched, and his Mum cuddled him. His Mum scolded "June! You're worse than Pam! I didn't realize!" as she laughed "I'm sure it won't hurt him and as we say, 'there's nothing wrong with a boy in an apron playing dollies!'" June laughed "I often see little Tina, wheeling her dollies about her drive or up and down the street!" adding "I'm sure she'd love to have Tom here, join her wheeling his dolly about the place!" as he sobbed "Please don't tell her! It would be terrible playing dollies with her and her friends!"

His Mum laughed "June! Don't you dare tell her on him!" as she laughed "Course I won't!" as she winked to Tom. Tom removed his headscarf and then pulled Pam's pinny off, to leave him in his own and said, "Please don't tell Tina, on me June?" as she laughed "Of course I won't!" as she kissed his cheek. Tom then realised, when doing the washing up, he would be on show through the kitchen windows and tried to close the curtains. However, his Mum pulled them open and said, "Don't be a ninny in a pinny, Tom!" but gasped as he pulled on the pink headscarf

again as June laughed "Oh! I see we've got Nancy back again!" as she held up, Pam's pink apron, for him and saw him pull it over his blue one again. She giggled, to his Mum "Not sure if you're a boy or a girl!" His Mum scolded "Now June! Stop that!" Tom started the washing up, but his Mum then handed him, Pam's pretty PVC pinny, as he cried "Oh no! Not fair Mum!" as she laughed "If Pam comes back, she'll tell you off for not protecting your apron!"

June laughed "Oh fab! What a pretty pinny!" as his Mum said, "He doesn't have a PVC boys one, so has to borrow Pam's!" adding "Pam's suggested I take him shopping for a boys PVC pinny, saying, if he doesn't join me shopping to get it, she'll choose the prettiest pinny in the shop!" June laughed "Well I hope you'll let him try on, lots of PVC pinnies and pretty aprons, in the shop too!" as he cried "Don't Mum! That would be terrible, if someone from school spied me!" as his Mum laughed. She then fetched the little PVC pinny, Pam had put him into before and said, "Pam threatens him, with this little PVC pinny, from when she was 4 of 5!" as June gurgled "I'd love to see him in that!" as he begged "Please don't make me!"

They stood there watching him and saw Baby Suzie on top of the washing machine. His Mum laughed "You'd never have seen him doing the washing up, last week" turning and asking, "Would she, Tom?" and saw him shake his head and say, "No Mummy!" June said, "Tom! You shouldn't be embarrassed helping your Mummy, with the housework or wearing an apron! We wear aprons all the time!" as he huffed "But you're ….!"

Pam hears of him outing himself to June, about his doll's pram and Jamie

He heard his Mum laugh "There goes that chauvinistic side again!" as Tom complained "I didn't say, it!" as she laughed "But you definitely thought it! Young man! Didn't you?" as he blushed and nodded. He carried on his washing up and then heard the bell go and cried "Oh no! Let me remove these? It might be a flaming mate!" His Mum looked up and laughed "I think it's Pam!" as he grimaced "That's worse!" June stood laughing "Aren't you going to let her in, Tom?" as his Mum went up and opened the door, saying, "June from next door is here!" as Pam giggled, "Is she?" as she called "Hello Mrs Makepeace!" as June giggled, "Call me Aunty June, children!" Pam asked, "What's my dolly pram, doing in the porch?" as they laughed and June said, "Oh somebody wanted to take his dolly for a test drive, around the garden!" as he sobbed "Don't tell her!" as she screeched "You didn't!" adding "I've been keeping Nancy and his dolly, indoors up till now!" as she giggled, "I thought you told me, Mummy, to keep Nancy a secret!" adding "You didn't out him to Aunty June?" as her Mum shook her head "Not at all dear!" His Mum laughed "He actually outed himself!" as she asked, "How?"

His Mum cuddled him and said, "He came around from school and I thought he'd just come in and get changed, to go out to play footy with his mates!" as Pam asked, "What did he do?" as his Mum laughed "I couldn't believe it!" and added "He came in the side door and asked, "Mum! Have you seen my baby doll? Pam's hidden it, beside her Wendy doll!" as June added "I was in the sitting room, speaking to your Mummy, when I suddenly heard him enter and call that out!" adding "I couldn't believe my ears!" Tom sobbed "She could have warned me, she had a visitor!" as Pam screeched "Oh fab! You told Aunty June, yourself!" adding "He probable just wanted someone else to know, how much fun he's having, playing dollies, as he sobbed "I'm not!" as they all laughed.

She saw his Suzie doll in the kitchen and giggled, "I see you've met his Baby Suzie doll!" as June nodded, "She is very sweet, isn't she Tom?" He nodded, "Yes Aunty June!" as Pam laughed "It still doesn't explain her doll's pram, in the porch!" as he cried "Don't tell her?"

June said, "I got Tom, I mean Nancy, to cuddle his dolly, but when he said, he didn't know how to play dollies, I got him to wheel her around the room and then, up the hall!" as Pam giggled, "Did she?" and saw him nod. He huffed "James nearly caught me!" adding "He called for me to play footy and she flaming made me join my Mum at the door, without Suzie and he'd just left down the drive, when she flaming called out!" as June giggled, "Tom!

You forgot your dolly!" as Pam screeched "Oh June! You outed him!" as she laughed "I wonder did Pete hear!" adding "You'll have to think of an excuse when you see him next!" as he blushed "It will be terrible if he Says, in front of the other guys!" Pam laughed "Tom! Just say, you suddenly realised how much fun dollies are!" as he huffed "Very funny!" as she laughed "You could say, you'll show them how to play!" as he sobbed "Mum stop her!" as his Mum cuddled him "Stop that Pam!" June added "I then cheekily, opened the inner door and he ran back to hide, but of course, I called "Oh Tom! You've forgotten your dolly!" and saw him run back, just in time, to see me, wheel his doll's pram, out, into the porch!"

Pam hears about him in the back which meant he can now do laundry

Pam giggled, "Oh what a fab trick!" June added "He had to pop out to get it and luckily no one, was there, but I closed the door on him and told him to wheel his dolly to the back-garden!" as Pam giggled, "Go on! I'm taking notes!" as he grimaced and begged "Please don't Pam!" at the thought of Pam making him do the same. His Mum then said, "I didn't think June would be so cruel to our Tom, sending him to wheel your doll's pram in the garden and so when he got there, I thought he'd prefer to be disguised as Nancy and so provided your pretty pinny and headscarf!" Pam screeched "Oh Mum! You could have given a better disguise and provided one of my frocks!" as his Mum blushed, and June screeched "Oh Pam! You are funny!"

Tom wailed "Not flaming fair! It was bad enough in the garden, but Tina nearly caught me twice!" as Pam gasped "How?" as he huffed "I wheeled the pram around the garden a few times and then they let me in, but she closed the door on me and made me wheel it back around the front again!" Pam laughed "You are naughty Aunty June! At least I've been keeping Nancy, a secret in doors!" and to Tom "Haven't I, dearie?" as they saw him nod, with a large blush on his face. Pam laughed "Mummy, as Nancy is ok, in the back garden, he can now help with the laundry, now!" as her Mum gasped "Oh Pam!" She looked at Tom and laughed, as the way she'd taught Pam to do the laundry was very girly.

He huffed "I'd wheeled the pram around the back garden a few times!" Adding "I was wheeling it back, up the drive, when Tina came out and saw me and asked if I wanted to play dollies with her, thinking I was you!" as Pam screeched "You mean Tina thinks I'm now pushing a dolls pram, about the place and will want me to play dollies with her and Julie?" as they all nodded. She gasped "Tom! That's going to be so embarrassing!" If my girlfriends see me, with my old dolly pram again! They'll tease me rotten!" June gurgled "Just a little bit less embarrassing, when Tina find's out about Tom and has Tom wheeling Baby Suzie with her about the streets!" He cried "Please Pam! Don't tell her? Please Aunty June don't?" as they all laughed, at the thought of big Tom, playing dollies with the little girl and her friends in the streets.

June said, "I told Tom it was good practice anyway for helping his wife with their children when he grows up! Pushing the pram in the streets, but then to the shops and around

town!" Pam gurgled "Well Nancy would need a proper disguise for the shops!" adding "Won't she, Mummy?" as she gripped her school dress and pinafore and bobbed a curtsy, as he wailed "I'm not wearing dresses to wheel a flaming pram around the town!" as his Mum scolded "Stop that, Pam!" adding "The two of you are getting too much for little Tom!" as he sobbed into her body. Pam said, "I'd have thought he'd be in his blue apron for the washing up!" asking "Did you make him wear mine?" as her Mum laughed "He didn't want to be recognised doing the washing up and so became Nancy again!" as Pam laughed "Now! Where's my pretty pink frock?" – not saying, the yellow frock, to put her Mum off the scent, that she knew about his dress up session, as he said, "No way, Pam!" as they laughed.

Pam has him giving and receiving complements and he's to curtsy

June and his Mum laughed, seeing Pam's control, over her big brother, as her Mum said, "Pam! He's had a bad time! We've had him pushing your dolly about in the pram!" Pam giggled, "It's his dolly! I've given Tom it, as an, early birthday present! Haven't I dear?" He nodded, "Yea!" and June laughed, "I know what some lucky boy will get from me, for his birthday too!" adding "Along with some pretty frocks!" as Pam and her Mum gasped, as she said, "I meant, for his dolly!" as his Mum laughed "Naughty girls!" Pam asked, "Do you like your dolly?" and heard him stammer "She's very pretty Pam!" adding "Like you!" hoping that would please her. She gasped, "Oh Tom!" as she gripped her pinafore and bobbed a curtsy to him "Thank you, Tom!" and reached out, she put her arms around him and gave him a kiss!" as he gasped "I don't like kisses!"

However, he was told to tell June and his Mum how pretty they were and received curtsies and kisses from them. She then said, "Tom! You look very sweet, in your pretty pink apron and floral pinny!" as he grimaced "Not funny!" as he gripped his apron and bobbed a curtsy to her "Thank you, Pammy!" and bending over, he gave her a kiss on the check, as she said, "Yuk!" to more laughter. Pam then asked, "What's that Baby Suzie?" as she took his dolly and said, in a small voice "I think Nancy's apron and pinny are nice too!" as he huffed "Funny!" but saw them look at him and he again gripped his apron and bobbed a curtsy "Thank you Baby Suzie!" as Pam said, "Don't forget her kiss!" as he took the doll and kissed it's lips again, to more laughter. Pam said, in the small voice "I also like her pretty headscarf!" adding "But think she'd look prettier in hair ribbons and bows!" as he cried "Oh no!" as June said, "Your dolly's waiting Nancy!" as he again bobbed a curtsy "Thank you Baby Suzie!" Pam said, "Tell Baby Suzie how pretty a dolly she is!"

Her Mum said, "Stop that Pam! Let him finish the dishes! He'll be here all afternoon if you don't stop!" June laughed "Oh Doreen! This is fun, playing curtsies!" adding "Although it's more fun in a skirt or a frock!" adding "Isn't it, Nancy?" as he said, "Funny!" but she said, "Isn't it, Tom!" He said, "Yes Aunty June!" as Pam laughed "I might be able to help you out later, Nancy!" He blushed and her Mum laughed "Don't you dare, Pam!" June said, "He said, he didn't know how to play dollies!" adding "You or your girlfriends must teach him!" as Pam giggled, "We don't normally play dollies, but Julie's little sister, Tina, loves playing and would love to show Tom, how to play!" He begged "Please Pam! Don't tell on me? It would be terrible if Tina and her friends, found out about me! They'd tell everyone and try to make me play outside!" to laughter. June giggled, "Is he shy?" as Pam nodded, "They all are, at first! He just needs some practice!" as Tom huffed "Ha!" as June laughed "At least he's not constrained to the house anymore and can play in the back garden!" as Pam nodded, "He definitely will get a lot of practice wheeling his dollies about the garden, from now on!" as her Mum laughed "Just because, I let June, doesn't mean I'll let you!" but Pam laughed "Mummy you know my Nancy, will do anything I want!" as they laughed.

Pam tells her Mum how she'd dressed him up, when she'd tied his hands

However, June then said, "I'm sure you could help teach him dollies too, Doreen!" as his Mum gasped and laughed "You are terrible June! It's bad enough Pam teasing him about his dollies!" Tom then cried "I've only got one dolly!" to laughter, as June laughed "Poor boy!" adding "I'm sure someone, will get more dollies, very soon from his sweet sister Pam!" adding "and of course new dollies from his Mummy and me, especially for all his birthdays and Christmas too!" as Pam gurgled "Oh fab!" and then said, "Mummy! At least that will take the guessing, out of what to get him, in future, along with some pretty skirts and frocks for him!" as her Mum gasped, as she paused and added "To dress his dollies in, I mean!" as he cried "Don't Mummy! I want a skateboard!" to more laughter.

Pam giggled, "Such a greedy boy – wanting dollies, skirts and frocks and a skateboard!" adding "And I wonder what else!" as she pointed to June's handbag. June laughed "Oh yes! Handbag's are such an important item, to a

girl's wardrobe!" as his Mum said, "Now you two! No handbags! He can't!" but then saw June slide her handbag around his neck, as Pam screeched "What a fab look, for my sweet sister, Nancy!" as her Mum took the bag back and said, "Right June! Off you go! He's had enough!" as she laughed "Poor boy!"

Pam said, "First time! I tied his apron in a knot and when he reached around to undo it, I tied his hands back with the apron ties and he was at my mercy!" as she added "Mum thought I was just in the front room, undoing the knot! but I took Nancy upstairs and played a little dress up with him!" as her Mum gasped "You didn't?" as she nodded "I took him upstairs and popped him into a little skirt!" as his Mum said "Pam you didn't?" as she nodded and then thought he'd suit some prettier underwear!" as they giggled "Never!" as he cried "She flaming took my trousers and undies down and saw my willy and then made me wear flaming panties!" as they screeched. Pam then laughed "I didn't have a magnifying glass and so couldn't see it!" as he blushed, and they laughed.

She then laughed "I finally added my pretty pink frock for him to bob some curtsies to me and a few curtsies to the street!" as her Mum scolded "That was naughty Pam!" as she laughed "I never realized!" as they laughed.

She continued "Then when he was released, I got him into my PVC pinny, but did suggest, he wear one of my little pinnies, from when I was 4 or 5!" adding "It would have looked fab on him!" It gave me lots of time, to tease him, He thinks my pink apron there, looks like a dress from the front!" as June giggled, "He might have a point!" as she looked at, the blushing boy, in the pink apron, with the floral pinny on top. Pam laughed "I was nice and let him remove his girly aprons and run on to play with his mates!" but then gurgled "Though he'd to keep my panties on to play footy!" as they screeched again. He cried "Mum! Let me go upstairs?" His Mum approached and hugged him, saying, "Now Tom! It's just your chauvinist ways, that makes all this worse! Just wash one more cup and then, I'll let Pam finish off!"

June leaves and Pam gets Tom to dress as schoolgirl Nancy

June went in to collect her handbag and called Tom in to say, goodbye. June picked her bag, as she laughed "I'd better get back, now! Thanks for the tea, Doreen and thanks Tom, for giving me a lot of fun!" as he grimaced and heard Pam say, "Come on Tom! Show Aunty June out!" He cried "I'm not going to the door, like this!" as June called "Bye Nancy!" as they laughed and Doreen showed June out, with Pam giggling "That sounded, a fun afternoon! Pam called "Bye Aunty June! See you later!" June called "Bye Pam! Bye Tom! Keep up the good housework!" as his Mum laughed "The poor boy! He's so embarrassed!" as June laughed "I'm sure it won't hurt and I'm sure it's improved his behaviour!" His Mum laughed "It certainly has! He does what he's told now and helps around the house, but I'm not sure about the girly bits to it, his dollies and pretty aprons!" June laughed "At his age, it won't hurt! Different if he was fifteen or something!" as his Mum giggled, "Hopefully he'll have grown out of it by then!" as June giggled, "Hopefully he'll have another pinny and lots more dollies, by then!" to more titters. He removed his headscarf and set it on the washing machine and entered the hallway in Pam's apron and pinny, holding his dolly and heard her say, "Sorry for teasing you Tom!" adding "You do look sweet in her aprons and carrying your dolly!" as he blushed and begged "Please don't tell anyone, Mrs?" as she reminded him "Aunty June!" as he huffed "Aunty June!" June entered her house and closed her front door, setting her handbag down, she sat down and laughed her head off. It was true she didn't have any children, but she had some nieces who loved playing dollies and dress up and thought it would be lovely for them to meet Tom, Pam and their dollies. She wondered if she should phone them but decided to postpone the event. She got up and popped on her apron, to prepare her dinner, giggling "Pity I don't have Tom in his pink pinny to help!"

Tom had removed Pam's pink apron and disappeared upstairs to his room, with his dolly of course, knowing it was too late to join his mates, for some football and lay down on his bed, quietly sobbing about his girly display in front of June. Meanwhile Pam was up in her room, changing out of her school uniform and into a skirt and blouse. She

laughed as she placed her school dress and pinafore on the hanger and hung it up on the outside of her wardrobe again, giggling at the prospect of seeing Tom, dressed as a schoolgirl.

She knocked on his door and heard him plead for her to leave him be, but she took him into her own room and locked her door and whispered "Just give me a giggle! Get into my school dress and pinafore before we go down to dinner!" He begged "Please don't?" but she said "Hurry up or its curtsies to the street too!" and saw him remove the jumper and then his shirt and take her dress and pull it over his head. She laughed and whispered in his ear "Let me Nancy!" as she undid his belt and then his trousers and then pulled them down, giggling at the small bulge in his panties but let the dress down, as she got him to step out of them. She then handed him her pinafore and giggled as he pulled it over his head and down over her dress, as she laughed "One day hopefully not too far off, Nancy can attend school like this!" as he blushed and said "No way Pam!" and hoped she was joking. She slid a few hair ribbons into his hair and gave him a kiss laughing away as he begged "Let me out of these?" as she said "Just a quicky!" and took a photo of schoolgirl Nancy!" She said "Sure you don't want to show Mummy?" adding "She might get you your own dress and pinafore for school!" as he cringed and changed back into his boys clothes.

Pam disguises herself as Nancy over to Tina and Julie to help Tom

Pam said "Don't worry! June won't tell!" as they exited his room. She bounded downstairs and offered to help her Mum with the dinner, as she popped on her pink pinny. Her Mum said, "Hi dear! How is he?" as Pam giggled, "I consoled the poor dear but did mention that Aunty June might increase his dolly collection on his birthday!" as his Mum scolded "Don't taunt him like that!" as they got on with the dinner. Pam told her Mum "I warned Tom he's to check who's about before shouting out, about his dollies!" as her Mum laughed "I couldn't believe it! I had just said, you weren't here, when he suddenly said, "Where's my dolly and that you had hidden it near to yours!" She continued "I gasped and laughed but then heard June laugh and realized she'd heard every word!" She added "Tom tried to make an excuse, saying, you had asked him to find your dolly for you, but I knew she'd heard and said, "June won't tell on you! and so his horrid time, with the dollies began!" with Pam giggling her head off.

Pam ran to the front room and looked out, giggling, as she saw Julie and her sister playing with her dollies and giggled, as she knew they'd love to have seen her big brother playing dollies and pushing his pram. However, she wanted to take things slowly with Tom wrt Julie and especially Tina, as far as Nancy goes. She still had to think of a way to go, without letting her Mum know, that she knew about her putting Tom in her frock.

Pam realized Tina had seen him, in her pretty apron and decided to play along, as she picked up his headscarf and pulled her apron on again and tied her headscarf around her and said, "Leave my pretty pinny back in the kitchen, Nancy, I mean Tom" as he huffed "Very funny Pam!"

She called "Mum! I'm just popping over to speak to Julie!" as her Mum said, "Fine dear!" as she saw her in her own pinny and the headscarf and asked, "What are you up to?" as she laughed "Saving somebody's bacon! So that Julie and Tina think it's been me, been prancing about, wheeling his dolly pram, around the place!" as his Mum laughed "Good girl!" as she asked "What about you Nancy?" as he cringed "Thanks Pammy!" as she gave him a kiss and taking her Wendy doll, she exited into the porch and popped her doll into the pram and lifting it down, she wheeled the pram out and across the street and heard Julie screech "Pam! When you said, you'd started playing dollies again, I never thought I'd see you wheel them across the street, in your doll's pram!" as Tina giggled, "Julie! It's fun to play dollies!" Pam said, "That's why I'm wearing the headscarf, to try and disguise me from being recognized by girls in the street!" as Julie laughed "Good thinking! but I'm not sure if I'd wheel Tina's dolly pram around the street!" as Tina laughed "It's fun looking like a Mummy!" to more laughter.

Pam said, "I can't stay long, I just came over to show you, that I've started playing dollies again!" as Julie laughed "Don't let me see you sucking your thumb or a baby's dummy?"

Tina gurgled and said, "Yes Julie! Let me see you, with a dummy in?" as her sister said, "Not a chance, you little imp!"

Tina thought he was Pam due to headscarf and Pam plans to use June's

Tina asked, "How come you wouldn't play earlier, when I saw you wheeling your pram up your drive and then carrying your dolly again later on?" as Pam laughed "Oh! Aunty June was around and played a trick on me!" as Julie laughed "What?" as Pam said, "It's a secret, but it was funny!" as Tina giggled, though, not understanding the joke. Julie asked, "You going to come over tonight to play?" as Pam nodded, "Though too many girls might see me, with my pram. So, I probably will only bring Wendy with me in a bag!" as Tina huffed "Oh bring your doll's pram, too!" Julie laughed "So you are worried about being seen by girls, who might tease you?" as Pam nodded, blushing a bit. Julie laughed "Mum's teased me a bit, since I started playing dollies again!" adding "And squirt hear keeps wanting me to play more and more!" as Pam laughed and said, "Though, it is fun!"

Pam realised that now with June as an accomplice, she can make Tom go around to hers and play lots of girly games with him, hidden from their Mum. He'd hate wearing skirts and frocks in June's front room and there's no way, she'll let him close the blinds, giggling "Poor boy!" She'd also have Nancy play dollies too, in his frocks, skipping about the place and doing ballet in skirts and tutus, dreading Julie, Tina or other girls or ladies recognize him, but then even worse, if one of his mates spied him.

She returned back home from Julie's and entered the kitchen and heard her Mum say, "Pam! Dinner's on the table!" and called "Tom! Dinner's ready!" as Pam went into the living room to eat and heard Tom's footsteps on the stairs and saw him enter, carrying his dolly, followed by his Mum. He huffed "Can't you let me off, carrying my dolly, till the weekend!"

Pam said, sternly "No way! You made my life hell, since I was a baby and you have to pay the price! Just get your pinny and eat your din-dins!" He got up and taking his doll, went into the kitchen to get his blue apron, as her Mum said, "Now Pam! No treating him like a baby!" Pam laughed "The thought never occurred to me, but now you've mentioned it, he would suit a dummy!" and heard her gasp and laugh.

Tom returned wearing the tabard and saw his Mum look at him and smile, as he asked, "What were you talking about?" as Pam giggled, "Nothing Tom! Just a possible future punishment, if you are very naughty again!" as her Mum tucked into her own dinner, to stop herself, continuing the baby conversation, which would have really embarrassed, Tom. She said, "Eat your dinner, Tom!" as he tucked in and heard Pam giggling at the thought of Tom with a dummy in his mouth or even better a baby bottle!" as she hiccupped and excused herself, as she went upstairs to stifle her giggling. She calmed herself and returned downstairs and asked "Got much homework, to do?" He huffed "No! I'm playing footy with my mates! I missed it after school, because of her next-door!" as Pam laughed "Now Tom! I might let you play footy for an hour, but after washing the dishes, I want you to play with me, for a while! I'll let you play from 6.30 till 7.30 ok?" as he grimaced and nodded, "Ok!" Knowing she knew about his being dressed up.

They finished their dinner and Pam helped Tom do the dishes.

TANIA'S PREPARES HER YOUNGER BROTHER PETER

Abi and Sandra tell at school about big Harry acting as a baby girl

At primary school both Abigale and Sandra got dressed in their school dress and pinafore and attended separate primary schools and of course, couldn't keep it in, as they burst out giggling, in their separate classes. Abi called out "I saw the funniest thing yesterday!" as the girls asked, "What?" as she said, "Come over here!" as she led them to a corner and said, "Mummy and me were walking back from a friend's house, when we saw a big ten year old boy, in two girly aprons and a girly headscarf with his Mummy!" as they laughed "He wasn't?" but she nodded adding "as we laughed our heads off at him! However, the lady next door, then called out 'Thanks for helping with the housework and I'm glad you liked your new pretty aprons!' as we giggled!" adding "However, she then called out to his Mummy "Let Harry remove his pretty girly aprons!" and his Mum said, "Ok Harry! You can remove them!" as the girls said, "No! He should have kept them on!" but gasped, as Abi said, "Next thing Harry said, he was enjoying his pretty aprons and wanted to keep them on!" as they gasped "Never?" as she laughed "I swear!"

Another asked, "Is he a sissy boy?" as she laughed "I don't know, but then she asked him, what age he started playing dollies from?" and next thing the big sissy was saying, "Since I was four or five!" as they gasped "He must have been a sissy!" as she laughed and said, "But next thing the lady was out the front door and at his gate, holding a big dolly and he took it and showed it to me and my giggling Mum!" as they gurgled "Oh fab!"

She continued "But the lady took us in and told us about Harry from a young age!" as they giggled, "Was he a sissy?" as she nodded but said, "At least that's what the lady June said, but Mummy thinks he might not have been and he's been made to sound like a sissy!" as they giggled, but the teacher then entered and told them to settle down. They all took their seats and the teacher Miss James told them to get their books out. The class took their seat, but the girls couldn't help giggling and she asked, "What is it girls?" as a girl called out "Abi met a big ten year old sissy, who wears pretty girly aprons and plays dollies!" as the teacher asked, "What?" as Abi called "and wears dresses and nappies too!" as the class gasped and the teacher giggled, "Now Abi stop fibbing!" as she laughed "Honest Miss, he does! He was given the chance of playing football, in his trousers or a frock and carrying a handbag and hair ribbons and he chose the frock!" She gasped "Oh Abi, he must be confused! Not knowing if he's a girl or a boy!" as they laughed. Some boys called "He sounds a right poofter!" and others called "Yea! A right girly!" as the teacher laughed "It's well we don't have any boys like that, in our class?"

Abi finds out which class Peter's sister nine-year old Tania is in

Abi giggled, "Funny you should say that, Miss! I was thinking how much fun, lots of our boys would have, playing dollies and dress up!" as they gasped and the girls giggled, and a girl Amanda called "Yes Miss, Johnny and David

would look fun in a dress and pinafore!" as they called "No way, bug off, Mandy!" as she gurgled "and skipping and playing dollies with us!" as the girls giggled, and another Penny called "Oh Marcus, Freddy and Pete would look sweet too!" as the boys said, "Stuff that!" One Dave said, "You girls try anything girly and my bro will do you!" as another Pete called "My sister will get you, if you try anything girly to me!" as Abi laughed and thought "I'm sure his sister would love it, if he started playing dolls and dress up!"

She found out which class, his sister Tania was in and approached her in the playground, saying, "Hi! I hear you're Pete's, big eight-year old sister Tania!" as she laughed "Yea! Who are you?" as she said, "I'm Abigale from his class!" as she asked, "What's up?" as she said, "I told my class a funny story, about seeing a big ten year old boy, in girly aprons, then panties and a frock!" as Tania screeched "You're joking?" as Abi shook her head and "Honest and nappies too!" as she gurgled "Never!" as she laughed "The girls and me were saying, it might be fun to have some boys, in our class in dresses and playing dollies!" as his sister gasped "You'd like me to help to get my Peter, to turn into a girly boy?" as Abi nodded, giggling. Tania said, "Well! I want to meet this big sissy of yours!" as Abi said, "Can you come back after school?" but Tania said, "You get out earlier than us, big girls!" but Abi said, "We'll meet you at the girls entrance to school at 3.45 as Tania agreed and ran to see her brother and saw him playing football, with his mates and said, "Pete! Come here a tick!" as he said, "Yea, what?" as she said, "Tell Mummy, I'm off to see a girlfriend after school, but will be home for dinner around five!" as Pete said, "Ok!" as she ran back and told Abi "Fine! I've told Pete to tell Mum, I'll be back around five!" as Abi laughed "You'll kill yourself!" as they ran on to their classes, with Tania laughing, at what might come to pass.

At three, a smiling Abi, met her Mum and laughed "Mummy! Did you get some girly things for baby?" as she nodded, "Big plastics and more baby stuff and some frocks too?" as she said, "Ok! We'd better go on home!" but Abi laughed "I've been a bit naughty and told the girls at school and then the class and have arranged to meet a big girl, after school here, at the gates!" as her Mum laughed "Oh Abi!" as she told them about school and Peter and his big sister. Tania exited her class, without telling her classmates, about Abi, but excitedly, made her way out and saw Abi and her Mum at the gates and called "Hi! I'm Tania!" as Abi's Mum laughed "I hope you have a spare pair of panties, you might wet yourself!" as Abi giggled, "I thought you only got enough nappies, for big Harry!" as Tania gurgled "So! She is serious, about the boy and his nappies, then?" as her Mum nodded, "It's all true, my dear!" as she told Tania, more about Harry, as they made their way back home, to Abi's.

Tania then sees Harry dressed up and hears he wore dresses to school

They had walked quite quickly and were pretty sure they'd made it back home, before Harry. Her Mum led them into the house and offered Tania and Abi a drink and some biscuits, but said, "Abi! Keep an eye out, for Harry returning from school! He might try to skip on bye!" They saw lots of older schoolboys and girls of various ages, most of Abi's schoolfriends, having left for home at 3pm and so were already home and some girls were out, pushing a doll's pram or skipping in the street. Abi pointed to a few boys and said, "There's some of sissy Harry's, football friends!" as Tania giggled, "They are big boys! Do they know about him?" as Abi shook her head, "I wanted to tell, but Mummy said, 'Not yet!'" as they laughed. Her Mum brought in some milk and an orange juice and some biscuit's, as they tucked in, when Abi gasped and giggled, "I think that's Harry in a dress and his aprons, Mummy!" as her Mum giggled, as did Tania, who looked at the two big girls, one in normal school dress, smiling and giggling a lot, but the other in more hair ribbons and mincing with her school shopper and a handbag, but also, other girls giggling at him.

Harry was escorted back home from school in his dress and pinafore, with the giggling Natalie and a few girlfriends. She was carrying his boy's clothes and he begged for them back, but she took him home and introduced him, to her laughing Mum, who'd seen him at lunch, but now realised, he'd had to attend classes, in her summer dress and pinafore, but gasped and her daughter raised them, to show his nappies too. She gasped "I hope you

didn't see or touch, his 'You know what'?" as her daughter giggled, "Us girls, must have some little secrets!" as her Mum slapped her hand, as she added "Anyway! It's good practice, for my babysitting experience, Mum!" as she laughed and heard him say, about Abi, as they giggled.

Natalie said, "I want to meet this little Abi and her Mum!" as he gasped "No! Not fair!" as she let him lead her to Abi's house, with him still wearing her dress and pinafore with the aprons on top, but having left their blazers at her house. He heard girls giggling, as they saw him in the dress and aprons and mincing with his girly bag, along with a handbag too. This was bad enough till he got to Abi's.

A smiling Abi was stood at her door and laughed "Oh Harry! Did you attend classes in a dress today?" He sobbed and saw her Mum and call "Its been terrible! This girl Natalie, saw me, trying to remove my aprons and at school tricked me, into wearing a pinafore and then a dress too!" as Natalie called "I loved it even more, when I realised you'd put Harry into nappies too!" as Harry called "Not so loud, Natalie!" as they all giggled. However, then Tania appeared and giggled, "Is this the big sissy?" as he sobbed "Who's this?" as they led him and Natalie into the house and into the living room and all sat down. Tania said, "I've a young bro in Abi's class and wondered, how I could get him to be a girly like you!" as he huffed "I'm not a sissy girly boy!" as they all laughed, as Abi's Mum said, "Tell her what happened to you?"

Harry Says, how he used to be a real macho boy till Sally tricked him

He huffed "It wasn't fair! I was like any other boy, not doing housework or wearing an apron and was a bit naughty, talking to Mum, when she happened to say, to our neighbour, Sally about my bad behaviour!" Tania asked, "What did she do?" as he huffed "Mum took me around to hers, for a cup of tea, saying, she'd a present for me!" as he huffed "It was a trick!" as Abi asked, "What did Aunty Sally do?" He continued "She pretended to have a new shirt for me and took me upstairs, to try it on! I removed my jumper and then the shirt, as she held up the shirt and got me to feed my arms, into the sleeves, but they were sewn together and my arms were held tight, behind my back!" adding "I called for Mum to help me, but Sally had told her to stay downstairs and ignore me!"

They giggled, "What did she do to you?" as he sobbed "She flaming dressed me up, in girly outfit's aprons, skirts, hair ribbons in my hair and took photos of me!" as he sobbed "She even took my underpants and put me in frilly panties!" as they gurgled. She warned me, not to play up, when released and soon had undone my shirt sleeves, or she'd show the photos!" adding "She then removed the shirt, but she then flaming put me into a nightdress and then slid my arms into the frock for more photos and then let me dress normally apart from the panties and nighty. However, she then popped the two aprons on me and asked me if I wanted to remove them, but you know what she'd done, she pulled my nighty out of my zip, so if I removed my aprons, Mum would see my nighty and panties and so I'd to keep the big apron on and say, I was enjoying my aprons!"

Adding "She took me downstairs and my Mum gasped as she saw me in the big girl's apron, but she then said, she was only joking, and I could remove my aprons. My Mum thought I'd jump at the chance, but couldn't believe it, when I said, I would keep my apron on, to do the dishes! With Mum wondering why, I wanted to wear the girly apron and thinking I'd been replaced with a robot ", to more laughter. He added "'However, when I offered to do the dishes, Sally pulled out, a little girl's PVC piny and tied it to my apron!' as Mum laughed at me, but I couldn't protest!"

He continued "However, then it was time to go home and I thought she'd take me into the living room, to let me hide my nighty and then remove them, but she didn't and I'd to go out with Mum and wear them out around home, when Abi and you, spied me and she made me sound, a right sissy boy, playing dollies and stuff!" as they screeched "fab!"

Tania laughed "I think I can arrange for my little brother, to become a real girly boy and start wearing my pretty aprons and then frocks!" as Abi screeched "Oh fab! Can you bring him around here to play dolly's and dress up, with me too?" as Tania nodded, "I don't see why not! In fact, I'll make him say, to boys in your class, that he fancies you!" Abi gurgled "Oh yes! I can have a sissy boyfriend and give him lots of sissy kissies!" as Tania screeched, but said, "Yuk!" Abi's Mum said, "You should give your bro lots of kisses, when he says 'how nice you are and how he likes your pretty skirt and dresses and complements your Mum too', with a nice curtsy and a kiss too for him!"

Tania, Natalie and the girls help change Harry's diapers

Tania gurgled and then asked, "Are you really wearing nappies?" He sobbed "Not fair, girls!" as Caroline asked, "Has baby wet his nappy, again?" as he shook his head, but knowing he had, as she laughed "If baby is lying, he'll be sorry!" He nodded, "It was when she appeared, and I thought you'd loads of girls, to see me!" as Tania gurgled "Oh you, big baby!" as she laughed "Can I help change his nappies?" He cried "No way!" but Caroline laughed "Well! My little girl can't see, but sure you want to see?" as she nodded, giggling with embarrassment, as Natalie laughed "A teacher and me changed his nappy earlier and put him into a diaper too!" Abi's Mum said, "Abi! You go up and change out of your school uniform, while we see to Harry!" as she called "Oh! Why can't I see?" as Tania laughed "I did used to see my little brother's willy, when he was a baby!"

Caroline asked, "So Harry! What do you call that, in your nappies?" as he blushed "It's my baby-pee-pee!" as Tania and Natalie gasped "It's not! What a fab name, for it!" as Caroline asked, "Ask him why he calls it that!" She giggled, and asked him and heard him stammer "Because it's only the size of a little baby boy's Baby-pee-pee!" as they all screeched and she said, "If it's that small, I don't see why little Abi, can't take a peek, at his tiny baby-pee-pee!" as her Mum said, "Well Abi! If you're quick!" as she ran up the stairs to change.

Her Mum got the baby changing mat and said, "We'll lay it down on the floor to change baby!" as he begged "Please don't, Aunty Caroline?" as she laid him down on his back and pulled up his dresses, to expose his nappies with the plastic bag pants, as Tania gurgled "Have you an apron to protect my school dresses?" as Caroline laughed "I think you can borrow Sissy Harry's aprons!"

She laughed and undid his PVC pinny and then his apron and pulled them on herself. She laughed "Oh fab!" as they giggled. Caroline laughed, as she pulled out the large plastic baby pants and said, "These baby pants should fit him!" as they all laughed. Caroline asked, "You sure Tania?" as she nodded, "Please!" as Caroline popped the dummy into Harry's mouth, but also the baby bonnet onto his head, to screeches, as Tania pulled some plastic gloves on, as did Caroline, but Natalie pulled some, on just in case. Caroline pulled the plastic bag down and then undid his diaper, pulling it down to expose his disposables, to more giggles. Caroline pulled his legs up and said, "Natalie! Can you hold his legs up and we can do his naughty botty!" as she held them and peering down into his face, laughed as Caroline pulled the disposable from his penis as the girls gurgled "Oh fab! It is a tiny baby-pee-pee!" He blushed at the two girls and Abi's Mum, looked down on him. She said, "Just pull baby up Natalie, to get his other nappy off!" as she pulled his legs up and laughed as they pulled the disposable from his bottom and laughed again. She took some wet wipes and asked, "Tania! Want to wipe baby clean?" as she nodded, and gurgled, as she started running the wipes over his bottom and then his front and giggled, as she wiped his willy, asking "Is baby all clean?" as he blushed.

The girls start tickling his willy and one even goosed his botty

However, then Abi came running down the stairs and screeched when she entered the kitchen and saw Harry with his bottom in the air and then gasped "What's that, Mummy?" Her Mum laughed "What is it, baby?" as she removed his dummy and he sobbed "It's my baby-pee-pee!" She screeched "Oh! It looks funny!" but she was

told to ask why he called it that and couldn't believe it, when he said, "because it's the size of a little baby boy's, baby-pee-pee!" as they all screeched and Abi's Mum, laughed "Fibber!" However, then a laughing Tania, tickled it and he cried "Oh no! Not fair!" as Natalie laughed "I'll have to try that, on my baby boyfriend, too!" She asked, "Can you hold his legs?" as she knelt down and started tickling his willy and tiny balls, as he started wriggling to more laughter and Abi asked, "Can I, Mummy?" but she shook her head "Sorry! Leave it to the big girls!" as she huffed "Not fair!" Tania laughed "She can give him a little tickle!" as her Mum laughed and said, "Just a little tickle!" as she bent down and reaching out she grabbed it, as he cried "Oh no!" as she tried to lift him with it. Her Mum gasped and giggled, and took her hand away and said, "Just tickle it!" as the little girl tickled his willy and laughed "It feels silly!"

Her Mum handed the gel and talcum powder to Tania, who gurgled as she spread some onto her glove and started rubbing it over his bottom and then between his legs and then his willy, as Caroline said, "Don't forget beside his baby-pee-pee!" as he blushed and felt her gel him again. She took the talcum powder and sprinkled it over his bottom and then front and heard Natalie, ask "Can I apply a disposable?" as they handed her one and saw her apply it over his bottom, but had taken some gel onto a finger and goosed him, saying, "We forgot his naughty botty!"

He cried "Not fair, Natalie!" as she applied his disposable again and then Tania applied the disposable over his willy. Next, they were rolling him onto the diaper and soon, it was pinned up, to laughter. Next came Caroline's new plastic baby pants and she laughed as she stood him up and pulled them up, over his diaper. Tania laughed "I can't wait to get my little bro, Peter, back into nappies and plastics!" as Caroline laughed "Oh! Wouldn't that be cruel?" but said "What about just making him, wear your aprons, to help you and your Mummy, with housework?" She shook her head "Oh! I might just let him off with dollies and dress up!" but Abi giggled, "Oh popping Peter into nappies and plastics, would be so much fun!" adding "If we can get him to attend school, like sissy Harry, in a dress and pinafore! It would be fab!" as Tania gasped and gurgled "Oh Abi!" as she then added "And then we might try to trap some other boys, in class, till the whole class of boys, end up in dresses and pinafores!" as Tania called out "And nappies!" as they all screeched.

But then Natalie had a thought and gasped "I know we can't do this, with big Harry here!" as they asked, "What?"

Natalie suggests a large pram to transport a big baby sissy boy about

Natalie gurgled "If your baby bro is small enough, like your Peter and the pram is big enough, you could maybe get him, into a girly pink pram, to wheel about the garden!" as the place erupted, in laughter. Caroline laughed "Who's a lucky boy, he's too big for a pram, or else he might be wheeled around the streets and town shopping, to be shown off, as a big baby!" Natalie screeched "Oh girls! It seems a shame to leave baby Harry out, of being put back into a pram!" as he begged "Please Natalie, Please girls! Don't put me into a big pram! That would be the worst!" Tania gurgled "I can imagine my little baby bro Peter, begging not to be wheeled about in a pretty girly pink, pram!" as Abi said, "and given his baby bottle!" Her Mum said, "Funny you should say, that! I'll just get baby's milk on, before we take him around to Sally's, for his sissy football with his Mummy!" He begged "Not milk!" as they giggled. Natalie knelt down and started tickling his plastics and was copied by the little girls. He sobbed "Not flaming fair!"

Natalie laughed "Your lucky you've a big girls dresses on and not a little girl's, that would show off baby's nappies to the street!" as he begged "Please make sure, I have big long skirts and dresses, when in nappies!" They all started kissing him and saying, "Keep up saying, girly things and we'll be nice to baby!" as he cringed. Caroline said, "We'd better get Harry back around to his Mum in his boy's clothes, or at least to Sally's where she'll pop him into a frock, for to play Sissy football with his Mummy again, before coming back to us!" He huffed "Not fair girls!" as they stood him up and pulled his dresses off, but then pulled his trousers and shirt and jumper on,

but undid his trousers, as they fed the girly aprons on again and had him mince around with the girly bags again, looking a real sissy. Natalie asked Tania, where she lived and said, "I'll take this little girl home!" as she took her hand, saying, "I want to meet your little brother!"

Harry's Mum was looking out and gasped as she saw him mincing around the corner in his boy's clothes, but the girly aprons with Abi and her Mum. She laughed, as Sally met them and took Harry inside and a few minutes later, her blushing boy, was skipping around the garden in a frock and aprons, over his trousers with his handbag again. When she came out to the back, Sally popped 2 chairs either side of the fence for him, to step over and start playing sissy football, with his laughing Mum. Abi and her Mum entered the garden with Caroline and asked, "So Harry! Do you want to remove your frock and play football with your sweet Mummy in your trousers, or your frock as a girly!" Of course, he had his trousers undone, to expose his nappies and plastics and so said, he wanted to wear his frock and so before climbing over, he removed his trousers and sounded a complete sissy, to his Mum again. She laughed "Oh Harry, I don't know how they've turned you into this sweet girly boy, but it is funny!" as he cringed and said, "Ha!" as he minced over with his handbag and kicked the ball, as they told him to show off his dribbling skills, to his Mummy. Next thing he was dribbling the ball, but with his arms outstretched with his handbag over one elbow as he extreme minced, to screeches of laughter.

Peter's Mum hears all the girly and baby things wrt Harry

Then Tania and Natalie came out and were introduced to his Mum, who gasped as Tania said, "We plan to trap my little brother Peter, who's in Abi's class and make him be Abi's sissy boyfriend!" She asked who Natalie was and she replied, "Oh! I'm in Harry's year at school, but a different class, but he said, he fancied me, and I'll let him be my sissy boyfriend!" as his Mum laughed "Lucky boy!" Natalie laughed "Lucky girly! but it is more fun having a sweet girly boyfriend, to play dollies, skipping and dress up with!" as his Mum laughed "Well! Keep him indoors and no showing him off, to too many of your friends!" as she laughed "Just a few!" Harry blushed, knowing the whole school knew, he wore a school dress and pinafore and even wore them home.

Natalie escorted Tania home and they entered their street, where they saw her little bro Peter, playing footy with his mates and laughed as Tania pointed Peter out. Pete saw his big sister with a bigger girl and saw them enter his house. She rang the bell and her Mum came out and Tania kissed her Mum and said, "Mummy! This is a girlfriend, who's just escorted me home!" as her Mum said, "Hi Natalie! Like to come in?" as she smiled and nodded, and said, "Tania's told me, all about her dollies and pretty clothes and I'd love to see!" Her Mum laughed "You still play dollies, at your age?" and led them up to her room and said, "I'll get you two some refreshments, then!" as she left them to it. Tania showed her lots of her dollies and some clothes to dress them up, as Natalie took one and undressed it, before dressing it in a new frock again.

She then showed her lots of her pretty dresses, but more importantly, those from when she was six, the same age as Peter and they gurgled, as they started selecting some pretty clothes and putting them away in carrier bags. They heard her Mum coming up and Natalie quickly took the dolly she had changed and sat there holding it. Her Mum brought up some refreshments and laughed, as she saw Natalie, with the doll and heard Tania laugh "Natalie couldn't resist, changing Cloie into a new frock!" as her Mum laughed "Gosh! I stopped playing dollies around 8 or 9! I'm sure you'll soon get tired of playing dollies Tania!" She laughed "Now Mummy! Dollies are fun!" as she laughed "Yea! When's the last time I saw you wheeling your dolly down the street, like you did, when you were a little girl?"

Tania talks about Peter playing dress up and pretty aprons

Natalie laughed "Oh Mummy Says, that even boys, should be taught to play dollies!" as Tania giggled, and her Mum laughed "She's got a brother Peter and you wouldn't get him playing dollies, in a million years!" Natalie explained

"It's so that, when he grows up and gets married and has children, he doesn't leave dressing and undressing his kids, to his wife and can help with dressing and undressing the baby and kids! Even changing the nappies"

Tania laughed "Hear that Mummy? You are being naughty, not teaching Peter to play dollies and change nappies too!" as her Mum laughed and slapped her wrist, saying, "Naughty girl!" Natalie asked her "What age is he?" as his Mum said, "He's five, almost six!" and took them into the front room and pointed to the young boys, playing football and said, "The one in the grey jumper with the ball, Peter!"

Natalie laughed "Well! It's not too late, for him to learn!" as his Mum laughed "Now I can't expect him to learn to play dollies! He'd scream, blue murder!" Natalie laughed "If you keep it a secret, I'm sure Tania wouldn't tell!" as his Mum laughed "Yea! See that flying pig! If he started playing with her dollies and what else?" Tania giggled, "You don't mean dress up and maybe wearing my pretty hair ribbons?" as her Mum said, "Shush! You'll make me wet myself! Any way, his Dad would go mad, if he started acting all girly!" as Natalie said, "There are ways to keep it a secret, when his Dad's in!" as Tania asked, "How?" She laughed "If you have a female neighbour, who's game for a laugh, he can go out to play football, but instead is sent down to hers, where you or Tania join her, to play dollies or dress up!" adding "or help peg out the laundry or do the ironing!" as she asked, "Do they both help you with housework?"

Peter's Mum answered, "Well Tania often helps me, with the washing up or some housework, pegging out the laundry or what not!" as Tania laughed "In my pretty aprons!" as her Mum said, "Not always! Though I do say, they protect your skirts or dresses!" Natalie asked, "What about Peter?" as his Mum said, "Once in a while, I get him to help with the dishes and very occasionally, to peg out his clothes, but he wouldn't go near her or my dresses and stuff!" as Tania laughed "I help peg out his silly boy's clothes and he should help peg out my frocks and stuff!" as her Mum laughed "Now! See that flying pig!" Natalie laughed "Oh! Abi showed me a fun way, to make the laundry or airing clothes, lots more fun!" as Tania asked, "How?" as she said, "I'll leave it till another day!" as they begged, but she wouldn't say.

141

PART D

JUNE GETS TOM A BOY DOLLY AND HE'S TO SUCK ITS DUMMY

June, Brenda and Claire head to town to get Dress up clothes

Pam plans for Tom to use June's house for dollies and dress-up

Pam loved that June had found out about Tom's dolly and aprons and seamed to tease Tom, as much as she did. She thought it would be fun to pop around to Junes, with Tom and play dollies or other girly things. She also loved the fact that neither her Mum nor Tom, realized that she'd instigated the full plan and June hadn't spilt the beans and kept it a secret. Pam then thought 'I'll get Tom to tell Mum he's going out to play footy, but instead he's to go next door, where, June will start him off, playing girly games with him, initially indoors, so Mummy doesn't see or realize. I'll of course pop out to join him and have fun with Nancy, without Mum realizing. When we let Tom go, I'll have him say, "I had a really fun time with a new guy Gordy!" as she laughed "Life with him is going to be so much fun!"

Pam slips around to June's to explain her plan and June readily agrees, but is annoyed she can't take him outside or expose him to other little girls and stuff, but Pam Says, "I want to take is slowly with Nancy, without Mummy knowing, what I've been doing to Tom!" as June laughed "It's going to be fun!" asking "What have you planned?" as she replied, "Oh Dollies of course, Curtsies, Ballet in a skirt or tutu and then dress up of course!" June laughed "You do realize, when playing dress up with him, you might spy his naughty bits?" as Pam gurgled "He's always told me to scat and threatened me, if Mum was changing his trousers or anything!" but I did happened to spy it the other night!" adding "although, I now make him wear my frilly panties, when he returns from school!" as June gasped "You don't?" as she nodded, as she added "and have noticed a little bulge in them, when I spy him in them! Though it's a very small bulge!" as she giggled, "I've thought of a wonderful name for his willy!" as June asked, "What?" as Pam laughed "His Baby-pee-pee!" as June screeched and heard her say, "and when asked 'why?' He's to explain 'because it's the size of a little baby boy's, baby-pee-pee!'" as June laughed her head off.

June then thinks about getting him a baby doll too, a girl one, but she knew how to modify it to turn it into a boy dolly, which would really embarrass Tom, when changing its nappies. Hence, she went out shopping and got another large baby dolly in nappies and plastics. She However, she went to Boots and got several baby dummies, for his dollies and then thought why not!" and got a range of baby stuff, with large plastic baby pants which she was sure would be useful for Baby Tom, sooner rather than later. She undressed the dolly out of his plastics and diaper and then it's disposables to be naked apart from its baby dress and laughed as she talked to it "Sorry girly, I'm just going to turn you into a Baby Tom, which needs a little addition!"

June gets Tom a baby dolly, but transforms it into a boy dolly for Tom

She took one of the baby dummies and selected a pink one and taking some glue, she stuck it to the front of the doll, so the teat was sticking up, but was movable with the stem stuck down to the dolly. Hence, the dummy was still suckable, but actually looked like a little baby boy's pee-pee. A few minutes later and it was stuck solid and she smiled as she added the disposables, diaper and plastic baby pants and saw no sign of the bulge in its nappies to give the surprise away. Hence, she asked Pam to get her baby dolly and nappy changing stuff ready, when she brought his new dolly around for him and Christened it "Baby Nancy!" but asked her to keep quiet about her present.

Pam giggled, and said, "Mummy! Aunty June wants to see Tom do his nappy changing trick again and has a new dolly for him!" as her Mum laughed "I think he'll be over the moon at that again!" Tom was watching TV when his Mum said, "Tom, I've got a little bit of bad news!" as he asked, "What?" as she laughed "June wants to see you changing dolly's nappies!" as he cried "Not again!" as then they heard the bell go and he wanted to run, but Pam stopped him and said, "Aunty June's got you a new dolly!" as he sobbed "Not fair!"

Pam had laid out the changing mat again and had her dolly Baby Jane laid on the carpet!" as June was shown in with her own diaper bag and stuff. She said, "Hit Tom! This time I think Tom should perform the nappy changing instead of Nancy!" as Pam laughed and he said, "Very funny!" as Pam said, "Sit down and show Aunty June how you change nappies!" as he cringed. However, then June said, "I take it you don't like changing Baby Jane's nappies!" and saw him nod, but she then produced another large dolly and said, "I've got you a present!" adding "I've christened her Baby Nancy!" as Pam and her Mum laughed and saw a dolly very similar to Baby Jane. Pam said, "If you do it right, then we'll let you go and play footy afterwards., but if you don't' then you also change Baby Jane too!" as he huffed "Ok! I'll change my flaming dolly, but no tricks and no putting that talc near my trousers!" as she said, "I Promise Tom!"

Tom took the dolly and pulling down it's plastic baby pants, he heard June say, "You should always kiss your dolly, when facing her, to reassure her you love her!" and saw him kiss the dolly's rubber lips to laughter, as she said, "Tell Baby Nancy you love her too!" as he said, "I love you Baby Nancy!" June added "And you'll give her lots of kisses in bed with you!" as he cringed "Not fair! Ok Yes! I'll sleep with her and give her lots of cuddles and kisses!" as his Mum laughed "Pam didn't even do that!" as he blushed. Pam laughed "Although I might add Baby Jane, so Nancy has three dollies to cuddle to sleep!" as June laughed "I know who'll be his favourite!" but left it at that.

He then turned it over and heard Pam say, "I want a commentary!" as he said, "I pulled down baby Nancy's plastic baby pants and turned her over onto the changing mat!" as June said, "Very good Tom!" and then said, "I'm now going to remove her diaper and undid the same type of Velcro fastening as before and saw the bottom with the disposable and heard Pam say, "Check if baby Nancy, has done a little pooh!" He pulled the disposable off and said, "No, she hasn't!" as Pam gurgled "So you sure you haven't done a poo, Nancy!" as her Mum said, "Less of that!" Tom then said, "I take the wet-wipe and wash baby Nancy's botty!" as he wiped it down and heard them laugh, as June said, "Unfortunately I don't think my dolly wets itself!" as Pam said, "Oh June! It's more realistic when they do!" as he blushed.

He then took the gel and rubbed it over the dolly's backside saying, "Just gelling baby Nancy's backside! and then adding talcum powder!" but Pam said, "Don't forget the crack!" as he huffed and rubbed gel into the crevice to laughter. He then sprinkled talc and replaced the disposable again. He then turned the doll over to face him and had to give it more kisses and tell her "I love you Baby Nancy!"

Tom then discovers its willy and June then makes him suck the dummy

He then pulled the disposable off and gasped and cried "Oh no!" as Pam let out a shriek of laughter, as did their Mum, as they looked down on the pink dummy, sitting up, on show, from the doll's front, as Pam gurgled "Oh Fab, Aunty June! What a fab trick, to play on Tom and you got him to kiss his boy dolly and he'll have to sleep with him too! Oh fab!"

Tom cried "No way! Mum don't make me?" as his Mum gave him a cuddle and kisses and said, "June! That's so naughty!" as Pam gurgled "Gosh Tom's got a boyfriend, before even I have!" as June giggled, and nodded, and her Mum said, "Less of that, Pam!" Pam laughed "Look Mum! It means we can get practice changing girl dollies and boy dollies, so we'll both be ready, for any kind of baby-sitting!" as he cried "No way, Pam!" as she gurgled "Tom's actually, even more embarrassed, as his baby dolly, has a bigger baby-pee-pee, than he has!" as he sobbed "Oh no! Not fair June!" and sobbed. June said, "Continue changing Baby Nancy's nappies!" as he cried "What! I've to continue with a flaming boy doll?" as they nodded, affirmatively and his Mum scolded "Oh June!" as she saw him take a wet wipe and start rubbing it over the doll's front as Pam said, "Now Tom! Make sure you clean your dolly's big pee-pee!" as he blushed and rubbed the clothe over it, to giggles. He then went to take the gel, but June asked, "Doreen, could you get some milk on the boil a tick!" as she said, "No! I want to see!" but she said, "Just, go out a tick!" as she asked, "Why?" but stood up and exited saying, "Don't be too, cruel!" as she took the baby bottle and put some milk on the stove.

However, June laughed "I don't think Tom will want to suck his dummy, when he's got gel and talc on it, as she turned it upside down and said, "Suck!" as he cried "Oh no!" as Pam saw him suck the dummy and screeched, as her Mum ran in and gasped "Oh no! Tom don't!" June took it out and said, "Just comforting little Tom!" as her Mum laughed "That's so naughty!" as she set the dolly back down and said, "Continue gelling your dolly!" A sobbing, blushing Tom, took the gel and applied it to the front of the doll and then it's dummy as Pam laughed "I'm taking notes, Tom, for when I have practice on Baby Tom!" as he cried "No Mum! Don't let her?" as his Mum said, "She'd better not!" as June laughed "Spoilt sport, Pauline!" Pam laughed "I think Tom will need some comforting in bed sucking his dummy!" as her Mum gasped "Don't make him, Pam!" as she gurgled at the thought of him sucking his boy dolly's, willy in bed.

Pam has Tom sing his doll a lullaby to sleep cradling a boy doll

Tom sprinkled talc over its front and then applied the same disposable, which he'd just removed before and then pulled the diaper on his dolly, sobbing "This has been ten times worse, than with Pam's dolly!" as his Mum cuddled him and said, "Just pop **'her'** plastics on again and you can go and play footy!" However, Pam gurgled "Mummy! I think you'll have to go back to school again, for the facts of life!" adding "Don't you know the difference between a baby boy and a baby girl?" adding "That's **'HIS'** boy dolly!" as June gurgled "She is right Doreen!" as she blushed and laughed "Pam, you are terrible!" – and nodded, and said, "Ok! Just pop his plastics on again and you can go and play footy!" as he swallowed "Not fair Mum!" His Mum let him go after he asked Pam to wear her panties out to play footy, but he'd to give his new dolly a kiss again. His Mum said, "I've a good idea to try and get that dummy off his dolly!" as Pam said, "Don't you dare, Mum!" June said, "It's just a little different to his other dollies!" as his Mum laughed "I never thought you'd get him a boy dolly and make him kiss and then suck on its, flaming, wllly!" as Pam screeched "Oh Mum! Isn't Aunty June marvellous?" Her Mum shook her head, violently "No! She is not! That was not funny for my poor boy, Tom!" as June apologized "Sorry Doreen, when I heard Pam say, about babysitting, only girls, I thought she might appreciate some practice with Baby Nancy!"

His Mum laughed "Well keep it away from Tom!" as Pam nodded, and called "See that flying pig, Mummy!" as she ran out of the room laughing, with her Mum running after her and catching her, giggling daughter. June asked,

"Will I go now?" adding "I just thought my idea for a boy dolly, might tickle someone's fancy!" as Pam laughed "I couldn't believe it, when he pulled the nappy off and we saw its willy and then when he sucked on his willy!" as her Mum said, "Now! Less of that talk!" as Pam said, "It was just his dolly's dummy!" She laughed "That's ok Mum, as long as you've given the go ahead, for our big Tom, to suck on a dummy, or suck on his thumb or have a baby bottle, as they all laughed at his embarrassments.

She then said, "I wonder what comes next and pretended to be Baby Nancy and call in a squeaky voice 'Nappies and plastic baby pants' as she said, "Clever boy!" as her Mum scolded "Don't either of you try it!" June laughed "Oh Tom! I'm sure you'd prefer something else, for your birthday! You could have your own dollies to play with, instead of having to borrow Pammy's!" as he cried "No way!" as his Mum laughed "June you are terrible!" as June laughed "At least I know what to get him along with some pretty frocks for it!" Pam then laughed and said, "Tom cradle your dolly in your arms like this, to sing them a lullaby to sleep!" as he cried "What?" as Pam demonstrated with her arms as she took her Baby Suzie doll and using both arms, cradled the dolly and swinging them left and right, sing "Lullaby Lullaby, Go to sleep sweet Baby Suzie! Lullaby Lullaby! Sweet dreams tonight!" as he cried "Oh no!" as June laughed "Try with your new dolly Tom!" as he blushed and took the large baby doll and cradled the boy dolly and grimaced, as he called "Lullaby Lullaby, Go to sleep sweet Baby Nancy! Lullaby Lullaby! Sweet dreams tonight!" as his Mum gasped "Oh June! Oh Pam!"

June asks her sister Florence for some dress up clothes for a young girl

Pam laughed "Don't forget HIS kiss!" adding "You should have a nice smile when singing your baby a lullaby!" followed by "You wouldn't want to scare her!" as he sobbed "Not fair Mummy!" as he kissed the boy doll, to laughter. His Mum laughed "I suppose it's not as bad as some of the things you've done tonight and over the last week!" as he had to repeat to more laughter. June said, "Don't forget to pop your dolly's dummy back in and then give it the baby bottle of milk!" as he blushed.

Hence, next thing Tom had popped a dummy into the doll's mouth and then went to pop it's baby bottle in, but Pam takes the bottle and Says, "Better check it's not too hot!" as her Mum said, "I haven't heated the milk!" but Pam Says, "It's the principle, Mummy!" as she got him to take the bottle into his mouth to giggles, before adding the bottle to the doll.

June took Pam aside into the hall and whispered "I think I'll be popping around the shops tomorrow, to buy Nancy some lovely pretty dress up clothes!" as Pam giggled, "Great!"

adding "They don't need to be new, some things from a charity shop or some relations, that have grown out of them will do, him!" as June gurgled "My young nieces would love to meet your Nancy and some older ones, would gladly donate some of their old frocks, to see him play dress up!" as Pam giggled, "Fab!" adding "Mum or no one local, should realize, what I'm doing to him!"

That night June phoned her sister Flo and explained that it was a sweet young 8 year old girl Nancy's birthday and she was after some presents for her, a pretty frock or something!" as she added "She hasn't many skirts or dresses?" as her sister asked, "Why's that?" as she said, "Oh she used to be a bit of a Tom boy, always playing footy and thinking skirts and frocks were silly!" as Flo laughed "I see!" as her sister said, "My Rachel is ten and has some lovely frocks and stuff from when she was eight!" as June asked, "Could you bring a selection for me to choose tomorrow. If we meet at Beckam's Bakery in West Street?" as her sister agreed.

That night Tom had three dolls in bed with him as his Mum read him a story, but when she'd left, Pam slipped in to see Tom had removed his PJs and got into the lacy nighty and was lying there with the three dolls. Pam removed

his Baby Nancy's plastics and nappies and turning the doll upside sown she shoved it down his nighty and said, "Suck on your dolly's baby-pee-pee!" as he cried "But it's got baby goo all over it!" as she laughed "You can add more in the morning before school!" and had him suck on the dummy, making a funny face, as she gurgled. She held it telling him to suck in and out.

The Monday, June set off early and went around a few charity shops first, to see if she could see anything pretty, that would fit Nancy and not be too expensive. She saw a few pretty frocks and skirts and bought a few of each, for about £15 and laughed.

She let slip to the lady "They're actually for an 8 year old boy, who for years never helped his Mummy, with any housework and was getting out of control!" as the lady gasped "Never!" as June said, "I'm meeting my sis who's, daughter is 10 and has outgrown, some lovely skirts and dresses and I'm going to get some of her stuff, too for him!"

June sees her sister arrive with her daughters' old pram

The lady gurgled "Fab! You couldn't bring him in some time, for me to see?" as June nodded, "I'll try!" adding "At the minute, his young sister and me, are trying to keep it a secret, from other girls and his mates and especially at school!" adding "She gets him to pretend to go out to play footy, but instead he runs around to me, to play dollies, ballet or dress up!" as the lady screeched "Oh fab!" as she exited to the bakery.

She had arrived early and had a coffee while she waited and suddenly gasped as Flo came in wheeling a large pink pram and laughed "I thought I might as well use Rachel's old pram! I doubt I'll be having any more children!" adding "although a lady friend spotted me and thought I'd had a new daughter!" as June giggled, and kissed her sister "Hi Fran, like a coffee first?" She peered in and saw lots of bags of clothing and a few dollies, as she added "I wasn't sure, if she was too old, for dollies!" but June laughed "She's dolly mad, my dear!" as they sat down. June asked, "What would you like?" as she said, "The all-day breaky, sounds fine!" as June ordered two for them and a smiling teenager serving, asked, "Can I see your daughter?" but they laughed and Fran said, "I'm just using it to transport, some of my daughter's old skirts and dresses and stuff around for my sister June, here!" as she laughed "Oh I see!" as they chatted. June then showed her a few skirts and dresses she'd got, and Fran said, "Oh I've much better than that! Watch this!" as she took one bag and pulled out some pretty skirts and dresses, as June laughed "I remember seeing Rachel in this beautiful dress here!" as her Mum nodded, "Yes she did look lovely!" as she showed her other skirts and dresses. She took another bag and said, "This was the bridesmaids dress she wore for our cousin Dianne's wedding!" as June gasped "Oh Nancy will adore that! She'd love to be a bridesmaid!" as a thought came into her head for Nancy. She then held up a tutu ballet dress and said, "She can borrow that, Rachel said, she might give that to a young girl she knows!" as June laughed "Fine I'm sure she'll be over the moon!"

She showed her some frilly panties and underwear and even a young girl's training bra, as June screeched "Oh fab!" as Fran laughed wondering why she was giggling so much.

She said, "I take it you'll want the pram, unless you want to get a taxi home?" as June gasped "I hope nobody think's I've got a baby?" as they laughed. June could keep it in no longer and said, "I've actually tricked you!" as she asked, "How?" as she said, "You know they're for a Tom boy?" as Flo nodded, "They're actually for the boy next door, who's called Tom!" as Flo screeched with laughter "Never!" as June said, "He used to be a real MSP and never help her, or his sister with any housework and be a bit of a bully to little Pam!" as her sister said, "No!" as she continued "However, Pam has the upper hand now and makes him carry a dolly around the house, from room to room and if he forgets it, she calls loudly "Oh Tom! You've forgotten your dolly!" as Flo screeched "Oh Fab!" as she said, "She even makes him change into panties, when he returns from school!" adding "Though his

Mum doesn't know that!" as she gasped "Never! Why would he do that?" as June laughed "She can tell on him, that he plays dollies, carries one about the house and wears her panties!" as Flo giggled, "Gosh!"

June explained how Pam is dressing big Tom up and want's June's help

She added "And she's extending it to dress up too, at my house" as Flo asked, "So his Mum won't know?" as June nodded. She added "Pam's taking things slowly with him and not outing him to girls or his mates!" as she laughed "Lucky boy!" as June said, "She doesn't want her Mum to know, what she's doing with Tom, around at my place!" as Flo asked, "Which is what?" as she laughed "She'll make him say, he's going out to play footy!" adding "But in fact he's to come around, to me, to play dollies, ballet and dress up!" as Flo screeched "Oh the poor boy!" asking "When can I come around to meet your little girly?" as she then thought "I doubt I'll be able to keep it a secret from my big girl, who will screech the place down!" as June said, "Don't tell her his name, call him Dave!" as she agreed.

June said, "She has kept Nancy indoors!" as Flo laughed "Oh doesn't she let him get some air in the back garden to play skipping?" as June laughed "That was until Tom accidentally let me into his secret!" as Flo asked, "How?" as she explained "Pam called around at my place before school, asking if I'd pop around to see her Mum around 4, just before her big bro, Tom was due to arrive home! Telling me I'd probably have a laugh!" June giggled, "I popped around to see his Mum later that day and she invited me into the sitting room to talk!" as Flo listened. She continued "Tom came home from school and his Mum exited the sitting room, to tell him, his little sister Pam was around at a girlfriends house and that he could go and play footy with his mates!" as Flo asked, "So what!" June gurgled "I couldn't believe it, when I heard him say, 'Do you know where my Suzie doll is, Pam Says, she's hidden it beside her Wendy dolly!'" as Flo gurgled and screeched "Never?" as June nodded, "Of course, I'd stayed hidden out of sight, listening as asked to by little Pam!" adding "I then exited and he nearly fell through the floor, trying to think of an excuse for his dolly!" as Flo laughed "Oh fab!" She said, "He stammered something about Pam asking him to get her Mum to find her dolly or something like that!" but soon was sobbing and telling his Mum off, for not warning him that I was around for a chat!" as Flo laughed and asked, "What did you do?" as June replied, "I gave him a cuddle and told him not to worry, that I won't tell!" as she added "See that flying pig?"

Flo laughed "You didn't tell on him?" as she laughed "Let's say, he's gradually having to show himself outside now, as Nancy, but so far it's been just in Pam's pretty aprons and her pretty headscarf as a disguise!" as Flo giggled, "Oh June! Not even a frock?" but June laughed "Well Pam's wanting to dress him up in skirts and frocks, but doesn't want her Mum to know and Hence, has roped me into her plan and scheme of things!" as Flo laughed "I see!" June explained "See Pam knows she can make him do anything that she wants, for fear she tells her friends!" adding "So she's going to get Tom to pretend to go and play footy with his mates, but instead to slip around to my place, where a short while later Pam will join us to play dress up and dollies!" as Flo screeched "Oh My daughter will definitely want to be introduced to your Nancy!" as June laughed "One step at a time!"

Pam returns, realizing he'd been outside so could do laundry

June explains how she made him wheel his dolly around the back garden as Nancy in a headscarf and pink apron. June added "Of course when Pam came back from her friend's house and heard that I'd had Nancy in the back garden, she then told her Mum that I'd set a president!" as Flo asked, "What do you mean?" as she explained "Up till then, he couldn't help with the laundry, as it was outdoors and her Mum didn't want Tom to be spied by Me or the other neighbours!" adding "But now I'd got him wheeling his dolly around the back garden as Nancy, she said, that Nancy could now help with the laundry!" as Flo laughed "Quite right sis! You or I don't mind pegging out the washing or clothes to air!" as June laughed "But Pam and her Mum have an extremely girly way to peg out the washing!" as Flo asked, "How?" as she laughed "They use a pretty handbag to hold the pegs and so he'll have to dip into the handbag and most probably mince around the garden carrying his handbag to lots of teasing

and blushes from him, dreading the neighbours in the back spying him!" as she added "And of course I'll have the help of my little housemaid Nancy too! but my house is more open to the back houses and he'll be more likely to be recognized, especially if some naughty girl removes his headscarf and replaces them with hair ribbons or even curtly grips!" as Flo gurgled again "Oh June!"

June then thinks of getting Tom into the pram, but dressed as a big baby

However, then Flo asked, "Could he fit in the pram?" as June shook, her head, saying, "His legs would be too long and have to sit out, over the handle, but June laughed "Pity! Pam would love it, if she could get her big brother back into a pram to wheel around the garden!" but added "Then the streets and then even around the shops!" as Flo screeched with laughter.

Flo laughed "If you are careful and do some needlework, I won't mind, if you want to make a hole at the end for baby's legs to stick out and hide them with a blanket or pop them into a basket or something!" June gurgled at the thought. June laughed "Oh Pam would wet herself, if she got Tom back into nappies and plastic baby pants, but especially if we got him into your pram! I don't know what he'd do as well!" adding "His Mum wouldn't stand for it! It's one thing dressing him up as a girl, but as a baby too!" as Flo gurgled "I'm sure Pam could keep it a secret!" as June laughed "See that flying pig?" as they continued eating their meal. June laughed "I'll maybe add a few items to my shopping list for today!" as Flo asked, "What?" as June laughed "Baby's dummy, bottle, bonnet, disposables, diaper, nappy pins, large baby pants!" as Flo laughed "Don't forget extra milk and some baby food too!" as June added "And a few bibs for baby!" as they both screeched into their handkerchief's. June then told her about getting him a big baby doll but turning it into a boy doll with a dummy glued to its' front and called it Baby Nancy. She gurgled "If you'd have seen his face when he spied it's willy, well baby-pee-pee as Pam calls it saying, it's bigger than his!" as they screeched.

Brenda and Clare head to the same bakery where June is

That same Monday, Brenda calls up at Claire's and they set off on their shopping trip. They giggle as they head along to the local shops and then get the bus to town. They enter a few charity shops where they purchase some skirts and dresses. Brenda said, "We should try to get elasticated waisted skirts, to make sure they will fit!" as Claire giggled, "It should also mean, they should last for several years!" as Brenda nodded, giggling. They then headed to Boots and got a selection of baby stuff for a big baby. Claire gasped "So you were serious about us actually diapering him?" as Brenda giggled, "Of course, I can't see him telling his Mum or Pam on us!" adding "I'm sure Pam will eventually baby him!" as Claire laughed "The poor boy!"

They get a large changing mat as Brenda Says, "We'll need to protect the carpet, when changing baby!" as Claire gurgled "We certainly will!" as she added "We'll have to see about some short baby dresses, that will show off baby's nappies and plastics!" as they giggled. They get baby wipes, disposables, diapers, diaper pins, large plastic baby pants, baby gel, talcum powder, a few dummies, blue and pink, baby bottles blue and pink, a few baby bonnets and are about to finish, when Brenda said, "We'll need baby reigns, for taking baby walkies!" as Claire gasped "We couldn't! Not out in the garden?" as Brenda laughed and nodded, "Eventually!" as she giggled, "Naughty girl!" However, they then realise they need two of each item, as they'd have baby in each of their houses and didn't want to have to carry it around between their houses every time, they had him in their respective houses. They buy the baby stuff and take around half each in their shopping bags and baskets and head on to more charity shops. In one they spy some ballet outfit's which should fit Tom and purchase the skirts and tutu ballet dress, giggling at the thought of Tom in them.

They also spy some dresses for a big young girl which were short enough to show off his nappies and eventually are happy with their selection of girly clothes for his dress up fun.

They exit the shop and head on to get some lunch. They pop into a bakery and happen to notice two ladies, but they also had a large pink pram with them. Brenda gasped "That's that lady, who lives next door to Tom!" as they listened and heard laughter and giggles from the two. They noticed that the pram didn't have a baby in it, but lots of shopping. Brenda laughed "I wonder is that lady, planning to do something the same as us to Tom!" as Claire gasped "Let's plead ignorance! It will be more of a surprise, if we do!" as Brenda looked away from June and her sister. Brenda laughed "I think we've spent enough on Lucy, any future dress up, should be available from our nieces who have out-grown their dresses and stuff!" as Claire agreed "Yes! Some of my nieces would be over the moon, especially if they could meet Lucy!" as they laughed quietly. Brenda said, "I'm sure we can make use of Lucy to help with housework!" as Claire agreed "We'll have to get him some sweet aprons and PVC pinnies!" as they decide where to go, to get his pretty aprons.

Brenda and Claire speaks to June on her way out with the pram

They saw June pay the shop girl and then wheel the pram out, chatting to Flo, but giving Claire a nod, as she thought, she recognised her, on her way out. Claire nodded, back and said, "You live down the street, don't you?" as she replied, "Yes I'm June! Just meeting up with my sister Flo here!" as Flo said, "Hi!" as Claire said, "My niece Lucy is coming over for a few weeks and so I'm getting some shopping for her, with my friend Brenda from the bottom of the Drive, as Brenda called "Hi June! I think I've seen you about!" as June said, "It's a nice café here isn't it?" as they agreed and called "Bye!" as they exited.

Brenda laughed "Do you think June was getting dress up things from her sister too?" as Claire gasped "Gosh the poor boy, will be dressed up at hers and our places!" adding "But whereas Pam will know about June, we'll try and keep ours a secret, so he'll be doubly worried!" as they continued with their meal. They finished their meal and after paying, June laughed "I take it you want me to wheel the pram home?" as Flo nodded, "That ok" as June laughed and taking hold of the handle started out of the shop, calling bye to the shop girls. They kissed each other bye and each went home, laughing at what was to come. June wheeled the pink pram home, calling at the charity shop where she showed the lady and said, "Guess which lucky boy has lots of dress up things from his cousin?" as the lady gurgled and looked at the bags and checked all the pretty clothes. However, then June mentions about the pram and what Flo had said, about turning him into a baby and maybe converting the pram to let his legs out the end so he could fit.

June heads home with Flo's pram of dress up clothes

June exited and wheels the big pram back and passing some shops, calls in and gets questioned about the pram and explains their just some clothes for a young relation to play dress up and Mummies at her place. She keeps Tom a secret for now and exits to wheel the pram home. Tom's Mum didn't spy June wheeling the pram around to her place and so June was able to hide the stuff away and pop the pram up the stairs into the spare room. She starts taking the clothes from the bags, giggling at how girly some of the skirts and dresses are, hanging them up on hangers and putting some underwear away in drawers ready for Nancy to play dress up. Brenda and Claire head on home and laugh at the prospect of getting Tom to enter and play dollies with them. They then realise they've forgotten some dolls and dress up clothes for them.

Hence, they pop into a toy shop and see a range of dolls and pretty dresses for them. They have a look at several dolls and eventually decide on two pretty dolls around the same size, so the dresses will fit both dollies. They select

about six dresses for the dolls and after trying a few dresses on both dolls, pay for the dollies and their clothes and exit, satisfied they'd everything for Lucy to play dollies properly.

Tom has to pretend to go out, but instead play at Junes

Over the next few days, Pam makes Tom pretend to go out with mates, but instead, the first night, when she told him "Right into my room for a chat!" as he entered wondering what she wanted. She said, "Look! Don't you dare tell Mummy!" as he asked, "What?" as she said, "I'm being good not letting on at school or to my friends about Nancy!" as he nodded, "Thanks!" as she continued "At times I want you to tell Mummy you're going out to play football, but in fact you'll slip around next door for some fun at Aunty June's where I'll join you later!" as he huffed "Not fair!" as she laughed "Don't worry I'll still let you go and play footy at times, it will just make Mummy think I'm letting you off playing dollies, a bit less, than she thinks!" as he blushed and sobbed "Not fair!" She said, "I'll let you off tonight, maybe tomorrow night!" Pam sends Tom around to June's with him calling "Right is it ok if I go to play football Pam?" as she said, "Fine! but be back here for about eight, ok?" as his Mum said, "Oh Pam! Let him stay out, till eight-thirty?" as Pam laughed "Ok! To show I'm not an Ogre!" as she smiled knowing it meant about two hours, for Nancy to play dress up and dollies!" He went out the door and wanted to join his mates but knew he'd to join June next door.

Pam distracted her Mum from seeing Tom at the front and said, "Mum did you see that?" pointing to an imaginary bird in the garden, as her Mum looked out the kitchen window and asked, "What?" as Pam said, "I thought I saw a beautiful bird at the end on the right!" but her Mum couldn't see the imaginary bird. Pam said, "I'll pop over to Julie's and then Alice the next street!" as her Mum said, "Thanks Pam for letting him out as a boy! It's not right making him play dollies all the time!" as Pam laughed "Though hasn't his attitude and housework improved?" as his Mum said, "Yes!, but you shouldn't make him look and sound so girly!" adding "And now June knows about him, I hope she won't tell anyone?" as Pam laughed "Don't worry Mum! All she might do is make use of him with some chores!"

adding "It will be nice to have our own maid!" as her Mum laughed "Now stop that Pam!" June heard the bell go and smiled as she saw Tom standing there at her door and said, "Come in Tom!" as she closed the door on him and led him up the stairs to her spare room. She said, "Now you must be quiet! We don't want your Mummy to realize you are here and so here's a clean handky to keep you quiet!" as he grimaced and took the handky and popped it into his own mouth. She said, "Before Pam comes in, let's get you undressed and into some pretties!" as his eyes opened in despair. He saw the large pink pram and dreaded what it was for. She laughed "Don't worry Tom, I just borrowed the pram to transport some of my niece's old clothes from my sister, who thought it was for a little Tom boy!" as he blushed and heard her giggle at the double entendre.

June pops Tom into nappies and baby pants, but hides them with a tutu

She gets him undressed down to Pam's panties, but then ties his hands behind his back, still with the gag in his mouth and then she removes the panties to leave him naked apart from his socks. He wondered what was to come but gasped as she then shows him the diaper bag and nappies, as his eyes widen in fear, but he then also sees the large baby plastic pants that she'd bought that day, in town. She gurgled "Before Pam comes around, we'll try and keep it a secret from her!" as he blushed and sobbed through the handky, with her saying, "I've something which should keep baby's nappies, hidden, even when trying on his pretty dresses, in front of Pammy!" She asked, "Is baby going to be quiet?" and saw him nod, as she removed the handkerchief to hear him sob "Not flaming fair, Aunty June!" as she popped a pink baby's dummy into his mouth, followed by a large white baby bonnet, saying, "Just till I get baby, dressed!" adding "Move those baby lips in and out, that's a good little baby!" to see him blush and motion with the dummy. She turned him over onto his front and wiped his botty and underneath with wet

wipes and then applies the gel, followed by adding the talcum powder, giggling "We don't want our little baby to get nappy rash!" as she applied the disposable and then turned him, giggling at his blushing, tear stained face, but also with his willy on show to her.

She laughed "I see your baby-pee-pee is still quite small!" as he grimaced and sucked on his dummy. She started wiping him with wet wipes and then gelled and applied the talcum powder and soon had the disposable nappy applied over him. She slid him into a diaper and pinned it up and then pulled up the plastic baby pants over them, as he sobbed in embarrassment. She led him over to a full length, mirror and showed him his reflection, with tears appearing in his eyes, at the big baby boy, on show as she laughed "Don't worry! We'll try and keep baby a secret from Pam, for a while!" as he felt her apply frilly panties over the plastics and then add white tights and pull them up his legs. She then showed him a turquoise ballet tutu and heard him huff "Not fair!" as she laughed "The good thing is that the tutu, should hide baby's nappies and plastic baby pants from Pam's view!" as she started pulling the tutu up his legs, over his nappies and then up his body and undoing his arms, she slid them into the sleeves of it. She laughed as she showed him his reflection in the mirror and saw him sob at the girly sight, as he begged "Please don't show Pam?" as she laughed "Oh Tom! Or Nancy should I say, will sound a sweet girly, especially when I ask in front of Pam, does she want to remove his tutu to go and play footy or stay and play ballerinas!" as he gasped and realized that Pam might think he likes being in the tutu and really consider taking him to ballet class, in it!"

She led him into the front bedroom and opened the wardrobe and said, "Look at all these pretty skirts and dresses, my sister and I got today while shopping in town!" as he blushed she said, "Take that turquoise frock out and try it on!" He cried softly as he saw the open window, with him still looking like a baby ballerina and "Close the blinds!" as she laughed and closed them a little.

June led him into the room, showing him the clothes and the big pram

He removed his dummy and the baby bonnet and hid his baby stuff away in his handbag, in case Pam came up and spied it. She heard him ask "Can we go downstairs?" as she laughed "Why?" as he huffed "I don't want Pam to see that!" as he pointed to the pram. She laughed "It belongs to my sister Flo!" as she gurgled "In case Pam thinks of popping baby into nappies herself!" as he nodded, and June took the handky he'd had and stuffed it into her own mouth, to stop herself screeching with laughter. She sat down on the bed and hugged him and removing the handky, she gave him a kiss, saying, "Ok! You'd better help me bring some pretty skirts and dresses down, so Pam doesn't spy your baby pram!"

Hence, Tom helps June, carry lots of pretty clothes, down the stairs for Pam to play dress, up with him. He begs her to close the door, to stop Pam seeing the pram and she closes it, knowing it will be fun, in the future, to tease him with it, or eventually show Pam. June gets him into a pretty frock over his tutu to surprise Pam and adds his trousers, to keep the tutu a complete surprise to Pam.

She starts him playing dollies in the living room, with him dreading the neighbours spy him dressed as a girl, or her bringing someone in. They then heard the bell and June exited to let her in and saw Pam, follow her into the sitting room and giggle when she saw Sissy Tom, in a dress, without ribbons, but also with lots of girly clothes. She laughed "Keep quiet so Mum doesn't hear or else!" as he nodded, "Ok! How long do you need me for?" as she laughed "Maybe just half an hour to an hour! It depends, what we are playing!" June turned up the volume on the TV, to try and stop his Mum, hearing any cries from Tom. He cried softly "Close the blinds!" as they gave in and pulled them closed as he blushed and saw June reach into a handbag and retrieve some hair ribbons and bows, handing them to Pam, saying, "I think he'll be wanting these!" and Pam added them to his head. June slid a handbag up his arm and over his shoulder and take a photo, as he cried "No photos!" but luckily, the volume of

the TV muffled the sound. Pam then slid the handbag down to his elbow and had him mince around the room to more laughter and more photos were taken.

She clapped "Oh Sissy Tom! You do look sweet!" but added "Come on! Off with those silly trousers!" but June laughed "Now Pam! Nancy's a little surprise for you!" adding "Can you wait a while and let him play in his skirts and dresses over his trousers?" as Pam laughed "What! Leave him as a half boy, half girl?" as June nodded but heard her say, "If he's wearing trousers, then we can remove these, till later!" and removed his ribbons again and popped them back into his handbag.

June gets some dolls and dresses for Sissy Tom to play dollies with

He cried "Not fair Pam! Leave my ribbons in?" as she giggled, and flicked her wrist to him saying, "Such a girly brother!" June gurgled "Oh Pam!" adding "I'm so pleased Tom outed himself to me about his dollies!" June then gets some dolls and dresses for him to play with and Pam instructs him how to remove the different dresses and then dress his dollies. Of course, more photos were taken of the sissy boy without ribbons or headscarf, in a pretty dress and holding dollies. Pam explained "Your dolly's dresses with Velcro are the easiest to remove, as you just have to pull on the back of your dolly to release dress and then gently pull its' arms out of the sleeves!" adding "Just the way you remove your own frocks Sissy Tom!" as June gurgled.

Pam explained "See! He's only Nancy when in ribbons or headscarf!" as June laughed "Oh Pam! I'm sure she can't wait to look more girly again!" as Pam laughed "You mean apart from his pretty frock and playing dollies!" as he sat there blushing and sobbing "Not fair, girls!" as he felt the awkwardness of the nappies, diapers and plastic baby pants, not to forget his tutu ballet dress.

Pam gets him to undo the Velcro and carefully remove the dolly's dress and then slip it into another similar dress, doing up with Velcro as they clapped and applauded him, quietly "Well done Sissy Tom!" as he blushed and got a kiss from his laughing sister and one from June, as he cried "I don't like kisses!" to more laughter. However, then heard Pam say, "Now Sissy Tom! You love your dolly, so give her a kiss and tell her how pretty she is!" as he blushed and picking up the dolly, he raised it up to his mouth and kissed it, saying, "I love you dolly!" as June said, "You can call your dolly Sissy Nancy!" to more laughter and heard him call "I love you Sissy Nancy! I think you're very pretty!" and saw Pam take the doll and bob a curtsy with its' dress, but then say, in a squeaky voice "Thank you Sissy Tom!" However, he then heard her say, "Sissy Tom! That's a pretty dress you are wearing!" as he realised what she wanted and so stood up and bob a curtsy with his dress and say, "Thank you Sissy Nancy!" as June laughed "I think we can leave the curtsies till after his dollies! When he's removed his trousers!" as Pam said, "Ok!" Pam then took another dress and said, "This frock is a bit more difficult with hooks and eyes to contend with and showed him what to do and soon he was trying to cope with them but found them more complex and guttery. He eventually had done the doll's dress back up to more applause and complements and of course got more kisses and then had to give it kisses too.

Pam asked, "Will I get my dolls pram around for him to wheel his dollies about the place!" as he begged "Please don't Pam? Mum will realize I'm around here!" as she laughed "Mummy knows I've taken up playing dollies again with Julie and Tina and so won't suspect anything!" but June said, "Leave his baby pram for another time!" as he blushed "Knowing she was referring to the large baby pram upstairs, which would give Pam ideas of turning him into a baby!" Pam gets him to carry each dolly around the room, telling each one he loves his dolly and giving it kisses, as she laughs.

She gurgled "Oh why didn't Sissy Tom or Nancy appear, years ago! I'd have had a sister to play lots of girly games and by his age now, he'd have been an expert at dollies, dress up and even ballet!" as him and June gasped as he

begged "Please Pam! Stop teasing about ballet!" June laughed "Oh Nancy! I'm sure you'd love joining Pam and the girls for ballet!" He huffed "Not fair!"

Pam Says, 'Pity Nancy didn't appear years ago' and then ballet and Tina

Pam scolded herself "Oh I should have brought one of my ballet, tutus around with me!"

June laughed "Now Pam! Let's leave that for another time!" adding "Let him just try a few skirts and dresses after he's finished with his dollies!" as he blushed more at the teasing about dollies, ballet and dress up, with June not wanting to spoil Pam's surprise, when he removed his trousers. Pam laughed "It's a pity about ballet! It would be fab having him join me as Sissy Tom or Nancy, on a Saturday morning!" as June giggled, at her keeping up the ballet conversation with him, begging "Please Pam stop teasing! You know Mummy won't let me do ballet!" adding "There's lots of girls from school, who know me, and they'd tell and then I dread what would happen in class!" Pam gurgled "You mean you might have to attend school as a girl, in a dress and pinafore!" as June gurgled "Oh he couldn't?" adding "Could he?" as Pam nodded, and Tom sobbed "No way! Please don't make me?" June cuddled him as Pam laughed "Oh what a lovely thing to consider in the future!" as she gurgled "Although not too far away!" He begged "Please Pam! Don't tell or let anyone see me or Nancy, especially Julie or Tina!" as she laughed "Julie would be ok!" adding "But Tina, doesn't like you much, since you called her, lots of names and threatened to hit her and her friends, for playing dollies, near your footy game and I dread to think what revenge, she'd want on my big sissy brother here!" as he blushed at the thought.

She gurgled "She loves wheeling her dollies up and down the driveway, but then often wheels them in the street!" as she gurgled "I could just imagine her making you wheel my doll's pram up and down the street!" as June laughed "Oh Pam!" as she laughed "Don't worry! I'd make sure she was kind and let it be Nancy in a pretty frock and hair ribbons to try and disguise herself and not Sissy Tom instead, without his ribbons or headscarf showing off as a complete sissy!" as June gurgled, but then heard Pam add "Thought Julie tells me she even sometimes takes her dollies for a ride with their Mummy around the shops in town!" adding as she gurgled "Could you imagine Nancy or even worse Sissy Tom wheeling his dollies around town in a pretty frock and having to use a handbag and purse in lots of shops with little Tina outing you to lots of ladies and girls and even boys too!" as he sobbed and begged "Please don't tell her, Pammy?" as she cuddled him and gave him a kiss, saying, "Don't worry! I want Sissy Tom and Nancy all to myself!" adding "Except for her playing with lovely Aunty June here!" as June bobbed a curtsy to them and saw Pam and then Tom grip their dresses and bob curtsies back again. He begged "Please Pam, make sure I'm hidden when Tina is about!" adding "Please Aunty June! You nearly let Tina see Nancy! Please don't play tricks and let her spy me!" as she giggled.

June apologised "Sorry Sissy Tom! I'll try and not be as naughty, as little Pam here!" as Pam opened the blinds and June held him on show, but luckily nobody was outside, but it did have a bad effect and he wet his nappies, with June half realizing, but Pam not having a clue. Pam pulled them closed again, but it was too late. June slid his handbag up over his shoulder to be ready for his curtsies and said, "Nancy, complement June on her outfit!"

They play curtsies with him as Sissy Tom, but Pam then sees his tutu

They heard him say, "Your dress is very pretty Aunty June!" and saw her grip her dress and bob a curtsy to him saying, "Thank you Sissy Tom!" and bending down she kissed him. Pam then said, "Now to me!" and heard Tom say, "You look very pretty Pam I like your pretty dress!" as she bobbed a curtsy, saying, "Thank you Sissy Tom!" and reaching out kissed him, as he blushed. Then Pam said, "What a pretty frock, Sissy Tom!" as he gripped his dress, still with his handbag over his shoulder and bobbing a curtsy, he called "Thank you, Pammy!" and

approaching her gave her a kiss on the cheek, to laughter from June who said, "Well done, Sissy Tom!" as he asked, "Is that it, then?"

However, then June Says, "I've a surprise Nancy has for Sissy Tom and you Pam!" as Pam asked her giggling "What, Aunty June?" as June said, "Stand up and remove your trousers and then we'll start playing curtsies properly!" as he huffed "Not fair!" but standing up, he reached under the dress and started undoing his trousers, heard June gurgled "Do it slowly Nancy!" adding to her "Nancy has a little surprise for you, Pammy!" as June handed her a handkerchief to stuff into her mouth, in cases she screeched and her Mum heard her.

She laughed and raising the handky, looking at her blushing brother, she saw him reach under his frock and slowly pull them down his thighs and let them fall, as she still didn't realize what was up. He stepped out of them and saw June bend down and pick them up as she threw them onto the sofa, out of the way. Pam then saw her take him back a bit away from Pam, as she then raised his dress and Pam rammed her handky into her mouth, as she saw his beautiful tutu ballet skirt and screamed with laughter "Oh fab!" as June removed his dress fully over his head. Pam removed the handky and ran to get a closer look, asking "Where did you get his tutu?" as she replied, "My sister brought it to town for me! It's one of her daughter's old ones and I thought Nancy would suit it and as you see, he looks a treat!" as she laughed "I was wanting to hold back and keep it as a surprise after his playing dress up, in lots of her skirts and dresses!" as Pam laughed "Oh! but he looks such a sweetie in it!" adding "Don't you Nancy?" as he blushed and nodded, "Not fair Pam!" She gurgled "I think those ballet classes, are getting closer every minute!" as June laughed "Now Pam, be nice and teach him some moves as ballerina Nancy around here for a while and only let him join you at ballet, after he's got some experience and can show off some ballet moves, to the girls!"

June has him in the tutu try on some more of Flo's skirts and dresses

Pam gurgled "Though I'll have to put him through his paces twice! Sometimes as Nancy and then get her to show Sissy Tom some ballet too!" as he sobbed "Oh no, Pam! Please don't?" as she kissed him and June said, "I think since he's removed his trousers, Nancy can appear again!" Pam laughed and taking his handbag, she removed some hair ribbons and slid them into his hair, laughing at him as Nancy, but in his tutu now. June Says, "Look Pam, before he does some ballet with you, let's try him in some of these skirts and dresses!" as Pam huffed "Ok! but I was looking forward to showing him lots of ballet moves that I've learnt over the years, at ballet classes!" adding "You've a lot of catching up dearie!" as he blushed and begged "Please Pam! Don't even joke about me doing ballet!"

as they laughed. Hence, next thing June took a skirt and blouse and slid the skirt up his legs over his tutu skirt, with him thinking "At least it stops the chance of Pam realizing I'm in nappies and baby pants!" She let Pam add his blouse, with her taking over when it came to tucking it in, just in case she felt his diaper or plastic baby pants and so next thing he was prancing about in the skirt and blouse, with Pam saying, "Nancy! It's so much fun wearing pretty skirts with a blouse!" as he blushed but heard June giggle "Now Pam! Stop teasing Nancy! You know she prefers pretty frocks, to a skirt and blouse!" adding "Don't you?" as he nodded. Pam laughed "I know what you'll get for a birthday present soon!" as he begged "Don't give me skirts or dresses?" as she laughed "Oh I wouldn't dare get those for Tom!" adding "See! It will be Nancy's birthday the same day and so it will be her, trying on lots of pretty skirts with a blouse and dresses and she'll probably be a lucky girl and get some pretty handbags too!" as June gurgled "Oh definitely! I hope she'll be a bit of an expert with her handbags, by then!" as Pam laughed "I hope so! I'm going to suggest Mummy helps me, teach her and play Shopping!" as he cried "Oh no!" as she laughed "Don't worry! It will be in doors where only Mummy and I will see Nancy practicing with his purse and handbag!" as June laughed "Oh can't I play too?" but Pam said, "I want to have fun with Nancy on my own!" as

June giggled, "Spoilt sport!" with Pam saying, "I'm sure you'll have lots of fun with her, too!" as Tom blushed at the thought of both of these.

June then laughed "What about a bra?" as Pam screeched "Oh fab!" as June said, "Quiet Pam! Your Mum will hear!" as she laughed softly Oh Yes! I remember playing dress up in Mummy's old clothes and trying on her bras when I was only four or five!" as she laughed "I'll have to suggest we play dress up with Nancy!" as he begged "Please don't Pam?" adding "That will be terrible!" June said, "They have some small training bras for young girls and I'm sure I could get him one to practice with till Nancy becomes a lady!" as Pam laughed "You mean when Tom becomes a man?" as June nodded, "Around ten or eleven normally!" and he cried "Please don't?" as Pam laughed "What exactly happens as she laughed "Well some things I'll leave out, but one thing is his voice gets deeper!" as she asked, "What else?" but she laughed "It will be better if we leave it as a surprise for you and Nancy!"

Nancy and then Sissy Tom in tutu does some ballet dance moves

Pam laughed "What about for Sissy Tom?" as June laughed "Oh he'll definitely be over the moon at what happens to him!" as Tom blushed "Half realizing what June was talking about!" having heard bigger boys talking about wanking and sex. They pop him into several other dresses and have him prancing about, still without Pam realising about his nappies or plastics and then June Says, it's time for ballerina Nancy.

Pam then has him raise his arms above his head and do some spins, like she learns at ballet classes. She has him splay his arms out effeminately to do more spins and do some moves on his toes, with June teasing him more about joining the ballet class or dancing in the street as a little fairy, with more photos and videos being taken. She has him do some pirouettes, spinning quickly around till he got dizzy. He complained and Pam laughed "Don't worry Nancy! A few years at my ballet classes will soon have you and even Sissy Tom, being expert in their tutus performing all kinds of ballerina moves without getting dizzy!" as he begged "Please Pammy! You show me the moves at Aunty June's or in my bedroom, but don't take me to ballet and show me off to the girls?" as she gurgled and gave him more kisses on the lips, saying, "Yuk!" but then said, "Only joking Nancy! I love kissing you!" adding "I'm not so fond of kissing your naughty brother Sissy Tom!" as he blushed, as June laughed. She has him to do more mincing and extreme mincing in the tutu, but all this has been with hair ribbons and an Alice band on his head.

June then Says, "I think Nancy has had enough fun in her tutu!" as Tom thought she was going to let him remove the tutu to head on!" with Pam too protesting that he should keep his tutu on for at least half an hour. However, he was dismayed, when she said, "I think Sissy Tom should have a go in his tutu now!" as he cried "Not fair!" as Pam giggled, "Oh yes!" as she removed his Alice band and then the hair slides to leave him looking a complete sissy. Hence, he had to repeat the various ballet moves that Pam had made him do before, but now without his hair ribbons and Alice band, with Pam gurgling "I think at ballet class, he'll want to attend as sweet little Nancy, rather than Sissy Tom!" as he sobbed "Not flaming fair, Pam!"

She then gets him to try and do the splits, which he finds really difficult, but she said, she'd try and get him to practice before bed each night to help his subtleness, as June laughed "It will be even more difficult for him in a few years!" as Pam asked, "Why?" and June laughed "When he becomes a man around eleven!" as Pam tried to enquire more, but she laughed "Your Mum or I will tell you in a few years!" as Pam shrugged her shoulders and Tom thought he knew, but wasn't sure. However, then June produced some fairy wings, as Pam gurgled "Oh fab, June!" as Tom cried "Not flaming fairy wings!" as June fed the elastic up his arms and around his back to hear him beg "Please add my ribbons back in! Pretty please?" as they gave in and Pam adds his ribbons and Alice band onto his hair, as he bobs a curtsy to her "Thanks Pammy?" as she bobs one back, with June taking more photos.

June adds fairy wings to his tutu for garden and Pam Says, about ballet

He has to prance about with the fairy wings around his back, with them giggling and teasing him about looking like a fairy. Pam has him repeat more dance moves and part way through, when he was looking away from the window, she opened the blinds to have him on show to the street, if anyone looked in. He turned and cried "Oh no! Close the blinds" and ducked down onto the floor, as he saw a big girl go past and peer in at him. However, she just thought it was a young girl practicing ballet, as June closed the blinds again. Pam Says, "If we get him to ballet, he wouldn't have to join my class or wear the same ballet outfit at me!" as he thought she meant his PE stuff or something but heard her gurgle "The young girls are called the fairies! They are allowed to wear a tutu and part way through the class, they end up in fairy wings, just like our little fairy is wearing now!" as June giggled, "Oh fab!" He begged "Please Pam don't take me to ballet class!" as they laughed and took more videos of him doing more dance moves, but now dressed as a fairy.

However, Pam then said, "I'm sure your little fairy would love some air about her tutu!" as June gasped "What about your Mum spying him?" as Pam said, "Look I'll pop around to keep Mum in and say, something to alert you if Mum comes out or goes upstairs where she might look out!" as he cried "I can't go out in this tutu and fairy wings!" but Pam scooted around to their place and a few minutes later, June led the blushing Tom out the side door and around the back, where he gasped at the more open garden on view to the houses at the back and ran to try and hide nearer the fence, out of sight. June then took the chance and asked, "How's baby Nancy's nappies?" as he sobbed "Not fair! I've wet them!" as she gurgled "Oh fab! I think I'll have to get some more practice changing baby!" adding "I've only helped some relations with their girl babies!" as he begged "Let me out of them and don't show Pam?" as she laughed "Oh Tom! What do you think Pam might do, if she found you in nappies?" as he blushed and sobbed as she giggled, "She wouldn't! Not change your nappies and actually gel your baby-pee-pee!" as he blushed and huffed "She'd better not!" adding "Mum would go mad if she touched my willy!" as she laughed "Your baby-pee-pee!" as he blushed and repeated. She laughs "Don't worry I'll make sure baby is dry for joining his mates!" as he cried "Please don't send me around in my nappies and especially my diaper! They'll see the bulge and wonder!" as she laughed "Oh what a predicament! We'll wait till Pam is out of the way and I'll see to baby's nappies!" as he blushed at the thought. He complained saying, "That was terrible showing Pam my tutu and I'm dreading her making me join her at ballet!" as she laughed "I'm sure she'll keep your practicing to here and your own house!" as he thought she meant, hidden away in her or his bedroom, from their Mum, but June had other ideas and that he'd get practice secretly at her, but also soon in front of his Mum, with Pam pretending not to realize.

Pam distracts her Mum while June has Fairy Nancy wheels his pram

He continues prancing about in his tutu and fairy wings and dreads being spied by neighbours, as June's garden is more open than his own. Pam chats away with her Mum half peeking out to June's, but can't see much of her fairy brother prancing about in her tutu and fairy wings, but then Says, "I think I'll wheel some dollies around the back garden, to practice for playing with Julie and Tina!" as her Mum laughed "You feeling all right! Don't let me see you suck your thumb, young lady?" as she screeched "Funny Mum!" as she brought a few dollies out with her and got her dolls pram from the garage, as she wheeled it the garden and smiled as she saw her brother prancing about like a fairy. Her Mum leaves the kitchen to pop upstairs and Pam Says, "Quick June! Hide our little fairy!" as she takes Tom back to the house wall, as he turned around and cried "Them out the back houses can see me!" as she laughed and Pam called "Such a shy little fairy!" adding "A few weeks with the fairies at ballet, will soon give him lots of confidence prancing about in his tutu!" as June laughed and he cringed "Stop teasing me about flaming ballet!"

She wheeled her pram on and gasped as her Mum looked out Tom's bedroom window as Pam smiled and waved up to her. She waved back and called out "You look very sweet pushing your doll's pram around the garden!" as Pam giggled, "Mum! You're making me blush!" Her Mum laughed and gasped as she saw Pam stick her thumb in her own mouth and heard her Mum screech "Pam! I'll just get your old dummy and baby bottle ready for you!" as they both screeched with laughter. Pam then called up "Mum! Tom's been showing me, how much fun sucking his thumb is!" adding "He's so looking forward to his dummy and baby bottle of milk, at breakfast and supper time!" as her Mum laughed as he heard and called "Now Pam! Stop saying, baby things about your big brother!" as he wanted to cry "I haven't!" but found June's hand across his mouth, whispering "Don't you dare Tom or else!" Pam carried on wheeling the pram and when her Mum came down said, "Coast is clear for our fairy again!" as June got Tom to turn again and return to the position he was in before to prance about as a fairy, saying, "That wasn't funny Pam!" as she continued wheeling her dolls around the garden. She then had a thought and when she saw her Mum pop into the living room and sit down to watch some TV, she popped the pram and dolls over the fence and said, "I'm sure our little fairy, will enjoy wheeling his doll's pram around and make sure he gets some practice sucking his thumb too!" as he sobbed "Not fair Pam!" as she opened the garage door and closed it with a bang, to pretend she'd left her pram back inside again. June said, "Right fairy Nancy! Start wheeling your dolls around the garden!" and saw him woefully take the doll's pram and start around the garden, but then heard Pam say, "Right baby Suck your thumb for each other around of the garden!" as he sobbed "Oh no!" and then had to wheel his pram with one hand and suck his thumb with the other. Pam returning indoors and joining her Mum to watch the TV and have a chat. She said, "I've left my doll's pram back inside!" Her Mum gurgled "I couldn't believe when I saw you suck your thumb in the garden!"

Her Mum scolds her, warning her not to treat Tom as a baby, but June is

Pam laughed "Mum! That might be a fun thing for Tom!" as she gasped "Don't you dare make him! It's bad enough you, dressing him up as a girl, but don't you dare as a …!" Pam screeched "You mean as a baby! Oh Mum! That would be wonderful, getting him back into nappies!" as her Mum scolded "Now Pam! Less talk, even if you're joking about Tom and nappies!" as she gurgled "Wouldn't it be fun?" as her Mum smacked her hand "Naughty girl! Don't you dare!" adding "Let's change the subject!" However, Pam hadn't realized that June had popped him into nappies and baby plastics and was teasing him about wetting his nappies. Meanwhile Tom was back prancing about in the tutu and fairy wings wheeling Pam's doll's pram about the garden, sucking his thumb between arounds, when June told him to continue as she ran inside and returned with a baby's dummy as he sobbed "Oh no! Not fair!" as she popped it into his mouth as he spat it out, but she said, "You do that again and it will be Pam or maybe little Tina pick it up!" as he sobbed "Not fair!" and picked the dummy up and popped it into his own mouth, as she giggled, and took more photos of him. She returned indoors and put some milk on the boil and returned to see him still with the dummy in his mouth wheeling the pram around her garden. She laughed "I think Baby Nancy has had her fun!" adding "I'm sure Baby Sissy Tom will enjoy it too!" as she removes his ribbons and Alice band as he cried "Oh no! The neighbours will recognise me!" as she said, "It's about time Sissy Tom discovers how much fun ballet class will be!" as she said, "Continue sucking your dummy around and bob a curtsy at the end here to the houses at the back!" as he sobbed "Not flaming fair! Them or Pam will see me!"

She returned to the house and filled up the baby bottle from the saucepan and soon had locked up again and exited to see him as Sissy Tom as a ballerina but sucking on the dummy. However, then he reached her and sobbed "Oh no!" as she produced the baby bottle and said, "Suck your bottle ever ten feet around the garden!" as he went to remove his dummy, but she said, "Just pop your baby bottle into your handbag and swap when you need a drink from it!" as he took the bottle and slid it into his handbag and heard her say, "Zip your handbag up between using it!" and saw him zip it closed again. He minced his pram around the garden, and stopped and unzipping his handbag, he took the baby bottle out and removing his dummy, he sucked on the bottle, as June said, "Ten seconds suck!" and saw him suck again, hating the milk. He took it from his mouth and replaced it into his handbag and zipped it up

again and popped his dummy back into his mouth, to wheel his pram around the garden again and then repeated. However, she said, "Just one more around and you can hide your baby stuff away!" as she then unclipped his tutu and raised it up, to show off his plastics. He cried "Oh no! Dreading the neighbours, or Pam spy his nappies and plastics. He wet his panties again, as he minced around, with his nappies and plastics on show to the garden, stopping to suck on his baby bottle a few times around the garden, but eventually was back to the laughing June, who said, "I wonder how many ladies have looked from the back houses!"

June let's him hide the baby stuff in a handbag, but Pam comes around

He sobbed "I hope nobody has seen me in my tutu and nappies and sucking a flaming dummy and baby bottle!" as she laughed and kissed him again. She quickly did his tutu together under his plastics and asked, "Baby's plastic pants holding ok?" and saw him nod "I think so!" as she laughed "Thank goodness for Pampers!" Luckily Pam hadn't gone out or upstairs to spy on her brother, sucking his thumb, as June laughed "As you've done well, I'll let you hide your baby dummy and bottle back in your handbag!" as he said, "Thanks Aunty June!" and popped them back into his handbag and zipped it up again, as she laughed "I think baby is learning how to use a handbag correctly!" as he begged "Please don't tell Pam, about baby and his handbag?" as she laughed "Don't worry! I'll try and keep baby a secret!"

Pam shot around to June's to let Tom finish his ballet class, but they realised they had to let him indoors again, in case her Mum, went upstairs and spied him in the back garden. She laughed "How was Fairy Nancy?" as June laughed "Oh! He's had fun wheeling his dolly around the garden and even playing with his handbag!" as Pam gurgled "Great! I was thinking he needs more practice with a handbag!" as June asked, "Want Pam to take your handbag or want to play with it some more?" as Pam laughed "Well you owe me!" reaching out, expecting him to ask her to take it, but she gasped as he huffed "Can Nancy play with her handbag some more?" as she gurgled "June! Are you making him say, that?" June shook her head "Honest Pam! He's shocked me, as much as you!" as she laughed "Maybe he is having fun with his handbag!" as Pam asked, "Are you Tom?" as he huffed "Nancy's enjoying her handbag!" as he dreaded Pam, spying his dummy and half full baby bottle and asked, "Can you leave it upstairs for me to play with later?"

Pam screeched and her Mum heard, as they quickly got him indoors and led him back into the sitting room. June got his trousers along with his shirt and jumper and said, "We'd better let him head around to play footy!" as Pam laughed "Oh June! I want to have more fun with ballerina Nancy with his handbag!" as he blushed and heard June say, "Well Tom, want to remove your tutu and get back into your silly boy's clothes or have another fifteen minutes playing ballerina with Pammy!" adding "I'm just getting you girlies some drinks!" as Pam said, "No! Don't let him go yet! I want ballerina Nancy to play a while more!" as he blushed and stammered "Can ballerina Nancy play for a while more!" as Pam gasped and gurgled "Did you make him, June?" as she shook her head "Honest Pam! I've a feeling he's actually kind of enjoying his ballet dress!" as she asked, "Are you Tom?" as Pam said, "I think we should have two answers!" as she laughed and asked, "So Nancy are you enjoying your tutu?" and saw him grip his tutu skirt and bob a curtsy "Yes Pammy! It's lots of fun, but just in doors with you and Aunty June!" as she gurgled "Great!" as she kissed him again. She then removed his hair slides and asked, "So Sissy Tom what about you?" as he gripped his skirt again and bobbed another curtsy "Yes! Pammy it's fun even more as Sissy Tom to play in his tutu, but just indoors with you and Aunty June!" as Pam nearly wet herself and kissed him again, as did June who laughed "I've a feeling it won't be long till he's an expert and can join you at ballet!"

Pam goes to distract her Mum and June changes Tom's nappies

Pam has fun making him do more ballet moves for ten minutes when June brings in some drinks and gives them to Pam and Tom and takes a glass of wine herself. She told Pam she'd better let Tom go now, but to make sure

their Mum doesn't spy him leaving and so sends Pam to keep her out of the way. June said, "Pam! Go over to Julie's telling her, you'll be there in a minute, but then back home to ensure your Mum, doesn't spy Tom, leaving here!" as Pam laughed "Good thinking!" as she slipped out and over to Julie's. Julie's Mum came to the door and saw Pam, but she said, "I just need to speak to Mum a tick and then will be back to play with them!" as her Mum said, "Fine Pam!"

Pam slipped across and her Mum let her in, as she said, "Mum! I've been over at Julie's and just wondered when it would be ok to tell her about Nancy, but not Tina!" as her Mum followed her into the kitchen and said, "No Pam! Don't! Please don't!" as she said, "Ok Mum! It was just a thought! Honest I won't say, yet!" as she slipped into the sitting room and watched as Tom slipped out June's gate. She got her Wendy doll and said, "Ok I promise Mum! I won't tell yet!" as her Mum said, "Thanks Pam!" as she kissed her Mum and taking the doll, she popped it in a carrier bag and called "Bye Mum! Love you!"

Meanwhile Tom was now alone with June and asked, "Now she's gone, can you get me out of these flaming nappies and baby things and my tutu?" as she laughed "Oh Baby! Come up and let me see to changing your nappy!" as he gasped "Can't I clean myself and get dressed?" but she led him upstairs and taking the diaper bag she undid his tutu and pulled it off over his head and slid his arms out of the sleeves and gurgled at him back with his nappies on show through the plastic baby pants. She laughed as she got him down onto a changing mat and then pulled on some rubber gloves and pulled his plastics down to his thighs. She then undid his diaper and pulled it off. She smelt the urine and called "Oh what a stink, baby!" as he blushed and begged "Please be quiet! Mum will hear!" She pulled the disposable off and laughed at his wet red willy and said, "Naughty baby-pee-pee!" adding "You know your Mummy should really be doing this!" as he blushed and she took the wet wipes and cleaned his front up, before applying the gel to his front and baby-pee-pee, as he blushed. She then added the talcum powder and then a clean disposable and went to apply the diaper, when he begged "Please don't add the diaper?" as she said, "Ok!" as she pulled the plastic baby pants up, laughing at the two disposables on show through the plastics as he sobbed "Not fair! I can't play in my plastic baby pants and nappies?" as she said, "Don't worry! Your tutu stays too!" as he cried "Not fair!" as she clipped it up again and then handed him his boy's clothes. He finally pulled his ribbons out and then pulled on his trousers, shirt and then his jumper as she asked, "Hasn't baby got something to ask me before he goes?" as she of course got him to ask again "Please Aunty! Can I go out to play footy in my nappies and plastic baby pants and tutu ballet dress?" to giggles from June again!" as she said, "Well Baby Tom! No playing swapsies with your friends and swapping nappies!"

Tom was let go to play with his mates in nappies and ballet tutu

She led him down and said, "Make sure you stay playing with your mates till they finish! No running back to change out of your ballet tutu, baby pants or nappies! When you've finished, you pop in here and I'll remove your tutu, but your baby pants and nappies stay till I remove them in the morning!" as he cried "Not fair! I hope Pam doesn't see or it will be terrible!" as she made sure his Mum wasn't about the front and they watched Pam slip over to Julie's and then back over to their Mum and after a minute, heard June say, "Pam should have distracted your Mum, by now, so shoot out the side door and slip up the street and around to your mates. Tom edged out the side door and June watched him walk down her drive and slip up the street and then shoot around the corner. He heard them down the next street and soon heard them call "Come on Tom, where have you been?" as he joined a team and soon was larking about playing football with his mates.

He felt really nervous in the tutu, nappies and plastic baby pants and hoped his mates wouldn't hear a noise from his plastics when he ran. Luckily there wasn't any and he had a reasonable time playing football in the street and even scored a few goals. They finished and he joined a few mates around home, but when they'd gone on, he slipped back around to June's and heard her laugh "How was baby football?" as he cried "It was terrible! I was dreading

them hear my plastic baby pants, but luckily they didn't!" as she laughed "I knew I should have added something else to make some noise!" as he begged her not to. She said, "Ok! Let's get our little ballerina out of his tutu!" and pulled his pullover off followed by his shirt to leave him with his tutu on show again. She pulled down his trousers and unclipped his tutu and pulled it off, over his head, laughing as his plastics with the two disposables were again on show. She said, "Ok baby! Here's Pam's panties! Just slide them into your pocket, for later!" adding "Pull up your trousers and get your shirt and jumper back on to return to your house!" and saw him quickly pull them up and pop back into his shirt and jumper as she gave him a kiss. He popped them into his pocket, with a handky on top to hide them from view. He returned home and his Mum let him back in, with Pam calling "Julie Tina and I had a lot of fun playing dollies!" adding "Nancy would have loved it!" as her Mum scolded "Now Pam! You've got to let Tom be himself and have fun playing with his friends!" as she laughed "Did you have fun today?" and saw him nod "Yes Pam! I scored a few goals and played pretty well!" His Mum said, "That's good!" but saw Pam smile and hold up her pretty apron and say, "Well since Tom has had his fun! We'd better let Nancy help with the supper and do the dishes after!" as he blushed and heard her ask "Mum have you got his pinny yet?" but she shook her head and saw Pam hold up her little girl's one, as he begged "Please Pammy! Let Nancy have one of your big pretty aprons!" as she screeched and through her arms around him and kissed his lips, as her Mum said, "Pam! Not on the lips!" as they both laughed. She said, "Just try this little pinny on for a minute to give us a laugh and saw him take the little PVC pinny and pull it around him over her apron, causing them to screech at the sight before he changed.

TANIA TRAPS HER BROTHER PETER 7

Peter finishes football and meets Natalie visiting Tania

Tania decides to trap her little seven-year old brother to become a girly and maybe a baby too. She has met Abi and makes Peter choose her as his girlfriend. They trap him and dress him up as a girl and take him down to the kinder garden school, to possibly be diapered.

Peter 7 comes in from Footy and meets Natalie visiting his sister Tania

Seven-year old Peter came in from footy and said, "That was a good game of footy, Mum!" as he saw his smiling sister, with the big girl and his Mum, at the front door. Natalie said, "Is this your sweet brother, Tania?" as he blushed as she said, "Isn't he adorable!" as she put her arms around him and he cowered away, as his Mum and sister giggled. She said, "I'm her friend Natalie!" adding "Tania has just been showing me her lovely dolls and dresses!" as he said, "Aren't you a bit old, to play stupid dolls?" as his Mum laughed and said, "Her Mummy Says, that even boys, should learn to play dollies!" He said, "You must be joking! I'll break them, if she puts her stupid dolls, near me!" as he stumped off and into the living room, as Tania laughed "See what me mean, Natalie! A right MSP!" as she kissed Tania and her Mum bye and said, "Why don't you try and work on him, tonight and get him to do more housework!"

His Mum laughed and she added "I'm sure you can find him a pretty apron and pinny, to protect his dresses, I mean trousers, from getting wet!" as Tania screeched, at her mistake.

They showed her out and swapped phone numbers, before she called bye and skipped off back home. Tania and her Mum went in and said, "Wasn't my friend Natalie sweet?" as he huffed and tried to concentrate on the TV. His Mum said, "She said, Boys too, should learn to play dollies, so when they grow up and have babies themselves, they can help their wives, dress and undress the children!" He huffed "Bug off! No way!" as a smiling Tania, went upstairs and returned down again, with a few dolls, but with the one Natalie had changed.

She sat down on the sofa with him in the armchair and said, "Natalie changed pretty Cloie into a new frock!" as he said, "Bring her over here and I'll rip her head off!" His Mum heard and said, "You break any of her dolls and you're for it, you'll be taken to town, to buy her a new one!" Tania laughed and said, "And I'd make sure you test drive lots of dollies first, in a dolls pram too!" as he said, "No way! I'll tell Dad!" as they scolded, "Now it's only if you're naughty and break one of her dolls!"

Tania makes Peter complement his Mum and her with dolly threats

He said, "Ok I promise I won't break any of them!" as Tania said, "Come over here! Sorry for teasing you, as she set her dolls on her side and said, "Sit here! As I want to ask you something!" He stood up and begged "Well please keep the dolls away from me?" as she said, "Ok! But they don't byte!" as he huffed "Ha!" as he sat down and she said, "I want you to do something for me!" as he asked, "What?" She smiled and whispered "Tell Mummy how pretty she looks and then the same to me!" as he gasped "No way!" but she said, "I could get my dollies to attack you!" as she took a doll and set it onto his lap, purposely touching his trousers, as he gasped "Tania! That's my willy, she just touched!" as she laughed "Oops!" as she said, "Just go in and say!" Peter blushed and standing up, he went into the kitchen and saw his Mum in her apron and PVC piny and said, "Mummy you look pretty!" Tania was behind and said, "Mummy isn't Peter sweet? I think that deserves a nice curtsy to him!" as her Mum curtsied and said, "Thanks Peter!" as Tania held him and said, "and a kiss too!" He cried "Oh no!" as she laughed and whispered, "My dollies could be kissing you, instead!" as his laughing Mum, bent down and gave him a kiss on the cheek. However she said, "Only the lips count, Mummy!" as he cried "Don't Mum!" as his laughing Mum, kissed his lips and he said, "Yuk!" as she laughed "It's been years, since I kissed you Peter!" as both her and Tania laughed.

Then she said, "Now for me!" as he huffed "Tania, you look pretty too!" as her Mum gurgled "Oh Tania!" as she gripped her skirt and curtsied too and said, "Thanks Peter! That deserves a sweet kiss!" as he begged "Please don't?" as she laughed "I think he'll want my kisses in future, as she ran in and got her big dolly, that Natalie had changed and said, "Give Cloie a kiss or else!" as he sobbed "Not fair!" as she held the doll up to his lips and he gave her a quick peck, to laughter from both of them.

He said, "There! Not fair!" as she took him into the living room and said, "Now tell Cloie, how pretty a dolly she is!" He said, "No way!" but she threatened "I could tell your mates you kissed my dolly!" He sobbed "Not fair! Take your dollies away please!" as she laughed "Just tell her!" as he said, to it "You're a very pretty dolly, Cloie!" as she added "And you love her!" as he sobbed "Not fair! And I love you!" She said, "Just one kiss each!" as he kissed the doll again and then gasped as Tania lowered the doll down to his trousers again, but she then pulled him over and kissed him on the lips. He said, "I don't like kisses!" as she laughed "We'll get these dollies, out of the room, before Dad comes!" as she held out her doll to him and he cried "Oh no!" as she took her other dolls and ushered him out, but turned him to show her Mum and say, "Mummy! Sweet Peter here, is bringing his new dolly Cloie, up to his room, till bed time!" He begged "Not to my room?" as his Mum laughed "Oh Tania! This better not get out, as she laughed "I'll try and keep his playing dollies, a secret, but he's to be a good little boy and promise to help you, with the dishes and housework!" He cried "Not fair!" as she led him up the stairs and said, "Just another kissy!" as he huffed and kissed the doll, but she said, "For me silly!" and saw him kiss her, as he huffed "Ha!"

Tania makes Toby admit to having played dollies since 4 or 5

She laughed "Now! You don't want me to tell the girls at school, or your friends?" as he begged "Please don't tell?" but she took the dress, Natalie had removed from her doll and said, "Just try and get your dolly, into her new frock!" He begged "Don't make me dress your dolly?" as she asked, "Who's dolly, is she?" as he said, "She's my dolly!" as she kissed him again. He took the doll and turned her, she said, "Just carefully undo the Velcro here and remove your pretty dolly's dress!" He sniffled "Please don't tell on me?" as she hugged him and kissed him again, causing him to blush, as she saw him, undo the material and then slide the doll's arms out of the dress and then pull it off. She giggled, "Well done Peter! You've done that very well!" as he blushed and she handed him the other dress and said, "Quick! Your pretty dolly doesn't like being undressed and wants into her frock, quickly!" as he took the dress and tried to put it on, but got it wrong. She scolded "Silly boy! You've to unbutton her frock at the top!" and saw him undo the, buttons and then pull the dress down its arms and over its head and then down

it's body, as she gurgled and said, "Just redo the, buttons, of your dress, I mean dolly's dress, Peter!" as he blushed and did the, buttons up.

She gurgled and called "Mummy! Come and see this!" as her Mum ran up and saw him holding the dolly and heard Tania gurgle "Mummy look! Peter changed his dolly, into its new frock!" as her Mum screeched "Oh Peter!" as he sobbed "Mum! She made me!" Tania laughed "Actually Mummy! I was surprised, how quickly, he actually changed his dolly's frock! I've a feeling it's not the first time, he's changed my dolly's!" as he cried "It is!" as she laughed "He let me into a secret Mummy!" as she asked, "What?" as she laughed "He's been secretly stealing my dollies, into his room and dressing and undressing them, for a few years now! Since he was 4 or 5!" as he cried "I haven't!" but she laughed "Now! Will I bring some young girls in, to join you playing dollies?" as he begged "Please don't?" Tania laughed "So what age did Patsy, start playing with my dollies?" as he huffed "Since I was 4 or 5!" as she scolded "Naughty boy! Without asking me!" as her Mum laughed "Naughty girl!" as Tania kissed him again.

She brought him downstairs and held out one of her old floral aprons and said, "Get that on, to show Mummy a tick!" as he sobbed "Oh no!" and pulled the apron on, as she giggled, and tied it behind him. She took him into the kitchen and heard their Mum giggle, as she saw him in the girly apron and said, "Oh Peter! I didn't think her dollies, would lead to this!" as they both giggled. Then their Dad came in from work and she said, "Not a word about dollies or else, ok?" as he sobbed and she took him into the bathroom and wiped his eyes and washed his face, removing his girly apron, as she gave him another kiss. She said, "Peter! I bet you'll have your own girlfriend soon!" as he huffed "I don't like girls!" as she laughed "We'll see!" She then asked, "Are there any girls you like in your class?" as he shook his head "They're all stupid little girls!"

Tania tells her Dad 'Pete's got a new girlfriend' – Cloie, but then has Abi

She laughed "I'll try and find you a girlfriend, in your class!" as he begged "Please don't?" as she laughed "I'll want you to tell your mates at school you fancy one of the girls and see how it goes!" He begged "Please don't, it will be terrible!" She laughed "What! Being all kissy-kissy with a sweet young girl and getting lots of kisses from her!" as he said, "Yuk!" as she laughed "So you'd rather kiss your dolly, Cloie then?" as he shook his head and heard her add "Right downstairs and not a word to Dad?" She waited a few minutes and slid Cloie between the pillows, on his bed, hidden away, in case his Dad saw and closed the door. She descended the stairs and said, "Hi Daddy!" as she kissed him and said, "Had a good day?" as he said, "Not bad dear! How was yours!" as they sat down at the dinner table and their Mum dished out the dinner.

They finished their dinner and sat down to watch TV, with him popping out to join his mates. Tania waited till he'd left and said, "I've heard a rumour that Pete's got a girlfriend!" as her Mum said, "Now Tania! He's too young!" His Dad laughed "A chip off, the old block!" as Tania said, "Now Mummy! You know kissing is fun!" as she laughed "I've heard her name is Cloie!" as her Mum heard and gasped and went into the kitchen, to have a giggle, at his girlfriend, being his big pretty dolly. The next day at school, Tania had let Pete wear his boy's clothes, but approached him in the canteen and said, "I've had a word around and checking which girls are in your class and I think Abigale can be your girlfriend!" He huffed "Not fair!" as she asked, "Which one is she?" as he pointed to a table of girls, eating their lunch and blushed and said, "The one with pigtails and a pink bow!" as she said, "The pretty girl with the plats?" as he nodded. She laughed "Oh! I think I've chosen well!"

She said, "Make sure you tell several different boys, you can start at lunch here and whisper to your mates, about liking Abi!" as he begged "Please don't?" She laughed "You could be here in a dress and pinafore!" as he huffed "Ha!" He cringed as his laughing sister, minced off and he went and got his dinner and sat down with some boys from class. He was eating away when he stammered "I quite like that Abi from class!" as a mate John said, "Peter loves Abi! Peter loves Abi!" as another guy heard and asked, "Do you?" He blushed and nodded, as he said, "Gosh

you could roast a pig on your face! It's red as a beetroot!" He went over to the girls and said, "See Peter from class?" as she nodded, he added "He Says, he fancies, Abi!" as the girls laughed "Oh Abi! You've got an admirer! Peter!" She blushed, but having known already, what Tania was planning, just giggled, and looked over to Pete's table and blew a kiss to him and said, "I'll see, what he Says!" His mates said, "She blew you a kiss, send her one back!" as he said, "No way!" as they laughed and blew her kisses themselves, calling "Pete Says, he loves her!" as he huffed "I don't!" as they laughed. She said, "I might invite him around to play at my place and see what he's like and if I want him, as my boyfriend or not!" An older girl heard and laughed "Aren't you 2 a bit young, to be all kissy-kissy!" as Abi laughed "Oh! Kissing is lots of fun!" adding "I've kissed a ten-year old boy, though he's not my boyfriend!" as they gasped "You have?" as she nodded.

After lunch in canteen and Abi takes Peter for a chat to the playground

However, then his sister Tania heard and went over to him and said, "Peter! What's this about you fancying a little girl in your class?" as he blushed, but then heard her say, "What about your girlfriend Cloie, and all the kisses you've given her, lately! Does she know?" adding "You little two timer you!" The boys gasped "Gosh! My brother doesn't even have 1 girlfriend and he's nine!" as he cringed, at his sister talking about his dolly, as he took another mouthful of food and she skipped off, to leave him to questions about Cloie. His mates said, "You kept quiet about Cloie, how long have you two been seeing each-other?" as he cringed "Not long!" as they laughed "How come you fancy Abi, if you've another girlfriend?" He huffed, trying to think of an answer and said, "Abi's prettier than her!" as they gasped "He must have it bad!" as his mate laughed and one said, "Girls Yuk!" as some others echoed with Pete wanting to call "I hate girls!" but couldn't and just blushed, as he finished his dinner. Abi had finished before him and picking up her pretty girly shopping bag of books, she was joined by a few other girls and minced over to his table and said, "What's this I hear about you fancying me, Peter?"

He gasped "I'm eating! Leave me alone!" as she said, "Finish your meal and we'll have a chat!" as the girls giggled. He huffed "Not fair!" as he looked up and saw his big sister, looking at him, sternly and stammered "Ok!" as he stood up and taking his satchel, said, "Bye guys! Catch you at footy!" Abi said, "He'll see you in class, I want a good talk with him and maybe give him some sweet kisses!" as the boys called "Yuk!" as she laughed "Watch it Alan, or you might get a girlfriend too!" as he huffed "No chance!" as her and the girls laughed. He joined Abi and the girls out of the canteen and said, "What do you want to chat about?" as she said, "What's this I've heard about you going with someone else, I think she's called Cloie!" He gasped and cried "Not fair! How did you hear about her?" as she laughed "Oh walls have ears!" as another girl scolded "Going after 2 girls! Greedy boy!" He blushed and stammered "I think you're prettier than her!" as she laughed and blushed and stopped and said, "I think that deserves a curtsy to my sweet boyfriend" as she gripped the skirt of her pinafore and dress and bobbed a curtsy to him, as her friends giggled, as she then added "and a kiss!" as she threw her arms around his neck and kissed his lips!" as he gasped "Oh no! I don't like kisses!" The girls laughed and he blushed, as a teacher saw and said, "Hey you two, less of the kissy-kissy in the corridor!" as Abi giggled, and called "Sorry Miss! It's just that my boyfriend Pete here, said I was pretty!" as she laughed "Did you?" as he nodded, as she said, "Mummy's taught me to give a curtsy and a kiss, for anyone complementing me!" as the teacher laughed. Abi whispered "Tell the teacher, she's very pretty!" as he gasped, as she laughed "Or I tell about Cloie!" as he gasped and stammered "Your pretty too Miss!" as she gasped and saw Abi bob a curtsy!" as the laughing teacher, curtsied to him "Thank you, young boy!" Abi laughed "He deserves a little kissy!" as she gasped "No way!" as she laughed "He'll hate it!" as she bent down and kissed his cheek!" as the girls screeched "Oh Abi!"

A prefect tells Pete off, for being in the girl's playground

She laughed "He prefers the lips!" as she said, "No way! I'll leave that to you, young lady!" as she said, "No more kissing in the corridor!" as she walked off laughing. He gasped again as Abi said, "What's this, I've heard about you

having another girl friend and giving her lots of kisses too?" He stammered "She's not as nice as you and she's not really my girlfriend!" as she asked, "I've heard someone has been all kissy with her!" as he blushed and said, "But I prefer you!" as she minced on down, with her shoulder bag dangling from her elbow, towards the playgrounds. He said, "I'm off to play football!" but she said, "No Patsy, you come and talk to me!" as the girls laughed, at her dominant attitude, to the boy. He huffed "Not fair!" as she led him down and he cried "It's the girl's playground! I can't go there!" as a girl laughed "If you want some kissy-kissy! You could go behind the bicycle sheds!" She led him on and soon was entering the girl's playground, where he saw all the girls, with most of them older than him, as his sister saw them and ran over and said, "Hi Peter, are you going to introduce me, to your sweet friend!" He cringed and said, "Tania's my big sister!" adding "This is Abi, from my class!" She said, "How come you're down here, with her?" as Abi said, "Oh Peter has said, he fancies me, but I don't want to be two timed, with some other girl, Cloie!" as Tania laughed "Cloie is sweet, so why do you prefer Abi to her?" as he huffed "Abi's prettier than her!" to more giggles, as she again bobbed a curtsy "Thanks Patsy!" as she again threw her arms around his neck and kissed his lips.

A prefect came over and said, "Now boy, you can't be down here! This is the girl's playground! You aren't a girl, are you?" as he blushed and heard Tania say, "Look these two, have just got together and you'll have a giggle soon, if you can let him stay! He can be an honorary girl!" She laughed "Ok! We'll let you be an honorary girl!" as Abi laughed "I could lend him a hair ribbon, as he cried "Please don't?" His sister grabbed him and said, "Just one, so you can stay, to chat to Abi!" as he sobbed "Not fair, Tania!" as Abi removed a ribbon and slid it into his hair, to giggles and screeches from the girls, but also the prefect, who said, "Next time, be prepared for a dress and pinafore dear!" as the girls screeched "Oh fab!" as he begged "Please don't, girls?" Abi laughed "Oh Patsy! It's fun being a girl and wearing pretty skirts and dresses!" adding "And you'll get more kisses from me!" as she again threw her arms, around him and gave him a kiss, to more giggles, but some girls called "Yuk!" as he begged "Please! Remove your ribbon?" as she shook her head and said, "If I do, then I'll replace it with my pinafore, for you to test drive, around the quad and maybe do some skipping!" as he gasped "Oh no! Don't please?" She said, "So you don't mind wearing some ribbons, to please me!" as another girl Karen said, "Oh you little sweetie!" as she removed her yellow Alice band and popped it onto his head, followed by another girl, removing 2 slides and giggled, as she slid them, into his hair too!" but then gave him a kiss too with Abi calling "Eh no stealing my girly Patsy!" as Tania laughed "Oh Patsy, I'd never have dared to put you into ribbons and bows!" adding "till now!" as the girls laughed. Abi said, "Oh Tania, you should give him some practice, playing as your little sister!"

Tania, Abi and the prefect dress Peter up as a girl but also panties

She gurgled "Oh Peter! What's it going to be like, back at our place?" The prefect gasped at the girly boy and said, "Well! If your girly boyfriend wants to stay, he can't be noticed in those trousers!" adding "Better get him into a pinafore!" as the girls giggled, and screeched "Oh fab!" as he called "Please don't? Tania help me?" as Abi removed her blazer and quickly pulled off her pinafore and held it out, to the prefect. He sobbed, as his sister took them around the side and said, "We'll do it here, out of site!" as she said, "Quick Patsy, remove your blazer and jumper a tick!" as he cried "Mum will give it to you, for dressing me up!" as she laughed "I'm sure Daddy will see the funny side too!" as he cringed at the thought. He removed the blazer and then the jumper and then took the dress, from the smiling prefect and pulled it over his head and slid his arms into the sleeves, to more giggles. Tania said, "I hope Abi won't mind, but I think that deserves a kiss, from all of us!" as one after the other gave him a kiss. Then the prefect asked, "Can I give your sissy, a kissy?" as Abi screeched "Oh yes!" as she too gave him a kiss. However, then Tania said, "He'd still look a boy in his trousers, as she reached under his pinafore and said, "Hold still or else!" as he cried "Leave my trousers, Tania!" as the girls screeched and soon she was undoing his trousers and zip and pulling them down, but then cried "Oh no!" as he felt his underpants, coming down, as the girls gasped, as she pulled them both down his legs and saw him try to hold his dress down.

Tania said, "Now Patsy, tell the girls, what was hiding inside your silly boy's undies?" as he cried "Oh no! Don't make me say?" as she nodded, and he blurted out "It's my baby-pee-pee!" as the girls gasped and giggled, Abi knew and said, "Why do you call it that Patsy?" as he sobbed "Because it's only the size of a little baby boys, baby-pee-pee!" as the girls screeched and his sister raised his pinafore, as he sobbed "Oh no!" as they all saw, his little willy and all cried "It is a little baby one!" as he sobbed "Not fair, Tania!" as she laughed "Anyone got spare panties?" as he cried "Don't put me into panties, girls?" as they all shook their heads, Lucy said, "I do have a pretty pair, for the ballet, after school!" as she rummaged into her dance case and held them up!" as the girls screeched. Abi said, "Ask Lucy to pop Patsy into her dance panties, or we mince you around, without your pretty ribbons!" as he asked, "Can I please wear your pretty pink panties, to hide my baby-pee-pee!" She gurgled and blushed as she bent down and said, "Lift your legs, Sissy!" as she fed the panties up his legs, as Abi raised her pinafore again, to giggles, as he begged "Please hide my baby-pee-pee!" as they all giggled, at the sight and eventually a laughing Lucy, raised the panties to cover him, but touched it, on the way up. She then said, "You'd better not wet my pretty panties girly!" as they giggled, and Abi laughed "Don't worry, if he does, then it's nappies and plastics pants, for my baby boyfriend!" He promised "Honest Lucy! I won't wet your panties!" as they laughed.

Peter is put into a carrier bag over nappies, but taken to the prep school

She heard Abi say, "I was going to use my carrier bag here, for something else, but I know a good way to protect panties!" as they looked at her and Tania knew, what she was going to do. She said, to him "Lucy! Remove your panties a tick!" The blushing girl reached up and pulled his panties down again, giving the girls another look at his willy. They then saw Abi take the girly pink carrier bag and make 2 holes in the corners, as she said, "Right baby! Step into your baby plastic bag!" as he sobbed "Oh no! Not fair!" as he fed his feet into the bag and felt her pull it up his legs, as his sister pulled his dress up and the saw her stretch it around his thighs and then up to hide his willy!" as she gurgled "That will offer a little protection, till we get some nappies for my baby boyfriend!" The girls gasped and gurgled "Oh fab!" as Lucy said, "Promise if I lend you my panties, you'll get some nappies, as soon as you can, to protect them!" as he looked at the laughing girls and nodded but she made him say, it, as she fed them back up over his plastic bag and gurgled "Oh fab!"

However, the prep school with younger girls was nearby and Tania whispered to the prefect, who said, "We won't be cruel and take our girly, to the big girl's playground!" as he felt her and Tania guide him down, out a side entrance and across the road, where they heard lots of little girls and boys playing separately, with a few lady teachers watching the proceedings. The teacher saw the group of girls and called "What's going on girls?" as they laughed and asked, "Would there be some babies or girls with spare nappies, one of our girls forgot hers and although, she has her plastics on, she needs some nappies to protect her pretty panties, just in case!" as the lady laughed, not realizing their trick. She saw all the girls in dresses and most in pinafores. She led them into another room, where some babies and their Mum's, were tending to them, giving them their bottles and some changing nappies.

She called "Grania! Would any of you ladies have some spare disposables, for a big girl, who sounds to have some trouble!" as one said, "Yes! Where is she?" and saw the big girls, guide Pete over, as she gasped "It's not! Is it?" Tania whispered in his ear, play along or I tell what Cloie is!" as she said, "My little girly brother, here has some problems, wetting himself and forgot his nappies and plastics today!" She gasped and then saw her raise his dress and show her, he's afraid of wetting his pretty panties, as the teacher gasped "Not very regulation?" as Tania laughed "He's a bit of a rebel and likes to wear, my pretty panties!", as the girls giggled. The woman asked, "Want to take him to the loo, to change, or do it here?" as he cried "The loo please?" Tania said, "Now tell the truth, how many times have you changed your own nappies?" as he said, "Never!" as she said, "It's left to Mummy and me to change him!" as she said, "Just lie down and we'll change baby!" as the girls gurgled "Oh fab!" She asked, "Tell the lady what's in your panties?" as he grimaced "My baby-pee-pee!" as she and some other Mum's

and little girls giggled, and was asked, "Why does baby call it that?" He sobbed "Because it's the size of a little baby boys, baby-pee-pee!" as they screeched, and the teacher came over and heard them say, "Oh the poor boy! I never realised it was a girly boy!"

Pete's treated as a baby sucking on a dummy whilst being diapered

Tania laughed "Can he borrow something to keep him quiet and pacify him!" as the mother gasped "You don't mean he?" as she took a pink baby's dummy from her daughter and handed it to Tania. She said, "Better suck and be quiet!" as she stuck it into his mouth, to more screeches, as her daughter called "I want my dummy back!" as her Mum laughed. She said, "Let the big sissy boy, borrow it a tick!" as they both laughed, but then heard her say, "He loves wearing his baby bonnet, when being diapered!" as he tried to cry through the dummy, but next a pretty frilled baby bonnet was slid onto his head and tied under his chin. They pulled down his pretty pink panties and the mother gasped "Whatever is that?" as Abi called "Baby was trying to protect his panties, with a girly plastic bag!" as they gurgled, but she then said, "Raise up baby!" a He raised his bum and she pulled down the plastic bag and they all giggled, at the big boy, showing his little pee-pee, as she laughed "It is a little baby one!" as she removed his dummy a tick and asked "What do you call that?" as he cringed and stammered "My baby pee pee!" as they all giggled. She replaced his dummy and said, "We'll see to baby's bottom first!" as they turned him over onto his front. She took some wet wipes and went to wash it!" Abi called "As he's my baby boyfriend "Can I? I've got experience!" as the lady handed her the wet wipes and saw the little girl, take them and wipe his bottom cheeks, first the left, then the right, but then underneath and then prodded his bottom, saying, "Mustn't forget baby's bull's eye!" as the mothers gasped, at her cheek.

The Mum asked, "Will I as I've got gloves for babying!" but Abi said, "I'll wash my hands, after seeing to my baby boyfriend!" as she was handed the gel, but brought her hand down on his bottom, as he cried "Oh no! Not fair!" as she said, "Naughty botty!" to more laughter. She started gelling his bottom, both cheeks and underneath and then said, "You couldn't make sure his botty is gelled?" as the Mum took a finger and gently prodded it, as Abi said, "Lucky baby, I'd prod you more than that!" as the Mum's gasped and gurgled. The lady sprinkled talcum powder over his bottom and Abi stuck the disposable down, to cover it. They said, "Now for his baby's pee-pee!" as they turned him over and he cried "Not fair!" as several Mum's and daughters, were looking down on him, laughing. She took more wet wipes and they gasped, as she took hold of it and rubbed it, as he said, "Be gentle with my baby pee!" to more laughter, as she then took some gel and rubbed it over his front and his penis, as the ladies and girls gasped. at her cheek.

Next talcum powder was being sprinkled with Lucy calling "Some fairy dust for baby!" as Abi popped his disposable on, as the lady asked them "A diaper too?" as they all nodded, and soon, he was being popped into a diaper to giggles. Another lady said, "My large baby girl here, has some big plastics, that might fit your baby!" as they nodded, and she took the clear pants, over to them, as he sobbed "Not flaming plastic baby pants too?" as he was stood up and they pulled the plastics around his diaper, to more laughter. Of course, Tania took some photos of him, in his nappies and plastic baby pants.

Abi feeds the girly carrier bag over his nappies, but then a pinafore

However, then Abi took his pink carrier shopping bag and said, "If you girls can get baby out of his dress and shirt, I've a fun way to ensure, baby stays in his nappies all afternoon!" They gasped and started removing his pinafore and then his shirt to leave him bare chested, as she made another 2 holes in the plastic carrier, at the front and back and said, "See if I feed it up his legs and over his nappies, but I then can feed the handles of the bag, up and feed his his arms in, to look like a leotard. They screeched "But the 2 holes in the corners, now showed his nappies too, as she fed it, up his body and up his arms to his shoulders as they gasped and a lady took a hair

ribbon and tied it around his neck, as they giggled, and saw the bag look like a leotard, around his chest, but partly hiding his nappies. She then fed the girly panties up his legs, over the bag and said, "Much prettier!" However, one of the girls had disappeared into the toilet's and removed her dress and pinafore and returned wearing her school pinafore and said, "I hope baby looks after my school dress!" He sobbed "Oh no!" as Abi nodded, "Perfect for my sissy boyfriend!" as they fed the dress up his arms and over his head and down to hide his plastic carrier bag and nappies. Next was Abi's pinafore and soon he was standing there, as a sissy girly boy, as the girls and ladies all giggled, at him, in the dress, baby bonnet and replaced his dummy again.

After having a baby-bottle they then give him baby food

However, then Tania saw a few mothers feeding their baby's and giving them their baby milk and said, "My brother is feeling a bit hungry!" as she saw the ladies smile and one laughed "Oh the poor boy!" as she took her daughter's bib and fed it onto Peter, as he cried "Not baby food!" as the lady laughed. She said, "If you can get your baby brother down here tomorrow, I'm sure one of two of us ladies, will have some more food, to satisfy baby's hunger!" as they all gurgled and he cried "No don't!" but next thing a little baby spoon of baby food, was held up and he tried to resist, but then took it in his mouth and cried "No, that's horrid!" as they all screeched. Abi called "Naughty baby! I'll make sure, my big baby boyfriend, has lots of baby food, from now on!" as Tania giggled, at the fear, in her brothers face, as she asked, "Baby, want his baby bottle?" He nodded, "Wanting to wash the horrid food, down!" as the lady fed the baby bottle, into his mouth and saw him suck, as she laughed "Such a big baby! Goo Goo Ga Ga" Tania laughed "I know what baby will have for breakfast and to drink, from now on!" as he cried "Not baby food?" as he said, "Mum, won't let you!" as she laughed "But I know some lady friends who will love feeding my little baby brother!" as she laughed "And your baby bottle!" as they all giggled.

Then another lady with a young girl asked, "Can I feed baby?" as they all nodded, and she fed the large spoon into his mouth. They saw his face change and cry "Oh no! That's worse Mrs!" adding "I hope his nappies and plastics hold!" as they screeched.

Peter dirties his nappies and has his botty smacked

He asked for the baby bottle, but the lady took another large spoonful and handed it to Abi, who fed it into his mouth and said, "Hold on baby, don't swallow yet!" as she fed his dummy back in and said, "Move that mush around baby's mouth and no swallowing yet!" as the girls laughed and gurgled and saw him suck on the dummy, but his eyes open, as he tasted the mush. She said, "Now swallow baby!" as he swallowed and his eyes closed, as he tasted the horrid mush, and all laughed. He begged again "Can baby have his baby bottle?" to more laughter, as they gave in and he swallowed the milk, which washed the horrid goo, down again. However, then he gasped "Oh no! Let me go to the loo?" as they asked, "a tiddle, or a poo poo!" as he sobbed "Both!" as they stood him up and got him to curtsy and dance about the room, to giggles as he cried "Oh no!" as he wet his nappy and then pooed them too. He cried "Not fair I've done both!" as a laughing lady took him across her lap and they all smacked his dresses, but Tania pulled them up and all smacked his legs and some of his nappies, as he cried "Oh no, it's spreading over my bum!" as they gurgled "Thank goodness for Pampers! Eh baby!" as he sobbed "Not fair girls!" as he was stood up and his baby bonnet and baby bib removed.

Pete is led out, past laughing ladies and teachers and little girls and boys. He begged for his hair ribbons and bows again but was led on. They asked the girls, not to tell the girls and boys about his nappies, or baby food and stuff, as it will be more fun tomorrow. He begged them not to show him off to girls and boys in his class, but Abi said, "I'm letting you wear your trousers again!" The girls said, "No! Keep him in his dresses!" but she said, "Wait and hear girls!" as she did them up his legs, but did his belt buckle, but not his trousers and said, "When, we ask girly,

if he wants to remove his trousers or frocks, in front of girls and teachers, my sissy girly boyfriend, will ask to keep his frocks on and sound a complete sissy girly boy!" to more screeches.

He sobbed "Oh no!" as they led him, to the big girl's playground again, where none recognised him, till there was a screech. A girl called "That's not your Pete, Abi?" as she said, "He surprised me by telling me, he likes playing dress up and dollies!" as they screeched, but said, "I think it would be too embarrassing, to show him off, in his dresses, to the boys in class, so I'll let him remove his dresses, to attend classes as a boy again!" They said, "No! Take him in his dress and pinafore!" as lots of girls gathered around, watching and listening and heard her say, "So Patsy! Want to attend class as a boy again, or please me and these girls and keep your dresses on and remove your silly trousers?" They said, "Go on Pete! Keep your dresses on!" not thinking he would, but gasped as he sobbed and called out "Can I keep my dresses on, Abi?" as she gasped "I never realized my macho boyfriend, was such a sissy girly boy?" but then asked, "Are you Patsy?" and saw him nod. She said, "So! If any of these girls, see you acting all macho in boy's clothes, again and have a spare frock for you, to play dress up in, you'll enjoy it more, slipping into their frock and handing over your silly trousers and underpants!" as they giggled. He cried "Not my undies too?"

Peter asks to keep his dress on and tells of his panties and led to the gym

She laughed "Tell the girls what you're wearing as undies today?" as he huffed "Some frilly turquoise panties!" as they screeched and she said, "Not very regulation, but we won't tell the teachers!" adding "Will we girls?" as they giggled, and nodded. They led him up to the girl's gym and into the corridor, where she warned Peter, to play along or else. She knocked on the door and heard the teachers call "Wait! Five minutes girls?" as she knocked again and the teacher opened it and saw the girls standing there, smiling as she asked, "Yes girls! What do you want?" as Tania laughed "My little girly brother here, Patsy, is wanting to do dance with the girls, instead of PE!", as she looked at the little boy standing there in the school dress and pinafore, as she gasped "You aren't a boy, are you?"

He bobbed a curtsy and said, "Yes Miss!" as her and another teacher gasped "Oh fab!" as Abi called "He's my new boyfriend from class and I've only just found out, he likes playing dollies and dress up, like me!" as they laughed "Oh you poor boy!" as she said, "We're giving Patsy the choice of, removing his dresses for class, or his silly trousers, but he's told the girls out in the quad, if they ever see him in silly trousers, again and have a pretty skirt or frock to wear, he'd prefer to swap into that, to play dollies with them!" as they asked, "You haven't?" as he nodded, "Yes Miss!" The teachers said it was fine for Pete to join the girls for dance as he cringed, dreading when the boys and the rest of the girls found out.

Tania laughed "You know me, Miss?" as one nodded, and she said, "He's my little girly brother and has been playing dollies and dress up, in my old skirts and frocks for years now!" as he gasped "Not fair!" as they laughed "You tease!" She laughed "Oh! He's just annoyed, that I've let his girly side, out of the bag!" as they asked, "Where will he change?" as Abi said, "He can't change with us girls! So! He will have to change into his dance skirt, with you sweet teachers!" as she asked, "Tell the teachers, what you think of them?" He bobbed a curtsy "You're both very pretty teachers!" as they screeched and heard her say, "That usually deserves a curtsy!" as they both curtsied to him, but then she said, "and a sissy kissy!" as they both gurgled and bending down, they both kissed him. Abi threw hare arms around him too and kissed his lips to more laughter as he cringed "I don't like kissing!" to more laughter. However, Abi then said "Pete! That's a pretty dress and pinafore you're wearing!" as they looked at him and he gripped his dresses and bobbed a curtsy back to her and stammered "Thank you, Abi!" and pursed his lips and Abi of course kissed him too, to more laughter and giggles.

However one of the teachers asked "What was that noise, when he bobbed his curtsy?" as they laughed and said "We just had him down to the kinder-garden section and realized that Patsy might have a little accident in my

friend Lucy's panties and so we had to protect him!" as the teacher gasped "You don't mean nappies?" as they nodded and tears appeared in Pete's eyes, with the place exploding with laughter, She continued "Before he had his diaper and large plastic baby pants, we used a plastic carrier bag to protect his panties!", as she raised his dresses to show them, adding "But now since baby's protected with proper baby things, we now added the carrier bag, as a protecting leotard!" as they gasped "Never!" as they saw the panties over the plastic leotard but with holes in it to show off his diaper and plastic baby pants too, as Tania gurgled "So my little baby brother makes a lovely plastic sound when he minces about the place or shows off his curtsies in his dresses!"

Peter asks to dance with the girls and is taken to needlework department

Tania said "Abi had heard Patsy has another girlfriend Cloie and had given her lots of hugs and kisses last night!" as the teachers laughed "You little two timer!" as Tania laughed "However she doesn't have to be too worried about Cloie!" as a teacher asked "Why?" as Tania gurgled "Cloie is one of my dollies which I've given to Patsie as an early birthday present!" as they all screeched as she laughed "He changed her into a new frock last night and slept with her too, in one of my old pretty nighties!" as he sobbed "Don't tell Tania!" to more screeches.

She said, to her "Just off to get him to request to join us girls in embroidery and needlework!" as they heard the door close and the ladies screech, at what they just heard and saw. Next, they led him along to the needlework and repeat to the teacher there.

She gasped "You aren't going to attend class in your dress and pinafore?" as they nodded, and Abi asked, "So Patsy! Do you want to attend class in your pretty dress and pinafore?" as he nodded, "yes Abi!" They said, "Let him attend as a boy!" as Abi removed his Alice band and ribbons, as they heard him beg "Please! Can I have my pretty ribbons, back?" as Tania laughed "He's always slipping into my hair ribbons, to play dress up in my old frocks at him and begs me and my girlfriends to play dollies with him!" adding "Pushing his dollies around the street, in my old pink dolls pram!" They all giggled, and said, "It's ok if he wants to do needlework, instead of being with the boys!" as they nodded. The girls called "Thanks Miss!" as she closed the door and they heard giggles again.

He begged "please replace my ribbons?" as they gave him some kisses and saw more girls appear and screech, at the girly boy, as Abi called "He's my boyfriend!" as they gasped, as she fed more ribbons and bows into his hair, to giggles. He was led along to the last 2 classes and heard giggles from the girls, but gasps, as the boys saw Peter in a dress and pinafore, over his trousers, but then saw the female teacher, Mrs Atkinson and she heard the commotion and said, "What's up girls and boys?" as the boys called "Peter's wearing dresses and ribbons Miss!" as the girls giggled, and pointed to the boy in dresses and trousers, but also ribbons, as she gasped "What on earth is this, girls?" Tania said, "Can you let the class in and I'll explain about my Sissy brother!" as he huffed "Not fair!" as she let them in and said, "Settle down girls and boys and get your books out!" as a boy called "You may have to say, Girly Boy, too, from now on!" as she smiled and closed the door. She saw Abi and said, "You too, Abi!" but she said, "Patsy is my new girly boyfriend and he's a bit embarrassed, at his dress up, has got out!" as the teacher laughed "Oh you poor boy!" Tania asked, "Want me to take your dresses and let you attend as a boy again, or are you having fun in your frocks, that Mummy got you, at the weekend!" The teacher gasped "She didn't?" as he swallowed and saw him grip his dress and bob a curtsy as he said, "I'm having fun in my dresses and ribbons Miss!" as she gasped and giggled, "Oh Peter!" as Abi said, "I'll just console him with some kisses, before I bring her in!" The laughing teacher entered and closed the door.

Abi quickly removed his trousers and popped them away in her bag, in case a teacher needed to hear Peter, sounding a complete sissy girly boy again. She opened the door, as Tania and a few girls went off to explain to their teachers, why they were late.

Abi threatens to turn any boy in class into a sissy

Abi said, "My girly Patsy can sit beside me!" as the girls giggled, and the boys called "Poofter!" and "Sissy!" Abi called "Any name calling or bullying My Patsy and the boy will join Patsy in dresses and ribbons, to apologise, maybe with a little sissy kissy!" but added "Understand?" as the boys said, "Watch it, or else!" as the teacher scolded her "Now Abi! Stop telling fibs and trying to threaten the boys!" She added "You know! You couldn't get them to dress up, like Peter!" as she laughed "Do any of the boys, want to bet, that me and some bigger girls, couldn't turn any single one of you, into a girly boy!" She stood up and pointed, to each boy in the class, as they gasped, as she said, "I swear Miss! I can turn any boy here, or any boy in the school, or my street into a sissy!" as the girls gasped and giggled, as the boys swallowed. They thought "Who to heck, is this little girl, who usually would run away timid, from any of them?" as one complained "You'd better not try anything Abi, or else, I'll tell my Mum and Dad!" as others echoed and heard her and the girls giggle. She laughed "Don't worry boys, it's fun to play dollies and dress up and help your Mummy's with housework, in pretty aprons!" as they said, "No way!" The girls giggled, and joined in saying, "Oh yes Abi! It's fun wearing pretty aprons, to help with housework and playing dollies and dress up!" Jenny called "Oh Dave, you'd look sweet, dressed like Patsy here!" as he said, "No way! Please don't?" as the girls giggled, at his timid response. Tania had excused herself from her last lesson, to explain to the female teacher her brother had let out, he liked to wear dresses and was attending school as a girl, as she gasped and let her go, to shepherd her little brother home.

Hence, she was waiting for the class, to break up and Abi and Peter to leave, as the door opened and the class dispersed with the boys saying, "I'm telling Dad on you Abi!" as did others and some said, "I'm telling Mum!" as the girls giggled, and patted Abi on the back "Well done, Abi! The boys were scared silly, about what you said!" as she laughed and said, "Ok Patsy! Get your shopping bag of books ready!" The teacher said, "Look Abi! Was this some trick and you've done this to poor Peter?" as he nodded, "Yes! It is!" adding "I'm not a girly boy!" as he saw his big sister, Tania, standing in the doorway, with her hand on her waist and say, "Sorry Miss! My sissy brother, sometimes likes to pretend he's a macho boy, but I told the girls earlier, he'd a girlfriend Cloie!" Abi said, "I wanted to meet this girl, that he kissed before me, but now realize I've nothing to be worried about!" as Tania said, "Tell Abi and the teacher, who Cloie is!" as he sobbed "Oh no! She's my dolly!" as the teacher gasped and they all broke down, giggling!" She asked, "And who gave her lots of kisses and changed her frocks yesterday?" as he sobbed "I did!" as she asked, "And who slept with her, in one of my prettiest nighties, last night?" as he sobbed "I did!" as the teacher held his head. Abi laughed "So I haven't another girl friend, to contend with and you've only me?" as he nodded, as she kissed his lips, causing the teacher, to gasp "Oh you, poor girly boy!"

PART E

PLASTIC CARRIER BAG SKIPPING AND DANCE WITH HANDBAGS

Nancy does the laundry and minces frocks around the garden

Tom dreads Pam or his Mum spying his plastics and nappies, but is ok

He goes to bed that night, again having to wear one of Pam's nighties, but dreading her spy his plastic baby pants and nappies. He of course got into the bathroom before bed and removed both the nappies and plastic baby pants, knowing June couldn't check on him and so hid them away slipping into his room and hiding them well away in a carrier bag and that at the bottom of his toy box. He quickly pulled her panties from his pocket and pulled them up over himself under his nighty and was relieved nothing was showing.

Pam came into his room and checked he was in her nighty, but also the panties. He tried to show her in bed, but she got him out and said, "Lift your nighty till I see!" and saw him pull the nighty up, but heard Pam gasp "What are those marks on your legs?" as she saw where the tight baby pants had dug into him for most of the night and asked, "What to heck caused that?" as he fibbed "Some of my underpants are a bit tight!" as she laughed "You'll maybe have to wear my panties to school, if that's the effects your silly boys underpants are having on your legs!"

Morning, Tom's goes around to June's to remove the baby stuff, but …

Next morning, Tom let Pam go on to school first and slips back into his nappies and plastic baby pants with his boy's undies over them, followed by his trousers as he heads around to June's. He rings the bell and saw the laughing June let him in and lead him into the sitting room, where she has the blinds open. He ask's "Can I go up and remove these?" as she laughs and hands him a girl's apron and said, "Don't worry! Your nappies and plastics will be hidden from the children going bye and if you wear that pinny, they'll be hidden from anyone looking from across the street!"

As he sobbed "Not fair!" as she said, "Just remove your blazer and don the pretty apron and then you can drop your trousers to remove your baby pants and nappies!" adding "Otherwise it's to school as a baby and I'll add something to make a lovely baby sound in your trousers!" as he quickly removed his blazer and tried to turn around as he donned the girly apron, but she turned him to face the houses and street.

He gasped as he saw children going by both girls' and boys' as he begged "Please let me turn when boys go by?" as she said, "Ok!" and saw him turn as a boy went past.

He turn to face the front as she took a changing mat and set it on the floor in front of him and said, "Just stand on that in case of accidents!" as he stammered "Funny!" as she saw him step forward and cry "But that's too near the window!" and start to undo his trousers under his girly apron.

June replaces plastic baby pants with a plastic carrier bag over his nappies

The underpants were around his ankles as she stepped behind him to peer at his plastics, but was disappointed to just see his boys underpants, as she laughed and pulled them down and off, as he whispered "Not fair!" as he knew his baby plastics and disposables were on show from the back. However, he gasped as he felt her turn him around and cried "Oh no!" knowing his nappies might be seen from across the street, as he wet his nappies again. She gasped "What a big baby boy you are Tom!" as she took her diaper bag and pulling him down onto the mat, she pulled his apron off to expose his plastics, causing him to cry "Please don't?" but then calmed down, as he realized he couldn't be seen in the nappies. She took some rubber gloves and pulling them on, she stuck a dummy into his mouth, as he sobbed "Not fair!" as she pulled down his plastics and then pulled his wet nappy off, giggling at his red willy again and started cleaning it and then gelled it as he cried "Not to school as a baby? Please don't make me wear the plastic baby pants to school!" as she laughed "I'll let baby off his plastic baby pants!" as he sighed but saw her apply the talcum powder and pull his plastics down and off.

He thought that's not too bad, with just nappies, which I can hide away at school, but then saw her take a pink plastic carrier bag and stick two holes in the corner, as she fed it up his legs and said, "Reach up baby!" as he did, she pulled the bag over his nappies as he cried "Oh no!" She took the apron and pulled it down his front again to hide his carrier bag and handed him his undies and trousers and said, "Better get your underpants and trousers on or I send you into the porch to play dress up!" He gasped as he saw a girl across the street and saw her momentarily look across and see a girl in an apron. He cried "Oh no!" and stepped into his trousers and pulled them up and as he got to his thighs, he turned and pulled them up over his plastic baby bag. He did them up and then pulled the apron off as she laughed.

She took him to the door and heard him cry "Oh no! You can hear my bag rustle as I walk!" as she laughed "Poor baby! Head on to school and see if you can get to the loo before someone hears your baby bag pants!" but added "Make sure baby wears his nappies and plastic bag pants home!" as he cried "Not fair!" and she gave him a kiss and sent him on his way. He managed to get to school, purposely not speaking to any mates, but saw the bigger girl, who'd looked into June's stop and say, "Hi! I think I saw your sister this morning!" as he blushed and said, "Yea! She's a year below me!" as she said, "Was she doing some housework for someone! I saw her in a flowery apron!" as he nodded, "Yea! She sometimes does some for extra pocket money!" as she nodded, "Me too!" as she went on her way and chatted to some girlfriends.

Tom gets to school and sees some friends who try to call him over, but he Says, "I'm dying to go!" and ran on to school. He gasped as he saw Pam ahead of him with some girlfriends and held back, till he saw her enter the girl's entrance.

Tom ran on and soon was near the boy's toilet's and slipped into the loos and seeing some boys there, he grimaced as he entered a cubicle, hoping to hear them and anyone else exit.

He pulled down his trousers and saw his underpants, but also the pink carrier bag on show and slowly pulled the plastic bag down and reached in, he pulled out the two disposables which he slid into his satchel. He slid the plastic bag inside his underpants, trying to hide the bag before pulling off his trousers and then the underpants.

Tom reaches school, entering the loo, removing nappies and plastic bag

He then heard a noise outside his cubicle and gasped, holding his breath as he pulled his trousers up and taking the bag from his underpants, he folded the bag up and slid it into his satchel. He quickly pulled his underpants back up and heard a bang on the door, with some guy calling "Hey! I'm bursting for the loo!" as Tom called "I'll be out in a second! Just finishing!" as he pulled his trousers up over his underpants and sighed as he lifted his satchel and exited and saw a guy rush in and close the cubicle, locking it behind him.

He made his way to the assembly and saw his mates gathered in their usual spot on the second level on the left. They called "Hi Tom!" and he went over, He looked around and saw Pam and some of her class chatting and saw her smile towards him and blushed, thinking of the dress up yesterday and wearing his tutu, playing ballerina for Pam and June, but of course being in the nappies and plastic baby pants. She looked up and laughed as she saw him blush and turn away from her. The assembly ended and the classes made their way to their classes and his day started and went ahead pretty much as normal, with him playing footy at break and lunch, although dreading someone peek in his satchel and spy the nappies and plastic carrier bag.

End of school, with him replacing his nappies and carrier bag for home

Pam passes Tom on his way from footy after lunch and checking he wasn't near a mate, she teases "Looking forward to more ballet?" as he blushed and said, "Ha!" as she minced on past him, with him glad, she didn't know about his nappies and carrier bag pants. His last two lessons follow on as usual and Tom has to head to the loo again to replace his nappies and carrier bag. He was glad that the loo was empty compared to that in the morning and soon was pulling down his trousers and underpants and pulls them off his legs. He removed the plastic carrier bag and blushed as he pulled it up his legs and stopped at his thighs, before taking the nappies he slid them into the bag and slid them down his front and back before pulling up his underpants and then his trousers. He sighed as he pulled on his blazer and picked up his satchel and exit's the loo and heads home, glad not to see Pam as he heads home. He heads home and grimaces as he hears his plastic bag rustling, hoping not to spy Pam, but also mates, who might hear something as he walked. He reached his home, but heard June call him in and he blushed, as he entered her house and sobbed "That was really embarrassing, having to change in and out of my nappies and that flaming bag at school!" as June laughed "Oh Tom! Just my little joke!"

Home, June hands him a carrier bag with handbag to disguise his pants

She held out a pretty apron and a pink headscarf and saw him slip it on as she tied it behind his back and tied the headscarf around his head, She then hands him a white plastic carrier bag and he looked in and gasped, as he saw a yellow handbag, as he asked, "What's this for Aunty June?" as she laughed "I think baby will want something to rustle, to disguise the noise in your panties!" as she slid his arm into the handles of the carrier bag and said, "Let's hear that bag rustle!" and shook his arm up and down and heard the bag rustle, as the handbag jumped about in the carrier bag.

Next thing, there was a ring of the bell and he gasped, as he saw a lady's silhouette through the inner porch door. June opened it and he gasped as he saw his Mum standing there with her handbag, as June called "Hi! Doreen! Come on in! I thought Tom might demonstrate his skipping skills!" as he gasped "What! I can't skip!" as his Mum laughed "Hi Tom! How was school?" as he huffed "Ok Mum! Where's Pam?" as she laughed "She popped around to the next street, to see a girlfriend!" and then asked him "What's in the bag?" as June laughed "Now Doreen! He's got to have a little secret or two!" as she said, "Come on Doreen and we'll go out to the garden.

She led them to the kitchen and Tom slipped out the door followed by his Mum as June exited and locked up. Tom went into the garden and blushed, as he heard his panty bag rustle, causing him to slide the bag along his arm and jerked it quickly, up and down to hear his carrier on his arm rustling too and then saw June with a skipping rope and said, "Tom! We want to see how you skip!" as he cried "No! I can't!" as she laughed "Just a few!"

Tom's to skip with carrier bag + handbag between his Mum and June

June handed his Mum one end of the rope as his Mum and her started to swing the rope around and around a few times and then keep it still on the ground, as he watched and heard June say, "Nancy! You step in and we'll start looping the rope, as you jump!" He tried a few times and eventually got himself into the middle and managed a few skips, but made sure his handbag bounced about in the carrier bag, causing his Mum to laugh "That's not a handbag in there?" as June nodded, and said, "Try again Nancy!" as he blushed and skipped again and quickly shook the carrier bag on his arm, causing him to grimace and heard laughter from his Mum and June. He tried a few more times and managed three or four before snagging the rope again. He then heard June say, "Tom want to try a few more times without your bags or else skip and mince around the garden with your carrier bag and handbag, as his Mum laughed and said, "Thanks June, for letting him leave his handbag down!"

Nancy asks to carry his carrier with handbag to mince around the garden

June asked, "So want me or your Mummy, to look after your carrier and handbag?" as she took the carrier bag with the handbag from him, but his Mum gasped, as he said, "No, Aunty June! I want to show off, skipping around the garden!" as next thing he took the carrier and slid it back up his arm again and started skipping around the garden, to laughter from his Mum and June. His Mum laughed "Now June! What have you threatened him with?" as she put her hand up and called "I swear Doreen!" adding "Have I threatened you with anything if you don't take your handbag back?" as he shook his head "No Mummy! As it's just you two, who can see me and I'm dressed as Nancy!" as he continued skipping around the garden, but made sure his carrier bag, shook to cover up the rustle from his trousers.

June laughed "It seems that Pam's making him play dollies has had a side effect of him, enjoying handbags!" as his Mum gasped "Now June! He's got his handbag hidden in a carrier bag!" adding "It's not like he's got it, dangling on his arm like us, when we go shopping!" as she had her own handbag, dangling from her elbow. June approached her and asked, "Can I prove something?" as she took her handbag from her arm and approaching him, slid it up his arm to trap his carrier bag and said, "Still want to skip around the garden with your handbags?" as he called "Yes! Aunty June!" as she patted him on the bottom and said, "Off you go Nancy!" and they saw him start running around the garden, but jerking his arm up and down causing his Mum's handbag and the carrier bag to rustle, as his Mum gurgled "Oh Tom! I mean Nancy! You are funny!" as June called "Now try to skip around!" and saw him change to skipping, still jerking the handbag and carrier up and down, to more laughter and giggles. He called "Don't tell Pam!" as they laughed.

June then said, "Swap your Mummy's handbag onto your other arm!" as he gasped "Not fair!" and took the light blue handbag and slid it up his left arm to the elbow, as he started to skip again around the garden, but she said, "Here you look to be uneven there!" as she slid the carrier off his arm and retrieved the yellow handbag, but then slid the carrier back up his arm and then slid the handbag up his arm to trap it. His Mum gasped as she saw him now with two handbags and the carrier, as June said, "Continue skipping Nancy!" and saw him resume skipping around the garden, but now having to jerk his right arm with the carrier even more, to make it rustle, without the handbag inside of it. He had both arms with his handbags jumping up and down on each, causing his Mum and June to laugh their heads off. However, then June said, "I think that's enough skipping around for Nancy!" as she whipped his headscarf off and said, "Sissy Tom should have a go, for a few minutes!" as his Mum gasped "Now

don't you dare, June!" as June patted his bottom and saw him resume skipping around, jerking his two handbags, although his right arm was jerking much more than his Mum's handbag. His Mum said, "Now Tom! Give me my good handbag!" June said, "Just once more around the garden Tom!" as he continued skipping and running around the garden. This caused his Mum to gurgle "Oh Tom! You do make me laugh!"

June takes him indoors and removes his trousers, but makes him dance

His Mum approached him and took her handbag back and laughed "I'll maybe find you one of my old bags to play with!" as he begged "Please don't Mum! Pam will tease me silly!" He begged "Don't tell Pam about this!" as they laughed. His Mum said, "I'd better go on June and she was shown out, with June saying, "I'll just see to Tom and send him around soon!" His Mum left and June brought Tom in and heard him huff "That was terrible! I was dreading Mum hear my plastic pants!" as she laughed "It turned out funnier than I'd planned, with you having one and then two handbags, to mince around the garden!" He said, "I hope Pam doesn't find out and realize about my plastic bag!" as June took him into the sitting room and shut the blinds to let him out of the apron and headscarf. She then undressed him down to the plastic bag over his nappies and was about to let him out of them, when she laughed "You know what we forgot?" as Tom shook his head.

She laughed "Have you learnt to dance, yet?" as he shook his head and gasped as she laughed "Just skip on the spot!" as she handed him back the handbag, but then fetched one of hers and slid it up his other arm, like he'd done with his Mum's. He resumed skipping, but now with the plastic carrier bag on show, causing her to gurgle "Oh I think your Mummy will laugh when she sees your dance!" as he gasped "Oh no! Don't let her see?" However, she then said, "When you get around, I want you and then Nancy to show your Mummy dance with two handbags!" as he sobbed "Oh no!" but she said, "Don't worry I'll remove baby's nappies and plastic bag pants!" as he sighed "Thanks Aunty June!" She of course took some photos of him dancing as Sissy Tom and Nancy with handbags with him begging not to tell Pam.

Tom goes around with his satchel, looking like his normal boy self and enters to see his Mum flick her wrist to him and laugh "That was funny this afternoon with you skipping with your two handbags and that carrier bag, making that rustling sound!" as he asked, "Is Pam out?" as she nodded, "I'll try not to tell her!" as he huffed "Thanks Mummy!" as she asked, "Do I get my kiss?" and saw the blushing boy reach up and kiss her as she laughed "Go up and change" but heard him stammer "While Pam's out, Aunty June wants me to give you another laugh!" as she asked, "How?" as he said, "I've to show you my sissy dance!" as he asked, "Have you got two handbags?" as his Mum fetched two of her old handbags and handed them to him and saw him slide one up each arm to the elbow and start skipping on the spot, as she gurgled "Oh Tom! I see you're skipping on the spot instead of around the garden, as she saw his arms move up and down with her handbags dangling from each. She laughed "Oh Tom! You are making me laugh today but then opened the cupboard and retrieved a girly carrier bag and handed it to him saying, "The carrier bag rustling, made it even funnier with your handbags!" as he cried "Mum!" as she laughed "I thought you'd have been more worried about being seen with two girly handbags than a silly carrier bag!" as he blushed and resumed skipping with his right arm making the bag rustle again, causing her to giggle and flick her wrist towards him effeminately.

His Mum suggests he should show Pam his dance and get her to join in

She laughed "You should be able to show Pammy!" as he gasped "Please don't Mum?" as he said, "Especially about the carrier bag?" as she couldn't understand why, but said, she wouldn't say. She said, "You can just do it, without my handbags!" adding "Anyway! It's about time you learnt to dance for school dances and stuff!" as he blushed at the thought of dancing with a girl. She removed her handbags and the carrier and said, "Have a go at dancing normally!" as he continued, but didn't move his arms so much and heard her laugh "It seems you need

your handbags to dance!" and added the two handbags to his arms and saw him move them more and laugh. He begged "Please take them back and I'll dance better!" as she took them again and saw him dance, jerking his arms, like he'd done with the handbags and carrier in the garden, causing her to laugh and giggle at the sight of him skipping and moving his arms up and down again.

She then took Pam's apron and tied it around him along with adding her headscarf around his head and laughed again as he danced, but then added the handbags and carrier and laughed even more at her blushing boy. Tom takes his dolly with him upstairs to his room and changes out of his trousers and replaces his underpants with cream and white lacy panties, Pam had left for him under his pillow. He thought to himself, at least they are better than nappies and that carrier bag or even plastic baby pants!" thinking "That flaming June is ten times worse than Pam!" as he stuck two fingers up towards her house and said, "Up you, you stilly stupid hag!"

Pam returns home and kisses her Mum hi, as she ask's "How was school, dear?" as she said, "Fun! I got a good score for my English homework!" adding "Is he in?" as her Mum nodded and gurgled "He has been making me laugh!" as Pam laughed "What! As Nancy?" as she said, "It was more that he's learnt to dance and showed me his new dance!" as Pam gasped "Has he?" and called "Tom come on downstairs and show me your dance!"

He heard and sobbed "Oh no!" but thought "I hope Mum doesn't say, about handbags or Pam think of it and add one or two to my arms!"

Hence, he came downstairs and heard Pam giggle "What's this I hear about you showing Mummy your new dance!" as he blushed "It's not very good Pam!" as she then saw him without his dolly and called "Oh Tom! You've forgotten your dolly!" and saw him run up the stairs again and pick it up from his bed, sobbing "Not flaming fair!" as he carried it back downstairs again and heard them laugh as he returned to the kitchen and set the dolly back down on the washing machine. Pam said, "Show me, Tom!" and saw him blush as he started skipping on the spot and moving his arms up and down, as Pam and her Mum screeched and he sobbed "It's not fair!" as his Mum cuddled him "Now Tom! You'll soon be attending dances at school and I'm sure if you practice here with Pam, the two of you will be quite good, by the time the school dance occurs!"

Pam wants to see Nancy dance, but then has his dollies dance too

Pam laughed "I'll have to think up some more moves for us to do!" adding "Oh Tom!" as she picked up her pink apron and called "I want to see Nancy dance too!" as he cringed "Mum! I knew she'd tease me and want Nancy to dance too!" as he took the pink apron and pull it on to giggles as he cried "She won't be dancing at school, Pam!" as she laughed "Oh Nancy! The girls would enjoy being taught dance by a sissy boy!" as her Mum scolded "Now Pam stop teasing Tom! Let Nancy show you her dance!" as he again started skipping on the spot and moving his arms up and down.

Pam then laughed and picking up his dolly, held it out and said, "Your dolly Baby Suzie wants to dance with you too!" and so next thing he took it and started dancing, moving his hand and arms up and down carrying his dolly as Pam and her Mum screeched with laughter.

Pam ran and fetched her Wendy dolly and handed him it, saying, "Take Wendy doll in your other hand and you can skip and dance with both dollies!" and saw him sob "Not fair!" as he took the doll and resume skipping both dolls in the room, with more laughing and gurgling. Pam laughed "The girls at school would love you to show them dance with your two dollies!" as her Mum said, "Now Pam! You've promised to keep Nancy a secret!" as he begged "Please Pammy don't tell on your sweet sister Nancy?" as she approached him and gave him a hug and

a kiss on the lips, laughing at his embarrassments of the kiss and how he looked. Pam then said, "I'll go and get changed and then we can play dance some more!" adding "In the garden!" as he cried "Oh no Pam!

Not outside!" as she laughed "Don't worry it will be Nancy, not sissy Tom! So! Get your headscarf on or hair ribbons in!" as he begged "Mum stop her!" as she laughed "It's better here where I can control her! It's better than next door or at Julies, even without your dollies or bags!" as he begged "Don't tell about my handbags or carrier?" as she laughed and bending down kissed his lips again.

Pam returned downstairs having changed into a skirt and blouse, with another two dollies and said, "I've brought two of my other dollies for us to dance with!" as she saw Tom in her headscarf and heard him beg "Please Pammy! Keep me indoors to dance, especially with these dollies!" as her Mum asked, "Go on Pam! Keep him indoors!" as she laughed "Well for a while!" as she laughed and said, "Ok! I'll be nice but swap the headscarf for hair ribbons!" as he cried "Not fair!" and pulled the headscarf off and waited for Pam. She ran back upstairs and fetched her handbag and slid some hair ribbons and bows inside and slid it over her shoulder. However, she remembered how his arms were jerking up and down, causing her to giggle, as she took another handbag, sliding it over her other elbow and minced along the landing and down the stairs. Tom waited in the living room with his Mum hoping it wouldn't be too long, as he saw Pam enter with two handbags and said, "Here take a handbag Nancy!" adding "I mean Sissy Tom!" as her Mum scolded, but she said, "Don't worry Mummy! She'll be Nancy again, after he's asked his sweet Mummy to pretty up Sissy Tom's head!"

Pam gets her Mum to slide ribbons in his hair, but then adds handbags

They both gasped and he stammered "Mummy! Will you please pretty up Sissy Tom's hair so she can become Nancy again to dance with her dollies!" as both Pam and her Mum screeched with laughter, at his request and Pam and then her Mum both kissed him, as tears appeared with him sobbing "Not fair! Pam!" He was still holding both dollies, when Pam slid her pink handbag up his arm and said, "Mummy better get some ribbons to pretty up my sissy brother's hair!" as she gasped and they both hoped she'd take her bag back when his hair was done up! His Mum slid her hand into the handbag and retrieved a few hair slides and smiled as she slid them both into his hair, one at either side. She reached in and got another few and slid them into the front and back of his hair, as Pam laughed "That will do now that you've transformed Sissy Tom into Nancy again, she can resume her dance demo!" He took the handbag and went to set it down, but she laughed "When I was upstairs I remembered how your arms jumped up and down and so thought you could give your handbags a dance too!" as he cried "Oh no!" and his Mum laughed "Oh Pam! You're getting worse!" even though it was the way his Mum and June had made him dance and skip around. She saw her take the other handbag and slide it up his other arm with his hands still holding the dollies as he sobbed "Not fair!"

She said, "Right Nancy be a sweet little sister and show me how to dance again!" and saw him resume dancing again with his knees jumping up and down, but especially both arms with the handbags and his dollies dancing too. His Mum sat down screeching the place down, as did Pam, as he tried to run out and up to his room, but Pam stopped him and threatened "I could take you around to Aunty June or over to show Julie and especially Tina!" as he lay down on the couch sobbing.

His Mum took the handbags off his arms and then the dolls and said, "Pam let him go out and play! This has been so embarrassing for him with dancing, but then with his dollies and then your handbags!" as Pam laughed "Spoilt sport! Though it will be a fantastic look to practice his! I mean her dancing some other time!" as he blushed and took the ribbons out of his hair and heard Pam say, "Pop your hair ribbons back into my handbag, Tom!" adding "I mean Nancy!" Her Mum scolded "Pam stop that!" as she laughed "Sorry Mum it's so difficult to remember if he's a sissy boy or a girl!" as he cringed and said, "Very funny Pam!" as he asked, "Mum have you her handbag?

I've to replace these hair ribbons!" and saw his Mum take the handbag, she'd taken from his arm and slide it up again, as Pam gurgled and he blushed and slid the two ribbons into the handbag, followed by the last two and hid them away in the handbag. Pam said, "Just take my two handbags back up to my room and no being nosy!" and saw him pick up the other handbag, but heard her say, "Make sure you mince with one over your shoulder and one from your elbow, Sissy Tom!" and ran ahead of him up the stairs to watch him mince up to her room.

He enters Pam's room to return 2 bags, but has to bob a curtsy in a frock

His Mum gasped "Pam!" but saw him slide the white handbag up his arm to his shoulder and slide the pink handbag up over his elbow and mince along as she gurgled "Tom you are getting good with your handbags!" as he blushed and huffed "Ha!" as he disappeared up the stairs and heard Pam gurgle "Good girly!" as he stumped up the stairs with them and along the landing and into her room.

He shot down on the floor and cried "Close the curtains Pam!" as she laughed "Oh Sissy Tom! Not want to play with me up here?" as he begged "Please let me out Pam, Mum wants you too!" as she laughed and said, "Just one curtsy to the street and I'll let you go! No complaining to Mummy!" as she took a pink frock and said, "Just slide it over your head and I'll do Nancy's hair ribbons!" as she handed him the dress and said, "Sit up facing my wardrobe, till your dressed for your curtsies!" as he sobbed "Not fair Pam!" but sat up on her bed and pulled the dress down over his head and down his body, as Pam gurgled and said, "I'll add your hair ribbons for your curtsies!" as he cried softly "You said, Only one!" but Pam said, "We'll make it five and you can then remove your frock and head on to join your mates!" She went behind him and said, "I'll just borrow your handbag!" but reached into the other bag and said, "Oops wrong handbag!" and slid it up his arm over his shoulder, as he begged "Please don't Pam! I'm not disguised as Nancy yet!" as she gurgled and gave him another kiss. she picked up her pink handbag and reached into it.

She pulled out a hair ribbon on a slide and showed him, but then hid it away and took a curly grip and slid it into his hair at the front side as she said, "I want you to thank me for prettying up your hair!" as he said, "Thanks Pammy for prettying up Sissy Tom's hair!" as she sat on his lap and throwing her arms around him kissed his lips, as he cried "Please don't kiss me Pam?" as she laughed and said, "Let me get a few more ribbons into Sissy Tom's hair so Nancy can bob her curtsies!" She of course showed him more ribbons and replaced each one with curly grips and so he thought he had lots of hair ribbons disguising him as a girl in a frock. She slid her pink handbag up his arm to his elbow and said, "You can raise your handbag to your shoulder to do your curtsy and then return it back to your elbow till the next curtsy!" as he huffed "Not fair Pam!" She said, "When I say, now!

Nancy has to bob her five curtsies slowly to the street" as he begged "Make sure Julie or Tina or anyone else can't see me!" as Pam laughed "Now you're sitting there in that sweet frock as Nancy, not as Sissy Tom!" She positioned herself to try and stop him seeing his reflection in the mirror and said, "Ok Nancy! Turn and start your curtsies!"

Tom turns to face the street in frock, with the handbags to bob curtsies

He turned and gasped as he saw the neighbour across the street, but then some of Julie's and Tina's windows, as he raised his pink handbag to his shoulder and gripping her dress he bobbed a curtsy, but heard Pam say, do it slowly or else!" and saw him grip the dress again and bob a slow curtsy, as she laughed, thinking "I wonder will either Julie or Tina or that lady next door spy my sissy brother in a frock?" as she said, "Well done Nancy just return your handbag again. He reached up and pulled the pink handbag back down to his elbow and peered out the window, dreading being recognized by the neighbours or Julie. Pam said, "Do your second curtsy, Nancy!" as he blushed and pulled his pink handbag up to his shoulder and then slowly gripped his dress and bobbed down to do his second curtsy to the street at Sissy Tom. The lady beside Julie's house was doing some housework at her back

rooms, but then went into her bedroom at the front and smiled as she peered across and saw Pam and a girlfriend playing, but she didn't pay much attention to them and soon had slipped back out again.

Tom gasped "Oh no! That woman beside Julie's saw me!" but Pam said, "Look you're disguised as Nancy and she'll just think you're one of my girlfriends!" and hear him huff "Can I have a headscarf too?" but she laughed "Maybe for your last curtsy!" and saw him raise his handbag again to bob his third curtsy, as she thought to herself "I'll have to speak to that lady and hint that it was Sissy Tom!" as she giggled, and watched her sissy brother exposing himself in her frock to the houses across the street.

Pam smiled as she saw Tina and a girlfriend wheeling their doll's prams in her driveway and wondered would they recognise Tom in his pink frock and Says, "Tom better turn around!" and saw him turn his back to the window as Pam said, "I'll wait till that lady is gone, but she actually wanted to try and attract Tina and her friend. Pam waved across to the two girls who initially didn't see, but then Lucy saw her and called "That big girl is waving out her window!" and Tina looked up and said, "Yea! That's Pammy! My big sister Julie's best friend and she's started playing dollies again and sometimes plays with me!" as she laughed "Will she join us now?" as Tina waved up and tried to beacon Pam down to play dollies with them.

She said, "Coast is clear Nancy!" and saw him turn as she tried to distract him from looking down to the girls but move over a bit to be more on show. She said, "You aren't quite curtsying correctly!" and moved to where he was standing, adding "Take one foot behind the other like this!" and showed him and pulled him beside her, to be more on show and said, "You try again!" He gripped his dress and bobbed another slow curtsy to the street and came up again, sliding his handbag back down to his elbow again. He huffed "That's three! Thank you for my pretty hair ribbons Pammy!" as she laughed "I think you can add an extra curtsy for that thank you!" as he huffed "Not fair!" but raised his handbag again and bobbed another curtsy, to laughter from Pam.

Lucy spies Tom in his frock, but thinks its Pam's big girlfriend playing

Lucy looked up and said, "She seems, to have a big girlfriend with her in a pink frock and carrying a handbag and they are bobbing curtsies!" as Tina looked up and waved again to try and get them over. She tried to see the girl's face. She said, "I don't recognize her friend! She seems to have very short hair!" as Lucy said, "There's only one or two girls in my class with short hair!" adding "Their Mum's are silly not letting them grow it to look pretty like us!" as Tina nodded, "Yes! Long hair is much more fun to add ribbons and play with!" adding "And our Mummy's, have fun doing it in pigtails or ponytails, as Lucy nodded, and they continued wheeling their prams around, forgetting about Pam and her girlfriend for a while.

Tom had slid his handbag up again over his shoulder and bobbed another curtsy and was constantly checking the bedroom windows across the street, when he was part way through his curtsy, when he saw the heads of the two girls come into view and cried "Oh no! Tina is in her driveway!" as he tried to step back, but Pam held him and said, "Look you've got your hair slides and so they won't recognize you as Sissy Tom!" as he cringed and checked again and saw the girls just tending to their prams and heard Pam say, "Just one more and I'll add your headscarf!" as he continued his curtsies and manipulating the pink handbag.

Their Mum called "Pam! What are you doing with Tom?" as she laughed "Mum! We'll be down in a few minutes and Tom can go out to play!" as she then thought "Oh yes! If he goes out, they might associate my girlfriend in a frock upstairs with my big sissy brother. He did another curtsy and although Tina didn't look, Lucy did and got a better look at the big girl and thought that the girl looked funny in some way or other and that there was something funny about her.

Pam adds a headscarf over his curtly grips and Tina sees the big girl again

Tom said, "You promised me a headscarf Pam!" as she huffed "Ok! but you then go down and show Mummy and let me remove your hair ribbons!" as he huffed "Not fair! She'll give it to you for putting me into a dress!" as she laughed and added a yellow and red floral headscarf over his curly grips. She said, "Just one more curtsy which this time had both girls looking up but didn't recognize him in the headscarf and so just continued playing dollies. She said, "Well done Nancy! Let's go down to give Mum a laugh!" as she led him halfway down, but said, "You don't move from this spot or else I'll have you dancing all night at Aunty June's!" as he gasped "Ok Pam!" as she said, "Mum! Come into the living room a tick!" as her Mum left the kitchen and entered and heard Pam whisper "Mummy! I've been a little naughty and got Nancy playing curtsies!" Her Mum gasped "Naughty girl!" but Pam said, "Only five that's all!" as her Mum said, "I suppose that's not too bad!" Pam said, "Please don't tell him the little trick I played on Nancy Mum?" as she laughed "What?" but she said, "Just smile when you realize and let me turn him into macho Tom again to go out to join his mates?" as she nodded, "Ok!"

Lucy sees Tom exit and asks will Pam and her friend join them at dollies

Pam returned to Tom and said, "Right Nancy down here!" as he descended the stairs to the hall and saw his headscarf in the mirror, glad he couldn't be recognized by the girls looking in. She led him into the living room and her Mum gasped "Pam! I told you no skirts or dresses! Leave it at your aprons and headscarf!" as she apologized "Sorry Mum! I couldn't resist!" adding "At least I've let her be Nancy, so she's not recognized by any of the neighbours as Sissy Tom!" as she laughed "I suppose that's not too bad!" as she said, "Right Nancy! I'll remove your hair slides for you to become Sissy Tom again and you can then let Mummy remove your frock and let you go and play with your mates Ok?" as he nodded, "Ok Pammy! Thanks!"

Pam then took both his handbags off and said, "Turn around, till I get your hair ribbons!" as he turned and she put her finger to her lips, for her Mum not to tell. She pulled off his headscarf and his Mum swallowed as she saw him as a boy, with just curly grips in his hair. Pam took two hair ribbons in her hand and removed a few curly grips and showed him the ribbons and did the same with the other two curly grips and said, "Mum! You can now remove Sissy Tom's frock, to let him run on to play with his mates!" as she laughed "Pam! You are naughty!" as she laughed and saw her Mum pull his frock up and over his head and off his arms and say, "Right Tom! Better run on to join your mates!" as he said, "Thanks Pam! Thanks Mum!" as he exited the side door and down the driveway.

Tina had popped into the house for something, leaving Lucy with her own doll's pram and dolly wheeling it up towards the gates. She looked up and saw the big boy coming down the driveway and called "Will Pam come and join us playing dollies with her friend?" as he blushed and said, "No! I think she's doing something at the minute!" as she called "She looked to just be playing curtsying, with her friend and maybe dress up!" as he did a beamer at her comments. Tom said, "Yes she's got her big cousin around playing with her!" He said, "I think she's too old for playing dollies!" as she said, "Tina Says, her and Julie are playing dollies again!" and stuck her tongue out to him, as young girls do when someone annoys them, or Says, something they don't like.

He heard Tina come out and he ran on up the street in case one or other of them recognized him, as the sissy in the dress and carrying a handbag. However, he thought "With the hair ribbons I should have been ok! I should have looked more like a girl" as he blushed at the afternoon's dancing with handbags and carrier bag.

Lucy Says, a big boy left Pam's house and I asked would Pam join us playing dollies!" Tina said, "Yea! That's Tom, her nasty big brother!" adding "He often calls us names and threatens us, if we play too near their silly football game!" as Lucy laughed "I'm surprised how much their cousin looked like both of them!" as Tina said, "I didn't

see her face that well!" as Lucy said, "I got a better look when you were seeing to your dolly and she did look really like them!" as Tina laughed. Lucy said, "For being naughty, he should play dollies instead of silly football!"

Tina laughs at the thought of Tom playing dollies and wheeling a pram

Tina laughed "I'd love to see him playing dollies and wheeling a doll's pram like us!" as Lucy laughed "In a frock like us!" as Tina screeched, but neither girl, never associated the girl with Tom. Meanwhile her Mum scolded Pam "Pam that was naughty putting him into a frock and then those curly grips!" adding "I hope he was at the back, playing?" but Pam laughed "He was ok, in my room, bobbing some curtsies!" as her Mum gasped "Now Pam keep Nancy secret!" adding "Especially Sissy Tom!" as they laughed. Pam said, "Although the lady beside Julie, did pop into her room, but was out again in a jiffy and didn't see anything of my sissy brother. She giggled, "However Tina had a girlfriend playing dollies in their driveway and they did wave up to me to try and get us down to play with them!" as her Mum gasped "She didn't recognize Tom?" but Pam shook her head "No! They'd have been over here in a flash, to get Nancy out to play with them if they even suspected!"

She laughed "I think her friend got more of a look at his face, than Tina and so when you sent him out to play with his mates, there's a slight chance she might just recognize the girly boy playing dress up in my room!" as her Mum gasped "Oh no! I hope she didn't recognize him!" as Pam laughed "I might just pop across to play dollies!" as her Mum said, "Don't Pam please?" adding "It would be terrible if Tina or Julie find out!"

Pam laughed "I don't think Julie finding out would be that bad! She'd go easy on him and keep Nancy a secret!" adding "But Tina would tell the whole place and have him playing dollies all about the street, with him wearing dear knows what?" as her Mum gasped "You don't mean a frock?" as Pam nodded, and gurgled "And shopping in town using a handbag and purse too!" adding "Probably as Sissy Tom and not even Nancy!" as her Mum gasped "She'd better not find out!" as Pam giggled, at the thought.

Pam exits to check if Tina and Lucy had recognized her brother, in her pink dress with handbags and bobbing curtsies to the window. She smiles as she sees the two young girls wheeling their prams in Tina's driveway and called "Hi Tina! Is Julie in?" and saw her nod and call "Where's your big girlfriend?" adding "I hear she's your cousin!" as Pam nodded, "Yes Nancy is a year older than me, but still plays dollies!" as Tina called "Go and bring her over, Lucy saw her and you playing curtsies or dress up!" as Pam laughed "Hi Lucy! Aren't you a pretty little girl?" adding "Just like Tina there!" as they laughed and heard her say, "When given complements, you should always bob a curtsy with a thank you!" as they both gripped their skirts and bobbed a curtsy saying, "Thanks Pammy!" as she bobbed one back "My pleasure girls!" She said, "Unfortunately Nancy left to speak with some friends, about something!" as Lucy said, "We never saw her go out! Just you and your nasty brother!" as Pam laughed "He's not that bad! Just footy mad!" as Lucy said, "You should make him play dollies instead of silly football!" as Pam laughed "You'll have to tell Julie what Lucy said, Tina!" as she nodded, "I will!"

Pam calls for Julie to join her with the young girls talking about Nancy

She rang the bell and Julie came to the door and saw Pam and asked her "Want to come in?" but Pam said, "Come on out! I was just chatting to Tina and her sweet friend Lucy here!" as Julie said, "Playing dollies again Tina?" as she said, "Come and join us Julie!" as she laughed and said, "I'll maybe play later Tina!" as she called "Just chatting to Pam, Mum!" and heard her say, "Ok dear!" but she came up the hall and looked out and said, "Hi Pam!" as she said, "I'm just chatting to Tina and her friend here!" as she smiled and closed the door. Lucy said, "We saw Pam and her cousin Nancy, playing dress up and curtsies!" as Julie laughed "What? Were you?" as Pam nodded, and said, "I just got Tina and Lucy to bob a curtsy when I complemented them!" as she laughed "Although it sometimes includes a kiss too!" as they laughed "Don't be silly!" as she giggled, "We'll leave that till another time!"

Julie said, "I don't know Nancy! Who is she? Where's she live?" as Pam said, "I don't know her as well as Tom, they're about the same age and in the same class at school!" adding "You should ask him about Nancy? He might be able to get her around to play dollies with you two!" as Tina called "I don't like Tom! He sometimes calls me and my friends names" as Pam laughed "Naughty boy! I'll have to tell him off!" as Julie laughed "Thinking he'll hit her if she does!" and said, "See that flying pig!" as Pam laughed.

Pam said, "You know what Lucy said?" as Julie shook her head and Pam replied, "That for being naughty, Tom should play dollies with them!" as Julie screeched "Lucy you definitely don't know big macho Tom! He'd run a mile from a dolly!" as Pam laughed "What do you mean Julie! Just this afternoon he was playing dance, with not one, but two of my dollies!" as she laughed "Oh yea! See that flying pig again?" as they laughed as Pam laughed "Not only that! but with two of my handbags dangling from each elbow as he skipped!" as they screeched with laughter and Julie laughed "It's well he can't hear you or you'd be dead meat!" as the girls laughed, but didn't actually believe her.

Pam said, "I can't be too long! I've to tidy up after Tom and Nancy playing dollies!" as they giggled, again as Julie laughed "What's got into you! You'd normally never have even dared to tease him, about playing dollies, yet alone have told us!" as Pam laughed "Just joking!" The girls giggled, but she said, "Wouldn't it be fab, to get a big boy to play dollies!" as Lucy gurgled "And wear a frock!" as Julie called "Stop that Lucy, I'm nearly wetting myself here!" as Tina called "I just did!" as they laughed and Pam said, "I'll have to tell my big bro off, for making you girls wet yourselves and maybe as a lesson put him back into nappies and plastic baby pants!"

Julie gasped and cried "Oh no! I've just wet my pants!" and ran around to her back door to change and tell her Mum about Pam's jokes about her big brother Tom. Tina laughed "Julie wet her panties! Julie wet her panties!" adding "I'll have to go and get Mummy's diaper bag to change her nappies!" as Lucy laughed "I'm nearly wetting my nappies too and don't even know him!" as Pam laughed "I thought you'd saw him earlier playing curtsies with Nancy!" as she gurgled "What in that pink frock and carrying a handbag?" as Pam nodded, and Lucy laughed "I've wet my panties too!"

Pam jokes about him playing dollies, causing all three to wet their pants

Tina laughed "Let's go in and I'll lend you some of my panties Lucy as she led them into her side door. However, Pam said, "I'd better go on Tina! Don't forget to ask Tom about getting Nancy around to join you girls playing dollies!" as Tina called "Ok Pam!" Julie, Tina and Lucy go in and have to wash and change into new panties and their Mum can't believe that all three had wet themselves, especially her big Julie and as a joke gets her diaper bag out for when they came from the bathroom. She saw them exit, having changed out of their wet pants and after washing themselves and changed into dry panties, with the wet ones in a carrier bag. The three girls exited the bathroom and she called them down into the kitchen and then showed the diaper bag and held up a pair of Tina's plastics and said, "Julie! I'm not sure if these plastic baby pants will still fit you!" as she laughed "Very funny Mummy!" as she said, to her "I can't believe Tina and Lucy wetting themselves, but especially you at your age!"

Julie laughed "It was that flaming Pam!" as her Mum asked her "Whatever did she do?" as Tina called "She fibbed about her big nasty brother being a sissy!" as she asked, "What Tom being a sissy?" as they nodded. She pretended that he played with her dollies and was dancing about with one in each hand and had a handbag on each elbow to skip!" as she laughed. Julie said, "It's well Tom wasn't around, or he'd have killed her!" She added "The last straw was when she said, 'She'd have to teach him a lesson for making Tina and Lucy wet their panties and put him back into nappies and plastic baby pants!'" as her Mum gasped "She didn't?" as they nodded but continued "She was so funny!" adding "And made us laugh so much we wet ourselves!" as her Mum laughed "What's got into her?" as Julie nodded, "I know! She'd normally be really scared of her big brother and we'd better not say, anything to him!"

Tina said, "Well apart from trying to get him to bring his cousin Nancy over to play dollies with Lucy and me!" as her Mum asked, "Nancy?" as Lucy said, "Apparently she's their cousin who Tina and I saw playing curtsies with Pam earlier!" adding "Apparently Nancy is in Tom's class at school! Pam said, he'd get Nancy around to play dollies with us!" Her Mum asked her "Isn't she too old to play dollies at Tom's age!" as Tina said, "apparently she still is playing dollies!" as they laughed. Their Mum asked her "What's she like?" as she replied, "We only saw her upstairs in the bedroom, playing curtsies and dress up! She was in a pretty pink dress and had a pink handbag over her shoulder!" adding "I saw her more than Tina, who was checking her dolly at the time! Though she had quite short hair!" She added "When Tom came out later, I was amazed at how much Nancy looked like Pam and Tom!" as they smiled. Their Mum wondered could Tom actually be a girly and play dollies, but didn't say, as she didn't want him to hit her girls, if they teased him about it. She said, "I think you should let Lucy head back home!" adding "Julie will you escort her and tell her Mum I'll wash her wet panties!" as she laughed "Imagine you three wetting your panties!" as they laughed. Lucy heads around to the next street with Julie and they both giggle as they see Tom playing footy, as Lucy Says, "He does really look like the same as Nancy did upstairs!" as Julie laughed.

Next day, Tom as Nancy has to help Pam and their Mum with laundry

The next morning Pam let's Tom head on to school, but then Says, to her Mum "Look Mum! I know you were trying to keep it a secret, from the neighbours about Tom, but seeing he actually outed himself to Aunty June and has been prancing about in the back garden, in my apron and headscarf, as Nancy, pushing his doll's pram!" adding "He should now be able to help with the laundry!" as her Mum said, "Now Pam! What about the neighbours out the back houses?" Pam giggled, "Mum! That's why Nancy, will want to peg out the laundry, not macho Tom, in my pretty apron and wearing my pretty headscarf!" as she giggled, "Or hair ribbons?" as her Mum gasped "Don't you dare! Make sure, he's got a headscarf to wear!" as Pam laughed "Just joking Mum!" as she kissed her and asked, "Could you have some girly washing for Nancy and I, to do this afternoon, when he returns from school?" Her Mum laughed "I take it, you want to make him, copy us, using a handbag for his pegs?" as Pam giggled, "Funny you should say, that, Mummy!"

as they laughed and she said, "Look it will be Nancy, pegging out the washing, not Tom and so adding a pretty handbag to his arm, shouldn't hurt!" as she laughed "I suppose so, but it's still not right Pam, treating him as your sister!" Pam gurgled "Mum! It's not like, I'm popping him into a frock!" as her Mum gasped "You'd better not! It was bad enough yesterday indoors, with Tina and her friend nearly recognizing him!" adding "I told you off, last time when you tricked him with those frilly shorts!" as she laughed "Sorry Mum, but he deserved a little payback!" She added "Look on the bright side! Helping with the laundry, using the peg-bag, will be good practice, for helping with the shopping!" as her Mum gasped "Don't you dare, Pam! I'm warning you?" as Pam laughed "Look I've not even hinted to Julie, Tina or anyone at school!" as her Mum said, "Keep it that way!"

Pam popped upstairs and came down with a dress on a hanger, around her neck, saying, "Mum! Alice showed me a fun way, to peg out pretty dresses!" as her Mum laughed "What?" as she replied, "You pop a dress onto a hanger and then slip the hanger around your neck, like this! Like we do in a dress shop, when we don't have time, to try them on!" as her Mum laughed "I think we can leave the hanger to you and me dear!" as Pam laughed "Oh shouldn't Nancy, have a go with a few?" Pam said, "Deal Mum! You mince around the garden, with all of yours and I'll do all of mine!" as her Mum laughed "Ok Pam!" as she said, "You promise, to let me mince with all my frocks around the garden, before pegging them up from my handbag?" as her Mum laughed "Ok Pam! Miss bossy boots!" as Pam laughed. His Mum laughed to herself, remembering Tom skipping with his handbag in the carrier bag and mincing around the garden with one, at June's yesterday and so thought, it no big thing and that only they would know.

Their Mum has the washing ready for Nancy and Tom to peg up

Pam picked up her pretty bag of books and sliding it up her elbow, she kissed her Mum bye, as she laughed "I'm sure we'll have a laugh, seeing Nancy mincing with his handbag this afternoon!" as her Mum saw her mince down the driveway, with her girly yellow shopping bag on her elbow and flicking her wrist, she laughed as she skipped on to school. Pam was good as her word again and didn't spill the beans on Tom, although she was so tempted to have fun at his expense, she thought to herself "I'll take it slowly, I've lots of time to expose little Nancy to the street and then the school!" as she broke down laughing, causing her girlfriends to ask why, but she giggled, "It's a secret!" as they probed, but she wouldn't tell. She finishes her lessons and heads home, entering the back door and kissed her Mum saying, "Hi Mum! I hope you've got the washing ready for the three of us!" as her Mum laughed and nodded but asked her to let Tom off, but Pam shook her head saying, "Look Mummy! It's a very important part of housework! What's he going to do when married! Leave all the laundry to his poor downtrodden wife?" as her laughed "No! but we could forgo the handbag and just pop the pegs into a plastic bag or bucket for Tom's first go!"

Tom gets home from school and is told he's to do some housework

She then reminded her "Anyway Mummy! It will be Nancy pegging out the washing!" as she then gasped "What a fab idea Mummy!" as her Mum asked, "What?" as she laughed "How's Tom to learn, if Nancy does all his stuff! He can peg an item up, as Nancy, but then become Sissy Tom to unpeg it and then reattach it to the line!" as her Mum laughed "Now Pam! Maybe just some items as Tom and others as Nancy, will that do?" as Pam nodded, and kissed her "Thanks Mum!" Her Mum reminded her, that most of the washing was hers. She laughed "Some is Tom's!" as Pam asked, "Have you included lots of my pretty frocks?" as her Mum nodded, saying, "I hope, you'll peg up most of them!" as she said, "No making Tom mince around with your frocks!" as she laughed "Mummy, as long as he pegs up his own quota, using our handbag!" as her Mum laughed "He'll die, when he realizes we use a handbag for the pegs!"

Tom having had an ok day, with his mates, playing footy at break and lunch and messing about, glad not to be teased by Pam. After school finished, he exited with his mates and joined them part way home, before carrying his satchel on home. He got in and heard his Mum say, "Hi dear! How was your day?" as he said, "Not bad! I'd some good games of footy with the guys and Pam's not told on me!" as his Mum held out his Baby Suzie doll and said, "Pam was thinking of hiding your doll again, but I stopped her!" as he said, "Thanks Mum!" He huffed "Do you think she'll let me play with my mates?" as she laughed "I think she's got a little housework, for you to help her with!" as he grimaced and said, "Can you have a word to stop her, teasing me?" as his Mum laughed "She did let you out to play with your mates last night?"

Tom asks to wear her headscarf as he realizes he's to do the laundry

He wanted to yell "She flaming-well, made me go around to June's for dress up and dollies!" but bit his tongue and exited up the hall and up to his own room. He took the doll but saw her smile as she handed him Pam's apron, but also Pam's headscarf, as he cried "Can I not wear my own blue apron?" but she laughed "Trust me Tom! It's better that Nancy do this housework!" as he grimaced and took them and his dolly. Pam called "Tom! Better come up and get changed!" He got up the stairs and heard Pam say, "Panties are under your pillow Nancy!" as he cringed and asked, "Mum Says, you want me to do a little housework!" as she smiled and said, "Get changed and we'll see!" as he locked his door and changed out of his school clothes and into his casual shirt, panties, trousers and jumper. She smiled as she saw Tom having just changed into her panties, come out in his normal trousers and jumper, carrying his dolly and her apron and headscarf, Pam said, "Nancy will need her pretty apron for the housework!" and saw him pull her pink apron around himself, as Pam tied it in a tight knot to hear him cry "Not a knot Pam?" as she laughed "Hi Nancy!" as he asked, "What housework do you want me to help with?" as she laughed and led

him down the stairs. She said, "Mum! I think we should share the washing between the three of us!" as he cried "But I'll be seen in the back garden! I thought you were keeping me indoors!" as she laughed "That was before Aunty June, had you wheeling your dolly around the garden!" His Mum said, "Tom it won't be too bad!

There's only a few of your things in the wash!" adding "Pam! You know most of the washing is yours and mine!" as she laughed "Mummy! We didn't mind pegging up his horrid clothes and so he shouldn't mind pegging out some of ours!" as he blushed. She said, "Don't worry! I'm sure, Mummy will let you, out of your pretty apron, once you've finished, helping her pegging out the laundry!" He blushed as he saw himself in the girly apron and saw Pam tie her own apron around herself as she laughed "It's fun to wear pretty aprons to help Mummy peg out the laundry!" as he huffed "Ha!" Pam laughed "Don't worry It will be Nancy not Tom for most of the wash!" adding "Just like you did, wheeling your dolly for Aunty June!" adding "We'll let you disguise Nancy, with my pretty headscarf too, so you won't look like a sissy boy!" Pam giggled, "Sure I can't offer some hair ribbons?" but her Mum took the pink headscarf and said, "Now Pam! Don't be naughty! No hair ribbons!" as she tied it, around his head, as Pam laughed "Oh look Mummy, it's my sister Nancy again!" as her Mum laughed. Her Mum smiled at Tom in the girly apron with the headscarf over his head, holding the dolly and said, "Pam! I know he's disguised, but there's still a chance someone will see him!" Pam took him upstairs a tick and said, "Look! I want you to make Mum laugh, a little!" as he asked, "How?" as she said, "Look for my clothes, mostly I just want you to peg them up, as normal, but for my dresses and blouses, I'll peg most of them out, but I want you to do a few!" adding "But we'll both carry them a special way!" as he asked, "How?"

Pam shows how she wants her frocks minced on a hanger over his neck

She said, "We will use a hanger and pop the frock onto it, but then we pop the hanger over our head and down to our neck, to mince around the garden, like this!" He then saw her slide a dress onto a hanger being slid over her head and cried "Oh no! Not around the garden?" but she said, "That's a definite, or I might bring Julie or Tina over to spy Nancy!" as he begged "Please don't, Pam?" as she laughed and gave him a kiss, knowing he hated it. She laughed "The nice thing about having the dress hanging down from the hanger is it leaves our hands free to peg up our frock!" adding "Or get the purse from our handbag in a dress shop too!" as he blushed "Ha!" She laughed "We'll mince once around the room, Ok Nancy?" as he huffed "Ok! Not fair!" She took the hanger from her head and slid it over his and down around the back of his neck and giggled, at the dress hanging down over his front and gurgled "I think it's such a girly way to mince around the garden, before pegging out our frocks!" as he blushed and huffed "Ha!" as she said, "Off you go Nancy!" She asked, "Need the loo?" and saw him nod and say, "I'll be down in a minute!" as he did his ablutions and washing his hands, he exited to see a smiling there. They went downstairs, with Pam holding three clothes hangers, where her Mum was getting the washing, out of the machine and soon had it all in the wash basket.

Tom as Nancy has to take the basket of washing out to the garden

Pam said, "Tom you take the basket of washing out to the back garden and wait for Mum and I!" and opened the door for him and said, "I'll check and call you!" as she stepped out and seeing a few children going down the street, she said, "Just turn away from the street and you'll be ok!" and saw him step out and turn quickly towards the garage and stepped quickly around the back and into the garden. He soon was at the line in the centre of the garden, turned away from the back houses. Pam said, "Mummy! Tom's agreed to share the laundry, with you and me!" as she laughed "Has he?" as Pam said, "Lock up Mummy!" and then, added "He's not to get in, till all the laundry is done!" She then took two pretty PVC floral pinnies and heard her Mum laugh "Oh Pam! A pinny too!" but she said, "This is the way you taught me, over the years, to help peg out the washing!" as she tied the floral PVC pinny around herself, but saw her Mum done her own PVC pinny and smile. Her Mum saw her take the three hangers and asked, "How come the hangers?" as Pam slid the spare PVC apron and slid it over the hanger and then

that over her neck to let the pinny hang down her front. Her Mum gasped as Pam laughed "Just for a few of my dresses Mummy?" as her Mum laughed. However, she then pulled the purple PVC handbag, from the cupboard and taking some more pegs, from a large bucket and popped them into the handbag. She swung the handbag over her elbow and said, "Mum you bring a handbag too and we can peg multiple things up at the same time, which should save time!"

Tom realises he's to use a handbag to hold the clothes pegs

Her Mum laughed and took an empty handbag herself and Pam popped pegs into her handbag. They exited and Pam got her Mum to lock up, as she looked across the street and smiled as she saw Tina in the driveway, but she was looking away from them, as her Mum laughing at what was to come, but it was going to get far worse than she was expecting. Pam slipped around to the garden after her Mum and Tom saw her in the PVC apron, but carrying another PVC pinny on a hanger and cry "I don't need another apron!" as Pam laughed "It's ok, Nancy! Look Mummy and I, don't worry about wearing PVC pinnies, to stop our pretty aprons getting wet and neither should you!" as he grimaced "Not fair!" He saw Pam with the hanger over her neck, to hang down her front, as she minced over to him and said, "I'll slide the hangers on the garage door, for our dresses!" as she removed the hanger and then the pinny and handed it to Tom. He took the PVC pinny and pulled it around his apron and felt Pam tie it, behind him. Tom then realised his Mum and Pam had handbags and asked, "Why have you the handbags?" as she laughed "Now Nancy! What do you need to peg out, the washing?" as he stammered "Clothes pegs!" as Pam opened the handbag and showed him, as he cried "Mum! Don't make me use a handbag, for the washing!" but his Mum laughed and said, "Look Tom! You don't look like a boy, in your apron and headscarf and it will just be us three!" adding "And between us all, we shouldn't take that long!"

Pam took the handbag with some pegs in it and demonstrated "Look Tom! All you have to do is slide the peg bag, up your arm like this!" as she slid the pretty handbag up her arm to the elbow and then reached into the basket and taking one of her skirts, she then unzipped the bag and taking two pegs, she zipped it up again and then pegged the skirt up on the line. Her Mum gasped "Pam! I think we can leave the bag open, for him to get to his pegs!" but Pam said, "Now Mummy! You taught me from a young age, to zip my handbag up between use around the shops, in case my purse, was stolen!" as her Mum laughed, saying, "Pam! He's not using a purse here! So, he should be ok!" as Pam laughed "Ok! but if he has a purse in his handbag, he's to promise to zip it up between use!" as his Mum laughed and he blushed and heard Pam say, "Ok Nancy?" as he huffed "Ok!" as she said, "Continue! See Tom! I mean Nancy! It's simple as that!" as he huffed "Why! Can't we just use a bucket for the pegs like everyone else?" as his Mum laughed "He has a point!" but then Pam said, "Watch it or I take your headscarf and you'll have the choice of looking like Sissy Tom, or I let you use hair ribbons!" as he blushed and sobbed "Not fair Pam!" She said, "Nancy! You have a quick go, with that pair of your silly underpants!" and saw him take the handbag and woefully slide it up his arm to the elbow. He unzipped it and reached down for the underpants and then dipped a hand into the handbag, he picked up a clothes-peg and pegged up his pants. His Mum said, "Well done Nancy!" as he blushed and said, "Not flaming fair! My mates don't need to do the laundry!"

His Mum has a go with a frock, but then Nancy has to peg out a frock too

Pam laughed "Mummy! Since Nancy's had a go, can't Tom have a quick go?" as she laughed "Now Pam! Don't be naughty! Tom's been a good boy! Or Nancy a good girl, so let him off!" as Pam gurgled "Mummy! You are funny mixing up the his and hers, with Sissy Tom and Nancy!" as he blushed and sobbed "Not flaming fair!" Her Mum asked, "Will I peg up something?" as Pam said, "You try with one of your frocks Mummy!" as her Mum laughed and reaching down into the basket, she pulled out a large dress and taking the handbag, she slid it up her arm over her elbow, as Pam handed her a coat hanger, as she laughed "Oh Pam! Do I need it?" but saw Pam nod, as she took the hanger and they saw her Mum slide the dress onto it and then dangle it, over her head and around her neck.

Her Mum asked, "Will I have a go?" as Pam said, "You try with one of your frocks Mummy!" as her Mum laughed and reaching down into the basket, she pulled out a large dress and taking the handbag, she slid it up her arm over her elbow, as Pam handed her a coat hanger, as she laughed "Oh Pam! Do I need it?" but saw Pam nod, as she took the hanger and they saw her Mum slide the dress onto it and then dangle it, over her head and around her neck. Pam gurgled "Mummy! Just the way I've seen you model a frock in a dress shop, when you've not time to actually try it on!" as she laughed "Yes Pam! but this will make the laundry take twice as long!" adding "Now don't forget to mince around the garden, like in a dress shop!" as her Mum laughed.

Her Mum started mincing around the garden, with the handbag on her arm and the dress hanging down her front, till she got back to the line and laughed as she removed the dress from the hanger and reaching into the handbag, she retrieved two pegs and pegged the dress up on the line, beside Tom's underpants and handed Pam the hanger. Pam then said, "I think Nancy can have another go now!" as he cried "But someone might come up the driveway!" as his Mum said, "I'll keep a look out!" as she moved down to the entrance of the garden to keep a lookout. He huffed "Ok! I'll peg out my trousers there!" and saw his Mum hand him the handbag, which he took and slid up his arm to his elbow, but was dismayed when Pam said, "I think my sweet sister can peg out one of my frocks!" as he gasped "Not fair Pam! Not like Mummy?" but she nodded and smiled "Just like Mummy or else it might be two or three times around the garden, maybe as Sissy Tom!"

Pam explains Tom worrying about someone coming up the drive

Hher Mum said, "No Pam! Just let Nancy do the mincing!" as she laughed and said, "Obey Mummy!" and reaching into the basket, she carefully pulled a pink and white floral dress and set it on top of the basket. He cried "Not fair!" as he lifted the dress and saw Pam hold out a hanger for him and they saw him slide the dress onto the hanger and woefully pull it over his head and around his neck, but then started mincing around the garden, with his Mum and Pam giggling at the spectacle. He was halfway around, when Pam laughed "I've a feeling Mummy, that Nancy could be helpful with us, around the dress shops!" as he said, "No way!" as his Mum laughed "Stop teasing Tom!"

Pam laughed "Is this my big macho brother, in a pink apron and mincing with a frock and handbag?" as her Mum laughed "Ok Nancy!" as he huffed "Very funny Pam!"

He continued on around the garden and reached the line again and dipping into the handbag on his arm, he retrieved two pegs and then removed the dress from the hanger, he pegged up each shoulder of it, as Pam and her Mum giggled, and his Mum said, "Well done Nancy! Pam or I couldn't have done that better!" as Pam laughed "Mummy! Just to think of all the wasted years, when Tom could have been helping us, with the laundry!" as he cried "It's not Tom here! It's flaming Nancy!" as he held out the hanger to her and saw her take it and hang it up on the garage door.

James comes up and goes to enter their driveway, but luckily Pam spied him and called "James! Tom has gone out!" adding "He'll probably see you later, tonight!" as he called "Ok Pam!" and walked on up the street. Tom heard Pam call out to James and cried "Oh no!" and ran to the back of the garage to hide, sobbing at the thought of James spying him dressed up as Nancy. Pam called "Come on Nancy, I've sent James around and saved you!" and saw Tom peer around the garage and call "He could have spied me!" as Pam said, "See! I'll protect my little Nancy!"

Pam said, "Tom's agreed to share pegging out the washing with you and me Mum!" as her Mum smiled and asked, "Has he dear?" as her Mum laughed "It won't hurt you as her Mum tried again "Not, let him off?" but Pam shook her head. He cringed "But! What if Julie or even Tina, comes over and spies me, or even my mate?" as she laughed "We'll tie the gate closed, to try and stop anyone coming in!" as he huffed "But they might climb over!" as she laughed "I'll try and think of a solution!"

Pam said, "Look Mummy!" Tom's really worried about Julie or even Tina coming over and spying him as Nancy and I think I have a solution!" as her Mum said, "What can you do?" as she said, "I'll go and tie the gate shut!" as Tom cried "But they might climb over and come in and it might be a mate!" as his Mum said, "You could run and hide behind the garage!" Pam said, to her "My solution is that I climb over the gate and pop across to play with them and make sure Julie and Tina in their driveway and are occupied and can even spot a mate, trying to climb over and spot Nancy!" Her Mum said, "What about you helping with the laundry!" as Pam laughed and said, "Mum! I think Nancy would rather me, stop Julie or Tina or a mate come over and see him, than me help with the laundry!" Her Mum laughed "You, naughty girl! So, we're having to do it all?" Pam shook her head "Of course not! It's Nancy and you!" as she laughed and removing her PVC pinny and then the apron said, "I'll go and make sure the gate is tied shut and nobody comes to see Nancy!" as he cried "Not fair! Let me go Mum?"

Tom's to do Pam's share and use a purse to hold six clothes pegs

His Mum cuddled him and said, "Pam will make sure you aren't spotted!" but added "Can you bare, with me a tick?" as she took Tom to the back, of the garage, said, "Hold still a tick or I might let slip to Julie or Tina!" He cried "Please! Don't Pam?" as she slid the handbag up his elbow, but then tied it to his apron and PVC pinny, as he cried "Oh no!" as she led him back to her Mum. She then said, "Mummy! Nancy can do my share of the laundry as her Mum laughed. Pam said, "Just let me see Nancy peg out another skirt and then another of my frocks!" as she perched herself at the garage entrance to check, nobody is coming up to spy Nancy whilst spying her brother pegging out the washing. His Mum took one of Pam's skirts and handed it to Tom and saw him reach into his handbag and take out two pegs as Pam called "Now close your handbag up, between use!" He grimaced and zipped the bag shut!" as her Mum laughed "Oh Pam!" and then saw Tom take the skirt and peg up each side of it to the line. Pam laughed "Well done Nancy!" as he grimaced.

She then minced around the garden laughing away as she minced with her handbag saying, "This is what we do in a dress shop, if we don't have time to try, our frocks on!" as Tom wailed "Don't you start, Mum!" Pam giggled, "I'd better run across to Julie's, before I wet myself!" as she ran and kissed Tom saying, "Be a good girl, Nancy!" adding "I'm probably going to have to spend the afternoon, playing dollies with Tina!" adding "Sure you don't want to take my place? Tina's lots of fun, wheeling her doll's pram up and down her driveway and in the streets too!" as he gasped and cried "No way!" as his Mum laughed.

His Mum then handed him, one of Pam's dresses, but Pam said, "Hold on a tick!" as she reached into her own apron and pulled out a large pink purse and approaching Tom said, "Open your handbag and pop six pegs into your purse to use!" as she ran back to keep lookout on the garden. His Mum gasped "Oh Pam! It's bad enough he's to carry a handbag!" but she said, "Mummy! It will be better practice for helping with the shopping!" as her Mum laughed, but heard Pam say, "Mummy! What did you say, Nancy has to do, when getting a purse in or out of his handbag?" as he blushed and heard his Mum say, "Oh Pam! He's to zip his handbag closed to stop his purse getting stolen!" as he sobbed "Not fair Pam!" She watched Tom open his handbag and taking some pegs, he popped some pegs into his purse, as her Mum laughed "You mean, he's to keep refilling his purse, from his handbag?" as she laughed and Pam said, "Right Nancy! Pick up my frock and reach into your handbag and get the purse out, to get your pegs. He picked up the frock and holding it, he found it difficult to open the handbag and get the purse out but heard Pam call "Now Nancy! Let me help you, with your frock!" She picked up the clothes hanger and slide the dress over it and then slid it around his neck, as her Mum giggled. She said, "There Nancy! You are ready to mince around the garden!" to more laughter. He cried "Not fair Pam!" as he started mincing around the garden, still with his handbag dangling from his elbow, to giggles from Pam and her Mum. She continued "When you've finished mincing around the garden, your arms will be free, to get your pegs, from your purse!" as her Mum gasped "Oh Pam!" as she ran back to the garage wall to keep look out.

Tom has minced around the garden before pegging the dress up

He minced back over to the line and reaching into his handbag, he removed his purse and removed the two pegs, before sliding the purse back into his handbag and zipping it up again. He took the dress from the hanger and hung it up, before using the two pegs, he pegged Pam's frock up. Tom had almost finished mincing around the garden, when Pam gasped, as she saw one of Tom's mates Pam called "Mum! Your turn to peg out something!" as her Mum called "Ok Miss bossy-boots!" and picked up a bra and reaching into her own handbag, she took out one peg and closed it up again. She took the bra and pegged it up, as Tom said, "Peg something else up Mum, I did two!" as his Mum laughed "I think you're getting into the swing of the laundry!" as he blushed "Ha!" standing there in the pink apron, with the pretty PVC pinny on top and a handbag dangling from his handbag from his elbow, as he stood back to watch his Mum do a few of her clothes. She then picked up a frock and said, "I suppose I'd better copy you!" as she picked up a hanger and slid her dress onto it and hung it around her neck, asking "Is this right?" as she looked at him and heard Pam screech "Good one Mummy!" as he blushed "Not funny!" Pam giggled, "So you've to peg up, all my stuff, as well as yours!" as he blushed "Not fair!" and saw her run out the garden. His Mum then reached into her handbag and got two pegs out and removing the dress from the hanger, she hung the hanger up and then zipped her bag closed. She then pegged up her dress and said, "This does slow down the laundry!" as he asked, "Can we just peg out the stuff normally?" but she said, "No!"

His Mum said, "Sorry Nancy! It does make it much more fun, especially with you helping me!" as he cringed and heard her say, "Your turn Nancy!" as he huffed "Ok!", pulling a face. Pam ran and didn't forget to tie the gate shut before she skipped over to Julie's. Julie's Mum came to the door and called "Julie! Pam is here!" as she giggled, "Hi Pam! You over to play dollies again?" as Pam blushed and giggled, "Now ask Tina! Dollies are fun!" as she heard Julie come down and ask, "Want to come up for a while?" as Pam said, "Can we play in the driveway? Mum wants me to keep an eye out for Tom coming home?" as she asked, "Why?" as Pam shrugged her shoulders "Not sure!" as Tina came and asked, "Want to play dollies again?" as Pam nodded, and Julie gasped "I thought you were just joking about playing dollies so much.

Julie said, "Ok Tina! Bring your doll's pram out and we'll wheel it up and down the driveway!" as Tina asked, "Can we play in the street?" but Julie said, "Pam and I might be teased by our friends!" as her Mum and Tina laughed "Spoilt sports!" as Julie joined Pam out the front door.

Meanwhile Tom had selected a pair of Pam's panties and soon had pegged it up, but his Mum then said, "Now for a skirt!" and saw him reach into the basket and select another skirt. He reached into his handbag and got his purse out and had just got two pegs, when June popped out to collect her washing. June gasped as she saw Tom dressed as Nancy again and laughed "Hi Doreen! You've got Nancy to help you with the washing?" as she nodded, "I was trying to keep Nancy in doors, till some naughty lady, had made him wheel his dolly around the garden!" as June bobbed a curtsy and laughed "I'm sure it didn't hurt!" His Mum laughed "It set a president for Pam, who said, he can then peg out the laundry too!" as June laughed.

SUZIE TRAPS HER NINE YEAR OLD BROTHER ROBBIE

Katie has her boyfriend Joey in a frock wheel a dolls pram

Fourteen year old Katie had trapped her boyfriend Joey into doing anything she wanted and he ends up in school in a dress and pinafore, but then is taken back to a class mate's Margy who takes them upstairs and pops him into a party frock, but also gets her old dolls pram for him to wheel home, with Katie. He's dreading being recognised as a sissy boy on his way home, but is ok, even when he passes some nine-year old boys who just think it's 2 big girls going past –, but Katie then sees a little seven year old girl Suzie who is introduced to her boyfriend Robbie and giggles as she calls for her Mum and Katie then tells them how easy it is to trap any boy into doing anything they want – like playing dollies and dress up. Suzie begs her Mum to trap her big nine-year old brother Robbie.

Details

They get Joey to wheel the dolls pram back around home, with Katie joining him to ensure he wasn't spotted by some boys and beaten up. He's in Margy's pretty frock over his nappies and wheeling the dolls pram, dreading being spied and recognised by anyone. They are wheeling the doll's pram along and then see some twelve-year old girls, they don't know and introduce Lucy aka joey, as the girls screech at realising that he's a sissy boy. However, Katie explains, he's not a sissy and she can do this to any boy, as the girls gasp and gave her their names and phone numbers, thinking they could do it to brothers or boys they know.

They continue on and then see some young six-year old girls, who gasp and can't believe it's a big boy in a dress and mincing with his handbag and shopper. They giggle and screech as Katie tells them they could have any boys they know to ask to wear a frock and play dollies with them. They bring Katie and Joey in to see their Mum, who gasps as she realises that Lucy is a boy. They giggle as Katie explains how easy it was to trap her boyfriend and explain about the shirt sleeves sewn together and say, about their big eight-year old brother and how they'd love to get him to play dollies and dress up. They again swap phone numbers as they head on home. Katie laughed "It seems your fame is going to spread to lots of other girls and girlies!" as he cringed and said, "Not fair Katie!" as they continued on. Then they saw some nine-year old boys playing footy in the street and he begged Katie not to expose him, as she smiled and made him wheel the pram on bye them. However, she saw a young seven-year old girl nearby and asked, "Do you know those boys playing footy?" as she said, "One's my big bro Robbie! He's nine and a bit of a bully!"

They meet Suzie and she shows her sissy boyfriend to her

Katie asked, "Does he not play with you?" as she asked, "What skipping and dollies?" as Katie nodded, as she screeched "Oh I could just imagine Robbie playing dollies with me or skipping with me and my girlfriends!" Katie added "With pretty ribbons in his hair and maybe wearing a skirt or frock!" as Suzie gurgled "Oh! That would be fab to see!" but saw her shake her head and laugh "You must be joking!" Katie explained "Can you put your hand in your mouth, to not screech?" as she raised her hand, to her mouth, as she asked, "Why?" as Katie asked, "See my big friend, Lucy here?" as she looked at the big girl, in pretty frock, with a shopping bag and pink handbag and ribbons in her hair. Katie explained "He's my sweet boyfriend!" as Suzie rammed her hand, into her mouth and screeched, but luckily her hand, stopped it getting to the boys, in the street playing footy. She removed her hand and asked, "How did you get him, dressed up?" as Katie explained "It's quite easy!" as Suzie brought her up the driveway, to the back door, to meet her Mum and knocking, called "Mummy! Have you got a tick?"

Her Mum came out the door and saw her young daughter with two big girls and asked, "Can I help you, girls?" as Suzie gurgled and Katie said, "I hear Suzie's big bro, is out playing football, in the street!" as her Mum nodded, "Why?" as Katie asked, "Does he ever help you or Suzie, with housework?" as his Mum said, "You must be joking!" as Katie asked, "What about slipping into one of Suzie's, pretty aprons to help you?" adding "Or playing dollies with Suzie?" as she gasped "You must be joking!" as Suzie laughed and heard Katie say, "My boyfriend Joey used to be just like that, a real MSP thinking only us girls, can do housework and the like and wear pretty aprons, to help their Mummy with housework!" Suzie giggled, at her Mum not realising that Joey was a boy, as Her Mum said, "Yes a lot of boys and men are like that!" as Katie said, "Weren't you Joey?"

Her Mum sees Joey and is told how easy it is to make a Sissy

Her Mum looked at the sweet big girl, with the doll's pram and gasped, as she put her hand to her mouth and asked, "You aren't a boy?" Katie and Suzie nodded, and asked, "How?" as Katie explained "Until yesterday, he was as macho as any boy in the world, but now is one of the most girly!" as her Mum asked, "How?" Katie explained "He's been at school today, wearing my dress and pinafore, for most of the day!" as they gasped and giggled, "Never!" adding "The teachers are letting him attend as a girl?" as she nodded, and giggled. She Says, "See! I can make him say, and do anything I want and so he sounds, a real girly boy to them, when wearing a dress over his trousers and asked, 'If he wants to remove his dresses', he Says, he wants to keep the dress on!" as Suzie and her Mum gasped "How and Why?" as Katie giggled, "I'd heard of ways to trap a boy and decided to try it out yesterday!" Suzie giggled, "Can we try it on Robbie, Mummy?" as her Mum laughed "I don't think, it would work on our Robbie!" Katie said, "All you have to do, is take one of his own shirts and sew the cuffs together, around the back" adding "And then pretend you have got him, a new shirt!" explaining "He pulls it on and slides his arms into the sleeves, as you do the front up and he's trapped and yours for dress up!" Suzie gasped "Please mummy! Let's try?"

Katie then secretly shows Suzie's Mum his nappies and plastics

Katie said, "I added some hair ribbons and photographed him and then added a girly apron and took more photos and then a skirt and handbag too!" as Suzie gurgled "Fab!" as she added and then made him promise to help with the washing, as he promised to help, but didn't realise I now use a handbag as a peg bag!" Her Mum gasped "I'd never thought of using a handbag as a peg bag! What a fab idea!" as Katie explained "If you make him mince around the garden between pegging up each item, it's fun!" She added "I replaced his undies with frilly panties!" as they screeched and her Mum said, "You naughty girl, you saw his naughty bits!" as Katie asked, "So Joey! What do you call, what's in your panties?" as he huffed "It's my baby-pee-pee!" as Suzie screeched, as did her Mum. She then asked, "Why do you call it that?" as he grimaced and said, "Because, it's only the size of a little baby boys, baby-pee-pee!" as her Mum gasped "Is it?" but Katie shook her head and said, "It's just really embarrassing for

him, to have to say that!" as Suzie asked, "What?" as her Mum said, "I haven't explained about boys yet!" as Suzie said "We get sex ed at school, but I haven't seen a boy's willy or anything!" as Katie laughed "You might have to explain abou boys, if you take it, as far as I have!" as her Mum asked, "What?" Katie said, "Suzie! Can you pop around the front of the house, a tick?" as she asked, "Why?" but Katie said, "Big girl talk, for just a minute!" as she huffed "Ok!" and skipped up the driveway.

Katie said, "Not a word for a while!" as her Mum asked, "What about?" as Katie took Joey's frock and said, "Look!" as she raised it up and the lady gasped, as she saw the plastic baby pants, over the diaper and gurgled "Oh, you poor boy!" as Katie laughed "Poor baby!" as Joey blushed and sobbed "Not flaming fair!" as Suzie's Mum, gave him a hug and a kiss on the cheek, to laughter from Katie.

Katie kissed him and said, "I let my girlfriends kiss my sissy!" as she bent down and kissed the sissy boy. Suzie ran back and asked, "What was it Mummy?" as her Mum laughed "the poor boy!" as Katie said, "that's why my big sissy boy, will do anything, I say, or ask!"

Suzie asked, "Mum! What was it?" as her Mum giggled, "I can't say, yet!" as Katie said, "Your Mummy and me have kissed my sissy!" adding "Want to give him one?" as her Mum said, "No way!" but Katie gave him a kiss and said, "It's fun to give a sissy, a kissy!" and her Mum gave in and said, "Just one!" as Suzie reached up and kissed the blushing boy. Katie laughed "Give me your number and if you need some help, I'll come around to give your big brother some fun!"

She took their number and gave them her phone number as she took Joey and skipped off with him wheeling the dolls pram again. Robbie finished the game of football and came in saying, "That was a good game!" and heard Suzie giggling and her Mum say, "Come in here Robbie!" as he entered the living room and saw his Mum and smiling sister, both in pretty aprons and asked, "What do you want, Mum?" She said, "Will you be a good boy and help me lay the table?" as he said, "No way!" as Suzie called "Robbie! I want someone to play with!" as she took a dolly and held it out to him and he said, "You must be joking" adding "You two can bug off!" as he left the room and stomped up the stairs.

Robbie 9 returns from footy and his Mum has a shirt ready

Suzie laughed "Come on Mummy and let's get one of his shirts, to sew up!" as her Mum laughed "Should we? Wouldn't that be cruel?" as she giggled, "Wouldn't it be funny seeing our Robbie, in one of my pretty aprons, playing dollies with me and maybe in a frock too!" Her Mum laughed "Now! We won't take it that far, but we'll maybe get him into your pinny, till he gets some for himself!" as Suzie called "and possibly playing dollies!" as she thought "If he doesn't want me to tell his mates, he'll wear a frock too!" adding "And play ballerina too!" Her Mum had one of his shirts that had just been washed and had already dried on the washing line, as she took it and said, "Let's go up and get my sewing box!" as Suzie giggled, "I'll go and get hair ribbons ready!" adding "Will my panties, fit her!" as her Mum said, "No panties dear! Maybe a wraparound skirt!" as Suzie screeched with laughter. Her Mum started sewing the cuffs together, behind the back and soon was satisfied with her handywork. She went up and called "Robbie! Have you got a tick?" as he exited his bedroom and called "What do you want Mum?" adding "It better not be about, helping with housework, or anything!" as he heard his Mum say, "I've got you a new shirt and want to check it will fit!" as he looked and said, "If it's the same size as my others, it should be ok!" but she said, "Just try it a minute!"

He said, "Ok, give it here!" but she said, "Just slide your arms in and check!" as she held it out for him. The trusting soul turned around and slid his arms into the sleeves and then felt them stop down his back, as his Mum did a few, buttons up at the front and heard him say, "Mum! There's something wrong! I can't get my arms out the sleeves!"

She gasped "Oh! Is there dear, let me see?" She turned him and smiled at his hands appear out the shirt sleeves at the bottom of his back and laughed "Oops! I think I see the problem!" His Mum laughed and said, "Now Robbie! You have been acting as such a MSP, and it would be nice to have you helping me and Suzie, with some housework!" He cried "No way Mum! Let me out of this shirt! Let my hands go!"

However, then a giggling Suzie appeared, with a handbag and said, "Mummy I've some hair ribbons for our sissy!" He cried "No way! You get away, brat!" as she giggled, "You'd better be nice to me, from now on, or I'll tell my girlfriends or your mates about you playing dollies with me!" as he cringed "No way! Mum don't let her?"

Suzie starts prettying up his hair and then adds her aprons

Suzie laughed "You've to promise to help Mummy and me with the washing, in the back garden!" as he gasped "What?" as he huffed "Ok! I've helped Mummy, once before!" as Suzie laughed "In one of my little pretty aprons!" as he cried "Oh no!" but not realizing it would be, much more embarrassing for him doing the laundry, than he could ever think off. He cried "But the neighbours will see me in your girly aprons, Suzie!" as she laughed "That's where hair ribbons or a pretty headscarf, come in to help your disguise!" as he cried "Please don't, do my hair up, like a girl?" as they laughed and his Mum said, "At least it might stop them, recognizing you!" He cried "No way Suzie, you can bug off!" as she laughed and said, "Here Mummy! Let me get some ribbons into Alice's hair!" as he cried "No Mum! Don't let her?" as his Mum led him into Suzie's room and sat him down on a chair, in front of the dressing table. Suzie giggled, as she took some hair ribbons and slid the first one into the front, as he looked in the mirror and sobbed "Oh No! Please Suzie! Don't do that to me!" as she giggled, "Mummy! I've always wanted a sister to play with!" as she took another one and added it to the left hand side!" as she gurgled and her Mum said, "Oh Suzie, that does look funny!" and then a matching one on the right!" as he cried "How could you let her, Mum?"

His Mum said, "Look Robbie! It's just to get you to do more about the house and be a sweeter boy, to Suzie!" as Suzie giggled, "Now Mummy! Alice has to promise to play with me, as my sister, just a few times a!" as he cried "Not a few times a week!" as Suzie giggled, "A day!" as he begged "Please only once a week?" as she shook her head "Don't worry, Alice! I'll try and keep you inside, for most of the time!" adding "though, you'll be in the back garden, to help with the washing!" as he sobbed "Not fair! Not in hair ribbons?" adding "Mummy! Don't let her?" as his Mum said, "Katie! Suzie's new girlfriend said, "You might actually ask Suzie for some ribbons, when doing the laundry!" as he said, "No way! I won't!" as Suzie laughed and said, "Hold on sweetie!" as she went over to a drawer and on opening it, she pulled out a frilly flowery apron and ran over to him, holding it up, as he cried "Oh no! Not a girly apron, please?" as her and her Mum both laughed at his pleas'. She said, "As you're his Mummy, you'd better pop him into his first of many pretty apron's!" Mummy!" as she held it out, to her Mum, as her Mum giggled, "Ok, Miss bossy boots!" as he begged "Please don't Mummy?" as his Mum took the little apron and fed it down his front and the ties around his back, to giggles from Suzie, as she clapped her hands with joy, as tears flowed down his cheeks. His Mum said, "Now Robbie! In a while, we'll be releasing your arms and letting you start helping Suzie and me, with some housework!" as he cried "Not fair, Mummy!" as Suzie said, "You must promise to wear that pretty little apron, for any housework!" as he sobbed "Not out the back?" as Suzie nodded, "Especially out the back garden!" as he cried "But the neighbours will see me and laugh at me!" as she laughed "Don't worry! We'll try and not let them realise you are a boy, in a pretty little apron!" as he cried "Not hair ribbons too?" as she nodded,

Little Suzie makes big Robbie be really girly

His Mum said, "Maybe just a headscarf to disguise you, if you're a good boy!" as his sister booed "Oh Mum! Hair ribbons look much sweeter on him!" as he cried "No Mum! Just a headscarf!" as Suzie giggled, "Oh Robbie! You'll look so sweet, wearing a ladies headscarf!" as she whispered "Mummy! Go and get him one!" as his Mum

slipped out of the room and downstairs, as Suzie whispered to him "When Mummy comes back, you'd better say, something to her, or I'll take you around next door as Alice, to show Aunty Helen, your pretty ribbons!" as he asked, "What?" as she said, "Ask to play dollies with me every day, in your pretty apron and ribbons!" as he gasped and cried "Oh no! Not fair, Suzie!" as they heard their Mum coming up the stairs. She said, "When I nod, or else it will be walkies!" as he cried "Please don't?" as his Mum entered the room holding a pretty floral headscarf, as he cried "Oh no, Mum! I thought it would be a plain headscarf! That one's too girly!" adding "Lleave it till were out in the garden?" as she laughed and Suzie said, "Hold on a tick, Mummy!" as she took her aside and whispered "I want to see Alice's ribbons, a while longer, before you hide them from show!" but then said, "I might let him off playing dollies and just leave him to helping us, with the housework!" as his Mum laughed "I think he'll appreciate that!" as she smiled to her and they returned to the dressing table.

Suzie said, "We might leave it, to just having you, help Mummy with the housework!" as she nodded. Robbie swallowed and then said, "Suzie!" as she said, "What do you want Robbie?" as he said, "Could I play dollies every day with you?" as she gasped "Oh Robbie, what would you wear?" as he sobbed "Your ribbons and this apron!" as she giggled, "Great! You'll want to play as my little sister, then?" as he nodded, with tears flowing down his cheeks, with embarrassment and he heard his Mum screech and throw her arms around his neck and gave him a kiss, causing him to gasp and cry "No kisses!" as Suzie said, "Let me give my sissy sister, a kissy too!" as she turned him, in the chair and threw her arms around his neck and kissed him on the lips, with him crying "No kisses! I don't like kisses! Not on the lips, Suzie!" She said, "Mummy! You missed sissy's lips!" as her Mum went around and kissed him on the lips too, as they both giggled, at him, sitting there in the little apron and hair ribbons.

Suzie realised she had her big brother, willing to say, and do anything as she said, "Every morning Robbie will come down with a big smile on his face and slip into his girly apron here, with a curtsy to Mummy with a cheery 'Morning Mummy' with a sweet kiss and then a curtsy to me 'Morning Suzie' with another kiss!" as he sobbed, "Not fair!" as she giggled, and then another curtsy to your dolly and 'Morning dolly Alice!' as you'll kiss your dolly too!" as he cried "a dolly?" She laughed "I'll give you a pressy from my collection of dollies!" as he grimaced, but heard her add "On leaving from school, you'll call "By Mummy with a kiss, Bye Suzie with a kiss and then in the porch, Bye dolly Alice with another kiss!" as he cried "Not the porch?" Her Mum said, "By the inner door, Suzie!" as she gurgled "But I think you'll want to do something else before you leave for school!" He asked, "What's that?" as she laughed "Remove your hair ribbons!" as her Mum gasped and giggled, as she added and maybe a frock!" as he sobbed "Not fair Mum! Don't let her turn me into a sissy!" as she gurgled "too late!" as her Mum laughed "Oh Suzie!"

Suzie tells Robbie to curtsy to her and her Mum every morning

His Mum said, "Let's try this on you, to hide your hair ribbons!" as she turned him back to face the mirror and folding the scarf in a triangle, she tied it around his hair over the ribbons, as Robbie cried "Mum! When I'm outside, make sure there's no ribbons in my hair?" as Suzie giggled, "Oh Robbie! It's fun to wear pretty hair ribbons to pretty you up!" as she whispered "Tell Mummy! You must have at least 3 ribbons in your hair, when wearing her headscarf!" as he gasped "Or else it's Aunty Helen!" as he cried "Not fair!" but said, "Mummy, can you make sure I've at least three ribbons in my hair, when wearing your headscarf?" to laughter. His Mum gurgled "Ok Robbie!" as she then took a camera and took some photos of him in the headscarf, as he sobbed "Not photos Mummy!" as Suzie took him around to face her and sat on his lap, with her arms around his neck and kissed him again, as her laughing Mum, took some more photos of him. She then removed the headscarf for another few photos, as he cried "Please Mummy! Don't show anyone?" as Suzie said, "My turn and you with Alice, Mummy!" as she ran over and took the camera from her smiling Mum, who went over to Robbie and lifting him up, she sat down on the chair, in her own apron and pulled him down onto her lap, saying, "Ups a Daisy!" as Suzie clicked some more photos,

of her big brother, sitting there in little hair ribbons and her little apron, as she said, "Mummy a kissy, for my little sissy!" as he sobbed "Not fair, Mummy!" as she turned him and kissed him again, with Suzie clicking away at him.

Suzie said, "Roby, now give me a nice sweet smile, to show you're having fun, as my sister!"

as he gasped "What?" as she said, "Smile or else!" as he swallowed again and mustered a smile, as his giggling sister put it on video and asked, "What did you ask me to do earlier, as he said, "I asked to play dollies with you, wearing this little apron and your hair ribbons, Suzie!" as she said, "Oh Alice! You'll be fun to play dollies and dress up with!" as he cried "Not dress up too, Suzie?" adding "Not dresses too? Please don't dress me up?" as his Mum hugged him and said, "Now Suzie! Leave it to just playing dollies with him!" adding "Anyway your clothes would be too small for him!" as Suzie gasped "Oh Mummy! What a fab idea!" as Robbie asked, "What?" as she gurgled "A lovely shopping trip for Robbie to get some dress up clothes to play with me!" as he cried "Don't Mum! Please don't get me any skirts or dresses?" Suzie screeched "Oh Robbie! It's so much fun wearing pretty skirts and dresses!" adding "You can play curtsies with them and skipping is so much more fun in a frock, to silly trousers!" as more tears flowed down his cheeks.

She still had the phone on video, as she said, "Promise to play dollies and dress up every day with me, or Mum will show the photos and I'll tell some girlfriends about my big sister!" as he said, "I promise to play dollies and dress up with you every day, Suzie?" as she asked "What as,?" as he said, "As your big sister, Alice!" as she laughed "Little sister, Alice!" as he replied, "Little sister, Alice!" as she giggled, and said, "Mummy you take over!"

They release Robbie's cuffs to let him dress and play dollies

Her Mum went and took the phone and saw Suzie said, "Just keep it pointing towards him Mummy!" as she took it and gasped, as she saw it was on video and giggled, "Oh Suzie! You, naughty girl!" as she said, "Robbie, it's fun to help Mummy shopping too!" as he asked, "What?" as she said, "Promise to help Mummy with her shopping from now on!" He said, "Mummy! I promise to help you with the shopping, from now on, as Suzie ran and took the handbag and slid it over his head and said, "It's fun using a handbag and purse around the shops!" as he cried "No Mum! Don't make me carry a handbag shopping?" as his Mum giggled, "Oh Suzie! You are a naughty girl!" as Suzie sat herself down on his lap and threw her arms around him and said, "Ask Mummy, to buy you a new handbag and purse?" as he sobbed "Mummy! Will you buy me a new handbag and purse?" as she added "And you'll select them yourself!" as he cried "Oh no, you mean I'll have to go in and try out a flipping handbag?" as she nodded, and he cried "Not fair, Mum! That will be terrible and the ladies in the shop will laugh their heads off at me, buying a handbag!" Suzie giggled, "I'm sure there won't be too many little girls there, to tease you too!" as her Mum laughed "Oh Suzie! You are pushing it!"

Suzie said, "Don't worry Robbie!" as she added "After Mummy has taken you around to try on a few frocks, the girls and lady's in the handbag shop won't recognise, that you're a sissy boy and so you'll be ok, buying your pretty handbag and purse!" as his Mum gasped and giggled, "I think that will do Suzie!" as she turned the video off. Suzie giggled, "Mummy we'll keep this a secret from Alice, for a while, ok?" as her Mum nodded, "He'll die when he finds out!" Robbie asked, "What?" as he didn't know about the five-minute video, of him looking and sounding a complete sissy, but Suzie just kissed him again and giggled, "Alice! You are going to be so much fun with me!" as he blushed and asked, "Can you cut my sleeves now?" as his Mum took some scissors and said, "Now no playing up or removing your ribbons or you'll be sorry and I'll let Suzie tell her friends!"

He begged "Please Suzie, don't tell any of your friends and especially my mates?" Suzie then took a wraparound skirt as he cried "Please Suzie, don't!" but saw her pull it around his waist, as he cried "Not a skirt too?" as she giggled, "Oh yes!" as she asked, "Mummy! Will you do his girly panties or will I?" as her Mum said, "No way,

young lady!" as she laughed and ran in and came back holding several pairs of frilly panties and asked, "I know they might be a bit small, but it would be funny to see photos of our Sissy in my panties!"

Robbie is put into panties, but Suzie puts him to bed in his Mum's nighty

Robbie cried "Mum! Don't let her?" as his Mum said, "Give me them Suzie and you go outside, a tick!" Suzie skipped out, down the stairs and looked out the front at the street. She giggled, "I wonder could I get another boy, in a frock!" Her Mum took Robbie over to the bed and said, "Better get these trousers off, before Suzie comes up!" as he gasped "Take me into my room to remove my trousers!" as his Mum took him in to his own room and locking the door, she removed his trousers, as he sobbed. He then gasped as she pulled down his Y-fronts, as he cried "Not my undies too?" He cried "Not fair!" as his Mum slid both pairs of Suzie's panties up his legs and giggled, as she spied his willy and giggled, "Oh Robbie! It's been years since I spied that! We'd better stop Suzie spying that little thing, in your panties!" as he sobbed "Not fair, Mum!" Suzie ran up the stairs again but holding one of her pretty aprons for him and saw her room was empty and called "Mummy! Where is Alice?" as her Mum laughed and opening Robbie's door, she led the blushing boy out in the skirt and said, "Just a quick peek, Suzie!" as she raised his skirt and heard Suzie screech and say, "Fab Mummy! Let's get Alice into my room to play dollies!" as he sobbed "Please don't make me, Suzie? That's not fair!" as his Mum said, "Now! You'll be nice Robbie, to little Suzie, as Suzie held up the pretty apron and said, "You promise to slip into my pretty apron and wear it to play dollies and then to help Mummy with housework and also peg out the washing?"

He cried "I can't go out the back in that girly apron!" as she said, "You promised to help with the washing, or I tell some girlfriends!" as he sobbed "Ok Suzie! Not fair!"

Her Mum said, "I'll undo your sleeves, but any hitting Suzie or being nasty, or not doing what we say, and Suzie will tell on you!" as he said, "Ok Mummy!" "Ok Suzie!" as his Mum cut the cuffs free and he brought his hands around and rubbed them.

He looked down and sobbed "Not fair! What do you want Suzie?" as she held out the apron to him and said, "Get your pinny on!" and saw him woefully take the apron and pull it on, sliding his arms into the arm holes and sobbed as he saw the girly apron, with Suzie clapping with joy and giggling "Come on Alice! I'll show you how to play dollies!" as her Mum said, "I'll get the dinner on!" adding "No being naughty!" as he said, "I won't!" but heard her giggle "I was talking to Suzie!" as she giggled, "What?" as she watched her Mum go.

She said, "Oh Alice! This is going to be so much fun!" as he asked, "How come, you did this to me, Suzie?" as she laughed "Two big girls were walking up the street and walked past you and your mates, playing footy!" as he said, "Yes! I did spy them!" as she laughed "One was a girl and the other was her boyfriend, she made dress up!" as he gasped, as Suzie gurgled "He was completely dressed up?" as he gasped as she gurgled "Wheeling a doll's pram along the street in a gorgeous frock, mincing with ribbons in his hair and with one of these!" as she held out a handbag to him and said, "Pop that over your neck!"

He cringed and begged "Please don't make me?" but she nodded, and saw him take the bag and slide it over his head and down his body, as she gurgled "Carrying a handbag, is lots of fun!" as she giggled, and held out a dolly to him.

Suzie suggests her Mum get him frock from shops or girlfriends

He took it, as Suzie laughed and said, "Oh! You are going to have lots of fun, playing dollies with me!" He blushed and begged "Please Suzie! Don't be naughty?" as she giggled, as he begged "Please don't tell any of your girlfriends, about me?" as she said, "Give me a kissy!" as he gasped and said, "No way!" but she asked, "Will I tell Doreen and Joanne and get them around, to play dollies with you?" as he cried "Ok! On the cheek!" as she

laughed and threw her arms around his neck and kissed his cheek and then the lips!" as he cried "Not on the lips, Suzie?" as she said, "Pop down and ask Mummy for a kissy for her sissy!" as he cried "Not fair!" as he exited in her skirt and apron, carrying the handbag and dolly and descending the stairs, he quickly entered the hall.

His Mum saw him and laughed "What is it dear? Nice handbag" as he huffed "Can you give your sissy a kissy!" as she screeched and bending down, she kissed his dolly and said, "Oops wrong sissy!" as she kissed him on the lips and said, "Back up to Suzie and ask her to go easy on you!" as he blushed and took the dolly again, as Suzie said, "Just undress dolly Alice, like you'd remove your own dress!" as he huffed "I don't wear a dress!" as she giggled, "You will soon, sissy!" as he begged "Please Suzie! Don't make me wear a dress?" She giggled, "Oh my dresses are too small for sissy, so either I ask a big girlfriend from ballet, to lend me some frocks, or you ask Mummy to take you out, to get you some frocks to play dress up with me!" as he cried "Not fair, Suzie! That's going to be terrible!" as she laughed "Mince down and do it, or it's my friend Caroline!" as he exited and went back downstairs as his Mum laughed, as he entered again, with the handbag and dolly and said, "Mummy! Will you please take me out and get me some frocks?" as his Mum screeched "Oh Suzie! Naughty girl!" as he huffed "Mum Suzie is threatening, to get some from a big girl, she knows from ballet!" His Mum giggled, "Oh the naughty girl! I never thought she'd take it this far!" as she laughed "I don't think, I can stop her, but will try and make sure she doesn't take it outside!" as he sobbed "Not fair, Mummy! It's going to be terrible having to be her big sister!" as his Mum hugged him and kissed him on the lips again. She called "Suzie dear!" as a giggling Suzie came down the stairs and said, "Yes sweet Mummy!" as she laughed "Can I get your big brother some frocks?" as she screeched "Oh You big sissy!" as he blushed "Not funny, Suzie! You know, you made me!" She giggled, "I just offered to save Mummy some money, by trying to get some, of my ballet friend, Caroline, who'd love to give my big sissy sister, some free-bees!" as her Mum screeched "Don't you dare tell her, Suzie! It would be terrible for Robbie!" as Suzie giggled, "I don't know why he's so worried! She'll see him anyway, when he joins me at ballet, on Saturday morning!" as he sobbed and cried "No! Not ballet!" and "Mum! Stop her, don't let her take me to ballet?" His Mum hugged and kissed him, saying, "She's just joking!" as Suzie giggled, "Am I?" as her Mum scolded "Naughty girl!" as she said, "You two back upstairs and I'll call when dinners ready!"

Suzie undresses big Robbie naked before adding his nighty

Later that night, before bed, Suzie went up to her Mum's bedroom and searching the drawers and wardrobe, giggled, as she found a pretty nighty and slipping downstairs, she hid it behind her back, as she entered the living room, where her big brother was still in her pinny and skirt with hair ribbons in his hair and holding a dolly and handbag. Suzie entered the room and smiled as she said, "Mummy! My nighties won't fit Alice, so can she borrow this?" as he looked and cried "Not a nighty?" as his Mum gasped "Oh Suzie! I can't believe we're doing this, to Robbie!" as she giggled, "Fab!" as he took the nighty and huffed "Not fair, Suzie!" She giggled, "Pity he won't fit any of your frocks!" as he cried "No way!" as her Mum said, "No way, Suzie! He's not going to dress up in my clothes! They'll be too big" as Suzie gurgled "Too late!" as he cringed at the thought.

Suzie giggled, "Mummy do you remember when I used to play dress up, in your clothes? We used your dress up box!" as her Mum screeched "Oh Suzie! We couldn't? Not in my old bra's and undies?" as Robbie begged "No! I can't!" as Suzie gurgled "Oh today just gets better and better!" as she ran over and kissed him again, on the lips. He cringed "I don't like kisses, Suzie!" as Suzie said, "Mummy he prepares your kisses!" as he blushed and his Mum kissed him again, laughing as she cuddled him.

It was Suzie's bedtime and she said, "Time for beddy byes!" as he said, "It's your bed time, not mine!" but Suzie asked, "Will I phone Caroline, to come and tuck my big sissy sister into bed?" as he cried "Oh no!" as he got up and took the nighty, dolly and handbag up the stairs and into his room. Suzie said, "Strip and I'll dress my sissy!" as he cried "What! Oh no!" as he went to call out "I wouldn't, if I were you!" and heard his Mum, say, "Clean your teeth and wash up!" as he called "Yes Mummy!" as she watched him go into the bathroom and do his ablutions.

Suzie entered after him and said, "Keep your clothes on and wait for me to undress you!" as he sobbed "Not fair, Suzie!" as she giggled, and entered the bathroom to wash and clean her teeth. She returned and smiled as she saw her sobbing brother and sat down and kissed him saying, "Don't cry! This will be fun!" as he sobbed "Not for me!" as she said, "Take your jumper and shirt off!" and smiled as he stripped down to his bare chest, as he asked, "Will I put Mummy's nighty on now?" as she gurgled "Oh Robbie! I mean Alice, it's so funny hearing you ask to wear Mummy's nighty!" as he blushed. He saw her shake her head and say, "I want to see sissy undressed!" as he cried "Not naked?" as she nodded, and giggled.

Suzie asks why the bulge in his panties and is told his baby-pee-pee

She said, "Let me undo your trousers!" as he sobbed again and felt her undo his belt and then his trouser, button and then blushed as she unzipped them and pulled them down, giggling at her two pairs of panties on show. She said, "Remove your trousers!" and he blushed as he pulled them down and off. She laughed "Why's there a bulge in your panties?" as he huffed "It's my willy!" but she laughed "No Robbie! From now on, you call it your baby-pee-pee!" as he gasped "What?" as she giggled, "Tell me!" He sobbed "It's my baby-pee-pee!" as she giggled, and then said, "Why's it called that?" as he shook his head, as she giggled, "Because it's just the size of a little baby boy's baby-pee-pee!" as he cried "Oh no! Not fair!" as she giggled, and said, "You'll call it that when you talk to Mummy!" He cried "Oh no!" as he said, "Stand up sissy!" as he stood up, as she sat down on the bed and giggled, as she said, "Not a word to Mummy!" as she reached out and slowly pulled the 1st pair down his legs and giggled, as she saw some of his willy hanging out from the 2nd pair. She gasped "Oh that does look funny!" as she pulled the 2nd pair down and giggled, "Oh fab!" and reaching out, touched it, saying, "What a sweet little baby-pee-pee!" as he cringed. He begged "Please can I put Mummy's nighty on?" as she giggled, and nodded, and saw him take the nighty and pull it over his head and down his body, but gasped as she reached out and grabbed hold of it, saying, "Oops!" as she let go and let it fall again to his knees. She laughed "Oh Robbie you are going to be so much fun as a big sister!" as she kissed him. She said, "Keep your nighty on all night! I'll check in the morning!" as she added "Right Sissy! Back to bed! Nighty night!" as he ran out and into his own bedroom, where he flung himself down on the bed sobbing "Oh no! How could her and Mum do that to me?"

Their Mum came up the stairs and opening Suzie's door, saw her lying, giggling in bed, as she said, "I put my big sister to bed!" as her Mum laughed "I hope he kept it hidden from you?" She shook her head "No he flashed it to me and said, how big it was!" as her Mum said, "Naughty boy! I'll have to think of a suitable punishment!" as Suzie gurgled "Fab!" as her Mum said, "I'll go and check he's ok!" Suzie handed her the fairy tale book, her Mum normally read her and giggled, as she said, "Read Alice a fairy tale!" as her Mum laughed and took the book into Robbie's room. He lay there and then saw his Mum enter and heard her say, "What do you mean by letting Suzie see your – you know what?" as he sobbed "She stripped me naked!" as his Mum gasped "She didn't!" as he sobbed and she touched my baby-pee-pee!" as his Mum gasped "The naughty girl!"

His Mum laughed "Just as well Suzie, didn't know what that Katie did to her boyfriend!" as he asked, "What?" as she laughed "And you thought Suzie was bad!" as he asked, "What did she do?" as she whispered "Nappies and plastic baby pants!" as he gasped and begged "Please don't tell, or even mention about baby things!" adding "She'll make me wear nappies and plastic baby pants!" as she laughed "She wouldn't, would she!" as he nodded, and she kissed him and said, "I'll read princess a fairy tale!" as she sat on the bed and started reading him the fairy tale.

Their Mum tells what Katie did to her boyfriend – nappies

His Mum finished and kissed him sweat dreams princess, as she turned out the light and closed the door. She entered Suzie's room and giggled, "Naughty girl! Stripping him and touching his pee-pee!" as Suzie gurgled, lying there in her frilly nighty and blushed "It did look really funny, like a big baby's dummy!" as her Mum gasped, at the

baby reference and hoped she didn't know about Joey's nappies, or she dreaded what she'd make him wear, even to school. She said, "I'll read you a fairy tale, but Suzie said, "Why don't you tell me about trapping my sissy brother today and things we can do with her tomorrow and in the future!" as her Mum gasped "Now Suzie! Don't tell on him! It would be terrible for him, if his friends or girls at school, hear about him dressing up or playing dollies!"

Suzie giggled, "Can I join you with Robbie tomorrow, to get him to try on lots of pretty dresses and skirts!" as his Mum gasped "Now Suzie! I was only joking!" but she said, "If you don't, then Caroline will love popping Robbie into lots of her frocks, to play dress up!" as his Mum gasped "Oh! You little tyrant!" Her Mum talked about meeting Katie and Joey and then Suzie meeting them and showing her the sissy boy. She then said, about them trapping Robbie, but Suzie asked, "Mummy! Yhy did you ask me to go around the front, to leave you with Katie and Joey?" as her Mum laughed "She told me a big secret about Joey!" as Suzie said, "Go on Mummy! Tell me!" but she shook her head, as Suzie asked, "Does Robbie know?" as her Mum fibbed and shook her head. Suzie laughed "I'll have to try and meet Katie and Joey again and find out the big secret!" as her Mum laughed "Naughty girl!" as she continued the story of Robbie playing dollies and dress up with his little sister and finally going to bed in a nighty.

Suzie arranges to meet Mum to take Robbie shopping for frocks

Suzie said, "Now for the future! Mummy! Tomorrow meet him at the school gates and I'll join you and we can go shopping for some new frocks!" as her Mum gasped "I couldn't!" as Suzie said, "It's either that, or Caroline dresses him up for me!" as she laughed "Oh the poor boy!" as she kissed her good night!" as she turned out the light, as Suzie called "Night Mummy!" and lay down to sleep.

In the morning Suzie got herself dressed for school in new panties, vest and then slipped into her dress and pinafore on top and giggled, as she wondered about her sissy brother and school clothes. She knocked on his door and told him, he could wear his normal shirt, jumper and school trousers, but he'd to wear her panties to school. He sobbed "Not fair, Suzie!" as she laughed "But I want you down in your nighty and small apron, carrying your dolly here and handbag, to ask Mummy 'Where's my good school dress and pinafore, I can't find them!'" adding before calling "Morning and giving us and your dolly kisses! PS don't forget your ribbons!"

He comes down to breakfast dressed in nighty and small apron

He cried "Oh no!" as she slipped downstairs to call "Morning Mummy! Today should be so much fun!" as she kissed her, they heard Robbie coming downstairs and at the bottom he turned into the hallway, dreading being seen through the frosted glass. His Mum gasped as she saw him, still in her nighty, but with the small pinny on top, carrying the dolly and handbag, with hair ribbons in, as his Mum screeched "Oh Suzie!" as she then saw him bob a curtsy and heard him ask, "Morning Mummy! Where's my good school dress and pinafore?" as his Mum screeched and ran and hugged him and gave him a kiss. He had tears in his eyes as he bobbed a curtsy with his apron and called "Morning Suzie!" as Suzie ran and kissed him and said, "that's a good big sissy brother!" as he sobbed "Not fair!", setting his dolly down on the top of the washing machine. Suzie handed him another half apron to tie around his front and saw him tie it around himself, crying "Mum! Close the curtains! Those in the back will see me, dressed as a girly!" Suzie giggled, "Oh Robbie! Wait till they see you in your school dress and pinafore!" as her Mum scolded "Now! Stop Suzie! Don't be cruel!" as she smiled "Would I?" as he cringed. She asked, "What about dolly, Alice!" He picked up his dolly and bobbing a curtsy with his apron, called "Morning dolly Alice!" as he kissed her too, to giggles from Suzie and her Mum, as Suzie asked, "Alice, I hope you had fun sleeping with dolly Alice?" as he nodded, "Yes Suzie it was good fun!" as she asked, "Did you give her lots of kisses?" as he grimaced and said, "Yes Suzie! She got lots of kisses to sleep!" as she pretended to be the dolly and said, "What did you say, dolly Alice?" and said, in a squeaky voice "I want to attend sissy school, with Sissy Alice!" as her Mum said, "Now Suzie! No making Robbie, carry a big dolly to school!" as he begged "Please Suzie

don't be naughty!" as she giggled "I remember when I was five or so and carrying my dolly Lulu to school with me and having her on my desk all day and showing her off to my girlfriends! It was great fun!" as he blushed and said "Ha!" as her Mum laughed. Their Mum dished out the breakfasts and soon the kids were eating away and when finished she said, "Upstairs and clean your teeth and get ready for school!"

Robbie went upstairs and got washed and his teeth cleaned and then removed his nighty and hair ribbons and slipped into his shirt and trousers over Suzie's panties, as he donned his jumper and blazer. Suzie whispered "Mummy! I'll meet you at Robbie's school, at about 3.50 for our shopping trip!" as her Mum gasped "Oh Suzie!" as she said, "Bring some pretty shopping baskets and a handbag for him!" as his Mum giggled. Robbie took his satchel of books downstairs Suzie asked, "What happened to your school dress and pinafore, Robbie, not to mention your shopper and handbag?" as he blushed and begged "Not at school!" adding "Mummy! Don't let her?" His Mum laughed "You go on" adding "And you stay here, Suzie!" as Suzie huffed "Oh! I wanted to escort him to school!" but her Mum laughed "You'll only make him carry your girly school bag or something girly!" as Suzie gasped "Are you a mind reader, Mummy?" as she said, "Right Robbie, kiss Mummy and then me!" as he kissed his Mum and then bent down and kissed her on the lips, to more giggles as he huffed "Not fair!" as he took his dolly up to the door and heard Suzie call "Robbie, be careful with your pretty hair ribbons at school!" as he huffed "Funny Suzie!" as he kissed his dolly, saying, "Bye, Dolly Alice" and removed his hair ribbons, as he exited with his satchel.

Morning Suzie tells 2 girls all about what Katie did to Joey

Suzie kisses her Mum bye, saying, "Isn't it fab, Mum, about Robbie and how girly he is acting?" as her Mum laughed "Yes! But don't tell on him at school! It will get back to someone, he knows!" as she giggled, "Oh Mum!" but added "Don't forget to meet at his school gates later!" as she skips along to school and joins some girls on their way, giggling away as she tells about Katie and Joey. She kisses her Mum bye and exit's with a girly shopper with her books and minces with it along the street, giggling to herself as she saw both girls and boys, thinking what the boys might look like in dresses and mincing along with a handbag on their arm or playing dollies.

She then spotted two girls from her school, who aren't actually in her class, but the same year. She Says, "Hi Fiona, Hi Naomi!" as they asked, "Why are you giggling?" as she said, "I saw the funniest thing yesterday!" as they asked, "what?" and she said, "I saw two big schoolgirls coming back after school, about 4.30 or so! One in school dress and pinafore and the other in a very pretty frock, mincing with her handbag, like so!" as she took her girly shopping bag of books and demonstrated. The girls shrugged their shoulders and said, "So what, lots of girls do that and even our Mummies too!"

Suzie giggled, "But the girl in the pretty frock was actually a fourteen year old boy!" as both girls screeched and cried with laughter "It wasn't?" as she nodded, "It was the other girl's boyfriend!" as they laughed and Naomi asked, "She has a sissy boyfriend?" as Suzie shook her head "That's the funny thing! Apparently Joey is as macho, as any boy in our class and she's making him, act as a girly boy!" as they screeched "She isn't?" and Fiona asked, "Why?" as Suzie laughed "Another girl told her how easy it was to transform a boy into a girly boy and she and his Mum decided to try it out on him. Apparently he has a little sister, who now loves to get him to play dollies and dress up and guess what, he's now attending school in these!" as she opened her blazer and bobbed curtsies with her dress and pinafore!" as they screeched "Never!" as they asked "The teachers are letting him go to school, in dresses?" as she nodded, to more laughter.

Naomi asked, "His Mum helped to turn him into a sissy?" Suzie laughed "Apparently Joey was a bit of a MSP! Never helping with housework or wearing an apron or helping with the shopping, leaving it all to his Mum and little sister. She apparently mentioned to them, when Robbie was out, wouldn't it be wonderful, if he started helping with housework!" as they giggled, "See that flying pig!" She added "But when his little sister went out, she got

his Mum, to get one of his shirts and sew the cuffs behind his back!" as they giggled, and asked, "Why?" as she said, "Just listen girls!" She explained "When he came back from his game of footy, Katy of course gave him a welcome kiss, putting him at his ease!" adding "His Mum said, she'd got him a new shirt and that Katie had it!" She said, "His Mum went out, leaving him and his girlfriend alone and he was surprised at being left alone and took her up to his room to kiss and maybe you know what, be naughty together!" as they laughed and asked, "What happened?" as she giggled, "They started kissing etc!"

She got him to try on a shirt and he was trapped for her to dress him up

She continued "However, she told him she'd the shirt and wanted him to try it on"

She got him to remove his jumper and shirt, to try the shirt on!" as they listened and heard her say, "But the naughty boy removed his trousers and asked her did she want a peek at his willy!" as they gasped "Naughty boy!" as they giggled. She said, "He wanted to show her, his baby-pee-pee!" as they asked, "What?" She laughed "You know boys have a willy to pee?" as they nodded, and Fiona said, "I've seen my little cousin having his nappy changed and it does look funny!" as Naomi said, "I haven't seen one, but Mum did tell me about boys and their naughty bit's and warned me to stay away from them and to tell her if any boy or man showed me his!" as they laughed. Suzie continued "Apparently big boys like their girlfriends to see or even touch their baby-pee-pee!" as they asked, "Why's it called that?" as Suzie laughed "When you get a boy under your thumb! It's funny and really embarrassing to make him call it his baby-pee-pee and when asked Why?",

Suzie explains about his hair ribbons and baby-pee-pee

He's to say, 'It's because it's the size of a little baby boys, baby-pee-pee!'" as they screeched "Oh fab!" Suzie continued "So Katie then showed him the shirt and said, "Let's try your new shirt on you!" as he saw the shirt looking like any other shirt and slid his arms into the sleeves!" They laughed "Didn't he realise the sleeves were tied up?" as she shook her head and said, "His girlfriend did a few, buttons up and he said, "There's something wrong, I can't get my arms out, the sleeves!" as she smiled and kissed him again, to put him at his ease, as he asked, "Was she into bondage?" as she took him over to the dressing table and sat him down.

Fiona asked, "What did she do next?" as Suzie giggled, she started to pop hair ribbons into his hair, as they gasped and screeched "Oh fab!" as she added and told him he was going to start helping his Mum and little sister with the housework, as he tried to say, "No way! I won't!" but next thing she took one of her girly aprons and slid it over his head and down his front!" as he sobbed "Oh no! It's too girly!" as they giggled, "great!" as she added "And she then produced her phone and took some photos of him in hair ribbons and pinny". They were giggling away, when some other girls from Suzie's class joined them and asked, "What's up, Suzie?" as Suzie said, "Look! I'm telling these girls here, a story, but will tell you and other girlx at the break! Can you just leave us, while I finish it with Naomi and Fiona?" as they said, "Ok Suzie! Catch you, in class!" as they heard more giggles and laughter from the three.

Suzie said, "She then asked, "Want me to pull your undies down and touch your little friend?" as he nodded, and said, "Will you Katie, fab?" and added "Let my hands go and I'll touch you?" as she laughed and standing him up, she pulled his undies down!"

She said, about having to complement his sister and agree to play dollies

They gasped "Naughty girl!" as she laughed "But she then showed him some very frilly panties!" as they giggled, "She didn't? Great!" as he cried "Oh no! Not panties!" as she took him over to the bed and sitting him down, she

pulled them up his legs and over his naughty bits. She then told him, what it was called and he'd to call it his baby-pee-pee from then on as she took photos of him in the frilly panties!" as they gurgled, as she said, "And some of them with the panties down his legs, to show off his little baby-pee-pee!" to more laughter.

She continued "He'd of course locked the door, to have his wicked way. with Katie and then heard his little sister come back and call for their Mum!" as they laughed "Did she let her in, to see her big brother in hair ribbons and apron?" Suzie laughed "Katie called 'Your Mum's gone next door and left Robbie and me, here!" as his little sister gasped "She's left you 2 alone in your room!" adding "I'm going to tell on you 2, if you don't let me in!" as she ran upstairs and tried his door!" as they laughed and Fiona said, "He must have been wetting himself, in case she let her in?" as she nodded. Suzie said, "Katie got him to tell her, how pretty his little sister was, through the door and that he'd start helping her and their Mum with housework. However, she then said, "His sister could provide any apron she wanted for him to wear and he'd to promise to wear it!" His sister gasped as he promised to wear one of her little aprons, to help her and their Mum with housework!" as she giggled and ran to fetch her prettiest pinny!" Suzie added "She got him to promise to help with the washing or to peg out some clothes to air and asked Suzie to get some of her and her Mum's clothes for him to peg out on the washing line!"

However, she then got him to promise to play dollies with Karen and she asked, "What age did you start playing with her dollies?" as he'd to say, "He used to steal her dollies and play with them in his room from the age of, 4 or 5 and he'd to promise to play dollies with Karen every day!" as Fiona and Naomi screeched "Oh fab! She made him do all that and sound a complete sissy?" as she nodded, "Isn't it fun?" as they gasped "It's not true, it's just a story? Isn't it?" but Suzie shook her head "It's all true!"

They gasped "You haven't tried it on your big bro?" as Suzie giggled, "Would I?" as they gasped and heard her giggle "My lips are sealed!" as they gasped and screeched. Especially when she said, "I'd never seen a baby-pee-pee, before last night, when I put him to bed in Mummy's nighty and my panties" as they screeched "You never did?" as she nodded, "It was such a laugh!" Suzie continued "Katie then said, she'd put his trousers on, with him whispering for her to remove his pretty apron, hair ribbons and panties!" as they laughed "She should have put him into a skirt or frock!" as Suzie laughed "Wait and hear!" She said, "She'd remove the ribbons, but he might ask for them later himself!" as he said, 'No way!' as she pushed him down on the bed and pulled up the trousers, to hide his frilly panties!" as he sighed and asked her to remove his girly apron. She then took him over to the window and opened the curtains, as he cried "Quick before the neighbours see me in these ribbons and your apron?" as she removed his hair ribbons to leave him on show in her girly apron!" as she then said, "I'll now remove your apron!" as she undid the ties and pulled it off!" but heard him cry "Oh no!" They asked, "What was it?" as she giggled, "They weren't his trousers but were from a charity shop and she'd cut a massive big hole at the front, to show off his frilly panties!" as they screeched and jumped about with joy.

She explains the charity shop trousers with a hole and frills

She laughed "So Joey ended up asking for her pretty apron back and knew he couldn't remove it, or his sister would see his frilly panties!" She hid the ribbons amd his smelly underpants away in a pink handbag and slid it over his neck. for some more photos!" as she said "If his sister looked in the handbag and saw his undies, she'd wonder what he was wearing instead and so he'd to keep the handbag too as she led him over to the door and told him she'd be cutting his sleeves in a second, but any playing up and she'd show him off to his sister!" as they laughed "Fab!" Hence, she cut his cuffs and unlocked his door and saw his little sister run up and screech at her big brother in a big girly apron, but also carrying a pink handbag, with I suppose his hair ribbons!" She asked him did he want his sister to take his handbag, but he said, he was enjoying it, not wanting her to see hair ribbons and undies!"

However, Katie had actually gone much further with Joey, than she'd told Suzie and had put him into nappies, gelling and applying baby powder to his baby pee pee and plastic baby pants and so it was a nappy and baby stuff in his handbag, that he dreaded his sister, Karen, spying. Whether she'd just threatened to show photos of him if he didn't carry it or what, but he'd not let Karen take it from him and minced with it on his elbow, looking a real sissy!" as they laughed.

However, his sister then held out her girly little apron, as he tried to say, that as he'd Katie's apron on, he didn't need her little one, but Katie reminded him, he did promise to wear her aprons!" as he woefully took it and pulled it on over her own big apron, making him look a real girly boy. They took him downstairs and said, "We'll delay taking you outside and you can play dollies for a while!" as they giggled "He didn't?" as she nodded and said "Of course, she offered to let him remove his girly aprons, but he said, he was having fun in them!" to more laughter. She said, "He played dollies with them for a while, but she then said, "Look Karen, I think we're being unkind to big Joey here, we'll let him remove his pinnies, as he's promised to peg out the clothes to air and be a good boy!" as Karen said, "No! Make him stay in his girly aprons!" Katie asked, "So Joey! Do you want to remove your pretty aprons, or are you having fun in them?" as he so wanted to remove the aprons, but dreaded Karen spy his frilly panties and so said, "No girls, I'm having fun in my aprons, but can I remove Karen's little one to go outside?" but she wouldn't, but a funny thing was Joey had a pink handbag, that he kept hold off and even when Katie asked him did he want Karen to look after it for him, he said, he wanted to carry it?" Hence, he minced out with a pink handbag, but also in the 2 pretty aprons, carrying the bowl of clothes to air, looking a complete sissy!" as they giggled, "Oh fab!" Suzie said, "Here's something you girls can try, to make the laundry with your Mummy's more fun!" as they asked, "What?" as she giggled, "Katie then told Karen to get a few more handbags!" and Karen obliged and fetched some, before locking up the back door. Katie then said, she used a handbag as a peg bag and that's what you can do now, to make helping your Mummy with the laundry, especially if you can get your brother or Daddy to promise to help with the washing!" as they giggled.

They listened on, as she said, "So Joey, had to take another handbag and fill it with clothes pegs and then mince back to Karen, who was holding the bowl of clothes peg out.

Suzie showed them mincing and extreme mincing

She added "See he couldn't use his pink handbag as he'd not want Karen to spy its contents of his underpants, again not realizing it contained his baby stuff. Hence he had two handbags to mince about with and look a complete sissy!" She laughed "Remember he still didn't have any ribbons or a headscarf to disguise him and so looked a sissy boy!" as they laughed "Oh fab!" Katie then said, about the neighbours spying him and recognising him and think he's a sissy and so offered him a disguise!" as they asked, "What?" as she giggled, "Hair ribbons!" as they screeched, as she continued "He'd to remove hair ribbons from his pink handbag and then hand them to Karen and ask her to pretty up his hair and she had great fun. sliding ribbons into her big bro's hair, one at a time!" She giggled, "However, his Mum and Jan were looking down, amazed at his girly look and taking photos or videos of his new girly look, in ribbons, girly aprons and two handbags, especially as Katie had him mince around the garden carrying them too. She had him do mincing, but then extreme mincing!" as they asked, "What?" as Suzie giggled, "this is mincing!" as she slid her shopper up her arm to the elbow and the other onto her waist, as he minced along. She then said, "This is extreme mincing!" as she slid both elbows, to her waist and extended her arms out to the side and minced along to screeches from the girls, as several others looked and laughed, not realising the situation and both girls copied her. Fiona then said, "I might try this on my bro! It would be fun getting him playing dress up and dollies with me!" as she laughed "Though I doubt if Mum, would let me dress him up in my frocks!" as Suzie laughed "That's where a neighbour, can be of help! Once you have him under your thumb with photos or what not, you can then get him to tell his Mum, he's going out to play footy, but instead, he's to run to

the neighbours where you have lots of dollies and frocks, or whatever you want for him to play girly games, maybe a dolls pram for him to push along and stuff!" as they giggled, "Our neighbour is Jan and she's really nice, I'm sure she'd help me dress him up!"

Naomi giggled, "Oh I wish I'd a little brother now! I've only a big sister" as Suzie laughed "You could maybe get a boy from the street!" as she laughed "Bob next door, who's eight and often calls me names. She said "I'll have a word with his Mum and ask if she'd like him to help with housework!" but add "whispering to her wearing one of my pretty aprons!" as she laughed "I'll try!" as they skipped along.

They were nearing the school, as she laughed "Katie said, his Mum was next door and she'd remove his little apron and pop a headscarf on his head, if he wanted to go around for his Mum to rescue him!" as he said, "Ok!" as she laughed "She removed his little sisters apron, to leave him in her apron, but again asked, "Did he want to remove it and go around as a boy!" but he shook his head and said, "He wanted to prove he wasn't a MSP anymore!" as they laughed and Katie showed him the headscarf, but then replaced it with a clear see through plastic rainhat, to show off his girly hair ribbons again, as he minced down the driveway, making sure none of his mates were about, as he minced along looking a complete sissy. She then said, "Look girls! Don't mention this to the boys, as we might play some tricks and maybe get the boys attend school in hair ribbons, girly bags and eventually maybe some of them in dresses and pinafores!" as they screeched "Fab!" as Naomi gasped "You're serious?" as Suzie and Fiona nodded. They separated with them calling "Bye!" as she skipped along to her class.

PART F

PAM SHOWS JULIE AND HER MUM SISSY LAUNDRY WITH A HANDBAG

Play shopping and her Mum finds out that Pam knows …

June makes Tom mince a dress around the garden using a hanger again

June then saw his Mum hand him another of Pam's dresses and said, "Show June the way to peg out your dress!" as he grimaced as he took a hanger and hung the dress over it, before pulling it around his neck as June giggled, "Oh fab!" but then saw him mince around the garden, with the frock hanging down his front. June gurgled "Doreen, he could be a treasure around the dress shops!" as his Mum laughed and then saw him reach into his handbag and retrieve his purse to get two pegs and then pegged it up.

June saw Doreen mince around the garden with her own frock and peg it out as she called him over to the fence and whispered something, but then pulled the headscarf from his head and said, "Shouldn't Sissy Tom have a go, at pegging up one item!" as his Mum gasped "June don't! The neighbours out back might spy him and think he's a sissy!" She said, "Just one item for Sissy Tom!" as he minced over to the basket and took a pair of Pam's panties and trying to hide his face behind the dresses, on the line, he reached into the handbag and got his purse.

He soon had pegged them up as June said, "Ok Tom, well done!" and calling him over, she tied the headscarf back around his head, as he minced back over to the basket. His Mum said, "I'll do a few of my frocks now and let you rest for a while!" as he sighed.

Meanwhile Julie and Pam were taking turns with Tina, wheeling a dolly each, up and down the driveway. Tina then wheeled the doll's pram out and said, "Come on girls, join me wheeling dolly down the street!" as they ran to catch her, carrying their dollies when a couple of girls from ballet spotted Pam and Julie and teased "Hi Julie! Hi Pam! Still playing dollies?" They blushed and Julie said, "My little sister, Tina here has roped us into joining her, playing dollies!" as the other girl called "Don't let us see you sucking your thumbs girls?" as they all laughed and Tina called "Dollies are fun!" as the girls laughed. Tina said, "Pam you go and get your dolly and her doll's pram!" as Pam laughed and said, "Ok!" thinking "I might be able to check on Nancy again!" as she slipped over and Julie wondered, why she had to climb over the gate.

Pam climbed the gate and quietly slipped up the driveway smiling as she saw Nancy and her Mum, but also a smiling June. She called "Come in Tina!" as Tom cried "Oh no!" and wet his panties, as she giggled, "Just joking Nancy! I've just come to fetch my doll's pram!" as Tom cried "I've flaming wet my panties!" as his Mum didn't realize he'd said, "Panties!" and Pam gurgled "Oh Mum! I knew Tom was out of his nappies, too soon!" as her

Mum scolded "Less of that, young lady!" June and his Mum laughed, but his Mum scolded "That was naughty Pam!" as she said, "Sorry Tom! Quick back of the garage and remove your wet panties!" as her Mum then gasped "Pam! He's not wearing your panties?" as she nodded but said, "Mummy! At least only us three, will know!"

She opened the garage door and pulled her doll's pram out, saying, "Tina's getting us, to wheel our dollies about in the street! Julie and I have just been teased silly, by two girls from ballet" as her Mum laughed "You, poor girl!" Pam laughed "Would you prefer to deputize for me, to save my blushes, beside little Tina, wheeling your dolly, up and down

Pam comes over and fetches her pram and scares Tom who wets himself

the street!" adding "dressed like now?" as her Mum gasped "No way Pam!" as he shook his head. She giggled, "Don't worry Nancy! I'll look after your dolly!" but then heard Pam call "Mummy! Will you get Baby Jamima too?" as he gasped "Why?" as she laughed "Tina wants me to wheel my own dolly around the street in its baby pram, here!" His Mum laughed as she exited the garden, to fetch a pair of Pam's panties and his dolly along with the washcloth and towel.

His Mum said, "I'll go in and get him some clean Y-fronts and a wash-clothe and towel to clean himself. Pam called "You know where, his panties are, or else I'm sure Aunty June, could find something, even more embarrassing, for baby to wear!" as his Mum gasped "You little tyrant, you!" His Mum had fetched a pair of Pam's yellow panties, along with his dolly and then a wash-clothe and a towel and exited, locking up again.

His Mum gets a cloth and panties, but June fetches him a tutu skirt

However, June ran inside too and returned with a tutu skirt, along with a plastic bag, for his wet panties and laughed "Tom! We'll let you off coming around, tonight and let you play footy, after tea!" as he said, "Great!" Pam laughed, but added "Pity, I was looking forward to more fun with Nancy" as he grimaced "Not fair!" but took the skirt and pulled it up, under his apron and PVC pinny.

His Mum gasped, as she saw her blushing Tom, now in a pretty tutu ballet skirt, making Pam's apron flayer out sweetly and giggled, "Oh June! You didn't?" as she laughed "It adds sweetly, to Nancy's disguise and he'll earn brownie points, from Pam and me, for giving us a giggle!" His Mum cuddled him and popping his dolly into the doll's pram, she said, "Down to the back of the garage and remove those wet things and here's a clean pair of Pam's panties!" as Pam said, "Nancy! Pop your panties into your handbag, Nancy!" and saw him open the handbag and zipping it up, he blushed as he minced off, to giggles. Pam laughed "Mummy! Aren't you going to clean baby Tom, up?" as her Mum laughed "Now Pam! That was a naughty trick!" as June laughed "But it was funny!" He huffed "Not fair!"

Tom went to the back of the garage but heard Pam call "Since Nancy's in her skirt, she can remove her wet trousers and panties and pop them into that bag June has supplied!" as he cringed "Not fair Mum!" He got around the back and reaching under his aprons and tutu skirt, he undid his trousers and pulled them down and off his legs. He then sighed, as he reached under the aprons again and pulled the wet panties down and off.

Tom slides a hanger with frock and mince the dolls pram around

He then took the cloth and started washing his front and some of his backside. He soon was drying himself and then reaching into his handbag, he retrieved his panties and pulled them up his legs, under his skirt, as he grimaced, looking down at the girly skirt, not without his trousers. He took his trousers and panties and popped them into the carrier bag along with the wet-cloth and towel and returned to his Mum, Pam said, "That's Nancy looking much

212

more girly, in his pretty ballet skirt, with a much better disguise, to mince around the garden, with my frocks!" June and his Mum then saw Pam, wheel the doll's pram, around and say, "See what I'm having to do for him, Mum!" as they laughed. It's so embarrassing!" as her Mum scolded "What about for Tom?" as June laughed "A little girly mincing and dress up won't hurt at his age!" adding "Quick before I go, let me see you peg out another frock!" He called "Not fair! Make sure Julie or Tina don't come and look for you!" as she wheeled the pram to the side of the house, peering out to Julie and Tina, who were still across the street in their driveway, as she said, "Don't worry Tom! They're still across at Julie's!" She then laughed "Actually for this one frock, you can have the pleasure of wheeling your pretty Baby Suzie dolly around in her pram too!" as he cried "Not fair Pam!"

Tom took a hanger and heard Pam say, "Nancy! Why don't you peg out my pretty yellow frock!" as her Mum gasped and blushed, realizing, it was the one, she'd made him wear, that night to change his ways and the one that, had got Tom, to play dollies and lead to him now prancing about in the garden in a skirt, Pam's aprons and a pretty handbag!" He bent down and rummaging through the basket he pulled the dress, but heard Pam say, "Be careful with your pretty frock, Nancy!" as he blushed bright red and June laughed "Not realizing the joke!" as he retrieved the dress and pulled it onto the hanger and then slid it, around his neck, to screeches from June "Oh fab!"

Tom went over to he took the pram from her and started mincing his doll's pram, wheeling it around the garden, with the yellow frock hanging down his front, but now in the ballet skirt and pretty apron, mincing with his handbag and looking really girly, with lots of teasing from June and Pam and laughter from his Mum. He gets back to the line and unzipping his handbag, he retrieves the purse and takes two pegs out for his dress.

He closes his purse and returns it to his handbag which he zips up and then removing his dress from the hanger, he pegs it up to laughter. Pam then said, "It's a good suggestion for him pegging out Aunty June's washing too!"

He begged "Please don't make me?" but June said, "It will give you lots of practice for helping your Mummy with the laundry!" Pam said, "I've always helped Mummy with the washing and now you will learn how much fun it is!"

Pam wheels her pram with his dolly over to Julie

She added "I want to see a nice smile on Nancy's face while helping Mummy with the laundry, no grimaces!" as he cringed, but then tried to muster a smile. Pam Says, "Just kiss your Baby Suzie dolly, bye and I'll wheel her over to Julie and Tina's house!" and saw him reach in and taking his dolly out, he kissed it's lips again, to cheers as he replaced it, back into the pram. Pam said, "Just once more around the garden Nancy and telling your baby doll you love her and will miss her madly!" as her Mum scolded "You are naughty Pam!" as he blushed and started wheeling his doll back around the garden again, but this time without his dress hanging down his front. Pam called "Bye! Don't worry Baby Suzie, your Mummy - Nancy, will take you walkies later!" as he gasped "No!" and his Mum laughed "No way Pam, don't be cruel!"

His Mum said, "This is taking so long Pam!" as she laughed "Oh, but it is giving Aunty June and me, so much fun!" as her Mum corrected her "Aunty June and I" as Pam gurgled "You having fun too, Mummy!" as they laughed, as he called "Not fair Mum!" as he looked at his girly look. Pam said, "Using his purse and handbag is good practicing for shopping!"

as his Mum said, "Now Pam he can't carry a handbag around the shops!" as Pam giggled, "Don't worry Mummy, we'd make sure it was Nancy using her handbag and purse, all around the town!" as he cried "Please don't Pam?" to more laughter.

Pam wheeled the dolly out the driveway and down, having to lift the pram over the gate, before climbing over herself. Julie called "Why's the gate tied shut Pam?" as she laughed "Oh! Too many of Tom's mates were calling

at our house and Mum's trying to deter them!" as Julie laughed "Won't they just climb over?" as Pam laughed "That's why I was keeping an eye out the front!" but added "I'm sure they're all around the street and won't call for him now!" She heard Julie call "We were, about to send a search party, over for you!" Pam called "Mum wanted a little help with the laundry and so I gave her some help pegging up the washing!" but added "I found a wonderful way to make it more fun!" as Julie asked, "How?" as Pam said, "You wheel your dolly around the garden, before pegging out each item of washing!" as Julie laughed "But that will take forever!" as Tina said, "That sounds fun!" Pam laughed "Even better when you've to peg out a frock!" as Julie asked, "Why?" as she giggled, "If you take a dress and slide it onto a clothes hanger and then pop that around your neck, like we do in a dress shop!" then we can mince around the garden wheeling our dolly before pegging out the frock!" as Julie and Tina screeched and Julie said, "I've never thought of doing that!" adding "Wait till I tell Mummy!" Pam then Says, "Mummy uses a pretty handbag to hold our clothes pegs to peg out the washing!" as Julie gasped "Gosh just like shopping?" as Pam added "Even better if we add a purse, to hold six pegs, at a time and keep on refilling the purse, to practice shopping properly!"

Pam tells them to use a handbag and purse to hold pegs for laundry

She added "And make sure you zip up your handbag before use!" She asked, "Tina, you know why?" as the little girl shook her head and heard her reply "So your purse isn't stolen from your handbag when mincing around the shops!" as she nodded, "I see!" Julie giggled, "Especially if you're pegging out a frock, like you said, "It would be just like in a dress shop, but actually in the back garden!" as Pam nodded, and Tina laughed "Will we try it now?" as Julie said, "I don't think Mummy has any washing ready!" but Pam said, "We can just peg up some clothes to air!" adding "It will stop us being seen about the street wheeling our dollies and being teased silly!" as Julie nodded, "Good one Pam!" June's Mum sees Julie bringing down, some of her and Tina's pretty dresses and asked, "What's up! I'm not doing the washing today!" as Julie said, "Pam's told us, a fun way to make the laundry or pegging out the clothes to air, more fun!" as her Mum laughed "That should get you to help me, more with the laundry!" as Julie laughed "I do a little!" as she said, "Not that much dear!" She then picked up three handbags, but also four clothes hangers, just in case her Mum wanted to join in and popped a purse into each bag and said, "Mum! We need a handbag and purse too!" as she laughed "What? For pegging out the washing?" as Julie nodded, "That's what Pammy Says!" as her Mum, laughed and followed her out. Julie joins her Mum out to see Pam who Says, "Julie we all need a pretty apron and if the washing is wet, then a PVC pinny too!" adding "But today! We only need a pretty apron! So, can you bring pretty aprons for you, Tina and me?" and saw her run back and fetch some aprons for the three of them.

Pam gets Julie to fetch 3 aprons, handbags and clothes hanger

Julie pulled her own apron around herself and tying it behind her back, before running out and handed Tina one of her own pretty aprons and then one of hers to Pam too. Soon they were all in pretty aprons. Julie handed the handbags and a hanger to Pam and Tina, but Pam said, "Julie the hanger's must be able to slide around your neck!" and Julie ran back and changed two of the hangers for the open type and ran back out, as her Mum brought out the basket of clothes. Julie handed the two hangers, to Tina and Pam, so they were ready. Pam asked, "Where's the clothes pegs?" as Julie pointed to a washbag on the line. Pam took it and opening it, she took lots of pegs and popped them into the three handbags as Julie, her Mum and Tina looked on. Pam said, "Now pop six pegs into each purse and return it to your handbag!" as Julie said, "Mum you want to join in?" but she said, "I'll watch and maybe try next time!" The three girls took a purse out, of their handbag's and opened them and then popped six pegs into each one. She said, "Now girls! Return your purses to your handbags!" and saw Julie and Tina return the purses to their handbags and closed them up, as Pam did too. Julie helped Tina close her handbag and Pam closed hers.

Pam demonstrates how to mince with a frock on the hanger with handbag

Pam laughed "Now girls select a pretty frock!" and saw Tina take one of hers, Julie take one and Pam, take one of Julies as Pam said, "Now slide your dress onto a hanger and then slide it around your neck with the dress hanging down your front. She saw them take their dresses and slide them onto the hangers and pop them around their necks. However, Tina had a problem and Julie helped her and soon all three girls were standing there with the dresses on hanger's around their necks. Pam then said, "Now take your handbags and slide them up your arm's to your elbow!" and Tina and Pam copied as their Mum laughed "You look just like me, when I go dress shopping in town!" as Pam laughed and said, "Now girls copy me, mincing around the garden!" and saw her start walking around the garden, followed by Tina and then Julie as their Mum laughed "You look very sweet girls!" We just peg up our dress after mincing around the garden!" as she got to the line and said, "Right girls, open your handbag and get your purse out and open it, to get your two pegs!" and saw the girls open their handbag's and get a purse out and open it and get two pegs and then close the purse and return it to their handbag. Her Mum helped Tina with her purse and handbag and soon they all had their pegs ready. Pam said, "Now! Slide the dress off your hanger and pet it up!" as Julie took her dress and removed it from the hander and pegged it up. Pam did the same, but Tina needed help as she slid her dress off the hanger but was too small to get to the line and so her Mum lifted her up and she managed to peg out her dress.

Pam laughed and said, "Normally that is it! but it makes it even more fun, if we wheel our dollies around the garden, while mincing around the garden with our dresses around our necks with our handbags dangling from our elbows!" as Julie's Mum laughed and said, "Oh Pam!" Pam said, "I'll pick another dress and demonstrate with my pram and dolly!" as she picked up another of Julie's dresses and sliding it onto a hanger, she slid it around her neck. She then took hold of her doll's pram with Baby Suzie in it and minced with her arm swinging as she minced her handbag around the garden, to giggles from Julie, Tina and their Mum at Pam's girly antics. Julie said, "I'll go next with Tina's pram and dolly!" as she picked up one of her frocks and sliding it, onto a hanger, pulled it over her neck and down her front. She then soon was wheeling Tina's doll's pram around the garden, again mincing with her handbag, before opening her handbag, getting her purse out and then taking two pegs and after returning her purse to her handbag. She then closed them up and pegged her dress up again. She laughed "Gosh Mum! Why didn't we think of this before?" as her Mum nodded, "It does look fun, although it will make the laundry take about twice as long!" as Pam laughed "Well with Julie and Tina helping you more, it shouldn't take that long!" as her Mum said, "So do you and Tom help your Mummy?" Julie and Tina screeched about Tom helping mince around the garden with the laundry. Finally, Tina picked up one of her own frocks and sliding it onto a hanger, Julie helped her slide it over her neck, so it was hanging down again.

Julies' Mum suggests Pam try to get Tom to copy them with the washing

Julie slid her handbag up her arm to her elbow and said, "Now Tina! Just push your dolly pram around the garden again!" and saw little Tina, start pushing her dolly, around the garden, with her little dress hanging around her neck, with her handbag on her elbow, mincing around the garden again. Pam said, "Well done, Tina!" as Julie and her Mum laughed and saw her return from mincing her pram around and then open her handbag to get her purse again to get the pegs. She then she lifted Tina up to peg out her dress again, as Pam said, "What do you think girls?" as Julie giggled, "It's great!" and Tina called "That's lots of fun, Pammy!"

However, then their Mum called "Pam! I hope you're teaching your Tom, to peg out his washing too?" as Pam gasped, knowing he was just across the street, mincing around the garden, with his pretty aprons and handbag and dresses. Pam laughed "Now he never usually even lifts a finger to help with the washing up!" Julie called "Yes Pam! You and your Mummy should show him how to mince like us!" as she laughed "We'll try! but he might take a bit longer for him to enjoy, compared to you girls!" adding "I might have to lend him my doll's pram and dolly,

Baby Suzie here! As I don't think he's got his own dollies!" to more screeches. Julie said, "Oh Pam! Your Mum should have bought him some dollies, when he was young!" as Pam laughed "I don't think he hid his dollies, away in his room from me!" as Julie and Tina both screeched, at the thought of macho Tom, mincing around the garden in a pretty apron, with a dress dangling down from a hanger along with a handbag, wheeling a doll's pram! Pam gurgled "Now girls! Could you imagine my big bro Tom, mincing around the garden like us!" adding "although I think it's wearing a pretty tutu skirt or frock, that he'd be more worried about!" to more laughter and giggles.

Meanwhile Tom is carrying on, pegging up the washing and when it came to dresses, mincing them around the garden, with his handbag, with June complaining "It's a pity Pam took your dolly pram, or you could wheeling her, around the garden too!" as he blushed saying, "Ha funny!" as he continued pegging out the wet clothes on the washing line. His Mum peered around the garage wall to the drive and over towards Julie's as she saw Pam, Julie and Tina disappear around to the back garden and thought "I hope none of Tom's mates climb the gate to check where he is!" but she was ok and his mates were engaged in footy around the next street. He eventually has finished, pegging out all the washing and sighs, as his Mum Says, "Right Tom! I'll go and open the back door, to let you in!" as June laughed "Well done Nancy! We're very pleased with you today!" as he huffed "At last!" adding "It's been terrible, having to peg out all that washing!" adding "But especially mincing with those frocks too!" as June laughed "At least Pam took her doll's pram and your dolly over to stop you having to mince your dolly around the garden!" as he nodded, and stammered "That's going to be terrible in future, for the laundry, if I've to mince that doll's pram around the garden!"

Tom has to go to June's and is sent home from June's in ballet tutu skirt

She laughed and said, "I'll let you keep your tutu skirt for now! Be careful as you pop around to your house!" as he stepped towards the edge of the garage, dreading, Julie or Tina, spy him in his tutu ballet skirt and Pam's aprons, mincing with a handbag on his elbow. Pam Julie and Tina finish pegging out the clothes from the basket, with their Mum thanking Pam for showing her girls how to make the laundry more fun. Pam removed Julie's handbag and pretty apron from around her and handed them back to Julie and wheeled Tom's dolly Baby Suzie over home. She called "Bye Julie! Bye Tina!" as they called bye to her and saw her mince her dolly pram over across the road. Of-course, Pam was spied by one of Tom's mates, who called "You still playing dollies Pam?" as she blushed but called "It's lots of fun! You boys miss out so much on playing dollies and wheeling their doll's pram!" as he huffed "Funny Pam!" and saw Pam lift the doll's pram and lift it over her gate and then climb back over and wheel the pram back up the drive.

Pam wheeled the pram around to the garage and left it inside, before taking his dolly and entering the side door. She called "Hi Mum!" and then "Tom! Come here a tick! I've got your Baby Suzie here!" as he called "Not so loud Pam!" as he came downstairs and saw her, holding his dolly, out to him. He took it, saying, "Thanks! I did all that flaming laundry this afternoon! It's been terrible!" Pam giggled, "I've just been showing Julie, Tina and their Mummy, how to mince washing around the garden, with a handbag, purse, clothes-hanger for their frocks and doll's pram, to make the laundry more fun!" as her Mum laughed "I suppose that was to stop Tina making you wheel your doll's pram about the street?" as Pam nodded but said, "One of his mates Jamie, flaming teased me when I wheeled my doll's pram back over!" adding "I'll have to try and get him back!" However, she gurgled "Their Mum suggested as a laugh, that Mummy should teach Tom, how to mince it around the garden!" as he cried "Oh no!" but added "Don't worry Tom! I kept Nancy, a complete secret, from them all!" as he sighed "Thanks Pammy!" as she laughed "For now!" as he cried "Mum! She said, 'For now!'" as her Mum scolded "Now Pam! No telling tails on him!"

However, then Pam took Tom upstairs and said, "I've thought of a way to stop you forgetting your dolly!" as he asked, "How?" as she handed him her pink apron and said, "Slide into my pinny again!" and saw him pull it on and

heard her ask "Can I just borrow your dolly a tick!" as he nodded, asking "Why?" as she said, "Stay in your room for a few minutes!" as she left. Pam took his dolly into her room and taking a pink handbag, she sewed the handle of the handbag, to the doll's hand. She checked and slid the handbag over her elbow and saw the dolly hang down, meaning she had to hold the dolly up and thought that will be brilliant, him mincing around the house with both the handbag and dolly! Pam returned to his room and heard him gasp, as he saw Pam mince in with the handbag, dangling from her arm, but also holding his dolly, attached to it.

Pam takes Tom and borrows his dolly to sew a handbag to it

She laughed "I've found a way that Nancy shouldn't forget her dolly anymore!" as he cried "Oh no!" as she giggled, "I've given your dolly a handbag, as a pressy and so as long as, you carry your pretty handbag here, you shouldn't forget your dolly!" He begged "Please don't? Mum won't let you!" but she removed it and then sliding it up his arm to the elbow, she tied it to his apron, as he cried "Oh no! Not the pinny too?" as she nodded. Pam then said, "Look Tom I don't want to get into trouble with Mummy!" as he said, "She'll give it to you if you try and make me carry a handbag all about the house and wear your flaming apron too!" as she laughed "Now I'm going to tell her and you that you don't have to carry Baby Suzie about any more and I won't even call out about you forgetting her!" He said, "So I don't need the bag then!" She laughed "See Tom! I'm deputizing Aunty June, to call down to you from her upstairs window! With you at the front window, holding your dolly and handbag!" adding "Imagine her calling down 'Oh Tom! You, naughty boy! You've forgotten your dolly and handbag!" adding "As a little girl or lady is passing by, looking in at my big sissy brother!" as he cringed "Not fair Pam!" He sobbed "Oh no! Someone will spy me!" as she nodded, "So just tell Mum! You've realized how much fun playing dollies is and especially carrying Baby Suzie about the house!" as he sobbed "Not flaming fair! I'll sound a right sissy!" as she nodded. She laughed "Look on the bright side "With your headscarf or ribbons, you shouldn't be recognized!" as he begged "Not ribbons too?" as she laughed "Not yet! I want to take it slowly with my sweet sister Nancy!" as she kissed his lips, causing him to gasp "Oh no!" as he asked, "Where is your headscarf?" as she laughed "Better get down to ask Mummy!"

Just head down and call out "Mummy! Pammy has thought of a way to stop me forgetting my dolly, when moving from room to room!" as he cringed and exited his bedroom followed by his smiling sister. His Mum heard footsteps on the stairs and Tom call "Mummy!" as she called "Yes Tom!" as she heard him continue "Pammy has thought of a way, to stop me forgetting my dolly, as I move from room to room!" as she called "Yes Tom! How?" but then saw him turn from the bottom of the stairs, into the hall, as she gasped "Oh no!" as she saw him in Pam's apron, but with a handbag, dangling from his elbow, but holding his dolly with the doll attached to it. Pam called "Look Mummy! I've given his Baby Suzie, a pressy! I've sewn her new handbag to dolly's hand! A pretty handbag, for her to carry about the place!" as her Mum, screeched and called "Pam! I said, no handbags, for Tom!" as he called "Not so loud Mum!" as they, laughed. Pam said, "Now Mummy! Seeing, that Nancy can carry her handbag, about the back garden, to peg out the laundry! That has set a president and so, she should be able to mince about the house, with her dolly's handbag too!" as her Mum laughed "Oh has it dear?" as she hugged him. She said, "Since her handbag is tied to his apron, it means that while in my apron, he won't forget his pretty dolly and I won't be able to call out to him!"

Pam pretends she's letting Tom off carrying his dolly and handbag

Pam then said, "I'm only joking Tom! I've decided it's a bit naughty, making you carry my baby dolly Baby Suzie, about the house and I won't even call out, if you forget, to bring it with you!" Her Mum said, "Thanks Pam! I'm sure he'll appreciate that! It must have been so embarrassing!" Pam smiled and said, "I'm off out for a few minutes to see Julie, Mum! I might need my pretty pink pinny and headscarf, to play dollies, with Julie and Tina!" His Mum said, "Ok Tom! You can sit down and watch TV!" expecting him to remove the apron and set his handbag

and dolly down and life about the house to return to normal. His Mum couldn't believe it, as the next thing he stammered "Pam! Can I keep your pinny on! Mummy where's the headscarf! I've decided, I'm enjoying playing dollies!" adding "and with Baby Suzie's handbag, it will stop me forgetting her!" as his Mum gasped, and Pam screeched "Oh Tom! You, big sissy!" He blushed and heard her say, "Ok! I'll get my other apron! but I want my headscarf!" as she pulled her turquoise floral apron on, adding "Maybe, Mummy will lend you one of hers, or you can pop some of my pretty ribbons, in your hair, to be Nancy again instead of looking like a Sissy Tom!" as she picked up her Wendy doll and the pink headscarf and skipped out. His Mum looked at him and scolded "I thought you'd jump at the chance of being able to leave your dolly down for a while! I hope you're not actually turning into a girly!" as he blushed "Ha!" as she laughed "Will I find you a headscarf then?" or want to try a few of Pammy's hair ribbons?" as she giggled, and flicked her wrist towards him. He huffed "Can you find me a headscarf Mum?", as she fetched her shopping bag and pulled it out of a side pocket and laughed as he took it and tied it around his head. She laughed "I take it Pam's making you, keep them out?" adding "But you can't tell me how!" as he nodded, and she laughed "She is naughty! Making you sound a right sissy in front of me!" as he nodded, and blushed "It's going to be very embarrassing, if I'm spotted, carrying a flaming handbag and dolly, by anyone, as she laughed "You do look very cute like that!" adding "You could be fun, to take shopping!"

Tom cringed and said, "Don't you start Mum! Pam's bad enough!" She asked, "Want to remove them, while she's out?" and saw him nod "Thanks!" and removed the apron and slide the handbag and dolly off, setting them down onto the sofa, beside him, relieved to be dressed as a boy again. His Mum went back into the kitchen and saw Tom go out and say, "Just, off to the loo!" and when he reached the stairs, she called quietly "Oh Tom! You've forgot your dolly!" as he cried "Not funny!" and ran back and picked the handbag and dolly up, trailing the apron with them, as she laughed "Just joking, Tom!" but saw him run up the hall and turn up the stairs to the toilet. He returned back down a few minutes later, still carrying them, to hear her laugh, as he went into the living room and setting them down, he resumed watching the TV. His Mum entered and saw his dolly, handbag and apron beside him and said, "I'll have a word with her!" as he blushed.

Pam sends Tom up without his dolly and handbag, but doesn't call out

Pam returned from Julie's after about ten minutes and entered past her smiling Mum and saw Tom out of her apron and his dolly on the sofa, as she laughed "I see you've removed your pretty pinny and set dolly and her handbag down for a while!" as he huffed "I'd to go to the loo and Mum flaming called out, to make me run back and bring them with me!" Pam screeched "Oh Mummy! You, naughty girl, teasing my big macho brother, about forgetting his dolly!" as her Mum laughed "I was just joking and said, it quietly!" as he huffed "It isn't funny!" Her Mum said, "Me naughty! What about you making him sound a right sissy, by asking to keep his apron and dolly with him!" as Pam laughed "I told him he could leave his dolly behind and I won't say!" as she said, "Go on Tom up to your room and listen!" as he tried to say, "I'm watching this program!" but she pulled him up and said, "Just for two minutes till I prove to Mummy!" Tom stood up and exited the room and his Mum laughed, as she saw him without the dolly and heard him run up the stairs, as Pam said, "See Mummy! I'm not calling anything out, to embarrass Tom!" as she said, "Good girl! It will be good, if he can forget about that doll and act like a normal boy!" Two minutes later he came down and she said, "See Tom! That wasn't too bad without your dolly?" as he nodded, and grimaced "Ha!" Pam whispered to him "After dinner, I want you to say, you're just popping up to your room to play for ten minutes, but if you forget then June will call!" as she added "Nancy's to be in her apron too!" as he huffed "Not fair!" as she said, "Mummy! I'll let Tom off the dishes after dinner!" as his Mum laughed "Thanks, Pam! I'm sure he'll appreciate some time out of that pink apron of yours!"

Their Mum dished out dinner with Pam wearing her apron, but Tom in just his boy's clothes, apart from her panties of course. They tucked in and had a normal chat.

Towards the end of their meal, his Mum laughed "Pam that isn't right and making him wear your panties too!" as Pam laughed "Oh Mum! No-one will know and it will just give Tom a little reminder, of his lovely sister, Pammy, while he kicks his silly ball about, with his mates!" causing his Mum to laugh. Pam added "It might be different, if I made Nancy play footy, like he was earlier!" as he cried "No way!" as she added "Mummy! Could you imagine Sissy Tom! I mean Nancy here, mincing his handbag and dolly, about the street, kicking the ball!" as she added "Playing Sissy Football!" She then gurgled "That might be a game, that we all could play in the back garden!" as he cried "Oh no! Not, Sissy football!" as she nodded, and giggled, "At least it would let Mummy and I join in playing football, not to mention Aunty June too!" as her Mum laughed "Pam you're getting worse!" adding "Since Mummy and I are showing you how much fun, playing house is!" as her Mum giggled, more and Tom huffed "Funny ha ha!"

However, after the meal Pam and her Mum brought the dinner things into the kitchen and started running the water to do the washing up, when Tom said, "I'm going to my room, to play for a short while!" as Pam said, "Don't forget about your homework!" as he nodded, "I've only a little maths!" as she asked, "What about you Pam, any homework?" as she said, "Just a little English!" as they continued the washing up.

Their Mum spy's Tom as Nancy with his dolly, but doing homework

Tom knew he'd have to do it and soon had slipped into Pam's pink apron and exited the living room. His Mum looked and saw him back dressed as Nancy apart from the headscarf, but still carrying his handbag and holding the dolly and gasped "Tom! Pam's told you that you can leave your dolly!" as he stammered "I'll just bring her up to my room!" as she laughed. Pam However, called "If Nancy is up playing upstairs or doing your homework, she'll need her pink headscarf!" adding "Her blinds stay open, is that clear?" as she held the pink scarf, she'd worn over to Julie's, out to him and saw him run back and take it and tie it around his head, as Pam flicked her wrist to him, with a large blush on his cheeks, as his Mum laughed. Pam screeched "Mummy! It sounds, like he's realized, how much fun, playing dollies is!" as her Mum laughed "Tom! Leave them back inside!" but he shook his head and ran up the stairs with laughter filling his ears. Pam laughed "Nancy's handbag, could give him practice, even when doing his homework!" as she added "I can't see why he can't dangle his handbag from his elbow, when writing!" adding "Although if he wants to swap his handbag onto his left arm for a change, I won't mind!" as her Mum gasped "He can't, Pam!" as she laughed "Baby Suzie, Says, she can help Tom, with his homework! She's quite clever, you know?" as her Mum laughed "Oh Pam!"

Pam then said, "I know what will give Nancy some practice with Tom's handbag, I mean Nancy's handbag, I mean Nancy's dolly's Baby Suzie's handbag some practice!" as her Mum asked, "What?" as she laughed "Play shopping!" Her Mum gasped "Oh no, Pam!" as her Mum said, "There's no way Tom will carry a handbag, shopping with us!" as Pam laughed "Mummy of course he won't!" adding "I meant when Nancy, joins us shopping in her frocks!" as her Mum gasped "Now Pam! Not a chance!" Tam has helped her Mum to do the washing up and then had popped around to June, while Tom was upstairs in his room, dreading being spied by the neighbours dressed as Nancy while he did his homework with the handbag dangling from his elbow, while doing his sums. Tom hated having the handbag dangling from his arm, as he wrote and heard his Mum come up and laugh, as she saw him dressed as Nancy, with the pink headscarf, on his head and said, "Pam Says, 'you can untie your handbag'!" as he huffed "Thanks!" and undid the lose knot, from his apron strings and set the handbag and dolly down, as he said, "That's better!" However, his Mum said, "Give me your handbag a tick!" as he handed it to her, but then saw her slide it up his left arm and tie it to the left hand side, of his apron again, as he cried "I thought, I could remove it!" as she laughed "At least that gives you some rest from, it bouncing on your arm, while you write!" as he nodded.

He looked in the mirror and blushed again, saying, "Every time I look in the flaming mirror, I see my girly look and cringe!" as she laughed "Especially with the blinds open!" although, not up and the possibility of the people at the back spying him. His Mum kissed him and gave him a hug as she returned downstairs and said, "I've let him change as you suggested!" as Pam laughed.

Tom asks to wear her pretty panties out to play footy

Pam went upstairs and laughed "Hi Tom! I see Mum took my suggestion and tied your dolly's handbag on your left hand, to give you some rest from her bouncing on your arm when you write!" as he nodded, "I thought she'd let me off, when she said, 'I could remove it!'" He finally said, "Finished! Can I get these off now and go down and play footy?" She laughed as Tom stammered "Pam! Can I please wear those pretty yellow panties, out to play footy, with my friends?" as Pam giggled, and said, "Downstairs a tick!" as he descended the stairs to where their Mum was, in the kitchen. Pam said, "Repeat to Mummy!" as he gasped "Oh no!" as his Mum listened and heard him repeat "Mum! Can I wear Pam's pretty yellow panties, out, to play footy with my mates?" as they both screeched and heard Pam say, "Well Tom! No playing swapsies" as her Mum gurgled "Oh Pam! Oh Tom!" as she hugged him and gave him a kiss, but Pam had other plans for the evening. She said, "Tom! I want you to stay in this evening with Mummy and me!" as he cried "But I thought, I could play footy!" as her Mum said, "Pam let him off?" but she said, "Look! You'll be dressed as a boy, although we might need Nancy later on!" adding "So remove your pretty apron and leave your handbag and dolly down on the sofa!" Pam saw him pull the apron over his head, removing the headscarf his Mum had found for him earlier and leave it and his handbag and dolly on the sofa.

Pam said, "Isn't that better Tom?" as he nodded, and his Mum hugged him again. Pam said, "Stay down here a tick!" as she bounded up the stairs and he protested "Mum! I thought doing all that girly laundry, this afternoon as Nancy, especially in that flaming skirt of June's, I could s be a boy again, to play footy?" as she laughed "Just play a little bit and I'll try and get her to let you off, to play with your mates!" She added "At least, in here, nobody should see you, dressed up, or acting girly!" as he said, "Hopefully as Tom, I won't look girly!" He removed his apron and saw the handbag and dolly slide off his elbow, as he handed them to Pam and said, "At last! That's been terrible Pam, having to carry a handbag too!" as she laughed "Now Tom! It keeps Nancy's pretty dolly near her, so Aunty June or Mummy, can't yell anything out and give the game away!" as he blushed. She laughed "Be back to let Nancy do your homework by 8.30 ok!" adding "With the help of her handbag and Baby Suzie of course!" as he blushed asking "Make it 9.00, but she shook her head. He checked he'd no ribbons in his hair or anything else girly, as he exited the side door calling "Bye!" and ran on down his drive. His Mum said, "Thanks Pam for letting him out to play with his mates and let him off, being Nancy!" Pam bobbed a curtsy saying, "I want Tom to sound and look his normal self to his mates, so when they do see Nancy, it will be such a shock the diff of big macho Tom to sweet little Nancy!" as her Mum gasped and said, "Now Pam! Don't tell, please?" as she laughed "Don't worry Mum! I'm not even hinting at school or to Julie and Tina!" as her Mum said, "Thanks!" giving her a hug and a kiss. Pam brings his apron, handbag and dolly up the stairs to her bedroom and locks her door, as she opened a drawer. She took a bag and retrieved lots of pretty hair slides and bows, along with an Alice band and slid them into his pink handbag and zipped it up again.

Pam can't wait for Mum to knows about her yellow frock

She thought "Don't worry Nancy! I'll let you remove your hair ribbons and I wonder where you'll have to put them while doing your homework! Pink panty brother Tom! I mean Nancy!" She took one of her own school notebooks and a pen and set them on her dressing table. She then pulled on, her pink apron and slides his handbag up her elbow and sat down at her bedroom table, before taking some ribbons and bows and sliding them into her hair and looked at herself in the bedroom mirror. She gurgled at the thought of Sissy Tom doing his homework, looking at himself as she started to write and felt the handbag dangle and dance on her elbow as she wrote out some homework.

Pam can't wait for her Mum to realize that she knew about her dressing Tom up in her yellow frock and apron to do the dishes, when he said, 'Washing up was girls work!'

She devises a way to let her know and suggests they teach Tom to do the shopping. Her Mum scolded "Now Pam! We aren't taking Tom out around the shops as a girl!" as Pam said, "Mummy! It's only going to be play shopping

in the house, with the three of us!" as her Mum Says, "Let me think on it?" as she Says, "Well no bringing anyone else in to see him?" Pam nods "Honest Mummy! It will only the four of us!" as her Mum asks "Four?" but Pam then giggles "Now Mummy! We'll let Tom do some of the shopping, but as he'll not enjoy using his handbag and purse that much, we'd better let Nancy take over so she can enjoy herself, more!" as her Mum laughed "You are naughty! He's going to hate that!" Pam thinks to herself "At the minute I'm able to dress Nancy up and do what I want with him, around at June's, but Mum is making me go easy on him!" as she added "But once Mummy knows, that I know and I've the re-enactment of that wonderful night, with her dressing him up, then the gloves are off!" She added "I'll be able to have Nancy more about the house, prancing about in my frocks, either in the house watching TV, playing dollies or doing embroidery or dressmaking"

She thought "Outside, I can have Julie over to join Nancy and me to skip in the back garden, with us all in frocks!" as she gurgled "Oh fab!" adding "I'm sure Nancy will love to practice skipping with us!" She laughed "It will be wonderful practice for when he eventually is outed in school and has to skip with the girls!" adding "I know that Serry who is always having a go at him, would love it, to have him join her and the girls skipping in the playground!" She then thought "I wonder how long it would be for her and me to get Tom into a dress and pinafore!" as she flicked her wrist at the imaginary Tom dressed up as Nancy and thinking how wonderful it would be. Then she laughed "I'm sure she'll enjoy doing the laundry or playing Sissy Football in the garden in one of my pretty frocks!" as she gurgled to herself "And then maybe the street for his Sissy Football!" She thought "Wouldn't it be fab if we could get him out in the street kicking the ball with us in a pretty frock and mincing with his handbag!" as she thought and gasped "He'd wet himself!" as she thought "Why not add nappies and plastic baby pants to his outfit and then he could play Baby Football in the back garden, but then nearly wet herself as she thought "the street! Kicking the ball about in a diaper!" and had to calm herself down.

Tom and Nancy do Play Shopping

After doing the dinner things, Pam runs around to June and Says, "Sorry I'm making Tom stay in and you'd better not come around, in case Mum guesses, your involvement and guess that he played around at yours!" as June laughed and said, "Ok Pam! Pity! I was looking forward, to seeing him playing dress up!" Pam laughed "I'm going to let him be Tom for a while, out of any kind of apron as June asked, "Why?" as Pam gurgled "I'm going to make him play shopping, but he'll be mincing sweetly, like he did this afternoon, getting clothes pegs from his handbag!" as June gasped "What, dressed as a boy?, but carrying a handbag and purse?" as Pam nodded, and they giggled. She added "You might hear a lot of giggling and shrieking later on!" as June asked, "Why?" but Pam wouldn't say. They heard Pam coming down the stairs and then saw her with another few handbags, but also with three dresses on hangers, as Tom gasped and her Mum laughed "What are you up to, young lady?" as Pam giggled, "You talking to me or Tom?" as he fumed and they laughed. She said, "Mummy! Since Nancy had a lot of practice this afternoon, getting pegs from her handbag and purse!" adding "She's told me, she's told Tom, how much fun it was and how useful it will be, when he goes shopping!" as he cried "No!" as his Mum laughed "What?" as Pam laughed "I thought it might be fun to play shopping tonight!" as he cried "Not fair Pam!" Pam laughed "I want Tom to get some practice with various types of shopping, food shopping, dolly shopping, etc.!" adding "Not to mention dress shopping!" as he cried "Oh no!" as his Mum hugged him and said, "Pam I hope this doesn't take too long, he should have time to play!" as she giggled, "He is Play Shopping, that is!" as he sobbed "Not flaming fair!" but she said, "Hopefully it won't take long!" Pam laughed "Tom your dolly can watch and give you complements!" as he cringed "Ha!" but she then opened a yellow handbag and showed him a pink purse and said, "This is your handbag and purse, to help you shopping!" as he cried "But I won't be carrying a handbag, to help Mum shop!" as she laughed "We're only in here Tom! It's just play shopping!" as he cringed, and their Mum laughed. She said, "Shopping position Tom!" and slid the yellow handbag, up his arm to the elbow!" as she laughed "Mummy! Just the way Nancy minced around the back garden, this afternoon, with her handbag and purse, full of clothes-pegs?"

as her Mum nodded and laughed "He'll need a shopping bag or basket too!" as he cringed "Not fair Mum! Not you too!" Pam then fetched one of her Mum's wicker shopping baskets and slung it over Tom's shoulder and got a shopping bag herself and said, "When you've paid for any shopping, just pop it away in your basket and mince off!" to more laughter. Pam went a fetched a tub of butter from the fridge and the Fairy washing up liquid bottle from the kitchen and said, "We'll play supermarket shopping first!" as her Mum gasped and said, "Better be quick! I don't want that, butter to melt!" as she laughed and said, "Mum! You be the shop girl, have you got some receipts for Nancy, I mean Tom, to pop into his purse or handbag?" as her Mum took her handbag and opening it, she took some receipts and said, "Here's some!" adding "and I'll use my purse, for the change!"

Tom has to use the handbag and purse to do the shopping

Pam said, "Tom and I will be shoppers, with our handbags and shopping bags and baskets!" as he huffed "Not fair!" as her Mum laughed. She said, "Tom take the, butter and Fairy over to Mum and say, you'd like to pay for them!" and saw him lift the two items and set them down in front of his Mum. His Mum took the, butter and made a beeping sound, as she ran it through the pretend scanner and the same with the Fairy liquid. She said, "That's, butter and Fairy! That will be 3.50 sir!" as he opened the handbag and retrieved the purse and opening it, took out a 10p piece and said, "There you are, Mum!" as Pam laughed "It's a shop girl Tom! Say, Miss!" as he said, "There you are, miss!" as his Mum took the 10p and then handed it back with a receipt and said, "There's your change and your receipt, sir! Just return them to your handbag!" and saw Tom take the coin the popped it back into his purse and close it up and then take the receipt and popped it into his handbag. Pam said, "Sir, you'd better close up your pretty handbag and then pop the shopping into your pretty basket!" and saw him close his handbag up, before popping the, butter and Fairy into his basket and walk away, as his Mum laughed "Well done Tom, you did that very well!" as Pam laughed "He could be of help, when we go shopping Mummy!" as he cried "Don't make me carry, a flaming handbag shopping?" as his Mum hugged him and said, "Quick Tom! Return that, butter, to the fridge, before it melts!" and the bottle to the sink!"

Pam laughed "Mum! He can keep the Fairy in his basket, as a little reminder, of how he looks?" as she flicked her wrist effeminately, at her blushing brother, with the handbag dangling, from his elbow, mincing out of the room. He cried "Mum she's calling me a fairy!" as Pam gurgled "If the frock fits!" as her Mum scolded "Stop that Pam! He's being a good boy, playing this!" as she called "Sorry Tom! Just my little joke!" Pam called "Tom! Do you know why you've to shut your handbag between use?" as he cried "Be quite Pam, someone will hear you!" as she laughed and asked again. He came back and said, "No!" as she replied, "So your purse isn't stolen by any thieves around the town!" as he cried "I won't be carrying a flaming handbag around town!" as she giggled, "You hope!" Tom enters the kitchen and returns the, butter to the fridge, but looks up, to see a lady in her bedroom, at the back and bolts back again. His Mum sees he's still got the Fairy liquid and asks didn't you want to return that dear?" as he cried "There was a lady in her bedroom at the back and she nearly saw me!" Pam took the bottle and said, "Miss can I have this Fairy!" as she then pushed Tom forward and this fairy too!" as her Mum giggled, "Now Pam! Stop calling your brother a fairy!" as he blushed "Very funny!" as her Mum said, "That will be £1.50 miss!"

Pam opened her handbag and purse to get her money and held it out to her Mum, who gave her change and a receipt and saw Pam return them, to her handbag and purse. She took the Fairy and popped it into her own shopper and minced off saying, "Thanks!" but then took the Fairy and popped it back into his basket saying, "I think this is yours sir!" as he grimaced "Very funny Pam!" and heard her giggle "A Fairy for a fairy!"

Tom's to buy three doll's dresses, but change a dolly's frock

Pam notices the liquid bottle is nearly empty and mentions it to her Mum, who Says, "I got a new one the other day Pam, it's under the sink!" as Pam smiled, and a thought came to her. She took Tom upstairs a tick and whispered to him "Tom I want you to do something, that only you and I and maybe Mummy will know about!" as he asked,

"What?" She laughed "See the Fairy liquid bottle is nearly empty?" and saw him nod. She said, "Next time you do the washing up! I want you to ask "Mummy! Can I have this empty bottle!" as he asked, "Why would I want that stupid bottle?" as she laughed "It will just about fit in your handbag!" as he cried "Oh no!" She laughed "Since Mummy won't let me call you a fairy!" adding "I will then ask you "So Tom what are you, when playing in your frocks?" as she said, "I'll then want you to say, "Mummy! I'm a!" adding "And at that point, you will open your handbag and hold the Fairy bottle up to Mummy for five seconds and then replace it back into your handbag again!" as he sobbed "Oh no! Not fair!"

She said, "Stay here!" as she ran out of the room and bounded up the stairs and got her Wendy doll and a few dresses for it and returned back down to show Tom and his Mum.

Pam said, "Tom! I think for being such a good boy and Nancy behaving herself and being a good girl! You can have my Wendy doll too!" as he cried "Not two dolls Mum?" as his Mum giggled, as Pam laughed "Now Tom, with Baby Suzie attached to her handbag, you can't dress and undress her into other dresses, but with Wendy you can play dress up!" adding "I mean with your dollies!" as he huffed "Ha! Funny!" as his Mum and Pam laughed. He saw her enter and cried "Not dollies?" as she laughed "You're just buying these three dresses for your dolly!" as he sobbed "Not fair Pam!" as her Mum laughed "Pam, you shouldn't?" but Pam said, "Look! By rights in the shop, he should check each frock fit's his dolly, but as we don't have time, I'm letting him just try one Flo. He blushed and took the dresses and she popped the doll into his basket, as he said, "Not fair!" He took the dresses over to his Mum and asked, "Can I have these three dresses for this dolly?" She said, "Repeat with My dolly!" but then pulled her doll, from his basket and heard him say, "Can I have these dresses for my dolly here?" Pam said, "Tom! Choose a pretty frock to try on!" as she laughed "Silly me! I meant for your dolly!" as she held a dress up to his neck and said, "I think that frock will be a tad small, for you sir!" as her Mum scolded "Stop that, Pam!" She said, "Choose one, Tom!" and saw him select a turquoise dress, as she said, "Good choice Sir! Right first remove your dolly's dress!" and saw him take, her Wendy doll and turn her over and ask "How do I get it off!" as she scolded "Your Mummy has been neglectful, not teaching you how to dress and undress your dollies, hasn't she?" as he nodded. His Mum said, "That sounded like a complaint! Watch it or you'll spend the next week, getting your dolly in and out of frocks!" as Pam screeched "I dare you Mummy!" as she laughed "Just joking! Carry on!" as Pam said, "Although he'd be much better with his dolly's skirts and dresses if he'd practice himself with some first!" as he cried "No! Don't Mum?" as she laughed.

Tom has to change his doll's dress in front of his Mum and Pam

Pam said, "Right turn your dolly onto her front and then gently pull the Velcro tabs to remove your frock!" as she added "I meant your dolly's frock!" as her Mum laughed "You tease Pam!" and saw him turn the doll over and check parts of the dress as Pam said, "That's right just there!" and saw him pull and soon was able to remove the dress to laughter and Pam said, "Well done Tom! Is that the first time you've removed a frock, from your dolly?" as he nodded. However, she knew he'd been getting practice with June's as she laughed "It's not is it?" as he shook his head "No!" remembering several times recently at June's, but heard her say, "You admitted that you, used to steal my dollies into your room to play without me knowing!" as he cried "I didn't?" as his Mum said, "Now Pam, he didn't!" but heard her say, "From the age you were 3 or 4!" as he shook his head, but heard her ask "Will I get June to ask you?" as he nodded, "Yes Pam I used to steal your dollies and dress them up without, you or Mummy knowing!" as her Mum gasped and giggled, "Tom! You little tinker!"

Pam then said, "Right Mr know it all! You should be good at getting Wendy into her new frock!" as his Mum laughed and saw him take the frock and slide it's arms into the sleeves and then slide the dress around the doll and press down on the Velcro as his Mum gasped "I thought you were joking! You did that quick, Tom! Have you played dollies before?"

as he blushed and nodded. Pam then said, "Right before you pay for your three frocks you've to get Wendy out of her new frock and back into her dress again!" as he huffed "Not fair!" as he took the doll and quickly undid the Velcro and soon had if off as Pam gasped "He is such a fast learner with frocks Mummy!" as she laughed and saw him quickly pop the other dress onto Wendy and said, "There!" as they both laughed. His Mum hugged him and said, "Gosh Tom! I am surprised!" as he blushed. Pam said, "Right Tom, you're ready to buy your three frocks again!" His Mum laughed and said, "Oh I say, Sir! What a pretty dolly!" as he blushed and said, "Ha!" Pam said, "Ask the girl how much your frocks are?" and heard him stammer "How much are my three frocks!" as his Mum held a dress up to his neck and gurgled "Somehow dear, I don't think you'd fit in this frock?"

Pam screeched "Fab Mum!" and then said, "Repeat, but say, about your dolly's dresses!" as he blushed and asked, "Miss! Can I have these three frocks for my dolly here?" as Pam giggled, "Mummy! He'll be fab when you take him with his Wendy doll, to buy her a new frock!" His Mum laughed "No way Pam!" as Tom wailed "I'm not going into the flaming doll's department!" as an idea hit Pam's mind and she giggled, "We'll see!"

His Mum took each doll and said, "Beep!" and "That one's £5 sir" and "Beep!" and "This one's £6" and "Beep!" again and "This one's £7.50" as she asked, "Can you guess how much you owe the shop?" as he tried to count and said, "£17.50" but she shook her head and asked, "Pam do you know?" as Pam laughed "Miss I don't know how you knew my name, but I think it was £18.50 for his frocks! I meant his dollies frocks, but it would be nice to see the little fairy here, shopping in a frock!" as he said, "Funny!"

Pam teases Tom about shopping for a new dress for his dolly

She said, "But! I'm sure it won't be too long, before we see him, shopping in pretty frocks and hair ribbons!" as his Mum laughed, and he protested "Mum! Stop her!" but she said, "Just joking!" as he blushed "Not flaming fair!" His Mum said, "Miss, that's 18.50 for your dollies 3 dresses please" and saw him open up his handbag and retrieve his purse again and opening it handed her another ten pence piece!" as she laughed "I think you need more money from your pretty purse!" As he reached in and handed her a 50p piece and said, "That better!" and handed him it back with a receipt and said, "Pop the receipt and change away in your handbag, sir!2 as he blushed and popped the receipt and coin back into his purse and then slid it back into his handbag and closed it up, to laughter from Pam "He's done very well with his handbag and purse Mum! Hasn't he?" as his Mum nodded, smiling and heard Pam say, "See Mum it's all the practice Nancy gets pegging out his pegs from his handbag and purse!" as he grimaced "Not funny Pam!" His Mum said, "Sir! There's your dolly's pretty dresses! Better pop them away in your shopping basket!" and saw him take the three dresses and pop them back into his basket. Pam then said, "Don't forget your dolly sir!" as he picked up the doll and slid it into his basket too. He said, "This is getting heavy Pam!" as she laughed "Mummy and I have had to lug heavy shopping all over town before, without your help!" adding "but now we will definitely have either Tom or Nancy to help with the shopping!" as his Mum laughed "Pam! Don't push it!" as she laughed "Who Moi?" as he blushed. Pam said, "Try sliding your basket and handbag over your shoulders for a while, that shouldn't make them so heavy!" and saw him slide the handbag up to his shoulder and then his basket over his other, as his Mum laughed "Gosh Pam! You are giving him some real practice at being a real shopper. Pam said, "Tom! You'll only need to lower your handbag down, when needing your purse!" adding "Or your basket down when you need to pop some shopping into it, or getting something like your dolly out of it!" as he blushed more and heard his Mum laugh as she said, "Once finished you can return them to your shoulder, Ok?" as he nodded.

Pam said, "Now Tom can try some dress shopping!" as her Mum laughed and saw her pick up a turquoise dress and hand it out to him on its hanger and said, "Tom you're after a new frock!" as he cried "Tom doesn't wear frocks!" as his Mum said, "Say, it's for your cousin Nancy!" as Pam laughed "Or he could, just be one of those boys, who likes slipping into his sister's frocks!" as he sobbed "Not funny Pam! You know I don't!" as his Mum ran and

cuddled him "Pam! You are naughty!" as she too hugged him, and he cried "Pam get off me!" Pam said, "Now for the frocks, you've to check in the mirror, just slide the hanger over your neck, like Nancy did in the garden, this afternoon!" as he cried "Mum stop her!" as she said, "Just pop upstairs to check in the mirror in Mum's room!"

Tom has to try three frocks on which includes the pretty yellow frock

He cried "But that's at the front!" as she said, "Ok your room, but you'd better give a curtsy or else!" as he blushed and taking the dress he slid the hanger over his head and exited the room to laughter as Pam ran and followed him. Pam followed Tom up the stairs and saw him enter his own room, but gasp as he saw the blinds open and completely up and duck down on the floor, but she said, "Don't ruin your dress Tom! Stand up now and I'll close the blinds a bit!" and slipped over and looking out smiled as she didn't see anyone and closed the blinds, but they were noticed by a lady in the back houses. Tom minced over to the mirror and gripping his dress, he bobbed a curtsy to himself as Pam giggled, and gave him a kiss saying, "Good boy Tom!" as he slipped back downstairs to his laughing Mum. She asked, "What happened?" as he cringed "My blinds were open, and I was nearly spotted with this flaming dress, but she closed my blinds so I could bob a curtsy to myself!" as his Mum laughed. She saw Pam enter and say, "Tom did a sweet little curtsy to himself with his frock!" adding "I mean Nancy's frock!" as her Mum giggled. He followed this by the next dress – a white one with pink flowers on it and blushed as he copied the same ritual as before, but this time was glad his blinds were closed. He returned down and heard his Mum say, "I must say, sir, that is a pretty dress!" as he blushed and stammered "I'm just checking these dresses out for my cousin Nancy!" as Pam gurgled "He should really take them for a test drive?" adding "Slid over his trousers to see how they look!" as his Mum said, "Now Pam!"

He then followed this by a shorter pink frock which was very little girly and he slid the hanger over his neck and repeated up the stairs to curtsy to himself before popping back down and heard Pam ask "Which of the three frocks do you think Nancy would like to wear?" as he blushed and said, "None!" but she said, "Hurry up and choose one for after this it will be Nancy's turn shopping!" as her Mum said, "Now Pam hasn't he had enough?" but she said, "Mum! I won't be mean! I'll only want him to do frock shopping as Nancy!" as he grimaced "Ha!" Pam Says, "I know which dress he thinks Nancy will like best!" as he looked at her and she said, "The pretty pink frock!" as he cried "It's too little girly!" as his Mum laughed, but Pam took him upstairs and said, "Remove your trousers a tick!" and heard him protest "Please let me keep them on?" but she shook her head. He pulled down his trousers and Pam handed him the short tutu skirt that June had given him that afternoon to peg out the laundry. He pulled the skirt up and heard her laugh as he pulled it around his waist and she gurgled "Oh tonight is going to be so much fun!" as he asked, "How much longer?" adding "Mum said, I could go and play footy soon!" as she laughed and flicked her wrist towards him. She said, "Hold on a tick!" as she returned with some hair slides and slid them into his hair, saying, "Nancy is now doing the shopping!" as he blushed. She then handed him the pink frock and saw him set his handbag and basket down on the bed, to then pull his arms into the sleeves and then pull it down over his head and down over his skirt. She clapped with join and kissed him again as he cried "No more kisses Pam!" as she handed him back his handbag and basket.

Pam pops him into the yellow frock as her Mum realizes she knows

His Mum looked up and said, "That frock suit's you Miss!" as Pam laughed "Miss! Don't you recognize this little fairy here! He's the same boy that's been shopping all over town using a handbag and purse!" as her Mum scolded "Stop teasing him Pam!" as Tom blushed more. She asked, "Do you want this frock?" and saw Tom nod and say, "I'll just remove this frock for you to detag!" as his Mum laughed and saw him set his shopping basket and handbag down and then pull the dress over his head as she then saw his tutu skirt and giggled, "I see Pam has dressed Nancy for the part!" as Pam curtsied back to her. His Mum took the dress and watched Tom pick up his handbag and shopping basket as she did a beep and say, "I think that is 19.99 Miss!" as he opened his handbag and

then take money from his purse and hand it over. She said, "There's your receipt and change!" as he took them and popped them back into his purse and then replaced it into his handbag and closed it shut. His Mum took a carrier and popped the dress into it, as she held it out to him and said, "There's your pretty frock Miss!" as Pam giggled, "Oh He should wear it out!" as his Mum laughed "Now Pam!"

But Pam had a trump card to play and said, "Almost finished!" as he cried "What now?" as she laughed "Just something to make Mummy giggle!" as she said, "I've hardly stopped Pam! This better be good!"

Pam took Tom in his tutu skirt out the door and up the stairs and into her own room. She said, "I want to blind fold Nancy for a moment!" and took a pair of pantie sand slid them down over his head and then tied a ribbon around it to make sure he couldn't see!" She asked, "Can you see?" and he shook his head. She then opened her wardrobe and retrieving the yellow frock from the first night, she took it from its hanger, she said, "Arms up Nancy!" and slid his arms into it and then it over his head and down over his tutu skirt. She smiled as she added the Alice band onto his head and then called "Mummy can you come here a tick?" Her Mum ran up the hall and up the stairs wondering what the surprise could be and on turning onto the landing she entered Pam's room and gasped as she saw Tom in the yellow frock with the yellow Alice band on his head, but Pam had opened the blinds on him to let neighbours spy him, if they happened to look over. She removed his ribbon from his eyes and the panties and saw him look down and gasp "Oh no!" as his Mum gasped "Do you know?" as she laughed "Of course!" as his Mum took him onto the bed and cuddled him. He still didn't realize he was on show to the neighbours. His Mum asked, "How did you find out! When from?" as Pam laughed "You know I made him sleep with Baby Suzie?" as her Mum nodded, and heard her add "Well in the morning I went in and checked he was still sleeping with her and was about to leave when I spied some yellow material from under his pillow!"

His Mum asks how Pam knew and she Says, of threatening re-enacting it

Her Mum gasped "You forgot to hide your panties away?" and saw him nod, it was terrible. She laughed "What did you do?" Pam giggled, "I couldn't believe my eyes and asked how come my panties got there!" adding "He tried to fib saying, you must have made a mistake, but I threatened to tell girlfriends if he didn't tell the truth and so the story came out about what his sweet Mummy did to him!" as his Mum laughed "You poor boy!" as he sobbed "It's terrible!" as Pam laughed "I ran in and fetched my nighty and another pair of pink panties for Nancy and so came back and he'd to slide into them for to tell me the wonderful story of Mummy and my frock!"

Pam said, "I told him he wouldn't want you to realize, what I knew?" as her Mum asked, "Why?" as Pam gurgled "Because then I will want a complete re-enactment of everything that happened that night, but this time with me standing right beside him!"

Her Mum shook her head "No way! I tripped him and smacked his bare bottom!" as Pam laughed "I've seen his baby-pee-pee lots of times since then!" as her Mum gasped "You haven't?" as Pam nodded, "Haven't I missy?" as he nodded, and heard her say, "It's ok Mummy!" and then to Tom "Tell Mummy why you call it your baby-pee-pee!" as he blushed and stammered "Because it only the size of a little baby boys baby-pee-pee!"

His Mum hugged her sobbing boy who cried "Not fair Mum Please don't!" as Pam laughed and hugged him and said, "Right Mummy! You go down and start the washing up – running the water into the bowl to be ready for Tom's naughty reply! I'll hang my frock here up, for you to dress Nancy later!" as her Mum giggled, "You really want me to go over it all?" as she nodded, "Oh yes!" adding "I'll stand beside you and then even pop out, to ring the bell as you bring him upstairs to wait for me!" His Mum went downstairs to wait and ran the water into the bowl but called up "Tom! I mean Nancy I need your Fairy liquid for the washing up!" as Pam giggled, "Mummy! The fairy will bring the Fairy down for you in a minute!" as she screeched "Funny Pam!" as he huffed "Please

don't call me a fairy?" as she kissed him and removed his dress, she hung it up in her wardrobe. She then pulled down the tutu skirt and handed him back his trousers again. He slipped back into them and turned and cried "Oh no! The blinds!" as he realized he'd been sitting on the bed and then undressed on show to anyone looking in.

He took the washing up liquid downstairs and held it out to his Mum who laughed "This is so naughty Tom!" as he huffed "You don't have to do it!" but she said, "She'd maybe tell on Nancy if I don't!" as he nodded, "yea! That would be terrible!" as she gave him a kiss too. She called "Pam we're ready!" as she popped some clean dishes into the bowl for the play acting and heard Pam on the stairs and then saw her enter the hall to stand beside Tom and pop her arm around his waist and say, "We're ready!" His Mum asked, "Tom would you be a good boy and help me with a few dishes here?" as he ran up the hall and up the stairs and shouted out "**No way! That's girls work!**"

Tom has to dress in the panties, tights, petticoat and frock in front of Pam

Pam giggled. His Mum gasped "You, naughty boy! Pam's helped me all afternoon!" as she ran up after him and followed him into his room, with Pam joining her and sitting on his bed, she watched. She said, "I pulled his trousers and pants down and off!" Pam laughed "I'm waiting Mummy!" and saw her undo his trousers and pull them and then his panties down!" as Pam giggled, at his little willy on show, saying, "Mum he's got such a little baby-pee-pee!" as he sobbed "Not funny!" His hands shot to cover it, but she said, "Pirouette position!" and saw him raise his hands, above his head to leave himself on show to them. His Mum added "I then took his undies in and got your panties, tights and petticoat, but left the frock as a surprise!" but Pam said, "Isn't Mummy missing out on an important fact?" as she tried to think. Pam pushed Tom down over his Mum's lap and smacked his bare bottom hard, as he cried "Oh no! That hurts!" as Pam laughed "Mummy you must completely copy, or we repeat over and over!" His Mum smacked his bare bottom hard and he sobbed "Not fair Mum! That hurts too!" as Pam smacked his other cheek and he was soon sobbing with a sore bottom. He sobbed "Sorry Mum! I didn't mean it!" as she asked, "What? I'll do the washing up for you in future!" as she said, "Too late!" and soon had brought him into Pam's room, but he cried "Oh no! The blinds!" as he saw the blinds up and his willy on show to the house across the street and even to Julies. She fetched a pair of yellow panties from Pam's drawer, white tights, the yellow frock and a petticoat, as Pam pushed him on to the window still with the Alice band on his head.

His Mum took the panties pulled them up his legs to hide his embarrassments. Next were the tights' and then the petticoat. His Mum said, "I then took him into your room and showed him the yellow frock. His Mum got him to remove his jumper and shirt and then pulled the frock over his head, but Pam removed his Alice band and pushed him to the window and when the dress came down, from his head, he found himself staring out the clear window, at the street, completely on show., but Pam slid down to the floor and pulling his panties down, she grabbed hold of his willy and held it there, pushing his bottom towards the window. He cried "Oh no! Don't Pam?" as his Mum saw her laughing daughter, on the floor, holding something under his dress and gasped "Pam you aren't! Let go of his willy!" as Pam laughed and held him still, as he cried "Oh no! A woman across the street, is looking over!" as she laughed and said, "Just a few curtsies with your dress!" and saw him grip the dress and bob curtsies quickly to the street. She let go and he turned quickly and pulled his panties up and ran back, to his room sobbing "Not fair Mum! I knew this would be terrible, when you found out!"

Pam laughed and adding her Alice band. She said, "Now down to the kitchen to don his pretty apron, for the washing up!" as her Mum laughed "You are wanting your pound of flesh! I hope Nina thinks it was you, playing curtsies to the street!" as Pam laughed "Pity he's so small, she couldn't actually see, his baby-pee-pee!" His Mum laughed as she went down followed by Tom and a smiling Pam, smiling at Tom in the yellow and enter into the kitchen, where he picked up Pam's apron.

Tom asks for an empty Fairy liquid bottle to call himself a fairy wrt mime

He pulled it around his dress, but this time, Pam had made sure his handbag and dolly were tied to the apron. Her Mum saw them and laughed "Last time Pam, he didn't have his handbag and dolly, attached to your apron!" Pam laughed "Just some poetic license!" as Tom pulled a face. He pulled the curtains, before he slid his arms into the apron and slid his right arm into the handbag handle, with his dolly hanging down in front of him. He ran the water and takes the Fairy liquid and squeezes the last drops into the water, as Pam smiles and saw him pull on the rubber gloves. She said, "Oh Mummy! It seems we've just used the last bit of the Fairy!" as her Mum said, "I told you earlier, there's a new one under the sink!" However, Tom knew what she wanted him to say, and stammered "Mummy! Can I have this empty washing up bottle, now!" as her Mum looked at him and said, "Yes Tom, Why?" as he blushed as he took the empty bottle and unzipping his handbag, slid it inside and then zipped it up again. His Mum laughed "Is it for a school project or something Tom?" as he shook his head and started washing the few cups and saucers, as she asked, "Tom! Why the bottle?" Pam said, "I'll pop out now to ring the bell Mummy! Wait till you hear it, Nancy!" as her Mum laughed "Ok dear!" Pam started to exit the kitchen when she called out "Mummy! Ask Tom what he is when wearing a frock?" as she looked back and saw Pam run out the kitchen, but close the kitchen door, saying, "I think this was closed, to stop me spying him, in my frock!" as his Mum nodded, "Yes! You're right!" His Mum asked, "So Tom! What are you when wearing Pam's frocks?" and saw him blush and sob "Not flaming fair!" as he took his hands out of the water and drying them on the tea towel, he unzipped his handbag and woefully pulled the Fairy liquid bottle from it and held it up to show his Mum, who gasped and giggled, "Oh Tom!" as she saw him hold it there for a few seconds and then replace it back into his handbag and zip it up again. She laughed "The naughty girl! Because I wouldn't let her call you a fairy! She made you do it by mime!" as he nodded, and stammered "That's terrible Mum!" adding "I hope she won't play any tricks on me, outside or in front of anyone else!" as she hugged him and gave him a kiss.

She laughed "Now Tom! She's kept you quiet and not told on you at school or anywhere apart from June who you outed yourself to, that afternoon. He blushed and stammered "June will screech the place down when she sees me with that flaming bottle in my handbag!" as his Mum laughed and nodded. She asked, "Will I take it back?" but saw him shake his head, saying, "If you do, she might tell on me!" as she laughed "Poor boy!" Pam ran up the hall and opening the door, she had a naughty thought. She left the inner porch door open and slipped out across to Julie's and rang her bell, saying, "Can Julie come over for a few minutes?" as her Mum called "Julie! Pam needs you a second!" Julie ran down and out to see Pam take her hand and say, "Can you keep, what you see a secret, from Tina and your Mummy?" as Julie asked, "What?" but heard her say, "Be quiet and just slip into the hall and hide at the bottom of the stairs, a tick!"

FRANCESCA HELPS TRANSFORM GERRY 9

They suggest his Mum trap Gerry and play dress up with him

The word spread about sissy Toby around the school, but also around the local streets where even bigger boys had heard about him and his dresses and handbags.

Some mothers got together and decide to transform their boys, but realized only one of them hadn't a hubby or man around and it was Gerry's Mum They got Francesca down with her brother Toby to ask her, how to bring their boys under control and she said, "It was so easy when the big girls came around and tied my bro into my girly aprons and then made him do curtsies and stuff and it gradually escalated!"

She said, "Toby used to hit me, for the slightest thing, if I annoyed him!" but then said, "Toby what do you say, to that?" as he said, "Sorry I hit you, Francesca and will never hit you again!" as they laughed and Gerry's Mum said, "I dare you to start off Rita with your Paul!" as she laughed "I'd dread to think what my hubby would say, if he caught him dressed up"

They then said, "Linda! You don't need to worry about that! Why don't we give it a try with your boy, Gerry!" She laughed and nodded, adding "I suppose, since I'm the only one of us without a man around, I'll let you ladies use my house, to trap your boys, if you'd like too" as they said, "Ok, but you go first Linda!"

Francesca giggled, "When their Dad's in, 'it's best to get him to call, he's going out, to play footy, but then send him around to a female neighbour, ie. Gerry's Mum to play dollies or dress up!'" as they gasped but then heard her add "Until you ladies, get your hubbies or boyfriends to play 'house' too!" as they gasped "We couldn't! They wouldn't!" as they giggled. She said, "Initially your girly boys, won't have too many skirts or frocks to play dress up with you!" but added "All little girls like playing dress up in their Mummy's old clothes and bras and nighties too!" as they screeched at the thought!"

For housework, a good idea is to have him wear a pretty apron with a PVC pinny over it for the washing up or laundry, but for homework you can dangle or tie a handbag to his elbow, to help his writing!" as they giggled. For the laundry, it makes it much more fun if you pop the pegs into a handbag and or purse and have him practice his shopping, while pegging out the clothes!" as they gasped, as she added "while mincing around the garden with the frock or bra …" She said, "Toby your aprons please?" as he removed both aprons to be left in his frock. She then handed his Mum a handbag and said, "Tie this string around his handbag, ready to slide up his arm and tie to his apron string, on his elbow!" as she gurgled. She then said, "Another way is to have one of his shirts with the cuffs sewn behind his back!" She asked, "Can you get one of his shirts and sew the sleeves together!" as she ran over and got one and got her Mum to sew the sleeves, together and taking it back over, to the ladies and Francesca.

Gerry is trapped by a shirt and Toby's sister Francesca dresses him up

They waited for the boys to finish their football, thinking it might be five o'clock finish, but Gerry needed to have a pee and so part way through the game, he ran around home and soon was walking down the street and entered his house. His Mum said "Had a good game of football dear!" as he said "Still playing Mum, I needed the loo!" and heard chatter in the sitting room. He peered in and saw some ladies and said, "Hi!" and heard them call "Hi Gerry!" as he ran upstairs to the toilet. He returned a minute later to see his Mum hold up a shirt and say "! got you a new shirt and wanted to make sure, it fitted!" adding "Just remove your jumper and shirt and I'll try it on you!" He looked at the shirt, which seemed similar to his other shirts and thought nothing of it, but said "I'll try it on after the footy!" but she said "I just wanted to show the ladies how it looked on you dear!" as she led him into the living room.

He quickly removed his jumper and then his shirt and said "Give it here, Mum!" She said "Turn around and slide your arms in!" as he turned and slid his arms into the sleeves and stretching them down and out the cuffs, he said, "Mum! There's something up! I can't get my arms out! They're stuck!" as she laughed "Are they? Let me see!" as he then saw the ladies, exit the sitting room and ask, "How do you like your new shirt, Gerry?" as he huffed "I can't get my arms out?" as they laughed, as he struggled to get free.

His Mum then waved across the street and a smiling Francesca crossed over and rang the bell and was let in. She entered the room and he gasped as he saw her enter the room asking them "What's, she doing here?" as she approached Gerry and called "Is there a big boy here, to play dollies and dress up with me?" as he cried "No way! You F off!" as his Mum scolded him and said, "Now Gerry! That's no way to talk, to a little girl!" A Mum handed her Toby's flowery apron and said, "You'd better see to his pinny!" as he cried "Keep that away from me, Mum!" as she laughed and taking the apron, she tied it around him and his back.

He sobbed "Not fair Mum! Not in front of these women and her?" as he gasped "Don't show me off, in this stupid apron?" as Fran then took her phone and photographed him, in the girly apron. However, she then opened her handbag and slid an Alice band and ribbons into his hair, as he cried "Don't do my hair up like a girl?" as they giggled at his new look. She said, "If you don't want the girls and maybe boys, around here or school, to see these photos, you've to promise to do what we say!" He sobbed "Not fair, Francesca! Not fair Mum!" as they laughed and she said, "You'll help your Mummy and me, with the washing and washing up, from now on! Won't you?" He sobbed "Not fair Mum!" but nodded "Ok!" but heard her add "In your pretty aprons?" as he cried "Mum! Don't make me!" as Fran fed a handbag around his neck, as the ladies giggled and his Mum laughed "I love your new look Gerry!" He sobbed "Not fair! Don't turn me into a sissy, like your big brother, Toby?"

Gerry complains about Franny stealing his big dolly and does curtsies

Francesca laughed "Oh Toby's not a sissy! He just has to do anything I want!" adding "or say, anything I want!" as he huffed "Ha!" His Mum and the ladies wondered what she meant, but then saw her approach him and whisper in his ear "When I nod, I want you to call out to your Mummy, 'Mummy! She stole my big dolly and I want to sleep with her!'" as he said, "No way!" but heard her ask, softly "Will I bring some girlfriends in, to see you?" as he gasped "Oh no!" He cried "Not fair!" as she waited and saw him nod "Ok!" as she smiled and heard his Mum ask, "What Franny?" but heard her say, "Oh! I was just telling Gerry here, that Toby isn't a sissy at all! Though he does tend to wear skirts and dresses more than trousers, these days!" as they laughed. The ladies were talking amongst themselves and had just asked, "Gerry something about housework, when Francesca nodded. He sobbed "Not fair, Francesca!" as she shrugged her shoulders and looked at him, with a smile on her face. He suddenly cried "Mummy! She stole, my big dolly and I want to sleep with her!" as his Mum gasped and giggled, and they heard screeches from the room.

His Mum ran over and gave him a kiss!" as he sobbed "I don't like kisses!" but soon, Francesca ran over and said "I think my sissy deserves a kissy too!" as he cried "No don't!" and threw her arms around his neck and kissed his lips, to laughter. She said "Ladies sissy deserves a kissy too!" and the soon the ladies, had all given him kisses.

She whispered complement your Mummy on her clothes and handbag!" as he stammered "Mum your dress and apron are very pretty and so is your handbag!"

She gurgled and bobbed a curtsy to him and then kissed him on the lips!" However, she then said, "Now to me!" as she bobbed a curtsy back and kissed him and then to each of the Mum's.

However, then Francesca said, "Gerry! Oh, what a pretty girly apron and hair ribbons you're wearing and that is a pretty handbag you carry too!" as he asked, "What?" as she laughed "A nice curtsy and kiss would be appreciated!" His Mum demonstrated and said, "Try and bob down like me, with a foot behind you!" as he sobbed "Oh no!" but obeyed and then pursed his lips for a kiss, as she kissed him. Then his Mum did the same followed by the laughing ladies!" She said, "We'll be letting you play football soon too!" as he said, "I can't wait to get out of these clothes and ribbons?" as she said, "You'll do what I say, or photos will be shown around?" as he nodded, as she asked "Can I borrow Gerry a tick?" as his Mum nodded and the smiling young girl led him in to the living room and locked the door.

She then retrieved a pair of frilly pink panties and said, "I just want you to wear these frilly panties for a laugh!" as he cried "Oh no!" She said, "Lift your legs a tick!" as he cried "Don't! But Mum and them will see!" as she fed them up his legs and up over his trousers and giggled, "So Sissy! Do you want to wear the panties over your trousers or under them?" He sobbed "Under them!" as she laughed, as she pulled the panties down, but then undid his belt and then trousers and pulled them down and laughed at his underpants on show!"

Francesca puts a bound Gerry into frilly panties under his open trousers

However, he then realized his predicament, sobbing "You wouldn't dare!" as she pulled his undies down and heard him cry "Don't!", as she giggled, "Oh your baby-pee-pee, is much bigger than Toby's!" She said, "Don't worry! I'll hide your baby-pee-pee, from show, in a second!" as she pulled the underpants off his legs and hid them away in his handbag and said, "Now for your frillies!" and he raised his legs and she slid the panties up, to hide his embarrassment. She photographed him some more, in the panties and said, "Now! I'm letting you wear your trousers again!" as he sighed "Thanks, Franny!" as she pulled them up over the panties and did up his belt again, but of course, left his trousers undone, with the apron hiding his frillies. She whispered "I've left your trousers open, so if you remove your apron, they'll spy your frillies!" as he cried "Oh no! Not fair!" She added "When offered to remove it, just say you're proving your not a MSP anymore!" as he sobbed.

She unlocked the door and led him out again and said, "I think we can let his hands go ladies!" and saw his Mum, cut the sleeves, to let him bring his hands around, to the front again, as he cried "Mum! That was a rotten trick!" as he looked at the little girl and heard her say "I think we've been cruel to Gerry and we'll let him out of his pretty apron and ribbons to go and play footy!" as the ladies said "No! He suits it!" with others saying, "He should keep it on!" as Fran added "I've told him, he'll earn browny points from me, if he wants to stay here and keep his pretty apron on to help with some washing up or housework!" as his Mum laughed "I think he'll be relieved to get out of it Franny!" as she went to undo his apron. However, she couldn't believe it, when he said "It's ok Mum! I'll keep it on, to prove I'm no longer a MSP!" as she gasped "What Gerry?" as the ladies giggled and patted him on the back and gave him kisses saying "Well done Gerry!" as more tears appeared in his eyes and a large blush at the thought of them spying his frilly panties, if he removed the apron.

She asked "Have you some washing up for Angela to do?" as he cried "Not Angela?" as the ladies laughed as his Mum said "Now Francesca! We can't!" but she laughed "Just while he's doing girly things for you!" adding "Disguising himself as a girl!" as he said "No way!" but heard her say "See! He'll want a pretty headscarf or hair ribbons to disguise him when helping you with the laundry, wearing a pretty apron and PVC pinny to stop it getting wet!" adding "And maybe with the washing up too, in case the neighbours recognize him looking a girly!" as they laughed. His Mum said "I''ve only a few things to wash up!" as Fran said "That's ok! Just to let him demonstrate how he'll help you in future with the dishes!" as he cried "Not fair!" but was led to the kitchen where his Mum ran the water and then added the washing up liquid and they removed his handbag, He approached the sink, but then saw Fran remove a small PVC pinny from her bag and hold it out to him, as he cried "I don't need that!" but she insisted and next his Mum was tying him into the girly PVC pinny. He then pulled on some rubber gloves and started the washing up with his Mum and ladies smiling at his new look. He washed the few cups and glasses with his Mum drying them and soon had finished.

They get Gerry to help with the laundry in a frilly apron and PVC pinny

Franny said "Now for some laundry!" as his Mum said "Sorry Fran! I don't have any ready!" but she laughed "Just get a few of his and your things to air in the garden!" as he cried "I can't go out into the garden, in these!" as Fran laughed and said "I suppose as long as he promises to help peg up a couple of his own clothes, we'll let him remove his girly aprons and hair slides to go and join his mates!" as she removed his Alice band and hair ribbons, to leave him looking very girly in the apron and pinny, to laughter from the ladies. His Mum took the wash basket and went upstairs and fetched a few of his things – shirt, trousers, underpants, socks and then into her bedroom for her own clothes and returned downstairs and heard Gerry protesting but heard Fran say "I've removed his hair slides and told him he can remove his pretty aprons to peg out a couple of his own clothes and then run on to play footy!" as his Mum laughed I'm sure he'll appreciate that Franny!" as she said "Ok Gerry! Hurry up and you can peg up a shirt and jumper for us!" as he stood there wanting to remove the stupid apron and pinny but knew he couldn't or they'd spy his frillies and so stammered "Its ok Mum! I'll keep them on to please you and the ladies, but can I have a headscarf?" as she gasped "Gosh! Gerry you sure?" as the ladies gasped and giggled and a laughing Fran said "Come here girly!" as she took a floral headscarf from the handbag and approaching him, tied it round his head to laughter and giggles.

His Mum got the bucket of pegs, she normally used when doing the laundry and handed it to another lady Lucy, she opened the side door and led the ladies out to the garden, where Gerry froze in fright, that he might be recognized in the girly aprons and headscarf. His Mum said to him "Come on Gerry, you're well disguised with Franny's pretty headscarf!" as she set the basket of clothing down on the ground in the center of the garden, but then ran and locked the side door. He went over and reaching into the basket, he retrieved a shirt and asked "Give me the pegs and I'll peg this up!" as his Mum took the bucket, but Fran asked "Can I have the bucket a tick?" as his Mum handed it to her and saw her disappear around the back of the garage, with her handbag around her neck. They wondered what she was up to as she returned with a large smile on her face and Gerry called "Right Fran! Give me the bucket for the pegs!" as she said "Some girls showed Mummy and me a way to make the laundry much more fun!" as they asked "How?" as she set the bucket down near the house.

She then approached him and removing the handbag from her neck, she said "We use a handbag to hold our pegs!" as he cried "Oh no! Not a handbag!" as the ladies all screeched with laughter, as she took the handbag and slid it up his arm to his elbow and said "Keep that there or I tie it to your pinny!" as he sobbed "Not fair Franny!" as his Mum gasped "Gosh Fran! That's such a girly look for doing the laundry!" as her and the ladies laughed and said, "I think we'll all be using a handbag to do the laundry in future!" as he cried "Not fair Fran!" He asked them "Can't I use the bucket?" but they shook their heads and Fran said "What makes it even funnier, is this!" as she whispered into his ear and heard him cry "No! Not fair!" as they wondered what she'd said.

Gerry has to use the handbag and purse to peg out the clothing

He reached into the handbag and retrieved about six pegs, but then reached in again and retrieved a purse and next thing had opened it and popped the pegs into the purse before closing it up again and retuning it to his handbag, to laughter and giggles. Fran said "See ladies, by using his handbag and purse, it should provide him with practice for helping his sweet Mummy around the shops!" as he cried "I'm not carrying a flaming handbag and purse around the shops!" as his Mum laughed "I couldn't Fran!" as she laughed "Just joking!" but added "Although if he's a naughty boy, it would serve as a good punishment to get him well behaved!" as they laughed and dared her.

He went to peg up the shirt, but Fran said "Gerry its good fun to mince your handbag a few times around the garden, before pegging up any clothes!" as he cried "Not fair!" as she laughed "The sooner you get the laundry done, the sooner you get to play footy!" as they saw him mince his handbag around the garden, blushing and sobbing as he walked around. However she then approached him and took his arms and said "Splay your arms out like this, Gerry!" as he cried "Not fair!" as she said "This is extreme mincing, ladies!" adding "To make carrying his handbag, even more girly than before!" as she said "Follow me Angela!" as they saw him extreme mince around the garden, following Fran with them both splaying their arms out to the sides causing the whole garden to explode in laughter. He got back to the line and picked up the shirt again and now reached into the handbag and retrieved the purse and got two pegs out. Fran said "Return your purse to your handbag and zip it closed, so when helping your sweet Mummy shopping, your purse isn't stolen from your handbag!" as he cried "No way!" as they all laughed at the implication of him joining her shopping. They saw him obey and put his purse away and zip the bag shut to be left holding the two pegs and the shirt, which he quickly pegged up on the line and heard his Mum and the ladies congratulate him saying "Well done Gerry!" as he blushed.

His Mum said "Just a pair of your trousers and we'll let you play football!" as he had to again mince and then extreme mince around the garden, joined by a giggling Francesca who said "Toby enjoys doing the laundry too!" as he cried "He's not about here, is he?" as she laughed "Oh Gerry! Wouldn't you like some help with the laundry?" as he cried "No Fran! Keep your sissy brother away from me!" as they all screeched again at his dreading meeting Toby, dressed in his aprons and headscarf, carrying a handbag too.

Fran said, "Tell your Mummy you'll help her with the laundry from now on!" as he repeated and heard her add "Wearing sweet pretty aprons and carrying your peg bag!"

as one Mum called "I think Gerry will be a treasure around the shops!" She giggled, "I'd never thought of him using a handbag or purse to peg out the laundry!" adding "or use shopping!" as the other ladies nodded, in agreement, as he begged "Please don't Mummy?" She laughed "Hear that girls?" as they asked, "What?" as she replied, "he'd never usually call me, Mummy!" as they laughed. They then watched his Mum peg out some of her clothing, of course using the handbag and purse but she gasped as she noticed a pair or boy's underpants inside.

Fran pops him into a dress and hair ribbons to show his Mum

Fran said "So Toby! Why did you want to wear that pretty headscarf?" as he huffed "So I'd not be recognized by the neighbours wearing these stupid aprons!" as they all laughed but then heard her ask "So Gerry! What are you disguising yourself as?" as he begged "Don't make me?" but she nodded and he huffed "A flaming girl!" as they all laughed but then asked "Can I borrow him for a minute?" as she took him down to the back of the garage and said, "Look! I just want to give your Mum and the ladies a laugh, for a few seconds and will then let you play silly football after!" as he asked, "Promise?" as she nodded but took another bag from the back of the garage and showed him the frock.

He gasped and cried, as he whispered, "Not a flipping dress?" as she laughed "Honest Gerry! Just for a few seconds or a minute and then you can remove, all your girly things and go around to play footy!" He huffed "Not fair!" as she undid his pinny and then the apron and fed the dress down over his arms and head and giggled, "Oh fab Gerry!" but she then pulled his headscarf off, with him begging "Please leave my scarf?" but she opened his handbag and retrieved some hair ribbons and the Alice band and soon had his hair nice and girly and then returned his handbag to his arm.

She then said, "Now for a little trick on your Mummy!" as he asked, "What?" She said, "Now not a word to anyone, as she raised his dress and said, "Let me?" as he gasped "Let me keep my trousers on?" as she lowered his panties and giggled, as she pulled his willy out of them, but kept the belt done up and whispered "You remove your dress and the ladies spy your frillies and your baby-pee-pee!" He sobbed "Oh no!" He then realized if he removed his frock, he'd show off his panties, but also his willy and sobbed "Not fair!" She added his apron back over his dress and then the PVC pinny again but then said "When you show your Mummy, tell her your Gerry's sister Angela who loves being girly!" as he sobbed "Not fair Franny!"

She led him out and heard screeches from the garden as she called "Ladies! I've done this just for a joke, to let you see how girly, he can look!" as they all saw him now in a dress and ribbons, as he sobbed "Mummy! I'm Gerry's sister Angela!" as he bobbed a curtsy to her, as his Mum gasped "Oh Gerry!" Fran said to his Mum "I've promised that he can remove his frock and girly things in a minute!" as he cringed and they laughed "He looks so cute! He should keep it on!" Fran laughed "It's so much fun running about in a pretty frock, you never know, he might start to enjoy it and not want to give me Toby's frock back!" He huffed "Funny!" as she laughed "Though if he wants to keep it, I'll want his kind Mummy to take him out, to get Toby a nice replacement frock and while he's there, his Mummy could get him some skirts and frocks, not forgetting nighties for himself!" as they laughed and he begged "Please don't Mummy!"

Gerry is told he's to play Sissy Football in his frock with a handbag

She then said "Ok Gerry! Since you've been a good sport and given your Mummy and these ladies a lot of fun, you can now remove your girly things and get back into your silly shirt and jumper to join your mates!" He blushed, realizing he couldn't, but heard her say "Or are you having fun and want to keep them on a while longer to please us?" as they expected him to remove the handbag, hair slides, aprons and frock. They did see him remove his handbag and say "I'll keep them on to please you Franny, but I don't need the handbag!" as she gasped "Gosh Gerry! I think like my Toby, you're realizing how much fun being a girly can be!" as he cried "I'm no!" to laughter.

Francesca Says, "As you're having fun in your dress and pretty aprons, but also enjoy playing football, we'll play football here with you, here in the garden!" as he huffed "What! You're joking?" as he added "Mum! You can't play footy!" adding "And you all can't play footy either!" as they laughed and his Mum said, "That's very sexist dear!" adding "We'll have to get those MSP views, out of that silly head of yours!" as Franny laughed "After lots of fun in his frocks, he'll be completely changed! I know how well it's worked on my bro, Toby!" as they all laughed at the thought. She laughed, but then said, "It's not normal football!" as he asked "What do you mean?" as she giggled, "It's Sissy Football! To play you need your aprons or frock, a handbag and ribbons are optional" as he cried "Oh no! You mean I've to play football as a girly, in a flaming frock?" as they laughed and nodded, with him sobbing away, as Fran slid the handbag back up his arm to his elbow, but then tied it to his apron, as he cried "Not fari!" as he was passed the ball.

He cried "But the neighbours might see me, in the garden and recognize me kicking the ball, as Franny laughed "Don't be silly! You're well disguised in your frock now with your hair ribbons and mincing with our pretty handbag too!" as they laughed, and he cringed "Not fair! Some mates houses overlook the garden here!" He kicked

the ball and was told to dribble it about in the garden, like he did when showing off with his mates. He started dribbling the ball and was told to dribble around the ladies and Francesca. However, when he got to her, she reached up and pulled his Alice band and ribbons out of his hair and he cried "Please leave my ribbons alone, someone will recognize me!" to laughter. He continued playing and after about five minutes Francesca said, "That's ok, Gerry! We've had our fun! You can now remove your frock and girly clothes and we'll let you back into your boys things to join your mates!" as all the ladies booed and some said, "Oh can't he stay in his frock and ribbons?" She added "Although! I think you'll please the ladies and your Mummy, if you want to stay and keep your pretty frock and things on to play footy with us!" He so wanted to remove them, especially his frock, but didn't want them spying his panties and especially his willy and so next thing, he then astounded his Mum and said, "It's ok Mummy! I'll keep my frock on, to play Sissy Football with you all!" His Mum gasped and giggled, "Oh you sweetie! I can't believe it! Are you actually having fun in Franny's frock and playing Sissy Football with us?" as he nodded, with tears in his eyes.

Tinkabelle - Toby is brought down to meet Gerry - Angela

She said, "I'll just get him back down!" as he sobbed "Oh no! Don't get Toby to play with me!" as she laughed and rang up home. Toby was out playing footy with his mates, but this time as a boy. Franny ran up with her Mum to give Toby the good news, that he was to come down the street for walkies in his frock. Franny ran around with another girlfriend and saw the boys playing footy in the next street and called "Toby! Mummy wants you!" as he looked up and called "Can't I stay out to play?" but she laughed "Maybe later!" as he called "Got to go, guys!" as a few of them called "Going to get back into your frocks and hair ribbons?" He cringed "Hope not!" adding "I'm not a sissy! My flaming sister makes me!" as they laughed "But she's only about five!" as he cringed "You can't understand! You'd do the same as me if she had you as a brother!" as they laughed "You must be joking! She'd get a thick ear, if she tried that on me!" as he huffed "Ha!" and ran off to join Fran and her girlfriend.

Meanwhile, his Mum and the ladies led a reluctant Gerry still in the frock, hair slides and aprons mincing across the road with his handbag on his elbow down to another lady's house. He was relieved there weren't any boys about, but did blush and begged for his Mum to hide him from girls and ladies who were nearby. They sat him down and chatted away with the lady asking how they had got him dressed up.

He huffed "I was enjoying that game of footy!" as his sister said, "Mummy wants you to meet a new girl!" as he huffed "What age is she and what's she called?" as she laughed "Oh she's pretty and about your age!" adding "And she's looking forward to giving you lots of kisses too!" She said, "She's called Angela!" as he shrugged his shoulders, not knowing any girl called Angela and has heard how you like to wear frocks and hair ribbons!" as he cried "I don't!" as her friend giggled, "Now Girly! I heard you admit to playing dollies and dress up, since you were 3 or 4!" as he blushed. He cringed "I don't like kisses!" as she got her friend Sharon to give him some kisses, as she giggled, "I love seeing your big brother in dresses and acting as a girly!" as he blushed.

He entered the house, apprehensive that the girl might be there, waiting for him, but his Mum said, "Come on and we'll get you into a pretty frock to meet Angela at her place!" as he said, "Fran said, she was called Angela!" asking "There aren't several girls there?" as she laughed "Just the one!"

His Mum took him into his room and removed his clothes, got him down to his panties and laughed as she slid him into his nighty and then the frock again, with ribbons in his hair and then handed him the handbag and took him back downstairs and heard his sister screech "There you are Tinkabelle I missed you!" as she threw her arms around him and gave him a kiss, causing him to blush. Hence, they brought him out and locked up, checked to make sure none of the other boys were about and minced him back down towards Gerry's. However, they knew that, Toby knew where Gerry lived and would smell a rat, if they took him in there! Hence, they'd arranged that

Gerry dressed up as a girl would be taken across the street to a lady, who hadn't any kids and so Toby wouldn't suspect anything

Both Toby and Gerry ask how long they've been dressing up

His Mum saw one of the smiling ladies Kathy, at her front door and heard her call "Are those your two sweet little girls?" as she nodded, "Yes! This is my sweet Francesca and Tinkabelle!" I love their dressse!" as he wondered, 'Did she know he was a boy?' She laughed "Angela is looking forward to meeting your girls and playing dollies with them!" as he blushed and heard Franny giggle "Oh! We both love playing dollies and dress up!" adding "Don't we Tinkabelle?" as he nodded, "Yes Franny!" as the lady led them into her driveway and up to the side door. She leads them in doors, with him ready to be teased, by yet another girl, laughing at his dress, hair ribbons or handbag, but thinks, it can't be that much worse, than the girls in the street or at school, teasing him about his girly look. Franny Says, before he enters "Make sure you give a nice curtsy and a kiss to Angela and tell her how pretty she is!" as he huffed "Ok!" He's led into the sitting room and sees several smiling ladies, some Mum's of his footy mates, but others, he doesn't know! but also, a little girl of about his age, in a pretty dress, that he thinks he's seen before, in ribbons and an Alice band, holding a dolly.

He grips his dress and bobbed a curtsy and calls "Hi Angela! You're pretty!" as the room filled with laughter and his mate called "Flaming Sissy!" as he cried "Oh no! It's not you, Gerry?" He sobbed as he gripped his dress and bobbed a curtsy back to the blusing boy. Toby asked, "What are you doing here?" as they laughed and his Mum said, "We didn't want to take you, to our place and you guess, Gerry might be there!" as he huffed "Not fair, Mum! Take me home?" but she shook her head. Franny laughed "You, girlies are going to learn to play dollies and dress up together!" as they asked, Toby asked, "How long have you been dressing up?" and heard Gerry say, "Just this afternoon! It wasn't fair! You know I was playing footy and needed a pee?" as he nodded, "Well when I entered Mum said she'd a new shirt for me, to try on!" as he said, "So what!" as Gerry cringed "It had its cuffs, sewn together and so when I pulled it on, I couldn't move my arms and was at her mercy and they dressed me up!" He gasped "What a rotten trick!" They suddenly saw the flash and sobbed, and both called "Mum! Don't let them take photos!" to more laughter and giggles from the room as Fran called "A nice smile girlies!" as another photo was taken.

Gerry asks, "Toby! How did you start dressing up?" as they laughed, and he sobbed "It's only been the other night!" as he cringed, as he remembered and said "We had a questionnaire from school on the internet, asking did we help with housework and stuff like that, but with a prize of £10 if I won!" He added "I got a phone call saying I'd won and three big girls came around to check my answers and give me the prize!" Gerry said "So what!" as he huffed "It was a trick! I tried to get her to leave the room, but they said she could stay and they got her to bring in some of her stupid aprons and pinnies!" as Fran giggled "Next thing they were trying my pretty aprons on but then got Toby into one too!" adding "I screeched the house down when I saw him in my pretty apron, but then they added a PVC pinny too!" and giggled "Just like you are wearing Gerry!" as he blushed. He sobbed "Next thing they'd me in hair slides, then made me play dollies and then I ended up in a pretty frock too!"

Toby and Gerry have to complement each other with curtsies

Gerry called "I heard girls say, you started playing dollies and dress up from the age of 3 or 4!" as the ladies gurgled and he cried "That's because she's making me!" as his sister bobbed a sweet curtsy, to them and explained "See I can make him do anything I want!" as he gasped "How?" as she laughed "Oh just threatening to tell some girls or your mates about him or even worse, let them see him dressed up, as a girly!" as he said, "But you can do that to me too!" as she said, "Exactly! So, be willing to do or say, anything I want!" as he cried "Not fair!" adding "Ok! I'll do what you want!" as she laughed and asked, "Anything?"

She thought a second and then giggled, as she whispered into his ear "Tell me how pretty I am and you like my pretty skirt and blouse!" and heard him stammer "Francesca! You're very pretty and I like your skirt and blouse!" and heard the ladies laugh and saw her grip her skirt and bob a curtsy to him and laugh "Thank you Angela! I think that deserves a Sissy Kissy!"

He gasped "What?" as she threw her arms around him and kissed him on the lips, as he cried "Eh!" and tried to push her off, adding "I don't like kisses!" as his Mum and the ladies all laughed. However, she then whispered to him again and heard him cry "Please don't Francesca?" as the ladies asked, "Whatever did she want you to say?" as he blushed and stammered "Toby! You look very pretty in your dress and ribbons!" as both Mum's said, "No Francesca! That's naughty!" as Toby cried "Oh no! Mum stop her!" as he looked at his smiling sister. Toby stands up and grips his dress and bobbed a curtsy to Gerry and said, "Thank you Angela!" but then sit down again, as Fran called "Angie's waiting or will I bring some girlfriends in to persuade you!" as he sobbed "Not fair!" as he went to give Toby a kiss, as he said, "You can f-ck right off! I'm not kissing you!" but was threatened with being taken around the street again, to show his mates and next thing sobbed, as he let Toby pull his arms around his neck and kiss him to giggles and screeches, as both boys sobbed "Not fair!"

She giggled, as she said, "One good turn deserves another!" saying, "Toby tell Gerry how pretty he is too, in his frock and ribbons!" as he cried "Mum! Make her stop!" but the ladies laughed "It's only fair, since Toby kissed him!" as his Mum laughed and nodded, and heard him say, "Toby! I mean Angela, you look very pretty in your frock and hair ribbons!" as Toby sobbed "Not fair Mum! I'm not a sissy!" to giggles, as he stood up and mumbled "Thank you Toby! I mean Tinkabelle!" and sitting down again, he kissed him, to more laughter.

They were told to sit down beside each other and take a dolly each. Franny said, "I hope you two will appreciate me, lending you my dollies and not break them. They both promised not to break her dollies and play properly. She got each boy to kiss his dolly to more laughter from the room, but then to swap dollies and give another kiss, which they hated as the other had kissed it.

The boys must play dollies and change their dresses and hold hands

Next thing she'd handed them both a frock and said, "Carefully remove your dolly's frock and then slip her into her new frock!" as they blushed and sobbed. She had to show Gerry a bit more than Toby having given him some practice at home with her dollies and dresses. Both boys were blushing, bright red as they tried to remove the doll's dress, but of course needed help from Franny, although Toby was a bit better due to the practice she'd given him since that first evening when the girls had come round.

They eventually got the dresses off their dollies. They again had to kiss their dollies and then swap again to kiss the other dolly and were then handed two frocks for the pop back onto the dolly. Gerry's was a simple Velcro connection and he soon with a bet of help had slid the frock back onto the dolly again, with his Mum laughing "Gosh Gerry I never realized you were such a dolly expert!" as Francesca laughed "Now Gerry tell your Mummy how long you've been secretly coming up to my house to play dollies with Toby and me!" as he cried "I haven't!" but she whispered "I could bring a few girls round to help you remember!" as he cried and whispered "Oh no! Not since I was 3 or 4?" as she nodded and heard him stammer "Not fair!" as she asked again "What age did you first play dollies with Toby and me?" as he stammered "Since I was 3 or 4 Franny!" as the room exploded with laughter and his Mum laughed "Oh you meany! You could have told me!" as Fran continued "He also told me he loves slipping into your clothes to play dress up too!" as he cried "I don't!" but heard Fran say "Now Gerry! You and Toby have been playing dress up with Mummy's dress up box for years now!" adding "Haven't you?" as her Mum laughed and his said "I think I'll have to get him a dress up box too!" as he begged "Please don't Mum?" as they laughed. Next was Toby's turn and she had a frock with more complicated connection which he needed more

help with. He said "I don't know how my dolly's dress does up!" to more screeches but then Francesca handed it to Gerry and said "Have a go Angela!" as he huffed "I haven't a flaming clue!" and his Mum helped him and he soon had it done up its back. However, then Fran said "I think the girlies are ok with playing dollies! Lets see how the sissies do!" as she removed both boys hair ribbons and slides to screeches and sobs from the boys saying "Please leave our ribbons and hair slides!" to more laughter, as the boys had to repeat undressing their dolly and then adding the frock again to more giggles and laughter, but now sitting in the frocks as sissy boys. Of course, Fran then said "Console each other, sissies!" as her Mum gasped "Not as sissies, Franny?" but she nodded and pushed their heads together and they then had to give each other kisses, to more laughter. Francesca said, "Now boys! I hope you two are going to be nice to each other and play together!" as they both gasped "Oh no!" as she whispered to Gerry's ear and heard him ask "Toby will you come down and play dollies with me tonight!" as he cried "Oh no! Don't make me Mum?" as the room broke down in laughter. Gerry had to curtsy and then kiss the blushing sobbing, Toby.

Fran suggests the boys could act as each other's dolly to play dress up

Francesca whispered, "Hold hands and mince around the room!" as the boys cried "Not fair!" and took hands and walked around with their handbags dangling. She added "Now extreme mince girlies!" as the boys minced with their arms, outstretched and then they had to link arms and mince again!" However she then laughed as she said "When you don't have a dolly nearby you two still can have fun playing dollies!" as her Mum asked "What do you mean Franny?" as she gurgled "They can act as each other's dolly and play dress up with it!" as the boys sobbed "Oh no!" and the ladies all screeched again. Fran knew that Gerry couldn't remove his frock, as her trick would be exposed to them but toby was in a frock over panties without his willy sticking out and so she said "Today only my big sister Tinkabelle will act as Angela's dolly!" as Toby sobbed "Oh no! Please don't, Franny?" as her Mum said "Now Fran! Stop that!" but she said "It's ok Mummy! She's got her petticoat on to hide her blushes!" as her Mum realized she meant his nightdress and laughed "Ok, miss bossy boots!" as she laughed "Right Angela, remove your big dolly's frock!" and heard the boys beg, but to no avail as she saw him pull the dress up his body and the ladies ask "Is it a petticoat?" but his Mum laughed "The girls provided him with a pretty nightdress to sleep in too!" as they screeched and saw Gerry pull the dress up over his head and then off his arms to leave him in the nighty, to laughter from the room, as Fran called "It's wonderful putting my big sissy brother to bed, in his nighty!" as they gasped "You don't?" as she nodded, as they laughed and one Mum Lucy asked "I hope you don't go near his you know what?"

Fran laughed and took Toby's hand and said to Lucy "Come with me a tick and you ladies stay here!" as her Mum asked her "What are you up to Francesca?" but she said "Just bare, with me Mummy!" She led Lucy out the room with Toby and whispered to him "What do you call, that in your panties?" as he blushed and sobbed "Not fair! It's my baby pee pee!" as Lucy gasped "Oh fab!" as Fran raised his nighty, to show her the frilly panties and then said "Ask him! Why she calls it that!" and heard her ask, as he blushed again and stammered "Because it's just the size of a baby boy's baby pee pee!" as Fran yanked his panties down, to show her and heard her screech, as Fran quickly let his nighty down and pulled his panties back up again, as the door opened and her Mum asked "What was the joke?" but Lucy laughed "We'll keep it a secret but it's very funny!" Fran then handed Gerry another frock and said "Pop dolly Tinkabelle into her new frock and saw him raise the dress over his head and slide his arms into the sleeves and pull it down his body over his nighty again to more laughter and giggles. Of course both boys were sobbing with embarrassment but then had to kiss each other again. When they had left, Gerry got home still in his frock, He'd to show his Mum what Francesca had done, as she asked, "Why could you not remove your frock, to join your mates, my little missy!" He sobbed "I couldn't believe what she did?" She asked, "What?" as he sobbed "Take me upstairs and close the blinds and look what she did! but said, "Just for a few minutes, but I want you back into your frock again!"

Gerry gets home showing his Mum the trick with his panties and willy

He added "Remove my frock and look!" as she led him upstairs to the bedroom and closed the blinds a bit, as she giggled, and took hold of his frock and raised it up and gasped as she screeched "Oh fab!" as she saw him in frilly pink panties, but with his willy on show!" and laughed "It's been years, since I saw that!" He then said, "She flaming, touched it!" as she gasped "She never did! Naughty girl" as he nodded, "Tell her off, Mummy, and say, she's not to touch my willy!" He blushed and stammered "Mum! It's not fair! You see how big it is?" She laughed "What a show-off!" as he huffed "Fran makes me call it something else!" adding "She's making me say, this!" She laughed "What?" as he huffed "It's my baby-pee-pee!" as she giggled, and asked, "Why's it called that?" as he stammered "It's the size of a little baby boys, baby-pee-pee!" as she giggled, "Fibber!"

Fran runs down again, to Gerry and asked his Mum "Can you let him out to play with his mates tonight?" as his Mum laughed "I thought you were wanting him to be a girly or even play with your brother again?" as she laughed and nodded. However, she said, "I don't want the other guys to realize anything is happening to him and so we'll let both Gerry and Toby, go around and play footy with their mates, so the other guys don't suspect, what we might be planning for them!" as his Mum laughed and nodded, "I see!" She laughed "Toby begged to be let him play with his mates and so I've let him!" Gerry said, "Mum! Let me play with them too?" as Francesca held out her hand, "Come on Gerry, you know they let Toby play footy with them, in his frock!" Gerry's Mum laughed and gasped "You aren't planning to get all the boys in the street, into frocks and carrying handbags?" as Francesca laughed and nodded. Francesca said, "I might even let some who ask sweetly, to wear hair ribbons too!" as she went over and removed his hair ribbons and Alice band. He sobbed "Please leave my hair ribbons in Francesca?" as his Mum gurgled "Oh fab!" as she asked, "It's fun to have him dressed in his school boys uniform, but with hair ribbons and carrying his dolly and handbag about the house, saying, girly things to you!" as he cried "Oh no!" as she held out a dolly and said, "here's Barbie!" adding "and here's some dresses to play dress up with her!" as his Mum gurgled "Oh fab!"

Hence, that evening they let Toby and Gerry both join the boys in boy's clothes to play footy with Gerry even being able to wear his underpants, in case Toby squeals on him and they debag him to check. They didn't suspect Gerry and just teased Toby a bit about his playing dollies and dressing up. Toby got some teasing from the guys, but not from Gerry, dreading him letting the guys know he was being dressed up too. He tried to lessen his teasing, saying, "Come on guys! We know his sister and Mum are making him act girly! Let him be and get on with the game!" As the others said, "Yea!"

She asked, "Now what's it called Missy!" as he huffed "It's my baby-pee-pee!" as she added "Oh fab!" and said, "Well you don't need your trousers, as you'll be in your frock all evening!" as he sobbed "Oh no! Not all evening!" as she laughed "Until bedtime, till I find Missy, a nice nighty to wear to bed!"

Franny brings down a nighty and then suggests a sleepover

He cried "You wouldn't make me, Mummy?" as she nodded. Francesca brings him down a pretty nighty to wear, but has her Mum there too, who giggled, "Gosh I see my Toby has become, a role model for Gerry too!" as his Mum laughed and said, "I can't believe how girly, the boys, are acting and he's helping me about the house, in his pretty aprons and ribbons!" Franny suggests he play dollies, dressing and undressing them and Says, "She'll lend him her doll's pram!" to prance about in his frocks, wheeling them about the garden and the street if he's naughty!" as he cried "Don't Franny! Please don't?" as they laughed. He cried "Toby's, not here too?" as his Mum nodded, "Come on Tinkabelle!" as he cried "Oh no!" and wet his panties as Fran giggled, "No! Just joking!" but then realized by his face and saw his hands shoot down to his dress. She gurgled "I think some naughty girly, has

239

just had a little accident in his panties!" adding "We might need to see about some nappies and plastic baby pants, for my little baby here!" as he begged "Please don't, Mummy?" as he sobbed "Not fair, Franny!"

However, she then added "If you pop your girly into nappies and plastic baby pants, I'm sure Francesca will have to do the same, with her big brother Toby, to stop baby Angela being too embarrassed!" as a kind of dare to his Mum. Franny and her Mum laugh as she said, "Wouldn't it be fab if we can get both boys into nappies and plastic baby pants, but also sleeping together, in nighties too!" as her Mum laughed "Oh Franny! Wouldn't that be too much?" as she shook her head. Franny laughed "I'll try and keep it a secret from the girls, although they did suggest nappies and plastics, to solve the problem of Tinkabelle, using the girl's toilets!" as her Mum gasped "Oh Fran! You didn't out him? Not at school?" as she nodded and gurgled "We put him into a dress and pinafore, almost as soon as he got there!" as she screeched "Oh the poor boy!"

They entered and heard her laugh "I heard you attended school today as a girl in dress and pinafore!" as he sobbed "It was terrible Mummy!" adding "She showed me off to the whole flaming school, in my dresses!" as she gave him a cuddle and a kiss, as Fran laughed "Sorry Toby! but it is much more fun to skip about in a dress and pinafore!" as he blushed and sobbed into his Mum's apron. They exited and his Mum said, "Let me tend to your accident!" as he huffed "I'll go up and clean myself Mummy!" but she shook her head and led him upstairs to the bathroom and removed his frock and laughed, at his wet panties with the largish bulge in them.

She took his frock and said, "Stay there, young man!" and exited out of the bathroom into the spare room, where after rummaging, eventually found what she was after. She took the bag and smiled as she popped along to the loo, where her Gerry looked and cried "Oh no! Please don't Mummy?" as he saw the diaper bag with Baby Gerry on it!"

He sobbed "Not fair!" as she gurgled "It's been years since I used this, apart from a few times on your nieces!" He cried "Please don't, Mummy? I won't wet myself again!" as she laughed "Now Baby! Either here or in the back garden or up at Toby's!" as he gasped and said, "Ok here!" as she set the bag down and got some rubber gloves out and slid them on.

Gerry's Mum puts him in a nappy, but adds a plastic carrier bag as pants

She looked into the bag and saw some dummies, baby bottle and even a bonnet, not as frilly as a girl's, but very babyish. She laughed as she took the dummy and washed it in the sink as he cried "Not a flaming dummy, too?" as she then popped it into his mouth and gurgled "Oh this is even better, than dressing you up as a girly!" as blushed. She removed his panties and laughed at his wet willy and soon was using wet wipes, to clean him and he asked, "Where's my undies?" but then saw her take a disposable as he cried "I'm not wearing nappies, Mum! Please don't?" but she laughed "Sorry I haven't any other girly panties!" She then said, "Tell you what! If you let me put these on you, I'll let you run up and ask Fran to borrow, some of hers, from her Mummy!" as he cried "Oh no!" as she nodded, and saw him nod "Not fair Mum!" as she said, "Mummy!" as he said, "Not fair Mummy!" as she added the disposable to his front and heard him huff "Not flaming fair!" as she looked at her big boy in the nappy. However, she laughed "Gosh it's been so long, I've forgotten hoe to change a baby's nappies!"

She then took the baby gel as he cried "Not gel too!" but she laughed "I don't want baby to get nappy rash!" as she pushed him back and pulled off his nappy and squeezed some gel into her hands. She started applying the gel over his front, laughing at his embarrassment, as he blushed. She adds talcum powder and then the disposable, asking "Do you think your botty is ok?" as he nodded, vigorously, to more laughter as she looked at his nappy. She laughed "Will I add the diaper yet?" but saw him shake his head and so she then pulled out his old plastic baby pants and gurgled, as she held them up, beside his nappy and laughed "Somehow! Even without baby's diaper! I

don't think these will fit baby!" as he shook his head, agreeing with her and begged "Please Mummy! Leave the baby pants off, me!" as she gurgled.

She then had a thought and said, "Wait here or it's a diaper too!" as she skipped out the room door and he wondered what she was up to. He hoped she wouldn't try to borrow some large plastics, from a Mum nearby, but was almost relieved when she entered a few seconds later with a pink girly carrier bag.

He asked, "What's in the carrier bag Mummy?" as she laughed "Hold on a tick!" as she exited and punching 2 holes in the corners, she returned and said, "Close your eyes for a minute and let me try something out!" as he closed them, but felt her raise his legs as she fed the bag up over his feet and then up his legs and gurgled as she pulled him up to stand. She quickly pulled the bag up, over his nappy and screeched. He looked down and gasped and cried "Oh no! Not fair, Mummy!" as she giggled, "I now can answer what's in the carrier bag!" adding "It's baby's nappy and is naughty bum-bum!" as he blushed "Get this off me, please?" but saw her slap his hands, saying, "Don't be a naughty baby!" She laughed and said, "Right get dressed and pop up, to ask for your pretty frilly panties!" as she added "You'd better use those exact words!" as he cried "But she'll hear my plastic bag rustle!" as she said, "Hurry up and get dressed till I listen!"

She went shopping for a lot of baby stuff – large baby plastics, diaper. etc.

The next day However, he had been wearing pretty aprons to help his Mum with housework, as soon as he'd got back from school and even a girly PVC pinny on top, for helping with the washing up. His Mum was enjoying the new helpful boy, helping with housework in a pretty apron and sometimes PVC pinny over a pretty skirt and blouse or frock!" The next evening, however, his Mum got her Gerry into nappies, but this time in proper plastic baby pants. He cried "Oh no! Not a diaper and plastic baby pants?" adding "But Toby and Franny will see!" as she laughed "Don't worry! Franny should be in bed by now!" adding "If Toby's not in nappies, we'll let you wear some panties instead!" as he huffed "It's going to be terrible, if she sees my nappies, Mummy!" as she hugged and kissed him, laughing. She said, "At least I'm letting you head up there as a boy in your normal clothes, hiding your baby stuff!" as he cringed. You could be prancing up the street in a big frock with your handbag!" as he begged "Please don't tease?" as she gurgled "Or a short baby dress to show off your nappies and plastics!" as he blushed even more.

They get Gerry to slip up to Toby's place and they then realize he's in nappies and plastic baby pants. Gerry was begging his Mum not to send him up to Toby and Francesca's in nappies and now proper plastic baby pants, but she threatened him with going up in a frock to their place and so he agreed.

Toby was unaware of any plan or sleepover, but was in a frock, with a handbag over his elbow, tied there doing some homework when the bell went. They checked the street and his Mum took the shopping bag up, taking Gerry' hand as she led him up to Toby's and making sure none of his mates were about, she led him up the drive and into the porch. She rang the bell and their Mum answered and giggled, as she let them in the door. She leads Gerry and his Mum into the sitting room with the blinds drawn and call a blushing Toby in his frock to join them. She Says, "Be quiet as Francesca is in bed asleep!" His Mum gets Gerry to slip up to the toilet and change out of his boy's clothes into a nighty and then a frock to come down to join them as Angela again. He was glad he didn't have to do it in front of Toby as he didn't want him or Franny to discover his nappies and plastic baby pants. He took the bag and slipped upstairs trying to keep as quiet as possible to not awake Franny and let her see him. He went into the bathroom and quickly undressed down to his nappies, not even closing the door, in case she awoke. He took the nighty and pulled it over his head, grimacing as he saw it was quite short and would show off his nappies. He then took the frock and was pleased as he checked and saw it was longer and pulled it over his head.

He popped his boy's clothes back into the bag and slipped back down the stairs again. he enters the room to see Toby in his frock bobbing a curtsy and quietly say, "Why Angela, don't you look pretty!" as he grimaces and gripping his own frock, he bobbed a curtsy back and said, "Thank you Tinkabelle!"

Their Mum's make both boys get into bed and complement each other

They approached each other and kissed to laughter from both Mums. Toby has just girly panties under his frock and doesn't realize the Gerry is in nappies and plastic baby pants. They are told to mince around the room using their handbags and say, sweet things to each other and their Mums, all the time trying to not awake Francesca asleep upstairs. However, his Mum wanted to see Gerry go back down in his frock and so said, "Right! One of you boys can come back down, as a boy – with boy's clothes over his nighty, but the other is to come in a frock!" They lead the two boys down to Gerry's place, both dressed in nighties, but Gerry in a frock and Toby in his boy's clothes, with him not realizing about their sleepover. They walked down having to hold their Mum's hand and glad that Francesca has been put to bed, to not tease either of them.

They are led into Gerry's house, where Toby's boy's clothes are removed and taken away, to leave the blushing boys sitting there in their nighties and Gerry still in his frock, dreading what was coming next. They were told to play dollies for a while and both set about changing the dolls in and out of a frock and then after a while, to play curtsies with more complements and the accompanied curtsies and kisses, between each other, to laughter and giggles. Gerry's Mum asked, 'What they wanted to drink!' and went off to sort out the tea and soft drinks while the boys played together. A few minutes later she brought the drinks and biscuit's in and they were part way through when Toby asked, "Mum! When can we go back home?" as she looked at him, smiling and said, "Not long now for beddy byes, dear!" as Gerry's Mum laughed and said, "You finished boys?" as they nodded, and she said, "Come upstairs a tick, both of you!" as they stood up and followed her up the stairs and into Gerry's bedroom. Next thing the smiling ladies pulled back the bedclothes and Gerry saw the plastic sheet in place of his normal bedsheet. He cried "What to heck is that, sheet for Mum?" as she laughed "Now Gerry! You've to just get into bed and be quiet or else!" adding "It's just to protect your bed, in case of accidents!" The embarrassed boy then removed his frock and Toby gasped, as he saw his nappies and plastic baby pants, under his short nighty. He asked, "Why the nappies?" as he blushed "Mum played a trick last night, pretending you were there, and I wet myself!" adding "She then put me into flaming nappies!" Gerry jumped into bed on top of the plastic sheet, saying, "That feels terrible Mum!" However, next Toby's Mum laughed "Toby! Don't you feel left out! Since Gerry is in nappies and plastic baby pants, shouldn't you?" as he begged "Please don't make me Mummy?" She laughed "Right Tinkabelle, into bed with Angela for to wish her sweet dreams!" as both boys sobbed "Oh no! Don't make us kiss in bed?" but next thing he was slipping into bed beside a very embarrassed Gerry. However, then his Mum laughed "Toby you do look sweet lying there in your pretty nighty!" as he huffed "Ha!" Gerry's Mum laughed and said, the same and so he got a kiss too. She laughed "Guess what come's next Gerry?" as he begged "Please Mummy don't make us kiss?" but she laughed "Angela tell Tinkabelle how sweet he looks in his nighty!"

Their Mum's then pop them into nappies for their sleepover

Next thing he said, "Tinkabelle! You look very pretty in that nightdress!" as Toby sobbed "Not fair Mum!" as he reached over, but saw Gerry pull away, as his Mum scolded "Now Gerry! That's not very sisterly!" However, next thing his Mum had got his left hand and tied a ribbon around it and then tied that to Toby's nighty around his neck, as he cried "Oh no!" This was followed by his right which was tied up around his neck too, so that he'd his hands tied up near to Toby's head. Toby's Mum did the same to him, as he cried "Mum! Don't!" but soon he was tied up too, as they took another string and tied it around the back of both boys neck, to stop them trying to break the ribbons. Toby said, "This better not take too long! I might need the loo soon!" as his Mum said, "Ok! Where's that kiss!" as both boys grimaced and kissed each other, as their Mum's laughed. However, then they reached under the

bedclothes and pulled them off, to leave both boys on show. However, they then reached up under their nighties and pulled down their panties, as they both cried "What are you up to?" Gerry called "I'll tell on you Mum!" as did Toby, who cried "Stop it Mum! Put them panties back on me!" to laughter from both of their Mums.

However, they then saw the diaper bag and cried "Oh no! Not nappies?" as both boys sobbed. They pulled their nighties up and then rolled the boys onto their sides, so that they were facing each other. However, it also meant that their willies were touching too, as their Mum laughed and pointed at the two of them, Toby's little one, but Gerry's a lot larger. Each Mum took the other boy to wash down and then apply the gel and talcum powder and then each had two disposable nappies on their front to separate their willies and then their bottom. Each lady then took a large pair of plastic baby pants that they'd got while shopping that day and pulled them up over each boy and smiled down at the sight of them both in nappies and plastics.

Toby sobbed "How could you Mummy?" as she laughed and said, "At least we've done it when Francesca's not here!" as Gerry begged "Please don't let her see us?" as his Mum's laughed "Would it be that bad, letting her see you babies?" as they nodded, and Toby's Mum then said, "Come in Franny!" Both boys cried "Oh no!" as she giggled, "Just joking!" but both had wet their nappies!" and sobbed "Not fair! I've wet myself" as Gerry's Mum laughed "Naughty girl!" but then checked both pairs of plastics and said, "I think their nappies and plastics are holding up ok, till the morning!" Gerry's said, "I think the plastic sheet will just be some added protection for the bedding, just in case there are any accidents, their nappies and plastics can't handle. They gasped and cried "Not the morning! We can't sleep together like this!" as their Mum's laughed "Now settle down boys!" as they took a dummy each and said, "Just another kissy before your dummies are added!" as both boys were facing each-other and blushed as they kissed. However, each dummy was attached to a girly frilly baby bonnet, by elastic and popped it into their boy's mouth and said, "Suck! Or we get Franny for real!" They applied the bonnets onto the boys head's and then fed the dummy on elastic into their mouths laughing at the sight.

PART G

JULIE AND THEN HER MUM DISCOVER NANCY

Pam deputizes her Mum to check he's in panties for football

Pam leads Julie across to spy Tom as Nancy and is told all

Julie asked, "Why?" but Pam said, "Wait and see!" Pam led Julie in and pointed to the bottom of the stairs, where Julie squatted down to wait. Pam closed the inner door on her and then rang the bell. Tom called "Oh no!" in pretend shock. His Mum removed his pinny and then opened the side door and called "Pam come in the side door!"

Tom opened the kitchen door and fled up the hall in Pam's frock, but on turning to the stairs gasped and cried "Oh no!" as Julie saw him in Pam's frock and an Alice band and screeched "Tom! What on earth are you wearing?" as he sobbed "Oh no! Not fair!" as his Mum ran up and gasped "Oh no! Julie! Pam didn't?" as she nodded, "She did!" and a giggling Pam came in and said, "Look! I've asked Julie to keep my sister Nancy a secret from Tina or her Mummy! Ok?" Her Mum laughed "I thought you were keeping him a secret!" as she laughed "It will be more fun with Julie and me playing with Nancy!" Tom sobbed "Not fair! I knew she'd tell on me!" as Julie put her arms around him and gave him a kiss saying, "Don't cry Tom! I mean Nancy! I think it's fab that Pam has a pretend sister and we can have fun together!" Pam laughed "She is so much more fun than my silly bro Tom ever was!" as her Mum asked, "Did you plan this Pam?" but she shook her head "It just came to me when I ran up the hall with the kitchen door closed that if Julie got in to see my sweet Nancy, then he'd have fun with both of us playing dollies and skipping and dress up!" Julie gurgled "I'll look forward to playing lots of little girly games with you!" as she gave him another kiss, but on the lips.

He cried "I don't like kisses!" as she kissed him again, sorry Nancy, you've to do what Pammy or I say, or else Tina might want to play with the new girl!" as he begged "Julie don't tell your Mum or Tina?" as she laughed "She's so much fun!" as Pam nodded.

Julie asks to see Tom aka Nancy playing dollies and Pam takes them into the living room where her Wendy doll is and hand's it to Tom and Says, "Nancy, get your new dolly out of her dress and into a new frock!" as Julie and her Mum giggled, and she asked, "Has he only one dolly?" However, then got up and brought in his apron, handbag and Baby Suzie attached to it and said, "Right Nancy get into your apron to show Julie!" as he cringed "Not fair Pam!" but took the apron and pulled his arms into the sleeves and then, it over his head.

Pam took the handbag with the doll attached and slid it up his arm to the elbow and then tied it there. Julie Says, "I'd better get back now, but I promise not to tell Mum or Tina about Nancy!" Adding "Although! I may break out into fits, of laughter causing them to wonder why!" as he blushed. She gave him a final kiss and called "Bye Pam, Bye Nancy!" and skipped down the stairs, as Pam said, "Nancy! See Julie out!" and he blushed as he descended

the stairs and saw Julie wait for him. Julie opened the inner door and saw him, step to the side and say, "Bye! Please don't tell!"

However, Pam then reached under his dress and pulled his panties down and reaching her hands to keep his shoulders up, she dared her "I dare you to take Nancy out, to the porch for a final kiss!" Pam whispered, "Just pull on his baby-pee-pee!" as Julie gurgled.

Julie brings Nancy out to the porch and makes him run to the backdoor

Julie checked her house and that her Mum wasn't looking and nobody seemed to be about, as she reached under his frock and took hold of his willy and laughed as she pulled and felt him join her and then out into the porch, as he cried "Not fair Pam!" who said, "Nancy can get around the side door!" as she pushed the door closed again and left him to Julie. A laughing Julie let go and threw her arms around him and gave him a kiss, before calling "Bye Nancy! I don't know if you'll want to wait, for your Mummy, or join me out and back around to the side!" as she slipped out the outer door and stood there, laughing at him. He gasped as he saw a light come on, in her front porch and shot out and around the side, to try and avoid being noticed, by her Mum or Tina. Julie saw the light and then her Mum appear and see her and call "I thought I'd to send a search party out for you!" as Julie called "Bye Pam! Bye Nancy!" as she skipped across the road to her Mum, laughing. Her Mum let her in, to hear her say, "Just popping up to the loo, Mum!" and ran up the stairs to the toilet, where she had to stick her hand in her mouth, to stop herself screeching with laughter.

She ran some water and washed her hands since they'd been holding his willy a few seconds ago and then her face, to calm herself down and said, "Right Julie! You've just met Pam's cousin Nancy and so will keep to that story, to try and keep some semblance of reality and so can mention Nancy to Tina and even maybe her Mum without giving the game away. She opened the bathroom door and went downstairs, where her Mum and Dad were in the living room, watching TV. Tina was sitting at the table, drawing on a scrapbook as she entered the room and said, "Pam introduced me, to her cousin, Nancy!" as her Mum asked, "Nancy? What age is she?" as Julie said, "Eight! About the same age as Tom!" Pam laughed and said, "But, she still loves playing dollies!" as Tina's ears heard and said, "Dollies! Good! She can play dollies with Pam, you and me!" as her Dad heard and said, "Julie's stopped playing dollies, Tina!" but then heard his wife say, "Actually Pam's started playing dollies again and so of course, our Julie has started too!" as he said, "Don't let me see you sucking your thumb Julie!" Tina screeched at his jokes!" as Julie blushed and said, "Oh Daddy! Dollies are lots of fun!" adding "I don't see why boys and men can't play dollies too!" as her Mum laughed

Julie asks for a sleepover taking her good nighty and panties over

Julie asks her Mum for a sleepover with Pam and her Mum Says, "I don't see why not!" adding "I take it you'll bring your PJs over and not want Tom to see you in your pretty nighty!" but surprised her Mum by saying, "Actually Pam has said, Tom shouldn't spy me and it should be ok!" adding "Apparently he's seen her several times in her nighty and is ok about it!" Hence, Julie brings her prettiest nighty and panties over.

Tom didn't like the fact that Julie was staying over at theirs and knew she'd tease him. Their Mum didn't see anything wrong with Julie staying over, knowing Tom wouldn't dare do anything nasty to her, but didn't realise how cheeky Pam and Julie might be. Julie joins Pam in bed for a cuddle, but part way through the night they make Tom join them and he has to get into bed with Pam and then Julie too, with them all in nighties and her giving him lots of kisses and cuddles, but also tickling his baby-pee-pee.

Morning Pam makes Tom wear Julie's good nighty and panties

She of course spends some time, sleeping with Tom in his nighty and panties, as does Pam too, with their Mum not realizing what was going on, till the morning. However, the next day, Julie asked Pam could she make Tom, wear her nighty and panties, under his boy's clothes next to his skin. Tom was told he could play footy with his mates, but then was told to strip and Pam dressed him in the pretty panties, with the pretty nighty over his chest and down over his panties. He blushed as she laughed "They're actually Julie's!" as he huffed "Not fair!" as she said, "After the footy, I want you to do something for me, unless you want to play dollies and dress up, all afternoon!" Tom asked, "What?" as she said, "Sprint up and down the street five times!" as he huffed "But I'll be tired!" as she laughed "Well try your best and run as fast as you can!" as he cringed "Ok!" as he dressed in his shirt, jumper and trousers over the frillies and headed down, to ask to wear the nighty and frilly panties, out to play footy with his mates.

Julie tells her Mum she's forgotten her nighty and panties

Julie returned home to her Mum and Tina and said, "I'd a nice time with Pammy last night!" as her Mum asked, "How was Tom?" as she laughed "Oh, the same MSP, refusing to do the washing up and housework for their Mum!" Julie Says, "Pam thinks that boys should be taught how to play dollies and is going to ask her Mum to teach big Tom!" as her Mum laughed "Now Julie, there's no way I could see big Tom playing dollies!" as she laughed "Thought I did hear Pam ask her Mum, to make him play dollies!" as Tina laughed "Yes she should! Then he could play with me!" as her Mum laughed "Now Tina, there's no way that big Tom would play dollies! Not in a million years!" as Julie laughed "It's playing dress up. he'd find it more difficult to do!" as Tina and her Mum both screeched with laughter. Tina had gone out to play dollies and Julie said, "Mum! I think I forgot my good nighty and panties from the sleepover, last night!" as her Mum said, "You'd better go and get them!" as she said, "I did ask Pam, but she Says, she can't find them!" but then added "I'm just wondering if her nasty brother, played a trick with them and hid them somewhere!" as her Mum laughed "I doubt Tom, would go anywhere near your pretty nighty and panties dear!" Julie laughed "I don't know! I was going to wear my PJs, because Tom was there, but then Pam persuaded me, that Tom wouldn't see me, in my nighty and so I wore it over!" She added "He did actually spy me, when I popped out to the loo and I saw him blush and stammer something, about me looking nice or it was a pretty nighty!"

Her Mum laughed "Yes! I'm sure Julie! I could just imagine a boy saying, something like that! Especially not big Tom!" Her Mum said, "Don't you dare tell Tina, or she might say!" as Julie laughed "We'll keep the joke, between the two of us!" as she watched him, play with his mates.

Julie hints Tom's wearing her nighty + panties, but her Mum disbelieves

She laughed "I don't know, if he's a thing about nighties!" adding "And pretty panties!" as she looked out and they saw him playing footy, in the street and she laughed "Pam Says, that she's looked everywhere in all her drawers and wardrobe and even in his room too!" as her Mum saw him playing footy with his mates in the street.

Julie added "You know what he might have done!" as her Mum shook her head and heard her say, "He might have hidden them on him!" as she pointed to him in the street, as her Mum laughed "Stop it, Julie! Stop trying to indicate that Tom is a sissy and is wearing your nighty and panties! What under his shirt and trousers" as she laughed "He'd better not be, they'd be smelly and sweaty, when I got them back!"

Her Mum laughed "Is this some joke, you and Pam have cooked up, to embarrass him or me!" as she laughed "Just because when we were pegging out the washing, yesterday, I suggested Pam show him how to peg up the laundry

using a handbag and purse!" as Julie laughed "Not to mention mincing around the garden, with any frocks hanging from his neck and pushing his dolly around the garden!" as her Mum screeched. Tina heard and ran in "What is it Mummy?" as she laughed "Something funny, that Julie said, but it's a secret!" as Julie laughed "Big girl talk! Isn't it, Mummy!" as she laughed "Yes dear!"

Tom finishes his footy and then runs up and down the street to get sweaty

Tom had fun playing with his mates and scored a few goals, although he didn't enjoy the fact, he was wearing Julie's stupid nighty and frilly panties. He finally finished his game and his mates went home. Tom remembered Pam's instructions and started running up and down the street, sometimes fast, but then slowed a bit, before speeding up again. Julie made sure she'd stayed in so her Mum couldn't suspect her of tampering with her nighty and panties. He finally finished and slipped up to the side door, where his Mum laughed "Had a good game Tom!" as he said, "Yea! It was great! I scored a few goals!" as she laughed "You look a bit flushed! You've ran a lot!" as he nodded but didn't expand on Pam's instructions. She said, "Pam's at ballet and is getting a lift from one of the other girls Mum's" as he said, "Ok!" Pam had told him that he'd to return from footy and running and to strip off out of Julie's things, into a pair of her pink panties for the afternoon, but to carefully pop the nighty and panties into a plastic carrier and she'd deal with it later!" and so he shot upstairs and locking his door, he stripped down and removed the nighty and then panties and popped them into the carrier, thinking "I'm glad Pam or Julie or even June didn't play a trick on me with that nighty and panties on!" as he popped Pam's pink panties on and dressed again for dinner!"

Julie's Mum collects the nighty and panties and realizes he did wear them

Julie had asked one of Tina's friends to take her to their house for dinner and so had her Mum to herself. Her Mum made their dinner with Julie laying the table, making sure she stayed in, so her Mum didn't suspect her of messing with the nighty or panties and said, "Mum! Could you pop over to try and get my things from Pam's!" adding "Tom might be nasty and not give them back!" as she added "I'll pop around to a friend Penny's house after dinner and then collect Tina and bring her back!" as her Mum said, "Ok dear!"

Her Mum laughed, but then heard her say, "Actually I think they might be still in Pam's room in a carrier bag!" as her Mum laughed "You little tease! Implying to me earlier that he'd been wearing them all morning to play footy!" as she dished out their dinner and they were soon eating away, chatting about this and that. They finished and washed up and then her and Julie went out the front door and she watched Julie go up the street to her friends and then to fetch Tina.

Her Mum crossed over the road and rang the bell and Tom's Mum came to the door and said, "Hi Dianne! You after Pam?" as she laughed "I hope my Julie wasn't any bother last night for the sleepover!" as she said, "No! Not at all! Any time!" as she said, "I think Julie forgot her favourite nighty and lacy panties and she said, she'd left them in Pam's room in a carrier bag!" as his Mum went up and opening Pam's door, she saw the bag and looking inside, brought it down, saying, "Pam's been at ballet all morning!" adding "Another Mum is bringing her home!" Julie's said, "Thanks dear!" as she took the carrier and looked inside, not checking, till she got over.

She sat down and opened the carrier bag and lifted the nighty out and let it fall and saw some sweat stains on the front of it and turning it around saw more on the back and laughed, as she wondered could it be true about Tom. She then pulled out the frilly panties, which looked ok, but she then turned them inside out and gasped as she saw not only sweat, but skid marks on them too and gasped and giggled, "Oh the naughty boy!"

and gurgled "She was right, the naughty boys been wearing her pretty nighty and panties to play footy with his mates! Wait till I get him!" as she laughed and put on some rubber gloves and said, "Yuk!" as she realised, she'd

touched the nighty and panties with her bare hands. She thought could Pam have orchestrated this or even Julie and thought "But she's ben at ballet and Julie has been here, all morning!" as she gurgled "The big sissy boy!" as she laughed "It might be fun, to get him to do the laundry for me!" as she laughed the place down and thought "Just as well, they aren't here! I must keep it a secret from Tina!" adding "But will quiz Julie when she's out!" as she laughed.

She ran the water and started gently hand washing the good nighties and frilly panties, thinking "I'd make him do this, if he was here!" as she thought "Why not!" as she slipped across the road again and rang the bell, asking "Can I see Tom for a few minutes?" Tom came out, from watching TV and heard her say, "Julie's Mum wants you a minute or two!" as he came out and asked, "What do you want?"

Julie's Mum knows Tom wore them and dresses him up

She said, "Julie, wants to speak to you, about something!" as he got his shoes on and huffed "Ok! Mum Says, dinner will be soon!" as she led him across the street and asked, "Did you have a good game of footy, this morning?" as he said, "Yea! I scored a few goals!" as she led him into the porch and opened the front door. He waited for Julie to appear, but heard her say, "Actually Tom! She's not here!" as he sighed with some relief, but saw her lead him into the kitchen and said, "Have a look, Tom!" as he looked into the sink and saw the nighty and frilly panties, that he'd just removed, ten minutes before!" as he started to tremble and shake and ask "What Mrs!" as she laughed "Look at the state, you've made of her favourite nighty and especially those panties!" as he sobbed "Pam made me wear them!" She laughed "Did she indeed?" as he nodded, continuing "And then she made me

run up and down the street, five times!" as she said, "I happen to know Pam was at ballet and my Julie and Tina were here for most of the morning too!"

He said, "Pam told me before she left!" as she said, "A fine story! So! You like wearing pretty nighties and panties?" adding "Follow me or else!" She took him up the stairs to Julie's room and said, "Get undressed girly!" as he cried "Oh no! Not fair!" but removed his jumper and shirt!" but she said, "Those too!" as he sobbed "Not fair!" and pulled the trousers down, as she gasped and screeched, as she saw Pam's panties with the small bulge.

She said, "Get the trousers off!" and saw him step out of them, as she took one of Julie's frocks and said, "Get this on girly!" as he sobbed "Not fair!" and pulled the dress over his head and down his body. She asked, "Does your Mummy know, you like to dress up?" as he huffed "I don't! Pam and June make me!" as she gasped "June, next door too?" as he nodded, and she laughed. She said, "Right girly! Downstairs and into an apron and PVC pinny to do the washing!" as he blushed and went down the stairs, begging "Please don't tell Tina?" She laughed "We'll see!" as she led him into the kitchen and handed him the pretty apron and saw him tie it around himself. He asked, "Can I have a headscarf?" as she laughed and shook her head and slid some hair ribbons, into his head and an Alice band on too. She said, "Now for your PVC pinny!" and slid a floral PVC pinny, but he then saw it was small and realised it was Tina's pinny, as he cried "Not, Tina's pinny?" as she laughed and nodded. She handed him some of Julie's pink gloves and said, "Gently start washing the nighty and panties, girly Tom!" as he sobbed "Not fair!"

He reached his hands into the sink and started rubbing at the nighty and then the panties, as she said, "Do the nighty first!" and saw him concentrate on it and ten minutes later he was done with the nighty. Next was the panties and he'd to rub harder on the bottom with the skid marks, as she laughed "It was those skid marks, that gave you away, girly!" as he blushed "Not fair!" He continued rubbing on the panties, as she said, "Be gentle with the frills! I'll have to supply you with, some really frilly outfits, to play in!" as he begged "Please don't, Mrs!" as she said, "Call me Aunty Dianne!"

Julie and Tina return and Nancy escapes back home in Julie's frock

She laughed and bent down and kissed him. He then heard the bell go and gasped "Oh no!" as she laughed "It's Julie and Tina!" but she then said, "I'll call them around the side and you shoot over to show your Mummy and tell about ruining Julies good nighty and panties!" adding "Or else stay and let Tina see!" She opened the side door and called around the side girls, as he saw them disappear, as she opened the side door said, "Right up and out the front girly!" She led him up to the front door and opened it, but held his apron strings, till she heard Julie and then Tina's voices and asked, "Coast clear!" A blushing Tom ran out the driveway, checking the street which had a few people, but with his hair ribbons to disguise him, he was ok and ran across the road and in through the gate, he ran up his driveway and opened the door, His Mum was about to say, something, when she gasped and giggled, "Oh Tom! Do they all know?" as he sobbed "Just Julie's Mum was there, and she complained about the state of Julie's nighty and panties!" as she laughed "Why?" He sobbed "Pam made me wear her nighty and panties playing footy under my clothes and then made me run up and down the street five times to get them really sweaty!" as she laughed "Oh no!" as he nodded, and explained "So when her Mum took them over, she saw the sweaty clothes with a flaming skid marks and knew, it was me who'd been wearing them!" as he sobbed "She had me washing them in the sink and then Julie and Tina came back and she brought them in the side door!" as she gasped "They know!" but he shook his head, adding "I escaped out the front and luckily no mates were about!"

She laughed "We don't want Tina to know!" as he shook his head and said, "No Mum!" as she laughed and said, "Stay here!" as he sobbed "But Pam might bring a girlfriend in and see me!" as she laughed "Ok! Up to your room, but keep everything on, or else!"

Tom's Mum laughed, at his outfit, saying, "Gosh that's a lovely frock, she put you in!"

She added "Better not ruin that!" Meanwhile Julie's Mum had spoken to the girls a bit, but then had shot upstairs and picked up his clothes and hid them away in her own wardrobe, to stop Julie and especially Tina spying them and realizing what she'd done to the poor girly Tom. She came down again and laughed as Julie asked, "Mummy! Was I right or not?" as her Mum laughed and nodded, as Tina asked, "About what?" as she said, "Big girl talk!" as Tina said, "I'm playing dollies! Want to play Julie?" as she laughed "Just for a short while!" Julie skipped back to her Mum who said, to her "Such a girly boy!" as Julie laughed.

His Mum went across the road and rang the bell at Julie's house and her Mum came to the door and blushed "Sorry Doreen!" as she laughed and whispered, "Not at all dear!" She laughed "It was me who should apologise and just was wondering, if those items are completely washed yet!" adding "If not! I'll bring them over and get the guilty party, to give them a gentle wash and rinse and then peg them out!" His Mum said, "Apparently Pam made him wear them all morning to play footy and then he'd to jog up and down the street to make it even more sweaty!"

Her Mum laughed "Julie was hinting to me, that he'd played a trick and hidden them under his clothes to play footy, but I thought she was joking, until I checked them and saw how sweaty the nighty was and especially when I saw the skid marks, on her frilly panties!" as his Mum said, "Such a naughty girly boy!"

His Mum collects the nighty and panties for Nancy to redo

Adding "Pam's been making him play dollies and dressing him up for a week now, but Julie only found out last night!" adding "But we'd better not let Tina know!" She said to her "Have you a bowl to take it over?" as her Mum led her into the kitchen. His Mum laughed and looked at the washing, in the bowl as Dianne said, "Take this one!" as she emptied the water out She can bring it over after he's finished, as long as she's dressed the same!" as she laughed and flicked her wrist to her. as his Mum said, "As long as Tina or his mates aren't about!" but "added "If you'd like to come over to see her peg out the washing, I'll give you a bell!" as she giggled, and nodded, "Fab!"

His Mum took the washing over in the bowl and checked and entering the side door, she took the bowl over to the sink and called "Nancy! Better come down and do this washing a bit better! The panties need more work!" as he blushed and came down the stairs, still in the dress, with Julie's apron on top and Tina's girly PVC pinny over it. His Mum laughed and said, "Seems you left the washing half finished!" as he sobbed "Not fair! Julie and Tina came back and nearly caught me!" adding "Does Tina know?" but she shook her head.

His Mum ran the water and added detergent and handed him some rubber gloves. He pulled them on and resumed washing with his Mum saying, "Go gently, especially on the nightdress'!" as he washed the nighty, some more and then tried to get the brown marks from the panties, helped by his Mum. She laughed "You're getting quite good Nancy!" as he cringed "I don't think her Mum realizes they call me Nancy!" adding "She just called me girly!" as she laughed. She threw the water out and then started rinsing them, helped by Tom of course.

She got Tom to wring them out gently and then rinsed them again and soon they were ready and seemed quite clean as she emptied the water from the bowl and said, "Ready to peg out the washing!" and saw him nod, but ask "Can I remove these silly things?" but saw her shake her head and say, "Julie's Mum is wanting to see you peg them out!" adding "Don't worry she's keeping Nancy a secret from Tina!"

His Mum phoned across and her Mum, Dianne answered the phone asking "Has he finished?" as she said, "I'll get Julie to take Tina, around to her friend's house!" as Julie whispered to her Mum "Make sure he wheel's his dolly around the garden in its' pram, before pegging up each item!" as her Mum laughed and nodded. Julie and Tina kissed her bye and Julie took Tina around to her friend's house again. Tina asked, "Why can't Jenny come here, and we play around here?" but Julie said, "Mum and I are going out and you can't be here on your own!" as she took her on around to her friend's house. She said, to her Mum that she'd pick her up later that afternoon, about four or so and her Mum said, that was fine.

Julie's Mum hears about June finding out and his Baby Suzie doll

Julie's Mum, Dianne picked up her handbag and went over to Tom's house, where she rang the bell and his Mum came to the door and let her in. She asked, "All finished?" as she was led into the living room, where she laughed "Don't you look sweet in Julie's prettiest frock?" but added "and her pretty apron, but also Tina's pretty pinny!" as he blushed and sobbed "Not fair! Tina doesn't know?" as his Mum laughed "He's so frightened of little Tina finding out!" as Dianne laughed "In case she makes him mince his dollies around the streets or even to the shops!" adding "Probably in a frock!" as they laughed again.

His Mum Says, "Right Nancy! Pick up the washing and let's show Julie's Mum how you peg out the laundry!" as she asked her "Where's his doll's pram?" as his Mum laughed "In the garage! It's open!" as he huffed "Dollies too?" as they laughed and she was handed his Baby Suzie doll and then saw the handbag attached to it, as his Mum explained "He's to carry his dolly all about the house, from room to room, with Pam's threats if he forgot it!" adding "She calls out very loudly 'Oh Tom! You've forgotten your dolly!'" as Dianne giggled, "What a fab tease!" as his Mum then said, "I was trying to keep Nancy in doors, but then he outed himself to June!"

She explained "June popped around to chat around 4pm just before he came in one day last week. He knew Pam wasn't around as she was playing at a friend's house. Hence, I just expected him to come in and change out of his school uniform, to play footy with his mates, when he called out "Mum have you seen my dolly?" and June heard and next thing was making him wheel his dolly in the back garden, with your Tina nearly catching him!" as her Mum gasped and laughed "What happened?" as he huffed "I was facing away from her in the driveway, wheeling the pram to the back garden, but I was wearing Pam's pink apron and a headscarf and so she thought I was Pam, when she called over for me to play dollies with her!" as they both giggled, "Lucky boy!"

His Mum continued "Pam then heard that Nancy had been out in the garden and said, it set a president and that meant he could now do the laundry too!" adding "But it's an extremely girly the way, I've shown her over the years, with a pretty handbag and she's even added a purse!" as Dianne laughed "Yes! She showed Julie and me the other day the girly way you peg out washing!" adding "Especially for frocks or blouses, mincing them around the garden!" as his Mum laughed "I'd told her no handbags for Tom, but seeing he carried one for the laundry, she said, it had set another president meaning she could add a handbag to his fun and so she then sewed a handbag to his dolly!" adding "She Says, it stops Nancy forgetting his dolly!" as she said, "Show her Tom!" and saw him blush "Not fair!" as he took the handbag and slid it up his arm to the elbow and then hold the doll in his left hand, as Dianne screeched "Oh fab!"

Nancy has to peg out the washing using a handbag and purse

She laughed "Mincing a frock or blouse on a hanger only came about last week, with Pam thinking it up to embarrass him even more!" adding "You especially love mincing your frocks and blouses around the garden!" adding "Don't you Tom?" as he grimaced and huffed "It won't be Tom! It will be Nancy mincing the nighty around!" as they gurgled. She continued "Although it does slow the laundry down, but with a girly boy, it does give us a good laugh!" as he cried "I'm not a girly boy!" to screeches from both of them, as he sat there in the girly frock and aprons, with ribbons in his hair, holding his handbag and dolly. He tried to run out, but his Mum caught him and apologized "Sorry Nancy! It just sounded so funny your protesting you're not a girly boy, looking so effeminate!" as he sobbed "Not flaming fair!"

His Mum handed him a handbag. Dianne laughed "You've taught him to use his purse and handbag like Pam!" as she nodded, and he cringed and heard Dianne laugh "Such a girly boy!" as her Mum laughed "So I see!" His Mum handed him a hanger for the nighty, to mince around the garden. His Mum led them out holding the bowl, with nighty and frilly panties, with Dianne following behind as she locked up. Dianne went and opened the garage door and saw the doll's pram and then popped his dolly into it and wheeled it over to him. His Mum said, "Right! Nancy time to take the nighty out of the bowl and then onto the hanger to mince it around the garden, as Dianne laughed "and mincing his dolly too!" as he cringed "Not fair!" He took the nighty from the bowl and slid it onto the hanger and popped it over his head to hang down his front to laughter from the garden.

He then took the doll's pram handle and started mincing it around the garden, before reaching into the handbag and pulled out a purse and got two pegs from it, before closing it again and returning it to his handbag. He took the two pegs and started to peg up the pretty nighty to laughter and clapping, especially from Dianne. He then opened his handbag again and got two pegs from his purse, before closing them up again and then picked up the frilly panties and pegged them up but was told to mince them around the garden with his dolly pram. He minced the doll's pram around the garden and soon was back to the line and pegged out the frilly panties, to more laughter.

Julie pretends Tina is there and Tom wets his panties

Dianne laughed "I hope I can borrow your little treasure to help peg out my laundry!" as his Mum laughed "I don't see why not!" as he cried "But not when Tina is there?" adding "It would be terrible and she'd tell everyone and make me play dollies with her!" as they laughed and giggled.

Julie came around from Jenny's house and went across to Tom's and slid quietly up the driveway and laughed and called "Hi Tina!" as he grabbed his dress and cried "Oh no!" as Julie laughed "Only joking Tom!" as she laughed "I think some naughty baby, has had an accident in Pam's panties!" as he sobbed "Not funny!" as her Mum scolded "Julie that was a naughty trick!" as she laughed "Anyone got nappies?" as they laughed. Julie gasped "I hope my good frock isn't wet? Otherwise I'll want Nancy to wash it gently by hand and will stand over her, to make sure

it's done right!" as he huffed "I don't think it's wet!" as she went over and checked and lifted it up, at the front and back, as her Mum said, "Watch it Julie! Don't go near his naughty bits!"

She gasped "I hope you haven't seen it?" as she laughed "Us girls must have some little secrets!" as her Mum **ran** after her, as she ran off giggling and her Mum said, "I hope you're joking young lady!" Julie laughed "Mum listen!" She laughed "Pam calls it his baby-pee-pee!" as her Mum asked, "What?" as she said, "Mummy! Ask him why he calls it that?" as her Mum asked, "Tom! Why do you call it your baby-pee-pee?" as he cringed "Because it's only the size of a little baby boys, baby-pee-pee!" as her Mum and they all screeched. Julie laughed "Pam and me did give Nancy a nice kiss good night last night!" as her Mum laughed "I hope he was downstairs!"

Julie giggled, "Unless his bed is downstairs!" as her Mum laughed "You'd better not have!" as she gurgled and ran off again saying, "We were only in bed with Nancy, for a short time, Mummy! About half an hour, either side of him!" as Pam's Mum laughed "I thought they were in their own room asleep and him in his!" His Mum said, "I'll go and fetch something to clean him up and some more panties!" as she disappeared into the house. She went in and got him a wash-clothes, towel and another pair of Pam's panties again and brought them down. She soon had sent him to the back of the garage, to remove his wet panties. Tom went around and his Mum took some rubber gloves and removed his wet panties, as she got him to hold up his dress as she washed and dried his front and back and he then pulled on the panties. He returned back around to cheers and the wet panties in a carrier bag. June then came out and laughed "Hi Nancy! Pretty frock!" as Julie's Mum giggled, "I heard you found out about Nancy, last week?" as she laughed "He kind of outed himself, about playing dollies to me, last week, when I popped around to speak to Doreen here!" Julie calls "Tom's just had his panties changed after wetting his panties again!" as June laughed "Excuse me a second!" as she went back into the house and returned back with two chairs, as they thought she was going to sit down. However, she set one chair on Tom's side of the fence and the other on her side and asked, "Can I have Nancy over the fence a tick Doreen?" His Mum nodded, as he gasped "Not fair Mum!" but stepped up onto the chair and was helped over by his Mum and June on her side.

June pops him back into nappies and plastic pants and shows him off

He jumped down and was led into the house and said, "Now! Tom, you know to do what I say, or little Tina finds out about Nancy!" as he begged "Don't tell Tina!" She led him into her house, as he cried "Oh no!" and felt his clean panties come down again but gasped as he saw the diaper bag. She pulled up his frock and turned him over and soon was applying the gel and then talc to his botty and then applied the disposable to it. She then smiled as she turned him over and started gelling and applying talc to his front and said, "We need to protect Julie's pretty frock!" as he blushed and sobbed "Not flaming fair! In front of Julie and her Mum!" She smiled and applied the disposable to his front.

She then laid the diaper down and sat him on top of it. She pulled up the sides and pinned them together and then pinned the front corner to it and soon he was snugly fitted into it and then saw the large baby plastic pants and felt her pull them up his legs and over his diaper. She pulled him up and let his dress down again.

June leads Tom out and locks up again as they asked, "What were you doing with Tom?" as she laughed "Just protecting your pretty frock, Julie!" as she raised his dress and heard screeches, as they saw his plastics and diaper, as she screeched "Oh fab!" and both his and her Mum gurgled "Oh June! That's so naughty!"

He sobbed "Not fair!" as his Mum said, "Now June that's taking it too far!" but she laughed "Now Doreen! He's in such a vulnerable position, with his frock, that any little joke, by the girls or me, is likely to make baby wet his panties! You'd be cleaning up baby and changing his pants all afternoon" as she said, "But there's only two items to peg up!" but she laughed "I'm sure I can add a few clothes to a basket for him to show off his laundry skills!"

He cried "Not flaming fair!" as they gurgled and she helped him over, raising his dress again to more laughter, as his Mum helped him down again. June said, "I think for any shopping trips with his Mummy or anyone else, nappies and plastics will be a necessity as his Mum laughed "Now June he won't need nappies around the shops!" as she laughed "With Pam willing to play subtle tricks on him and embarrassing him with handbags and dresses, all over the place, his trousers or frock would soon be soaked!" as Julie's Mum laughed "I think June might have a point, Doreen!"

Pam returns and see his nappies and makes Tom wear her tutu

However, then Pam returned from ballet class in her friend Jenny's Mum's car and got out wondering what Tom had got up to and if Julie's plan, to inform her Mum had worked. She decided not to invite Jenny in to meet her Nancy brother, but would in due course, several weeks or months later. She got out and called "Bye Jenny!" as Jenny and her Mum waved bye and drove off. Pam ran up and heard laughter from her garden and entered and screeched and called "Come in girls!" as he cried "Oh no!" Tom wet himself again, as June had expected, but this time, he didn't have as big a reaction.

Pam laughed "Oh what a pretty frock, is it new?" as Julie laughed "It's my prettiest frock that Mum put Tom in for slipping into my pretty nighty and panties this morning to enjoy his football and getting them all sweaty!" as Pam laughed "Such a girly brother!"

However, June laughed "It's ok Pam! I've made sure baby's pretty frock, is protected as Julie ran and pulled up his dress to show off his nappies, as Pam screeched "Oh fab girls!" adding "Oh Tom! Nappies and plastic baby pants?" She set her ballet case down and asked, "Are your nappies and plastics holding?" and saw him nod, as she said, "Follow me Baby Nancy!" as her Mum asked her "What are you up to young lady?" as she picked up her ballet case and took Tom to the back of the garage and said, "Can you girls bare-with me a tick, for some fun!"

Pam took Tom around the back and opening her case, she pulled out her tutu which she often brought, just in case she had a chance to show off, instead of her leotard and skirt, like the other girls. She said, "Just step into it!" and saw him step into the tutu dress and pull it up his legs, as Pam removed the aprons and then his frock a tick and slid his arms into the sleeves, before adding Julie's frock again to give them a surprise!" They heard "Why are we waiting?" from the garden and Pam closed her case and escorted him out with him looking the same, till she then raised his frock and the place exploded with laughter, with him dressed as a little ballerina for them.

She got him to remove his frock to be left in the tutu ballet dress. Of course, Pam had him prance around the garden as a fairy and said, "Mum! The girls at ballet would love to see Nancy prancing about!" as he cried "No Mum! Don't! There'll be girls from school there too!" as Pam giggled, "You wouldn't have to wear the same as me!" as he huffed "Still in my trousers or something they'd still tease me!" as she laughed "The big girls like me, wear a leotard and short skirt!"

She However, added "But they let the young girls like you, some still in nappies like you!" and paused as she explained "They're allowed to wear a tutu like you!" as he cringed Funny Pam!" as she gurgled "And are called the fairies like you!" as they place erupted with laughter at her joke, as her Mum scolded "Stop calling your big brother a fairy!" as they laughed and hugged him and Julie ran and kissed him, saying, "Pam I don't know if I want my big boyfriend to be a fairy!" as she kissed him, as her Mum laughed "You better be joking dear!" Julie said, "So Nancy! Every morning you shall come down to breakfast in Pam's pink pinny, without your trousers and wearing your tutu skirt and bob sweet curtsies!"

Tom hears he's going to be given lots of baby bottles of milk before bed

Pam added "And how much he adores his tutu skirt too!" as they laughed. As Julie added "Before he skips around the garden mincing with his handbag and dolly of course, till the breakfast is ready!" as Pam screeched "Oh Julie!" She laughed "That's unless he'd prefer to pop across to us and tell us how nice we look too!" as Pam gurgled "Tian would screech the place down, if Tom popped over in a skirt to bob curtsies to her!" as he sobbed "Not fair! Stop teasing girls!" to laughter, as Pam However, Julie then Says, "Now, I hope his pretty tutu skirt will still be protected, with his nappies and plastics before Aunty June let's him change out of them for school?" as Pam screeched "What a fab idea!" as he heard and cried "No! Don't make me wear nappies to bed!" Pam gurgled "At least they'll protect the bed and your nighty and not risk wetting any of my pretty panties!" to laughter from the garden. He cried "Mum! Pam's saying, "I've to wear nappies and baby pants to bed too!" as she gasped "Pam he can't!" as she laughed "Mummy! Look at the advantages! Baby will be well protected in the night and it will keep his bed dry, in case of accidents!"

Her Mum laughed "Now Pam! He hasn't wet the bed in years!" as Pam gurgled "But that was before Big Sissy Nancy! Became a baby again and needs lots of baby bottles, before bed and dear knows how many bottles, baby will have, if Julie, Aunty June, me and maybe you too, all give him a baby bottle each!" adding "I'd say, baby will be peeing his nappies most nights!" His Mum gasped "I'm not giving your big brother a baby bottle!" as she heard June giggle "I'm sure one of us can provide one on your behalf!" as she gasped and giggled, "Oh you poor boy!" as he sobbed "Not fair! I'm not having baby bottles!" Pam laughed "If you don't want Nancy's secret out to little Tina, you'd better ask for a baby bottle before bed!" as he sobbed "Now fair!" Tom gripped his tutu and bobbed a curtsy and asked, "Can I have my baby bottle before bed?" as they all laughed "But then heard Pam say, "To each of us!" as he gasped and cried "Not fair Pam!" Tom went up to June and bobbed a curtsy, asking for a baby bottle, as she bobbed one back and giving him a kiss and said, "Of course Baby Nancy!" as he blushed.

Then he approached Julie and asked the same, as she copied June and then her Mum who laughed "I hope you don't drain us out of milk! Tina still likes her milk and get suspicious about why it's all gone!" adding "Whatever excuse will we have to come up with?" as they all laughed. He then asked, "Pam and then his Mum who said, "I'll only give you a little!" as they all laughed, but Pam said, "I'll double up for Mummy!" as he pulled a face and huffed "Not fair!" Pam laughed "I think Baby Nancy can pop into the shop on his way home from school and do some shopping to get us some milk!" as Julie said, "If he hasn't got a baby bottle with him, we can leave one in with the girls in the shop that he can top up and have a quick suck!" as he cried "Please don't make me girls?" as they giggled. Julie laughed "Just joking!" as Pam laughed "You are cruel!" as Julie laughed "I'm not!" but added "If and when Tina finds out, she might make him pick one up from the chemists, and slip into a frock and using his handbag too!"

Julie's Mum worries about Tina spying his baby-pee-pee

Her Mum said, "When I fetched her pretty nighty and frilly panties, I couldn't believe my eyes, they were so sweaty, as if someone had been doing some very strenuous exercise in them!" Julie had hinted "Tom might have hidden them under his clothes to play footy, in them!" as Pam gasped "You weren't, were you?" as he cried "You made me!" as they laughed. She added "I take it, Tina doesn't know about Nancy?" as they shook their heads and Julie laughed "He's dreading her find out and make him push his doll's pram around the streets or even the shops!" as they laughed and he cried "Please don't tell on Nancy! I'll be a good boy!" Julie laughed "I doubt she'd want to play dress up with him!" as Pam laughed "What Julie?" adding "Use him, as her big dolly?" as they laughed, as her Mum laughed "Hey! She might spy, his baby-pee-pee!" Pam laughed "She'd be ok unless she had a magnifying glass!" as he cried "Not fair Pam!" as she giggled, "You've heard about his little baby-pee-pee?" as her Mum laughed and said, "She'd better not spy his baby-pee-pee, Julie!" as she laughed "It's not my fault if some naughty

boy shows off his baby-pee-pee and you have to explain about boys and their baby-pee-pee!" as they laughed "You poor girl!" as she laughed.

Julie's Mum giggled, "When Pam showed us how to mince our washing and especially our

dresses around the garden, I actually joked about you teaching him to peg out the washing too!" His Mum laughed "He was actually pegging out the laundry, in one of Pam's frocks, mincing his dresses around the garden at the same time as you were being shown by Pam!" She added "and just before she took her doll's pram over to you, she made him mince her dolly around the garden, like now, with a frock around his neck!" as they laughed and giggled. She said, "It is so funny using a handbag and purse, even though it takes a lot longer to get the washing done!" as June laughed "I'm sure with Nancy's help, you'll soon have the washing pegged up!" adding "If not the laundry, you can get some clothes to air in the garden and get Nancy to give you some fun!" as they laughed.

After the fun in the garden, with Tom as a ballerina prancing about in Pam's tutu, he was led back inside to have something to eat and get out of his nappies and plastic baby pants. Of course, Pam said, "Aren't you worried about having a little accident in your panties playing footy with you mates!" He went upstairs, taking a pair of Pam's panties with him, but his Mum ran up and said, "Be careful Tom! Do it in the bathroom, not your bedroom!" adding "Do you want me to help you change, since you had an accident this afternoon, when Pam teased you?" as he cringed "No way Mum!" as she added "I'll find you wet wipes, for you to clean the wee, gel and talc off and get you a baby towel!" as he cringed and waited for her to hand him the stuff. She fetched Pam's diaper bag and heard Pam screech "Are you going to change his nappies, Mum?" adding "Can I help?" as he cried "No way!" as Tom cried "I'm not! I'm just removing the flaming things!" as Pam screeched "You, big baby you! Don't let me see you sucking your thumb or a dummy!" as her Mum laughed "Stop that Pam!" as she too laughed. Her Mum scolded "He's not wearing nappies and baby pants to play football with his mates!"

Tom's let go to play footy, but Brenda and Claire trap him

Pam laughed "He could play Sissy football with you and me in the garden! We wouldn't mind if he wanted to keep his nappies on to play footy with us!" Her Mum laughed "Now Pam he's got to have some time as a boy!" as Pam pooed and said, "Oh Mum! Nancy loves being a girly and prancing about in a frock and aprons!"

After dinner and Pam and Tom have done the washing up. Pam and June are good as their word and Pam Says, "For being a good boy this afternoon and pegging up the washing for Mummy and me, June Says, I've to let you go and play footy!" as Tom said, "Thanks Pammy!" as she kissed him and said, "Have fun!" but added "Now what do you want to ask me?" Tom stammered "Pam can I please wear those pretty yellow panties out to play footy with my friends?"

Pam giggled, and said, "Downstairs a tick!" as he descended the stairs to where their Mum was in the kitchen. Pam said, "Repeat to Mummy!" as he gasped "Oh no!" as his Mum listened and heard him repeat "Mum! Can I wear Pam's pretty yellow panties, out to play footy with my mates?" as they both screeched and heard Pam say, "Well Tom! No playing swapsies with your mates!" as her Mum gurgled "Oh Pam! Oh Tom!" as she hugged him and gave him a kiss, saying, "Go on and enjoy yourself!"

However, the first night Claire had spotted Tom, slipping up the other side of the street to go around to play, with his mates, although she'd missed him, entering or leaving June's.

She phoned Brenda to say, "I've just spotted that sweet boy Tom, running past to play footy, with his mates! Will we try to trap him tomorrow night?" as Brenda giggled, "Fab! I'll be up after tea and if he tries to go around, we'll corner him and try and keep it a secret from Pam and his Mum!"

Hence, the next night, when Tom slipped up the street, to join his mates, he then heard Brenda call "Oh Tom! Have you got a minute?" as he went across to the lady, who was joined by another woman. Brenda asked, "We were wondering, if little Tina, knew who was wearing Pam's pretty apron and a headscarf the other day!" as he gasped "Oh no! How did you know?" as she laughed "Oh we were chatting, when we noticed the sweet boy, playing dollies with his doll's pram!" He gasped "You didn't?" as tears appeared in his eyes and she said, "You'd better come in, dearie and dry your eyes!" as he huffed "Not fair!" Tom checked down the street, but Pam nor June, realized where he was going, thinking he was playing footy, with his mates. Tom entered and was led into the sitting room, where he gasped "Oh no!" as he saw plastic sheet on the floor and heard them say, "Just undress and we'll play a game of dress up!" as he cried "Not fair! I've just been playing with Pam and June" as they laughed. He removed his jumper and then his shirt, to leave himself bare chested again. He asked, "Where's the dress?" but heard Brenda say, "Trousers too, Missy!" as he cringed and said, "They let me hide my undies with a dress before I remove my trousers!" but removed his trousers, to leave himself in socks and Pam's turquoise frilly panties, as Claire laughed "I'm sure the boys would be dead jealous of your panties!" as he blushed. Tom explains all about Pam and his dollies and then June and dress up.

Brenda and Claire pop tom into nappies and plastic pants

Brenda and Claire were next wiping his front down with wet wipes but then do his willy too. They then add the baby gel and laughed "What a tiny little willy!" as he huffed "Pam makes me call it my baby-pee-pee!" as they giggled, "Oh fab!" as they finally sprinkle talc over him and add his disposable nappy. They giggled, as they then lift him, onto the towel, folded in a triangle and pin it into place. He sobbed "Oh no! This is ten times worse than playing dress up or dollies!" as the ladies gave him kisses. Of course he huffed "Not more kisses!" as they asked, "Who's kissed you?" as he huffed "Pam and June make me complement them about their skirts and dresses and I'm then rewarded with curtsies and a kiss!" to more giggles as they laughed "We'll have to play that later!" as he grimaced. Of course, more photos were taken of the blushing boy with a dummy replaced in his mouth and then his bonnet was removed to make him more recognizable as a sissy boy.

Then plastic baby pants were pulled up over his diaper and they were pleased as it fitted perfectly and took more photos as Brenda said, "At least that will protect baby, in case he has a little tinkle in his nappies, around the house!" as he cried "Not fair! Don't show me off to anyone in my nappies!" as they kissed him again. Brenda laughed "Pity I don't have a pram for you to play with!" adding "That's right! When we went shopping for some of your frocks and baby stuff, we went for a meal in a café and spotted June with her sister and she'd a large pink pram!" as he gulped and said, "Yes I saw it last night when she got me to bring skirts and dresses down to play with Pam!" as they laughed "And Pammy doesn't realize that June had it upstairs?" as he shook her head, as they added "You're afraid of her dressing baby up too?" as he nodded, "That would be terrible!"

They asked, "Has she spied your baby-pee-pee?" as he nodded, "Several flaming times!" adding "When she told me she'd get Mum to re-enact everything she'd done to me, but with her standing beside me, I protested, but she'd see my willy! And next thing she'd pulled my panties down and pulled me over to the window to do curtsies to the back houses!" as they screeched. He added as he blushed "June pulled my panties down to show her, my baby-pee-pee too!" as they laughed.

Brenda giggled, "We'll maybe have to try and get a large pram for baby Lucy here!" as Claire screeched "What for him to push?" but Brenda laughed "If it's big enough and we can modify it, we could maybe pop Lucy into it, to get the full look and feel of his baby pram!" as she screeched "Oh that would be fab, taking baby walkies, around the garden, then the street, then to the shops!" as Brenda gurgled "Not to mention shopping around the town to use his handbag and purse around the shops, in a lovely baby dress!" as Claire screeched "Oh that would be fun!"

as he sobbed "Please don't expose big baby Tom?" as he got more hugs and kisses from them. They eventually get him out of his nappies and back into the panties and dressed as a boy again to join his mates.

Pam deputizes her Mum to check he's wearing panties to play footy

Although Tom had been wearing Pam's panties for a few weeks now, she had thought of a new embarrassment for him, for when she was out, and he wanted to go and play football with his mates. Tom still found it embarrassing having to ask Pam when he wanted to go out to play with his mates, "Please Pammy! Can I wear your pretty panties out to play football, with my friends!" with her giving the reply "As long as you don't play too rough or play swapsies, with them!" to more laughter. Pam said, to her Mum, "Mummy please pretty please?" as her Mum laughed "What dear?" as one day when Tom was out, having of course, already asked to wear her pretty pink panties out to play.

Pam said, "You know my sweet big sissy brother, is having to ask Moi, to wear my panties out, to play with his mates?" as her Mum nodded, laughing. Pam said, "Well, I'm not always here for him to ask, and am wondering, if you would deputise for me as her Mum laughed "What? He's to ask me, to go out and play in your panties?" as Pam nodded but said, "It would be good, when he does, you say, 'Well let me see them!' and have him drop his trousers, to let you see his pretties!" as her Mum gasped and giggled.

She said, "Isn't it embarrassing enough for him asking you?" but Pam said, "I'm sure you'll have a giggle, at my macho big brother, asking to play in my panties!" adding "You could ask 'Is he sure, he doesn't want to slip into something pretty like my skirts or frocks to play football!'" as her Mum gasped and giggled, again. His Mum laughed "I'll think about it, Miss Bossy Boots!" as Pam kissed her and said, "Thanks Mummy! I'm sure it will be a laugh for both of us, especially, if you look out and see him playing in the street, with his mates and know how pretty the panties he's wearing. You could shout out "Tom! Don't be getting too sweaty! I've just washed those things!" as her Mum said, "No way! I wouldn't do that in front of his mates!" as Pam giggled, "Spoilt sport!" Anyway a few days later, Pam Says, to Tom "Upstairs a tick?" as he followed her up to her room, of course mincing with his handbag and carrying his dolly, as she asked, "Are you wearing my pretty yellow panties?" and saw him blush and nod "Yes Pammy!" as she laughed "Well I just realized! I might not always be here, for you to ask, to go out and play in your pretties with your mates!" as he looked at her smiling face, as she said, "From now on, if I'm not here, you'll ask Mummy "Please Mummy! Can I wear Pam's pretty pink or frilly panties out, to play with my mates?" as he cried "No Pam! Don't make me, ask Mummy?" She added "You must always be holding your handbag and dolly, on your arm, when you ask and wearing my pretty apron!" as he cried "Not fair!" Pam laughed "I'm out now! So if you want to have a go today!" as said, "Wait 5 minutes and I'll let you slip downstairs to ask her!" as he cried "Not fair!" as she laughed "At lease, you'll be able to play footy, with your mates, for a while, as he huffed "Ok!" but she said, "Don't be getting my pinny dirty, or lose your handbag, or dolly, while playing footy!" as he cringed "Very funny!" as she giggled, and left and descended the stairs.

He asks to wear panties for footy, but his Mum wants to see them

Tom hated asking Pam to wear her panties out, but now he was going to have to ask his Mum. Pam said, "Mummy I'm just popping across to Julies for a while!" as her Mum kissed her bye and resumed her housework. A few minutes later Tom came down the stairs and she smiled, as she saw him in Pam's pretty apron, but not only carrying his dolly, but also Pam's pink handbag. She laughed "You off shopping Tom?" as he cringed "Very funny Mummy!" as he stammered "Mummy! Can I please wear Pam's pretty yellow panties out, to play with my mates?" as she screeched "Oh Tom! Well don't be getting her apron or handbag or your pretty dolly dirty!" as he huffed "Very funny!" and went to remove the apron. She said, "I will! but let me see them first!" as he gasped "What?" as she laughed "Just drop your trousers, a tick, till I inspect!" as he cried "Mum! Pam doesn't even make me do that!"

as she laughed "Quick! In case she comes back! Just by the living room door!" and saw him stand by the door, to stop anyone looking in and see.

He undid his trousers and holding down his apron, he let the drop, as she stepped forward and pulling his apron up, giggled, at the frilly yellow panties and laughed "You look very sweet Nancy! I'm sure they improve Tom's, football prowess!" as he cringed "Can I get my trousers up again?" and she nodded, and saw him quickly grip his trousers and pull them back up to hide his panties, as she giggled, and he blushed bright red. She said, "Off you go! Have fun and don't get them too sweaty!" as he cringed. He blushed as he pulled his trousers up and huffed "Not flaming fair, she's getting worse, embarrassing me more and more!" as his Mum hugged him and gave him a kiss on the cheek, saying, "She does have some funny ideas, to make you blush!" as he nodded, "Please stop her!" his mum laughed "What can I do! Dress her in your trousers!" as he huffed "Ha!" He removed his apron and hanging it up, as he set the handbag and dolly back on the top of the washing machine!" as his Mum teased "You didn't fancy wearing your apron or handbag out to play footy with your mates?" as he called "Don't tease Mum! She's bad enough!" as he exited. He left and his mates started playing football in the street and his Mum had a giggle as she looked out and saw him playing football, wondering whether to say, anything like "Don't get your undies too sweaty, but left it be!" His mates said, "Gosh your face is very red Tom!" as he huffed "I ran home from school as I was late!" and was looking forward to our football game.

Over the next week Pam had him doing the same thing, feeling really embarrassed and her Mum had got quite used, to seeing him drop his trousers to expose, frilly lacy panties of various colours!" However, one day Pam called Tom to her room and said, "Don't you want to wear pretty panties today?" as he said, "Are you letting me off?" but she giggled, "For that I'll pop them in your handbag here and you can get Mummy, to put them on you!" as he cried "Not fair!" She said, "Just ask Mummy the same thing as usual "Can you go out to play in Pam's pretty panties?" but when she gets you to drop your trousers, to show off your baby-pee-pee!" as he gasped and cried "Not fair Pam!"

Tom asks to wear her frilly panties, but the next day he's not to look

She continued "Just say, Pam's, put them into my handbag and you've to put them on me!" as he huffed "Not fair Pam!" as she kissed him bye and left him to it. Hence, a few minutes later, he descended the stairs and his Mum saw him in Pam's apron, carrying the handbag and dolly again and giggled, "What colour has she got you wearing today Missy!" as he cringed "Mummy! Can I please wear Pam's pretty red and white frilled panties, out to play today?" as she said, "Let me see dear!" and saw him drop his trousers as she gasped and giggled, as she saw his willy and he'd none on!" as he blushed. He huffed "She's flaming put them, into my handbag and Says, 'you've to dress me in them!'" as she screeched and said, "Come into the living room and I'll close the blinds, dearie!" She giggled, "It's been so many years since I put you into your pants and trousers!" adding with a chuckle "Although only a few weeks, since I popped you into Pam's frock, panties and apron for being a naughty boy!" as he blushed.

She laughed "But we're keeping that from Pam, aren't we?" as he nodded, vigorously, even though Pam had made him tell her all that she'd done. Tom followed her in, and he lay down on the carpet!" She laughed "I'll get your trousers off and get them from your handbag, Missy!" and saw him remove the panties from his bag and she giggled, at the ultra girly pink frilly panties. She laughed "I can't believe I'm doing this young man!" as she pulled his raised his apron and laughed at his penis on show.

She removed his trousers and giggled, as she took the panties from his handbag and fed them up his legs and then pulling him up, she pulled them up to hide his blushes. She said, "Sure you don't want a skirt or frock, to match your panties and handbag!" as he cringed "I knew she was getting worse, Mum!" as she laughed "Ok get your trousers up and you'll be ready again!" as he wondered what she meant. He pulled them up and had just zipped them

259

up and did his belt, when she laughed "Have you something to ask me Nancy?" as he gasped "Can I wear Pam's pretty red and white frilly panties to go out to play footy with my mates?" as she giggled, "Let me see sweetie!" and saw him undo his trousers and drop them again, as she giggled, "Ok! I suppose so! but no playing swapsies!" as he blushed and heard her giggle more. He pulled his trousers up again and removing Pam's apron and handbag, he set them on the washing machine, as he called "Bye Mum!" and left to join his mates. Pam has his Mum pop him into various panties over the next few days, with her Mum telling her how embarrassed Tom is at having her put the panties onto him and her spying his baby-pee-pee. Pam giggled, "You could tease Nancy about the size of his baby-pee-pee and ask why he calls it that for a bit more fun!" as she slapped her wrist "Naughty girl!" but took Pam up on her suggestion and so next day she asked, "So Tom! Why do you call this, 'your baby-pee-pee'?" as he cried "Not you Mummy!" He stammered "Because it's only the size of a little baby boys, baby-pee-pee!" as her Mum screeched "Oh Tom!" and kissed his pouting lips, with him begging "Please don't ask me that!" as she laughed at his embarrassment, saying, "Pam is so naughty!" as he nodded.

Next thing his panties hidden in his handbag are actually baby pants

The next day Pam said, "Same as yesterday, but I don't want you to see, what colour panties, Mummy is putting on you, from your handbag. Just lay back and say, "Pam doesn't want me to see, the colour panties, you're putting on me Mummy!" as he cringed "Not fair!" He huffed "I bet their ultra girly!" as she laughed "I'm sure, Mummy will tell you at some time?", but promise me, you'll wear them out to play, with your mates or else someone might let slip at school!" as he begged "Please don't Pammy?" She giggled, "Ok Missy!" as she pulled him up and said, "Wait till I've gone and then down with my handbag and ask Mummy!" as she kissed him bye and descended the stairs, kissing her Mum bye, as she sped over to Julies. Tom descended in her apron carrying his handbag and dolly and said, to his giggling Mum "Mum! She's getting worse!" adding "She doesn't want me to know, what colour panties, you're putting on me and Says, I'm not to look!" Her Mum laughed "Oh Tom!" as she took his handbag and said, "Get into the living room, close the curtains and get your trousers down and off!" as he entered the living toom and got himself ready. She opened the handbag and reaching in, saw a lacy pair of turquoise, panties and said, "Just lie back dolly!" as he huffed "Funny! I bet they're really girly!" She smiled and pulled them up his legs, laughing "I remember pulling your underpants up as a little boy!"

He blushed, at her raising the panties up his legs and over his penis, blushing herself, as she spied his little baby-pee-pee. She laughed "They're something similar to what you've worn before!" as he blushed and felt her pull his trousers up, saying, reach up as she pulled them over his panties and did them up for him. He stood up and asked, "Can I please wear those panties out to play footy with my mates?" as she laughed "Repeat, but say, 'pretty lacy turquoise panties' Ok!" and heard him say, "Can I please wear my pretty lacy turquoise panties out to play footy with my mates?" as she laughed and kissed him and said, "Off you go sweetie!" as he blushed and sped out.

The next day, Tom had entered the living room to wait with his trousers down, still in the apron with his handbag and dolly, when his Mum opened the handbag and reaching in, she gasped, as she saw a large pair of plastic baby pants and giggled, "Oh Pam!" Tom cried "She's not there, is she Mummy?" as she laughed "No dear!" wondering whether she should run up and get a proper pair of Pam's panties or not. She wondered should she embarrass her son, with the baby pants. She laughed "Wait till I get her, but peering into the bag, saw rubber gloves in her size, nappies, gel and talcum powder, wondering would she have the nerve or not!" She entered and saw Tom lying there with the pink apron covering his naked lower body and said, "No peeking darling!" as he saw her enter, with the handbag dangling from her elbow, but not seeing the panties!" as he huffed "Hurry up and I'll get my trousers on!" He called "Hurry up!" as she giggled, "Patients dear!" adding "I've never heard a big boy plead to get back into girly panties!" as he blushed.

His Mum decides to keep him indoors in his nappies and plastic pants

She smiled "Look away dear!" and saw him look to the ceiling, as she took the plastics and stretching them, pulled them up his legs and giggled, as she fed them to his thighs!"

She said, "Just reach your botty up and I'll get them over your baby-pee-pee!"

Tom huffed "Please don't call it that and hurry up!" as he felt her pulling the panties up over his bum and penis. She laughed "There you're covered!" as she looked and laughed at his penis, on show, through the see through, plastic baby pants. She added "Though! I think you'll need some extra bits, to hide your baby-pee-pee!" Tom pulled himself up and then cried "Oh no! The witch! Not baby pants!" as she giggled, and pulling the nappies out of the handbag, said, "You mustn't call your sweet sister, that name!" She said, "Lay back down and I'll see to hiding and protecting your pee-pee!" as he sobbed "Not fair, Mum! Don't put me into nappies! Please don't?" as she laughed "Just to hide, in case someone looks!" as he cried "They'd better not see me!" She pushed him back down and pulling the plastics down, to his thighs and laughed as she took rubber gloves and pulled them onto her hands and said, "And there I thought my nappy changing days were over!" as he blushed sobbing "Not flaming fair!" She took the gel and spreading some onto her hands, she applied it to his loins and penis, as he gasped "Not baby gel, too!" as she giggled, "I can't remember the last time I diapered you, young man!"

He blushed "Not flaming fair!" but she took a dummy, out of his handbag and popped it into his mouth, laughing "I can't believe, I'm doing this! It's well you're still young and still have a tiny pee-pee!" as he cringed and sobbed "Not fair!" through the dummy.

She took some talcum powder and shook it over his front, laughing at his penis with the gel and powder over it, as she took a disposable and stuck it down over him, saying, "At least that hides baby's pee-pee or is it baby's baby-pee-pee and taking his dummy out looked at him, as he cringed "It's baby's baby-pee-pee, Mummy!" to more giggles and laughter.

She rolled him over and said, "I'd better get some gloves on for Baby's botty!" and taking the plastic gloves couldn't believe they fitted, but took more gel and applied it to his bottom cheeks and underneath laughing "This is funny, Tom!" as he blushed "Not for me!" as she sprinkled more gel, over his bottom and then added the powder and finally the disposable nappy. She asked, "What about the diaper?" as he pleaded "Please don't Mum! They'll see the bulge in my trousers!" as she laughed. She then pulled his plastic baby pants up over the two disposables and saw him make a face as he saw them through the clear plastic material. He However, surprised her by pulling on the panties, he'd on earlier and heard her laugh "I suppose they hide your plastics and nappies!" as he nodded, not thinking that they'd help protect his trousers too. She laughed "Let's get baby Tom's trousers up, over his nappies and we'll let baby go, but you'd better not play with your little mates!" as Pam might let something slip, so I think that while in nappies, you'd better play as Nancy and help me in the house or back garden.

Pam and June wonder if her Mum will diaper him and June pops around

However, she then asked, "Isn't baby going to ask me something?" as he cringed and said, "Please Mummy, can baby Tom go out and play footy with his mates in his nappy and plastic baby pants?" She screeched "Oh Tom! You are funny!" as she kissed his pouting lips, saying, "It's been years since I kissed you properly!" He blushed and she said, "Sorry! Baby Tom! You'd better not go out in your nappies and plastics and just stay dressed as Nancy, to help me with housework or play dollies!"

He cringed and said, "Thanks Mummy!" He was relieved that he'd not to join his mates playing, as he was sure Pam had a trick to play on him and embarrass him in front of his mates. She handed him Pam's yellow frock and said,

"Just pull that on over your boy's clothes!" and saw him take the dress and pull it over his head and slide his arms into the sleeves. However, he then surprised her by pulling on Pam's apron with his handbag and dolly attached as she laughed "I thought Pam was letting you off your dolly!" as he said, "Ha!" as she smiled at him now back in the pink apron, with the handbag dangling from his arm and holding the dolly in the other hand.

Of course, Pam was giggling away, this time at June next door's, wondering if her Mum had actually taken the bate and babied her big brother, or just ran upstairs and stolen a pair of her panties, to replace the baby things, she'd left him. She waited, but didn't see any sign of him exiting to join his mates and said, "I don't know if this is a good sign or not!" adding "If Mummy did actually diaper my big brother, she wouldn't be mean and make him go and play footy with his mates and would keep him in doors!" as June laughed and nodded. June said, "I'll pop around to speak to your Mum and see what's happening with baby!" as Pam laughed "I'll pop over to Julie but keep an eye out to see if he goes out, to play or not!" His Mum heard a bell ring and said, "Upstairs, but no changing till I say!" as he scampered up the stairs. He threw himself down on the bed sobbing at the trick, Pam had played, but that his Mum had actually, babied him. He wanted to pull the trousers down and rip the baby pants and nappies off but dreaded what his Mum might do or let Pam do.

His Mum opened the door to see June standing there, asking "How's things been going with Tom and Pam recently? I missed them both when they returned from school!" as his Mum invited her in, wondering had Pam told, what she'd done. She took her into the sitting room and June asked, "Is he here?" as his Mum called "Tom! June is here!" and heard him mince down the stairs, still wearing Pam's apron with his handbag and dolly over his arms and entered crying "Mum close the blinds?" as his Mum said, "Down on the floor!" as June giggled, "Oh I see Pam has added a handbag to his dolly to mince about the house!" His Mum nodded, "Because you made him wheel his dolly out back as Nancy and then that meant he could do the laundry with his handbag, she argued he could carry a handbag too!" as June laughed "Quite right Tom! I mean Nancy! You look so much sweeter, mincing with your handbag and dolly!" His Mum laughed "She also argued, he wouldn't lose his dolly, so much, with his handbag tied to his apron and so we won't be tempted to call out, about him and his dolly!"

June sends Tom out in his nappies to play without his Mum realizing

June added "Or Handbag now!" as his Mum laughed and nodded, as she added "Pam's such a thoughtful girl!" He blushed and stammered "To please you and Aunty June, I'll stay and play dollies with you!" June gasped "Gosh I thought he was footy mad!" as his Mum laughed "I think that's waning and he sees how much fun, dollies and helping with housework is!" as he blushed even more.

Then Pam came in the side door and laughed as she entered and saw June there as her Mum laughed "That wasn't funny young lady!" as Tom looked at her scowling as Pam laughed "Mum! Did you or not?" and said, to June "I played a trick on Tom and Mummy earlier, but can't say, what it is yet!" June laughed "What?" as Pam pretended to keep it a secret from her "Sorry Mum's the word!" and his Mum said, "He's wearing the panties you supplied earlier today!" She laughed "Spoilt sport!" but as June's here 'He's said, he'll stay and play dollies inside, instead of joining his mates outside'!" Pam laughed "Funny you should say, that! I'm going over to play dollies with Julie and Tina! Want to join us Nancy!" as he said, "Not a flaming chance!" as she laughed "Suit yourself and shot off to join the girls.

His Mum asked, "Can I get you something to drink?" as June smiled "A coffee dear!" as she asked Tom and heard him say, "A Coke Mum!" as she left the room. She put the kettle on and then said, "Just off to the loo a tick!" as she ran up the stairs and into the bathroom. June said, "Here Tom! I think your Mummy's being a bit cruel!" as she took Pam's apron and pulled it over his head, as he gasped "What?" as he felt his apron coming over his head, followed by the frock, and felt her lead him out the room and up to the front door, as she said, "Make sure you play

with your mates, for at least half an hour! Ok or else I let slip to Tina!" as he sobbed "Oh no!" He saw her open the door and felt her shove him out into the porch. He gasped as he saw the outer door and his mates playing. He shot out the door to the front!" as he gasped "Oh no!" as he froze, but heard June say, "Ten seconds to join your mates or else!" She saw him blush, as he ran down the driveway and heard his mates call "Right Tom! Come and join us for footy!" as June quietly closed the inner front door and slipped back into the sitting room, closing the door partly. His Mum came downstairs and called "Drinks will be just a minute!" as she entered the kitchen and got their coffees and a glass of Coke for Tom. She heard June say, "That is a pretty apron and even better with the handbag and dolly", teasing Tom, thinking he was still there. She poured the coffee out into the two cups and got the Coke out to pour for Tom and soon was wheeling the trolley into the room. She looked and saw June who said, "He said, he'd to go to the loo or up to his room for something!" as she handed June her coffee and sat down to drink her own. She called "Tom your Coke and biscuits are here!" as June said, "How's things been progressing Doreen?" as she said, "Oh Pam is such a tease and loves embarrassing him! but I don't think I should let her be so naughty!" as June laughed "It won't help and he seems to be so much better behaved, these days, with helping with the housework and playing dollies and stuff!" as his Mum laughed and nodded.

Pam wheels her dolly bye and tells him to stay out playing footy till 5pm

Meanwhile Tom was playing away with his mates, hating the feel of the gel on the plastic baby pants and hoping they wouldn't hear any sound from them as he ran about the street. He was playing ok, kicking the ball and even scoring, when he heard Pam's voice nearby. She called "Tom! Mum Says, for being a good boy, you can play till 5 today!" as he blushed at having to play even longer in his baby pants and nappies. However, he then saw her with her pink doll's pram and another baby doll in it. His mates teased "Pam you still playing dollies?" as she laughed "You boys don't know what you're missing out, playing dollies!" as they laughed "Bug off Pam!" She then took a dummy and put it into the doll's mouth and said, loudly "Baby Nancy, I'm sure you're Mummy will come around later to play with you and wheel you about!" as she smiled, to the boys and said, "Don't worry! I'll change baby Nancy's nappies later!" as he tried, not to look over to her with her gurgling with laughter at his embarrassment, wondering had their Mum actually put him into plastic baby pants and nappies or not. However, she wheeled the pram away from the boys, but then said, "Tom! Come here a tick!" as he gasped and said, "Pam! Mum said, you'd to leave me alone, when playing footy!" as his mates wondered, why he wasn't hitting her, or calling her names. She said, "Just a minute!" as he said, "I'll be back in a minute!" as they called "Tell her to scram!" as she smiled and saw him walk over to her.

She asked, "Did Mummy like my little joke! Turn around a tick!" as he begged "Please don't embarrass me?" as she reached her hand down and felt the plastic baby pants and gasped "Oh fab! Did Mummy completely diaper you?" as he said, "Just 1 disposable on my front and plastics!" as she whispered, "Why don't you ask me softly, to play footy?"

as he gasped and cried "Not fair Pam!" as he looked away from his mates and stammered "Can I please play footy in my baby plastics and nappy?" as she reached her hand down and felt his front, as she gurgled "Oh fab!" and reaching up kissed his lips, as one mate spied her and called "Yuk! Pam kissed Tom on the lips!" as they called "Yuk!" as she laughed "Sure you boys don't want a kissy, too?" as they said, "You'd better watch it Pam or else!" His mates called "Tom! Tell your stupid little sister to bug off and get away from our game, with her stupid doll!" as she laughed "What was that Tom?" You know Mummy told you off the last time you were nasty to me!" as he blushed bright red and said, "Leave her guys she's more trouble than she's worth!" as she smiled and left him be, wheeling her doll's pram over to Julie's house. Pam then came in and called "Hi Mummy!" as her Mum said, "Pam June's here!" as she called "Hi! Aunty June!" as June kissed her saying, "Hi Pam!" as her Mum laughed and heard her say, "Mum here a tick!" as she took her out to the kitchen, asking "Did you like my joke?" as her Mum

said, "That wasn't funny! I hope you didn't expect me to – you know what?" as she whispered "I got a pair from your drawer and put them onto him!" as Pam laughed "Spoilt sport!" as she said, "I hope he asked sweetly?" as her Mum nodded, "We'll continue when June's not here!"

His Mum realizes Tom's out playing and tries to get him in

His Mum returned to the room and saw June go over to the window and said, "There he is playing stupid footy again!" as her Mum gasped "He's not?" as she asked, "Why not?" as she said, "I thought he'd gone up to his room and was staying in today!" as she looked out at the boys playing footy and spotted Tom. June asked, "What's up dear?" as she said, "Tom wasn't meant to go out today!" as June laughed "Did you want to punish him and stop him playing with his mates?" as his Mum blushed "Something like that!" as June laughed "Do you want me to go and bring him back in?" as her Mum nodded. His Mum then saw June exit, but a few minutes later. She laughed "She's taking her time!" as she saw her call him over. She said, "Your Mum wants you back, but I want you out, till 5! Just tell her, you wanted to play on, and she can have a word with you, later!" as he blushed and she said, "No matter what! You stay playing baby football till 5, ok?" and saw her return back in. She called "I told you wanted him back now, but the naughty boy, said, he was having fun and you can have a word with him later!" as her Mum gasped.

His Mum said, "I'll pop out and get him in!" as June said, "Oh Doreen don't be mean!" as she exited and opening the front door she stood in the porch and shouted "Tom come on! I've Coke and stuff you wanted!" as he heard and knew he couldn't and called "It's ok Mum! I'm playing here till five!" as she gasped wondering and then realized Pam was making him. June asked, "Wouldn't he come in for you?" as his Mum smiled and shook her head, as June asked, "Want me to have a stern word and try and get him in?" as his Mum said, "Better not! I think Pam's given him orders to stay out, no matter what!" as June gasped "The little tyrant!" His Mum nodded, "I know! He's scared stiff of her!" as they laughed. Pam better not out him to them!" as June laughed "Look she hasn't said, a word at school and nobody around here, not even Tina know about Nancy!" as she laughed "I know, but he must be so embarrassed!" as they both sat down. She rang the bell and Julie's Mum answered and saw Pam with her doll's pram and giggled, "I'll just get Julie and Tina!" as Pam laughed "I just tried to get my big bro Tom there to play, but he said, maybe after his footy, him and his mates, will join us for dollies!" as her Mum screeched and looking out spied Tom, playing with his mates in the street. She laughed "He isn't half red!" Pam laughed "He wouldn't get so red if he joined Tina and us playing dollies!" as her Mum laughed "Wonderful tease Pam!" as she saw a different baby doll and saw Pam take it's dummy out and pop a baby bottle into its mouth. She laughed "What's your dolly called and heard her say, "Baby Nancy!" as she then heard Tina call "Hi Pam! I'll just get my doll's pram too!" as Julie laughed "Mummy's trying to borrow another dolly pram for me, so the three of us can play Mummy's better together!" Pam got Julie and Tina then to wheel their dollies, but especially got them to carry or wheel baby dolls with nappies and baby plastics and talk loudly about changing their nappies later!" as she mentioned changing Baby Nancy's nappies later too. Tom was hating every minute and wet his disposable at least once on the front, hoping his plastic baby pants wouldn't show the wet patch.

SOME GIRLS ENTRAP SOME SIX YEAR OLD BOYS

A group of girls plan to entrap some young boys to play Sissy football

Summary

A group of young girls hear about sissy Tom in his frocks and nappies and decide to try and get some big six-year old boys who normally play footy together in the street to be sissies too. They enlist some bigger girls to help them and ask each boy to show them how to play football. One by one they are trapped into frocks and some eventually nappies.

Details

Then **a group of young 5 and 6-year old girls** hear about Tom's dressing up and think it would be fun to see the boys they know playing dollies and dress-up and under their control. They see about **6 boys, the same age as them, playing football in the street** and decide to try and get them all to be under their thumb. They wait for one Saturday morning and seeing one boy in the street, a couple of girls ask him to show them how to play football. He asks, "Are you forming a team or something?" and they giggle and nod. They say, they've a ball in the back garden of their friend's house. He joins them and see a couple of other young girls in aprons with their handbags. He sees the ball and running over to it tries to show them how to play football, with dribbling and passing the ball. However, then some slightly older girls appear from the house and get him down onto his back. He then sees a girly apron and soon it's tied around him, but then a handbag is slid up and tied around his arm. He's sobbing away trying to get them off, but to no avail. They let him up and he's given the choice of playing Sissy football with the girls or being taken into the street. He of course wants to stay and is given a disguise of a headscarf, but then ribbons and then a skirt. He's taken into the house to play dollies and more dress up.

However, he's then threatened with much more embarrassments, if he makes a noise to warns him, as a mate is taken out the back for the same treatment. This continues until all six boys are in the house in frocks and aprons, holding handbags and they are then taken out to the back garden to play Sissy football with the giggling girls.

When let go and allowed to dress in their own clothes, except for a pair of panties each, they all run home, really embarrassed and realizing they're under the control of all those girls but keep it quiet from their Mum's and Dad's. However, one boy runs home and blurts out to his Mum what the girls did. He wants her to tell the girls off, but she just laughs and when told, she gets him to show her the panties, giggling away. She ends up treating him as a part-time daughter, even introducing him to the little girl next door to play dollies and dress up with. She even brings one or two of the boys in to play dress-up with her boy, but then tells them she knows about the girl's trick and has them play dress up and dollies with her new daughter. Eventually she takes her boy and the young girl

next-door and a few aprons around to the other boys Mum's to tell them what happened to their macho boys. The girl threatens the boy with telling lots of their mates and other girls on him and get the boy to slip into the girly apron in front of his Mum.

One group of girls took it one step further and decided to get about 6 or 7 young boys dressed up as girls and acting as sissies. They waited till one Saturday when they knew the boys normally played footy in the streets, letting their parents go shopping in town.

The girls trap James

A few young girls saw a boy James and approached him, saying, "Could you spare a few minutes to show us how to play football?" as he laughed "You girls playing football?" as they nodded, and said, "Just in our back garden over the road?" They said, "Some of the other boys have been trying to teach us, but say, you're better!" as he smiled and said, "Just a few minutes I've to play footy around the corner!" as he followed them down the street a bit and then over to a house and entered the garden.

He took the ball that was there and started kicking it and dribbling with in and said, "All you do is take the ball and pass it to some boys, or girls on your team!" adding "Or dribble it past them!" as he then saw some other girls appear in aprons and heard some giggles. He said, "Oh! There's more of you wanting to play?" as he said, "You girls don't need those flipping aprons to play football!" as the girls say, "Oh what about protecting your pretty skirts or dresses!"

However, he saw some more and was just kicking the ball again, when he felt some arms around him and he was soon down on the ground, calling "What's going on girls?" but next thing felt something being fed over his neck and up his arm and saw them tying some string around him and then was let up and cried "What's this girls?" as he saw a frilly apron down his body, but a handbag dangling from his elbow, tied to the apron. He tried to get them off, but to no avail.

He heard the girls giggling and sobbed "Please get it off me?" but then heard the young girls calling "We're playing Sissy Football!" adding "Do you want to stay here and play Sissy Football with us girls, with handbags and aprons, or will we take you out to show your friends?" as he gasped and cried "No don't show me off!" as they giggled, "So you want to play Sissy football with us?" as he nodded, and soon they added ribbons and bows to his hair, followed by a skirt and then removed his trousers and pants to add panties causing him to sob some more.

They had him kicking the ball a bit and then led him into the house where a mother laughed "Oh James! What have they done to you?" as he sobbed "Look! Please take it off me Mrs!" as she laughed "Oh now! Just sit down and no one will see you?"

She then asked, "So James! Do you have a sister?" as he huffed "No!" as they giggled, and asked, "Do you normally help your Mummy with housework?" and shook his head, as the girls giggled, saying, "We normally slip into a pretty apron to help Mummy!"

The girls then said, "You are going to ask your Mum to help you with housework and to get you an apron?" as he cried "No way!" as he huffed "Daddy nor me don't help!" as they laughed "Maybe we should do this to his Dad too!" as he huffed "He'll give it to you, when he finds out what you've done to me!" as they laughed.

However, then saw lots of dollies and cried "Don't make me play dollies?" as they giggled, and a young girl held one out and said, "If you are naughty and don't play dollies or do what we say, then we have a few extras to help

you obey!" A bigger girl then said, "At some point we will pop your dummy in and you've to be quiet! If you drop it or call out, then it will probably be nappies for you!" as he nodded, "Ok I won't say!" as they laughed and handed him another doll to play with. The girls had got lots of frocks together, in varying sizes, some from their wardrobes, others from younger girls dress up boxes, donated by their cousins and some older girls, from when they were younger.

The girls trap Clive

They then held up a pretty frock in his size and he cried "Not a dress too?" but soon was handed a petticoat and the handbag and apron removed, threatening him with nappies, if he tried to run and soon, he was in the frock. He huffed "What?" as one girl opened a handbag and removed a pink baby's dummy as he cried "Oh no!" as she said, "Suck or else!" and soon had it in his mouth, with the girls giggling and tears rolling down his cheeks. She then produced a baby bottle with milk, and he cried "No not that! Not fair!" as the dummy was removed and they said, "Drink baby!" and soon he was drinking from the baby bottle as they giggled, "Can baby guess what the next thing is!" as they removed his bottle and he huffed "You wouldn't dare?" as they nodded, "Diaper our little baby girl in nappies and plastic baby pants!" as he sobbed "You wouldn't dare! You'd see my willy!" as they laughed and nodded, However, most of the girls had gone out to trap their next victim.

John had joined up with his mate Martin and they were walking up the street together. The girls saw them and decided to wait, as they saw another guy on his own Clive further down wave to them. They approached him and said, "Hi what's your name?" He said, I'm Clive why?" as they said, "Us girls are wanting an expert to show us how to play football?" as he shook his head "Why don't you girls come and watch us boys playing and we'll show you!" as one girl said, "Your friend James showed us a bit, but said, "You would be better at it! Just for a few minutes!" as he heard and said, "Have you a ball?" as one girl said, "It's in our back garden!" as he said, "Ok! Where?" as they led him to the bottom of the street and around the bend.

He was asking "You girls forming a team or something?" as they laughed "Yea!" as he walked up the driveway and around the back. He saw a few girls there and the ball. He ran over to the ball and said, "All you do is this!" as he started kicking the ball about. He then saw some girls in aprons and said, "You don't need those aprons!" as he heard laughter and then felt arms around him and soon again was draped in a frilly apron and a handbag on his elbow, sobbing and saying, "I'll tell Mummy!" as he was given the choice of Sissy Football or going out to show off in the street. Once again, he was put into hair ribbons, a skirt and then his trousers and pants removed and replaced by panties. He was sobbing "Not fair girls!" as he had to kick the football about to girls all with aprons and carrying handbags too. However, then he was taken into the house and saw the girl's Mummy who laughed "Oh I see they have you dressed up!" as he initially into the front room away from James and shown dollies and asked, "Do you have a sister?" as he nodded, Amanda, she's only four! She's not here! Is she?" as they laughed and a girl shouted, "Come in Amanda!" as he huffed "Funny! She went shopping with Mum!" as they laughed. They told him he was going to start helping his Mum and sister with housework and get an apron to wear, as he tried to say, "No way!" He was then taken into the back room and gasped as he saw James sitting there in an apron, ribbons and frock carrying a handbag and huffed "they got you too?" as he nodded, "Not flaming fair!" He huffed "You could have warned me?" as the girls giggled, "James said, they threatened me, if I was bad!" as he huffed "What with? You're already in a frock and ribbons!" as the girls laughed and heard James say, "They're threatening to treat us as flaming babies!" as he gasped and cried "What?" Next thing a girl took a dummy and said,

The girls trap Andy

"Suck or else!" and soon he had a dummy in his mouth, but then a baby bottle was taken from a handbag and shoved in his mouth to more giggles. They then laughed "Can you guess what is next for any naughty baby?" as he cried

"Not nappies?" as they laughed and "Baby plastics!" as they showed both boys the baby pants as they cringed at the thought. One of them said, "We have a name for your thingy!" as he huffed "What?" and they giggled, "From now on you call it your baby-pee-pee!" as he cried "No don't! Not fair!" as they added "And when asked why? you must say, 'Because it's the size of a little baby boys, baby-pee-pee!'" to more giggles and screeches. He sobbed "Not flaming fair!" He then was shown the frock and begging them to no avail, ended up in the dress too. A girl called "Guess what's next for baby if he's naughty! Here in front of all us girls and some of your mates?" as he cried "Not nappies?" to screeches of laughter. They soon had him out of his skirt and into a frock and so the two boys were now sitting beside each other in pretty frocks, with ribbons in their hair and holding a handbag and dolly each.

The Mum left the room and a little girl said, "Little girls, like kissy-kissy!" as she kissed 1st one boy and then the other!" as both of them said, "Get off!" but she then said, "So you didn't like kissing me?" but then made them gasp, as she said, "If you don't want to be taken out the front, to the street, give each other a kissy-kissy!" as they cried "Please don't!" to screeches from the bigger girls and then saw them tentatively approach each other and kiss on the cheek, but the girls called "On the lips!" and soon had given each other a quick peck to cheers!" as she called "10 seconds or it's the front!" and soon had given each other a long kiss to more laughter. Meanwhile the girls saw another boy Larry and tried to get him to teach them footy, but he said, "Bug off girls! I'm off to play footy with my mates!" as he ran on away from them. They laughed "We'll have to punish Larry, for not joining us to play Sissy Football!"

However, they saw another boy Andy and said, "We're trying to learn football and your friends James and Clive, both showed us a bit, but said, you were better at it than them!" as he smiled "Did they?" He had his own ball and said, "Just watch me!" as he kicked the ball, but heard them say, "Another girl is in our back garden, wanting to learn!" as he asked, "Where?" and followed them down and into the garden. The same events followed and he was eventually led into the front room and asked did he have any brothers or sisters and said, an older brother and he'd give it to them girls for dressing him up, as a flaming sissy!" as the girls giggled, and soon he was slid into a pretty frock. Andy is then led into the back room and gasps "Oh no!" as he saw the other two boys in frocks and ribbons. He too was handed a handbag like the other two.

The girls asked, "Well boys what do you think of your pretty ribbons and handbags?" as they huffed "Please take them?" as the girls giggled, and removed all three boys ribbons, as the boys were even more embarrassed at sitting there in frocks as boys. The girls laughed "See boys! If we take you outside now! You'll look a real sissy, and everyone will recognise your faces, but at least with ribbons or headscarves, you'll just look like us girls and probably not be recognised!" They asked, "Want your hair ribbons back?" and saw the embarrassed blushing boys nod and then have to ask for their hair to be prettied up!" in the room of giggling girls, who delighted in telling them to pretty each other's hair up, for their girlfriends and laughed as they adding ribbons to each other's hair.

The girls trap Larry, but he gets it worse

The little girl then said, "Now tell each other you're a big sissy boy, who loves to play sissy football!" as they gasped "Oh no!" as she said, "It could be walkies!" as they said, "I'm a big sissy, who loves to play sissy football!" as they girls screeched again. She of course then got all three boys to kiss each other, to sobs from the boys, but screeches from the girls at the boys kissing each other and telling each other how pretty they were. The guys wondered where the other three were and one guy, Fred said, "I'll go and call at Pete's and James!" and Larry said, "I'll call at Andy's!" as they said, "They might have had to go to town, with their parents!" as they nodded. Larry again saw the girls and asked, "You girls seen our friends, as they said, "They came down to show us, how to play footy!" as he huffed "Yea sure!" as they nodded, "If you don't believe us, come and see?" as one girl ran on, to try and spring the trap. He followed the girl asking, "How come, you've started playing football?" as she laughed "Oh we've seen you boys, playing and think we can do better!" as he laughed "You must be joking! In your skirts and dresses! No

chance!" as she laughed. She led him in and up to the back garden, where he saw some girls kicking the ball about and thought "Where's the guys?" as one said, "Mum's got them some tea and biscuits, for helping us play footy!"

He was passed the ball and soon was saying, "All you do is this!" The door opened and he thought it would be his mates, but then saw some older girls in aprons and said, "Get the guys out and we'll show you girls, how it's done?" but soon was down on his back trying to kick out, but to no avail and soon was tied into the apron and handbag, threatening them when he got out of it they were dead. They gave him the choice of taken out or stay to play sissy football and of course he said, "Sissy Football!" He was kicking the ball to the girls in aprons and handbags, but still threatening them, when he got out and dressed, he'd get them. They decided to teach him a lesson for his threats and he was led into the front room, as the guys all with dummies in their mouths, realized it was Larry and he was soon sitting down amongst the dolls and had to play with a couple, initially throwing them away saying, "Bug off! I'm not playing dolls!" as they laughed and soon his hands were tied up to his apron and he huffed "What now?" They said, "See we've a worse punishment for any naughty boy, who threatens us!" as he huffed "What?" as a little girl opened a handbag and removed the dummy!" as he cried "No way!" but soon had it in his mouth, followed by the baby bottle, as he cried "Not fair!" and broke down in tears. The girls then said, "Guess what's next!" as he huffed "Not nappies?" as they nodded but whereas the other boys were only threatened, they then showed him the nappies and plastic baby pants and he cried "No please don't?" as he sobbed. He was laid back and his panties removed, to giggles, as the Mum wondered about the young girls seeing him but was assured it would be fun. He was told to call it his baby-pee-pee, when asked and then to say, it's the size of a little babies. Next the bigger girls and the Mum were rubbing baby gel into his bottom and after applying talc to him, they applied the disposable nappy. They then turned him over and he'd the same thing done, to his front, blushing away as the gel and talk were applied and then the disposable and then the diaper and finally large plastic baby pants. They all cheered and he was threatened with being taken out in his nappies, if he played up and he promised to be good, as he was told his string

Larry in his nappies and plastic is led in to see the other 3 boys in dresses

will be cut, for a dress and he huffed "Ok not fair!" as he was shown a big dress, but then on holding his arms up, to be undressed down to the nappies, felt the dress being fed down his arms and over his head, but then cried "Oh no!" as he saw the dress was really short and showed off his nappies and plastic baby pants. His hands were tied up and he was stood up and led into the next room where he cried "Oh no! Not fair girls!" as he saw the 3 boys gasp and giggle at his nappies and baby pants, on show, under the short dress. They laughed and teased "Whose a big sissy baby?" as the girls screeched and said, "See what happens when a boy is naughty!" as she asked, "tell the boys Larry or should we call him Baby Lisa!" as the girls giggled. He huffed "You flaming treated me as a baby and put me back into flaming nappies and baby pants!" as the guys gasped "You mean they even rubbed gel and powdered you?" as the girls nodded, and held up their little fingers. The girls asked him "What do you call your thingy in your nappies?" as he cried "Don't make me girls?" but sobbed "It's my baby-pee-pee!" Why as he sobbed it's just the size of a little baby boys!" to more giggles from the girls and laughter from the boys. She said, "Any playing up and we change baby Lisa's nappy in the back garden with your friends looking on and maybe even helping to change your nappy!" as him and the boys gasped "No way!" to more laughter and Larry saying, "I'll be a good baby!" as they all giggled. He huffed "How did they get you guys into frocks?" as they cringed the same way as you. The girls said, "You boys are all going to start helping your Mummies about the house in a pretty apron!" as the guys gasped "Not fair!" as the girls giggled.

The girls trap Ian and Freddy

Then the little girl said, "Ribbons out girls!" and the boys all had their ribbons removed and begged for them back and each boy had to take turns putting ribbons into the other boys hair, until they were all looking girly again!"

as the little girl said, "Kissy time!" as she kissed the 4 boys, to more laughter, as Larry said, "yuk!" but the others knew something worse was to come, as the girl giggled, "Oh Larry I mean Lisa, You don't like kissing a girl! You can have fun kissing your other sissies!" as he gasped and cried "No don't!" but she said, "Some big baby might be taken out into the street, if they're naughty to show off their nappies!" as he cringed and soon the 4 boys were kissing each-other to more giggles and screeches from the girls and the Mum. The girl then said, "tell each other you're a sissy boy and love playing sissy football!" as the boys cringed and started telling each-other they were sissy boys.

Meanwhile the girls had gone to try and get the other two Ian and Freddy. The boys had called at the houses, with one Dad, answering the door and saying, Peter was out playing footy somewhere!" as the boys said, "Yea he normally plays with us, but we haven't seen him!" as the dad shut the door. The two boys were walking back, when the girls saw them and heard them ask "You, seen, any of our friends?" as the girls said, "Yea some of them are teaching us girls, to play football!" as they said, "Yea sure! You girls playing football?"

as the girls whispered among each-other and nodded, whispering "We should be able to do 2 at once!" Hence, the boys were led up to the garden, where they saw some girls, kicking the ball about and ran over and Ian said, "You girls don't know anything! You just do this!

Come on Freddy let's show them!" as Fred ran to the other end and was passed the ball, as Ian asked, "Where's the other guys?" as the girls said, "Mum's invited them in for cake and biscuits!" not realizing the boys were inside, sucking dummies and Larry being given a baby bottle of milk, by a giggling young girl, occasionally tapping his plastics at the front, making him blush. The boys saw several girls appear in aprons and called "You don't need aprons and it's easier to play footy in trousers, than those silly skirts or dresses!" as the girls laughed "Oh is it!" and then first Ian and then Fred were pulled down to the ground and cried "Hey girls get off!" as the aprons were tied around them and then let up and they saw the handbags on their elbows, tied to their aprons and both sobbed "Not fair girls!" as they were threatened with going out to show their friends, or would they like to stay and play Sissy football!" as they nodded, and soon were in ribbons and skirt and panties, One girl giggled, "I bet you'll enjoy those panties, when you realize the alternative!" as another girl giggled, "Nothing!" as the boys gasped and cried "No don't show off our willies?" to more giggles and screeches.

Some boys are in frocks, but others end up in nappies

They played more football with the girls in aprons and carrying their handbags and eventually led into the house to the front room. They heard laughter from the front room wondering how many girls were there, to see them. One of the guys asked, "You don't have my big sister Rachel there?" as they giggled, "Maybe!" as he sobbed "Oh no! Not fair" but then were threatened with the dummy and baby bottle and nappies, before being put into frocks and then led into the back room and gasped and then giggled, at Larry, in his baby dress and nappies, but also their other mates. All the girls giggled, and hugged themselves, with several kissing each-other. They then told the boys they could either go out to the back garden to play Sissy football in their frocks and carrying handbags, or giggling said, "Play kissy-kissy!" as the boys gasped and sobbed as Larry begged "Please girls! Get me into a big dress like them? Let me hide my nappies?" as the place erupted with laughter!" as the young girls giggled, "So you'd like to stay and play kissy-kissy, rather than go out in your nappies?" as he looked down and nodded. One guy Ian said, "Poof!" as the girls gasped and said, "For that Ian will stay and play kissy-kissy with Larry I mean Lisa!" as he cried "I didn't mean it! Sorry girls!" as they said, "Sit beside Larry and give him a nice kiss!" as he sobbed "Not in front of my mates?" as they laughed and she asked, "So girlies! Hold up your hands if you want to pop out, to play Sissy football, since your sweetly disguised as sissies! Or do you want to stay and play kissy-kissy with these two sissies here!" as they saw 3 guys hold up their hands and eventually a fourth to leave Ian and Larry in the room. The other four left and went out the back kicking the football and feeling really embarrassed at having

to play in frocks and carrying a handbag. Eventually having to mince around the garden with their handbags. The girls inside said, "Now naughty Ian what do you want to do to this sweet sissy baby here?" as he begged "Please don't make me! Sorry I called him a poof!" as they giggled, and said, "You'd better start kissy-kissy or you'll end up the same adorable outfit as baby here!" as he gasped "No way!" and soon had leaned over and kissed Larry on the cheek, but the girls called "Oh the lips!" as they both sobbed "Not fair girls!" but soon had kissed on the lips, with the girls saying, keep going till we say, stop.

The boys have to act as sissies and hold hands around the garden

Soon the boys were kissing, as a giggling Sandra removed their ribbons they sobbed "Please replace our ribbons?" to more giggles. The girls gave in and let them take ribbons and bows from their handbags to pretty up each other's hair, with more kissy-kissy, afterwards. They had to hold hands, like sweet little girls and were going to take them out to see the others, when they decided to be kind to Larry and add a longer frock to hide his nappies and plastics. However, they were told to hold hands and mince around the garden and back again. They hated it but had to then enter the garden and mince around hand in hand to gasps and giggles from the boys and girls there. Pete couldn't resist it and teased "You got your boyfriend there Ian?" as he heard giggles, but next thing he was being led into the house and tied up and the girls laughed and asked, "Well girls what should we do with our little naughty girly here?" as one girl said, "He should definitely kiss the other two!" but then heard a few girls say, "I think Pete will do it better as a baby!" as he cried "No girls don't please Not fair!" as he sobbed, but soon his frock was raised and his panties removed, to expose him to not only the giggling girls, but also his mates. The baby bag was brought over and a dummy placed in his mouth, threatening to do this in the front garden, if he drops it!" as he was put onto his front and felt the oil, being gelled over him and then the talcum powder and a disposable applied.

He was then turned to see his 2 mates looking down, laughing, but then had to tell them, it was his baby-pee-pee and the size of a little baby boys!" to more laughter. Some bigger girls then applied the gel to his front and then applied the talc, but then handed the disposable to Larry, saying, "As you're the baby expert! Apply his disposable!" as he cried "Oh no! Not fair!" as he knelt down and went to pop the nappy on!" but one of the girls giggled, and whispered to the bigger one, saying, "I'm sure the boys didn't like kissy-kissy on their lips!"

The girl screeched and told them "Alice has suggested the boys kiss his baby-pee-pee!" to a gasp from the Mother and some girls, but then nodded, and said, "Right Ian, you first or it's nappies for you too!" as he sobbed "Not fair! It's got that goo over it too.

He knelt down and soon had given it a little kiss, as he pulled back "Yuk!" as he sobbed "Not fair!" as they said, "Lisa's turn!" as he sobbed "Not flaming fair girls! Nobody better hear about this!" as they giggled, and he knelt down and gave it a little kiss, but Sara said, "For that threat, give it a lovely lick all over!" as he sobbed "Not fair!" and soon was licking his mates willy, hating every second and heard Alice "One last little kiss, as if it's your baby dummy!!" as she held it up in the air and he'd to suck it, to giggles as he was let up to apply the disposable. They said, "We'll not tell the others about your baby-pee-pee, kissy-kissy, unless you babies are naughty!" as they sighed. They said, "Ok Miss!" as a diaper was pinned around him and he sobbed "Not fair girls!" as his plastics were pulled around him and he waited for the dress, but was pulled out and into the kitchen, sobbing and crying and then out into the back garden "Not fair girls, give me my frock!" to more screeches, as he'd to mince around the garden and hold some of the boys hands who giggled, at him, in the nappies, even though they were in pretty frocks, but he was eventually given a large pretty frock and they then started mincing around the garden, holding hands and then playing more sissy football. They were photographed and warned to do anything the girls wanted, or they'd be told on.

The boys are let go, but have to wear frilly panties and keep them on

They'd to keep their panties on, with the babies allowed to change from nappies, back into frilly panties, but all being threatened with more nappies, if they were naughty and disobedient. They were told to tell their parents, or friends, they had just had a game of footy in the street and not to say, anything about what happened to their Mums.

Anyway, they didn't know all the girls, who were involved and dreaded it getting out in school, with the possibility of ending up wearing a dress and gymslip to school – which is exactly what happened to one or two of the boys. The girls then plan to get Clive's little sister to control him and so approach Clive and hand him a large girly apron in his size, with a PVC pinny which was slightly smaller and tell him he's to wear it down in the morning, to offer to help his Mum with the housework and dishes. They said, "You'll say, Mummy! Can I help you with the washing up and any housework! Sorry for being a MSP, and I'll be good in future!" as he cringed "That's going to be terrible!" but she then added "With a curtsy with your pretty aprons!" as he cried "Oh no! Not a curtsy?" as he saw them smiled and demonstrate to him with their skirts and dresses. One said, "Pity you aren't in your aprons now or you could bob a sweet curtsy back to us!" as he begged "Please don't make me girls?" as they laughed and said, "Ok You promise to do what we want?" as he nodded, "Ok!" He sobbed saying, "But Amanda will see me too!" as they laughed and said, "Oh how sweet!" as he cringed at the thought. They threatened "You know Clive!

We have some wonderful photos of you, in a frock and worse!" as he asked, "What?" but they just giggled, "You don't want us to show anyone, especially your Amanda!" as he blushed "Not fair!"

However, they then said, "In the evening, you've to ask Amanda to hide your aprons away for the morning!" as he asked, "Why?" as Sharon giggled, "You then ask Amanda to wear one of her aprons and a PVC pinny, instead!" as he cried "Oh no! That will be worse!" as they said, "You'd better do what we ask or else!" adding "We'll be checking!" and ran off leaving him holding the plain white carrier bag. He entered his house that afternoon and his Mum asked, "What have you got there dear?" as he said, "Nothing Mum! It's a surprise!" as she wondered what it could be. Amanda was her normal self, playing with her dollies and wheeling them about the garden and drive in the pink doll's pram. He entered his room and hid the girly apron and PVC pinny away, dreading the reaction in the morning. After dinner he joined the boys playing football, dreading what might come tomorrow. He asked, "Have any of those flaming girls contacted you over our dress up the other day?" and saw them shake their heads. They all said, how terrible an experience it had been and hoped the girls wouldn't show any photos or tell on them. One guy asked, "What have you guys done with their panties?" as another said, "I threw mine in the bin later that night!" as others said, "Yea!" even though they'd actually hidden them away in case the girls might punish them. Ian said, "I kind of blabbed to Mum about them, expecting her to explode at them, but she didn't and just laughed and wanted to see my flaming panties!" as they laughed. Larry gasped as he dreaded Ian mention his Mum making them both play dress up and be babies with the little girl next door – see a later.

Five girls enter the street in pretty aprons with handbags

However, the boys then saw some girls come out, in their pretty frocks, with girly aprons over them and with handbags dangling from their elbow and start kicking a ball about in the street. The guys blushed and moved away saying, "We'll go around the next street to get away from them!" and went to go, but a girl ran over and said, "You boys must play in the same street as us!" as he cried "Oh no!" as he told the other guys, what she'd said, and they moved up a bit and carried on their game, but all blushing at the girls, playing Sissy Football, reminding them of them having to play in frocks and some in nappies in the back garden. However, when a girl or lady walked by the girls, they would say "We're trying to demonstrate to those boys up there, a different way to play, footy!" as the girl or woman looked and laughed "I could just imagine those boys, running about with handbags and pretty aprons!" as the girl said, "What about in frocks too?" as they screeched with laughter.

Claire, one of the footy girls Mum's came out and gasped as she saw her eight-year old daughter, playing football and giggled, "What's up with you girls, playing football?" as she laughed "How come the handbags and aprons?" as Claire gurgled "Oh Mum! We're trying to teach those boys, how to play football!" as her Mum laughed "Now dear! I'm sure they know, how to play football, better than you girls!" as she saw the girls mincing about with their handbags and only kicking the ball, between each other, with some skewing the ball, as they kicked it, causing her to laugh "I think you girls need a bit more practice at footy!" but her daughter laughed "Mummy! We aren't playing silly football!" Her Mum looked queryingly at her, but then heard her say, "We're playing Sissy Football!" as her Mum screeched "Sissy Football?" as her daughter giggled, and nodded, as another girl Sandy said, "Sissy football is so much more fun than normal football!"

Claire explains to her Mum they are playing Sissy Football

She explained "To play it, you need a uniform! A pretty apron, a handbag and hair ribbons or a headscarf, are optional" adding "A skirt or frock is optional too!" as another girl said, "We're trying to get those boys up the street, to learn it!" adding "Wouldn't they look nicer dressed like us!" as her Mum screeched and flicked her wrist towards the younger boys, laughing, as they played proper football. She then said, "Mummy! Why don't you stay and play?" but her Mum laughed "Count me out! What in these shoes!" as she pointed to the silver slightly high heeled shoes, saying, "I don't want these ruined!" adding "I don't know what your Dad would say, if he found out about us, playing football with our handbags and aprons!" adding "He'd think we'd gone, off our rocker!" Claire laughed "Just give the ball a little kick!" as she called "Fiona! Pass the ball to my Mummy Janet, for her to have a go!" as the nine-year old girl, minced over to the ball and passed it towards her Mum. Her Mum walked to the ball and heard Claire say, "Just steady yourself and kick the ball!" as her Mum laughed asking "Who to?" She replied, "Just anywhere!" and saw her hold her handbag out to Claire and say, "Just hold my bag!" but she shook her head and slid her handbag up her Mum's arm to the elbow and said, "You're now in position Mummy!" as she kicked the ball and saw it skew off, but she said, "Well done, Mummy!" as she laughed and heard her daughter say, "Just mince on up with your

Janet approaches the boys and teases them about Football

handbag like that, Mummy and mention to the young boys, how much fun Sissy Football is!" as her Mum laughed "Oh Claire! I don't know what they'd do or say, to me, if I did that!" Hence, she called "Bye darling!" and minced on up the street. She passed a friend Terisa who was in her garden, wheeling her lawn mower about, when she saw Janet, who laughed "My daughter, Claire there, has just let me have a go at football!" as Terisa laughed "I did see girls playing with a ball, in the street and thought it a bit funny!" as Janet said, "Apparently they aren't playing normal football!" as she looked down and asked, "What is it, then?" as she gurgled "It's called, Sissy Football and you need to mince with a handbag and wear an apron over a skirt or dress to play!" as she screeched "Never!" Janet said, "I'd better head on! I'm to ask those young boys, if they want to learn Sissy Football up there!" as Terisa screeched "You wouldn't dare?"

Hence, the boys were playing away in the street, when they saw the lady mincing up the street towards them. They ignored her, but then heard her say, "Hi boys! The girls down there say, 'Their football game is more fun, than yours!" and Ian said, "They can't play proper football!" as she laughed "Oh, but don't you think their uniform is much nicer than you boys!" as they realized what she meant, with them in the apron and handbag" as she laughed "I even had a go, myself!" as Jamie said, "They're flaming playing Sissy Football!" as she gasped "How on earth, do any of you boys know about that?" as they all blushed.

Some boys looked away and one Clive stammered "It was just once!" as the other five called "Don't flaming tell her, Clive!" as she gurgled "Oh boys! Were you all in aprons?"

as one or two blushed and nodded, as she giggled, "Not carrying a handbag each, too?" as a few nodded, and she gasped "Oh fab! Why did you want to play like that?" as they gasped "We didn't! A group of girls tricked us and got us into the back garden, one at a time, to show them how to play football!" as she laughed "What?" as he added "And they then got us onto our backs and slid a flaming girly apron around us and tied one of those stupid bags, up our arm to it and we were trapped!" as she gasped "Naughty girls!"

She then looked down at her daughter and gasped "Was my Claire there?" and saw Claire laugh and waving up to her, as she laughed "Naughty girl!" adding "What did they do to you?" as one of the boys Ian said, "Oh just made us prance about the garden, kicking the ball as sissies!" as she laughed "So you all were prancing around the garden carrying a handbag and wearing a pretty apron!" as she laughed "Not in hair ribbons?" as several shook their head, but others nodded, as she gasped "Not in frocks?" as a few nodded, and she screeched "Oh fab!" Claire laughed "I think Mummy has realised, what we did to those little boys!" as they all flicked their wrists to her!" and saw her laugh and return the effeminate flick. She heard several of the boys, begging "Please don't tell on us Mrs!" as she laughed "Let me think?" as she laughed "I think I've got it! I want you boys around at my house to demonstrate your Sissy Football skills!" as they gasped and cried "Not fair! Please don't, Mrs!" as she laughed "Call me Aunty Janet!" adding "I'm sure I can find a few of Claire's old frocks to fit you girlies!" as they cried "Not fair!" as she said, "Number 5 The gardens at 4.15 ok?" as they all nodded, as she giggled, and asked, "Is this the way you boys mince?" as she popped her right hand onto her hip and her arm up in front of her as she minced up the street with her handbag, laughing. A guy called "Why did you have to squeal on us, Ian?" as he huffed "Her daughter Claire is bound to tell her later and so it

Next morning Clive isn't looking forward to wearing aprons

would be out, anyway!" as Larry said, "I hope she keeps it to dresses and not include the baby stuff!" as Clive and him blushed and some laughed "Big babies!" as they ran to hit them, you watch it! Another said, "We all had it bad in dresses and flaming handbags!" as another said, "Let's continue the game and try to forget about tomorrow night!" as they all realized their time as girlies, was far from over. Several bigger boys went past and thought the girls were stupid, trying to play football in their aprons and with handbags, on their elbows. A few of the girls said, "We might try and trap some bigger boys, next, eh girls!" as they looked at the bigger boy going up the street and laughed "Wouldn't he look sweet, in a pretty apron and mincing with his handbag?" as they laughed at the thought. Another said, "Oh Deardry! You'll soon be thinking of transforming the hole street of boys, into sissies!" as she gurgled "Funny you should think that! Great minds think alike!" as they laughed.

The next morning Clive wakes up and hears his Dad leave for work and gets dressed and washed ready for breakfast. He hears his Mum come up and get his sister up and dressed and brings her down to breaky. She then calls him to get up and he woefully gets the pretty apron and pinny, from his wardrobe. He turns from the stairs into the hall and hears his Mum say, something to him, not looking, as she sets his breakfast down on the table. Amanda is sitting at the table, eating her breaky, when she looks up and screeches "Mummy look!" as her Mum looked up and gasped "What on earth, Clive!" as he sobbed "Some girl, is making me wear these flaming things!" as she ran and looked at him and gave him a cuddle, asking "Who?" but he said, "I'm not allowed to say!" Clive then amazed them by gripping his apron and bobbing a curtsy, to his Mum and said, "Morning Mum!" as she screeched and then gripped his apron again and called "Morning Amanda!" as she screeched too, laughing "I learn to curtsy at ballet class!" adding "Where did you learn?" as he blushed and said, "I just copied what I'd seen you doing!" as his Mum laughed "I never realised you were paying such attention, to her ballet!" as Mandy laughed "Maybe Mummy! He could join me at ballet!" as he cried "Please don't, Mum?" as she laughed "She's just, teasing you!" as Mandy laughed "Mummy! You'll have to get him a tutu, to join me!" as she laughed "Now Mandy stop!" She laughed "It's much easier to curtsy in skirts or dresses, isn't it Mummy?" as her Mum nodded,

and saw her daughter stand up and grip her dress and bob a curtsy to him and say, "Clive! You suit your pretty aprons!" as her Mum laughed and said, "Clive! I think you should curtsy back and say, thank you to your sweet sister!" as he blushed and sobbed as he gripped his apron and said, "Not fair! Thank you, Mandy!" to more laughter. Mandy called "Tell Mummy how nice she looks with another curtsy or I tell!" as he gripped his apron again said, "You look very nice Mummy, in your pretty dress and apron!" as she again bobbed another curtsy back. He then stammered "Mummy! Can I help you with the washing up and some housework?" as Amanda and her Mum both screeched and she gave him a kiss as she laughed "Come on, dear!" as Amanda gurgled and laughed "Doesn't Clive suit his pretty apron, Mummy?" as she nodded, "He does look very cute!" as he blushed and cried "Close the curtains, Mummy!" as she laughed and shook her head. Sorry dear "Mandy and I don't mind being seen in our pretty aprons and neither should you!" as he blushed and sat down to eat his breakfast.

Clive asks Amanda to hide his apron and pinny to trick him

After breakfast his Mum ran the water and said, "You wash, and I'll dry!" as he huffed "Not fair!" as she gave him a cuddle. He said, "Mandy! Don't tell anyone on me!" as she laughed "Oh I was going to tell the whole class at kinder garden!" as he begged, but then saw her bring in a dolly and said, "Kiss my dolly or I tell!" as her Mum gasped "Now Mandy! You can't make him, play dollies!" as she laughed "He can, or I tell!" as she laughed "She's only joking!" as he said, "She's not!" and took the doll and gave it a kiss, to screeches from his sister and laughter from his Mum.

However, that evening he said, to Amanda "Hi Mandy! Will you play a trick on me?" as she asked, "What?" as he said, "Hide my apron and pinny away!" as she shook her head "I like you wearing those girly aprons, especially to play dollies with me!" as he begged "Please don't make me?" but he said, "It will make you and Mummy laugh even more!" as she couldn't think why! Hence, that night before bed, she took his apron and pinny up to her room to hide them away and the next morning he came down without either.

His Mum saw him without his aprons and said, "Not in your pretty aprons, dear!" as he huffed "Someone hid them away!" as Amanda giggled, as her Mum looked at her and asked, "Why dear?" as she shrugged her shoulders, but then heard him ask "Mandy can I borrow one of your pretty aprons and PVC pinny?" as she screeched "Oh fab!" as she ran and fetched the girliest apron she could find along with a floral PVC pinny, as her Mum gasped "Oh dear!" as she said, "Mummy tie her, into my apron!" as her Mum laughed and took the little apron and giggled, as she fed it over his head and down his body, stopping at his waist, as she tied it behind his back, to giggles from both of them.

Hence after washing the breakfast things, he'd to play dollies with his giggling sister in her little apron and PVC pinny with her calling "Mummy! We'll have to get some dress up clothes for my big sister here!" as her Mum laughed "Oh Mandy!" as Clive begged "Please don't get me any frocks Mummy?" to screeches from both of them. Mandy ran and got one of her little handbags and fed it round his neck as he begged "Oh no! Not a handbag as she laughed "Mummy! Wont Clive be fun to take shopping?" as her Mum gasped "Now Mandy, we can't show him off outside as a girly boy!" as she laughed "Don't worry Mummy! I'll disguise him!" as she took some of her own hair slides from her head and said "Wear these or I tell!" and heard him sob as she slid some slides into his hair and gurgled "Oh fab, Mummy! We'll have to get him lots of skirts and dresses to play with me!" as he sobbed "Oh no!"

Mandy was out when his Mum said "Tell me how this came about, Missy!" as he sobbed "Us boys went out to play footy on Saturday and you had taken Mandy to town shopping!" as she nodded "Yea! So what?" as he continued "A few girls saw me and asked me to teach them, to play footy!" as she asked "Girls were wanting to learn to play football?" as he shook his head "It was a trick!" as she asked "How?" as he huffed "I followed them into a back garden down the street and saw the football and ran over to it, saying "You just do this as I demonstrated dribbling

and stuff!" as she listened and he said "Then some bigger girls appeared and suddenly I was on my back with a girly apron tied around me, but then a stupid bag fed up my arm and tied to the apron and I was trapped and couldn't leave or I'd be seen!" She gasped and gurgled "Naughty girls! What did they do?" as he sobbed "They flaming dressed us up?" as she gasped "Who's Us?" as he huffed "All my mates!",

PART H

PAM MAKES TOM WET HIMSELF AND HIS MUM CHANGES HIS NAPPY

Sissy Football and then Baby Football in the street

Tom needs the loo, but Pam makes him use his nappies

His mates called "Now there's flaming three of them with flaming dolls prams!" as Dave called "Julie! I'd expect Tina to play, but not you or Pam!" as she laughed "We just realized how much fun dollies are after giving them up last year!" Tom wants to go to the loo. He wait's till Pam's head is turned and tries to run off, but Pam turned and saw him called "Tom here a second!" and saw him blush and run over to her. He whispered "Pam! I've to go to the loo!" as she asked, "one's or two's baby Tom!" as he said, "Not so loud!" She laughed and heard him say, "Just one's!" as she laughed and whispered "I think Baby Tom is protected well enough, to be able to use his own nappies!" as he gasped "But I don't have a diaper!" as she gurgled "Sorry Baby!" but added "When you are about to pee, call out to me 'Pam! I'll give it to you later'" as he gasped. His mates called "Hurry up Tom! We need you back in the game!" as he blushed, still listening to Pam's instructions.

He then heard her say, softly "But when baby gets in, he's to promise, to ask Mummy, to change his nappies and stay in them till bed time!" as he cringed "Not fair, Pam!" as he walked back to the guys and resumed his football game. Tom returns back to his game, feeling really embarrassed at what Pam was making him do in front of his mates. He kicked the ball, but then felt the pee shoot out into his nappy and called out "Pam I'll get you later!" He wanted to turn away from his mates, as he did his wee, but realized that Pam was behind them and so had to stand facing his mates, as he peed his nappy!" and a large blush hit his face, as he turned away to try and hide his face. A guy called "Gosh, you haven't half gone red!" as he huffed "Yea! I do that sometimes!" as Pam called "You'd not go so red Tom if you played dollies with us instead of stupid football!" as Julie and Tina both laughed and he called "You bug off!" as his mates called "Yea! Tell her Tom!" as she laughed. He felt the pee soak into his disposable and hoped it would hold and not leak into his trousers and then thought, thank goodness I've got her panties on, as well!" However, it was even more embarrassing, as he ran about and kicked the ball, with the wet nappy on his front, feeling horrid. However, Pam had a new dolly in her pram and when they were nearby Tom, she called out loudly "My new dolly is called "Baby Nancy!" and added "She wets her nappies too!" as Tina called "Gosh mine doesn't even do that!" as Julie laughed, but didn't get the joke, except that Pam was talking about Nancy wetting her nappies, to embarrass Tom. Thankfully he didn't need to do a poo, at any time while playing footy or it would have been much worse, running about with a sore bum, which would probably have smarted. Tom eventually finished his game and ran in doors, sobbing as he entered the side door. His Mum was alone, June having left, having cornved her purpose of getting Baby Tom out to play football in his nappies and plastic baby pants.

He tells Mum Pam made him use his nappies and she's to change baby

His Mum asked, "What's wrong! Pam didn't let anything slip?" He shook his head, but cried "I needed to go to the loo!" but she saw me try to run off and called me over and when I said, it was number ones, she told me to use my flaming nappies!" as his Mum gasped "The naughty girl!" adding "You mean you were kicking the ball about the street and suddenly wee'd in your nappies?" She gurgled "That naughty girl!" as he nodded but then sobbed "She's making me ask this!" as she asked, "What?" and saw him sniffle and sob "Will you change Baby Tom's nappies?" as she screeched "Where is she?" but he said, "Still playing flaming dollies with Julie and Tina!" as she laughed. She led him up the stairs into her room and she pulled the blinds shut, as he removed his jumper and shirt. She then reached for his trousers and helped him undress down to only his nappies and baby plastics, as she took the diaper bag and reaching in, she took the rubber gloves and pulled them on. She laughed at the sight of her big boy, in nappies and laughed "Gosh Tom, you do look a sight!" as he blushed "You shouldn't have put me into these flaming nappies!" adding "When you saw Pam's trick, you should have ran up and got a pair of her panties for me to wear instead!" as she laughed "I was tempted, but thought, if I kept you in-doors it would be funny!"

He huffed "When you went upstairs, June flaming made me go out, to play with my mates!" as she gasped "When I came down stairs, I heard her talking and assumed you were still in the room and Hence, didn't realize you'd gone out!" adding "I thought you'd gone out on your own!" He gasped "What! In flaming nappies and plastics! No way! I'm not that big a sissy!" as she screeched, at his comment, as she said, "No Tom!" as she said, "After I've changed your nappies, which frock do you want Nancy to wear!" as she flicked her wrist to him, laughing her head off at his comment and his baby look. She took a dummy from her bag and said, "Better keep baby quiet!" as he blushed bright red and sucked on the dummy. Pam had seen the boys had finished their footy match and saw Tom run back indoors and knew he'd have to ask his Mum to change his nappies, as she giggled, but didn't let on to Julie or Tina. She carried on playing dollies, pushing her doll's pram and occasionally taking the doll out to cuddle and kiss, as did a laughing Julie and Tina, till about five minutes later, she said, "I'd better go home!" as they complained, but she called "Bye girls!" and ran off. She entered the side door and didn't see any sign of her Mum or Tom and then tip-toed upstairs and heard her Mum in her bedroom talking to Tom. She went back down quietly and had a baby bottle from June's place and a dummy and frilled baby bonnet, in her bag and taking the milk from the fridge, she heated some up and poured it into the baby bottle for Baby Tom. She returned upstairs and listened at the door and heard her Mum saying, about "I thought you'd gone out on your own!" and then Tom's outburst about not being that big a sissy and then his Mum's reply as she tried the door, but it was locked.

Pam sneaks in filling a baby bottle while his Mum's changing baby Tom

Tom cried "Oh no!" as he wet himself again. Pam stay out, I'm just changing Tom's nappies!" as he cried "Mum! Not so loud!" as Pam giggled, "Oh Mummy! Can't I come in to help change baby Tom!" but she said, "No way young lady!" as he called "Pam be quiet please, someone will hear!" as they both laughed. His Mum laughed "You haven't wet yourself again?" as he sobbed "Not fair!" as she laughed "Just as well, you were still in your nappies or I might have got a mouthful!" as Pam screeched "Mum, you could wait and take baby Tom downstairs and out the back to play Sissy Footy with us in his wet nappies and then change baby in the back garden for being a naught boy!" as her Mum laughed "Make him run about in his wet nappy! Like you did in the street!" Pam laughed "What a fab suggestion Mummy!" adding "Instead of Sissy Football, remove his frock after a while and play Baby Football, with Baby Tom running about the garden kicking his ball in his nappies and plastic baby pants!" as her Mum screeched and he sobbed "No don't!" as they both giggled, at her comments.

Pam said, "Mummy, can I have a running commentary, since I can't see you changing Tom's nappy" as he cried "Please Pam! Be quiet! Someone will hear!" She laughed "Sorry Baby Tom! I've to call out as the door is between you and me, unless someone asks his lovely sweet Mummy to let Pammy in to help change his nappy!" Mummy I

take it that since we had Baby Tom in his nappies playing footy it will be Baby Nancy this evening!" as her Mum laughed "Maybe!" as he blushed at his smiling Mum. Pam checked her own room and laughed "My good yellow frock is missing! Baby Tom better look after it and not get any baby gel or talcum powder onto it, or even worse, some of his baby pee!" as he cringed "Ha!" His Mum looked at him and smiled as she asked, "Well Tom! Do you want Pammy. to come in and help me with your nappies!" Tom didn't want her calling out anymore and nodded, "Not flaming fair!" as his Mum stood up and unlocked the door to let a giggling Pam in.

Pam entered and saw her frock on the bed and her blushing brother on the floor in his nappies and plastic baby pants, with the blinds closed and her Mum with the rubber gloves on. Of course, Pam asked, "Will I get my gloves Mummy?" as she shook her head and said, "I'll see to changing Tom's nappy this time!" as he again begged them not to speak too loudly, as Pam laughed "Spoiled sport!" She laughed "I still want the commentary while we change Tom's nappies, but at least this time, it's a lot quieter than when I was locked outside the door. His Mum said, "I'd better get the changing mat for Baby!" as Pam giggled, "I think we can call him 'Baby Nancy' when in his nappies!" He blushed and sobbed "Not flaming fair!" as his Mum said, "Naughty girl!" as she stood up and took the changing mat over to him, she said, "Just roll over till I get this mat underneath you!" as Pam saw him roll over and her Mum set the mat down. Pam stood up and said, "I think Wendy doll should watch too, along with his Baby Suzie!"

Pam opens the blinds fully so Baby can be seen

She added "Wait for me Mum before starting on Baby Tom!" as she exited and fetched his apron, handbag and the two dolls, but also her and her Mum's waterproof PVC aprons. She entered and set the dolls down beside Tom, who was now lying on the changing mat. She handed her Mum her PVC apron, as her Mum said, "Good thinking Pam!" as Pam pulled her own pinny on and said, "Just in case of Baby Tom having more accidents with his baby-pee-pee!", as he said, "Ha Ha!" She took her Wendy doll and handed it to him and said, "Give Wendy a kiss and tell her you're a naughty big baby who wet his nappies and has asked his Mummy to change his nappies!" as he blushed and threw the doll over the bed. Pam said, "Naughty baby!" as she went to fetch the doll, but then at the window, she reached up and opened the blinds, but also pulled them up, quietly without Tom or her Mum knowing. She returned and said, "Apologise to Wendy doll!" as he blushed and said, "Sorry Wendy!" and gave her a kiss, as they both laughed. His Mum said, "First I'm pulling down baby Tom's plastics!" as Pam saw her pull them down to his knees as Pam said, "Let me get Tom's diaper off!" Tom cried "Too loud, Pam!" as she laughed "Oops! Sorry Baby!" as she unpinned the triangle and then the sides and smiled as she pulled them off, saying, "Reach up baby!" and saw him raise his hunches and she pulled it off, smiling as he was left in the two disposables. His Mum said, "As I've the rubber gloves I'll do his wet nappy!" adding "Thank goodness, it wasn't number two's, you made him run about the street in, playing football, or you'd have been for the high jump, young lady!" as Pam gurgled "Lucky Baby Tom!" as he blushed and sobbed "Not fair!" as his Mum took a plastic bag and pulled the wet nappy off. Pam gurgled "Oh Tom! What do you call that?" as he yelled "Bug off?" as she laughed "Will I run over or out the door and call very loudly?" as he sobbed "It's my baby-pee-pee!" as her Mum said, "Stop teasing Pam! This mush must be bad enough for him!" as she asked, "Why do you call that little thing, your baby-pee-pee?" as he blushed "Because it's only the size of a little baby boys baby-pee-pee!" as they both laughed and looked at his little willy. Pam then laughed as she saw her Mum take the wet wipes and start rubbing his front and his willy as she gurgled "What a silly looking thing! Isn't it Mummy?" as her Mum laughed and continued, cleaning Tom up, taking some of the disposable around his bottom, off to wipe it, asking "Is your bum wet?" as he shook his head. He said, "I think it's just on the front Mum!" as Pam smiled. His Mum then took the baby gel and asked, "Sure you don't want to just get into Pam's panties?" but Pam looked at Tom and stared at him, as he blushed and shook his head "It's ok Mum! I'm doing it to please Pammy!" as she smiled and leaned over and kissed his lips to laughter from his Mum.

Pam pretends Tina is there and he pees over his Mum's pinny

His Mum took the gel and applied it to his willy and front, as Pam laughed "Don't forget his botty! Just in case!" as her Mum laughed, but then heard Pam say, "Actually I've been a little naughty Tom!" as she called "Come in Tina!" Both Tom and his Mum gasped as Pam stood up and ran back in case her Mum smacked her. Tom cried out sobbing "No! Not fair!" but also let out pee, as his Mum saw the urine squirt out, from his willy and shoot over her apron, as she scolded "Pam!" and looked to the door, but nobody was there. Pam laughed "Lucky boy! She must have had to go back home!" as he cried "You witch! You made me wet Mummy!" She gurgled "Sorry Mum!" as she laughed "Just as well I'd this PVC pinny or it would have ruined my dress!" as Pam laughed "I told you Baby Tom, might have another accident, with his baby-pee-pee!" adding "That's why I was a clever girl and brought up your PVC pinny!" as they both laughed. His Mum took another wet-wipe and rubbed him down, as Pam laughed "It looks a bit like de-ja-vu' as her Mum laughed "Very clever young lady" as she continued cleaning both her pinny and the changing mat. She then took the gel and re-applied it to his willy and front again. Pam said, "Let me apply baby Tom's fairy dust!" as she took it and sprinkled it over his front and his willy, but then reached out and lifted it up, as her Mum said, "Leave that Pam!" but saw her sprinkle underneath as she laughed "Mummy! We don't want baby Tom to get nappy rash!"

Pam laughed "Whatever would the nurse or doctor say, when he dropped his trousers and removed his nappies to show off a red willy!" as he cried "You bug off Pam, that's not funny!" Pam took the clean disposable as her Mum said, "I'll do his nappy, Pam!" but she shook her head and said, "No Mummy! I'll do it properly!" as she laughed and said, "Ok! Miss know it all!" as she watched Pam, undo the sticky bit's and pop it onto his front and stick it down. She smiled at Tom and saw him blush. She said, "Aren't Mummy and I nice, changing naughty baby Tom's nappy?" as he blushed and said, "Thank you Mummy, Thank you Pammy for changing Baby Tom's nappies!" as Pam stood up and bobbed a curtsy to him "Thank you Baby Nancy!" as he grimaced.

However, she then reached into her apron pocket and pulled out her pink dummy and whispered in Tom's ear, just while Mummy is changing baby!" as he gasped but let her pop it into his mouth. His Mum gasped as she saw the dummy in his mouth, but Pam then moved her lips in and out and her Mum laughed as Tom moved the dummy in and out, like a baby. Her Mum said, "Pam! It's embarrassing enough that we're putting him into nappies at his age but sucking a dummy!" Pam laughed "Just for a few minutes Mummy to give you a laugh!" as he grimaced, and his Mum laughed.

Pam adds a baby bonnet, dummy and gives him a baby bottle

However, Pam then said, "Close your eyes Mummy for ten seconds!" and Tom gasped as he felt something being pulled onto his head and when she opened them screeched as he was now in a baby girl's frilled bonnet and along with the dummy was really funny looking. He pulled it off, but Pam said, "You could be running about the garden in it!" and saw let her retie it under his chin. She gurgled "Pam! You are so naughty!" as she laughed "Just one more thing!" as she then produced the baby bottle as Tom spat the dummy out and cried "Not fair Mum! This is terrible as Pam handed it to her Mum and said, "You start off first Mummy!" His Mum checked the temperature was ok and fed the bottle into Tom's mouth and then handed it to Pam and said, "I'll get his diaper back on!" as Pam giggled, "I know Baby Nancy loves her baby bottle!" as she looked into Tom's face and smiled, as he pulled a face, at the milk trickling down his throat.

His Mum took the diaper and said, "Reach up Tom!" and slid it under him and then pinned it back into place, as she said, "When Pam has finished giving Baby his bottle, I'll stand him up and pull his plastic baby pants up again!"

However, Pam said, "Baby Nancy can hold the bottle herself!" and saw him take it and hold it in his mouth, as she pulled him up and Tom stood up, with Pam speaking to him to keep him looking away from the window.

She looked past him and saw Nina, the lady across the street at her window, looking over at him, in his diaper and with the plastics down his legs, but then saw him pull them up over his diaper. Nina gasped as she realized it was big Tom pulling plastic baby pants over his diaper and gurgled "Why the big baby!" bug she couldn't see his face or the baby bottle, due to his head hiding it, but did see his baby bonnet too.

Pam said, "Keep sucking Baby!" and saw him swallow the milk down, as she giggled, "Such a greedy baby!"

However, Julie had also been primed by Pam to be in the front bedroom looking over to see in case she could get Nancy on show, but didn't say, why. She again asked her not to tell Tina, but to maybe get her Mum to see too. Hence, Julie asked her Mum to take her into her bedroom for a talk. Tina stayed downstairs watching TV and playing with her dolly. Hence, both Julie and her Mum were watching too and gasped, as they saw Tom and Pam stand up, but Tom now in nappies and then watched him pull up his plastic baby pants, with him still unaware that he's on show to the street. Julie screeched "Mum did you see that?" as her Mum nodded, "Nappies and plastic baby pants and a baby bonnet too!" but then saw his head move to the side a little and she cried out "A baby bottle of milk too!" as her Mum said, "Quiet Julie!" as they saw he was sucking on a baby bottle too.

Julie and her Mum spy Baby Tom's nappies and plastics

They wondered, "Was it Pam changing his nappies or not?" Julie gurgled "You don't think Pam's doing it on her own!" as she laughed "And as I copy everything that Pammy does!" but her Mum said, "No chance! Don't you dare, young lady!" Julie laughed "I do need some experience for baby-sitting Mummy!" adding "And you can be there, to make sure, I'm not naughty and do something, I shouldn't to baby Tom!" She gurgled "I have slept with Nancy before in his nighty!" as her Mum gasped "Oh Julie!" as she added "Well only for half an hour, with Pammy on one side and me the other, giving him cuddles and tickles!" as her Mum gasped again. Julie said, "Although that was before, he grew down to become Baby Nancy in nappies and plastic baby pants!" but added "Not to mention having his dummy and baby bottle!" She said, "It means I can then advertise to do babysitting for both boy and girl babies!" as she laughed "I might use Tom to Nancy as a role model!" as her Mum giggled, and heard her continue "It might be fun to slip a little boy, into a frock to play dress up!" Her Mum laughed "Don't you dare! Her Mum and Dad would go mad if they heard!" as she laughed "I'm sure the ones that are old enough to tell, I'll take some photos to keep them silent!" as they both laughed. She laughed "Could you imagine having a whole street of girly boys in frocks playing dollies and dress up!" as her Mum gasped "You wouldn't?" as she nodded, "I'll have to sort out pretty frocks for the boys dress up sessions with me and Tina.

She laughed "Talking about Tina, I know we don't want her spying Tom, but she's not able to see over the window, as she's too small. However, we could lift her up and you spin her around, so she can't see big Tom!" as her Mum gasped and she added "He'll wet himself if he sees her, with us and thinks she knows, about him dressing up and his nappies!" Hence, she unlocked the door and called "Tina!" as she called "What do you want?" as she ran up the stairs and saw Julie and her Mum in the bedroom. Julie said, "I'm just checking how tall you are!" adding "Just come over here!" adding "and check can you see, out the window?" as Tina walked into the room, but back by the door said, "I can see out back here!" as she looked out, but luckily she was looking across at Tom's neighbours and not his house. She walked around the bed and said, "I can still see out across the street, but didn't try and concentrate on anything and so didn't spy Tom with his nappies and plastics being pulled up. She then stood by the window and said, "I can't see out much now! Hopefully in a few months-time, I'll be big enough to see out the window, without jumping or Mummy lifting me!" as her Mum laughed and lifted her up and spun her around before setting her back down on her feet, with Julie waving, to Tom while behind Tina's back. His Mum was still on the floor and took Pam's yellow frock, off the bed and handed it to him and said, "I'm sure, for once, you're looking forward to slipping into a pretty frock!" as he nodded, "Thanks Mum!"

Pam makes Tom ask to wear her frock, but takes it to window

Pam gurgled "Sure you want to wear this?" as he nodded, and she said, "You must promise to take it from me, on penance that I tell Tina!" He huffed "Ok Pam! I'll wear your frock!" as she continued "When you've asked me to wear it out in the garden, to play Sissy Football!" as her Mum gasped "Pam! You are pushing it!" as he nodded, "Ok Pam! Not fair!" as she laughed, but then added "And then Baby Football for ten minutes!" He cried "Oh no! Not running about the garden in my nappies and plastic baby pants?" as she nodded, and her Mum gasped "Now Pam, that wouldn't be fair! Someone at the back might see!" as she laughed "I'll try and keep him in the area near the fence, where Baby Nancy won't be seen!" as he sobbed "Not flaming fair!" as she said, "I'm waiting!" He grimaced as he asked, "Please Pammy can I wear your pretty yellow frock to go out to the back garden to play Sissy Football and then later on!" as Pam said, "!I think one hour of Sissy Football!" as he cried "A full hour!" as she nodded, and he continued "After one hour, I'll remove your frock to play Baby Football in my nappies and plastics as Baby Nancy!" She gurgled and threw her arms around him and gave him a kiss!" as she ran and quietly locked the door, taking the key and hiding it away.

Tom turned with the dress in his hands and cried "Oh no! The blinds are up!" as he remembered his baby bonnet and pulled it off, flinging it down on the floor, as Pam laughed "Oh I thought Baby Nancy suited her frilly baby bonnet!" as she gurgled at the thought of him now sleeping in nappies too and a baby bonnet, maybe sucking on a dummy! His Mum gasped "Pam you didn't! When we were changing Tom into his nappies!" as she nodded, and giggled, and scrambled across the bed and took the dress from him and held it up in the air by the window. Tom went to run out, but then gasped as he tried the door and gasped "Oh no! Where's the key?" as his Mum said, "The key now or else!" as she laughed "All you have to do is take my frock and pull it on and I'll let Baby Nancy out to play Sissy Football!" as he sobbed "Not flaming fair!" She said, "Just mince around the bed and take my pretty frock and in fact I'll be nice and put it on you!" as he huffed "Not fair Pam, I'm in my nappies and baby pants and will be seen!" She laughed "I doubt you'll be that unlucky!" as her Mum said, "Pam! He might be spied!" as she laughed "Look I'm sure the neighbours across the street and Julie have seen him girlied up lots of times and it's not that big a change to see him in his nappies and plastic baby pants!" Her Mum watched her big boy slip past her, wailing "Not fair!" as she said, "If you look away, they mightn't know who it is and might think you're a niece over visiting" as she giggled, "Or even Nancy slipping into my frocks again!" as he pulled a face and she saw him turn away from the window, as he turned and walked backwards towards her. He dreaded someone else spying him in her dress again, especially his mates and hoped they'd all gone home and wouldn't spy him, getting into his frock. However, Pam had other ideas for Baby Tom or Baby Nancy to show off his nappies to the street.

Nancy has to walk in his nappies to the window to get the frock

His Mum said, "Pam! Close the blinds!" but saw her shake her head and she asked, "Will I check nobody's looking?" but Pam said, "If Mummy's there, then it's two hours of Sissy Football and half an hour as Baby!" as he said, "It's ok Mum!" as he ducked down to try and not be recognised. Pam laughed "You do look silly Tom!" He moved slowly towards the window and tried to reach out for the yellow dress, but Pam swapped it to her other hand and held it high again. He cringed "Not fair Pam and slowly turned his head to try and look past her at the street and sighed as he didn't see anybody about.

He then looked up and gasped as he saw a lady across the street looking right over at him and cried "Oh no! Some lady across the street is looking over at me!" as Pam said, "Tom! It's just your imagination! Your nappies are below the window and can't be seen!" as he checked and realized she was right. Her Mum said, "She is right Tom! They are below the window ledge!" She added "If you act like a girl, they'll just think it's our cousin or even Nancy just slipping into one of my frocks again!" as he blushed and said, "Ha!"

Here Tom! Let me!" as she took the dress and said, "Arms up dearie!" and saw him raise his arms, still at the window looking backwards. She got behind Tom and smiled as she looked out into the street and fed the dress down over his head and fed his arms into the sleeves but turned him to be now facing the window and the street, with his nappies still hidden, although just. She fed the dress, down so his face was now on view, as Sissy Tom, still without any hair ribbons, as he looked and cried "Oh no! Julie and her Mum are laughing at me!" He cried "That woman is still there and laughing at me! Let me go!" as his Mum said, "Pam let him go, he'll be seen in your dress! Give him some ribbons!" as Pam took her Alice band and slid it onto his head! There you are big Nancy again, instead of Sissy Tom!" as he blushed and tried to move, but she held him still. However, Tom then gasped as he looked over to Julie's and saw Tina there and cried "Oh no! Tina's there too!" as he wet his nappies again, as his hands shot over his plastics and Pam gurgled "Mummy seems our little baby has wet his nappies again!" as his Mum gasped "You haven't Tom!" as he nodded, and they laughed. Pam looked over and said, "Tom! She's so small, she can't see you!" adding "I'm sure Julie and her Mum are keeping you secret!" as he looked again and saw part of her head, but her eyes were hidden from view. He huffed "I hope they don't show me off!" but gasped as he saw her Mum lift her up and spin her around as Pam held him on show, but luckily Tina didn't see him. Tom cried "Oh no! They've lifted her up!" as his Mum gasps "They haven't?" as Pam laughed "It's ok Mum, her Mum spun her around and set her down again, quickly to tease Tom!" as her Mum laughed "They are naughty!" Pam then pulled his dress up and fed her arms under his shoulders and lifted him up as high as she could. He cried "Oh no! Pam!" as his plastics and nappies were on show, for a few seconds and he saw both Julie and her Mum, but also Nina point at him.

Julie and her Mum lift Tina up and Pam pinches his arm to make a face

Her Mum scolded "Let him down Pam! He's on show, to the street!" as she could hold him no longer and let go of the blushing boy as he cried "Oh no! Let me go Pam! I'm on show in your frock!" She laughed "Ten curtsies Sissy Tom! While none of your mates are about!" as she held him on show, and he started to do the curtsies. Their Mum stood up having finished putting the baby stuff away and went over and peered out first and laughed as she saw Nina and then Julie and her Mum!" as Julie called "There's Pam's Mummy, Tina!" and lifted her up, but held her there, as Pam saw little Tina looking over and pinched his arm and heard Tom cry "Oh no!" but open his mouth to be more noticeable than before. His Mum spied Tina looking over at him and quickly closed the blinds, scolding Pam for nearly outing Tom to Tina. Tom cried "Oh no! Tina saw me!" as Pam gurgled "Now Tom! She just saw a big girl with me playing curtsies and Julie will say, it's my cousin Nancy visiting us!" as he sat down sobbing "Not fair! I knew wearing nappies, would be terrible today!" as his Mum cuddled him and said, "Pam you are so naughty!" Tina called "I saw Pammy and another big girl in a yellow dress!" as Julie laughed "That's Nancy! She's Pammy's cousin, who must be playing curtsies, with her!" adding "She apparently loves to play dollies too!" as she laughed "Goody! Will she play tonight?" but Julie said, "I think Pam said, she's busy tonight, but will play soon!" as her Mum laughed.

Tina said, "I'm sure I've seen her before, especially when she opened her mouth and said, something!" as Julie guessed Pam had done something to Tom and made him shout something out. Julie said, "Now Tina, she's their cousin and is bound to look something like Pam and Tom!" Tina said, "She actually looked more like Tom that Pammy!" as Julie gurgled "Now Tina! Somehow, I don't think big Tom, would play curtsies with Pammy in one of her frocks!" as her Mum gasped, at her giving the game away. She heard Tina say, "He's always such a nasty boy, calling us names and hitting us, if we play near their silly football!" as her Mum said, "You tell me, if he hit's you Tina!" as Julie giggled, "What would you do Mummy?" adding "Not pop him over your lap and give his botty, a good spanking!" as Tina called "Yes Mummy! Do that! Smack his botty!" to more laughter. Julie giggled, "Though, Pam has told me, her Mummy sometimes smacks his botty, but it doesn't do, any good!" as she added "He must have some kind of padding, for when his Mummy smacks his botty!" as her Mum laughed "Knowing

she was talking about his diaper. Julie said, "Tina can you think what type of padding, might stop Tom, feeling a hand smacking his trousers?" as she shook her head and heard Julie giggle "Think when you were very young, what did you wear?" as Tina gasped "Nappies!" as she nodded. Her Mum laughed "Oh Julie! You are funny, talking about big Tom in nappies and plastic baby pants!" as Tina screeched "Oh that would look funny, if I could see big Tom in nappies!" Julie quipped and Nancy's yellow frock too!" as Tina gurgled and gasped "I think I've just wet myself Julie!" as her Mum took her hand and led her into the bathroom. Tina laughed "Oh that would be fab!" as her Mum cleaned her up and popped her into clean panties.

Julie tells Tina things she can make a boy do if she has him scared of her

She returned to Julie who said, "If you ever find out that about any boy, Tina!" as she asked, "What?" as she laughed "that he wears a dress!" as she nodded, and heard her continue "Well any boy, would be dreading you tell other girls and especially his mates about him and a frock and so will do anything you want!" as she asked, "What do you mean Julie?" She laughed "Like what do you like to play?" as she called out "Dollies!" as she laughed "Yes! I'd make him push a doll's pram!" as Julie gasped "Not outside?" as she nodded. She added "Not in the back garden?" as she nodded but then said, "I'd make him push his dollies in the drive and then the streets too!" as her Mum gasped at Julie making it even worse, for big Tom, when Tina finds out about him. Julie gasped "Oh Tina, you wouldn't?" as she laughed "No you wouldn't?" as Tina asked, "What?" as she laughed "You wouldn't get Mummy to take us and him around the shops in town, wheeling your doll's pram!" as Tina gasped and giggled, "Yes Mummy! That would be fab! To make a boy, push my doll's pram about the shops!" as Julie gurgled "Not in his frock!" Tina nodded, "Oh yes! Wearing a frock!" as Julie picked up a handbag and said, "Not mincing around the shops carrying a handbag, like this!" as she swung the handbag over her elbow and minced to show Tina, who nodded, "Yes! That would be fab!" as her Mum laughed at the conversation between them.

Julie then runs upstairs and rummaging in the old toys she had as a young girl, finds what she was after and taking another of the dolls, she pops the straps around her body and does it up at the back. She then pops the dolly securely into the pink girly baby carrier and minces downstairs. Her Mum looks up and screeches at her big daughter now with the doll attached to her front and laughs "Oh Julie! Tina will screech the place down and Tom will die if he has to wear that to carry his dollies about the place!" as she nodded, "Oh Mum! Why didn't we think of this before?" She exit's the side door and sees Tina wheeling her doll's pram up the driveway and then turn. She looked and gasped "Oh Julie! I'd forgotten that baby carrier! Give it here, so I can try it!" as Julie laughs "Hold on a tick! I just want to surprise Pam!" Julie minces over to Pam's house with the dolly carrier hanging down her front and rings the bell. Pam's Mum called "I think that's Julie Pam!" as she opens the door and gasps as she sees the little girl with the dolly carrier and then said, "Oh no!" Knowing the girls would want Tom to wear that and his embarrassment at being seen by any girls or ladies in the street. Pam came out of the living room and up the hall and is about to say, when she spies Julie with the doll in the sling around her front and gurgles "Oh fab Julie! I know someone who will be thrilled at the prospect of trying out that baby carrier!" as her Mum begged "Don't you dare Pam! He'll be mortified!" as they laughed. Julie then said, "And we could then join him, playing football!" as Julie shook her head "I don't like silly football!" as Julie said, "Not normal football, we'd all be in frocks kicking the ball about the garden and carrying a handbag too!" as Tina screeched and heard her sister call out "It would be Sissy Football!" as they all laughed.

Pam gets Baby Nancy prepared for the Sissy Football

Tina laughed "It would be fun to see big Tom, in our back garden in a frock, carrying a handbag, kicking the ball about!" as Julie laughed "In hair ribbons too?" as Tina nodded. However, Julie said, "Though when in hair ribbons he'd be disguised as a girl!" but added "But without ribbons or any disguise, he'd look like Sissy Tom running about in a frock!" as her Mum laughed "Julie you are a tease! You know big Tom isn't like that?" as Tina said, "No

Mummy! but it is funny thinking about him dressed in a frock and prancing about!" Julie laughed "Though the best would be you know what?" as Tina shook her head and heard her say, "Eventually let his friends know!" as Tina asked, "Tell them!" as Julie giggled, "Show them!" as she added "Take him down with his hands tied behind his back in a frock to play as a Sissy, in the street with his mates!"

Tina screeched "That would be the best! Tom running about in a frock kicking the ball to play with his mates!" as Julie had a thought. She said, "Eventually get all his mates into frocks too and so they'll all be prancing about playing Sissy Football!" as her Mum gasped "Gosh Julie! You'd better stop!" adding "I'm nearly wetting my pants!" as they all giggled.

However, then Julie said, "You know what he'd hate even more than that Tina?" as she shook her head "Worse than a boy wearing a frock? I don't know anything!" as Julie gurgled "A big boy in nappies and plastic baby pants!"

Tina gurgled "Oh that would be even better!" as she said, "And a frock!" but heard Julie say, "No! Either just as a baby or a nice short baby frock!" adding "So that his nappies and plastics are on show everywhere. Tina screeched and said, "Mummy I need a change again! I've just wet my panties again!" as her Mum took her hand and led her off to be cleaned up again. Her Mum laughed at the thought of Tom in a dress, playing dollies with her Tina and then worse in his nappies!" as she gasped "She might spy his tinkle and Julie better not show her his either!" as she got Tina to pop downstairs.

She said, to Julie "Look Julie I know Tina doesn't know about Nancy yet, but when she does, I don't want her spying anything in his panties or nappies!" as Julie gurgled "What ever might she find there?" as she laughed "You know very well young lady!" as they both laughed and Julie said, "You mean his baby-pee-pee?"

Her Mum nodded, and Julie said, "I won't, but I'm not counting on Pammy! I think she'll be a naughty girl and show off his little baby-pee-pee!" as her Mum laughed "Gosh to think I never saw one till I was in my twenties!" Julie laughed "Who's was it?" as her Mum scolded "Never you mind dear! And no mentioning it to your Daddy either!" as her Mum blushed, and she laughed. Pam and her Mum take Nancy downstairs in her yellow dress, with her apron on top with his handbag tied to it and his dolly in his other hand to mince about the garden.

Pam brings Julie's neighbour Nina to join Nancy at football

Tom and his Mum pleaded for her to keep him indoors, but Pam was adamant, that Nancy play Sissy Football for an hour. His Mum said, "Pam provide some ribbons, or I'll add a headscarf!" as Pam booed "Mummy! Ok!" as she slid several ribbons and bows into his hair as she giggled, "Looking forward to playing Sissy Football Nancy?" as he nodded, and she kissed him and bobbed a curtsy to him. Hence, he took his ball and opening the side door, he nervously slipped out and around to play in the garden. Pam and her Mum slipped into aprons and picked up their handbags to follow him out to play and saw him dressed as Nancy kick the ball to his Mum, who kicked the ball over to Tom, but it went askew, to laughter. He asked, "Mum! Where should I stand to stop the neighbours in the back spying me?" as she laughed "Probably near the end of the garden Tom! I mean Nancy!" as he moved down a bit further and said, "I hope the neighbours up and down the street don't recognise me!" Pam giggled, "If you're worried now completely disguised as Nancy kicking the ball about, what's it going to be like later when Baby Tom has to prance around the garden in his nappies and plastics!" as he gasped "I'll have my ribbons in!" but she shook her head and her Mum said, "I'll find a headscarf for you!" as Pam laughed "Spoilt sport!" as she thought of a cunning plan, to stop her Mum spoiling her fun. She said, "I want Nancy to bob lots of sweet curtsies while kicking the ball about tonight!" as he cried "Not curtsies too!" as her Mum bobbed one to him and laughed. Pam laughed "I'd better get over to ask Nina from across the street to not tell on Nancy!" as Tom gasped "What?" Pam laughed "Nina definitely spotted you and could tell if I don't ask her not to!" as he grimaced and said, "Ok!" as

she skipped across the street still in her apron to Nina's. She rang the bell and Nina came out from the living room and giggled, as she opened the door to little Pam, asking "How's Baby Tom?" as she laughed "Could you keep him a secret, especially from little Tina next door!" adding "Julie and her Mummy know about my big sissy brother, but Tina doesn't and he's absolutely dreading her find out about him, in case she makes him wheel her doll's pram all over the place!" as Nina gurgled at the thought of it. She laughed "Can you spare an hour or so! I've got Nancy out the back to play football!" as she gasped "Does your Mum know?" as Pam nodded, and she said, "I suppose it could be fun to see him dressed up, as a girly, to kick his ball about!" as she fetched her keys, but Pam said, "Can you bring a pretty handbag too?" as she asked, "Why?" but Pam said, "Part of the surprise!" However, Pam said, "Can you also wear a pretty apron too?" as she laughed and Pam said, "You'll find out when you come across!" as she picked up a floral apron, she pulled it on over her dress and locking up, she joined Pam across the street. However, she said, "Can you wait a minute and then come in, to surprise my baby brother?" as Nina hid behind the chimney and waited, and Pam skipped into the back garden. Tom looked up and saw Pam enter and say, "I've asked her, not to tell Tina, or anyone else, about my Sissy Baby brother!" as he cringed and said, "Ha!" as Pam asked, "Where's that curtsy and thanks?" and saw him grip his dress and bob a curtsy to her, saying, "Thanks!"

Nina comes over to see Tom and he wets himself again

His Mum laughed and asked, "What did she say?" as Pam giggled, "She did ask how the big baby was!" as she was about to say, more, when in walked Nina, as Tom cried "Oh no!" as Nina saw him and gurgled "Oh! Doesn't he look sweet?" as Tom sobbed "Not fair Pam! I knew you'd tell!" as Nina ran over and cuddled him "I must say! You look adorable, in your frock and apron and I love your pretty handbag and dolly, not to mention your pretty hair ribbons!" Pam laughed "What does that deserve Baby Nancy?" as Nina let go of him and saw him grip his dress and bob a curtsy and say, "Thank you Mrs!" as she bobbed a curtsy back, as Pam laughed "He's normally also rewarded with a kiss!" as she hugged him and gave him a kiss on the cheek, but Pam said, "Next time on the lips!" as he grimaced and Nina laughed. Nina gasped "I see you are actually playing football with Tom!" as Pam giggled, "It's not normal football! You need to wear an apron or frock, mince with a pretty handbag and hair ribbons are optional!" and asked, "What's it called Tom?" as he cringed "It's Sissy Football!"

Nina gurgled "What a fab name for it!" as Pam said, "I think in your nappies you can call it Sissy Baby Football!" as he blushed and said, "Very funny!" She laughed "Though I thought him giving lots of curtsies too, will add to his fun tonight!" as they laughed.

Pam laughed "I suppose Baby has wet his nappy again!" as Nina said, "Again!"

Pam laughed "It's so easy to make him, have a little accident!" adding "Just the mention of Tina, coming in to see him, dressed up, has a torrential rain downpour, in his nappies!" as Nine screeched and her Mum said, "Stop embarrassing your brother Pam!" as she gurgled "Mummy! At least baby is protected"

Pam giggled, "Though I did pacify him with a pink dummy, frilly baby bonnet and then his baby bottle of milk, while Mummy was changing his nappy!" as Nina gasped and screeched "I couldn't see that?" adding "Baby had his head turned away from me, in the bedroom and although I did spy something on his head!" as she giggled, "I suppose we couldn't see Baby in his bonnet and with his dummy now?" His Mum said, "Now Nina, it's embarrassing enough!" but Pam giggled, and said, "Just for the encore Mummy, for the last ten minutes!" as he cringed at the thought of playing Baby Football in just his nappies and plastics, sucking on a dummy with the baby bonnet on his head as her Mum laughed "You are terrible to your big brother Pam!" as she gripped her skirt and bobbed a curtsy "Thank you Mummy!" as they all laughed and continued kicking the ball about, between each other. He cried "First off June sent me out to play in my flaming nappies and when I needed the loo, Pam told me I'd to use my nappies!" as his Mum said, "Thankfully it wasn't a jobby or some young lady would have been for

it!" Pam added "After we changed his nappies earlier!" as Nina gasped "You both changed him?" as Pam laughed and raised his frock and aprons to show the plastic baby pants over his diaper. Pam added "And some naughty baby did a wee over Mummy when she was changing his nappy!" as Nina screeched "Oh you, naughty boy!"

Pam gets Julie to come over and pretend Tina's there

Pam laughed "Lucky for Mum, I'd brought up her PVC pinny to protect her dress!" as they all laughed. He cringed and cried "She pretended Tina, was there and made me wet myself!" to more laughter. Pam looked up and said, "Talking about June, I'm sure she'll enjoy joining us for footy!" as Tom cried "Don't bring anyone else Pam?" but she skipped out of the garden. Pam laughed "Tom is so glad he's got his Pampers and diaper, not to mention his baby plastic pants to protect him!" as Nina laughed "Oh fab!" as she raised his frock and checked "Are your nappies doing the trick Tom?" and saw him nod "I think so!" as Pam giggled, "If he has any leaks, Mummy might have to change baby in the garden here!" as her Mum said, "No way Pam! Though he might be soaked by the time we finish here, with you girls teasing him!" Pam then laughed "What about if he needs a pooh?" as Nina gasped and his Mum said, "I think we can let him indoors, to use the toilet for that!" as Pam laughed and took him to the end of the garden and said, "Same deal as earlier, if you need a pooh, just call out "Pam! I'll get you for this!" He cringed and cried softly "What! I can't even go to the flaming toilet?" as she shook her head "I'm sure you'll be ok, it's just over an hour to last out!" and giggled, as she gave him a kiss on the lips. Her Mum asked, "What was that about Pam?" as Pam giggled, "Us girls like to have little secrets!" as they laughed and saw Tom pull a face. Pam skips next door and rang the bell and June came to the door and giggled, as she was told of Nancy playing Sissy Baby Football in the back garden, as they both slipped up the stairs and peered out to see Tom prancing about in his dress, hair ribbons and apron, with the handbag dangling and his dolly kicking the ball about.

June called out loudly "Hi Tom! What a pretty frock and apron!" as he cried "Not so loud!" as she added "I love your dolly handbag and hair ribbons too!" as he cringed and said, "Not flaming fair!" They went downstairs and June locked up and took a pretty handbag around to the garden, while Pam went over to get Julie, but not Tina. She rang the bell and their Mum answered and called "Julie! Pam's here!" as Julie exited, but with Tina behind who called "Hi Pammy! Are you playing dollies?" as Pam laughed, but shook her head and said, "Tina! You can get too much of a good thing! A break from dollies would do you good!" as she laughed "No I always play dollies!" to more laughter.

Pam asks can you come over as Julie nods, but mentions her cousin Nancy, saying, "We happened to see you playing curtsies with your cousin Nancy earlier!" as Tina called "Can I come too Julie?" but heard her Mum say, "It's past your bed time Missy!" as she called "Oh pooh!" as Pam giggled, at her statement wondering would Tom do one, while out playing Sissy Baby Football?" She replied, "Did you see Nancy indeed?" as Tina called "She's older than you Pam, isn't she?" as she nodded, "Yes just about a year older!" as Julie laughed, wondering would Tina twig that it was Tom, but she didn't.

Tina tells Pam about Julie's joke about Tom wearing nappies

Tina called "Mummy Says, she'll put Tom across her lap if he hit's me or calls me names anymore!" Pam gurgled "I'd love to see that Tina!" Her Mum laughed "Though I hear your Mum sometimes smacks him, but it doesn't hurt!" as Tina giggled, "Julie said, he might be wearing nappies!" Pam screeched "Oh Tina! Oh Julie! Could you imagine my big macho brother wearing nappies and plastic baby pants?" as they shook their head, as she continued "In a frilled baby bonnet and sucking on a dummy, or baby bottle of milk!" as they all giggled, and screeched., but Tina shook her head "I know we couldn't see him like that, but it's so funny, just hearing you and Julie tease about that!" with Pam knowing if she just walked across the street to her back garden, she'd see her sissy baby brother prancing about in a wet nappy and baby plastics. Pam asked their Mum, "Can I have a word a tick!" as she

took her in and saw her hubby watching TV and asked, "Can you come over a bit later, say, in half an hour or so's time, to see our cousin Nancy?" as she laughed "Dave you'll be ok looking after Tina when I put her to bed, if I pop out for half an hour!" as he said, "Yea Fine! She doesn't normally get up in the night!" Meanwhile June had just walked around and in with her handbag, wearing her apron to join his laughing Mum and Nina, who greeted her and asked, "How many girls or ladies know about his being a girly?" as his Mum said, "Only a few! Pam's been good and not outed her brother to too many!" adding "Just Aunty June here, who found out when Tom came home from school and shouted out "Mum do you know where my dolly is?" as June nodded, and said, "I was in the sitting room with his Mum, when he returned from school and couldn't believe what I heard!" as Nina screeched as she asked, "What about Julie and her Mum?" as they laughed "Pam wanted Julie to know and waited till I was re-enacting his first dress up session!" as June laughed "Listen to what our wonderful Doreen did to her naughty MSP son Tom, who'd never help with even the washing up considering it girl's work!" as Nina laughed "Naughty boy!" as they laughed.

His Mum said, "Pam had made me realise his hatred of dresses when she sewed some frills to his shorts and it ended up him dressed up in front of some of her girlfriends from the next street!" as they laughed as she said, "However, I got them to stop and not continue that!" as they booed. She laughed "That was until I asked one Saturday night of some token help to dry the dishes and the little MSP said, "No it's girl's work!" and something just snapped and I took him up and smacked his bare bottom, but then took him into Pam's room and dressed him in panties, petticoat and frock and took him down to done a pretty apron here and do his girl's work!" as they screeched "Fab!" as she bobbed a curtsy back. She said, "Anyway I didn't intend Pam to find out what I'd done and when she got back early from Julie's I let him run upstairs and change into his boys things again, but I made him keep the panties on!" adding "Knowing I just had to mention or show Pam and he'd be for it!" as they laughed. However, I made him stay in and Pam couldn't believe the change in her once nasty brother now saying, nice things to her and sitting near her and she eventually brought her dolls down to tease him silly.

His Mum tells how Pam knew she'd something on Tom who was scared

She ended up hiding a dolly between his pillows and when he rolled over in the night, found the doll and cried out as we came running!" She said, "Pam then knew she had something on him and made him carry Baby Suzie there, all around the house!" as they said, "How cute his dolly was!" as he blushed "Not fair Mum!" His Mum said, "You take over Nancy!" as they laughed and heard him say, "However, when she came into my room in the morning, to check if I was still sleeping with her dolly, she spied the panties sticking out from under my pillow and wouldn't accept any excuse and made me tell the whole story of what Mum did to me!" as his Mum bobbed another curtsy "My pleasure Tom!" as they laughed. He then said, "I'd not to tell Mum, that she knew, because when she found out, then Mum had to re-enact everything, stripping me and everything with Pam standing right beside her!" as they screeched "Did you?" as his Mum nodded, "She's very insistent and even gave him some smacks on his botty herself!" as they laughed. He huffed "Everything was the same, except for her standing there, until it came to the kitchen, with me in this flaming frock and apron here doing the washing up!" as they giggled. He added "She went out to ring the bell and Mum to call her around the side, for me to escape upstairs to my room!" as they listened as he huffed "She'd left the front door open and slipped over to Julies and brought her over and hid her at the bottom of the stairs, not realizing what she'd see!" as they cuddled him. He cringed "I then heard the bell and ran up the hall and wet my pants when I saw Julie hidden and heard her screech as I sobbed at being outed to her!"

Nina asked, "Did she tell her Mum?" but they shook their head and he said, "Julie asked for a sleepover with Pam and brought her favourite pretty nighty and panties!" as they laughed. His Mum laughed "Ever since that day Pam found his panties, she's made him wear a nighty to bed and panties too!" as they giggled. He continued "She stayed the night, but the two of them slipped in and slept with me for half an hour, without Mum knowing!" as they laughed. He added "Julie however, purposely left her nighty and panties at our place and Pam made me wear them

under my boy's clothes to play footy and then made me run up and down the street five times to get her things really sweaty!" as they laughed. His Mum said, "Her Mum came over to collect them and couldn't believe how sweaty they were with even skid marks on the panties!" and Julie had hinted that Tom might have hidden them, on his person!" as they laughed "Next thing she'd him over and striped down to see his panties and dressed him up again to do the washing and then sent him over to me in his frock!" as they cheered. Pam took Julie across and whispered, "Stay here for a minute and then come into surprise Tom!" as she hid again behind the chimney stack. Pam entered and said, "Don't worry Tom! I mean Nancy! They've said, Tina doesn't know about Nancy and so you're safe for now, as he gripped his dress and bobbed a curtsy to her as she laughed "You do curtsy very well for a sissy boy!" as in walked Julie.

Pam hides Julie to surprise Nancy and he does a poo

Tom cried "Not fair!" but then heard her say, "Come on Tina and see big sissy Tom!"

Tom gasped and pooed his nappies and cried "Oh no!" as Pam looked and wondered and couldn't believe as he cried out "Pam! I'll get you for that!" as her Mum thought he was threatening her and said, "Now Tom! I don't think she's there!" and to Julie "Is she?" and saw Julie shake her head "It's just a girly joke!" as she threw her arms around him and kissed his lips!" as Pam took the key of her Mum and slipped into the kitchen to get a chair. Nina took a photo of the blushing boy mincing around the garden in the apron, over Pam's frock and with a handbag and ribbons in. Pam brought the chair out and after locking up, she sat it down near the house itself, so he was viewable by neighbours in the back houses if they looked out. She the whispered to June, as his Mum asked, "What are you up to young lady!" as June went over to Tom and pulled him over to the chair as she sat down and pulled him across her lap, raising his frock to show off his plastics and diaper, as she said, "I think for that naughty outcry for threatening his lovely sister, he should have his botty smacked!"

Tom cried "Oh no! Stop her Mum" as Pam laughed "I think two smacks on the legs or one smack on his plastics!" as she said, "I'll be nice and not hurt baby!" as she smacked his plastics hard and he felt the pooh squish a bit, on his nappy and cried "Not fair!" as Nina said, "I'll go next and she too smacked his plastics, laughing as he sobbed "Not fair!" as she laughed "I'm sure with your diaper, you can hardly feel those smacks!" as Pam said, "Aren't the ladies nice, not wanting to smack Baby Nancy's, legs so his diaper takes the pain!" They laughed and his Mum said, "I'm sure you're right!" as she too smacked his plastics with the pooh now spreading much more about his bottom, as he sobbed "Not flaming fair Mum!" Just before June smacked him, Pam removed his ribbons and said, "I think it sounded like my nasty Sissy Brother Tom who yelled at me!" as they laughed, and he cried "No Pam! I'm sorry! Give Nancy her ribbons back!" as June smacked him twice and then a third time and said, "One for luck!" as he sobbed "That wasn't funny as she pulled him up, but he gasped and cried "Oh no! Those windows can see me dressed up!" but Pam held him and said, "Ten curtsies or else!" and saw him bob curtsies one after the other and finally had reached ten. Nina took more photos of him without his ribbons and knew they'd come in handy at a future time, whether it be days, weeks, months or years she couldn't tell. She thought to herself, imagine Tom in five or ten years-time, dreading his photo being shown and be willing to do anything she wanted. Pam then said, "Now skip twice around the garden and I'll get Nancy back again!" as he cringed "Not fair!" as he started skipping around the garden but felt the pooh on his bottom and cringed as he skipped around to more laughter. However, then his Mum gasped "Oh no! You haven't! Have you?" as he sobbed and nodded, "She made me yell that out when I was doing a pooh!" as they screeched and Pam gripped her skirt and bobbed a curtsy "Any time Tom!"

Doreen complains how awful a job to change his dirty nappies

She said, "For my naughty trick I'll add your ribbons back! Come here!" and stood on view and saw her sobbing brother let her add his ribbons, but with at least one lady spying him being turned into Nancy again. She asked,

"Do I get a curtsy and thanks?" as he gripped his dress and bobbed a curtsy, but then saw a lady laugh from her window and bob a curtsy to him back. He ran back up the garden and cried "Some flaming woman saw me and is sure to have recognized me!" as they laughed "Poor boy!" His Mum gasped "You know that's going to be a terrible job for me changing his nappies later! It was bad enough with him wetting his nappy, but now with a pooh, especially now that we've all smacked his plastics and it will be terrible!" as June said, "Look Doreen, for giving us such a laugh "I'll help clean baby up!" as he cried "No Mum, you do it! She'll want Nancy to go around to her house dressed up!" as his Mum laughed. His Mum said, "Pam that's a terrible trick to play on your brother!" as she laughed "Sorry Mum! How was I to know that just mentioning Tina, would cause him to do a pooh!" adding "He's such a big baby boy!" as they laughed and she added "I've a feeling baby will be needing his nappies and plastic baby pants in bed too!" adding "Under his pretty nighty!" as her Mum said, "No way Pam!" as she laughed "In a lovely frilly baby bonnet too!" as they screeched and he cried "No Pam! Don't make me! That will be terrible!" as she gurgled "Won't it, baby?" as she bobbed another curtsy. June asked, "Will I take him now?" but Pam said, "After the final event, in about half an hour and so they continued playing, kicking the ball about. Then Julie's Mum arrived but didn't trick him and he sighed as she said, "I've put Tina to bed and her Dad's looking after her!"

Julie laughed "I was a bit naughty and pretended Tina was here and he did a pooh!" as her Mum gasped "You didn't?" and saw them all, with their handbags and in aprons and the blushing boy, sobbing "It wasn't fair!" Julie laughed "Pam was brilliant! She had him wail "I'm going to get you Pam!" and so she brought out a chair, there and said, "For that outburst, he deserved a smacked bottom!" adding "And we all gave him smacks on his plastic baby pants, not realizing we were spreading his pooh, about his botty for him!" Her Mum gasped "Pam that was really naughty!" as she thought she was complaining, but then heard her say, "You should have waited for me!" and saw her take Tom over, to the chair and pop him over her own legs, as she smacked his plastics six times hard!" as he cried "Not flaming fair, this is getting worse!" Pam asked, "Want to bring the last ten minute and stop for, Sissy Baby Football!" as they complained "Oh we were enjoying the game!" as Pam laughed and said, "Arms up Baby!" and she pulled his apron off and held him there on show in her yellow frock with at least one lady, laughing at the obvious boy, in a pretty yellow frock. However, they couldn't believe it when she pulled his yellow frock up and over his head to leave him in the plastic baby pants over his diaper, as the place erupted with laughter of Baby Tom in his plastic baby pants and they all ran over and kissed him. She handed him, her own handbag, as he cried "Not fair!"

Pam laughed "He's got ten minutes as Baby Football, to look forward to, when I remove his frock!" as they all screeched, but she said, "I know he's loving standing here, on show as baby Tom again, with his ribbons!" as they laughed. Tom cried "Oh no! That woman is laughing at me from her bedroom!" as they all looked up and waved back to her, but didn't see her take some photos of him, as Nina took some more photos of Nancy again.

Pam removes his ribbons to show off as Baby Tom and adds a dummy

She then removed his ribbons and held him on show as Sissy Tom and repeated with more photos being taken of the poor boy. She then took him and removed her frock, saying, "I don't want my good frock ruined by you! You, big naughty baby boy!" as he sobbed, as he was left in his nappies and plastics. She handed him back his handbag and popped the dummy back into his mouth to more laughter and held him on show to the laughing lady again, but this time as a big baby. She gasped as she saw the boy with a dummy in his mouth and plastics over his nappies and screeched and took more photos of him, without him realizing, as he was busy mincing around and kicking the ball and being teased by the ladies and girls in the garden. They couldn't believe it that Tom was now skipping around the garden in the dirty nappy and plastics, but with the handbag on his elbow, occasionally kicking the ball and having to show off his dribbling skills but mincing with his handbag and with his nappies on show. However, Pam then remembered and slipped inside and locking up again, she slipped back out and held up his baby bonnet

and pink dummy to screeches. Tom cried "No Pam! Don't please?" but she stuck it into his mouth and then tied the bonnet around his head. She said, "I think five minutes with his bonnet and then five without with his face on show!" as they laughed and saw him skip on around and kick the ball a few times to more laughter.

He got to five minutes, when she removed his bonnet and said, "Another five minutes showing off your lovely baby face, but keep moving those lips in and out!" as she laughed and whispered "Every 30 seconds or so remove your dummy and suck your thumb saying, 'I want my dummy!' before replacing your dummy!" as he cried "Not fair!" Of course, photos were being taken think and fast of the blushing boy by both Nina and the lady at the back. However, she exited her bedroom and skipped downstairs and out to slip down to the end of the garden, to get a better look.

Tom was really embarrassed as he started skipping around the garden in the nappies with the handbag dangling from his mouth, kicking the ball occasionally, but knew he was going to have the garden in stitches as he reached up and took the dummy out. They watched Tom skip around the garden sucking the dummy in and out, but then stop and remove it and gasped as he stuck his thumb in his mouth and pulling it out, call "I want my dummy!" as the place erupted with laughter as he stuck the dummy back into his mouth to continue on around. He again was passed the ball to kick to one of the ladies who kicked it back again. They gasped "What a fab idea!" as she gripped her skirt and bobbed another curtsy to more laughter. Nina laughed "I think I know her, to chat to, around the shops! I'll ask her not to out Baby!" as he grimaced "Not fair!" Her Mum laughed "Pam you are terrible to your big brother!" as she held him for a minute and then got him to skip around the garden as Nancy again a couple of times before she removed his ribbons. June whispered something to Pam who slipped back in doors and soon had brought out about six chairs for the ladies, but also her Mum's diaper bag.

Her Mum asked, "What are you up to now Pam?" as June said, "I don't think our little baby, will want to run around to my place, in his nappies or even in his frock, if Pammy will let him, wear it!" as she shook her head "I don't want my good frock ruined!"

He begged "Please don't make me?" as she laughed "You're in luck, young man!" as she took two of the kitchen chairs and popped one chair on her side of the fence and the other

Ten minutes shows his skills at Baby Football in his nappies

on theirs and said, "Climb over and you can hop over to my garden, to have your nappies changed!" as he huffed "Mum! Will you do it? Please?" but she laughed "I'll let June have the honour this time!" June laughed "Thanks Doreen!" He cried "Ok! Make sure I'm not seen! Can I get my ribbons in!" as they laughed, but Pam said, "We'll see baby!"

The lady called out from her garden, Sorry I couldn't help noticing your sweetie playing dress up!" as his Mum gasped and laughed "Sorry My daughter Pam here has been very naughty and made her big brother Tom play dollies and dress up!" Nina called "Hi Yvonne! You couldn't keep Tom's dressing up a secret from the local girls and especially the boys!" as she laughed "Of course I will! Whatever is he in now?" as she gurgled "Not plastic baby pants and a diaper?" They laughed and nodded and heard her add "And this lady June has volunteered to clean baby Tom up at hers!" as she laughed "I hope it's only number ones!" as they shook their heads as she gasped "Oh dear! He is a big baby!" Nina laughed "His little sister wouldn't let him go to the loo and made him call out a threat, when he was about to go!" as she laughed as she continued "And then got us all to smack his botty and so it's spread all over his naughty bum-bum!" as she screech "Oh fab!" Yvonne laughed "Didn't baby want to mince around the front to show off his nappies and handbag?" as they shook their heads and Nina called "Baby Tom is a bit shy!" but added "I'm sure his confidence will increase to the point where he'll think nothing off popping out

into the street, in his frock, to join his mates playing footy and eventually join them as he is now as Baby Tom!" as they all screeched with laughter. Tom was at the fence in the nappies and plastics without the dummy and handbag over his arm, as he stood up on the chair and reached one foot over the fence, when Pam of course ran and held him and said, "Aunty June, you can pop around and help baby over!" However, she held up his dummy again and he'd to pop it into his mouth, now on show to lots of the houses now, without any ribbons to disguise him.

June changes Tom's dirty nappies in her back garden

He cried "I'm on show to the back Pam, let me down!" but saw her shake her head as her Mum went over and said, "Pam don't be cruel!" as she laughed and let go, as Tom reached his other leg over and jumped down again, feeling the horrid goo again in his nappies as well as the wet nappy on his front. However, Pam said, "Here Baby!" as she handed him the handbag again and said, "Baby needs his handbag!" to more laughter and then handed the diaper bag to Tom and said, "There's your diaper bag baby!"

Pam said, "I don't think Baby Nancy would want to go to bed in his dirty nappy!" as they laughed as she added "He might get nappy rash and have to go to see the nurse at school!" as they screeched and he sobbed "Ok! Not fair!" Tom took the diaper bag and motioned towards the side exit to get into June's house for his nappies to be changed, but saw her return up the driveway and heard her threaten to tell Tina, if he didn't do, what she wanted and saw him nod "Ok!"

Next thing June tied his hands together behind his back and said, "Stand still baby!" as she went in and got some newspapers and bags for his dirty and wet nappies. June said, "Right ladies and girls! If you can just line the chairs horizontal to get a good view of me, changing Baby Tom!" as he cried "no don't!" as she added "I think I have everything here in the garden!" He cried "Don't change me in the flaming garden!" as they screeched and positioned the chairs to best view. Yvonne too tried to get herself and good view of Baby Tom being changed, but due to the fence, she couldn't get as good a view of him in June's garden. She laughed as she wondered whether to chance slipping next door to ask could she take a peek at baby being changed, but knew it was a young girl next door, with her Mum and they'd laugh the place down.

June approached Tom and pulled down his plastics and then called out "Oh what a pong!" as they all screeched at the sobbing boy. She pulled them down his legs and off, to more laughter as he stood in the diaper. She said, "Mince around my garden too, Sissy Baby Tom!" as he started off mincing around the garden, which was more on view to the back houses, than his own. He cried "Oh no! the houses are on show from here!" as he cried "Can we do it in our garden, but she pulled him down onto his back and soon had pulled his diaper down, saying, again "Oh that smell's worse!" as she laughed "Any one got a clothes-peg?" as they all screeched. Tom was now left in both disposables, the one on his front half hanging off, showing off part of his little willy. The one at the back had completely come off onto the grass, as she took it and popped it into a newspaper and wrapped it up before putting it into a carrier bag and tying it up. She kept his bottom hidden from the ladies and said, "I'll keep baby's naughty botty hidden! I don't think you'll want to see me clean him up!" but then pulled the disposable from his front and Pam said, "If anyone has a magnifying glass, they might spy my big baby brother's baby-pee-pee!" as she called out "Why do you call it that Tom?" as he cringed and said, "Because it's only the size of a little baby boys baby-pee-pee!" as the garden exploded in laughter.

June cleans baby up and puts him back into clean nappies

June took some newspaper and tried to clean Tom's bottom, saying, "What a mess!" adding "It must have been all that smacking that we all did to his baby plastics!" as they laughed and nodded, "Poor you!" as she put some dirty newspaper away in a bag.

She said, "Now for the wet wipes!" as she started cleaning him up and said, "I'm getting there! I can almost see a bit of pink!" to laughter as she wiped him clean, as he huffed "Be gentle, My bum hurts!" Pam laughed "Is Baby Tom's botty hurting?" as he cried "You've been horrid today Pam!" as she laughed "Who's fault was it that he wouldn't help Mummy and I with housework and was a nasty bully to me for many years!" as Nina and Yvonne bot gasped "You mean it's only happened recently?" as they nodded, and said, "Just a few weeks ago!" as they laughed.

She soon had it almost clean and used some more wet wipes and was satisfied at her job and turned him around and stood him up to show the ladies and girls his bare pink bottom, with him whispering, "I need my botty wiped too!" as she took a wet wipe and poked his bottom to wipe it clean, as the girls and ladies laughed and said, "Yuk!" She then turned got him down again and applied the baby gel and then the powder to his bottom and then a clean disposable and stuck it down, saying, "Baby's botty is nice and clean and into a new nappy!" She then started wiping his front and cleaned it up with wet wipes with Pam calling "You keep missing his baby-pee-pee, it's so hard to see!" as they all laughed and he cringed "Not fair, Pam!" She wiped a few more times and applied the gel and powder and then the disposable and then pulled his diaper up for him, as they cheered. She soon was pulling his plastics up over the diaper. June put the dirty newspapers away into a bin bag and that into the bin, before seeing to the diaper bag and saw Baby Tom standing there in his plastic baby pants over his diaper. He begged for Pam's frock and his hair ribbons and heard Pam say, "Just skip around the garden as a Sissy Baby!" adding "Here's your handbag!" Then a cheeky Pam, reached over and took the chair back and holding out her frock "As Baby Nancy, is back into a clean state, here's his frock and some ribbons!" as he cried "Oh no! Let me get back Pam?" as her Mum said, "Pam! Don't!" She laughed "At least, he won't be on show to the back houses!" as she took the chair, as June held out Pam's dress to him and took his handbag back over the fence. He woefully took the dress and pulled it over his head and slid his arms into the sleeves as he finally had it back on and begged "Don't take me out into the street?"

Nancy minces around from June's in a frock, but Pam's his football ready

Pam called "We'll keep look out that your mates aren't about and it's safe!" as June said, "Here's Nancy's ribbons!" as she added his ribbons and then returned his handbag again. He took Pam's dress and pulled it over his head as they laughed and heard Pam say, "Oh we've got a nice clean Sissy Tom in clean nappies!" as he blushed and said, "Ha!" June led him up her driveway, but kept him behind her, as she checked the street and didn't see any boys or girls about, but saw the girls and ladies standing at Tom's porch laughing and waiting for him. She said, "Come on Nancy! Let's get you back, around home!" as she led him down the driveway. Pam slipped back into the garden and picked up his football, she giggled, as she joined her Mum and the ladies at the front of their house, said, "I knew Nancy would be fine playing football in the street, as she threw his ball into the street, as he saw his ball and cried "Oh no! Not in the street, Pam!" as she called "If Nancy, wants back in, she's to mince with her handbag and kick his ball, back in to Mummy and score in our gates!" as he cried "Not fair!!" Her Mum gasped "Pam! Nancy can't play footy in the street, in your frock and mincing with your handbag!" as they all laughed and nodded, "Wonderful idea, Pammy!" Tom tried to run back into June's, but she blocked his way and said, "Don't worry! If any boys come around, we'll run and hide you and get you back inside!" as he sobbed "Not flaming fair Pam!"

Tom minced out and saw his ball across the street and had to quickly cross, checking up and down and sighed as he saw it seemed clear. He ran across to his ball and turned guiding it, towards his own house, as he gasped and saw Pam and Julie and Nina standing, blocking him from scoring, in the gates, as he sighed "Not the three of you?" as Nina said, "If you promise to fetch the ball, if only Pam and Julie are in goal, I'll go back in!" Tom cringed and nodded, "Not fair! I'll be spied by someone!" He saw the smiling Julie and Pam in his gates and approached them, dribbling the ball towards them, but heard Pam say, "Hey no getting too close, shoot from there!" as he cried "But that's too far!" as he stood about halfway across the street. Of course, all the ladies and girls thought it

wonderful that, there was Tom dressed as Nancy, standing in the street, kicking the football, but with the added embarrassment, of nappies and plastic baby pants underneath.

Nancy scores a goal, but they remove his frock for Baby Football outside

He steadied himself and shoots hard, but it hit's Julie on the leg and goes to the right down the street and heard Pam gurgle "Right! Fetch your ball or else!" as she giggled, "It will be Baby Nancy or even Baby Tom without my frock and ribbons to kick his ball about!" as he cried "Not fair Pam! My mates or someone will see me!" as he sobbed and ran down the street, but Nina said, "I'll pop down to try and stop anyone recognising him or catching him!" as she skipped past Julie and Pam, who tried to stop her. She ran down and saw him get to the ball, as a lady came up the street, but laughed as it's was Brenda, Alice's friend and heard her giggle "Gosh Nancy! You are brave playing football in the street!" as Nina laughed "You know about Sissy Tom?" as Brenda laughed "I did spy him with his doll's pram!" as he kicked the ball up the street trying to get inside again. He kicked it up to nearby his gate and saw Pam and Julie run back to guard the gate and saw him get nearer as Pam said, "Back Tom, but saw him kick and score past them and said, "Goal! Let me in Pam!" as he minced towards them but gasped as he felt them take hold of his frock and pull it over his head and off, as he cried "Oh no!" as he was now in his nappies again. Nina and Brenda screeched "Oh girls! You haven't! Not outside in his nappies?" as Doreen said, "Pam! Let Tom in again!" but Julie called "Mummy throw his ball back!" and saw her laughing Mum pick up the ball and throw it, out above his Mum and out into the street, as the girls pushed Baby Nancy, out into the street and said, "Baby Nancy can now try and score and we'll let her back inside!" Tom saw the ball now across the street again, but near Julie's house and gasped as he ran down, now in his nappies and plastic baby pants, to get it, as Brenda and Nina gasped "Oh girls! You are naughty!" The noise outside with Brenda and Nina giggling about his nappies, awoke Tina, who happened to wake up and call "Daddy! I'm thirsty! Can I have some water?" as she exited her room door in her nighty and called again. Her Dad heard her and said, "Ok dear! I hope you don't wet your bed again!" as he fetched her, a glass of water.

He went upstairs and handed it to her, saying, "Your Mummy and Julie are not returned yet!" as he returned downstairs to watch TV again. Tina returned to her bedroom and turned on the light to drink her water and sat up on the bed at the small front bedroom, happened to hear some chatter and laughing from the street and she had got onto her bed and reaching up, peered out. Tom had just got to the ball, when he saw a light, come on, at Julie's house and looked up, as he cried "Oh no! It's not Tina?" and kicked the ball back up the street and ran after it, in his nappies. Julie and her Mum gasped, as they saw a light on in Tina's room and Julie gurgled "Mummy! I think Tina's up!" as they saw a face appear at the window looking out, Tina saw her Mum and Julie across the street at Pam's, but gasped as she saw a girl in ribbons, but also in nappies and baby plastics, kicking a ball up the street and over towards Pam's house and kick the ball in, with Pam at the gate. Julie was distracted by Tina and so it was just Pam in the gateway to try and block Tom from scoring and so Tom scored past her, as she cried "Julie! You let Baby Nancy score!" Tina then saw the girl kick the ball in, past Pam at her gate and run in through the gate, but she then saw Pam, pull her ribbons out and wondered, could that be her cousin Nancy in nappies and baby pants. However, she then saw Pam's Mum take Nancy in and into the back door and out of sight, with Pam and Julie laughing.

STORY 09

IAN COMPLAINS TO HIS MUM ABOUT THE GIRLS

Ian tells his Mum about the girls dressing him up

Hence, after dressing as boys again, and sat there being warned not to be naughty and offer to help their Mum's and sisters with housework. Asking their Mum's for an apron.

Most had then run on home and up to their rooms to cry and wonder what to do and reflect, on the horrid morning's events. However, Ian had ran in and sobbed to his Mum "Not flaming fair! He decided to tell some, but not all to her. She cuddled him and asked, "What on earth is wrong dear?" as she sat him down and he told about going to join his mates and the girls asking them to teach them, how to play football?" as his Mum laughed "Nothing wrong with that!" as he huffed "It was a trick!" as she laughed "What?" He continued "I followed them to their back garden, around the next street and saw some other girls of varying ages, some in aprons as his Mum showed him hers and the ball and started kicking it about, to show them.

However, next thing they flaming-well, got me down on the ground, as she gasped "What did they do! Not undress you?" as he huffed "Worse!" as she laughed "What?" as he cringed. He Says, "They tied a flaming frilly apron around me and slid a handbag up my arm and tied it there!" as she gasped and giggled, "They didn't!" as he nodded, "Then they got me up and made me an offer!"

His Mum giggled, "What?" as he sobbed "Stay and play Sissy Football!" or be taken out to show my mates!" as she giggled, "Oh the naughty girls!" as he huffed "Of course I didn't want to be shown off as a sissy, so stayed there and they then popped ribbons into my hair and then added a skirt and flaming panties too!"

She screeched "They never and showed off your little willy?" as he huffed and held his head in his hands" They made me call it my baby-pee-pee!" as she gasped, as he added "and say, it was the size of a little baby boy's, baby-pee-pee!" as she gasped "So! I might have a daughter here, too!" as he cried "Don't you start, Mum!" as she giggled.

He continued "They then joined me in their aprons and carrying handbags, to kick the ball about in the garden and then took me into the house, where some other girls were there. He huffed "They then got me into a frock!" as she giggled, "Didn't you try to run?"

He huffed "They threatened even worse, if we were naughty?" as his Mum asked, "What?" as he huffed "1st off, a baby's dummy to suck on!" as she gasped "Then they produced a baby bottle of milk, which I'd to suck from!" but then they said, "You know what's next?" She gasped and giggled, "Nappies! Oh wonderful!" He cried "No it wasn't!" as she giggled, "You aren't wearing, anything girly, now?" as he nodded, "Panties!" as she said, "Let me see! Please?" as he gasped "Don't Mum! Dad might come in!" as she giggled, and locking the back door, she brought him up to his room and locked the door, However, she then exited and returned holding a handbag and

ribbons as he cried "Don't make me Mum?" She said, "trousers off, missy!" and soon he had removed them and she giggled, at his frilly yellow panties!" saying, "At least they aren't pink!" as he huffed "Not fair!" and fed the handbag over his head and ribbons into his hair and said, "Continue Missy!" as he sobbed "Not fair, Mum!" She asked, "Was that it?" but saw him shake his head and say, "I was led into the next room and saw 2 of my mates in dresses too, carrying a handbag and with hair in ribbons, as she giggled, "Who?" as he huffed "James and Pete!"

Ian also tells his Mum about the other five boys in frocks

She giggled, "Wait till I tease the little girlies!" as he begged "Please don't Mum?" as she giggled. We had to sit there and suck dummies and play dollies, when we heard another boy in the back, but were warned, not to make a noise. She giggled, "How many did you end up?" as he huffed "6" but it was worse for big Larry and Pete!" as she gasped and giggled, "Why?" as he laughed "They ended up in nappies and plastic baby pants!" as his Mum had tears, running down her cheeks laughing "The girls actually diapered the big boys!" He nodded, "but then added "Well Larry, but Pete got it worse!" and said, "He was diapered in front of Larry and me!" as she gasped and giggled, "The poor girlies! I mean babies!" as she giggled, "I might have some of your old baby stuff, around in the box-room!" Ian gasped "Mum! You wouldn't!" as she gurgled "It's been years since I changed your nappies and baby pants!" as he gasped and blushed "Not funny, Mummy!" He continued "They say, we've to ask to help our Mummies with housework and wear an apron too!" He added "A girly one!" as she giggled, "Is that over a skirt or frock?" as he huffed "Funny, Mum! Ha!"

She giggled, "It would be nice to have another pair of hands, to help me around the house!" adding "And fun, if you were in a frilly apron!" as he gasped "Mum! You wouldn't!" as she giggled, "At least, if it was an apron dress, it would hide baby's nappies and plastics!" as he huffed "Not funny, Mum!" She laughed "Where can I get a pretty apron, for you?" as he begged "Please don't, Mum? Let me wear my school apron if anything?" as she laughed "I suppose I could speak to your cousin and get a few!" as he begged "Don't Mum. They'd want to see me dressed up, as she gurgled "What as Larry?" as he blushed.

He added "Some of the boys looked really silly in their aprons!" as she asked, "Why?" as he added "They were little girl's aprons, from a 3 or 4 year old's, especially initially Larry's and then in his nappies, with a short dress!" as she laughed "Rosie! Next door is 4 or 5 and hers might fit you!" as he begged "Please don't Mum? Hers would be too girly!"

His Mum pops next-door to Rosie's to get some aprons and dollies

She let him rest in his room and exited the house, popping around to Rosie's, as she saw her Mum and said, "I'll have a couple of young nieces staying soon and was wondering could I borrow a couple of Rosie's aprons?" as her Mum laughed and said, "I don't see why not!" as she asked, "What ages for!" as his Mum said, "A 5 year old and 3 or 4 year old!" as she added "And possibly a couple of Rosie's old dollies and dress up clothes!" adding "I'll buy her a new dolly, for helping me!" Her Mum called the little girl and said, "Aunty Irene here is wanting to borrow a few aprons?" as she asked, "What for big Ian?" as her Mum laughed and Irene screeched "Oh Rosie I could just imagine my Ian in your sweet aprons!" as she laughed too. Her Mum said, "She's having a couple of little nieces over to stay and would you have a pinny for a 5 year old and then one for a 3 or 4 year old!" adding and some of your old dollies and clothes for them, adding Aunty Irene will buy you a new dolly if you can. Rosie giggled, "Ok I'll bring them around in a while! I don't want them having my good dollies and breaking them!" as Irene laughed "I'll keep an eye on them!" but then Rosie said, "Me too! I want to be there when the girls are playing with my dollies!" as Irene called thanks and went back around next door.

296

She giggled, to herself at Ian's reaction on seeing the aprons and then the dollies and having to play dolls and wondering if to let Rosie play with him. Hence, Rosie set about finding a few pretty aprons and then some dolls and dolls clothes to fit, aided by her Mummy and popped the clothes into a sweet handbag. About an hour later she wheeled her dolls pram around and knocking on the side door, saw Irene open the door and called "I've got those aprons here!" as his Mum, took his arm and led him to stand by the door looking down at the little girl, saying, "Ian just come and see what little Rosie has supplied for your cousins! Lucy and Alice" as she led him out and he gasped at seeing Rosie with her dolls pram and holding up some aprons. He gasped "Oh no Mum!" as she said, "Just take the aprons from Rosie and thank her!" as he gasped "What?" She held out the aprons and saw the big boy take hold of them as his Mum led him out to the driveway beside the girl and said, "Hold them up and let me see Ian!"

He cried "Don't Mum!" as Rosie laughed at the big boy holding them. His Mum took the little one and said, "Oh Rosie isn't that a pretty apron?" as Rosie replied, "That's from when I was only 3 or 4" as she then said, "Hold yours up Ian and tell Rosie thanks!" as he tried to get back inside, but his Mum said, "Now what happens to naughty boys!" Rosie laughed "They get a spanked botty!" as his Mum laughed and are put into their nappies and baby pants!"

Rosie then realizes the girly aprons and dollies are for him

Rosie screeched with laughter at the joke and the blushing boy. He then held up one of Rosie's new aprons and saw it was a bit bigger and might fit him and hoped his Mum wouldn't let slip. He said, "There!" as his Mum laughed "Don't you like that one Ian?" Rosie laughed and then heard his Mum say, "I think he's saying, he'd prefer this one Rosie!" as she fed it down his front and tied it quickly behind him, causing him to cry "Don't Mum!" as Rosie screeched "Oh that pretty apron suit's you Ian!" as his Mum said, "Thank Rosie for her aprons!" as she then said, "Here's the dollies and dolls clothes for your nieces!" but then added "And Ian!" His Mum then said, "Take the dollies Ian!" as he cried "don't Mum! Please get this pinny off me!" as Rosie held up the dolls and saw the boy take them. She said, "Don't break them Iany!" His Mum laughed. "Now promise not to be too rough with her dollies when playing with your cousins and their dollies!" as Rosie giggled, and asked, "Will you be playing dollies?" as he cried "No way!" Rosie laughed "He should play in that little girls apron!" as she held out a handbag and said, "I've got their dollies clothes in here to dress his dollies!" as his Mum laughed "Take the dolls clothes!" as he sobbed "No don't make me! Not fair!" as his Mum took the handbag and fed it over his head and down his body as Rosie clapped and laughed "I love his new look!"

Rosie asked, "Can I play dollies with him?" His Mum laughed "In doors! Or out dearie?" as he cried "Not like this! In doors!" as Rosie laughed "What can I do with my dolly pram?" as his Mum laughed "We might let you play dollies in doors, if some sweet boy wheels Rosie's dolly pram around the back and into the garage, in case it rains. He cried "Not fair Mum!" as she said, "Better be quick before some girly friends come by! Hint, hint!" as he sobbed "Not fair!" and stepping out he took hold of the dolls pram handles and wheeled it out the back with a laughing Rosie and his Mum following him. He wheeled the pink pram around to the garage and then saw it was locked and he cried "Oh no where's the key?" She laughed "I'll go and fetch the key if some sweet boy wheels his dollies around the garden with Rosie!" as he cried "Not fair! Let me get these off?" as she laughed "If you remove your apron and handbag, it's 10 times around the garden with Rosie or only 5 with them as Rosie giggled, "OH playing Mummy's with my dolls pram is more fun in the street!" as his Mum laughed "Well Ian! Here or the street!" Rosie giggled, "Go on Ian! Wheel your dollies into the street as he sobbed "Not fair! Ok here!" He wheeled the dolls pram around with a giggling Rosie beside him and part way around she said, "Hold your dollies with one hand and heard him beg "Please don't tell Rosie!" as she giggled. His Mum looked out and saw him sweetly mincing around as she opened the window and laughed "Ian! Take the handbag and slide it over your elbow!" as Rosie giggled, "He wants to go shopping too!" as he cried "No way!"

Rosie's Mum spies Ian wheeling a dolly, mincing around with handbag

He was around the gardens 3 times when Lucy's Mum looked out and gasped and giggled, from the upstairs window and opening it called down "Rosie! You teaching Ian how to play dollies?" Rosie shouted, "He's just practicing before we play in the street and then go to the shops!" as her mum laughed "I love your handbag and little pinny!" as Rosie giggled. He sobbed "Not fair!" as his Mum appeared and waving up laughed "Hi Irene! You see what your little Rosie has made my big Ian do!" as she laughed "She's such a bully!" to more laughter and asked, "Want to come around for a cuppa?" as she nodded, "I thought you were taking him and Rosie shopping!" His Mum laughed "He's well prepared with his pinny and handbag!" as he threw it down and cried "I'm going!" and setting the dolls into the pram tried to run back in. However, his Mum had locked the door and waited with Rosie saying, doors locked "My sweet Ian must be wanting to play dollies in the street!" Rosie pushed the pram on and out to see him at the back door and call "Ian your Mummy Says, your wanting to play dollies in the street!" as he cried "No please don't?" His Mum handed the handbag back to Rosie and say, "See if you can find a suitable place for his handbag Rosie!" as she saw him trying to get the apron off. Her Mum then appeared with her handbag and laughed at Ian in the apron and then Rosie holding up the handbag and say, "Get your handbag on your arm sissy or it's shopping instead of the street!"

He cried "not in the street please?" as they giggled. His Mum whispered and saw Rosie take the handbag and run down to her Mum and said, "Sissy Ian wants his handbag tied to the gate!" adding "He'll be wheeling his dollies, down to get his handbag!"

Her Mum took it and tied it around the gate saying, "There Ian! Your pretty handbag is ready!" as he cried "Have you some hair ribbons or a scarf?" as Rosie removed a couple of slides and held them out to him. He woefully put them into his hair. His Mum said, "If sweetie doesn't want to be taken shopping, then better wheel his dolly down and mince back with his handbag!" He cried "Not fair! I wish I'd not told you about the dress up this morning!" as his Mum laughed and pushed him on. Rosie giggled, at the sissy boy wheeling her dolly down the driveway and he called "Make sure nobody is about!" as her Mum looked up and down and giggled, as she saw a lady coming up with her shopping bag and handbag! She said, "Coast Is clear Alice!" as his Mum laughed and pushed him on.

He wheeled the pram down and was at the gate when he heard the gate open and her Mum pushed him out and closed it. She lifted the pram and popped it back over the gate as he cried "Not fair!" as he was threatened with being taken to town and joined Rosie pushing the dolls pram down with the handbag on his arm. They were led back in to Lucy's with his Mum had they any dress up clothes for his size, and they nodded, saying, her cousin gave her some skirts and frocks to play dress up in and heard Ian beg "Please don't dress me up?" as they giggled.

Ian wheels the pram around to Rosie's where Larry joins them

They were playing away when his Mum laughed "Oh there's one of his little mates!" as Irene laughed "I bet he doesn't want him to come and join in!" His Mum laughed "Would you like some company, it should be even funnier for Rosie!" as she joined her down, but Irene asked, "Will he come over?" Hariet laughed "I'll see if I can persuade him!" as she exited the house and called Larry have you got a moment?" as he saw Ian's Mum and huffed "Is he about?" adding "to play footy!" as she laughed "I heard a few rumours about your fun and games with the girls this morning!" as he cried "He didn't tell did he! Not fair!" as she said, "I'll try and keep quiet if you come and play!" as he huffed "Not fair!" as he followed her inside. He was led upstairs and then Ian cried "Oh no not you too!" Rosie giggled, "Is he going to play dollies too?" as Larry called "I'm not playing dollies!" and tried to run, but Irene was behind and whispered "We could tell her about a big baby boy!" as he begged "Please don't tell on me!" She said, "Just go up and ask Rosie to play dollies with her and Ian!" and saw the boy go up and ask, "Can I come up and play dollies with you and Ian!" as she clapped with joy "Oh fab! 2 sissies to play dress up with!" as

he cried "I thought it was just dollies!" to more laughter. His Mum then whispered to Irene "Can you think any punishment, worse than making them dress up in frocks?" as she shook her head "Apart from showing them off around the shops, as sissy boys in frocks!" Irene laughed "Sounds some girls had them dressed up this morning at a girls house, but then to punish a few naughty boys, they produces a dummy and then a baby bottle and then guess what?" She gasped and giggled, "Not nappies?" as she asked, "Would you have any of Rosie's old ones?" as she giggled, "Old ones! She still wears them sometimes!" as they giggled, "Oh I haven't diapered a little boy since I was a teenager, but not a 6 or 7-year old! That would be so funny!"

His Mum laughed and nodded. She laughed "keep them amused!" as she went to fetch the nappy bag!" She returned holding it and heard Rosie say, "Mummy I'm not wearing nappies in front of them!" as her Mum laughed "Don't worry darling! It's for a couple of naughty girlies if they are naughty!" Ian and Larry called "Please don't Mrs?" as they laughed. Rosie giggled, "It would be wonderful to play babies with these 2 sissy boys!" as they cringed and heard Larry call "Not again?" as Rosie asked again "Who put you into nappies?" as he huffed "Some girls tricked us, this morning!" as Ian called "I didn't wear nappies! I only had to wear a frock!" to screeches from Rosie and her Mummy. Rosie laughed "Well Mummy I'm sure our girlies would like to play babies, instead of big girls! See big girls like to go shopping in town around the shops, whereas little or big babies only have to go around the street!" as they cried "We can't go out in our nappies!" as Ian begged "Please Mummy don't let them put us into nappies and baby plastics!" as her Mum laughed "I don't think Rosie's baby plastics will fit you boys, possibly Ian, but not you Larry!" Rosie giggled, and whispered "Then we should go at least to the local shops to get babies some big plastic baby pants!" as she giggled, "Oh Rosie you are naughty!" as she whispered to his Mum what Rosie suggested.

His Mum pops Ian and Larry into nappies in front of Rosie

His Mum said, "suggesting the shops!" as they called no don't!" but heard her say, "If our baby's ask to be diapered here now, we'll not go shopping!" as they called not fair, but heard them call "We're waiting!" and soon were asking to be put into nappies to screeches from the ladies and Rosie. Her Mum said, "Now Rosie you can't see when we diaper the boys!" as she asked, "Why?" as his Mum laughed they call them their baby-pee-pees!" as she asked, "Tell us Larry Why!" as he stammered because their just the size of a baby boys!" as Irene screeched "Oh you poor boy!" but then heard his Mum whisper if any of them are lying they might need to be punished "As she gasped and giggled!" and said, "Right baby's get undressed and we'll find you some frocks to slip into, before seeing to baby's nappies and plastics!" to more giggles. The boys were down to their underpants and Rosie was told to look away when Hariet took 2 disposables and removing their pants, applied them to the front of each blushing boy. Rosie turned back and screeched and asked, "What's that sticking out from their nappies?" adding "Why's Larry's, sticking out more?" as the ladies giggled, and her Mum laughed "I think some big baby, was lying about his baby-pee-pee!" as she took a dummy and stuck it in Ian and then Larry's mouths. Rosie giggled, and pulled the nappy off, as her Mum gasped and she giggled, "What's that there, Mummy?" as Larry sobbed "Not fair!" Her Mum handed some plastic gloves to his and said, "Let's see to baby's and turned them over to do their bottoms. They were soon gelling their bottoms, as Rosie giggled, and then turned them and she screeched, at seeing Ian's little one and giggled, "Ian's got a little baby one!" as he blushed and his Mummy laughed "I never realized, till today!" as Irene laughed "Didn't he let you dress him?" His Mum laughed "Not for years!" as they laughed and she said, "I think I'll be seeing it lot more from now on, to do his nappies and plastic baby pants!" as Rosie giggled, "especially with Mummy and me playing dollies with baby!" as he sobbed "Not fair Mummy!" Irene laughed "Rosie! You'll let him wear a frock!" as Rosie laughed "A nice short baby dress! I want to see baby's nappies!" to more laughter.

She huffed "Larry can come around to play babies too!" as he huffed "Not fair!" as her Mum laughed "Some boys like to come around to have a sleep over with their mates!" as they cried "No Mummy don't make us sleep

together?" to screeches from the girl and ladies. His Mum said, "I couldn't get it passed his Dad!" but then her Mum laughed "Well if they do have one, they could come around here and sleep together in nighties and baby plastics in our spare room!" as the boys cried "No don't!" as they all screeched and laughed and Rosie laughed "I hope our babies give each other nice kissy-kissy, before sleep!" to giggles, as she said, "Right babies! Give each other a nice kissy!" as the Mum's gasped and Pete cried "Not again!" as the Mum's gasped "They didn't make you earlier?" as they nodded, and blushed. The boys were soon having to give each other little kisses. Rosie tried to make them kiss longer, but Ian's Mum said, "No just a little peck will do!" as they gave each other a little kiss. However, then Ian's Mum had to go to the loo and

PART I

TINA REALIZES TOM IS NANCY AND PLANS FUN WITH HIM

June gets Baby Nancy into her large pram
Pam gets Nancy to school in dress and pinafore

Julie and her Mum return and tell her Dad they've been playing football

He ran in, but heard Pam say, "Shouldn't Baby Tom, score too, as she pulled his ribbons out of his hair!" as he cried "Pam! Tina's there looking out!" as she gasped and giggled, and waved over to the little girl who waved back smiling and laughing. Julie and her Mum realize they'll have to keep it a secret from her Dad and hopefully Tina for a while. They get in and her Dad asked, "What have you two been up to?" as she laughed "Just over at Julie's friend Pam's and had a laugh with her Mum!" Her Mum asked, "How was Tina?" as Julie smiled and heard her Dad say, "She woke up and wanted some water!" and added "I brought her up a small glass!" as she asked, "What have you been up to?" He said, "Just watching some football and then a film!" as Julie laughed "We've actually played football too!" as her Dad laughed "Yea! Sure! You two playing football, that's a laugh!" as Julie laughed "Such a MSP!" They had their supper and kissed their Mum's good night and returned upstairs to their bedrooms, but Pam slipped the baby bonnet onto his head and stuck the dummy into his mouth and said, "Just let Mummy see baby and see what she Says,!" adding "I might let you off, one of them later!" as he grimaced. His Mum went upstairs to read them both their fairy tales and gasped as she entered Tom's room and saw him sucking on the dummy and with a baby bonnet on his head and laughed "She does push it! Although here, it should be only the two of us, who spy Baby Nancy!" He cringed "Mum! Try and get her to let me off, especially those flaming nappies and plastics! It's terrible!" as she laughed "At least you can actually leave and use the toilet normally!" adding "Just pull down your plastics, diaper and pull the disposables off!" as he cringed "Now fair! I'm not going to school in those flaming things! I know that much!"

In the morning Tina thinks it's a dream about Baby Nancy

Tina wakes in the morning and assumes it was a funny dream she'd had. Her Mum gets her dressed and she joins Julie down to breakfast. Julie called "Hi Tina!" as she said, "I had a really funny dream last night!" as they laughed "Did you?" as she said, "I dreamt I looked out and saw that Nancy running about the street carrying her handbag, but kicking a football!" as Julie laughed "Still in that yellow dress?" Tina gurgled "No! She was in plastic baby pants and nappies!" as her and her Mum screeched as she laughed "What a funny dream Tina!" adding "Somehow I don't think a big 8 or 9 year old girl, would run about the street, in nappies, nor want to play silly football!" adding "Why would she carry a handbag to play football?" as Tina shook her head, saying, "I could only see the back

of her head, with her hair ribbons in!" Tina said, "Yes! You're right! but it seemed so real!" as her Mum laughed "Some dreams are very real! Maybe it was due, to you having that glass of water?" as Tina said, "It seemed to be, at the same time, that Daddy brought me up, the water and I peered out to see her, kicking the ball about!" She added "I saw you

Tina mentions Nancy looking more like Tom in nappies playing footy

and Mummy too!" as she laughed "Mummy and I were in your dreams?" as she nodded, adding "and Pammy too!" as they laughed as she said, "You were all waving up to me and when Nancy got in, Pam seemed to remove her hair ribbons, but then her Mummy, took Nancy up and into the house!" Julie laughed "Why would Pam want to take her ribbons out?" as Tina laughed "Maybe part of a game or something!" as she nodded. Tina then said, "Though that Nancy, has very short hair for a girl!" as Julie laughed "We have some girls in our class at school with short hair!" adding "It's not just boys who have short hair!" as Tina said, "We've only one girl in play school, who has short hair!" She then said, "How come if she's their cousin, she's living over with Pam and nasty Tom!" as Julie laughed "We'll have to ask Pam when we see her!" as Tina nodded. Her Mum then said, "Maybe because she has so short hair, she likes to wear ribbons to stop looking like a boy!" as Tina nodded, "Yes! She did look very boyish and you remember me saying, 'Nancy looked more like nasty Tom'!" Julie screeched "You weren't dreaming about big Tom running about the street, in nappies and plastic baby pants?" as her Mum laughed "Oh Tina! That would look funny!" as she laughed and nodded, "I'd love to see him in nappies!" as they laughed "Oh Tina!" In the morning Tom awoke and grimaced, remembering last night's terrible time in nappies and plastic baby pants and then also realized he was still in them under his nighty, with the baby bonnet tied under his chin and a dummy on the pillow beside him, as he blushed. He reached down and felt the plastic pants and said, "No way am I going to school in these!" as he then heard Pam knock and opening his door "Just checking Baby Tom is still in his nappies and plastic baby pants!" and saw him nod "I am! Honest!" as she laughed "Aunty June wants you to wear them around this morning under your school uniform!" He cried "I'm getting out of them now!" but she shook her head, you do and I bet you'll end up attending classes in a diaper too!" as he sobbed "Not fair!" as she laughed "See Baby at breakfast! No squealing to Mummy! Bring a pair of your boy's undies with you in your handbag!" correcting herself, "I meant Satchel!" as she slipped back to her bedroom to giggle.

They headed down to breakfast and his Mum saw him in his school uniform and smiled "I see you're back as a boy again!" but handed him his apron, handbag and dolly and saw him pull them on. He huffed as she laughed "I take it you're out of your nappies!" and saw him fib, saying, "Pam took them back!" as she laughed "I hope you didn't have an accident in the night!" as he shook his head, blushing away. Pam came down in her school dress and pinafore and called "Morning Nancy! What a fab night that was!" as he cringed once more. Julie ran over and gurgled "How is Baby Tom!" as she saw him in the apron with his handbag and carrying his dolly and gurgled "Oh it's Nancy again!" as Pam took her into the living room. Pam called him into the living room and without her Mum knowing, she pulled him across her lap and smacked his trousers and they laughed as they heard the sound of plastic baby pants and gurgled "Good baby!" as she let him go. Julie gasped and whispered, "Baby Tom's not wearing his nappies to school?" and saw Pam shake her head and say, "No! He's to pop next door and let June remove them and bring around his undies in his satchel!" as June laughed "Oh wouldn't you prefer to be protected at school?" as Pam laughed.

Julie Says, Tina thought it a dream about seeing baby Nancy play footy

Julie joined them for a few minutes in with their Mum and laughed "We think you're ok Tom! Tina thinks it was just a dream she had in bed!" adding "She did make us laugh talking about, seeing Nancy mincing about the street, kicking a football about the street!" adding "As I said, in her yellow frock, but she then said, Nappies and baby plastic pants as we all screeched!" as they laughed. Her Mum laughed "I'm sure Tom's glad to be back out of those

nappies!" as the girls giggled, and he pulled a face. She said, about her short hair, but I said, that's maybe why she had hair ribbons!" and we said, about girls in school having short hair!" as she said, "The dream all seemed so real!" but Mum was a bit naughty, when she thought Nancy looked more like Tom than Pam she said, "You couldn't imagine Tom running about the street playing footy in nappies and plastic baby pants!" as they all laughed and he sighed "Not fair!" Julie slips over and Says, to her Mum and Tina, I've to pop over to Aunty June's a tick, can you two head on and I'll catch you up!" as they called "Bye!" and saw her skip out over to June's. June laughed as she saw Julie and she laughed "I hear you're letting Baby Tom out of his nappies for school!" as June nodded, "It might be cruel, especially if he had to wear his diapers around kicking the ball! The padding might be spied!" as Julie laughed "I'm sure I can change Baby's mind!" as she said, "I'll hide till you're changing baby!" as June laughed "Naughty girl!" as they waited for Tom. Tom got himself ready with his satchel and popped a pair of his undies away for when out of his nappies and plastics.

He removed his aprons, handbag and dolly setting them onto the washing before kissing his Mum and Pam bye as he pulled on his blazer and picking up his satchel, he slipped around to June's, unaware of Julie's presence. He rang the bell and a smiling Julie answered and called "Any accidents in your nappies Tom?" as he cried "Be quiet! please?" and stepped inside and saw the changing mat in the centre of the living room floor. He begged "Please close the windows!" a, but she shook her head. He laid down and pulled his trousers down and she laughed at his plastics and diapers, as she then handed him a girly apron which he pulled around him and said, "I've got my undies in my satchel!" as June approached and pulled down his plastics then undid his diaper pins and pulled it off. She smiled at his disposables and said, "Oh Tom! Your disposables, do look sweet!" as he blushed and she said, "Aren't I being kind letting you out of your nappies for school!" as he nodded, "Thanks' Aunty June for letting me out of them!" as she laughed "That deserves a curtsy!" as he sighed "Close the curtains!" but she shook her head and pulled him up to stand in the short apron and saw him bob a curtsy to her, as she laughed "Raise your pinny a bit higher Baby!" She saw him bob another curtsy, but raise his apron a bit higher, but then Julie came behind and raised his apron up to show off his disposable nappies to the window and he cried to no!" and let out a little pee into the disposable!" June realized and gasped "You big baby!" adding "Sorry it seems baby is going to need his disposables to school!" as he sobbed "Not fair!" as she asked, "Want to attend school in your wet nappy or want Julie and I to change baby Tom!"

He cringed and bobbing a curtsy, asked, "Will you change Baby Tom's nappies please?" but gasped as he ducked down again, as he saw girls and boys going bye, as they giggled. June handed Julie some rubber gloves and took some herself.

June adds a plastic carrier bag over disposables for school

He cringed as they removed his wet nappy and popped it away in a carrier bag for later, with Julie giggling as she lifted it and said, "What a funny looking thing!" as he blushed. They soon were cleaning it with wet wipes and then applied the gel, as he begged "Not flaming gel and talcum powder and plastic baby pants?" as June had an idea and asked, "Does baby not want his plastic baby pants?" and saw him say, "No!" not wanting the plastic to make a sound, when he headed to school before he could remove it. Julie had applied the gel and sprinkled talcum powder over his front, before sticking down another disposable nappy and smiling into his face teasing and laughing. She heard June say, "Not a sound you two!"

as she took a plastic carrier bag and Julie gasped as she saw her make two holes in the sides and then slide it up his legs in place of his baby pants as Julie laughed "Oh fab! That bag makes an even louder noise when he walks!"

Tom sobbed "No! Not fair! That's going to be terrible!" as they both laughed and heard Julie say, "Right baby get your trousers up, if you don't want a diaper on top!" as he quickly pulled them up and gasped "Not fair!" as he

heard the sound. Pam was waiting for Tom to leave, wondering would June let him out of his nappies for school or not and then saw Tina and her Mum exiting. Pam called "Hi Tina!" as she called "Hi Pammy!" as Pam laughed "I hear you had a funny dream!" as she nodded, "It was about your big cousin Nancy who was running about the street in nappies and plastic baby pants!" as she screeched and her Mum said, "It made Julie and I laugh too!" as they walked on up, but Pam said, "I think Julie's still over with Aunty June next door if you want to wait!" as her Mum laughed "How's your nasty brother these days?" as she nodded, "The same as usual!" Julie looked out and saw her Mum with Tina and thought she'd get Tom over to them and see if they hear anything from his plastics. She said, "Right Tom! I want you to go straight across the road, before walking quickly up the pavement and head on to school, where you can change out of the plastic baby pant bag!" adding "If you try and cross the road or go off the pavement then I might tell!" Tom huffed "Ok! Not fair!" as he exited the house and gasped as he saw Tina and her Mum there walking ahead of him. He took his satchel and exited June's and crossed the road, behind them, unknown by them. Pam saw him and called "Hi Tom! Wait for me?" as he cringed and got over the street to be joined by Pam. He said, "Julie wants me to head on quickly to school!" as she asked, "Julie?" as he nodded, "She's there!" and saw Julie and June wave and Julie exit to run over and join them, calling "Hi Pam! Hi Tom!" as Tina heard and called "Julie join us here!"

Tom has to walk past Tina, but then they smack his trousers

Tom started walking quickly up the street and Pam gasped, as she heard a rustle from his trousers, as he walked and joined Julie trying to match his pace. He blushed as he got behind Tina and her Mum and saw them turn and look at him, but also Julie and Pam too. He called "Bye Pam! I'd better head on!" as he tried to walk quickly past Tina and her Mum and they heard a noise, as Tina asked, "What's that noise, Mummy?" as Julie called "Hi Tina! Did you not tell Tom and Pam about your dream, last night!" as she said, "Well Tom wasn't in it! Just you two and Pammy!" as Tom blushed, and Pam called "Tom!

Come here and listen to Tina's dream! It's a funny story!" as Julie gasped as Pam didn't realize June's trick on him!" They saw him stop and turn around and wait, as they walked and caught him up, as he asked, "What was it?" as Tina asked, "Where's your cousin Nancy?" as he stammered "Her Mum came and collected her early this morning!" as Pam laughed "Did she indeed?" Tina said, "I had a dream about Nancy last night!" as he asked, "What about?" as she said, "I saw her kicking a football about the streets!" as Julie said, "Well Tom likes playing football too, don't you?" as he nodded, and said, "I think she sometimes likes to play too!" and heard Pam laugh "Maybe, Nancy could teach Tom, how to play, the same as her!" as Tom tried to ask "What do you mean?"

Tina then gurgled "What, he wouldn't, in nappies and plastic baby pants!" as they screeched and he said, "Funny Tina!" as she added "I'd love to see you playing football in nappies!" as he blushed and huffed "Ha! Some chance!" and walked off quickly.

However Tina then heard the same rustling and called "Why is Tom making a rustling noise when he walks?" as they all laughed and Pam asked, "Will I let him go?" as Julie laughed and waited for Tom to get up thirty yards from Tina and asked, "You remember, Tom threatening you last night?" Pam gasped and wondering, was he still in plastic baby pants and ran up with Julie and both smacked the back of his trousers as Tom gasped and cried "Oh no!" as Julie laughed and said, "Run on Baby!" as Pam giggled, and saw him run on up the street to get away from them. They came back and Tina asked, "Why did you smack Tom's trousers?" as she hadn't heard the noise, apart from when he walked past. Julie laughed "I think Aunty June, played a naughty trick on him and attached a plastic carrier bag, to his undies and that's the sound, he's making before he gets to school and removes it!" Tina asked, "What?" adding "A plastic bag!" as Julie said, "An Etam's, carrier bag!" as they all screeched, as she said, "Oh fab! What a funny trick to play on nasty Tom!" as her Mum laughed "Especially if he'd to play football in the street with his mates!" as they laughed. Julie then thought "You know! It could have been worse!" as her Mum

asked, "how?" as she gurgled "The bag could have been, on the outside of his trousers!" as Tina gurgled "That would look even funnier, seeing big Tom run about, playing football in a carrier bag!"

Julie giggles that the bag could have been over his trousers

Pam laughed "You know what would be even funnier?" as they shook their heads and heard her say, as she took a carrier bag with her own stuff in it for embroidery and showed them "Instead of making holes in the corner to act as pretend baby pants!" as Tina screeched "That's right! They would be like baby pants he's wearing!" Pam laughed "But if you make the holes here and here in the bottom, centre instead of the corners, you can then pull it all the way up and slide the handles into his shoulders to act like a ballet leotard!" as they screeched some more. Tina gurgled "It would be fab to see big Tom in either of those!" Julie let the conversation subside a bit, but then added "I bet if he had a bag on show, he'd want to hide it!" as she laughed and bobbed a curtsy, with her dress and pinafore and Tina gurgled "Yes! We'd let him wear a dress, over his plastic bag!" as Pam laughed "And wear hair ribbons too!" as Tina called "Like Nancy!" as they all laughed.

Julie added "After you get him doing all that Tina, I'm sure he'd play dollies with you and then you can play Sissy Football with him!" as she gurgled "In his frock over a plastic bag?"

They laughed and nodded, with Pam saying, "Don't forget adding an Alice band or hair ribbons!" to laughter. Pam asked, "In the back garden?" as Julie laughed "Initially, but then the street!" as Tina gurgled and then heard Julie add "and then you might want to replace his silly plastic carrier bag, with something else!" Tina asked, "What?" as she gurgled "Plastic baby pants and a diaper over his disposables!" as Tina screeched "Oh fab! He'd do anything I wanted, and I could get him back for being so nasty!" as they all laughed and nodded, to her.

Tom gets to school and removes trousers and carrier bag

Her Mum then said, "Now Tina, I don't want you going anywhere near big Tom's trousers! Is that understood?" as she laughed "You're too young, little lady!" as the girls giggled. Tom headed, towards the school, trying to avoid his mates, when he saw one of them, he made an excuse and ran on, to stop them hearing the rustle from his trousers. He occasionally turned around to make sure Pam or Julie weren't there, to tease him or play another trick on him. A few mates mentioned about his red face, but he just said, he'd been in a hurry to get to school to finish a homework. He got to school and quickly hit the toilet's and removed his trousers, the plastic carrier bag and the disposables, wiping his front and back with some tissue paper, before getting the undies from his satchel and pulling them back up and then his trousers to feel safer. He then hid his nappies and plastic carrier bag inside his satchel, thinking in future I'll bring a non-girly carrier bag with me to wrap anything girly up in. He was dreading either nappies or bag be spied in his satchel or either of them be smelt by his class in the lessons and would say, he farted, if anyone mentioned the smell. Pam reached the school and waited till break time and caught him, saying, "I take it you still have the plastic carrier bag in your bag?"

Pam makes him get into the plastic bag as a leotard to wear home

He cringed "Does Tina know?" as she partially fibbed and shook her head, saying, she just wondered why we were smacking baby's botty!" as he blushed. She said, "Julie has asked you to do something, or she tells!" as he cried "What?" as she laughed "Now you didn't like, wearing that bag, as baby pants?" as he shook his head and asked, "What?"

At the end of school, Julie wants you "Make 2 holes in the bottom middle of the bag and then slide the bag up your legs and pull it all the way up, to pull the bag handles up over your shoulders to act as a plastic leotard!" as he cried

"Not fair Pam! That will be terrible!" as she laughed "You know to have your nappies on underneath too!" as he cringed "Not fair!" Tom cried "But someone might be in the loo!" but Pam gurgled "You could always use the girls loos!" adding "But you might need to slip into something more comfortable, as she bobbed a curtsy, with her dress and pinafore, as he blushed "Ha! Funny!" She asked, "Where's your last lesson?" and he said, "Art in 4G" as she said, "Ok! Make sure you're wearing your plastic leotard, baby!" as he cringed "Not fair!" Hence, Tom finishes school and slips into the loo and enters a cubicle to strip off, down to his underpants and then blushes as he puts on his disposable panties around his front and back, but gasps as he hears some guys enter the cubicle. However, Pam had noticed Tom enter the loo, realizing he'd be in the cubicle scared silly in case someone spotted him and watched two guys leave the loo, chatting together, as they exited. Tom waited and soon heard them leave and pulled the bag out of his satchel and woefully stuck his fist into the bag to made 2 holes and soon was pulling the plastic carrier up his legs and up his body and slid his arms into the carrier handles, blushing away, as he tried to keep the bag from rustling as much as possible. Tom slid his trousers on and then his shirt and jumper and finally his blazer, picking up his satchel to go, when he heard a noise outside his loo door. He thought it was another guy and tried to keep as silent as possible. Pam saw no guys leave and checked nobody seemed about and accidentally entered the boy's toilet and knocked and said, "Tom! Hurry up, with your leotard!" as Tom cried "Oh no!" and wet his nappy as she laughed "Catch you back home, Nancy!" as she ran out and gurgled, realizing Tom would have wet his nappy and have to wear a wet nappy all the way home. Tom sobbed "That witch!" as he felt the pee in the disposable, around his front and reached down, to the hole at the front, which had been up his legs, that morning and taking some tissue paper, he shoved it into the hole, under his nappy, cringing as he felt the wet disposable. He exited and checked nobody was there and washed his hands and exited, expecting Pam to be there and tease him silly. However, she wasn't and so he walked out of the school, hating the feel of the wet nappy on his front and the rustle of the plastic bag all over his body, as he walked along.

Pam makes Tom slip over to Tina's to play with her still in the leotard

He soon was walking along home, but then saw a few guys from his year, but said, "Sorry Guys I'm in a hurry!" and ran back past them, not wanting them to hear the rustle.

However, he had reached the top of his street, when he gasped as he saw Tina out her front with her dolly, but also Julie and Pam in dresses beside her. Tina saw Tom and called "Hi Tom! Come and play!" as he said, "No way!" and tried to slip across the road, but Tina wheeled her dolly across and said, "If baby doesn't play with me, I tell his mates about his plastic baby bag and saw Pam and Julie stand by the gate, smiling at him. He cried "Please let me in Pam?" She laughed "Now Tom! Just slip across to Tina's and play with her and she won't tell on you!" as he sobbed "Not fair!" as Tina called "What a big cry baby!" as Julie said, "Come on and she won't tell on baby!" as he joined her across the road. Tina wheeled her dolly across and they were soon entering her drive to her back garden and he felt Tina smack his trousers and laugh as she heard the plastic carrier bag and laugh "I want to see his nappy bag!" as Pam laughed "Oh Tom no longer has a nappy bag, have you?" adding "He's now a big sissy and has a plastic leotard instead!" as Julie and Tina screeched and called "Show us Baby Tom!" as he cringed "Not fair Pam! This is going to be terrible!" Their Mum then exit's and laughs as she heard Tina call "Baby Tom is now in his plastic leotard and has worn it all the way home! Listen Mummy!" as she ran and smacked his trousers and her Mum, heard the plastic bag and laughed "Oh Tom! You are such a baby!" as he sobbed "Pam made me!" as she laughed "Well it was your wonderful Julie's idea!" Adding "Did you like my joke, when I slipped into the boys loo before you came out!" as their Mum gasped "You didn't?" as she laughed "He must have wet himself!" as Julie screeched "You mean Baby Tom had to walk all the way home in a wet nappy!" as Tina gasped "Is he wearing nappies?" as they nodded.

She gurgled "I want to see!" as Pam called "Have you got a diaper bag ready?" as Julie ran inside and appeared a minute later with their one, as Pam laughed "I think Baby needs his nappies changed!" as Tina screeched "Oh fab!"

but her Mum said, "Now Pam! My little Tina can't see us change his nappy!" Pam said, "Hurry up and remove your shirt and jumper and then the trousers!" as he cried "I'm not removing them out here! Not outside!" as they laughed at his pleading, as their Mum took him down to the bottom of the garden. She said, "If we try it here, he mightn't be spied by too many neighbours!" as she helped him off with his jumper and then his shirt and heard screeches as they saw the plastic carrier on show like a leotard. Pam took them and handed them to Julie to hide indoors. She then removed his trousers and Tina screeched as she saw the full leotard, but with the disposables on show and gurgled "I can see baby Tom's nappies!" as her Mum said, "Now Pam, don't remove his plastic bag, Tina might see!" as Julie took his trousers to hide away too.

Tom removes his wet nappy and Tina realizes Tom is Nancy

Pam then had an idea and asked, "Can you get baby down a tick?" and the lady pulled him down onto his back on the grass, as Tina laughed and taking a dummy, stuck it in his mouth causing her to screech, as Pam then took her baby bonnet and tied it around his head to more laughter. Julie's Mum then took a diaper and folded it into the triangle and laughed "We'll add his diaper over his carrier bag!" as he gasped "Not fair!" Tom then cried "What about my wet nappy?" as they laughed and she said, "If you can get Tina to turn away, I'm sure Baby can remove his wet nappy and add a dry one in its place as he cried "Not fair!" Tina laughed "Can't I see?" but her Mum took her and led her up the garden. Pam handed Tom some plastic gloves and saw him pull them on and said, "Just pull off that wet nappy a tick!" as he reached into the hole at the front and pulled the wet nappy off!" as her and Julie spied his baby-pee-pee, peaking out through the hole and laughed at the sight. She handed him the dry disposable and stuck it down over his willy and heard Julie call "Baby Tom's back in a dry nappy!" as he heard Tina and her Mum running back towards him. Pam said, "We can now apply his diaper over his plastic bag!" as he cried "Not fair Pam!" as they sat him down on the diaper and started pinning him into it, with Tine screeching "Oh fab!" and called "Even funnier than with Nancy in her plastics and diaper!" They then pulled the large plastic baby pants over his diaper, that Julie's Mum had got for Tom that day since, she now knew about Baby Tom and that Tina or Julie's plastics wouldn't fit him.

He was pulled up and cried "Oh no! I'll be seen!" as Julie laughed "I suppose Baby wants something to hide his leotard!" as she called "Julie would you supply something to hide Baby Tom's leotard!" and saw Julie run in, but Pam had her yellow frock over and so next, Julie had exited and held up her yellow frock, but also had something behind her back. Tom cried "Not fair Pam!" as Tina saw and cried "What are you girls doing with Nancy's frock?" They laughed and fed it over Tom's head and fed his arms back into the sleeves as Tina gasped "He looks just like Nancy did, the other night and in my dream!" as Julie gurgled "Tom is Nancy!" as they all screeched. Tom sobbed as Tina screamed "Oh fabulous!" as she laughed "So Big Sissy Tom is Nancy and wears frocks!" as they nodded, and her Mum laughed "We were playing last night in Pam's house, while you were asleep and then Julie giggled, "Pam and I made Nancy play footy in the street!" as Tina gurgled "Fab! That means he can now play dollies with me in the street too!", as they laughed, but couldn't believe when Julie added "but then we removed his frock and he was left in his nappies and plastics to fetch his ball from outside our house, to be spied by my lovely little sister!" as she screeched "You mean is wasn't a dream?" as they shook their head laughing.

Tom must wear the baby carrier with a dolly in it over his frock

Pam said, "Tina, you made my big Sissy Brother wet his panties and then nappies loads of times!" as she asked, "Why?" Pam explained "Tom wasn't too worried about Julie knowing!" adding "But he hated the thought of you, making him wheel dollies up and down the streets and to dear knows, where?" Tina laughed "Oh Yes Tom! I mean Nancy! You are going to have lots of fun playing dollies with me around the shops!" as the girls screeched and Tom sobbed "Please Tina, Just let me play in the garden here?" adding "Keep me hidden from the boys and don't take me around the shops, that would be terrible!" to more laughter. Pam laughed "I'll go and get Tom's ball for

her, to play Sissy Football in the garden here!" as he cried "Please don't?" as Julie called "Hear that Tina! I think Nancy is dolly mad and prefers dollies, to his horrid football!" as he cringed. Pam goes upstairs and fetches some hair ribbons, but also his baby bonnet and dummy, but also picks up a baby bottle for Tom and pops them into a handbag. She went into the cupboard under the stairs and picks up his ball and pops out the side door. She takes it down the driveway, but at the gate, she takes a ribbon from her handbag and ties the gate shut, just in case he tries to escape up the drive and home quickly takes it out over to him. She giggled, as she saw Tina by the garage door at the end of the drive, with part of Tom's dress peeking out, with Julie and her Mum pushing him out of the garden, as he begged for some hair ribbons, as still looking like Sissy Tom.

Pam laughed "Now girls, let my Sissy Brother Tom have some hair ribbons. She opened her handbag and said, "Here Nancy!" as Tina gurgled as she saw Pam hold out, an Alice band and some hair ribbons, as Tom came out and meekly took them from her. He quickly popped them into his hair, as she laughed "I think that deserves a thank you and a curtsy!" as he gripped his skirts and bobbed a curtsy saying, "Thanks' Pammy, for Nancy's ribbons and Alice band!" as Tina screeched "Fabulous Pam!" as she then handed him her handbag and they saw him take it and slide it up his arm as usual. However, Julie then said, "I think we're being cruel making Tom carry his dolly about the place!" as Julie and Pam said, "No Julie, it's fun seeing him carry his dollies about!" as she laughed "So Tom, don't you want to carry your dollies about?" and saw him shake his head "No!" However, Julie then pulled the baby carrier from behind her and Tina screeched "That's my baby carrier! I'd forgotten about that! It will be perfect for Sissy Tom to carry his dolly about the street!" as he begged "Please don't make me?" but soon they were feeding the baby carrier around his dress and tying it behind his back, to laughter and giggles, as Tina fed one of her dollies into the carrier and said, "Perfect for our bit baby Nany!" as he sobbed "Not fair!" Tom as Nancy, now with the dolly carrier over his frock, has to still wheel Tina's doll's pram around the garden, sobbing at Tina now knowing about him and all she might make him do, with her doll's pram and dressi up.

Pam Says, Tina will want a re-enactment of last night's football

Pam went over and ran in doors again and said, to her Mum "Sorry Mummy! Tina has guessed who Nancy is and so his secret is out!" as her Mum scolded "How did she realize?" adding "Did Julie or her Mum let it slip?" She said, "Partly due to Tina, spying Baby Nancy, in his nappies and plastics, last night and wasn't convinced, when Julie and her Mum let on, she had just had a dream!" She continued "Also when she watched Tom pass her and her Mum on the way to school and he must have given the game away by blushing or something and I don't think Julie and her Mum could keep a straight face!" as she laughed "The poor boy! Ask her to not be mean to him!" Pam laughed "I think Tina is wanting her pound of flesh, for Tom being naughty and calling her names and stuff!" as she said, "You know I wanted the re-enactment of you first dressing Nancy up?" as her Mum laughed and nodded. Pam then gurgled "I've a feeling Tina might want last night's Nancy Football in the street, but then even Baby Football in the street!" as her Mum gasped as Pam laughed "With her standing right beside him screeching her head off!"

Her Mum gasped "Don't you let her, Pam! That would be terrible and lots of kids and people would come out to see him as a girly and then a baby!" as she laughed and nodded. Pam laughed "I'm afraid Tina is such a bully and made me bring my yellow frock, over for him to become, the same Nancy she'd spied from upstairs looking over at Nancy in your room Mummy!" She laughed "So! She's of course, got him in my pretty yellow frock, wheeling Tina's dolly, around her garden with a massive blush on his cheek, with Tina teasing and giggling at him. However, I'm afraid she'll probably want, Baby Nancy in his nappies and plastic baby pants like she saw in the street last night too, but I'll try and make sure not too many are about to spy Baby Nancy!" as her Mum laughed and said, "Try and stop her!" but Pam then gurgled "She might even want Baby Tom without his ribbons playing in the street!" as her Mum gasped "Oh no! Don't let her!"

Julie pushed the doll's pram out to him, and Tina called "Pam! Get your doll's pram!" as she laughed "Oh! but Pam said, "Now girl's we're going to play Sissy Football first!" as she threw his ball to him and he huffed "Back

in the garden, but they shook their head and Julie said, "Here in the driveway or the street!" as he huffed "Not fair girls!" Pam kicked the ball to Tom, who kicked it to Julie, who tried to kick it to Tina, but it skewed off her foot and Tina ran and kicked it back and then kicked it to Tom and called "Come on Nancy, kick it to me!" as he kicked it back to her. They carry on kicking the ball about, but Julie gasps as she sees a couple of Tom's mates coming down the street past and laughed "Nancy, don't turn around!" but Tina saw them and said, "Turn around, Nancy!" as he begged "Please Tina, don't be mean?" His mates go down and hear a ball being kicked, in the drive, but just see, three girls and a lady in the driveway and one bigger girl in a yellow frock and think "Stupid girls trying to play football!" as they walk on down the street.

Pam said, "It's ok Nancy! They've gone!" as Tina pulled his Alice band off and then his ribbons!" and called "Come on Tom!" as he gasped, but luckily his mates were out of range and didn't hear, as he sobbed "Not fair Tina!" Julie laughed "Oh Tina! Give Nancy his Alice band and ribbons back!" as she laughed and kicked the ball up the drive and into

Tom as Nancy kicks the ball in the street when two older girls appear

the street and said, "Only if Nancy runs to fetch the ball!" as he saw the ball go up into the street. Julie laughed "Well Tom want to go as Nancy or Sissy Tom?" as he took the Alice band and slid it into his hair, followed by the hair ribbons and cried "I hope my mates aren't still down there!" Tom edged up the driveway and peered around the edge of the house and checked his two mates, but they seemed to be gone. He looked out and saw his ball had rolled down about five feet, towards their houses. He timidly walked out towards the gate, checking up and down, with the girls slipping up behind him, smiling at him edging out in the dress and ribbons, mincing with his handbag out the drive. He checked the street and saw the ball, but also his gates across the street and ran over to get in and escape from the girls and their teasing and dress up. However, he then saw the gates were tied shut and cried "No! Not fair!" as he felt Julie and Pam take hold of him and turn him and Pam said, "Naughty girly, get your ball and kick it to Tina!" as he cried "In the street?" as they smiled and nodded.

He then saw a couple of older schoolgirls coming around and down towards him, as he cried "Oh no! Not in front of big school girls?" as they laughed "Just mince and they'll think you're a real girly!" as he cringed and got the ball and kicked it, to a laughing Tina in the street with her Mum who laughed at Tom now mincing in the street playing Sissy Football as Nancy. Tina kicked the ball to Julie and Pam and saw Julie run and kick the ball towards him, but it went up towards the two bigger girls.

He cried "No Julie!" as Pam giggled, at whether to expose her big brother as a sissy in frock and mincing with his handbag. However, one of the big girls saw the ball and went over and kicked it, towards the young girls playing football and Gena said, to Poly, that's unusual seeing young girls playing football in the streets. They continued down to the girls and saw a slightly bigger one in a yellow frock and with her handbag and called "That's unusual girls! You all playing football, in the street?"

Tina called "Our friend Sissy Tom is showing us!" Julie turned him and they gasped and screeched at the young boy in the pretty dress, hair ribbons and carrying a handbag, as he sobbed "Not fair Tina! Don't tell everyone on me?" as they ran and looked at him and giggled and held him. Pam laughed "He's my big brother Tom, who was a bit naughty and has ended up paying the price by having to join us playing dollies and dress up. The girls call "He looks adorable, in that pretty frock and with his ribbons and handbag!" Pam laughed "That's my best frock that he stole the first night!" as he cried "I didn't! Mum put me in it for being naughty!" as the girls screeched. However, then Tina ran up and said, "He has even more fun, when playing in his nappies!" as they saw her raise his dress and gasp and screech as they spy his diaper and plastic baby pants. She gurgled "Oh fab! You treat him as a baby too?" as the girls nodded. Julie asked, "Will we, while the coast is clear?" as Pam nodded, and suddenly they raised

his frock over his head, to screeches as the girls saw the diaper, but also the plastic bag leotard and screeched at the sight of the little boy, in the diaper and plastics, but especially the carrier bag as a leotard.

Tom cried "Oh no! Not in the street!" as Pam said, "Just run and fetch the ball and kick it up and score past me!" as he sobbed "Not flaming fair!" as he checked the street and ran down to get the ball, with Tina screeching her head off at the big baby boy as Julie said, "Tina try and tackle baby Tom!" and saw the little girl run towards him as Pam called

They remove his frock to let him play baby footy in leotard and nappies

"Tom show us your footy skills, dribble past Tina!" as he cried "Oh no!" as he had to concentrate on the ball and ignore who might come out to laugh at him. He saw Tina go to get the ball, but easily kick the ball past her, but she turned and grabbed hold of his plastic baby pants to giggles and screeches as he cried "You can't do that Tina!" as she gurgled at him held on show in the street. No men or boys spied him, but several ladies gasped and laughed as they saw Tom in nappies and plastic leotard and couldn't believe their eyes. However, Julie's Mum spied him and called Tina to let go, as Tom broke free, with her calling "Girls! You are so naughty!" but Pam had seen at least one lady, Annabelle, at her window and wanted her to know about his frocks. She asked one of the girls to borrow her handbag for Tom to mince and then took her yellow frock and said, "Before you go in, pop your frock back on and mince with this handbag, or we hold you on show!" as he woefully took the frock and pulled it over his head and then took the handbag and slid it up his arm to the elbow as Pam giggled, and kissed him and let Tom go and mince over to the gate, where Pam got him to turn and curtsy to the street and the girl took her handbag back, giving him a kiss, as she let him escape up the driveway and into Julie's house. Of course, several of the onlooking ladies, gasped and laughed even more at spying him mincing in the yellow frock with the handbag on his elbow.

The girls gasped "Why the plastic bag?" as Pam laughed "June next door put him into it as baby pants, when he didn't want to go to school in plastic baby pants!" as the girls laughed. Pam continued "However, naughty Julie said, she wanted him to put it back on, for his trip home, but wear it as a leotard as you saw girls!" as they laughed "What a fab trick to play with a boy!" Pam laughed "There's no reason, you can't do similar things with bigger boys or even your boyfriends, as they screeched as Poly thought of her boyfriend Danny, wearing a pretty frock. The girls join them into Julie's back garden and are told how Tom became Nancy and all about the panties and then his dolly Baby, Brenda and then him outing himself to June next-door, as they laughed. She told how her Mum, then realised that she knew about her trick with Tom, but then had to re-enact it, with Pam standing right beside them, as the girls giggled, more.

June put him into nappies, but she plans to use her pram

After dinner that evening Tom said, he was going out to play football with his mates, but again had to go next door to June's for more dress up. He slipped into June's and was let in and woefully undressed down to her panties, but was shown a blouse, but when he slid his arms into it, he realized the cuffs were sewn or tied together and his arms were trapped behind his back, so he was at her commands.

She popped a clean handky into his mouth and tied it with a ribbon, as she pulled his panties down and off to leave him naked apart from his socks. She then said, "I want Nancy to play dollies, but need to protect my good dresses, in case baby has another accident, with Pam or me here, pretending to bring Julie or Tina or some of your mates in and you wetting yourself again!" as he cried through the gag "Not nappies again?" as her and June smiled and nodded.

June pulled some rubber gloves on as the next things, he was lying on top, of a changing mat and turned onto his front, as wet wipes were used to wash his bottom before his bottom, was gelled and talcum powder was sprinkled

over him. Then the disposable was stuck down, and he was turned over onto a diaper. She smiled at his willy on show. She removed the handky and stuck a dummy into his mouth along with a baby bonnet onto his head, with him blushing away, as she pulled him to lay back facing up. Then she took some wet wipes and wiped his front down, before she took some gel on her hand and started rubbing it over his front and penis, saying, "We don't want baby to get nappy rash!" adding "Maybe we'll let baby Tom play with his mates again in his nappies!" as he begged through his dummy, "Please don't! Especially not in my diaper?" as she laughed. She then sprinkled talcum powder, over him and then the disposable was added, and he was ready for the diaper. June pulled his diaper up and pin it together, before his large plastic baby pants were pulled up his legs and over the diaper.

She got him up and said, "Right we'll release Baby Tom's hands now, but no playing up! Ok?" as he nodded and felt them cut his cuffs and he brought his arms around to his front and cringed "Not fair Pam! Why can't I just wear a dress?" as she laughed "It seems you wet yourself too easily, when Pam or I play a joke on you!" She said, "I'll undo your blouse and we'll get Nancy into his dress!" as he undid the blouse and pulled it off and soon was just in his nappies and baby bonnet. She eventually finished and got him out of her dress.

Meanwhile Pam had popped down to one of the ladies, Annabelle who'd spied Baby, Sissy Tom in the street in diapers and then frock, mincing with a handbag and knew she didn't have any children at school or anything and lived alone. She rang the bell and the lady answered and launched "Was that your big brother in the street earlier?" as Pam giggled, and nodded, as she was led into the living room. Pam laughed "He used to be such a MSP, and bully me, but now I'm getting lots of payback and am gradually increasing his girly outings!" They discussed some girly fun for Nancy without his Mum knowing.

June gets Tom upstairs into her sister's pram without Pam realizing

Pam gurgled "Oh June! Can't we send him to play footy in his nappies and plastics again!" Tom pleaded "Please don't send me around to play in my nappies and plastics again?" as they laughed and Pam kissed his pouting lips and said, "Thanks for the ballet class Nancy!" as he huffed "Not fair, Pam, turning me into a flaming sissy!" as she laughed "It wasn't me who shouted out to Aunty June, 'have you seen my dolly?'"

June nodded, "You did out yourself, didn't you Tom?" as he nodded, "Not fair!"

She said, "Hasn't baby got something to ask me before I go?" as she of course got him to ask again "Please Pammy! Can I go out to play footy with my mates in my nappies and plastic baby pants?" to giggles from Pam and June again!" as Pam said, "Well Baby Tom! No playing swapsies with your friends and changing each other's nappies!" as June giggled, again. Pam of course said, "June! If or when you have baby back out of his nappies and into my panties, can you get him to ask again to pop out to play footy in his panties again?" as June laughed and kissed Pam bye.

June showed Pam out and she slipped around to her house to keep her Mum in the back. June then said, to Tom "Look Tom, I want you to keep your nappies on for a while!" as he cried "Oh no! Not fair! Don't send me around to play footy in my diaper?" as she cuddled him and said, "Don't worry I won't! I want baby to stay here till I check something, but you've to be quiet or else!" as he huffed "Ok, what do you want?" as she first said, "Arms up!" and as he raised them, she slid him into a short baby dress, with baby reigns attached. He blushed as he saw his nappies in the plastic baby pants show beneath the short skirt of the dress. She said, "We'll keep this a secret from your Mum, but Pam too?" as he nodded, "Ok!" However, she then led him up the stairs and into the spare room, where his dresses and the pram were, and he cried "Close the blinds!" as she laughed and ran over and closed them. She turned on the light and took him over to the pram and pulled the pram handle down to the floor, so it's back end with the canopy cantilevered up, into the air, by the front wheels. She said, "Come over here Tom

and he walked over to stand where she wanted. She said, "Just stand on the handle here to keep the pram down!" but she then took the handky from before and popped it back into his mouth to keep him quiet.

She saw him mince over and stand on the handle, as she raised the body of the pram up a bit, but then pushed him back and he suddenly felt himself, overbalance and toppled back, into the body of the pram, as she took hold of the handle, as it automatically raised up off the ground and the wheels fell down, but she took the weight as she pulled down on the handle and next thing Tom was lying back, in the pram, with his legs up over the handle, as she gurgled "Oh fab!" He cried "Not fair!" through the handky. She removed it and replaced it, with a pink dummy and laughed "I wondered if you'd fit!"

Tom is given his bottle, but then fed some baby food

Tom begged "Please get me out of this!" but she slid a handbag, over one hand and then tied his hands to the side of the pram. She handed him a dolly and asked, "How does it feel?" adding "Is it comfier?" as he said, "It's horrid!" but then felt her, turn the pram around, but then saw her open the blinds as he cried "Oh no!" and tried to keep low. However, she then pulled up, the baby reigns and tied him sitting up right, as he cried "Oh no!" as he raised his dolly, to hide his face. She smiled into the pram, canopy and laughed "Oh! You look a wonderful baby!" as he looked out the window and saw both Julie's house, but other houses, to the left and part of the street, where people or children might spy him. He begged "Let me down Aunty June! Baby will be seen!" adding "Julie and Tina might spy me!" as she laughed and looked out the window towards their house.

Luckily neither Julie or Tina nor their Mum, were looking over and their Mum was in the back of the house. Pam too had stayed in the back, watching TV with her and her Mum, thinking Tom was out playing footy with his mates. However, Claire was in her room looking out for Tom coming up and maybe getting him in and then phoning Brenda again, when she happened to look up to June's windows. Claire gasped, as she spied a pink pram at the window, with two feet sticking up on top of the pram handle and part of a big baby on show sat up in a baby dress. She couldn't see his face but was pretty sure it was Baby Tom and gurgled as she ran and phoned Brenda. Brenda came on and asked, "Is he there, Claire?" as she giggled, "No! but you remember seeing that lady from next door to Tom, June in town with a large pink pram?" Brenda said, "Yea, why?" as she continued "I just happened to look down the street to see if Tom was coming up to play footy, when I peered up to June's windows and there were two feet in the air, on top of the pram handle and I'm pretty sure, she had baby Tom in his pram!" Brenda screeched "Oh fab! Wouldn't it be fab if we could borrow baby and take him walkies up and down the street?" as Claire screeched "Oh fab!" as Brenda said, "I'll just get my bag and pop around and see if baby's still in his pram!" as she hung up. June asked, "Is baby thirsty?" as he shook his head, but a few minutes later, she returned to the spare room with the baby bottle and removing his dummy, she popped the bottle teat into his mouth and smiled as he sucked the milk down. He begged "Please don't?" as she removed it a tick and then replaced it and saw him suck more. However, he'd forgotten to raise his dolly up and his face was on show, although hidden a bit by his baby bottle, as she removed it and stuck his dummy back into his mouth. He thought it was bad enough with the baby bottle but gasped as he then saw a bowl and realized she was going to feed him. He begged "Please don't?" as he then gasped as she produced a plastic bowl of baby food and laughed as she took a bib and tied it around him and then fed him. She raised a small spoon to his mouth. He cried "Oh no! That's horrid!" as she laughed "Oh fab!" as she took a bigger spoon and soon it was emptied into his mouth and he pulled such a funny face that she took some photos and videos of him.

Claire and Brenda go down to June's to feed baby

Five minutes later, Claire heard Brenda at her door and let her in. Brenda had quickly minced up the street and when part way up the street, managed to see part of the top of the pram and some of his baby bonnet peeking from

inside the canopy. She smiled and skipped quickly up to Claire's and rang the bell. Claire let her in and closing the door, she took her up to her bedroom and pointed out and sure enough, Tom was still in the pram at the window. Brenda laughed "Oh look Baby is being given his baby bottle and then a dummy!" as Claire laughed "I wonder could we borrow the pram to take baby walkies?" as Brenda gurgled "Where? In the street?" as she nodded, and they laughed. Brenda joins Claire and they spy June giving baby his bottle, but then his baby food and wonder could they take baby walkies. They take a baby bottle of milk and head down towards June's.

They head down and peer up at the window, as they enter June's and ring the bell laughing their head off. June hears the bell and think's it's Pam and Says, "Keep quiet! We don't want Pam to know about baby Tom in his pram!" as he nodded, and she stuck a dummy into his mouth again. She descended the stairs and opening the door, wondering who it was. She then recognized Claire and then Brenda from the bakery and laughed as she asked, "Yes Claire, Can I help?" as she laughed "I couldn't help noticing baby upstairs and phoned Brenda to join me and we've brought baby Tom some more milk, if that's ok!" June nodded, "Keep quiet and we'll surprise baby!" as they entered and she called "Bye Pam!" as she closed the door and said, "Stay there a minute and then come up! Baby might have a little accident!" as they laughed quietly. June ascended the stairs and slipped back into the room where Tom was sucking on his dummy. She said, "Don't worry I sent Pam back around!" as he sighed and saw her pop the baby bottle back into his mouth and he resumed sucking, but then heard footsteps on the stairs and she smiled as she saw his eyes open wide and he wet himself.

He was expecting Pam to bound in and tease him silly, when he saw Brenda and Claire enter and laugh "What a lovely baby pram for a big baby boy!" as he sobbed "Not fair!" but then he did his nappy – number twos and sobbed "I want to go home!" as June asked Brenda "Want to feed baby first?" as she giggled, and nodded, "Please!" as she took the bowl and slid a large spoon back into his mouth and saw him make a funny face in the canopy, causing them all to laugh. June said, "Try not to be loud, as I'm keeping it secret from Pam and her Mum too!" as they laughed "We see?" Then Claire took her baby bottle and said, "Let me, wash baby's food down!" as he nodded, and heard Brenda laugh "I think baby liked that too much!" adding "Give him more food between his baby bottles!" Claire asked, "Has baby done a tinkle yet?" and saw him nod as Brenda asked, "What about poo poos?" but they gasped as he nodded, to that too,

Pam calls around at June's while Nancy is upstairs in the large pram

June laughed "Thank goodness for nappies and plastic baby pants!" as he blushed bright red. Brenda laughed "We were wondering could we borrow baby's pram to have fun with him?" as he cried "Oh no! Don't take baby walkies?" as they laughed and she said, "Don't worry we'll keep baby hidden and let him lie down so nobody will see!" as June said, "Not at the minute!" as he sighed and they protested "Oh pooh!" June explained "I'm going to ask my sister Flo, if I can cut a hole for baby's legs!" adding "I'm thinking of cutting a hole in the back, to hide baby's feet, from show and if we can hide them in a basket, then baby should be able to hide down low in the pram from show!" Claire laughed "We saw him raise his dolly to hide his face!" as June gurgled "He loves dollies so much!" as they laughed and saw him blush "Not fair!" However, they then heard the bell go again. June laughed "I wonder is that Pam again, try not to say, and Baby better be quiet!" as she stuck a dummy into his mouth again. Brenda laughed "We'll stay up with baby!" as he swallowed. Brenda laughed "Does she not want Pam to know you're here?" as he shook his head and said, "I don't want her to know about the pram?" as they giggled, at his plight. June went down the stairs and saw Pam again at her door. She opened the door and heard Pam say, "Can I come in a tick!" as June invited her in, but said, "You can't stay long! I'm expecting some visitors tonight!" Pam laughed "I just wanted a chat! I can't mention it to Mummy!" as June smiled, wondering if Tom could hear as she brought her into her sitting room. Pam said, "He's still not back yet from his silly football?" as she said, "I take it you popped him into some panties and let him ask sweetly to play in his pretties with his mates?" as June nodded,

and smiled. Meanwhile Brenda started wheeling the pram about the room as Tom pleaded "Please don't?" as she quietly, asked, "Does baby not want to be wheeled along in his pram?" and saw him shake his head. However, she then whispered to Claire and next thing they'd lifted him out of the pram, though felt his hands stick, as he was still tied to the pram. They had him out and standing up in his baby frock and nappies and Claire gurgled "Oh what a fab look for baby!" However, then Brenda took the string and untied him from the pram, as she led him over to the window so he was now on show to the street as he cried "Oh no!" as he saw the whole street on show and hoped he wouldn't be recognised by anyone. His nappies couldn't be seen, but his baby dress and bonnet and face could be seen from anyone looking up or across from the houses across the street. She then saw a chair in the corner and lifted it over by the

Tom realized Nina across the street open her blinds and wave to him

window, whispering to Claire and next thing a smiling Claire and Brenda had lifted Tom up and said, "Quiet baby!" Stand on the chair baby or we bring Pam up!" as he cried "Oh no!" as he realised his nappies and frock were now, fully on show to the street. He wet himself again and sobbed "Not fair!" but luckily his nappies and plastics did the trick.

However, then a naughty Claire removed his bonnet to show off his face to anyone looking and he gasped as he did another pooh, which they heard. Nina, across the street, beside Julie's, happened to be looking out her bedroom window and gasped as she saw a big baby across the street in a baby dress, but also nappies and then saw someone remove his baby bonnet and gasped as she realized it was big Tom dressed as a baby. She gasped as she watched over.

Tom was sobbing when he saw her open her blinds, fully and wave over, as he cried "Oh no! Nina has seen me and recognized me!" as they waved back, laughing their heads off to her. He sobbed "I hope she doesn't tell Tina, as they said, "Oh you, poor boy! Would it be that bad?" has he cried "Yes it would be terrible!" as they giggled. Nina wondered "Why's big Tom dressed up as a baby girl?" as she laughed and flicked her wrist towards him. Brenda fed a handbag over his head and down his side, as Nina ran and got a handbag herself and slid it over her arm and laughed. Pam heard voices from upstairs and June said, "Some of my visitors are here already!" as she said, "I'd better go! but it was good to have a giggle about showing sissy Tom or Nancy off, to a girlfriend or two!" as June laughed "Naughty girl!" as they stood up and June led her to the door, saying, "Try your best to keep Nancy a secret for a while?" as Pam laughed "I'll try! but it will be so much fun when other girls get to play dollies, skipping and dress up with her!" She opened it and Pam exited and walked down the driveway. Tom was still stood up, when he gasped and saw his sister appear in the drive and quickly tried to step down, as he cried "Oh no! That's Pam!" as Brenda let go and let him step down off the chair. He'd just got down out of sight, when Pam looked up and saw two ladies peer down and wave to her. She smiled and waved back and skipped along and up her drive and rang her bell. Pam turned around and saw a lady across the street wave and she waved back, not realizing, it was something to do with baby Tom, or anything. Her Mum let her in, asking "No sign of Tom yet?" as she said, "No! He must be taking advantage of enjoying his footy with his mates!" adding "Away from being sweet little Nancy!" as her Mum laughed and nodded.

June laughed "Let's sit down and we'll tell you, how this all came about! Can I get you girls some tea or coffee?" as they nodded, and she skipped downstairs, but then came up with the diaper bag and some newspapers and said, "We'll maybe have to change baby later!"

Nina gurgled "Oh fab!" as she shook her head "It's not! It's a very nasty job with a big sissy baby boy like Tom here!" adding "I think we'll need lots of clothes pegs for our noses!" as they laughed.

He blushed as Brenda asked, "How many tinkle's has baby Nancy done?" as he said, three, as Nina screeched "Oh fab!" and then heard add "Any pooh poo's?" as he huffed "two!" as she giggled, "Why you big baby!" as they laughed. He cried "Please close the blinds, Julie or someone will spy baby!" as they laughed and she said, "I couldn't believe it when I peered across the road and saw a big baby girl in her pretty baby bonnet, baby dress and nappies on a chair!"

The ladies lift Baby Tom into the pram in June's driveway

They laughed, but then heard her say, "But nearly died when his bonnet was removed, and I saw baby Tom!" as he sobbed "It was terrible! I knew someone would spy me!" as she cuddled him and saw the ladies give him a kiss and so she said, "Poor baby!" as she gave him a kiss too. They beg June to let them have baby Tom in his pram just out the front of the house, where his legs shouldn't be seen, especially if they pop a blanket over them to hide his feet. She giggles as she wheels the pram down the stairs, with him begging "Please don't take baby outside in his pram?" adding "That will be terrible!" as they laughed. She got the large pram down to the front doors and is as she opened up and checking the street for Pam or Julie, she then wheeled it out into the porch and then quickly around the side of the house and up to the side door.

However, she got a large plastic sheet and laid it into the body of the pram, saying, "Just in case baby's nappies and baby pants don't do the trick! We mustn't wet my sister's pram!" The ladies hustled Baby Tom down the stairs and out the side door to stand in his nappies and baby dress on show for a minute, till they got him down onto his back and then lifted him up and slid him into the pram, with his legs sticking up over the handle, as he sobbed "Not flaming fair!" as they looked at his teary eyed face in the baby bonnet lying down inside the pram canopy and June laughed "Wonderful girls!" She again pulled the baby reigns up and soon Tom's head was part way up out of the canopy, but not fully raised on show and popped a pillow under him to support his upper body more on show. He was wheeled towards the front of the house, with him begging "Please don't take baby out ladies?" as they giggled, and dared June. She stopped at the front of the house and popped a dummy into his mouth. However, then Brenda popped the baby bottle and said, to them "I'm sure baby is thirsty!" as they laughed and checked the street.

June cuts a hole in the pram for Tom's feet and he's wheeled out

However, then June said, "Bugger it! I'll do it!" as she went in her back door and came out with her handbag, but also a large sharp knife. They wondered what she was going to do, as she locked up and approached the blushing boy sitting up in the pram. She said, "I'm sure my sister Flo will understand, as she took the knife and cut into the back of the pram underneath where his feet were lying and smiled as she cut into material. She said, "I'll try and make room for baby's feet!" as they laughed and giggled, "Wonderful June! That means we should be able to take baby around in his new pram!" as he sobbed "Oh no!

Please don't ladies! I'll be seen!" as they laughed "Shush baby!" and stuck the dummy back in. She cut more to make a kind of square section and soon was satisfied that his feet would fit out of it. They took his legs and bent them a bit and then fed one foot after the other into the pram and out the hole again, as they gasped and Brenda laughed "Oh great!"

as Tom's feet were pulled out and a blanket fed over them to hide them. June asked, "Is baby comfy?" as he sobbed "Oh no girls!" as she said, "If someone looks or you think might see you, you can use your dolly to hide baby's face!" She then thought "Look if Pam or Julie see me with a pram they might realize, so would you two or three take Baby, across the street and down past Julie's or even up and I'll keep a lookout from here!" as they laughed and nodded.

Brenda and Claire wheel him down past Pam's and he cringes as he peers up at first June's house and then his own, but luckily nobody sees him. They say, "Who's a lovely big baby girl!" as Brenda Says, "Oh there's one of your little friends!" but then added "Only joking!" as Tom wets himself again and cries "Not fair!" as Claire laughed "You've not done another tinkle?" as he nods, to more laughter, as they wheeled him on down his street.

They are wheeling baby on down the street and Brenda said, "Pity June had to ruin the pram there, but am sure her or one of her friends here can use our needlework skills to help pretty up the hole adding lace and what not!" She then said, "Talking about needlework, I don't think it amiss if Nancy learns some needlework skills!" as Claire laughed and nodded, "Oh yes! I know you're quite good at dressmaking Brenda!" as she nodded, adding "And embroidery and knitting!" Claire laughed "I'll be able to teach Nancy needlework if someone here, can escort her down to me!" as he cried "Oh no!" He cried "But everyone will see me dressed as Nancy, as Brenda laughed "There is an alternative if Baby wants to be wheeled down to my place disguised in her baby pram!" as he begged "Please don't Aunty Brenda?" but added although "Naughty Brenda might make Baby wheel his pram back up in his nappies and baby plastics on show to the street!" as Claire screeched "Oh Brenda! You are naughty!" as she laughed "Guilty as charged my dear!" as Tom scowled.

They wheel the pram past Jamie's house, but see him exit without spying

They go past his friend's house and Brenda asks "Sure baby doesn't want to pop in to play with his little friend?" as he begged "Please don't show baby Tom off?" as Claire gasps as she sees his mate exit up the driveway, just in front of them. James saw two ladies wheeling a large pink pram and ignored them as most boys would, as they wheeled Tom on past him. Tom was wheeled down past his house, when he peers up to see the back of James head just walk on, out his gate and up the street past them, as he tried to pull his dolly up to hide his face, but Brenda smiled and held his doll so he couldn't use it to hide, but also said, loudly "Naughty big baby Tom!" as Claire and him gasped. He cried softly to himself dreading James turn and did another pooh in his nappies and wets himself at the same time, dreading him turn and see him in the baby pram. He waited till he was out of earshot and cried "He just had to turn around and he'd have flaming spied me in the pram!" as Claire laughed "Oh Brenda! You are naughty!" but added "Did baby wet himself again?" as he huffed "I flaming-well, did a pooh too!" as they gurgled "Oh fab! Naughty baby!"

Brenda laughed "It might be an idea for Baby Tom to always have a diaper bag to hand as it seems he can't control himself, when playing in the street!" as Claire laughed "What even when playing with his mates?" as she nodded, and he said, "Ha! No way!" She then added "We might be nice and let him hide his nappies and baby stuff away in his needlework bag!" as Claire laughed "Oh fab! He will look cute" They reach the bottom and hear some girls playing skipping and see the pink pram and as most young girls do, ran and said, "Oh a little baby!" as he quickly pulled the dolly up to try and hide his face, but Claire saved his bacon and called "Just a dolly in the pram!" as they stopped "Oh pooh!" and returned to their game on the footpath across the street. Tom again thought he was going to be spied and wet himself. She laughed "Crisis over! You didn't do another poo?" but he shook his head "Just number ones again!" as they laughed "as Brenda laughed You see my point Claire?" who nodded. They turn the pram across the road, and he heard the girls, voices getting nearer, as Claire laughed "Now Brenda! Let baby down! They might see and recognize him!" as she said, "Baby Nancy! This here is my house! Number 79!" as she turned his pram and showed him her house with the pink paintwork and saw him nod "Ok!" as she turned him back around towards the young girls skipping.

Brenda raises Tom's reigns up to show him off without bonnet

Claire said, "Brenda, June doesn't want him outed yet!" as she laughed "Ok!" as she gave in and untied the baby reigns, but he was still held high due to the pillow under his upper body, as Claire removed it and Brenda said,

"Spoilt sport!" said, "There just use your dolly to play hide and seek baby!" and saw Brenda wheel the pram on up towards the girls. The girls were quite small and could just about see part of the pram as the ladies wheeled the pram on bye. They did look and see a large dolly in the canopy, but as the pram was about twelve feet away, one little girl Naomi saw it appear to move!"

She said, "I think those ladies had a baby in their pram! I saw its dolly move!" but her friend just said, "Yea! Maybe their baby was asleep, and they didn't want us to waken her up!" as she said, "Yea!" as they continued on with their skipping. Tom heard them get further away and was relieved they hadn't checked the pram for baby. Brenda laughed "Who's a lucky baby?" as Claire giggled, "You are pushing it Brenda with Baby Tom!" as she took over from Brenda wheeling baby. However, then he heard Tina's voice and another little girl too. He was dreading them peer in and hoped Brenda or play a joke and show them baby Tom. Even though Tina now knew that Tom was Nancy and about him in nappies and plastics. However, June didn't want Pam to know yet about his pram and so they'd to try and get by without them realizing. Claire wheeled the pram up towards them and again heard the girls see the pink canopy approach them and say, "Oh a baby!" and run to see, but she said, "Now girls our baby is asleep, so maybe another day!" as they said, "Sorry ok!" as they returned to Tina's to play with their doll's prams.

Claire laughed "Wasn't I kind Baby Tom?" as he nodded but then Brenda pulled his reigns up to raise his head up high on show and tied him off, but also removed his baby bonnet too, as she ran over, laughing to June and Nina!" Tom cried "Oh no!" as he saw her take his bonnet to leave him as a baby boy sitting proud in the pram, with no disguise to the street. Claire gasped and tried to use her body, to shield the poor boy, from being outed to Tina and her friend, but possibly the two girls down the street, but also to Julie or Pam who might be about. She wheels it over across the street to June's house and sees the laughing ladies, who could just see the pink canopy of the pram come towards them. Claire had hidden Baby Tom from Tina and her friend, but he was on show to the two girls further down the street who looked up and saw one lady run across the street, but then the other lady wheel the pram, but now the baby was sitting up in her pram. Naomi said, "Gosh that looks a big baby in her pram!" as her friend looked and nodded, "She must be

They take baby Tom out the back to change his nappies

at least 4 or 5!" as her friend nodded but added "I've heard that some girls stay in nappies till that!" as they laughed "Poor baby!" and continued their game. Claire gets the pram back up June's driveway and they gasp as they spy Tom up high, completely on show without his bonnet as Brenda holds it up laughing as she said, "Just my little joke on baby Tom!" as he sobbed "Those girls and Tina could have spied me!" as they laughed.

June said, "Just as well Pam or Julie weren't out to spy baby in his pram!" as they gurgled. Nina added "If Tina had spied baby, she'd have probably wanted to take him to town around the shops and most like up on high like he is now, without even a baby bonnet to disguise him!" as they laughed and nodded. They decide to change Tom's nappies and Claire volunteers Brenda since she caused him to wet and poo himself so much in the street. She laughed "She even wheeled him past his mate, as he was coming out the house, but luckily didn't look into the pram. Tom cried "And she held my flaming dolly down, to stop me hiding from show! All he had to do was turn or his Mum to call him back for something and I'd have been completely outed to him!" Brenda laughed "I bet his mates wouldn't believe him!" adding "Imagine a story of big macho Tom dressed as a baby in baby dress and bonnet in an actual girl's pram with a dummy in his mouth and baby bonnet on his head!" She then laughed "Who on earth would believe that?" as they laughed and he cringed, with annoyance. They take him into the garden to change his nappies by the wall, with one lady standing guard in case Pam spies.

Pam gets Tom to slip into her dress and pinafore to head to breakfast

Pam had chatted to the lady Annabelle who had spied him in nappies, frock and mincing with a handbag and suggested that she trap him one morning. She actually planned two mornings – one a school-day to out him completely as a schoolgirl but the other on a Saturday morning when Nancy could mince around lots of girly shops too.

Annabelle had been shopping and got lots of baby stuff for baby Nancy and so was ready for baby Tom or baby Nancy. Hence on a Friday morning, Pam had sneaked into Tom's room in her skirt and blouse and said "Lets give Mummy a giggle!" as he asked "How?" as she held up her dress and pinafore to hear him beg "No Pam! Don't!" as she laughed "Now when you're dressed I'll hand Nancy some yellow and pink ribbons and I want you down to ask Mummy which you should wear to school?" as he sobbed "Not funny!" as she laughed "It will just be for a joke!" as he huffed "Not funny!" as she left and he eventually removed her nighty and got into his underpants for school. He woefully pulled on her dress and then her pinafore and got himself cleaned up in the bathroom for breakfast. He exited, holding his dolly as usual and saw Pam standing there holding a lot of hair ribbons, some pink and some yellow as she slid a few of each into his hair, as she kissed his lips and slipped downstairs to wait with her Mum.

Her Mum saw her and kissed her "Morning Pam!" but noticed she was in her skirt and blouse instead of her dress and pinafore and said "You wearing your skirt today, dear?" as Pam said "I couldn't find my school dresses, did you put them in the wash?" as she said "No! You know I wouldn't during the week!"

Nancy asks her Mum if he should wear pink or yellow ribbons to school

Pam laughed "Mummy! Please don't blow up, as its just a joke - Nancy is going to play on you and pretend its nothing unusual!" as they heard footsteps on the stairs and soon saw Tom come into the hall and then enter the kitchen, in Pam's dress and pinafore holding the hair ribbons and his dolly.

He asked "Mummy! Should I wear the pink or yellow ribbons to school today?" as her Mum gasped and smiled "I think you can wear both!" as Pam said "I'll help pop your ribbons in Nancy!" as she took them and slid them into his hair. She took her apron and said "Here Nancy! You'd better protect your school dress and pinafore!" and saw him take her pink floral apron and pull it on, saying "Thank's Pammy!" as her and her Mum just smiled and his Mum set their breakfasts out on the table. He tucked in, wondering when his Mum would burst out laughing at him but Pam and her just tucked into their food and Pam said "Don't worry Nancy I'll do the dishes for you today!" as he bobbed a curtsy to her "Thank's Pammy!" as she asked "Want to bring my pinny to school or will you be careful and protect your pretty dresses!" as he finished his breakfast and said "I'll protect my dresses!" as he stood up and left the kitchen as his Mum burst out into giggles "Oh Pam you are naughty!" Pam said "Its ok Tom! I'll let you change!" as she joined him up the hall, but closed the kitchen door but then showed him her blazer and said "Let's see Mum, how you'd look in a blazer too!" as he huffed "That's not funny, Pam!" as she held it up and said "Just slide your arms in!" The trusting boy slid his arms into the sleeves but then realized they were pinned behind him as Pam shuved a handky into his mouth and dragged him up to the door. She quietly opened it and reaching under his dresses, she took hold of his willy and pulled him out and saw him quickly follow her out into the porch. There was another lady he'd not seen before who took his arms and led him out the porch and as Pam closed the inner and outer doors she removed his gag and said "Just down to my place to let Pam play a little joke!" as he gasped at being on show to the school girls and boys, dressed up as a schoolgirl.

Annabelle leads Nancy down to diaper him and take her to school

She led him out his gates and down the street, where he saw some girls and boys and at least one or two of the girls gasped as they asked "That's not Tom in a school dress?" as she nodded, as he sobbed and wondered where

they were going, when she led him into her house and into her sitting room. He gasped as he saw the diaper bag and cried "Oh no! Not nappies to school?" as she laughed "Don't worry Nancy! If you're a good girl and attend as Pam's sister, they wont realize about baby Nancy!" as he cried "I can't attend school in dresses!" but she laughed "Nonsense!" as she set about removing his underpants, as she giggled at his small willy and asked "So what's that baby Nancy?" as he cringed "My baby pee pee!" as she kissed him and then applied the gel and talcum powder before popping him into nappies, a diaper and large plastic baby pants. She laughed "Don't worry Pam will get the girls to protect you and if Nancy is a good girl, she'll enjoy herself. He cried "But the boys will give it to me!" but she said "Don't worry, the girls will deal with anyone who is nasty to you!"

Pam says he'd dressed and gone on to school, but he was being diapered

Pam meanwhile had returned downstairs with her schoolbag and blazer, but also another girls dress and pinafore as her Mum laughed "He let you have your dresses back!" as Pam laughed "I had such a struggle getting them back of him! I think Nancy is getting gallous of the girls at school!" as her Mum laughed "Naughty girl!" as Pam laughed "She is Mummy!"

as they both laughed. Her Mum asked "Is he still upstairs?" but Pam said "He came down a few minutes ago! Didn't he even say bye!" as her Mum shook her head "No!" and looked out the sitting room window but didn't see him. Her Mum checked and saw his school outfit gone, but Pam had taken it and his satchel and hidden them at Annabelles.

She however had taken his trousers with her to make Tom sound a complete girly to the whole school and even the teachers and so hopefully he'd be a schoolgirl from then on for a while anyway until their Mum discovered her trick on him.

Annabelle led a blushing Tom out dressed as Nancy but with a black wig on to disguise him till Pam had caught up with them. She led him down the street instead of his normal path up the street but down and out a house at the bottom of the cul-de-sac. His Mum actually did spy him but with the wig and dressed as a schoolgirl didn't associate the mother and daughter with Tom.

A lady in the bottom house, laughed as she saw the blushing boy dressed as a schoolgirl being led in her front gate and out through her back gate to head to the shops and bus stop via the back road. She came out and laughed "Doesn't he look sweet, as she saw the boy with his hands still pinned back behind him. Annabelle laughed "His sister Pam, is hoping he'll be able to be a schoolgirl, from now on! She's been dressing him up and making him play dollies, for several weeks now!" as the lady laughed "Oh fab!" as she removed his wig a tick and they both laughed, at the blushing boy.

Pam was waiting with some girls from school and some from Tom's class and laughed as she saw him being led along, by Annabelle. She'd warned Lucy, from his class that a new girl would be joining her, but she was shy and needed lots of cuddles and kisses, as Lucy laughed "Well! I don't normally kiss girls, Pammy!" but Pam said "I assure you'll enjoy her kisses!" as she saw the lady and young girl in long hair, come along the back road.

Lucy looked and didn't recognize the new girl, but as he got closer she saw something familiar about her, but then his wig was removed and her and the other girls gasped gasped and screeched as Pam laughed "It's my sissy brother Tom but he prefers to be called Nancy, when wearing a frock!" as they all ran towards him, as he sobbed "Not fair, Pam!"

She said "Right, Nancy, were going to cut your bound blazer, in a tick and add your trousers to let you decide if you want to dress as a boy or remove your dresses for school!" as the girls said "Go on Tom! Attend as a schoolgirl! Its

so much fun!" as Pam took his trousers and handed them to Annabelle, saying "Just pop him into his silly trousers!" and saw the laughing lady take them and slipped over to the back of a house and slid him into the trousers over his nappies, but of course just did his belt up and whispered "They're undone, so remove your dress and be outed as baby!" as he cringed and sobbed "Not fair!" as he was led back to the giggling girls. Pam said "Right here is the scissors to release your hands!" as she cut the bound blazer and they saw Tom pull his arms around to his front and say "That was a horrid trick Pam!"

Tom's released and is put into trousers but asks to keep his dresses on

She laughed and said "So Tom! Want to remove your pretty dress and pinafore to be a boring boy or ask to keep your dresses on to attend as my big lovely sister Nancy!" as they pleaded "Go on Nancy attend as a girl! Its lots of fun!" as he cringed and said "Ok! I'll keep my dresses on!" as they screeched an Pam threw her arms around his neck and kissed his lips, as the girls said "Yuk!" but she said "Go on Lucy, you'll really have fun with my Nancy from now on!" as she laughed and kissed his cheek, but Pam said "Only the lips count!" as she said "Ok Nancy! You owe me!" as she kissed his lips as he cringed "I don't like kisses!" but blushed as he quite liked Lucy's looks and the way she acted. Some other girls from Pam's class and year kissed him too as Pam laughed "He's great fun to play dollies and dress up with!" as they screeched. Pam said "We'll add his wig while on the bus to stop causing a racket, but we'll have to get some female teachers to sanction him attending classes as a girl in my dresses as they giggled. She said, "When you came down to breakfast in your dress and pinafore, carrying your baby Suzie dolly what did you ask Mummy?" as he blushed and stammered "Which colour hair ribbon should I wear the pink or yellow ones!" as they screeched as she asked "What did Mummy reply!" as he said "Both!" as they gurgled as Pam said "He's been stealing my dollies for years and dressing them up, as he knew he couldn't protest or his nappies and plastics might be exposed.

They waited together at the bus stop and he blushed as he saw some boys and girls he recognized but with his wig, they didn't realize it was him in his dresses. He got on the bus and sat down on the inside with a smiling Lucy beside him, with Annabelle and Pam behind him and the other giggling girls scattered about the bus, but having sworn not to tell on him yet. He was handed a girly bag with his books but also a pink handbag too to enjoy school just a little bit more. They arrived at the stop and girls and boys got off with him almost freezing with fear. However Lucy kissed him again as Pam giggled "Gosh Lucy! I think you're getting to enjoy Nancy's company!" as they led him off the bus.

They led him along to the school and in the gates, without him being recognized, but soon his wig was removed and replaced with some pink and yellow hair ribbons, as they entered the girl's entrance and soon were heading towards the dance teachers room and heard some girls giggle "That's not your brother, Pam?" as she giggled and nodded as several girls ran over and laughed at him dressed as a schoolgirl, but mincing with his shopper and handbag too. Pam led them to the teacher's room and knocked on the door and of course got Tom to say he wanted to dress as a schoolgirl as the teachers laughed but agreed he could and change to join the girls at dance. He was led along to the needlework teachers and again asked could he attend as a schoolgirl and was granted his request. Then to the girls playground where Pam and Lucy introduced him to lots of giggling girls and again he was offered to attend as a boy, but said he wanted to dress as a schoolgirl to screeches.

However then Serry from his class was told of the girly boy and screeched "Tom is that you in dresses?" as he sobbed "Oh no!" as Lucy said "Now Serry! Us girls must protect little Nancy and stop the boys being nasty to him! I mean her!" as she ssked "Is this some trick?" but Pam said "He's been playing dress up and with my dollies for years now!" but added "He's just got bored with his silly boys clothes and is enjoying my dress and pinafore!" as she screeched but then saw Lucy and then Pam kiss him as she gasped "Yuk!"

Pam giggled as she thought to herself "Next step is Nancy at ballet with the fairies!"

TV NEWS STORY ABOUT SISSY BOYS

News story about girls forcing boys of various ages, but also men to be sissies
Thousands of girls and their Mums and ladies hear and giggle about the story of sissies
They hear from a Mum of a boy who was turned into a sissy by some girls

News Story about girls forcing boys of various ages to be sissies

Several boys had been trapped by their sisters or girl neighbours into acting girly and playing dollies and dress up, due to being held down by bigger girls and a pretty apron and handbag tied around them and made to play Sissy Football.

However, then there was a TV news story and lots more girls and Mum's, heard about the boys, being made to play dollies and dress up. There was a news story and it said, "Reports are coming in, that quite a few boys, have been coerced, into dressing up by sisters or girls from school and then under the threat of telling or showing their mates, they then have had to agree to play dollies, dress up and wear pretty aprons to help with housework and some even shopping too with handbags and purses. Some boys even attending school, dressed as schoolgirls, in a dress and pinafore!"

Girls and their Mum's and other ladies couldn't believe the story and wanted to learn more about what happened to the little boys. They assumed this was all happening to young boys, but then heard the reports go on and mention boys as old as ten or eleven, but then about teenagers and even some men, as they screeched with laughter at the thought of their big boys or husbands being dressed up and playing dollies.

Even some teenage boys and reports have come in of some husbands too, being embarrassed into having to wear their wives' frocks, to do the housework and go shopping in girly outfits.

Report Says, of boys doing housework in girly aprons + pinnies

The report said, that boys who would not normally help with housework, were ending up in pretty aprons and offering to help their Mums and sisters with the washing up, but also other housework. The report continued – with the boys often wearing their sister's pretty aprons and even PVC pinnies but also having to bob curtsies with them too.

Sisters say, to their Mum's – "Mummy! Could you imagine, my brother wearing my pretty little apron here? Or this little PVC pinny?" as their Mum's laughed and shook their head.

The boys help with laundry, but using a handbag for the pegs

However, then the boys helping with the laundry in the back garden often in their sisters aprons and or PVC pinnies., but this situation was made worse by the fact that their Mum's used a handbag to hold the clothes-pegs and the boy initially having to dip into a handbag to get any pegs they needed to peg out the washing.

Then the boys being handed the handbag to hold and use, which is really embarrassing for them, so they often beg for a headscarf and or hair ribbons to disguise them from being recognised by the neighbours., but an addition to their embarrassment, is adding a large purse to their handbag and having to pop six pegs from the handbag into the purse, then close them both up, between pegging up each item of washing. Then the sister or Mum can say, to their boy "It's good practice for helping with the shopping!" However, the boys then start playing with their sisters, skipping, dollies and even some dress up too. The female reporter didn't know how the boys, had been coerced into helping with housework and then playing with his sisters, but reports have indicated there have been quite a few incidents of boys of various ages. Once the sisters have them playing dollies or dress up then the boys inevitably end up wearing pretty nightdresses to bed, often cuddling a dolly too. You may worry about the young girls spying something naughty, but the report mentioned calling it his baby-pee-pee to lessen the embarrassment on both sides and varying ways to hide it. There were giggles and screeches as girls and their Mum's heard the report and sisters said, "Oh Mum! We'll have to get our little or big brother John or Alex.

The boy joining the girls to play football –, but it's Sissy Football

The report then mentioned about girls joining boys to play football, which she couldn't understand. However, then said, "Actually it turned out, it was a boy joining girls playing football!" but said, "Actually it wasn't normal football!" adding "It turned out to be Sissy Football!" as she laughed "With all members of the team wearing pretty aprons, but also mincing about the back garden with handbags too!"

more girls said, "Mummy! You could join me playing Sissy Football with Frank!" as she laughed "No way Claire! I couldn't!" adding "We couldn't make him play Sissy Football!" as the girls nod vigorously and say, "At least it's a way to get us to play sweetly together. She then said, "Although they are kind and offer the boy a disguise to stop him looking like a sissy!" adding "Either a headscarf and or hair ribbons!" as more girls screeched at the thought of their brother wearing their hair ribbons.

The report then went on that after a while the boys then asked why he wanted hair ribbons and he of course makes an excuse, but then he's asked, "What are you disguising yourself as?" and he has to say, a girl with obvious consequences. As girls gurgled "Oh fab!"

At school, boys doing dance, needlework or attend as schoolgirl

There have also been stories of boys attending school having to carry their schoolbooks in girly shopping bags and being teased rotten. Often having to mince with the girly bags between classes but this has sometimes led to them having to join the girls at dance, needlework, etc. and in some cases the boys are even attending school in a dress and pinafore. This has led to teasing and name calling, especially among the boys with some threats and sometimes bullying. However, the boys concerned are then threatened with being dressed up the same as a schoolgirl and are soon very subdued at the thought of attending lessons in a skirt or dress. This again brought giggles and screeches from listening girls and their Mums. Boys who dared to listen to this thought it was a big joke and no way would any boy in their class or school attend classes in a dress and pinafore, However, then gasped as sometime later, it actually happened and one or two boys in varying age groups started mincing around school in a dress and pinafore.

Hundreds if not thousands of girls gasped and giggled, and almost as many Mum's heard and broke into giggles of the story and those girls with brothers, begged their Mum's to treat their brothers, as a girly and make him play dollies and dress up with them.

But it wasn't just little girls, trying to get their Mum's to dress their brother's up, but also teenage girls thinking about also trying to trap their brothers, or even boyfriends. However, then there were grown up women thinking of trapping their boyfriends and husbands, but also their nephews or neighbour's boys, who were bullies to their sisters and/or male chauvinists. Some Aunties knew their sister's boy was a real MSP

They even had one Mum come on, with her face and voice disguised and say, she was a bit shocked when she found out, what some girls down the street had done, to her young boy, first of all asking him to show them how to play football. Him a keen footballer, of course never thought anything of it and joined a few girls around their back garden.

He took the ball and started to dribble about the garden, saying, "See! You just do this and can pass the ball or dribble around the opposing players!" He then saw a couple of young girls, some his age and a few younger, but then some older girls appeared, and they all had aprons on, and he still didn't worry, telling them "You don't need aprons to play footy!" However, then some of the bigger girls got him down, on his back and suddenly a pretty frilly apron was tied around him, but also a girly handbag, was fed up his arm and tied to his elbow and the apron. He was let up and realized he couldn't get the apron or handbag, off and the little girls said, "We want you to show us how to play Sissy Football" as all the girls grabbed their handbags and said, "You have to wear a pretty apron and carry a handbag, while kicking the ball!" as my poor boy sobbed to let him out of it. However, the little girls said, "He could either stay, to play Sissy Football, or be taken out into the street to show to his friends!" with some of the listening girls thinking "I might get interested in football, now!"

They say, about Sissy Football in headscarf, but ask what's his disguise

She continued "Hence, next thing he was asking to play Sissy Football and then they said, 'Someone might recognise him as a boy in the pretty apron' and so next thing had ribbons and bows in his hair and a floral headscarf tied around them!" adding "He thought at least nobody would recognise him in the headscarf. So, there he was playing away at Sissy football!" When after 10 minutes they asked him "Why did you need the headscarf?" adding "He said, to stop looking like a little sissy!" as she giggled, and said, "But they pressed him more as to what he was wanting to disguise himself as and he eventually had to say, "To look like a girl'" to more giggles from the listening girls.

She laughed and said, "Then a skirt was pulled up under his pinny and then even one of the big girls took his trousers and then I think they made him wear some frilly panties!" to screeches from the girls and Mum's. She added "Although it has had some advantages! It has got him slipping into aprons, to help me with the housework and joining me shopping too!" to more laughter and giggles. She said, "One young girl came around and said, her brother started played skipping with her and her friends and even helped with housework!" as I gasped to my boy "You never!" thinking "How come! He'd never normally agree to play skipping with these 2 young girls and even do housework!"

A girl came around to say, her boy played skipping and did housework

She said "A girl then asked him, if he'd rather play footy in the back, or stay with her and help me with some housework. She of course was meaning Sissy football and so he reluctantly said, he'd stay and help me with some housework. She then produced 2 frilly aprons and I gasped as he pulled one on!" and it's meant he's now helping

me with housework and washing and even shopping!" as he blushed and said, "They promised not to tell!" but then the girl said, "He said, he used to help me, with the washing up and housework!" as I gasped "You little fibber!" - That was the end of the report, but off camera the Mum had continued to the reporter.

She continued "The girl said, 'He borrowed one of my pretty aprons to help Mummy with the washing up and then him and me helped her with some housework!'" as I gasped "He never!" and he stood there unable to protest, dreading them tell a lot more of what they'd made him do!" as he huffed "You promised not to tell!" as me and the girl giggled, and said, "Mummies don't count! They won't tell!" as he huffed "Not fair!"

She added "Unless you promise to help her with housework in one of my pretty aprons!" as he cried "Oh no! Don't! That will be too small and frilly!" as she added "And don't forget, to help your Mummy hang out the washing!" as he cried "Not fair!" as I laughed "You don't mean wearing your girly apron, outside to hang out washing?"

She giggled, and nodded, "He's helped Mummy with that too! but Mummy uses a handbag as a peg bag and tells me that will help me learn to carry the handbag, when I help her shopping!" I screeched "You didn't have my big boy here carry a handbag, around your back, whilst pegging up some washing?" as she giggled.

Reports of cheating/MSP husbands coming under the thumb

She laughed "Initially Mummy only had me and him dip into a handbag on her arm, to get some clothes pegs!, but then she had him take her handbag and carry it, whilst she dipped into it to get pegs!" as I giggled, "So someone could be useful helping me around the shops with shopping bags and handbags!" I giggled, and he protested "Please don't Mummy! That's not fair! Someone will see!" as they both giggled. The girl suggested "He should help you hang out washing every day!" but I said, "I only do the washing once a week!" as she laughed "You can give some undies and pretty frocks an airing and get him to peg them up to practice, with his handbag and apron on other days!" I giggled, and he begged "Please don't!" as Lucy laughed "Can you phone me, when he's about to go out, so I can pop upstairs and watch him use his handbag, or maybe pop out to encourage him, to enjoy mincing around the garden in his hair ribbons!" as she giggled, and he cried "Not fair Mum!"

A report mentioned, another lady whose husband had played around and left her for another woman, but then came back for an evening of drinks, was allowed to stay the night and after passing out with drink, awoke to find himself in a pretty nightdress and panties. His wife having told him she'd a home help, when in the morning a woman in an apron entered, with the wife's breakfast, and gasped and giggled, at seeing the ex-husband in a frilly nighty, as he suddenly realized what he was wearing and begged them not to tell. Anyway, he ended up being exposed, in not only a frock, but nappies and baby pants to hundreds of ladies and girls on an evening entitled "Ladies Only! How to get your partner or husband to wear an apron, to help with housework!"

They explained "He apparently ended up him shopping in a pretty apron dress and carrying a handbag!" as more women screeched, at the thought of partners or ex-boyfriends, being dressed up and having to do whatever they wanted. Carrying a shopping basket and handbag around the shops, going up to the till to remove a purse from his handbag to pay for a bra or frock. And some even thinking of them wearing a frock around town to help them shop.

See the full book …

PART J

NANCY ATTENDS TINA'S FRIEND BECKY'S BIRTHDAY PARTY

Becky takes Baby Tom walkies in his nappies and baby frock

Tina asks Becky if she can have her birthday party at hers

Tina knew her friend Becky was having a 6ᵗʰ Birthday party and was inviting lots of girls from her class and a few others from ballet etc. However, Tina asked could she actually hold it at her house and got their Mum's to agree as Tina wanted to introduce big Sissy boy Tom to all her girlfriends and embarrass him some more. Hence, Pam had made sure he was in 2 sets of panties one normal, but the next were very silky and had frills down to his thighs. Tom was dressed in her yellow lacy frock that he'd been put into the 1ˢᵗ night by his Mum and this time they washed his hair and put pink and yellow rollers in his hair and then tied a headscarf around it, but this was soon replaced by a plastic rainhat to show off his rollers. He was handed a pink handbag and told to make sure he minced with it the whole time while he was Nancy.

They made sure the coast was clear and Pam and Julie escorted him over, wheeling his dollies in Pam's pink pram, across the road, where a giggling Tina called "Come on Sissy Tom, I want to play dollies and dress up!" He huffed "I'm Nancy!" as Her Mum saw him and laughed "Oh Tina! Julie! You aren't bringing Tom over in his frock and rollers?" as they took him into the living room and sat him down, to play dollies with him begging "Don't tell anyone?" Pam said, "Tell Tina what you think of her pretty frock!" as he saw the girl in a beautiful pink frock and said, "You look very pretty Tina! I love your pretty frock! Is it new?" as Tina bobbed a curtsy to him and said, "Thanks Nancy!" She giggled, "Your frocks very pretty too!" as Pam said, "Bob a curtsy back to Tina and thank her for her comment about your frock!" as he gripped his frocks and bobbed several curtsies to the giggling girl, saying, "Thanks Tina!" Tina said, "I want a kissy Sissy!" as he grimaced and bending down, let her give him a kiss on the lips, to giggles from Pam and Julie.

He was sitting down dressing some dollies when they then heard the bell ring and he cried "Don't bring anyone in to see me, please?" as her Mum went to the door and smiled as she saw the birthday girl Becky and her Mum, with lots of bags and called "Tina! Becky's here!"

Tom is in Tina's when he hears the bell go and Becky arrives

Tina giggled, and left the room and saw her friend and called "Hi Becky come on in!" and saw the birthday girl in a pretty pink party frock, carrying a dolly and handbag enter and Tina ran and gave her a kiss, a bit to her surprise!" as she said, "Happy Birthday Becky!"

Tom then gasped "Oh no! Not fair!" as he realized it was a little girl's birthday!" and then cried "Not a birthday party?" as Pam and Julie giggled, and tears started to appear in his eyes. Her Mum said, "Happy birthday Becky!"

Becky called "Thanks! Pretty frock Tina!" as Tina giggled, and bobbed a curtsy back to her and said, "I've got one girl Nancy here, along with my sister and her friend Pammy!"

as she took Becky by the hand and led her into the living room.

Becky entered and saw Pam, Julie and Tom and called "Oh goody, Dollies!" as Tina said, "This is my big Sis Julie and saw Julie bob a curtsy "Happy birthday Becky!" and bending down gave her a kiss. Tina giggled, "This is her friend Pammy from across the road!" as Pam called "Happy birthday Becky!" and bending down gave her a kiss too, as Tina called "This big girl is Nancy, Pammy's cousin, who loves playing dollies and dress up with me!" as Pam said, "Nancy! Say, Happy birthday to Becky and give her a kiss!"

Tom said, "Happy birthday Becky!" and kneeling up, he kissed her and heard Becky say, "Why's Nancy in rollers!" as Pam said, "She wanted her hair to look pretty, in curls and only washed it 10 minutes ago!" Tina said, "The big girls will be going soon, to leave us little girls, to play dollies and stuff!" as Becky said, "I still don't know why, you wanted my party around here and not at our house!" as Tom realized, she was having a party and cried "Oh no!" as Becky asked, "What's wrong with Nancy?" as the girls giggled, and he turned away from Becky and begged "Please don't Pam! Tina?"

Pam said, "Big Nancy doesn't like lots of people know, she still likes playing dollies at her age!" as Becky laughed "Dollies is fun!" as did Tina, who said, "Nancy loves playing dress up and dollies with me! Show Becky, how well you play dollies!" and saw him take a dolly and undressing it, he added a frock back on it to giggles from the girls, as Becky said, "It's fun to play dollies!" as she sat down and started removing her own dolls dress and then opening her handbag popped it into a new dress!"

Then the door opened and in walked "Becky's Mum and Tina's who said, "This here is Tina from Becky's class!" and saw Tina bob a curtsy and call "Hi!" as she reached up for a kiss!" as the lady in her pretty floral apron bent down and kissed her "Thanks for letting us use your place for the party!" Her Mum Caroline said, "This is Julie Tina's big sis!" as Julie said, "Hi!" and bobbing a curtsy gave her a kiss too, This is Julie's friend Pammy from across the street!" as Pam bobbed a curtsy and gave her a kiss and finally this is her cousin Nancy "as he called Hi from sitting beside Becky and Tina and tried to not look at her. Pam said, "Stand up Nancy and give the lady a curtsy and kiss!" and saw him stand up and bob a curtsy and then the lady bent down and kissed him to giggles from Pam, Julie and Tina. Julies Mum said, "Don't I get a kiss too?" as she took Tom and kissed his lips to more giggles from the girls.

They ask why the rainhat and curlers and still don't realize about Tom

Becky's Mum said, "All you girls seem very affectionate, with all your kisses!" as they laughed "It's a kind of joke!" as she asked, "What?" as Pam said, "All will be revealed in due course!" Pam said, "Us big girls will be going soon!" as he sighed, hoping it would be soon, not wanting to be at a little girl's party.

She asked, "What's the itinerary for today!" as Becky called "Dollies and dress up!" and Tina called "We'll be playing Sissy Tag!" as the girls laughed "What?" as she said, "We run about in our pretty aprons and use our handbags to tag each other!" as she laughed and then heard her say, "Football too!" She asked, "Football?" as Becky called "I don't want football!" as her Mum called "I hope there's no boys coming?" as Becky called "No! I don't like boys!" as the girls laughed and giggled, and Tina said, "I bet you'll enjoy football the way we play it!"

as she shrugged her shoulders and wondered why. Then there was another ring of the bell and he whispered "Can we go soon Pam?" as Pam shook her head and said, "We'll be going soon!" as Tina ran to see her Mum at the door and ushering another 2 girls and their Mum in and called "Becky it's Laura and Clara!" as Becky ran "Hi girls!" She took the presents and popping them into the sitting room, ran and gave them a kiss each and then their Mum too as they giggled, a bit surprised at the kisses, but then Tina too and they entered with their handbags and pretty frocks and removing their coats let Becky lead them into the living room. Pam called "Hi girls!" as she bent down and gave them a kiss each, followed by Julie and then the blushing Nancy. Tina introduced them all. Julie said, "Us big girls will be going soon to leave you young girls to play dollies and games!" as Tom thought great. Their Mum came in and saw the older girls and said, "Hi girls! You supervising the young girls at the party!" as Julie and Pam giggled, "Oh we'll probably have to go soon to let the young girls have fun with their dollies and dress-up!" as she laughed "You big girls too old for dollies and dress up?" Pam giggled, "My big cousin Nancy here is dolly mad and loves playing dress up too!" as the girls and Mum laughed at the older girl in the pretty yellow frock playing with the dollies, but with the handbag dangling from her arm and still in curlers and a rainhat.

She laughed "Why the rainhat and curlers!" and was explained she washed her hair a bit late. She went back into the kitchen where she donned her own apron to help with the cakes and sandwiches and fruit juices. She laughed "That big girl Nancy playing dollies, at her age!" as Tina's Mum laughed and said, "It's only recently we discovered that she likes playing dollies and dress up with my Tina! She continued "See, she was a bit of a Tom boy till recently, always playing football with the boys and even wearing more trousers than skirts and frocks" as they laughed and continued with the preparations. She laughed "They'll probably be playing football today too!" as several Mums said, "I don't think my girls will want to play football!" as she laughed "I think they'll like the way Tina and the girls play!" as she added "You might even want to join in too!"

Ten-year old Gale escorting her little sister calls at the door

She laughed "No way!" as she giggled, "See it involves aprons and handbags!" as they laughed "What?" She giggled, "Don't mention anything to the girls yet?" as they continued with the tea. Then another couple of girls arrived with their Mums and were greeted with the same kisses and after depositing their presents into the sitting room, then led into the living room to be kissed and greeted by the rest of the big girls, who loved that Nancy's secret hadn't been discovered. Becky laughed "I can't wait till after tea and we open my pressies!" to laughter from the girls and then Lara said, "I hope you'll come to Clara and my party! Since we're twins, we have a double party!" as Tina said, "Can I come too?" as they said, "Of course Tina!" as she asked, "Can I bring my friend Nancy here too? I know you'll love her present too!" as they looked at the big girl paying dollies

They asked, "Isn't she too old for little girl parties?" as Pam and Julie laughed "She didn't used to get invited to little girls parties, even her sisters!" as Julie giggled, as she said, "see she used to be a bit of a Tom boy!" as Tina screeched with laughter, as the girls looked at her and asked, "What do you mean?" Pam asked, "Don't you know what a Tom boy is?" as they shook their heads and she said, "It's the opposite of a Sissy boy!" as she added "You know what a Sissy boy is?" as they asked, "Is it a boy who likes some girly things?" as she nodded, "Like playing dollies and some even like plying dress up?"

They giggled, "You mean wearing frocks?" as she nodded, and they all laughed as she said, "See a Tom boy is a girl who likes to play football and wear silly trousers!" as they said, "Yuk!" She added "See Nancy used to love playing footy with the boys and they wouldn't let her play in skirts or frocks!" as they asked, "Why did you like football! Dollies are more fun!" as Pam laughed "It's only recently that Nancy turned all girly and realizes what fun she was missing playing dollies and dress up and wearing skirts and frocks!" to more giggles from Julie and Tina.

Though she has recently combined her 2 loves football and handbags and aprons!" They asked, "How?" as she said, "Wait till later and we'll show you!" adding "I hope you all have your pretty aprons to protect your frocks!" as they all nodded. Then there was another ring and her Mum opened the door to see a young girl, but instead of her Mum it was her older sister Gale a girl of 10 years old "Just a year above Tom, as her Mum invited her in and saw Becky and Tina run to greet her!" Tina giggled, as she saw the 10=year old girl and realized it would be doubly more embarrassing for Tom. They all kissed, and she left the present into the front room. Gale was led into the living room and got lots of kisses from the girls and then Nancy, as she sat down to play dollies asking the arrangement and when they'd be having cakes. Meanwhile her older sister was chatting to the ladies saying, she was deputising for her Mum to look after Loraine and had brought her apron and handbag as instructed and asked did they need a hand, but was told they were ok and she should introduce herself to the girls.

Gale shows Sissy Tom off to the Mum's as he wants to go

Hence, she entered the room and Tom gasped as he heard a girl of his or a bit older enter in a skirt and blouse as Pam and Julie smiled knowing Tom might be exposed to the girls very soon. She had some kisses from Pam and Julie and the other young girls and then Pam said, "Nancy stand up and give Gale a nice kiss!" as she pulled him up and bobbing a curtsy went to kiss the big girl, who gasped and cried "Nancy! Oh fab!" She kissed him "You naughty girly!" as Tina and Julie and Pam all giggled, and heard Becky ask "What?" as Gale ran and giggled, "Oh fabulous, I never realised today would be so much fun!" as they asked, "Why?" Her Mum Caroline giggled, "Well ladies! You know there are some boys, who are real male chauvinists, who never help with washing up or housework?" as they nodded, and a couple said, "Yes my Dave's like that!" as another said, "My hubby is just like that!" as she continued "What would be the worst could happen to a MSP like that?" as they said, "Smacked bottom!"

She laughed "His sister suggested something or else his Mum just came up with the plan?" as they asked, "What?" as she laughed "She asked him to help with the dishes!" and he gave the usual reply "It's girls work!" They gasped "The naughty boy!" as she continued "She took him upstairs for a smacked bottom and removing his trousers and pants smacked him!" adding "but then fetched a petticoat and frock, from his sister's room and next thing had him dressed in them!" to screeches of laughter. She said, "She then brought him down to don a pretty apron and do the dishes, as it was girls work!" as they giggled, "Never!" as she added "Pam in there's his sister!" as they giggled, "Never! Where is he? Is he coming?" Gale ran in and taking him by the hand, dragged a reluctant Tom, into the kitchen to screeches, as they saw it was a boy in a yellow frock, as a laughing Pam and Julie appeared and raised his frock, to show off, his pretty pink panties!" to more screeches.

Becky gasped and cried "That's a boy!" as they all giggled, and he sobbed "Not fair girls!" as he was taken back into the room, to calls of "Sissy Tom wears a frock!" "Sissy Tom plays dollies!" He sobbed "You said, Us big girls could go!" as Pam laughed "Julie and I are big girls!" adding "But you're a big Sissy boy, who had better stay till the end, or we show your mates!" as he sobbed "Not flaming fair!" Gale gave him a kiss and said, "Girls! Console the poor Sissy! Give him a kiss!" They cried "No way! We already kissed him earlier!" but Pam laughed "He'll hate kissing you, fifty times more than you will" and so next thing all the little girls and then some Mums, were kissing him on the lips, to giggles and some of the Mums saying, "You naughty boy! Tricking me and my girl into kissing you!" adding "Thinking you were a little girl!" to more laughter.

Pam said, "I'm sure you can think of a way, to punish my Sissy brother for tricking you!" as he huffed "You make me dress up!" to more laughter. Pam said, "Ok We'd better get some ribbons in Sissy Tom's hair!" as the girls said, "No we want him to play as Sissy Tom!" as she got him to sit down and said, "You've to wheel your dollies around as Nancy when you get your ribbons in ok?"

Julie offers Sissy Tom as Becky's big dolly to dress up

He nodded, "Ok!" as she showed him a pink ribbon and said, "We'll start from the back and then the sides and then the front!" as she took the ribbon and dropping it back into her handbag replaced it with a curly grip in his back. She showed him a yellow flower and he nodded, as she again popped a curly grip into the side of his hair. She continued and the girls giggled, as he was soon stood there, again as Sissy Tom, but thinking he had loads of flowers in his hair.

She then took his hand and tied it to her doll's pram, to giggles from the girls, but she then tied his other to the top of his apron. She said, to Becky "You can take your dolly for a walk!" Becky giggled, and started pushing Tom around the garden, with him thinking he looked like a big girl, but was actually mincing around as a complete sissy boy on show to all the neighbours without any disguise. The girls were giggling their heads off as were several of the Mums as they were told of Pam's trick as one approached with a ribbon and asked, "Can I add a ribbon to Sissy Tom's hair?" as he cringed and said, "Please don't, take any out?" as she laughed "Oh you like wearing pretty ribbons do you?" and saw him nod, to more giggles. Soon the ladies were bringing out the cakes and things and the girls donned their aprons again and were sat down to enjoy their cakes, as the presents were taken out, all in their pretty wrapping paper. After the cakes and juices, came the presents with Tom having to make pretty comments about each one saying, to Becky how lucky she was getting such a pretty dolly or frock or nighty.

She ended up getting 2 nighties, 1 frock, 2 handbags, 2 shopping baskets, 1 purse and 1 tutu. When it came to nighties Pam giggled, "What colour Nighty did I put you into last night Sissy Tom?" to more laughter as he said, "turquoise!" as she added "I hope you cuddled your dollies to sleep!" as he nodded, to more giggles.

Julie then said, "As Sissy Tom hasn't brought you a present yet! I think he can act as your dolly for today!" as Becky and the girls giggled, and some mothers screeched and she asked, "What?" Julie asked, "What do you normally do with your dollies?" as she laughed "Dress and undress them?" Take them walkies in their pram!" adding "to the shops!" as he cried "Please don't take me outside like this, girls?" They giggled, wondering if she would. Tom's hands for the cakes, but Pam and Julie had a naughty plan for him. They had some dresses pegged up along with a large bag and said, "There's some dresses for you to dress your dolly Tom up in!" Some Mum's gasped "They might see a bulge, or something else!" as Pam laughed "He's just got a baby-pee-pee!" and to Tom "Why do you call it, your baby-pee-pee?" as he cringed "It's the size of a little baby boys!" as the mothers laughed and said, "I still don't want my daughter to see!" Pam said, "we'll try and hide him from them!" as Gale helped Becky, take a frock over to Tom and say, "Right Dolly Tom lie down for Becky!" and saw him lie down on the blanket, as she said, "Remove sissy's frock!" and saw the giggling girl, remove his frock over his head as they screeched at his pretty pink frilly panties.

Pam pulled down his panties to show and they diaper Baby Nancy

They quickly, buttoned the short dress up his front and then handed Becky, the large carrier bag and ran to say, to the ladies "Tom's hands are tied behind his back, so he can't struggle!" adding "Becky wants to change his panties!" as they gasped "Oh you naughty girls! What colour are they?" Pam laughed "Just white! but I'm sure you've seen them before!" as Becky ran up and showed her, as she gasped and screeched, as she removed a baby bonnet and dummy. Becky took the dummy and then a baby bottle and begged "Please Mummy! Let me change baby? It would be the best birthday ever!" as her Mum tittered, However, next thing Pam and Julie stood Tom up in the short dress, showing off his panties and said, "So Tom! Don't you like wearing frilly panties?"

Tom shook his head and gasped, when he felt them pulling both panties down, as the mothers and girls screeched and one or two said, "Don't look girls!" but next thing he was turned and they all giggled, at his small penis, on

show and Becky's Mum laughed "As it is a little baby one! It will be good practice for their babysitting!" as they saw the girls sit him down, on show to the whole garden of giggling girls, especially the new girls who'd arrived and gasped "You going to put him into nappies?" Becky nodded, "He's going to be my big baby dolly today!" as they screeched and one said, "I don't think Mummy thought, I'd see that!" as he had to tell them, it was his baby-pee-pee, the size of a baby boys!" Soon the bonnet was popped on his head and then a baby bottle was put into his mouth and he had to drink the horrid milk with his pee-pee still on show. The baby talc and gel were produced and some plastic gloves for Becky's Mum and little Becky and Tina.

Becky takes Baby Tom walkies in the street in nappies

He cringed and felt hands applying the gel to his front and then over his penis as Becky laughed "This is the best ever!" as she felt his penis and her Mum said, gently dear!" as she applied talc and then a disposable applied and he was rolled over and felt several hands smack his bottom. He cried "Not fair girls!" as he felt the gel and applied talc, followed by the disposable. The diaper was then folded into a triangle and he was sat on top of it and laid back as it was pinned into place and then the plastic baby pants were added.

Julie said, "Mum! There's something in the fridge which needs heated up for baby!" as her Mum opened it and gasped at the bowl of baby food and heated it up as she and he cried "Oh no not baby food!" A giggling Becky fed him loads of baby appeared food and then the baby bottle saying, "Definitely best party ever! Thanks Tina!" as Tina bobbed a curtsy and then "Thanks Pammy and Julie for exposing Sissy Tom to me!" They curtsied back and said, "Thanks Sissy Tom for showing yourself, as a big baby Sissy to us all!" as he was let up, but the bonnet removed and was told "Curtsy baby!" as he tried to bob a curtsy, to them to laughter, as his nappies and plastics were on show.

Tom was ushered up the street in nappies without a disguise

However, then Pam undid the baby reigns and said, "Becky here's some baby reigns, for to take your big baby walkies!" as the giggling girl went to pull them back, but Pam said, "If you pull them around his front, baby will walk normally!" Becky asked, "In the garden or the street!" Pam said, "I'll distract Mummy and if you can get him up the street and around the corner I'll join you as she giggled, and said, to one of the girls "Do you live the next street as she asked Want to help me bring Sissy baby around to show your Mummy?" as she nodded, "Great!" Pam shot over and her Mum asked, "I hope you aren't being too cruel to your big brother?" as Pam laughed "He's actually enjoyed the birthday cake and they even played some football for him!" as his Mum laughed and asked, "What time will it finish?" as Pam said, "He said, he'll be back in another few hours!" as his Mum laughed "Do they all know?" Pam laughed "It took forever! He was a natural!" Meanwhile Becky was pulling Tom in the short dress and nappies around the garden, but Becky explained to the mothers, Pam's distracting their Mum, while Becky and the girls get Tom up the street and around to play at little Susan's in the next street!" They gasped "Oh the poor boy!" as they saw Becky "Come on Sissy Baby dolly! Follow me or it's the shops!" as she lifted a shopping basket and handbag and popping his baby bottle which had been topped up and a dummy and said, "Bring his baby food around Mummy!" as her Mum laughed and took the half full bowl of mush around, with her saying, "The poor boy!"

Tom was ushered out and cried "Not in the street in my nappies!" to screeches of laughter from the girls as the mum's collected their handbags and joined behind the sissy boy and little girls pushing him up the street without any disguise and thinking he had ribbons in!" He was led out past the garage but didn't see himself in the garage window.

He begged "Can baby Tom have a headscarf to cover his ribbons girls!" as they screeched "Oh you, big sissy boy!" as he was ushered out the driveway without noticing the reflection in the garage window. He said, "Let me go over

home, girls? I'll tell!" but was pulled on up the street, fully on show, as a big sissy boy, in nappies and baby pants!" Tina said, "I might give baby his headscarf, if he sucks his dummy!" and soon a reluctant Tom, was sucking on his baby dummy, edging up the street, on show to all. A lady was walking back towards them and when she was about 5 feet away heard Julie ask, "Would you like to see our big baby Sissy Tom?" She gasped "Tom! Is that you?" as he blushed and cried "Oh no! It's James Mum!" as he cried "Oh no! I've wet myself!" as the girls screeched, even more and called "Baby Tom's wet his nappies?" He cried "Please don't tell James, or anyone on me?" as she giggled, "Oh what a pretty frock Tom! I hope James doesn't play dollies and dress up with you, too!" as he huffed "Ha!"

June supplies a pram for Baby to be wheeled around the streets

However, worse was to follow as the ladies asked would she like to join them around to a little girl's house, to play dollies with Sissy Baby Tom. She found herself nodding and saying, "It might be fun to play dress up with my James! It should help him get used to housework!" Julie explained how it keeps a boy under control and willing to help with housework, shopping etc. She laughed "What about the nappies?" as she explained "Pam thought the birthday girl and her friends, would love it, even more, if she treated him as a dolly and then we thought about nappies, for him and the girls diapering her big brother. They reached the corner and turned and gasped as they saw one of Tom's mate s coming around and Julie's Mum ran and stood in front of him and his baby bonnet was replaced before Andy could notice. Several other ladies helped shield him from view, as Andy saw James Mum and asked, "Is Andy home?" as she giggled, "Yes I think so! He might be playing with Tom, as she minced on and added to Tom "Soon! Very soon girly!" adding "It would be nice to have you and my James playing dollies together in frocks!" as he cried "Please don't Mrs!" as Tina said, "Say, that will be lots of fun baby! Playing dollies with all your mates in frocks!" as he had to obey. Pam sneaked into the living room and giggled, as she saw James Mum join them, but gasped as she saw Andy and realized he'd not spotted her baby brother, in his frock and nappies. She said, "I'd better get back to the party, Mum?" as she heard her ask "Will I come over and check?"

She gasped "Mummy! You don't want to be seen to condone what's happening to him! It's better if you have deniability and say, it's all due to naughty little me!" as her Mum kissed her bye and watched her go across the road, but then shoot up the street, to join them. June had noticed the girls taking Tom as Baby girl walkies and wheels his pram out to join them. She had cut a large hole at the front of the pram for Tom's legs with a frill sewn around it and also a shopping basket to hide his legs away and Hence, big Tom was able to fit in the pram without his legs being spied. She wheeled the large pink pram around called "Hi Girls!" and as the ladies and girls turned and a few called "Goody a little baby!" and ran to look inside the pram, but only saw some dollies and other baby items. She called "Girls! Does your baby girl want a ride in her pram?" as they looked and screeched "Will he fit?" as she nodded, and said, "I've cut a section for his legs at the front here!" as they looked and gasped "Fab!" and heard him bag "Please don't take baby around in his pram?" June laughed "At least your face will be hidden in the canopy of the pram, as he huffed "Not fair girls!"

The ladies helped get Tom into the pram and slide his feet through the hole and down into the shopping basket tied to the pram handle. Then a shawl was slid over his knees and they were set to take baby walkies. June took the reins and pulled him up as the girls screeched and Becky called "Oh fab!" as he was sat up on show in the girly pram as June laughed "You can then add or remove his baby bonnet, stick a dummy in his mouth or give him his baby bottle or even feed baby some baby food!" as they screeched and he cried "Oh no! Please don't girls?" as they all laughed. Becky popped a dummy into his mouth, gurgling at her captive baby dolly and then fed a frilled baby bonnet onto his head, to screeches of laughter, as Tom could do nothing about it.

Annabelle a lady who'd spied Baby Tom takes him shopping as Nancy

Pam suggested that she'd go to lots of girly shops and try on some really pretty dresses and that she'd ask for the dresses to be kept aside for her sister Nancy to try on ten minutes later. She can text Annabelle the shop and then

he has to try all the dresses on and hopefully she will photograph him in each, as will her Mum do with Pam. Then when we get back it would be wonderful to see Nancy modelling the same frocks as her. Pam then said, "Would it be possible to find a long wig for my sissy brother to help disguise him, to try and stop him being recognized by school girls or even his mates!" as Annabelle gurgled "I should be able to procure one!" as Pam added "Baby will of course need to be well protected from accidents and so nappies, a diaper and plastic baby pants are essential!" as she screeched "Oh Pam! You want me to put him into nappies?" as she nodded, "It's so much fun!" adding "Especially if you add a baby bonnet for him and a dummy or baby bottle while changing his nappies!" as she giggled, "You can make him suck his thumb if you like!" as they laughed.

She then said, "You can hide his nappies with a pretty tutu I can supply and so his nappies won't be spied while changing in and out of his frocks!" as she laughed "You are coming up with some fab ideas!" as Pam said, "You should take him to try modelling a few handbags and so I'll get Mum to take me along to a few bag shops and get her to photograph me, but then ten minutes later you can mince Nancy in and possibly also have Sissy Tom model them without his wig, which will be wonderfully embarrassing for him, especially if some young girls are there to tease him silly!" She then said, "Try and call him Dave or something so if it gets around school, they won't associate it with him yet!" he also supplied her with one of her pink girly coats, but she'd sewn the sleeves together around the back and so when he slid his arms into them, he'd be trapped and not able to escape till let go on the way to town.

June then produced a baby bottle of milk and the girls took turns popping it into his mouth to give baby a drink, with June saying, "Not too much girls, he might wet his nappies!" to screeches of laughter and sobs from him. Pam teased "Hi Davy!" as Tom wet his nappies again "Oh no Pam! I've wet myself again!" as she gurgled "Seems were going to have to change baby Tom!" but added "In a while!" as she laughed "It's good to give baby a nice feel of his wet nappies!" as they giggled. She laughed "Gosh Tom! There you were thinking you were too big for your pram and look at you now, dressed as a baby girl and ready to be taken to town around the shops!" as the ladies gasped "We couldn't! Your Mum would go mad!" but she shook her head, she's taken my Sissy Brother Nancy shopping in a frock and got him his own handbag and dresses too!" as he cried "They were only for my dolly!" to screeches from the group at his girly comment. He was wheeled around, and they saw a teenage girl, who couldn't believe it when she spied Tom in the pram, but also in his frock and nappies and joined the girls and ladies around the streets.

Hence, one Friday, she had supplied her tutu and her pink coat to Annabelle, who made sure she'd gone shopping for lots of baby stuff for him, along with a long black wig and then told Tom he was going to do some chores for a lady friend. However, Pam had slid a black patent handbag up the right arm to the coat elbow and sewed one handle there, meaning to open the bag, he'd to pull the other handle along to open it. However, she'd also added another pink handbag inside a shopping basket too. She had taken him to

Friday, Pam show's Nancy off again to Annabelle in frock and nappies

June's to be diapered and so had his plastic baby pants on top of the diaper, but then added her yellow frock again as he blushed. However, he was handed his shirt and trousers again and pulled them on over the dress, as they exited June's and a smiling Pam led him down the street. He asked, "Where are we going, Pam?" but she just laughed and said, "You've to do what Annabelle Says! Ok Baby?" as he huffed "Ok!" as she led him into the house about three houses down. She rang the bell and Annabelle came to the door and said, "Ah Pam! And this must be your sweet big brother Tom?" as Pam nodded, "He didn't used to be that nice, but now is adorable!" as she led them into the living room. Pam said, "Right Tom! Let us show Annabelle Nancy!" as he pleaded "Please don't?", but she laughed "I saw you in the street in your nappies and then mincing in that lovely frock with a handbag too!" as he cried "You didn't?" as she nodded, and heard Pam say, "She's been nice and not told your friends or anyone!" as he cringed and started unbuttoning his shirt as Pam undid his trousers. Annabelle gurgled "Oh fab!" as she saw

him in the frock again, but Pam then raised his dress, to show the plastic baby pants, as Tom cried "Not fair!" as he cried "Close, the blinds!" as they laughed and she pulled them partially closed. Pam said, "Help me, off with his frock!" as he cried "Don't! Please!" but soon felt them pull the dress up, over his head and so he was left in the nappies and baby pants.

Pam asked, "Have you the diaper bag ready?" as she gurgled and fetched it and took the changing mat, she laid it down on the floor. Pam then got Tom onto his back and said, "Right let us pop some rubber gloves on and see to changing baby Tom!" as he blushed.

They both pulled he gloves on and Pam got her to pull down his plastic pants and then the diaper, as she laughed at the disposable with the small bulge in it. Pam asked, "Tom what do you call that in your nappy?" as he blushed and stammered "It's my baby-pee-pee!" as Annabelle gasped and then said, "Ask why he calls it that?" as she did so and heard him call "Because it's only the size of a little baby's baby-pee-pee!" causing her to gurgle with delight. Pam said, "Now before we remove his disposable nappy!" She called "Come on in James!" as Tom cried "Oh no!" and they saw the nappy change shape as he wet himself!" as they screeched, and he cried "Not flaming fair Pam! Making me pee my nappy again!" Pam asked, "Is baby all finished wetting his nappy?" and saw him nod as a laughing Annabelle pulled the wet nappy from him and popped it into a carrier bag, as she blushed herself at seeing his little willy. Pam took a baby bonnet and slid it onto his head and then taking a dummy popped it into his mouth.

They clean botty, but Pam and then adds nappies, tutu and frock

Annabelle gurgled "What a fab look for baby!" She said, "Right take some wet wipes and clean baby up!" and saw her take one and start wiping his front and then his willy and giggled, as she remembered changing her niece's nappies, but never a boy's. Pam said, "Get the gel!" and soon she'd rubbed some gel over his front and then sprinkled the talcum powder over as Pam said, "Baby is well protected!" Annabelle asked her "Is that it?" but Pam said, "Better do his botty too! Baby has a tendency to do a little poo when embarrassed too much and he thinks a mate or girl he knows, might spy his nappies or frock or handbag!" as they laughed.

They turned him over and she asked, "Is baby Tom's botty clean?" and saw him nod, but she pulled the disposable off to see his bare bottom. Of course, Pam took her hand and brought it down hard on his left cheek, as he cried "Pam that hurt!" but she then did the same on his right, as he started sobbing "Not flaming fair Pam! That stung!" as Annabelle scolded her "Now Pam! Don't be cruel to your lovely baby!" as she said, "Ok! See to protecting baby's botty!" but added "Don't forget to protect his crevice!" and pointed to the crack and said, "We don't want baby to get nappy rash!" as he huffed "Funny Pam!"

A blushing Annabelle cleaned his botty with wet wipes, then added the gel to each cheek, but then applied a bit to his crack, but Pam took some and taking a finger, she goosed him, as he cried "Oh no! That might make me poo!" as they laughed and she copied her, as he sobbed "Not fair!" as she applied the talc and then added a clean disposable again. They pulled him up, but then Pam opened the blinds as he cried "Don't Pam!" as a laughing Annabelle pulled the diaper and then the plastic baby pants up over them.

Pam made her laugh as she said, "When I had baby in his nighty without any panties or nappies I was able to take him over to the open window and make him bob curtsies to the houses at the back!" as Annabelle asked, "How?" as Pam laughed "I took hold of his little baby-pee-pee and pulled him over and then sat down on the floor, still holding it out of sight, as he was left and had to do curtsies, half as Nancy, but then I stood up and removed his ribbons to have baby Tom do them too!" as Annabelle screeched "Oh Pam! That is naughty!" Pam then produced her tutu and said, "At least the tutu hides your nappies from show!" and saw him clamber into it as Annabelle

laughed "He seems an expert getting into his tutu!" as Pam laughed and nodded, saying, "I can't wait to have her join me at ballet classes on Saturday mornings!" as he begged "Please don't Pam!" as they both laughed. She then handed him her yellow frock and saw him scramble into it, preferring it to the tutu dress. Pam asked her for a handbag and purse and soon she'd handed them to Tom, and he was mincing and then extreme mincing around the room, blushing away.

Saturday, Pam gets June to help Annabelle to get Nancy to town

He had to take the purse from the handbag and Pam told Annabelle how her and Tom used a purse and handbag for clothes pegs while doing the laundry, as Annabelle said, she'd have to try using them for her laundry, but especially if she has Tom to help her too.

Pam then told how he also used them for playing Sissy football in his frock and then also Baby football in his nappies. Pam told how Julie and her had made him play in the back garden, then the street where Julie's little sister Tina spied him and thought it was a dream, but then when he returned from school in the plastic leotard bag and nappies and then Tina discovered Tom was Nancy and wanted a re-enactment of his Sissy and then Baby football, as Annabelle had seen.

Pam said, "Tom! Tomorrow when I've gone to ballet, you've to come down here to be dressed like now!" as he sobbed "Not fair!" as she said, "Annabelle wants you to help her with some housework and you've to promise to do what she Says,!" adding "Ok!" as he protested "But I usually play footy tomorrow!" as they laughed and Pam said, "That's fine Tom, as long as you're dressed as you are now!" as Annabelle laughed "I'm sure his mates would be dead jealous if Tom was playing football dressed in your frock!" as he blushed and said, "Ha Ha!" They played dollies for a while and had Tom doing some mincing and pegging out some washing with a headscarf around his head.

June pops him into nappies and leads him to Annabelle's to get dressed

Saturday, Pam gets ready for ballet and after kissing her Mum bye, she is picked up by her friend Sally's Mum and heads on to the ballet class. Pam joked about bringing Tom with her to join them shopping for frocks, but her Mum said, she'd let him play football with his mates. Tom had breakfast and his Mum gave him some money for a burger or fish n chips and headed off to town, around 10.30am. She led him out but took Tom with her and made sure he had some money for a burger or fish and chips. Tom had been warned to head around to June's once his Mum had gone. He saw a mate James, but said, he'd catch him a bit later. Tom headed around to June's, who got him ready for Annabelle's. However, she waited to see his Mum head off and once she was satisfied, she'd left, she got Tom ready and down to Annabelle's house. She gets him into nappies and plastics and brings him down, where they are let in and Annabelle protests she was looking forward to diapering Tom, but is told she can change his nappies on his return from town, when he's sure to have a wet and possibly dirty nappy, as he laughs "Yuk!" He cries "Not town!" but then was shown the wig and heard her say, "Pam's asked me to disguise you and so nobody should recognize you!" as he huffed "Ha!" She pops him into the tutu and then June helped pop him into the yellow frock as he blushed and saw his reflection in the mirror. Annabelle pops the long black wig on Tom's head and June then adds some hair slides and an Alice band onto his head.

They take Nancy to town, but keep him away from his Mum and Pam

June laughed "Gosh that wig, and those ribbons really disguise you Tom!" He huffed "Can't I stay here?" but they shook their heads. However, Annabelle removed his wig and laughed "I just wanted to see Sissy Tom again!" as June laughed, as he begged for it back again. She then replaced the wig in a few seconds and was pleased that she

could turn Tom to Nancy and back again to Tom so quickly. Annabelle popped him into the coat with the black handbag dangling from his elbow and he cringed as he saw the pink coat, with the black patent handbag, sewn to it. She then added a pretty basket but added another pink handbag into the basket so he could have a handbag once out of the coat, showing off the frock.

They head on to town, with Tom dreading being recognized by girls and ladies or his mates. June didn't know the whole plan of what Pam and Annabelle had planned.

They head to the local bus stop as he gasps at seeing a local girl he recognizes and cries "Don't take me over there! A girl knows me!" but June laughed "Keep cool and she shouldn't recognize you!" as his face reddens. They lead him onto the bus and quickly sit him down, with Annabelle sitting beside him, with June behind sitting beside a lady. She leaned forward and said, "Nancy! Check how much you have in your purse!" and heard Annabelle laugh, as he took he black handbag and unzipped it, but then pulled the handle along his sleeve to open it and retrieve a pink purse and opening it up, he reached in and checked and said, "Ten pounds, Aunty June!" as Annabelle said, "Do your purse up Nancy and pop it away in your new handbag!" and saw him clip up his purse and pop it back into his handbag and zipped it shut again. However, she then undid the, buttons of his coat, to show off the yellow frock, as he blushed and heard her say, "That's a pretty frock and handbag Nancy!" as he said, "Thanks Aunty Annabelle!" trying to sound really girly.

June sit's there chatting to the lady, with Tom hating the fact she might out him any second and be teased by her and lots of others on the bus. However, he was ok, till they had almost reached their bus stop and the girl who he recognized, stood up and was passing him and Annabelle said, "Nancy! That's a girlfriend isn't it?" as he gasped and saw the ten-year old girl smile and look down on the young black haired, girl in yellow frock with handbag, but didn't recognize her and just turned back and walked on and got off the bus. He cringed and cried softly "She nearly recognized me!" as she laughed "We told you, she wouldn't recognize you!" as June laughed and the lady asked, "What's up with the young girl?" as she wondered what to say, and laughed "She's a bit shy!" as he heard and blushed. It was time to get off and Annabelle stood up, as he tried to do up his coat, but she stopped him and said, "Now Nancy, be proud of your new frock!" as June stood up and said, "All set Nancy!" and saw him look back and the lady Alison, look up and look and then smile and giggle "Oh! It's not!" as June put her finger to her mouth and smiled. The lady saw the young boy in a wig, walk along with his girly basket and black patent handbag, dangling from his elbow and get off the bus. She waited and saw other passengers get off the bus and thought to herself "Why not!"

Tom's taken to a café while his Mum goes to meet Pam at ballet

The lady joined along, keeping an eye on where they were going, as she got off the bus and joined following behind. He said, "That wasn't fair June! That lady realized I was a boy!" as Annabelle scolded "Oh June! You didn't tell?" as she shook her head, but said, "Unfortunately Nancy looked right at her and made a funny face! She's going to have to practice making more girly faces!" as he huffed "Funny!"

They take him to a café around eleven thirty as June said, "His Mum will be collecting Pam from ballet around midday!" as he cringed and cried "You aren't showing me off to Pam and Mum around town or even worse at ballet!" as they laughed and shook their heads and Annabelle said, "Don't worry Nancy! We'll try and ensure your Mummy doesn't see you around town today!" They entered and he gasped as he saw several girls and their Mums and a few men there, but mostly women and they sat down towards the back and studied the menu. June took his coat off, leaving him in the yellow frock as Annabelle removed her own coat and set it over her chair, as did June. He tried to concentrate on the menu and not look at the other customers. His Mum arrived at the ballet class around 11.30 and watched Pam and the bigger girls doing various movements and dances. She also saw the

fairy group with the young girls and their fairy wings and laughed as she thought of Pam's suggestion that Nancy join it and the reaction the girls would have to discovering a girly boy in a tutu ballet dress and fairy wings. Pam eventually ran up and kissed her Mum and said, "Ballet was great today!" but added "Not bring Nancy?" as another girl asked, "Who's Nancy?" as her Mum laughed and said, "It's her cousin!" as Pam giggled, "She's such a laugh! Mum's thinking of getting her to join our ballet class!" as her Mum gasped and blushed as she said, "Now Pam! Her Mum isn't keen on her doing ballet!" as Pam laughed "Oh Mum! I'm sure Jenny and I can persuade her how much fun ballet is!" adding "Nancy especially loves dancing in her tutu dress and fairy wings!" as Jenny asked, "What age is she?" as Pam laughed "Eight almost Nine!" as Jenny laughed "Isn't she a bit old to wear the same outfit at the fairies!" as Pam gurgled "Oh I do tease her about joining them, due to her just being a beginner!" but she'd probably join us in our leotards and dance skirts!" as she took Jenny's hand and ran in to have a shower and change, with her Mum hoping she'd not spill the beans to Jenny or the other girls. Pam eventually exited in her dress and coat, carrying her handbag and a basket, along with her ballet case, but with Jenny beside her. She asked, "Mummy! Would it be ok if Jenny and her Mummy join us, to look at the frocks around town?" as her Mum said, "We'll need to check with her Mummy!" as Jenny ran to speak to hers and she said, "Well Pam! Promise to stop talking about Nancy and hinting to Jenny about him! It would be terrible if all the girls at ballet found out about him!" as she said, "Promise Mum! He's probably having fun playing at the minute!" but added "You are a meany not letting Nancy join us shopping!" as she laughed. Jenny's Mum came over and said, "Is it ok if we join you! I'll leave my car here and give you a lift back later!" as they exited the door.

Pam and Jenny enter Harriet's, trying on 2 frocks each and photographed

Pam and Jenny were able to pop their ballet cases in the car boot, to lighten their load, before they headed to the shops. Pam said, "I've a specific set of shops I've thought of looking around!" as Jenny laughed "I love New Look and Debenhams!" as Pam said, "There's a few more exclusive ones that I want to look at!" as her Mum said, "They'll be too expensive, but Pam laughed "Mum! We're just window shopping!" as they laughed.

They set off around the shops and hit one of Pam's shops 'Harriet's' and they entered and started looking around the skirts and dresses and even their Mum's had a look at some frocks too. There were several other girls there with their Mum's and one Dad too. Pam and Jenny selected a couple of frocks each and entered the changing room, past a salesgirl, giggling, to try them on. Pam tried the first frock on and exited the cubicle, with her handbag to show her Mum. Her Mum smiled and said, "That looks lovely Pam!" as she asked, "Mum take a photo!" as her Mum took her phone and took a photo of her in it, as Jenny exited and both Mum's took photos of each girl. Pam said, to her "I'll try the other one on!" as she went back and removing her frock, she tried the other frock on. Jenny tried her other frock and they exited holding hands, as their Mum's said, how pretty they looked, and her more photos were taken. They said, "Ok girls! Go and get changed and we'll try the next shop!" as they removed their frocks and got back into their own dresses and coats and bags. Pam However, texted Annabelle with the words 'Harriet's in East Street – leaving at 12.15 to North Street' as she took the two frocks over to the salesgirl, while her Mum was chatting away and asked, "Could you keep these two frocks aside for my sister Nancy who'll be coming in with my Aunties soon and loves slipping into the same frocks as me!" as the girl nodded, and hung them up for her. Jenny asked what she was doing, and Pam said, "We might be back here to have another look or maybe even swap dresses!" as she laughed "Fine by me!" as they exited out to see their Mums.

Meanwhile June, Annabelle and Nancy were finishing their meals in the café, with Nancy worrying about girls laughing at him, but nobody noticed. Annabelle got the text from Pam and said, "Right we're off to Harriet's dress shop in East Street, but have to avoid North Street, as they exited and made their way to the clothes shop.

Alison didn't want them to know she was following them and had popped into a bar nearby and had a coffee while waiting for them to leave. She smiled as she saw them exit and head into the centre of town and towards

East Street. They eventually reached it and entered the shop, with Tom dreading being recognized as he minced into the shop, with his handbag and basket dangling from his elbows. He saw several young girls there with their Mum's and luckily no boys. Annabelle said, "They have some lovely skirts and dresses here, don't they June?" as she laughed and said, "Yes! I don't normally come here, as it's a bit pricy!" as she asked, "What about you Nancy?" as he shook his head.

Nancy is handed a dress and has to mince to the mirror to

Tom was led over to a rail of pretty dresses and heard Annabelle say, "Take off your coat Nancy and we'll try a few frocks on you!" as he begged "Please don't?" but next thing June was pulling his arms out of the coat and June said, "I'll hold your coat for you!" as he was left standing there in the pretty yellow frock, blushing as he saw a young girl and her Mum approach the dresses near him. However, then Annabelle took the pink handbag from his basket and slid it up his arm and said, "Select a pretty frock in your size = you're a size-six, aren't you?" as he huffed "I don't know!" as they laughed.

Annabelle said, "That's a pretty dress Nancy!" as she selected a size six and taking the hanger slid it over his head and down the back of his neck, as June laughed "What's that remind you off Nancy?" as he stammered "Pegging out frocks, when doing the laundry!" as Annabelle giggled, "Does she?" as June nodded, and laughed "Once around the garden before pegging her frock up!" She said, "Right young missy! Mince up to the mirror and a curtsy and smile, to see how you look!" and saw him look and gasp as another girl around his age was there and begged "Let me wait till she finishes!" as they said, "Ok!" but saw the girl go back to her Mum as she said, "Ok! Coast is clear, Nancy!" and saw him nervously mince with his handbag up to the mirror and look at himself in the black wig and ribbons, with the frocks hanging down and his handbag, realizing how girly he did look. He tried to muster a smile to himself and bob a curtsy, when a young girl came up and held her dress up to her neck with her Mummy who said, "Tracey walk towards the mirror and back to see how your frock flows!" as they both looked in the mirror and saw the bigger girl with the dress around her neck, blush. He went to return, but then saw a smiling Annabelle behind him and felt her hold him and say, "Nancy! That is a pretty frock!" adding "What do you think?" as he said, softly "It's a really pretty dress Aunty Annabelle!" as the mother smiled and saw her own daughter walk towards the mirror, holding the dress to her neck and then turn and walk back again. Her Mum said, "Tracey copy this big girl and slide the hanger over your neck so your hands are free!" and took the dress from her daughter and slide it over her head as she took her daughters handbag and slid it up her arm like Nancy. The girl minced towards the mirror and back again. Annabelle said, "Nancy you try the same! Mince to the mirror and back!" and he started towards the mirror with a red face!" as the Mum was luckily tending to her daughter, as he turned and saw the flash of a camera as Annabelle took his photograph. She said, "Let's pop you into the cubicle to try your dress on!" as he cringed at the thought. June approached and said, "Nancy! That frock does suit you!" as Annabelle said, "She's just going to try it on!" He tried to stammer a protest, but next was being guided to the changing room with the salesgirl saying, "Ok! Just one frock!" Annabelle said, "Actually her sister Pam was in earlier and tried two frocks on and put them aside!" as the girl said, "Yes! Here they are here!" as she picked the two dresses that Pam had worn and asked, "Nancy is it?" as she nodded, and smiled "Yes! That's right!" as she guided Tom into a cubicle at the end.

Nancy is led out in the frocks to show June how she looks

She hung the other two frocks up and took the dress from his neck and hung it up on top, saying, "Right Nancy out of your dress!" as he cried "Can I pull it up?" but she shook her head and helped him off with Pam's yellow frock to leave him in the tutu, as she laughed. She said, "Right try this first dress on and we'll take it to show Aunty June!" and saw him pull the dress over his head and sliding his arms in, pulled it down his body, as she smiled and

taking her camera took a photo of him. However, he gasped as she pulled his wig off and handed him his handbag as she took a photo of Sissy Tom, as he gasped, but she quickly replaced it again.

Next thing the smiling Annabelle was leading Nancy out again past the salesgirl, who said, "Oh that dress looks lovely on her!" as she saw the young girl in the frock, mincing with her handbag out the changing room. June was standing there, holding Tom's coat, chatting to the mother of the young girl, who was holding the first dress for her daughter to try, but the girl had then selected another dress and asked, "Can I try this pretty dress too Mummy?" as she nodded, and laughed, as she took it. Next thing they saw the big girl come out with Annabelle as June laughed "That's a lovely frock Nancy!" as the mother nodded, "Yes! Tracey why don't you get a dress like hers!" as the girl asked, "Where did you get your dress?" as Tom pointed "Over there!" as the girl looked at the big girl with long hair and said, "Thanks!" as she ran over and selected one her size and ran back again to show her Mum, who said, "Try in the mirror again!" and saw the girl mince the dress up and down.

Her Mum then said, "Go and try it on Tracey!" as June said, "Nancy! Mine up and down a few times to the mirror to see how it feels!" as he blushed and walked over to the mirror. He walked forward and gasped as he saw an older girl checking a skirt against herself. She looked in the mirror, not paying much attention to the young girl in the dress mincing with her handbag. However, Tom had wet his nappies and was still peeing as he returned facing her, with a very red face. She asked, "You ok dear?" as he nodded, and Annabelle called "She's just a bit shy!" as they all laughed.

Next thing Tracey was out having removed her own dress, had slipped into a similar dress to Nancy. Her Mum laughed "I thought you'd suit that frock!" as Tracey said, "It's nice Mum! Can I have it?" as her Mum checked the price and nodded but said, "Wait till you try the other two frocks dear!" However, June asked, "Can we see yours and our Nancy mincing up to the mirror together and back?" as she said, "Tracey just take Nancy's hand and walk to the mirror and back, since you're both in similar frocks!" as he gasped, but then saw the girl hold out her hand and he'd to take it with his left hand and then start to mince towards the mirror, with the girl saying, "It's a really pretty dress, isn't it?" He nodded, "Yea!" as they turned and minced back again, with June taking another photo of him, but this time with the little girl. She apologized, but said, "I hope you don't mind the photo?" as her Mum said, "No fine!" She said, "Your girl is blushing a lot!" as they laughed and said, "She is very shy!" Her Mum said, "Try another dress on to see how it looks!" and they saw the little girl skip off to the changing rooms.

Nancy gets into next frock for photos as Sissy and Baby Tom too

Next thing he was being led in too, past the salesgirl and up to the cubicle, where he gasped as Tracey was changing next to him. Annabelle said, "Let's get this dress off you Nancy and try the 2nd one on!" as she pulled the dress off him, to leave him in the tutu again. However, she then removed his wig, causing him to gasp in case the girl peered in, but then reached underneath and unclipped his tutu and pulled it up, as he gasped at his nappies and plastic baby pants on show, as she smiled and took a photo of him. She laughed as she did up his tutu, but left his wig off and said, "Right into your next frock!"

He took the next frock which Pam had tried on and pulled it over his head and down, as he stood there as Sissy Tom and heard the girl say, "Darn I can't get my arm in!" as luckily his wig was added, just before the girl poked her head in and asked, "Can you help me with my frock?" and saw the red faced girl in another dress as Annabelle said, "Here let me help you dearie!" as she helped the girl into her next dress. She got him to pick up his handbag and then had both him and the girl mince out the changing room hand in hand, as they heard laughter from June and her Mum as Annabelle said, "Your daughter had a little problem getting into her dress and I'd to help, as her Mum said, "Thanks!" adding "Don't you two look sweet in your new frocks?" as they all nodded.

He again had to mince to the mirror and back and then with Tracey again, who said, "I like this frock too?" as her Mum said, "Check the third dress and I'll decide how many you can have!" as her daughter ran back to the cubicle and she asked, "You getting her any of hers?" as they laughed "We're more window shopping today, but might get her one or two frocks for being a good girl!" as she laughed "Poor girl!" as they laughed.

Again, photos were taken of Nancy and the little girl in the new frocks and then he was led back to try the third dress. He passed the girl in her cubicle and led him into his, with a smiling Annabelle removing his wig to take his photograph in the dress, as Sissy Tom, causing him to gasp in case the little girl saw him as a sissy boy. Next thing she had undone his tutu and raised it up and whispered, "Curtsy high!" and saw him raise his dress to show off his nappies for another photograph, as he dreaded Tracey peering in. She then removed his frock to leave him in the raised tutu and his wig was added again and his tutu was done up again, but she then said, "Show Tracey your pretty tutu, Nancy!" as she asked, "You decent Tracey?" as she poked her head out and saw the big girl in her red tutu ballet dress and said, "I do ballet too! That's a pretty ballet dress, as Annabelle said, "Now Nancy what do you do for a complement?"

Nancy Says, how he likes his tutu and is shown off to do ballet moves

He knew what she wanted and gripping his tutu, he bobbed a curtsy to her!" as the girl laughed and bobbed one back, but heard Annabelle say, "Nancy's been taught to give a kiss too!" as the girl laughed "Ok!" and saw the big girl bend down and kiss her lips, as she laughed "I'll have to do that with Mummy!" as she returned to her cubicle.

Next, he was trying on the third dress and pulled it down over his head and soon Tracey had popped her last dress on and had joined them to mince out again holding hands.

Again, they were photographed with the mother asking could you send me a copy of the photos, as she gave June her email address and phone number, saying, "I forgot my phone today, leaving it in my other handbag!" They were mincing again in front of the mirror when Tracey called out "Nancy has a really pretty ballet tutu on under her frock!" as they all laughed and June whispered "Show Tracey's Mummy!" and he blushed as he raised his dress to show it with several ladies and girls smiling as they saw the little girl in the pretty red tutu under her frock. Tracey asked, "Can I have all three frocks Mummy?" as her Mum laughed "Such a greedy girl!" as she nodded.

She then asked, "Want to remove your pretty tutu?" whispering "or tell me out loud you love your pretty tutu ballet dress!" but saw him shake his head and say, "I love my pretty tutu ballet dress!" as they gurgled and she said, "Show the girls some moves you learn at ballet!" as he gasped and raised his arms like Pam had shown him in June's garden and he then splayed his arms our with his handbag still dangling from his arm as they laughed and saw Tracey try to copy him. However, then June raised his dress and pulled it over his head, luckily not removing the wig, as she handed him back his handbag, to leave him in the tutu and said, "Repeat in front of the mirror!" and saw him blush again as he minced to the mirror followed by the little girl who did some better moves than him as the mothers laughed and more photos were taken.

Annabelle laughed "You are naughty June!" as she led him back into the changing rooms, where he'd more photos taken as Sissy Tom in the dress and then his nappies on show again, when they heard Tracey coming back again. She then heard her phone go and got the text that they had been in Sallsbury Handbags and so knew where to head next. He cried "Not fair!" She laughed as she did his tutu up again and added his own yellow frock, but then removed his wig, as he gasped "Oh no!" as she slid the Alice band and hair ribbons into his own hair and said, "Tracey, Nancy's trying to grow her hair and is using a wig till it grows a bit longer!" as she pulled him out and Tracey looked and gasped "Gosh she looks completely different with her short hair!" as he blushed and heard Annabelle say, "Tell Tracey how pretty she looks!" as he stammered "You look very pretty Tracey!" as she laughed

and heard Annabelle ask "What happens when we get a complement!" as Tracy laughed and gripping her dress, she bobbed a curtsy and then said, "Oh yes!" and kissed the big girl in short hair and laughed.

They exit and Tracey buys 3 dresses, but Alison enters to tell on Nancy

He was led back into the cubicle and his Alice band and ribbons removed as his wig was added again and the hair slides replaced. She called "Right pick up your handbag again and let's get out and onto the next shop!" as he picked it up and slid it over his elbow.

She called "Bye Tracey!" as she poked her head out and saw Nancy in her wig again and said, "She does look completely different like that!" as he grimaced and minced out to June and the mother. June took his handbag and slid it into his basket, before adding his coat and the Mum saw he'd a black handbag too. June explained "We like to see Nancy mince and so when she's her coat on, she has her handbag sewn to it, so she can use her handbag and purse properly at the till!" She saw the handles of the handbag sewn to the coat and laughed. June then said, "We also give her practice with her purse and handbag doing the laundry!" as she asked, "What?" as she laughed "You add six pegs into the purse and then pop it into the handbag and then use them to get the pegs for pegging out the washing!" as her Mum laughed "I'll try and teach Tracey that! It's extremely girly!" to laughter. They called "Bye! We'll send you copies of the photos!" as she called "Bye Thanks, girls!" and they exited and headed to the next dress shop. Next Tracey came out in her dress and coat, holding her handbag and the third frock as her Mum asked, "Want to go up and buy your own dresses using your handbag and purse?" as she nodded, and saw her Mum take her own purse and pop it into Tracey's handbag and zip it up and slid it up her arm to the elbow like Tom had carried his. She laughed and said, "That's the way Nancy carries her handbag!" but added "Apparently she even carries her handbag and uses her purse for the laundry!" as Tracey asked, "The laundry?" as her Mum nodded, and said, "They pop some clothes pegs into the purse and pop it back into the handbag and then it gives her practice for shopping too and looks very girly!" as she laughed "Ok!" as she approached the queue and waited to get to the till. Tracey said, "Mummy! That girl Nancy actually had quite short hair!" as her Mum laughed "Was it a wig then?" as she nodded, "Her Mum showed me her without the wig and she looked completely different!" as her Mum laughed, as she said, "Really short hair, but with the Alice band and ribbons too!" as her Mum said, "Why the wig?" as she said, "I think she's trying to grow her hair!"

Alison had gone into a few other shops nearby when she saw them enter the dress shop and wondered whether to go in or wait. She decided to wait and enter when they'd left the shop. Hence, on seeing them leave, she entered and saw a few girls and their Mum's there as she went up and saw the girl on the door of the changing room and said, "I think boys miss out on pretty skirts and dresses!" as the girl Gene laughed "Somehow I don't think many would want to try a skirt or frock on!" as Alison laughed "No!" adding "I happened to spy a sweet girl on the bus today in lovely black hair!" adding "And a pink coat with black handbag!" as the girl said, "Yes she was just trying on some pretty frocks here, with her Mum or some ladies!" as Alison giggled, "It was a wig and I'm quite sure she was a he!" as the girl gasped "You're joking! I saw she'd a very red face, but never realized it was a little boy trying on those frocks!" She looked over and saw Tracey and her Mum in the queue about to be served and said, "See the little girl at the till with her Mum?" as she nodded, and she continued "The little girl and him were trying on similar frocks and I bet she'll have a giggle if you tell them!" as she went over and waited for them to be served.

Tracey discovers Nancy is a boy and tells her Mum she kissed him

She saw the sales girl wrapping three pretty dresses and then the young girl reach into her handbag and retrieve a purse and pay for the dresses and then take the receipt and change and return them to the purse and then it back to her handbag, before her Mum took it back again. Her Mum picked up the bag with the 3 frocks and said, "Happy Tracey?" as she nodded. They left the sales area and saw a smiling lady approach and say, "I hear that your girl

was trying her dresses on with another big girl Nancy?" as her Mum laughed and said, "Yes! They did look very sweet together mincing up and down in matching frocks and with their handbags!" Alison laughed "Well I was on the bus behind them today and when they got off, I then realized why the sweet girl in front was blushing so much!" as her Mum asked, "Why?" as she laughed "She was a he!" as her Mum gasped and gurgled "He wasn't?" as Tracey asked, "What?" Her Mum laughed and asked her, "You know your girlfriend, Nancy?" as she nodded, "Yes! She was nice!" as her Mum laughed "Well it appears she was playing a joke on you and me darling!" as her daughter asked, "What joke?" as she laughed "Apparently she was a he!" as Tracey gasped "He was a boy?" as her Mum and Alison gurgled and nodded but then she called out "But I kissed him on the lips!" as they screeched "You didn't?" as she nodded, as her Mum asked, "Why?" as she said, "Mummy you look very pretty!" as her Mum said, "Thanks dear!" but Tracey said, "That deserves a curtsy!" and saw her Mum laugh and gripping her skirt bobbed a curtsy!" to her, but then said, "And a kiss!" as her Mum laughed and bending down kissed her young daughter and laughed "So he complemented you and you'd to bob a curtsy and give him a kiss?" as she nodded, "Wait till I see that big Sissy boy! I'll give it to him!" adding "I'll remove his wig to show him off as a big sissy boy!" as they laughed.

The salesgirl came over and laughed "I think his sister and her Mum were in here earlier and she tried on two of his frocks on and then got me to leave them aside for him to come in and try later, telling me she was her sister!" as they laughed "You think she's making him?" as she laughed "She looked younger, but I don't know!" adding "That's right she had a right beamer of a red face for most of the time she was trying on the frocks!" and said, "His Aunts said, she was just shy!" Her Mum laughed "You think they were forcing him to dress up?" as they laughed "Yea!" as Tracey called "Mummy! I want to play dress up with him!" as Alison laughed "You might have to explain to her about boys and their difference!" as she gasped "He'd better not show her anything or else he'll be for the high jump!" as Alison laughed "If he's under his young sisters thumb! He'd probably soon be under Tracey's thumb and they could do whatever they wanted with him!" adding "Including stripping him!" as her Mum laughed "The poor boy!" Tracey said, "I heard them talking about going to Sallsbury Handbag's shop next!" as they laughed and asked, "Should we?" as they nodded, and set off out of the shop to try and find Nancy and the ladies. They headed along but had to wait for Pam to tell them she'd left the shop. Her and Jenny tried out a few handbags and she saw Pam mincing up and down with several bags of different colours and types, with Jenny copying her, but her Mum said, "You've enough handbags till your birthday!" as they exited. However, Pam said, "I forgot something!" and returned to the shop and said, "My sister Nancy will be in later, with long black hair!" adding "Tell her she's to mince around the shop with at least ten handbags!" as she laughed "Ok dear! We'll tell her!"

Salesgirl tells her Manageress about the sissy boy trying on frocks

Pam called "Thanks!" and texted Annabelle to say, "Next to Debenhams!" and exited the shop. However, then Jenny said, "Let's try this shop here!" as she took Pam in and she saw the accessories and was joined by their Mums. The sales girl went back to the door, but then called a few colleagues over and told them and heard screeches from them as they then told the manageress who gasped "You didn't let a boy in to try on dresses?" as the girl laughed "How am I to know it's a young boy when he's wearing a long wig and frock?" adding "I can't exactly pull down his undies to check!" as they both giggled, and her boss said, "I suppose that's true!" and laughed "I'll have to run through the security tapes later for a laugh and to check how he looked. The girl laughed "Didn't you see the two girls, one in a tutu and other there doing ballet?" as she nodded, and gasped "Was that him in the red tutu?" as she nodded and heard her boss screech "Oh fab!"

They led Nancy along to the handbag shop and just missed his Mum, but she probably wouldn't have noticed him in his wig, as he was minced along in Pam's pink coat with his handbag. They saw the shop and crossed the street and led him in, with him gasping as there were several ladies there and a couple of girls around his age. He

quickly turned away to pretend to look at some bags and baskets, as Annabelle said, "Those are pretty handbags and baskets!" as he nodded. The two sales ladies were busy with one Gloria attending to a lady on her own who was buying a pale blue handbag and the other lady Lucy attending a mother of one of the girls, who was buying a large red snap purse.

The one serving the mother and daughter was finished and asked, "Can I help you ladies?" as they turned Tom and said, "Our niece Nancy is after a new handbag!" as she smiled and said, "Yes her sister was in earlier and said, she'd to try at least ten handbags and mince them around the shop!" adding "Is it some game you girls are playing?" as he nodded. Annabelle heard her phone go and the message saying, "Wallace's!" and smiled. June handed him one yellow handbag and said, "Try this first Nancy!" and saw him take it and slide it up over his left shoulder beside his basket, as they smiled. He then proceeded to mince around the shop with his black handbag dangling from his elbow and saw the other girl and her Mum look, but not wonder too much that a girl was trying out a handbag in the shop. Annabelle said, "Lower your handbag onto your elbow to mince now!" and saw him lower it and mince around the shop again. The sales lady said, "That looks very sweet on her!" as they laughed. Next Annabelle had selected a wicker basket and said, "Have a go with this Nancy! It could be useful for school when doing cookery or needlework!" as he blushed and minced on around the shop again with them saying, how sweet she looked walking with it on his elbow. The other girl Belinda was trying out a few handbags, looking in the mirror and spotted the girl of a similar age, with her basket and her Mum asked, "Want a basket for school too?"

Tracy comes into the handbag shop and removes his wig to show him off

She shook her head and said, "Maybe one of those larger baskets Mummy! That's a bit old fashioned!" as June said, "But they are so feminine!" as she nodded, and heard her laugh "Like you couldn't imagine a boy carrying one?" as Belinda laughed "I couldn't imagine a boy carrying any of the bags of baskets in here! He would look a sissy!"

Annabelle then said, "Remove your coat Nancy! We'll look after it!" adding "That way you'll only have one pretty handbag or basket to carry!" and saw June take his basket a tick and then help him off with the coat to leave him in his yellow frock and his basket was returned to him and they saw him slide it up his arm to the elbow again, but then June handed him his pink handbag and saw him slide it over his shoulder and then mince around the shop. He was blushing away now that he was out of the coat and on show to the shop, dreading the girl or ladies realize who and what he was.

However, then the door opened and in walked a smiling Tracey with her Mum and Alison and they saw him in the pretty yellow frock with the basket over his elbow and the pink handbag over his shoulder, as June and Annabelle both laughed, but Tom initially didn't look, dreading it be some more girls or ladies that might realize what he was. However, then Tracey laughed "What a naughty big sissy boy!" as she pulled his wig off, as he cried "Oh no!" as Belinda screeched "You aren't?" as her Mum laughed and said, "It's not a boy is it?" as he sobbed "Not fair girls!" as Tracey went over and put her arms around him and said, "Don't cry Sissy! It just came as a bit of a shock that I'd kissed a big sissy boy!" as she reached up and kissed him, as the other girl his own age went over and hugged him and said, "Don't cry! We think it's fab you like to dress up!" as he cried "I don't! My sister and them make me!" as he pointed to the two ladies and heard them laugh. His sister Pam seems to like dressing him up and is such a bully!" as they laughed "You, poor boy!" but then heard her say, "Pam's only seven and a lot smaller than him!"

They gasped "How does she make you!" as he huffed "I'm afraid my friends discover what she does to me!" as they gurgled and asked, "What?" as he huffed "Play dollies!" as they screeched and then heard him stammer "And flaming dress up!" as they all ran and cuddled him and gave him kisses. June explained "Up till recently Dave was a really macho boy, playing footy with his mates and being a bit of a MSP to his Mum and sister not helping with housework considering it girl's work!"

They laughed "Never?" as she added "And he used to bully Pam and her friends, too!" as several said, "Naughty boy!" as she explained "However, Pam played a trick on him and then his Mum taught him a lesson for his MSP ways!" as they asked, "What?" as she laughed "Apparently Pam took a pair of his shorts and sewed frilly and lace to the legs inside and so he didn't notice as he pulled them on and ran out to play footy!" adding "Next thing Pam and a little girl were watching for Frilly Knickers T/ Dave to prance about with his frills showing!" as they screeched "Oh fab!" She said, "His Mum forbid her telling her friends on him, but she laughed "Then he refused to help his Mummy with the

He's popped into his trousers, but tells them he wants to stay as a girl

washing up saying, it was girl's work and next thing she'd smacked his botty and made him stay in and be nice to Pam, but she ended up somehow making him play dollies!" as they laughed "Well done Pam!" She laughed "I was around one day visiting his Mum when he returned home from school and called out "Mummy! Have you seen my dolly?" adding "apparently Pam had hidden his dolly beside her own!" and he couldn't find it. He huffed "Not fair!" as she added "They were both in his doll's pram in the sitting room where I was sitting!" as they screeched. She then laughed "He then outed himself to Pam's friend Julie and then her Mum and then her little sister Tian who he's really afraid off!" as they asked, "Why?" as she laughed "She loves playing dollies in the street and he's afraid of her making him wheel a dolls pram around the streets and his mates spy him!" as Annabelle laughed "In a frock!" as they screeched and Tracey laughed "Oh wearing pretty frocks is fun! Isn't it Nancy?" as he nodded, "Yes Tracey!" as she whispered in his ear and said, "Tell Belinda how pretty she is!" as he gasped and said, "You're very pretty Belinda!" as she laughed and heard Tracey say, "That deserves a curtsy! "as the girl gripped her dress and bobbed a curtsy as Tracey gurgled and said, "And a sweet sissy kiss!" as she said, "No way!" but they egged her on and next thing she'd thrown her arms around him and kissed his lips as he blushed and said, "I don't like kisses!"

However, then June asked a saleslady "Can I take him out the back a tick to play a trick on him?" as she nodded and led them out into the back of the shop, with them wondering what was up. She took a pair of his trousers from her basket and said, "Tom you've had enough "Here get into your trousers!" as the lady said, "Oh he suit's his frock!" as she saw him step into them and June pull the trousers up his leg, but at the top, she asked, "Can you turn around a tick he's a bit shy!" as the lady turned and she unclipped his tutu to expose his nappies and plastic baby pants. She then did his belt up but didn't do his trousers to show off his nappies if he removed them. She led him back and said, "I'm afraid this has been a bit too much for Dave and We're letting him remove his frock for the rest of our shopping trip and won't even make him carry a basket or handbag!" as they booed her, with Tracey saying, "Oh please Nancy stay as a girl!" with Belinda laughing "You'll get more kisses if you do!" He blushed and heard June ask, "Want to get back into your boy's clothes or stay in your frock and show the girls how much you enjoy your handbags and baskets!" They heard the girls plead, but they couldn't believe it when he said, "It's ok! I'm enjoying my frock and will keep it on!" as they screeched, and both gave him kisses with him sobbing "Not fair!" as they laughed thinking he didn't like the kisses. She said, "Turn around girls and saw them turn as she undid his belt and pulled them down and off, to leave him in the dress, but she did his tutu up to hide his nappies again, as he sighed.

They say, about him joining ballet and then school as a schoolgirl

Tracey called "He's wearing a beautiful tutu too!" as they all screeched as she pulled up his dress to show them and they gurgled at the sight of his ballet tutu on show as she called "Him and me were doing ballet moves in the dress shop and we tried on three frocks each!" as they gasped "Never?" as her Mum nodded, "We couldn't believe it after when Alison came in and told us he was a boy wearing frocks!" Annabelle laughed "It seems the dollies and dress up is growing on him and he realizes how much fun they are to wear and handbags to carry!" as she asked, "Isn't that right Nancy?" as he nodded.

June and Annabelle then got him to bob curtsies with the two girls and then all the ladies, with him begging for his wig back, but Tracey shook her head and said, "We'll maybe add your Alice band and hair ribbons later, if sissy if a good girly!" as he huffed "I have been! Sissy asked to wear his frock and handbag!" as they laughed and she said, "Ok!" as she handed it back to him. He quickly pulled it on and had more photos with the girls and ladies, who begged for copies and she promised with Tom begging her not to.

Tom as Nancy has to mince around in the tutu but find his nappies

They then removed his frock to have him mince around in the tutu with him dreading they realize he was wearing nappies and plastic baby pants. He had just got back into the frock, when the door opened again, and a few more ladies entered and heard laughter as Tom had to mince around with more handbags in his frock with them saying, how sweet he looked. The ladies didn't get it till his wig was removed and they too started laughing and flicking their wrists but hearing how he was offered to wear his boy's clothes but had refused. One lady laughed "Some boys will be girls!" as they all laughed. Tracey called "I hope he'll join me at ballet class!" as Belinda gurgled "I hope he'll join mine too!" as he cried "I can't join ballet! Pam was wanting me to, but Mum won't let me!" as they laughed and he cried "There's bound to be girls at school there and they'd all know!" as June laughed "I thought due to you carrying some girly bags to school yesterday Pam had outed you and you'll soon be wearing a dress and pinafore to school!" as he cried "No way ! I hope not!" as Belinda said, "Oh Nancy! Wearing a pretty dress and pinafore to school is lots of fun!" adding "Isn't it, Tracey?" as she nodded, "Oh yes!"

Annabelle gets him the wicker basket which he has to carry on his elbow trapping his pink handbag either on his elbow or over his shoulder to more laughter. The girls and their Mum's along with Alison join him to the next shop where Pam and Jenny and their Mum's have been. However, Pam and her Mum were delayed in a few of Jenny's dress shops with trying on various accessories and then some dresses and so it was a bit later that they proceeded to Wallace's. They entered and Pam and Jenny of course headed for the pretty dresses and soon had selected some of the prettiest to try on in the changing rooms. Their Mum's looked at a few dresses themselves and ended up entering the changing rooms to try theme on too.

Pam and then Jenny then sees Nancy in a similar frock as her

The giggling girls had Nancy out of his coat and in his wig, selecting several of the prettiest frocks to try on. Beforehand of course, they had him with the frocks on hangers around his neck bobbing curtsies at the mirror, with the girls beside him also bobbing curtsies and taking a hand each, they minced him up and back with other girls and ladies, wondering the joke was. Jenny exited first before Pam who was checking her dress in the mirror and didn't quite liked it and so had changed into another one, as Jenny headed out. She saw a few giggling girls at the mirror and proceeded towards them to check out her own frock. She was looking in the mirror in the same dress that Nancy had been handed to model down his front, when she spotted it and said, "Snap!" as the girls said, "Nancy mince to the mirror and back!" and saw the girl in long black hair and pretty yellow frock mince forwards as Jenny checked herself in the mirror. Annabelle said, "Let's go and check these frocks girls!" and so they headed to the changing rooms, with Tm dreading being spied by anyone else, or worse exposed by Tracey or Belinda. They entered the changing rooms and heard Annabelle say, "Just try that frock on!" and saw him set his handbag and basket down and remove his frock and then take the new frock and pull it over his head, as she laughed and handed him back his basket and handbag to mince out again.

Pam tells her Mum of a surprise and pretends June is it while shopping

Pam heard a voice and realised it might be Annabelle's, as she peeked out and gasped "Oh no! Drat! They've come early and Mum will spy him!" as she tried to think of a solution to stop her. She heard her and Jenny's Mum,

chatting in the changing room and said, "Mum! Can you stay in there! I've a surprise for you!" as her Mum asked, "What?" but she said, "Hold on!" as she exited and saw Jenny and Tom in the same dress and gurgled and then saw Annabelle and said, "Quick Get Nancy down to behind a pillar till Mum goes!" but said, "I might have to show her June, but then saw June with the pink coat and took it and handed it to Annabelle. Jenny was standing beside Nancy saying, how pretty the dresses were when she saw a lady take her hand and said, "This way Nancy!" as she led her down to look at some frocks or something. Pam said, to June "Mum's needing a surprise and so you're it! It's just a coincidence that you've turned up here!" Her Mum came out and then laughed "Heh June!" as she laughed "I know a Beatles song called that!" as she asked, "What are you doing here?" as she replied, "Just shopping!" as she said, "My Pam is here with her ballet chum and they've tried on loads of dresses around town!" June laughed and saw Pam and said, "Hi Pam!" as Pam introduced her friend Jenny and her Mum. Jenny said, "There was a bigger girl here, in the same dress as me, but she looked a bit funny!" as her Mum asked, "How?" as she laughed "I don't know! I don't think I knew her!" adding "She had long black hair with ribbons, but something wasn't quite right!" as they asked, "What?" as she said, "I can't put my finger on it!" as she looked around, but couldn't see her and said, "Her Mum took her over to look at some skirts or something!" as her Mum shrugged her shoulders.

Jenny then discovers Nancy, but then Baby Nancy and tells the girls

June asked, "I take it you didn't bring Nancy along with you!" as his Mum laughed and shook her head saying, "Pam would have loved him to join us, but I couldn't take him around the dress shops, with Pam and maybe her friend Jenny teasing him silly!" as Pam laughed "Who me?" as Jenny heard and asked, "Who's Nancy?" as Pam laughed "She's my older cousin!" as her Mum said, "Pam don't!" as she took Pam's hand and led her back to the changing rooms and said, "No squealing about Tom!" as she laughed "Who moi?" as her Mum laughed "Yea!" However, little Tracey heard her ask about Nancy and laughed "Have you met him?" as Jenny laughed "I'm talking about my girlfriend Pam, who's got a cousin Nancy!" as she then asked, "What do you mean HIM?" as she gurgled and called "Belinda! Here a tick!" as the bigger girl went over and asked, "What Tracey?" as she laughed "This girl here is asking about Nancy!" adding "Apparently, she's her friend Pam's, cousin!" as she took Jenny's hand and called "Mummy! We're just going to look at some skirts down here!" as she asked, "Can you bare-with-us a tick!" as she led her out of that area and asked, "Tracey! Did you see where he went?" as Jenny laughed "What do you mean HE?" adding "Surely there's not a boy called Nancy?" as they giggled, and on heading down, spotted Nancy and Annabelle behind a pillar, hiding. Tom saw Tracey, Belinda and then the other girl and cried "Oh no! Don't girls!" as they giggled, and Jenny then saw the big girl, in the same dress as her and gasped "You're not a boy?" as he sobbed "Not fair!" as Belinda laughed and cuddled him, saying, "Console the poor boy!"

Jenny from ballet discovers Tom's in nappies and plastics under his tutu

A laughing Jenny said "I don't know about his kiss!" but Tracey said, "I kissed him, when I thought she was a sweet girl!" as she kissed him and he cried "Not fair! I don't like kisses!" as they laughed. Jenny said, "I must show my friend from ballet, Pam!" as he cried "Oh no!" as they laughed and said, "He's her brother!" as she screeched "Never?" but then Tracey raised his dress to show off his red tutu ballet dress, as Jenny gurgled "Oh! d So you're Tom!" as they said, "He told us Dave!" but Jenny said, "I know Pam's only one nasty brother Tom!" as he sobbed "Not fair!" but she put her hands around his bottom and laughed, but then gasped, as she felt the bulky material and asked, "You aren't?" as he cried "Oh no!" as they asked, "What Jenny?" as she gurgled and looked into his face and gave him a real snog!" as Belinda saw what she'd done and copied her and she too felt and gurgled "You're not! Are you?" as he nodded, as Tracey asked as she said, "Tell me or else!" as he sobbed "Nappies and baby plastic pants!" as they all gurgled and kissed him with tears running down their cheeks. However, next thing Jenny said, "Hold his arms girls!" as she reached under his tutu and released it and soon had the nappies and plastics on show under his dress, as it was raised and they giggled, into their hands, at the sight of the boy as a baby girl. Jenny

gasped "Who puts you into nappies?" and gasped "Not Pam?" as he nodded, and she gurgled "The naughty girl!" Annabelle said, "Now! Don't draw too much attention to baby!" as the girls giggled. She did his tutu ballet dress up and Jenny headed back to the changing rooms to join Pam and their Mums.

Jenny returns to change, but takes his frock to leave him in the tutu

They leave him there with Annabelle and run giggling up to their Mum's and hear them ask "What's the big joke?" as Jenny said, "Oh Belinda told Tracey and me the funniest joke, but we can't tell yet!" as her Mum probed "Go on tell!" but they shook their head. Pam and her Mum had changed out of their frocks and into their own dresses and her Mum said, "I'm sure your hungry girls! Change out of your frock Jenny and we'll head back to a café to get something to eat and drink!" Jenny ran and went to the changing room to her cubicle to change, she then spied Tom's yellow frock and wondered should she take it or not to leave him to prance around the shops in his tutu and then replaced it with a short frilly blouse, she sometimes wore after ballet. She changed out of her frock and back into her dress again and pulling on her coat and picking up her basket and handbag she exited. Her Mum asked, "Got everything?" as Jenny ran to Pam and whispered "You lucky girl!" as Pam laughed "How much to you know?" as she laughed and whispered "Baby Nancy must have wet herself, when I discovered her diaper!" as Pam asked, "Did you see?" but she nodded, and Pam laughed "I'll let you change baby's nappies sometimes!" as she screeched and heard her Mum call "Is it that joke again!" as her Mum said, "Pam don't be naughty!" thinking she'd told on Tom.

His Mum takes Pam, Jenny and her Mum along with June to the café, where they sit down!" as Jenny said, "I've a surprise to show you!" as she entered the toilet's with her bag and changed out of her pretty frock, but into Pam's yellow frock and exited to a gasp from Pam and her Mum, as Pam thought quickly and said, "I wanted Jenny to see how she 437looked in my favourite frock, Mummy!"

Her Mum promises to bring Tom shopping Saturday after coming to dance

She laughed at it being the same one, that she'd put Tom into and her Mum said, "You look lovely dear! That is a pretty frock Pam!" as she laughed "Oh! Mummy and us two love it!" Her Mum said, "Don't Pam!" as she laughed "I promise not to mention anything as long as you promise me something too!" as her Mum asked, "What?" and she laughed "To bring Tom shopping with us, next Saturday!" as her Mum said, "Ok! I promise!" Pam gurgled "After bringing him along as Tom, to watch me dance at 11am!" as her Mum gasped "Well! He won't be coming as you know who?" as Pam said, "Deal!" Meanwhile Annabelle had escorted Nancy back to try another frock on and led him into the changing room, as he entered and cried "Oh no! It's gone!" as he said, "That witch!" as Annabelle looked and saw the small frilly top and gasped and giggled, "You think Pam took that and left you to prance around town in your tutu instead!" as she said, "But Pam had already changed out of her dress back into her pink one!" adding "But Jenny had to change!" as she gurgled "I think Jenny was the culprit!" as she laughed "I hope the girls leave your tutu done up in the shops and don't show off baby's plastic baby pants and nappies!" as he sobbed "Oh no! Let me wear my trousers?" but she shook her head and laughed. She removed the frock to leave him in the tutu and said, "Better get into another frock or it's ballerina Nancy to mince around to the next shops!" as he cringed and cried "Try and get my frock back or buy me a new one!" as she laughed.

They finish in the shop and the girls then realize he's no frock and just has the frilly blouse to wear over his red frilly ballet tutu, while mincing with his handbags and baskets. He of course was begging them "Please get Nancy a frock or skirt, to hide his tutu?" to more laughter from them all, with Belinda saying, "I'm sure prancing about in your tutu today, will be good practice for joining Pam and Jenny at ballet next week!" as he begged "Oh no! but I'll be seen by girls from school and it will be terrible!" as she gurgled "You mean they might pop you into a dress and pinafore for school?" as he nodded, sobbing. They were about to leave when Tracey spies a mother with two

young girls of about five and six and gets Belinda to guide the blushing boy over to the two little girls and Tracey asked, "Do you girls do ballet?" as they nodded, and said, "We were dancing this morning!" as they said, "We love her tutu!" as next thing Tracey pulled his wig off, as Tom cried "Oh no! Please give it back!" as their Mum gasped "That's not a boy?" as her girls giggled, "Oh great! Does he do ballet?" as they all laughed, as she said, "Not yet! but probably will do from next week, with his sister Pam's ballet class at the Church hall in Swallow Street!" but the girls called "That's where we do ballet too!" as she laughed "You know little Pam who's seven?" as they giggled, and their Mum laughed "That's not her brother?" as they nodded. Annabelle and the girls Mum's joined them and laughed "Oh Tracey! Give Dave his wig back!" but she laughed and said, "Baby Nancy or Tom, gets his wig back, if he unclips his tutu, to show the little girls and their Mummy!" as he begged "Not here! Everyone can see!" she said, "Over by these skirts girls!" as they followed the big sissy boy, mincing over to the rail and beg "Please don't tell?" as he unclipped his tutu and pulled if up, as the girls and their Mum's gurgled "Oh fab! Nappies and plastic baby pants!" as a laughing "Belinda stepped behind him and fed her arms under his to hold them up, as a giggling Tracey raised his tutu further up to giggles and screeches from the girls and their Mum.

Tom and Nancy. To be Continued

CONTENTS

Girls – Have a giggle

Once you have the boy under your thumb, you then then make him carry
one of your dolly's, all about the house, from room to room
and any time he forgets, you take his dolly to the window and opening it,
you wait till a lady or girl is coming up towards you
and call out loudly "Oh Harry! You've forgotten your dolly!"
causing him to run back, still in your apron, to get his dolly and
the lady or girl laugh, as he approaches the window and
has to kiss his dolly on show.

The book has an unusual Full Index
Each page has one or more titles to identify what happens -
This means you can quickly discover the main summary of each story

If your Mummy won't let you have fun with your brother in the house,
then female neighbours can be useful to play with your pretend sister!

You can increase his fun by sewing a handbag, to his dolly's hand, so he's
to mince about the place, carrying a handbag on one arm and his dolly in
his other hand. You can have fun making him play dress up, in frocks,
ballet tutus and mincing about with handbags to play shopping.

Laundry can be a lot more fun than any of you think – What if instead of
using a bucket or plastic bag, for the clothes pegs, instead use a shopping
basket, shopping bag or handbag to hold the pegs.

This book contains various stories of boys, who end up controlled by
their sisters, neighbours, girlfriends or even Mums.

There are various ways to turn your macho, male chauvinist, controlling,
bullying boy, to be completely obedient and fun to play with.